Georgian

Georgian: A Comprehensive Grammar constitutes a complete reference work addressing all major elements of modern Georgian grammar and usage.

It provides a systematic and accessible description of the language's phonology, orthography, morphology, and syntax. The focus is on contemporary spoken and written usage, with attention devoted throughout to differences in register and genre. Points are illustrated with examples drawn from a range of authentic written and recorded sources, such as press, radio, and television.

The grammar is designed for a wide readership, including students of Georgian, particularly at the intermediate and advanced levels, as well as scholars of Georgian and theoretical linguistics.

Tinatin Bolkvadze is Professor at the Department of Theoretical and Applied Linguistics of Ivane Javakhishvili Tbilisi State University, Tbilisi, Georgia.

Dodona Kiziria is Professor at Indiana University, Indiana, Bloomington, USA.

Routledge Comprehensive Grammars

Titles in this series:

Dutch
A Comprehensive Grammar, 3rd Edition
Bruce Donaldson

Finnish
A Comprehensive Grammar
Fred Karlsson

Persian
A Comprehensive Grammar
Saeed Yousef

Norwegian
A Comprehensive Grammar
Philip Holmes, Hans-Olav Enger

Korean
A Comprehensive Grammar, 2nd edition
Jaehoon Yeon, Lucien Brown

Modern Irish
A Comprehensive Grammar
Nancy Stenson

Lithuanian
A Comprehensive Grammar
Meilutė Ramonienė, Joana Pribušauskaitė, Jogilė Teresa Ramonaitė and Loreta Vilkienė

Máku
A Comprehensive Grammar
Chris Rogers

Emirati Arabic
A Comprehensive Grammar
Tommi Tsz-Cheung Leung, Dimitrios Ntelitheos and Meera Al Kaabi

Georgian
A Comprehensive Grammar
Tinatin Bolkvadze and Dodona Kiziria

For more information on this series, please visit: www.routledge.com/Routledge-Comprehensive-Grammars/book-series/SE0550

Georgian

A Comprehensive Grammar

Tinatin Bolkvadze
and Dodona Kiziria

LONDON AND NEW YORK

First published 2023
by Routledge
4 Park Square, Milton Park, Abingdon, Oxon OX14 4RN

and by Routledge
605 Third Avenue, New York, NY 10158

Routledge is an imprint of the Taylor & Francis Group, an informa business

British Library Cataloguing-in-Publication Data
A catalogue record for this book is available from the British Library

ISBN: 978-1-138-24112-1 (hbk)
ISBN: 978-1-138-24118-3 (pbk)
ISBN: 978-1-315-28113-1 (ebk)

DOI: 10.4324/9781315281131

Typeset in Sabon
by Apex CoVantage, LLC

Contents

Acknowledgements **xiv**

Georgian language and alphabet 1

Chapter 1 Place of the Georgian language among the South Caucasian languages **3**

Chapter 2 The Georgian alphabet **7**

Phonology 13

Chapter 3 Sound system of the Georgian language **15**

3.1 Classification of consonants 15
3.1.1 Consonant triples 15
3.1.2 Consonant pairs 16
3.1.3 Single consonants 16
3.1.4 Structure of consonant clusters 17
3.2 Classification of vowels 18
3.2.1 Backness 18
3.2.2 Height 19
3.2.3 Triangle of vowels 19

Morphology 21

Chapter 4 Nouns 23

4.1 Noun groups 23
4.1.1 Animate and inanimate nouns 23
4.1.2 Concrete and abstract nouns 24
4.1.3 Proper and common nouns 25
4.1.4 Collective nouns 26
4.1.5 Noncount nouns 27
4.2 Grammatical categories of nouns 27
4.2.1 Case and number markers 28
4.2.2 Function of cases 29
4.3 Declension of nouns 32
4.3.1 Declension of common nouns 32
4.3.1.1 Declension of consonant-stem non-syncopating common nouns 32
4.3.1.2 Declension of consonant-stem syncopating common nouns 33
4.3.1.3 Consonant-stem common nouns with irregular syncopation patterns 39
4.3.1.4 Declension of vowel-stem common nouns 42
4.3.1.5 Declension of vowel-stem non-truncating common nouns 42
4.3.1.6 Declension of vowel-stem truncating common nouns 45
4.3.1.7 Vowel-stem common nouns with irregular declension patterns 49
4.3.1.8 Declension of vowel-stem truncating common nouns with syncope 50
4.4 Declension of proper names 51
4.4.1 Declension of consonant-stem personal names 51
4.4.2 Declension of consonant-stem geographic names 53
4.4.3 Declension of vowel-stem given names 54
4.4.4 Declension of vowel-stem family names 55

4.4.5 Declension of given and family names together 58
4.4.6 Vowel-stem geographic names 58
4.4.6.1 Non-truncating geographic names 58
4.4.6.2 Truncating geographic names 60

Chapter 5 Adjectives 63

5.1 Groups of adjectives 63
5.1.1 Derivative adjectives 64
5.2 Comparative and superlative adjectives 67
5.3 Declension of adjectives 71
5.3.1 Declension of adjectives without nouns 71
5.3.2 Declension of adjectives preceding nouns 72
5.3.2.1 Declension of vowel-stem adjectives preceding nouns 72
5.3.2.2 Declension of consonant stem adjectives preceding nouns 75

Chapter 6 Numerals 77

6.1 Types of numerals 77
6.1.1 Cardinal numerals 78
6.1.2 Spelling of cardinal numerals 79
6.2 Ordinal and fractional numerals 80
6.3 Declension of numerals 82
6.3.1 Declension of consonant-stem cardinal numerals 82
6.3.1.1 Declension of consonant-stem cardinal numerals 82
6.3.1.2 Declension of consonant-stem quantifiers 85
6.3.2 Declension of vowel-stem numerals 86
6.3.2.1 Declension of vowel-stem cardinal numerals 86
6.3.2.2 Declension of vowel-stem quantifiers 87
6.3.2.3 Declension of vowel stem ordinal numerals 87

6.3.3 Declension of cardinal numerals extended by particles 89
6.3.4 Declension of numerals followed by nouns 92
6.3.4.1 Declension of vowel-stem numerals followed by nouns 92
6.3.4.2 Declension of consonant-stem cardinal numerals followed by nouns 94
6.3.5 Declension of numerals followed by numerals 98

Chapter 7 Pronouns 101

7.1 Personal pronouns and their declension 101
7.2 Reflexive pronouns 104
7.3 Possessive pronouns and their declension 105
7.3.1 Declension of possessive pronouns with nouns 107
7.4 Demonstrative pronouns 110
7.4.1 Declension of demonstrative pronouns 111
7.4.2 Declension of demonstrative pronouns preceding nouns 112
7.4.3 Declension of demonstrative pronouns with added particles separately and with nouns 114
7.5 Interrogative pronouns and their declension 115
7.5.1 Declension of interrogative pronouns preceding nouns 119
7.6 Possessive-interrogative pronouns and their declension 120
7.6.1 Declension of possessive-interrogative pronouns preceding nouns 120
7.7 Negative pronouns and their declension 121
7.8 Definite pronouns and their declension 124
7.8.1 Declension of definite pronouns preceding nouns 126
7.9 Indefinite pronouns and their declension 127
7.9.1 Declension of indefinite pronouns preceding nouns 132
7.10 Reciprocal pronouns and their declension 134
7.11 Relative pronouns and their declension 135

Chapter 8 Compounds 137

8.1 Semantics of compounds 137
8.2 Structure of compounds 137
8.2.1 Compounds with reduplicated stems 138
8.2.2 Compounds with different stems 139
8.2.3 Closed compounds 144

Chapter 9 Verbs 147

9.1 Person and number of the verb 147
9.1.1 Persons and actants 147
9.1.2 Subject and number markers 150
9.1.3 Direct/indirect object and number markers 152
9.1.4 Subject and object cases 155
9.1.5 Inversion of subject and object markers 157
9.1.6 Grammatical and actual verb persons 157
9.2 Preverbs 158
9.2.1 Structure of preverbs 158
9.2.2 Functions of preverbs 163
9.3 Voice and transitivity of verbs 168
9.3.1 Active voice 168
9.3.2 Passive voice 170
9.3.2.1 Suffixal passive voice verbs 171
9.3.2.2 Prefixal passive voice verbs 172
9.3.2.3 Root passive voice verbs 175
9.3.3 Medial verbs 177
9.3.3.1 Medio-active verbs 177
9.3.3.2 Medio-passive verbs 179
9.4 Version 180
9.4.1 Neutral and locative versions 182
9.4.2 Subjective version 183
9.4.3 Objective version 185
9.5 Tense and its subcategories 188
9.5.1 Mood 189
9.5.2 Aspect 191
9.6 Conjugation of verbs 193
9.6.1 I series 193
9.6.1.1 Present subseries 193
9.6.1.2 Future subseries 218
9.6.2 II series 237
9.6.2.1 Aorist 237
9.6.2.2 Optative 251

9.6.3 III series 265
9.6.3.1 Perfect 265
9.6.3.2 Pluperfect 284
9.6.3.3 Perfect subjunctive 297
9.7 Irregular verbs 312
9.7.1 Irregular verbs with changing stems in agreement with a plural subject 312
9.7.2 Irregular verbs with changing stems in agreement with a plural direct object 328
9.7.3 Honorific verbs of polite conversation 345
9.7.4 Irregular verbs with changing stems by tense 350
9.7.5 Irregular verbs with changing stems by aspect 379
9.8 Verbal nouns 385
9.8.1 Gerund and its derivation 385
9.8.2 Participles 389
9.8.2.1 Active voice participles 389
9.8.2.2 Passive voice participles 391
9.8.2.3 Medial voice participles 395

Chapter 10 Adverbs 397

10.1 Primary and derivative adverbs 397
10.2 Semantic groups of adverbs 401

Chapter 11 Postpositions 407

Chapter 12 Conjunctions 416

12.1 Coordinating conjunctions 416
12.1.1 Correlative conjunctions 416
12.1.2 Separating conjunctions 418
12.1.3 Contrastive conjunctions 420
12.1.4 Equating conjunctions 421
12.2 Subordinating conjunctions 421

Chapter 13 Particles 425

13.1 Interrogative particles 426
13.2 Limiting particles 427
13.3 Negation particles 428

13.4 Affirmative particles 430
13.5 Reported speech particles 430
13.6 Approximating particles 431
13.7 Emphasizing particles 432
13.8 Particles expressing wish or desire 433
13.9 Selective particles 434
13.10 Particles expressing possibility or supposition 434
13.11 Imitative particles 434
13.12 Indicative particles 435
13.13 Particle denoting frequency of action 435
13.14 Particle denoting not witnessed action 436
13.15 Parts of speech functioning as particles 436

Chapter 14 Interjections 437

Syntactic structures 443

Chapter 15 Noun phrase 445

15.1 Noun/subject 445
15.2 Noun/direct and indirect objects 446
15.3 Adjectives 448
15.3.1 Attributive adjectives 448
15.3.2 Genitive modifier 450

Chapter 16 Verb phrase 452

16.1 Predicate 452
16.1.1 Simple predicate 452
16.1.2 Compound predicate and its structure 453
16.2 Adjunct object 456
16.3 Predicative adjective 459
16.4 Adverbial modifiers 461

Chapter 17 Syntactic pairs 466

17.1 Number of syntactic pairs in a sentence 466
17.2 Types of word relations within syntactic pairs 467
17.2.1 Coordination 468
17.2.2 Subordination 469
17.3 Increasing and decreasing basic parts of a sentence 470

17.3.1 Increasing the number of actants in a sentence 471
17.3.1.1 Increasing the number of actants with causative verbs 471
17.3.1.2 Increasing the number of actants by changing version 472
17.3.1.3 Increasing the number of actants with preverbs 472
17.3.2 Decreasing the number of actants in a sentence 473
17.3.2.1 Conversion 473

Chapter 18 Modality of sentences 476

18.1 Declarative sentence 476
18.2 Interrogative sentence 477
18.3 Imperative and exclamative sentences 479
18.4 Interrogative-exclamative sentence 481

Chapter 19 Structure of sentences 482

19.1 Simple sentences 482
19.1.1 Unextended and extended sentences 482
19.1.2 Complete and incomplete sentences 483
19.1.3 Sentences without or with omitted subjects 484
19.1.4 Noun-sentence 484
19.2 Sentence with coordinated parts 484
19.2.1 Coordinated parts 484
19.2.1.1 Joining coordinated parts 485
19.3 Coordinated parts in syntactic pairs 488
19.3.1 Compound predicates 488
19.3.2 Compound subjects 489
19.3.3 Coordinated direct objects 489
19.3.4 Coordinated indirect objects 490
19.4 Parenthetical words and phrases 491
19.4.1 Appositive 491
19.4.2 Free modifiers 493
19.4.3 Asides 493
19.4.4 Addressing formulas and expressions 495

Chapter 20 Complex sentences **497**

20.1 Complex coordinate sentence 498
20.2 Complex subordinate sentence 498
20.3 Adverbial clause of condition 506
20.4 Adverbial clause of concession 506
20.5 Adverbial clause of result 507
20.6 The compound-complex sentence 508
20.6.1 Compound sentence with several subordinate clauses 508
20.6.2 Mixed sentences 510
20.7 Direct and indirect speech 511

Bibliography **513**

Index **527**

Acknowledgements

This book is the result of several years of work. We, the authors of this work, belonging to different generations and living in different countries – Tinatin Bolkvadze in Georgia and Dodona Kiziria in the US – were brought together both by our shared interest and experience in teaching Georgian for many years and by our desire to write a comprehensive grammar useful to those studying the language for either practical or theoretical purposes.

Tinatin Bolkvadze's contribution is not limited only to the latest studies in theoretical linguistics, which she teaches as a professor at Tbilisi State University, but also the experience she acquired working in various countries in Europe and US, where she taught the Georgian language to university students.

Dodona Kiziria, Professor at Indiana University, has a 30-year-long experience in teaching Georgian at the University of Chicago, Duke University, and Indiana University, which was particularly useful for dealing with the difficulties of presenting the complex subject of this book in a lucid and succinct manner. Dr Dodona Kiziria collaborated with Professor Howard Aronson, author of *Georgian: A Reading Grammar* (1982, Slavica Publishers, Bloomington), the very first fundamental textbook for English speakers wishing to learn Georgian. Later, Professor Dodona Kiziria became the co-author of another of Professor Aronson's books, *Georgian Language and Culture: A Continuing Course* (1999, Slavica Publishers, Bloomington).

In his introductory note to his first book, Professor Aronson wrote, "An extensive and significant scholarly literature exists in modern Georgian, covering all areas of knowledge from anatomy to zoology. No one can hope to be an expert in the fields such as history, prehistory, ethnology, art, music, linguistics, folklore, etc. of the Caucasus without consulting the extensive scholarly literature on these topics written in Georgian." After the breakup of the Soviet Union, more and more foreigners are learning Georgian. The number of foreign scholars doing research in various aspects of Caucasian studies has also grown, and many scholarly works in foreign languages have appeared in this field. However, this does not diminish the importance of Georgian language documents and scholarly works published in Georgian.

We want to thank Professor Mzekala Shanidze, with whom Tinatin Bolkvadze had many conversations on various aspects of Georgian morphology during our work on this book.

A special contribution to the formation of the book in this way is made by Professor Yasuhiro Kojima, whose work we will always mention with special gratitude. His perceptive remarks helped in bringing the book to its final stage.

We are thankful to the students Patrick Norén and Isaac Eaton, who studied Georgian at Leiden University with Tinatin Bolkvadze, for their helpful advice.

Our heartfelt thanks go to our colleague and friend and a professor at George Mason University, Julie Christensen, for her many practical suggestions and comments.

We hope that this book, which covers exhaustively every aspect of the phonology, morphology, and syntax of Georgian, will be helpful to those wishing to master this complex and fascinating language.

Tinatin Bolkvadze
Dodona Kiziria

Georgian language and alphabet

Chapter 1

Place of the Georgian language among the South Caucasian languages

Kartvelian languages are a language family of the southern Caucasus, consisting of four related languages: Georgian (with texts going back to the fifth century AD), Megrelian, Laz (or Chan), and Svan. However, some scholars believe that Laz and Megrelian cannot be regarded as separate languages and they should be considered as the dialects of one language Zan (or Colchian). However, since Laz is predominantly spoken in the territory of modern Turkey, the political distance increases the linguistic distinction of these languages.

According to the theory of T. Gamkrelidze and V. Ivanov, the phonetic system of the proto-Georgian languages is closely related to the Indo-European initial phonetic system. The reconstructed Indo-European stop system finds a very close typological parallel in Caucasian languages. In particular, the stop system posited for Proto-Kartvelian (South Caucasian) shows the same number of series and orders and approximately the same phonological oppositions among the series and orders as the Indo-European system does. Proto-Kartvelian had a stop system consisting of three series (I, glottalized; II, half-voiced; III, voiceless aspirated) and four points of articulation (labial, dental, velar, postvelar). The postvelar order had a gap in the most marked, voiced slot. The half-voiced stops, which were phonetically distinct from true voiced stops in their lower degree of sonority and characterized by intensivity, can be compared to the Indo-European voiced aspirates. Analogously, glottalization spread in the Caucasus to late Indo-European languages, such as Ossetic. The Kartvelian language family also shows a distinctive isomorphic structure in consonantism with Semitic languages. Besides that, Kartvelian and Indo-European have identical structural canon for root and affixal morphemes and the rules for combining them, which involved ablaut alternations of vowels. Such similarity, complete down to

DOI: 10.4324/9781315281131-2

isomorphism of structures and root canons, would be the result of long interaction of these languages in a linguistic area and their allogenetic association with one another.

Gamkrelidze and Ivanov thought that Proto-Kartvelian (South Caucasian) dates to the fourth to third millennia BC. Glottochronological evidence puts the beginning of its differentiation in the very early second millennium BC (and possibly much earlier), at which time Svan separated out and Proto-Kartvelian separated into two different areas, Svan and Georgian-Zan, the latter subsequently splitting into Georgian and Zan (or Colchian): Proto-Kartvelian prior to its breakup must be placed, on the evidence of archaic lexical and toponymic data, in the mountainous regions of the western and central part of the Little Caucasus (the Transcaucasian foothills). The first wave of Kartvelian migrations to the west and northwest, in the direction of the Colchian plains, must have begun with one of the western dialects in the third millennium BC and led to the formation of Svan, which spread to the western Transcaucasia and was superimposed on local languages, probably of the Northwest Caucasian type, which thus became substrate to Svan. Svan was gradually displaced to the north, to the Great Caucasus range, by the next wave of migrations, which occurred approximately nine centuries later (on glottochronological evidence) and removed the westernmost remaining dialect as far as the Black Sea coast. This western dialect gave rise to the later Colchian or Zan, or Megrelian-Laz, language, one of the languages of ancient Colchis. The dialects which remained in the ancient Kartvelian homeland underlie Georgian. In historical times, speakers of Georgian spread to the west, to part of the Colchian territory, splitting the Colchian language into two dialects and setting up the development of Megrelian and Laz (Chan) into independent languages. They also spread to the north and northeast, displacing languages of the Northeast Caucasian type. These Kartvelian migrations triggered the breakup of Proto-Kartvelian and the expansion of its dialects beyond the original territory.

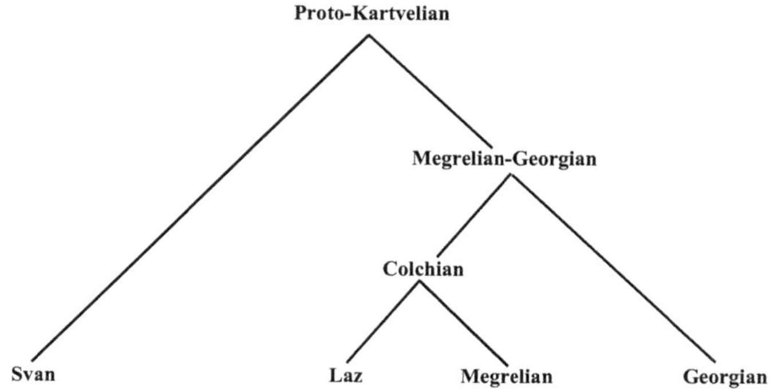

By the fifth century AD, Georgian was already a literary language, and it was taken care of. For the time, Georgian had the features of integration and unification necessary for wide communication; it was a modernized language, accepted and recognized by the Georgian Christian elite. Georgian had already been equipped with the special vocabulary, associated with Christianity and relevant discourses: translated books of the Old and New Testaments, hagiography, hymnography, and both original and translated literature. As investigations have shown, by the beginning of the fifth century, Georgian had already gained a significant social function – a means for *national identification* and *cultural self-establishment*.

Beside standardization, another aspect of language development is *modernization*. It is aimed at making a language similar to other developed languages, to make possible such forms of discourse relevant to a society's interests and goals. In the very initial period of the history of the literary language, significant intrinsic features of Georgian were salient: *flexible stability*, enabling culture-specific modifications, and *intellectualization*, as far as the codified variety of Georgian is different from its vernacular one, and is distinct from other Kartvelian languages in terms of a high degree of artificiality, normally peculiar to normalized languages. The earliest samples of the Georgian literary language demonstrate that, by that period, the language already had functions of *uniting the speech community*, and simultaneously, of *defence and distinction* from other speech communities. Georgian is a standardized language with a centuries-long literary tradition.

The status of Georgian, as of the state language, has never been debatable. Normally, the development of the social role of a literary language has been characterized by two tendencies. They are (1) the tendency of expansion and koineization and (2) establishment of a dominant role and performance of the function of a national feature. It is the common national function that is performed by the Georgian language as far as it has become a foundation of Georgian statehood. It was the Georgian language that was a reason for the establishment of political borders and their change and the localization of centres. It, in turn, was influenced by the migration of Kartvelian tribes and their mutual interference. These were the factors that conditioned the transformation of *Kartli* into *Sakartvelo* "Georgia" and the meaning of *Kartveli* "Georgian." Kartvelian diglossia has a centuries-long history. Kartvelian diglossia started many centuries ago, and the state prestige, as well as the sense of pride in this stable language, has always been associated with Georgian. Diglossia is a stable linguistic situation in which the kin languages cohabit and differ by functions, prestige, literary heritage, standardization, and other characteristics. The relationship between Georgian-Megrelian and Georgian-Svan is an example of the stable, centuries-old sociolinguistic situation called diglossia.

The Georgian literary language can be observed since the 5th century AD. Three periods can be distinguished in its history: Old Georgian literary language (5th–12th centuries), Middle Georgian literary language (12th–18th centuries), and New Georgian literary language (from 19th century onwards).

The Georgian language has de jure determined codified norms that are accepted and shared by the existing community of speakers; hence, it also has factual norms. Modern Georgian is homogeneous (i.e., its vocabulary, phonetics, and syntax arose as a result of the previous stages of its development). The old, middle, and modern Georgian literary languages are only working terms; they do not denote three languages which are different form one another. The Georgian language has a history whose origins are lost in the labyrinths of centuries; it is used by the existing community, and it is homogeneous. The range of the Georgian language is created by literary Georgian and the territorial and social dialects of the language. The Georgian language comprises dialects of western and eastern Georgia. The dialects of the Georgian language used beyond its borders are Ingilo (in Azerbaijan), Imerkheuli (Turkey), Phereidanian (Iran), and Mozdokian and Plastunkian (Russia).

Chapter 2

The Georgian alphabet

There are several theories concerning the origins the Georgian alphabet; the most widely accepted among them attributes its provenance to the Greek alphabet. Historical Georgian documents contain information about the time it was created and the person who created it. *The Life of Kings* provides the following evidence: "This Parnavaz was the first king of Kartli, one of the relatives of Kartlos. He gave popularity to the Georgian language and no other language was spoken in Kartli but Georgian. He also created Georgian writing." The statement presents a logical sequence of events: Parnavaz established the first Georgian principality, legitimized its state language, and consequently, created its writing system, the means for conducting state business. However, no written records of the third century BC and following several centuries have survived, and therefore, this claim is not supported as indisputable fact. If at that time there indeed existed written documents in Georgian, then its alphabet must have originated from the Phoenicians. From this perspective the bilingual stone with Greek and Aramaic texts discovered by Giorgi Tsereteli in East Georgia, near the city of Mtskheta, is of particular interest. The Aramaic letters differ to some extent from the ancient Semitic alphabet; some of its features resembled the Pahlavi (one of the Middle Iranian languages) writings, and some seem closer to the Parthian (also known as Arsacid Pahlavi). In order to establish the origin of this alphabet, the scholar looked at ancient Aramaic and even Phoenician but, finding it different from the both, named it the Armazi writing system.

According to Giorgi Tsereteli, the shape of some Armazi signs resemble Georgian letters. He therefore assumed that the Armazi and Georgian writing systems had a common origin in the Phoenician and ancient Aramaic, as had been suggested by Ivane Javakhishvili. On the basis of palaeographic analysis of Armazi bilingual texts and the known identity of historical personalities mentioned in them, Giorgi Tsereteli concluded that they were created in the

DOI: 10.4324/9781315281131-3

second half (around the '80s) of the first century AD. Since for various reasons the scholar could not decide whether the text was indeed Aramaic, we may assume that the Aramaic words in it are heterograms from some other language. This could have been the widely spread language in Kartli at that time – namely, Persian, which often used Aramaic heterograms. There are some Persian words in the text as well, but the text itself can hardly be defined as Persian. G. Tsereteli assumed that the Armazi text represented a stage of development of Middle Persian before its literary rules were defined. His conclusions come close to the proposition made by Ivane Javakhishvili according to whom Georgian writing system may have been of Semitic origin. It is possible that future archaeological findings will be able to provide the relevant material for this theory.

Another Georgian scholar Ramaz Pataridze considered the information provided by Leonti Mroveli reliable. Parnavaz gave the impetus to the development of a Georgian writing system, but it did not necessarily mean that the alphabet was created during his lifetime. It was possible that Parnavaz popularized some writing system that was in existence before his time. The scholar does not believe that the Georgian alphabet belongs to the western group of writing systems based on the Greek alphabet, since the ideographic and calendar symbolism, which is the property of Georgian letters, is absent in Greek. According to R. Pataridze, the Georgian alphabet, like Aramaic and Greek, is derived directly from Phoenician. *Asomtavruli* (the oldest type of the Georgian alphabet) was formed in semblance to the Phoenician alphabet but with straighter, linear shapes. The ideographic and calendar denotations of graphemes typical for a Semitic writing system support this theory. However, as was mentioned earlier, the best developed and generally accepted theory is the one that posits the Greek origin of the Georgian alphabet. It is convincingly elucidated in the work of Thomas Gamkrelidze in which the author analysis the typology of linear alphabets, comparing each of them to the ancient Greek writing system. In addition to Georgian, a whole range of alphabets, such as Coptic, Gothic, Armenian, and old Slavic, have features similar to the Greek. In the Georgian alphabet, as in the Coptic and Gothic, the sequence of letters followed that of the Greek alphabet with certain phonetic "adjustments" until the point when the sounds, specific to the "recipient" language were introduced. The order and meaning of the Greek graphemes designating numeric value were also preserved in these host languages. Accordingly, the paradigm of the prototype language and the numeric meaning of its graphemes remained basically intact. In the Gothic alphabet, phonetic adjustments to the

Greek letters were sufficient to cover all its specific sounds that were to be represented by graphic symbols. In the Georgian and Coptic alphabets, however, it was necessary to add graphemes corresponding to the specific sounds of these languages. As Ivane Javakhishvili pointed out, the Greek alphabet itself was created in the same manner; the letters designating specifically Greek sounds were added at the end of the Semitic alphabet, on its part adapted from the Phoenician.

The Georgian alphabet went through three stages of transformation: *Asomtavruli* (*Mrgvlovani*), *Nuskhuri*, and *Mkhedruli*. These three types of letters represent a single, unified cycle of graphic development of the graphemes during which the transitions from one type to another happened gradually. In Mrgvlovani, each letter is written between two parallel lines and has a round shape – hence the name Mrgvlovani. In Nuskhuri, the letters are written between four lines and have an angular shape. The alphabet used in modern Georgian is called Mkhedruli. It inherited the round configuration from Mrgvlovani and the distribution of letters between four lines from Nuskhuri.

Asomtavruli (Mrgvlovani)	**Nuskhuri**	**Mkhedruli**
Ⴀ Ⴁ Ⴂ Ⴃ Ⴄ	ⴀ ⴁ ⴂ ⴃ ⴄ	ა ბ გ დ ე

Winfried Boeder and Elene Machavariani focus on the graphic forms of the Georgian alphabet. The letters of Georgian Asomtavruli consist of lines and circles that are joined in such a manner that the shape of any individual grapheme can fit a square. No Georgian grapheme was designed as a certain ideogram, except for the letters Ⴕ (ქ, k^h) and Ⴟ (ჯ, dʒ). Ⴕ is the symbol of the cross on which Christ was crucified, while Ⴟ graphically combines the initial letters of the name იესო ქრისტე (Jesus Christ) in Georgian: Ⴈ + Ⴕ = Ⴟ. It was both the symbol of the crucifixion and the first letter of the word ჯუარი (cross), reflecting its shape and meaning in Mrgvlovani.

Ⴟ ⴈ ⴕ ⴟ

About the same time the letter ჯ came into existence, the graphemes ჳაე and ჳოე must have been created. These three changes most probably happened simultaneously at the time when the Georgian alphabet was reformed in connection with the Christianization of the population living on the territory of Kartli.

There is another theory that suggests the Armenian origin of the Georgian alphabet, but it has been long rejected for a number of reasons. The creator of the Armenian alphabet used an entirely different principle for arranging the graphemes. This discrepancy was noted by Friedrich Muller in spite of the fact that he himself considered Mesrop-Mashtots to be the creator of both alphabets. Muller pointed out that in the Georgian alphabet the specific sounds of Georgian were grouped at the end while in the Armenian alphabet they were distributed throughout. Because of such an arrangement, it is impossible to differentiate the graphemes designating specifically Armenian sounds from the order of the letters corresponding to the Greek original. In addition, all the graphemes designating numeric value of the prototype alphabet (i.e., Old Greek) are left out. All the graphemes of specifically Greek sounds that are absent in Armenian are also ignored; these are Ξ ξὶ (phonetic value *ks*), Ψ πσὶ (phonetic value *ps*), Ω ὠ μέγά (phonetic value *ō*). Thus, instead of the phonetic adjustments to the specifically Greek graphemes, the prototype alphabet was initially cut down so that the remaining letters could correspond to the Armenian sound symbols. It was this skeletal base upon which the ancient Armenian writing system was built. The distribution of the graphemes designating specifically Armenian sounds throughout the alphabet produces an illusion that the Armenian alphabet was not derived from the Greek and obscures its prototype writing system. On the other hand, the Georgian, Coptic, and Gothic alphabets strictly followed the principle of their respective model languages, including their designating numeric value, which was completely ignored by the creator of the Armenian alphabet. It should be mentioned as well that although historical Armenian documents name Mesrop-Mashtots as the creator of the Georgian (in addition to Armenian and Albanian) alphabet, the same documents reveal that he did not know Georgian, thus repudiating the theory that he could have created its writing system. Creating a new alphabet does not amount to inventing graphic symbols; it requires thorough linguistic analysis of the target language and the ability to divide speech into separate sound elements that would be identified by corresponding graphic symbols. It is hardly feasible that a person not fluent in a given language could have come up with an alphabet adequately reflecting its sound system. Ivane Javakhishvili conducted a critical analysis of Coriun's theory about Mesrop-Mashtots' authorship of the three alphabets for Armenian, Georgian, and Albanian languages, and concluded that this assertion must have been a later addition to his text. Javakhishvili referred to the Armenian historian Lazar Parpets' rebuttal of Coriun's work, identifying Mashtots as the author of only the Armenian alphabet. Thus, one of the main flaws of the Armenian theory is rooted in the very historical documents upon which it is based.

Georgian Alphabet and Pronunciation of Sounds

Letters			Name	IPA	Numeric value
Asomtavruli	Nuskhuri	Mkhedruli			
Ⴀ	ⴀ	ა	ani	/a/	1
Ⴁ	ⴁ	ბ	bani	/b/	2
Ⴂ	ⴂ	გ	gani	/g/	3
Ⴃ	ⴃ	დ	doni	/d/	4
Ⴄ	ⴄ	ე	eni	/ɛ/	5
Ⴅ	ⴅ	ვ	vini	/v/	6
Ⴆ	ⴆ	ზ	zeni	/z/	7
Ⴡ	ⴡ	[ჱ]	he	/eɪ/	8
Ⴇ	ⴇ	თ	tani	/$t^{(h)}$/	9
Ⴈ	ⴈ	ი	ini	/i/	10
Ⴉ	ⴉ	კ	k'ani	/k'/	20
Ⴊ	ⴊ	ლ	lasi	/l/	30
Ⴋ	ⴋ	მ	mani	/m/	40
Ⴌ	ⴌ	ნ	nari	/n/	50
Ⴢ	ⴢ	[ჲ]	hie	/je/	60
Ⴍ	ⴍ	ო	oni	/ɔ/	70
Ⴎ	ⴎ	პ	p'ari	/p'/	80
Ⴏ	ⴏ	ჟ	zhani	/ʒ/	90
Ⴐ	ⴐ	რ	rae	/r/	100
Ⴑ	ⴑ	ს	sani	/s/	200
Ⴒ	ⴒ	ტ	t'ari	/t'/	300
Ⴣ		[ჳ]	vie	/uɪ/	400
Ⴓ	ⴓ	უ	uni	/u/	400
Ⴔ	ⴔ	ფ	pari	/$p^{(h)}$/	500
Ⴕ	ⴕ	ქ	kani	/$k^{(h)}$/	600
Ⴖ	ⴖ	ღ	ghani	/ɣ/	700
Ⴗ	ⴗ	ყ	q'ari	/q'/	800
Ⴘ	ⴘ	შ	shini	/ʃ/	900
Ⴙ	ⴙ	ჩ	chini	/$tʃ^{(h)}$/	1000
Ⴚ	ⴚ	ც	tsani	/$ts^{(h)}$/	2000
Ⴛ	ⴛ	ძ	dzili	/dz/	3000
Ⴜ	ⴜ	წ	ts'ili	/ts'/	4000
Ⴝ	ⴝ	ჭ	ch'ari	/tʃ'/	5000
Ⴞ	ⴞ	ხ	klani	/χ/	6000
Ⴤ	ⴤ	[ჴ]	qari, hari	/$q^{(h)}$/	7000
Ⴟ	ⴟ	ჯ	jani	/dʒ/	8000
Ⴠ	ⴠ	ჰ	hae	/h/	9000
Ⴥ	ⴥ	[ჵ]	hoe	/o:/	10000

Phonology

Chapter 3

Sound system of the Georgian language

There are two groups of sounds in the Georgian language: consonants, which never form syllables, and vowels, which always form syllables. Some scholars assume that in the proto-Kartvelian there were sonant sounds that sometimes-formed syllables. Such sounds do not exist in contemporary Georgian (see discussion on this subject in the following section).

3.1 Classification of consonants

The Georgian language consonants are distinguished by the three main phonological combinations: point of articulation, manner of articulations and their voiced or voiceless character. There are no phonologically defined hard or soft consonants in Georgian. They are divided into three groups – triples, pairs and singles.

3.1.1 *Consonant triples*

The triple consonants represent the property that differentiates Georgian from Indo-Germanic languages. The latter have two types of pairs; one consists of the stops and affricates: b – p, d – t, g – k, dʒ (j) – tʃʰ (ch). The other group is composed of fricatives: v – f, z – s.

The Georgian consonant triples consist of stops and affricate consonants, while pairs involve just fricatives. Each set of triple represents a correlation bundle whose members are in phonological opposition to more than one consonant. One type of opposition is between the voiced and voiceless consonants. For example, voiced ბ /b/ can be in opposition both to the voiceless ფ /pʰ/ and პ /p'/. On the other hand, the voiceless consonants oppose each other as aspirated and glottalized consonants, like pʰ-p'. Thus, one consonant enters into more than one phonological opposition: **b-pʰ, b-p', pʰ-p'.**

DOI: 10.4324/9781315281131-5

Articulation manner	Articulation point	Voiced		Voiceless			
				Aspirated		Glottalized	
Stop	Bilabial	ბ	b	ფ	p^h	პ	p'
Stop	Dental	დ	d	თ	t^h	ტ	t'
Affricate	Prealveolar	ძ	dz	ც	ts^h	წ	ts'
Affricate	Postalveolar	ჯ	dʒ	ჩ	$tʃ^h$	ჭ	tʃ'
Stop	Velar	გ	g	ქ	k^h	კ	k'
Stop	Pharyngeal	–		–		ყ	q'

3.1.2 Consonant pairs

The Georgian consonant pairs are composed of fricatives. Within each group, the phonological opposition is based on the voiced and voiceless consonants.

Articulation manner	Articulation point	Voiced		Voiceless	
Fricatives	Labiodental	ვ	v	–	
	Prealveolar	ზ	z	ს	s
	Postalveolar	ჟ	ʒ	შ	ʃ
	Velar	ღ	ʁ	ხ	x
	Laryngeal	–		ჰ	h

3.1.3 Single consonants

There are several consonants that do not enter into either the triple or pair oppositions: რ /r/, ლ /l/, მ /m/, ნ /n/. They used to have sonant character in ancient and proto-Georgian language and in some cases could form syllables.

რ /r/ is a resonant consonant; vocal cords are vibrating during the articulations of this sound.

ლ /l/ is a lateral. During the articulation of this sound, the tongue is shaped like a spoon, and its tip is pushed against the teeth just under the alveolar ridge and retracted again. The air flows between the sides of the tongue and inner walls of the cheeks.

მ /m/ and ნ /n/ are partly nasal sounds. During articulation of these sounds the air flow coming from the lungs is divided, one part coming out from the mouth, the other from the nose.

ჟ /ʒ/ is the least frequently used sound; often it is derivate from the j sonant: ჲ /j/ > ჟ /ʒ/. For example, ჲორდანია *(jordania)* > ჟორდანია *(ʒordania)*.

ჰ /h/ has limited use in Georgian. Words with this consonant in their root are of non-Georgian origin. For example, ჰაერი (air), ჰავა (climate), ჰალოგენი (halogen), რეჰანი (basil) and others. ჰ has only a morphological value and is used as the second-person subject (in Old Georgian) or the third-person object marker: შენ მას ის ჰ-კითხე (you sked him/her about that); მან მას ის ჰ-კითხა (he asked him/her about that) – ჰ-marks the third-person object.

At the root of Georgian original or borrowed words, there are no geminated (i.e. double) consonants. Foreign words used in the Georgian language lose one of their geminated consonants: გრამატიკა (grammar), ესეი (essay), ილუზია (illusion), etc. However, double consonants appear at the junction of morphemes – for example, გემ-ი (ship, nominative), გემ-მა (ergative); კომშ-ი (quince, nominative), კომშ-ში (**in** quince -ში postposition); თბილისი (nominative), and თბილის-ს (to Tbilisi, dative). Double consonants are pronounced as one geminated sound.

3.1.4 Structure of consonant clusters

In Georgian there are two types of consonant clusters in which the front-row consonants occupy the first place followed by the back-row consonants. This can be illustrated with the words like დგას (he is standing) and the compound დგ or თქეში (downpour) with თქ. Such consonant order is also called *harmonious complex*. There are two systems of harmonious complexes in Georgian. Each group consists of four sets of triples. In group A they are followed by the fifth triple (გ – ქ – კ), while in group B the components of the fourth pairs (ღ – ხ) are combined with the consonant ყ since the sixth triple is deficient.

A system

1. ბგ – ფქ – პკ   ბგერა (sound) – ფქვილი (flour) – აპკი (membrane)
2. დგ – თქ – ტკ   დგომა (standing) – თქეში (downpour) – ტკბილი (sweet)
3. ძგ – ცქ – წკ   ძგიდე (edge) – ცქერა (looking) – წკმუტუნი (whimpering)
4. ჯგ – ჩქ – ჭკ   ჯგუფი (group) – ჩქარა (quickly) – ჭკვიანი (intelligent)

B system

1. ბღ – ფხ – პყ   ბღუჯა (handful) – გაზაფხული (spring) – პყრობა (ruling)
2. დღ – თხ – ტყ   დღე (day) – თხილი (hazelnut) – ტყუილი (lie)
3. ძ ღ- ცხ – წყ   ძღვენი (gift) – ცხვირი (nose) – წყლული (wound)
4. ჯღ – ჩხ – ჭყ   ჯღანი (rag) – ჩხავილი (screeching) – ჭყივილი (shrieking)

Georgian is permissive of consonant clustering. Clusters of four, five, or six consonants are usual – for example, **ფხვნ**ილი (crumbled, powder), **ფსკვნ**ილი (knot), and **ფცქვნ**ა peeling (fruits). The maximum number of consonants clustering in a single morpheme is six: **ბრდღვნ**ა (plucking). The number of consonants can increase due to phonetic changes or at the junction of morphemes.

Consonant clustering as a result of syncopation:

მგელი (wolf) → **მგლ**ის (genitive)
ნა**მცხვ**არი (cake) → ნა**მცხვრ**ის (genitive)

Grouping of consonants at the junction of morphemes:

ბრდღვნა (plucking) → **გვბრდღვნ**ის (pinching us)
წვრთნა (to train) → **მწვრთნ**ელი (trainer)

3.2 Classification of vowels

The vowel system of contemporary Georgian is quite simple. It consists of vowels, and the absence of diphthongs makes it even simpler. The vowels are differentiated by the position of the tongue during their articulation: elevated (vertical dimension), back (horizontal dimension), and labialized or rounded.

3.2.1 *Backness*

There are three types of vowels that differ from each other by the position of the tongue relative to the back of the mouth during their articulation.

1. **Front vowels**
   To pronounce the front or palatal vowels ე and ი, the front part of the tongue should rise towards the hard palate.

2. **Middle vowels**
   The vowels of this type are pronounced with the tongue in neutral position. Such is the vowel ა.
3. **Back vowels**
   The back vowels are უ and ო. To articulate these vowels the tongue is positioned as far back as possible in the mouth and raised towards the soft palate. That is why they are called velar vowels. These vowels are labials at the same time.

3.2.2 *Height*

The height of the vowels is measured by the degree of the tongue's elevation to the roof of the mouth or the aperture of the jaw. Accordingly, there are three types of high vowels.

1. **High vowels**
   The high vowels are ი and უ. The front part of the tongue is raised for pronouncing ი and the back part of it for უ. For these vowels, the tongue is positioned as close as possible to the roof of the mouth.
2. **Mid-high vowels**
   The mid-high vowels are ე and ო. The front part of the tongue is raised for pronouncing ე and the back part for ო. By the degree of the tongue's elevation towards the roof of the mouth, these vowels occupy the middle place between the high and low vowels.
3. **Low vowel**
   The low vowel is ა. It is the most open vowel of the Georgian language. To articulate it the tongue is positioned as far as possible from the roof of the mouth.

3.2.3 *Triangle of vowels*

The phonologists often use geometrical figures to illustrate the interrelationship of the vowels within any given system. The vowel system of the Georgian language can be best demonstrated by an upside-down triangle. Its lowest point represents the tip of the tongue where the low vowel ა is placed; to the left are the front vowels ე and ი, and to its right the back vowels ო and უ. The chart shows the vowel height presented with the dotted lines. ე and ო are the middle vowels, while ი and უ are the high vowels. The following triangle indicates also the roundedness of the vowels ო and უ.

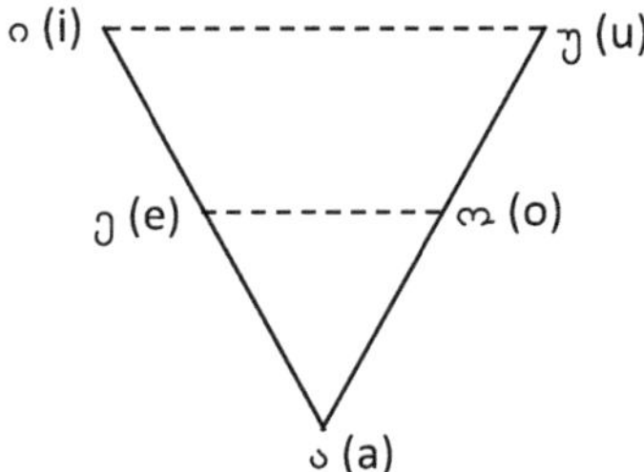

The phonological system of the Georgian language does not include long vowels. However, many vowels can occur side by side at the junction of morphemes – for example, გააკეთა (he did, did). Two ა vowels pronounced as a long ა (a:). Similarly, in მეექვსე (sixth), the double ე is pronounced as one long ე (e:). The word დააარსა (he founded) has three identical vowels. The first vowel retains its length, while the other two are pronounced as one long vowel ა (a:). The clusters of vowels form at the junction of morphemes, especially if the stem of a word begins with several vowels: აიოლებს (it makes it easier), გაუიოლებს (it will make it easier for him), and გააიოლებინა (he helped him to facilitate this).

Morphology

Chapter 4

Nouns

4.1 Noun groups

4.1.1 *Animate and inanimate nouns*

Nouns in Georgian language can be divided into three groups, denoting humans, other animate beings, and inanimate objects. The first group answers to the question ვინ (*who)*, the remaining two to the question რა (what).

ვინ? Who? Whom? Nouns denoting humans		*რა? What? Nouns denoting animate beings*		*რა? What? Nouns denoting inanimate objects*	
კაცი	man	მცენარე	plant	ჰაერი	air
ქალი	woman	ცხოველი	animal	წყალი	water
ბავშვი	child	ფრინველი	bird	ვარსკვლავი	star
სტუდენტი	student	თევზი	fish	შენობა	building
მოსწავლე	pupil	მწერი	insect	სკამი	chair

The category of a noun also determines which of the two possible versions of the verb *to have* should be used with it: ***ყოლა*** (*მ-ყავ-ს*, I have someone or something animate) or ***ქონ(ებ)ა*** (*მ-აქვ-ს*, I have something inanimate). The former refers to humans, as well as everything animate, the latter only to inanimate objects.

*მე **მყავს** მეგობარი.* – Who?
I have a friend.
*შენ **გყავს** ძაღლი.* – What?
You have a dog.
*მას **აქვს** დიდი ბინა.* – What?
He has a large apartment.

DOI: 10.4324/9781315281131-7

Similarly, the verb *to take* (in, out, over, etc.) with stems **ყვან-**, **ტან-**, or **ღებ-** is used, depending on the category of a noun to which it refers; the first one (**ყვან-**) is for an *animate* object and the last two (**ტან-**and **ღებ-**) for an *inanimate* object.

*დედა ბავშვს სკოლაში წაი**ყვან**ს.* – Whom?
Mother will take her child to school.
*დედა წიგნს სკოლაში წაი**ღებ**ს.* – What?
Mother will take the book to school.
*ბებიამ კატა ოთახში შეი**ყვან**ა.* – What?
Grandmother took the cat into the room.
*ბიჭმა ბურთი სახლში შეი**ტან**ა.* – What?
The boy took his ball into the house.

The exception to this rule is words denoting different kind of the vehicles (e.g. a car, a bicycle, a boat, etc.). They are often used with the verb ***to have*** for animate beings. However, the interrogative pronoun referring to these nouns should be **რა**, not **ვინ**.

*მე ორი მანქანა მ**ყავ**ს.*
I have two cars.
*შენ **რა გყავს**, ფორდი თუ ტოიოტა?*
What do you have, Ford or Toyota?
*გიამ ველოსიპედი გარაჟში შეი**ყვან**ა.*
Gia took/drove the bicycle into the garage.

4.1.2 Concrete and abstract nouns

Concrete nouns refer to material objects, both the animate and inanimate – child, mountain, river, etc.; abstract nouns represent ideas, notions, concepts, etc. – fear, pressure, philosophy, etc. Abstract nouns can be formed by using suffixes and circumfixes, mostly with -ობა, -ება, სი-ე, and სი-ო, added to various nouns and adjectives:

-ობა	-ება	სი-ე	სი-ო
მშვიდ-ობა peace	ბედნიერ-ება happiness	სი-მწარ-ე bitterness	სი-თბ-ო warmth
გრძნ-ობა feeling	ძლიერ-ება strength	სი-ლამაზ-ე beauty	სი-ტკბ-ო sweetness
ახალგაზრდ-ობა youth	აღტაც -ება excitement	სი-მდიდრ-ე wealth	სი-ლბ-ო softness

1. If the stem of a noun ends with the consonant -ვ preceded with a vowel, the -ვ will be dropped when followed by the suffix -ობა:

   თავ-ი (head)   თა-ობა (generation)   but ბავშვი ბავშვ-ობა

2. If a noun ends with the vowels -ა or -ე, the consonant -ვ- will be added to its stem when the circumfix სი-ე is used to form an abstract noun:

	კოხტა comely	სი-კოხტა ვ-ე comeliness
but	ყრუ deaf	სი-ყრუ-ე deafness
	ფართო wide	სი-ფართო ვ-ე width
	ცრუ liar	სი-ცრუ-ე lie

Unlike concrete nouns, abstract nouns do not have plural forms.

4.1.3 *Proper and common nouns*

Proper nouns designate a specific object or human being. They include the personal names, pseudonyms, geographic names, names of the newspapers, book titles, planets, etc. Common nouns refer to a class of entities designating people, places, concepts, organisations, etc.

Common nouns	*Proper nouns*
ქვეყანა country	საქართველო Georgia
ქალაქი city	თბილისი, ქუთაისი, სოხუმი Tbilisi, Kutaisi, Sokhumi
მდინარე river	მტკვარი, რიონი, ენგური Mtkvari/Kura, Rioni, Enguri
სახელი given name	ლუკა, ილია, აკაკი Luka, Ilia, Akaki
გვარი last name	ჭავჭავაძე, წერეთელი Chavchavadze, Tsereteli
ფსევდონიმი pseudonym	ვაჟა-ფშაველა Vazha-Pshavela

(Continued)

(Continued)

Common nouns	*Proper nouns*
ნაწარმოები literary work	„ვეფხისტყაოსანი" "The Knight in Panther's Skin"
გაზეთი newspaper	„ივერია", „დროება" "Iveria", "Droeba"

The titles and names of newspapers, magazines, specific TV programs, cafés, etc. are put in quotation marks:

> *ჩვენს ქუჩაზე არის კაფე* ***„მაია."***
> There is a café "Maya" on our street.
> ***„ვეფხისტყაოსანი"*** *დაწერა შოთა რუსთაველმა.*
> Shota Rustaveli wrote "The Knight in the Panther's Skin."

4.1.4 Collective nouns

A collective noun is a word for a group of specific items, animals, or people.

Noun denoting a single object	*Collective nouns*
ადამიანი human being	ხალხი people
მოსწავლე pupil	კლასი class
მსახიობი actor	დასი cast
ძროხა cow	ნახირი herd
ღორი pig	კოლტი drove of pigs
თხა goat	არვე trip of goats
ჩიტი bird	გუნდი flock
გემი ship	ფლოტი fleet

Collective nouns require verbs in singular form.

> *გუშინ თეატრში ბევრი* ***ხალხი იყო.***
> Yesterday there were a lot of people in the theatre.
> ***პოლიციამ*** *დამნაშავე* ***დააპატიმრა.***
> The police arrested the perpetrator.

If a collective noun is in its plural form, the verb correlated to it is also in plural.

> *ზოგიერთი თეორიის მიხედვით,* ***ერები*** *მეცხრამეტე საუკუნეში ჩამოყალიბდნენ.*
> According to some theories, **the nations** were formed in the nineteenth century.

Abstract nouns may be used to express an idea of a collective:

> *მე ხშირად ვფიქრობ ჩემს* ***ახალგაზრდობაზე.***
> I often think about my **youth.**
> *საქართველოს* ***ახალგაზრდობა*** *დემოკრატიისათვის იბრძვის.*
> **The youth** of Georgia is fighting for democracy.

In the second sentence, the abstract noun "youth" is used as a collective noun.

4.1.5 Noncount nouns

There is a group of nouns that denote the concrete objects, but they cannot be counted: ***წყალი*** (water), ***პური*** (bread), ***ფქვილი*** (flour), ***მარილი*** (salt), ***შაქარი*** (sugar), ***ღვინო*** (wine), and other similar entities. They require verbs in a singular form and are not used in a plural form except in some specific cases, such as in the following:

> *ქართული* ***ღვინოები*** *მსოფლიოში ცნობილია.*
> Georgian **wines** are famous throughout the world.

4.2 Grammatical categories of nouns

The nouns in Georgian have two grammatical categories: case and number. In archaic Georgian it had the category of definiteness denoted with articles. It has not completely disappeared and can be expressed with various means. For example, *ერთი კაცი* literally means *one man*, but in some contexts, it may mean *a man*, *a certain man*, or *a person*, not necessarily referring to the number of men. The indefinite pronoun ვიღაც (someone, some) also functions as an indefinite article:

ვიღაც კაცმა ჩაიარა.
Some man/a man passed by.

4.2.1 Case and number markers

In contemporary Georgian the noun forms correspond to the principles of agglutinative languages – i.e. the cases of nouns and their plural forms both have their corresponding markers. There are seven cases, all based on the stem of a noun. The suffix **-ებ** added to the stem of a noun changes it from a singular to plural form:

კაც-ი // **კაც-ებ-ი** (man/men)
სახლ-**ი** // სახლ-**ებ-ი** (house/s)
კატ-ა // კატ-**ებ-ი** (cat/s)

The case markers of nouns in plural follow the suffix -ებ. In addition, the archaic plural forms are still used in modern Georgian. Their declension markers differ from the regular plural forms; the suffix -ნ marks the plural in the nominative and vocative cases, and the suffix -თა indicates both the number and case in the ergative, dative, and genitive cases.

Case names in Georgian	*Case names in English*	*Case endings in singular*	*Endings of case and plural*	*Endings of case and archaic plural*
სახელობითი	Nominative	-ი	-ებ-ი	-ნ-ი
მოთხრობითი	Ergative	-მა/მ-	-ებ-მა	-თა
მიცემითი	Dative	-ს	-ებ-ს	-თა
ნათესაობითი	Genitive	-ის/-ს	-ებ-ის	-თა
მოქმედებითი	Instrumental	-ით/-თ(ი)	-ებ-ით	–
ვითარებითი	Adverbial	-ად/-დ	-ებ-ად	–
წოდებითი	Vocative	-ო	-ებ -ო	-ნ-ო

The stem of a noun can be determined by putting it in the ergative or dative case since here the stem is constant and does not change. The type of the stem and its declension pattern can be determined by removing the case markers. For example, the noun **წიგნ-ი** (book) in the ergative case is **წიგნ-მა**. Thus, its stem has consonant ending, and therefore, it is not syncopated. The noun

მაგიდა (table) in the ergative case is *მაგიდა-მ*. Here we have a vowel-ending stem which is truncated – i.e. the final vowel will be dropped in two cases, the genitive and instrumental.

4.2.2 *Function of cases*

The **nominative case** designates the following:

1. Subject of all conjugation verbs in I series (See 9.6.1.)

   ბავშვ-ი ხატავს სახლს.
   The child paints/is painting a house

2. Subject of II and IV conjugation verbs in all series

   ბანკ-ი შარშან გაკოტრდა.
   The bank went bankrupt last year.

3. Direct object of I conjugation verbs in II and III series (See 9.6.2.)

   მომღერალმა იმღერა ***სიმღერა.***
   The singer sang the song.

   ბავშვ-მა დახატა ***სახლ-ი.***
   The child painted a house.

The **ergative case** designates the subject of I and III conjugations verbs in II series.

> ***პროფესორ-მა*** *ლექცია* ***დაიწყო.***
> The professor started his lecture.
> ***მამა-მ*** *ბილეთები უკვე* ***იყიდა.***
> Father already bought the tickets.
> ***ბებია-მ*** *დიდ ხანს იცოცხლა.*
> Grandmother lived long.

The **dative case** designates the following:

1. The subject of the I and III conjugation verbs in III series

   ბავშვ-ს *სახლი დაუხატავს.*
   The child has painted a house.
   ბავშვ-ს *სათამაშო გაუტეხავს.*
   The child has broken a toy.

2. The direct objects of I conjugation verbs in I series

   ბავშვ-ი ხატავს ***სახლ-ს.***
   The child paints/is painting a house.

3. The indirect objects of I conjugation verbs in I and II series

   ბავშვი ***მეგობარ-ს*** *უხატავს სახლს.*
   The child paints/is painting a house for a friend.
   ბავშვ-მა ***მეგობარ-ს*** *დაუხატა სახლი.*
   The child has painted a house for a friend.

4. The indirect objects of II and IV conjugation verbs in all series

   დედა ***ბავშვ-ს*** *ეთამაშება* (II conjugation)
   დედა-ს ბავშვი უყვარს (Conjugation IV)

The **genitive case** designates the following:

1. Ownership

   მწერლ-ის ნაწარმოებ-ი
   Works of the writer
   წიგნ-ის ავტორ-ი
   The author of the book (the modified noun belongs to the modifier)

2. Material

   აგურ-ის სახლ-ი
   A brick house (house of brick)

3. Function

   ჩაი-ს ჭიქა
   Teacup (a cup for tea)
   მე თბილის-ის უნივერსიტეტ-ის *სტუდენტი ვარ.*
   I am a student at the Tbilisi University
   ბანკ-ის დირექტორ-ის მეგობრ-ის *სახელი იცი?*
   Do you know the name of the friend of the bank director ([the] bank's director's friend's name)?

The instrumental case

Generally, the nouns in the instrumental case indicate tools or other implements that are used to perform an action. In English, these nouns require use of the prepositions *with* or *by*.

ჩიკაგოში ***მატარებლ-ით*** *მივდივარ.*
I am going to Chicago **by train**.
ეს ხალიჩა ***ხელ-ით*** *არის მოქსოვილი.*
This rug is handmade (i.e. woven **by hand**).

მეტროს სადგურამდე **ფეხ-ით** მივდივართ.
I walk (i.e. go **on foot**) till the subway station.
Instrumental case is also used to form adverbs of time.
დილ-ით წვიმდა, ახლა კი მზეა.
It rained in the morning, now it's sunny.
არ მიყვარს **ღამ-ით** მგზავრობა.
I do not like travelling **by night**.

The adverbial case

1. This case ending may be added to nouns, adjectives, numerals, and pronouns to form various types of adverbs.

   ამ ქალს ყოველთვის **ლამაზ-ად** (ლამაზ-ი) აცვია.
   This woman is always dressed beautifully.
   ჩვენ **ერთ-ად** (ერთ-ი) წავალთ თეატრში.
   We will go to the theatre together.
   ისინი **ხშირ-ად** (ხშირ-ი) მოდიან ჩვენთან.
   They often visit us.
   ჩუმ-ად (ჩუმ-ი) იყავით!
   Be quiet!

2. In addition, the adverbial case is used to denote a transformation.

   ჩვენი სოფელი **ქალაქ-ად** იქცა.
   Our village turned **into a town.**
   ტყე **მინდვრ-ად** იქცა.
   The forest has turned **into a field.**
   ირაკლი **დირექტორ-ად** დანიშნეს.
   (They) appointed Irakli **as the director**.
   ეს ფიცარი **მაგიდ-ად** გამოვიყენე.
   (I) used this wooden board **as a table.**

The vocative case

This case is used when addressing a person.

მეგობარო, სადა ხარ?
Friend, where are you?
დედა, აქა ხარ?
Mom, are you here?

Given names do not take the vocative marker – ო (o). The nouns *mother* (დედა) and *father* (მამა) behave also like proper nouns. The Georgian word for *mother* in the vocative case with a vocative case marker has a very specific application. It is used only while addressing a nun or, in prayers, to Virgin Mary.

Nom. დედა Voc. **დედა-ო** *v* Mother

დედა-ო ღვთისა-ვ, წმინდა-ო მარიამ!
Mother of God, Saint Mary!

Nom. მამა Voc. **მამა-ო** Father

მამა, დედა სად არის?
Dad, where is Mom?

The vocative form of this word is used only when addressing a priest.

*შემინდე, **მამაო!***
Forgive (my sins), Father!

Nom. *ღმერთ-ი* Voc. ***ღმერთ-ო***! God!

Apart from prayers, the most frequently used expression with this form is **ღმერთო ჩემო!** *My God!* The word order in this expression is always reversed.

4.3 Declension of nouns

4.3.1 Declension of common nouns

4.3.1.1 Declension of consonant-stem non-syncopating common nouns

In Georgian, the consonant-stem non-syncopating nouns do not have any distinguishing features except when their final consonant is the same as the initial consonant of a case marker. Such nouns will have their stem ending consonant doubled: ***სკამ-მა, თას-ს.***

	Singular		*Plural*	
Case names	*chair*	*cup*	*chairs*	*cups*
Nominative	სკამ-ი	თას-ი	სკამ-ებ ი	თას-ებ-ი
Ergative	**სკამ-მა**	თას-მა	სკამ-ებ-მა	თას-ებ-მა
Dative	სკამ-ს	**თას-ს**	სკამ-ებ-ს	თას-ებ-ს
Genitive	სკამ-ის	თას-ის	სკამ-ებ-ის	თას-ებ-ის
Instrumental	სკამ-ით	თას-ით	სკამ-ებ-ით	თას-ებ-ით
Adverbial	სკამ-ად	თას-ად	სკამ-ებ-ად	თას-ებ-ად
Vocative	სკამ-ო	თას-ო	სკამ-ებ -ო	თას-ებ-ო

4.3.1.2 *Declension of consonant-stem syncopating common nouns*

The consonant-stem nouns are syncopated – i.e. the vowel in the last syllable of their root is dropped, mostly if they end with the following syllables:

ალ: ბ-ალ, წყ-ალ, ჩანგ-ალ, თებერვ-ალ, ხერხემ-ალ
ამ: კალ-ამ, ქათ-ამ, ვახშ-ამ
ან: საგ-ან, უბ-ან, მტევ-ან, მოედ-ან, ქოთ-ან
არ: სტუმ-არ, ჯვ-არ, ჭიშკ-არ, სიზმ-არ

ელ: სოფ-ელ, ტანსაცმ-ელ, სავარცხ-ელ, კურდღ-ელ
ემ: ირ-ემ, ურ-ემ
ენ: შევარდ-ენ, ყურძ-ენ
ერ: მტ-ერ, ოფიც-ერ, კის-ერ, მწყ-ერ, საც-ერ

ოლ: ობ-ოლ, ფოთ-ოლ, გოდ-ოლ
ონ: საპ-ონ
ორ: გოდ-ორ, ქოჩ-ორ, კოკ-ორ

The nouns ending with the syllables listed here are syncopated only in three cases when declined in singular forms – the genitive, instrumental, and adverbial – and in all cases in plural forms.

სოფელი → სოფ□ლ-ის[1] *სოფ□ლ-ებ-ი* *სოფ□ლ-ებ-ის*
საპონ-ი → საპ□ნ-ის *საპ□ნ-ებ-ი* *საპ□ნ-ებ-ის*
გოდორ-ი → გოდ□რ-ის *გოდ□რ-ებ-ი* *გოდ□რ-ებ-ის*

There are a few nouns with the stem syllables **-ონ** and **-ორ** in which the vowel **ო** may undergo reduction and change into the consonant *-ვ* in the same three cases, the genitive, instrumental, and adverbial:

მონაზონ → მონაზვ ნ-ის *მონაზვნ-ებ-ის*
მაწონ-ი → მაწვნ-ის *მაწ ვნ-ებ-ის*
მინდორ-ი → მინდვრ-ის *მინდვრ-ებ-ის*
ნიგოზ-ი → ნიგვზ-ის *ნიგვზ-ებ-ის*

Syncopating syllables

	-ალ *water*	*-ამ* *pen*	*-ან* *object*	*-არ* *guest*
Nom.	წყალ-ი	კალამ-ი	საგან-ი	სტუმარ-ი
Gen.	წყ□ლ-ის	კალ□მ-ის	საგ□ნ-ის	სტუმ□რ-ის

[1] Here and in the following cases, □ marks the sound dropped because of phonetic changes.

	-ალ	-ამ	-ან	-არ
	water	*pen*	*object*	*guest*
Instr.	წყ□ლ-ით	კალ□მ-ით	საგ□ნ-ით	სტუმ□რ-ით
Adv.	წყ□ლ-ად	კალ□მ-ად	საგ□ნ-ად	სტუმ□რ-ად

	-ელ	-ემ	-ენ	-ერ
	village	*deer*	*grape*	*enemy*
Nom.	სოფელ-ი	ირემ-ი	ყურძენ-ი	მტერ-ი
Gen.	სოფ□ლ-ის	ირ□მ-ის	ყურძ□ნ-ის	მტ□რ-ის
Instr.	სოფ□ლ-ით	ირ□მ-ით	ყურძ□ნ-ით	მტ□რ-ით
Adv.	სოფ□ლ-ად	ირმ□ად	ყურძ□ნ-ად	მტ□რ-ად

	-ოლ	-ორ		-ონ
	orphan	*basket*	*field*	*nun*
Nom.	ობოლ-ი	გოდორ-ი	მინდორ-ი	მონაზონ-ი
Gen.	ობ□ლ-ის	გოდ□რ-ის	მინდ ვ რ-ის	მონაზ ვ ნ-ის
Instr.	ობ□ლ-ით	გოდ□რ-ით	მინდ ვ რ-ით	მონაზ ვ ნ-ით
Adv.	ობ□ლ-ად	გოდ□რ-ად	მინდ ვ რ-ად	მონაზ ვ ნ-ად

Declension of syncopating nouns

	Singular *peach*	*Plural* *peaches*	*Archaic* *plural*
Nom.	ატამ-ი	ატ□მ-ებ ი	ატამ-ნ-ი
Erg.	ატამ-მა	ატ□მ-ებ-მა	ატამ-თა
Dat.	ატამ-ს	ატ□მ-ებ-ს	ატამ-თა
Gen.	ატ□მ-ის	ატ□მ-ებ-ის	ატამ-თა
Instr.	ატ□მ-ით	ატ□მ-ებ-ით	–
Adv.	ატ□მ-ად	ატ□მ-ებ-ად	–
Voc.	ატამ-ო	ატ□მ-ებ -ო	ატამ-ნ-ო

	Singular *leaf*	*Plural* *leaves*	*Archaic* *plural*
Nom.	ფოთოლ-ი	ფოთ□ლ-ებ-ი	ფოთოლ-ნ-ი
Erg.	ფოთოლ-მა	ფოთ□ლ-ებ-მა	ფოთოლ-თა
Dat.	ფოთოლ-ს	ფოთ□ლ-ებ-ს	ფოთოლ-თა
Gen.	ფოთ□ლ-ის	ფოთ□ლ-ებ-ის	ფოთოლ-თა
Instr.	ფოთ□ლ-ით	ფოთ□ლ-ებ-ით	–
Adv.	ფოთ□ლ-ად	ფოთ□ლ -ებ-ად	–
Voc.	ფოთოლ-ო	ფოთ□ლ-ებ-ო	ფოთოლ-ნ-ო

	Singular	
	garlic	*yogurt*
Nom.	ნიორ-ი	მაწონ-ი
Erg.	ნიორ-მა	მაწონ-მა
Dat.	ნიორ-ს	მაწონ-ს
Gen.	ნივრ-ის	მაწვნ-ის
Instr.	ნივრ-ით	მაწვნ-ით
Adv.	ნივრ-ად	მაწვნ--ად
Voc.	ნიორ-ო	მაწონ-ო

There are a few nouns that undergo syncopation even when they do not fit the structural pattern of syncopating stems. Thus, the vowel ***-ე*** is syncopated in the noun ***ბეჭედ-ი*** (ring, stamp), although it does not end with any of the syllables listed earlier. Another such exception is the noun ***კარავ-ი*** (tent), which has the vowel -ა syncopating stem.

	Singular *ring, stamp*	*Plural* *rings, stamps*	*Archaic* *plural*
Nom.	ბეჭედ-ი	ბეჭ□დ-ებ-ი	ბეჭედ-ნ-ი
Erg.	ბეჭედ-მა	ბეჭ□დ-ებ-მა	ბეჭედ-თა
Dat.	ბეჭედ-ს	ბეჭ□დ-ებ-ს	ბეჭედ-თა
Gen.	ბეჭ□დ-ის	ბეჭ□დ-ებ-ის	ბეჭედ-თა
Instr.	ბეჭ□დ-ით	ბეჭ□დ-ებ-ით	–
Adv.	ბეჭ□დ-ად	ბეჭ□დ -ებ-ად	–
Voc.	ბეჭედ-ო	ბეჭ□დ-ებ-ო	ბეჭედ-ნ-ო

	Singular *tent*	*Plural* *tents*	*Archaic* *plural*
Nom.	კარავ-ი	კარ□ვ-ებ-ი	კარავ-ნ-ი
Erg.	კარავ-მა	კარ□ვ-ებ-მა	კარავ-თა
Dat.	კარავ-ს	კარ□ვ-ებ-ს	კარავ-თა
Gen.	კარ□ვ-ის	კარ□ვ-ებ-ის	კარავ-თა
Instr.	კარ□ვ-ით	კარ□ვ-ებ-ით	–
Adv.	კარ□ვ-ად	კარ□ვ -ებ-ად	–
Voc.	კარავ-ო	კარ□ვ-ებ-ო	კარავ-ნ-ო

Not all nouns with the listed stem syllables are syncopating:

ხელ-ი: *ხელ-ის, ხელ-ით, ხელ-ად (hand)*
ფერ-ი: *ფერ-ის, ფერ-ით, ფერ-ად (colour)*
ტან-ი: *ტან-ის, ტან-ით, ტან-ად (body)*
ქარ-ი: *ქარ-ის, ქარ-ით, ქარ-ად (wind)*
წერილ-ი: *წერ-ილ-ის, წერ-ილ-ით, წერ-ილ-ად (letter)*
გამზრდელ-ი: *გამზრდელ-ის, გამზრდელ-ით, გამზრდელ-ად (nurse)*

The majority of one-syllable stems with consonant-vowel-consonant (CVC) structure do not have a syncope:

ქალ-ი	სარ-ი	ბარ-ი
woman	*stick, stake*	*spade*

However, there are some exceptions:

წელ-ი – წ□ლ-ის	ხან-ი – ხ□ნ-ის	ბალ-ი – ბ□ლ-ის
year	*period*	*cherry*

The same happens with the stems where these syllables are preceded with VV configuration:

როიალი	**ბოდიალი**	**გრიალი**
grand piano	*incoherent speech*	*thundering*

No syncopation occurs in the reduplicated stems:

ჩანჩალი	**ჯაყჯაყი**
dragging feet	*riding in a dilapidated vehicle*

It is possible that the stem syncopation depends on the stress and changing number of syllables in any given word. The following words illustrate this rule – *კარი* (door) and *დარი* (weather). Their stems do not syncopate but when they become a part of composite words, the increased number of syllables and movable stress of the Georgian language causes syncopation to occur. *კარი* and *დარი* are two-syllable words, and stress is on their stem vowel. In three-syllable composites like *ცისკარი* (dawn) and *ავდარი* (increment weather), stress is on the first syllable, and thus, the syllable *არ* loses its defence.

ცის+კარ-ი → ცისკ□რ-ის, ცისკ□რ-ით, ცისკ□რ-ად;
ავ+დარ-ი → ავდ□რ-ის, ავდ□რ-ით, ავდ□რ-ად.

The same rule applies to the following nouns:

ჭიშ+კარ-ი (gate) → *ჭიშკ□რ-ის, ჭიშკ□რ-ით, ჭიშკ□რ-ად*
დედა+ბერ-ი (old woman) → *დედაბ□რ-ის, დედაბ□რ-ით, დედაბ□რ-ად*
ნია+ღვარ-ი (torent) → *ნიაღვ□რ-ის, ნიაღვ□რ-ით, ნიაღვ□რ-ად*

Accordingly, it seems logical that *ალუბალ-ი* (sour cherry) is syncopated in the genitive, instrumental, and adverbial, but it is difficult to explain why *ბალ-ი* (cherry) is syncopating *(ბლ-ის, ბლ-ით, ბლ-ად)*, while *ქალ-ი* (woman) is not, and therefore, we have *ქალ-ის, ქალ-ით, ქალ-ად.*

There are many examples when the usually syncopating syllables in the consonant-stem nouns do not follow the rule. This happens with the native Georgian and borrowed stems alike.

- **ალ:** ქ-ალ (woman), ვ-ალ (debt), გრიგ-ალ (hurricane), მწვერვ-ალ (summit), დეტ-ალ (detail)
- **ამ:** წ-ამ (second), გრ-ამ (gram), გვ-ამ (corpse), სკ-ამ (chair), ქრთ-ამ (bribe)
- **ან:** ბ-ან (bass), ბან-ან (banana), ინტრიგ-ან (intrigant)
- **არ:** ბ-არ (spade), გვ-არ (last name), ლ-არ (standard monetary unit of Georgia)
- **ელ:** ვ-ელ (field), ფრინვ-ელ (bird), სახ-ელ (name), აკვარ-ელ (watercolour)
- **ემ:** გ-ემ (ship), თ-ემ (tribe), ჯ-ემ (jam), კრ-ემ (cream), აქლ-ემ (camel), ტოტ-ემ (totem)
- **ენ:** ცხ-ენ (horse), წვ-ენ (juice), ზვიგ-ენ (shark), ორდ-ენ (order), აბორიგ-ენ (aborigine)

– **ერ:** ბ-ერ (monk), გ-ერ (stepchild), წვ-ერ (beard), შპალ-ერ (wallpaper)
– **ოლ:** რგ-ოლ (circle), ბრ-ოლ (crystal), საწ-ოლ (bed), ბანდერ-ოლ (package)
– **ონ:** გარმ-ონ (accordion), ლით-ონ (steel), კოც-ონ (bonfire), იად-ონ (canary)
– **ორ:** ლ-ორ (ham), ამბ-ორ (kiss), ტბ-ორ (puddle), ავტ-ორ (author), ინკუბატ-ორ (incubator)

	Singular woman	*Plural women*	*Archaic plural*
Nom.	ქალ-ი	ქალ-ებ-ი	ქალ-ნ-ი
Erg.	ქალ-მა	ქალ-ებ-მა	ქალ-თა
Dat.	ქალ-ს	ქალ-ებ-ს	ქალ-თა
Gen.	ქალ-ის	ქალ-ებ-ის	ქალ-თა
Instr.	ქალ-ით	ქალ-ებ-ით	–
Adv.	ქალ-ად	ქალ-ებ-ად	–
Voc.	ქალ-ო	ქალ-ებ-ო	ქალ-ნ-ო

	Singular horse	*Plural horses*	*Archaic plural*
Nom.	ცხენ-ი	ცხენ-ებ ი	ცხენ-ნ-ი
Erg.	ცხენ-მა	ცხენ-ებ-მა	ცხენ-თა
Dat.	ცხენ-ს	ცხენ-ებ-ს	ცხენ-თა
Gen.	ცხენ-ის	ცხენ-ებ-ის	ცხენ-თა
Instr.	ცხენ-ით	ცხენ-ებ-ით	–
Adv.	ცხენ-ად	ცხენ-ებ-ად	–
Voc.	ცხენ-ო	ცხენ-ებ -ო	ცხენ-ნ-ო

It is possible that the word **კოცონი** does not syncopate because it would be confused with the noun კოცნა (kiss) in its genitive, instrumental, and adverbial cases: კოცნ-ის, კოცნ-ით, კოცნ-ად.

	Singular bonfire	*Plural bonfires*	*Archaic plural*
Nom.	კოცონ-ი	კოცონ-ებ-ი	კოცონ-ნ-ი
Erg.	კოცონ-მა	კოცონ-ებ-მა	კოცონ-თა
Dat.	კოცონ-ს	კოცონ-ებ-ს	კოცონ-თა
Gen.	კოცონ-ის	კოცონ-ებ-ის	კოცონ-თა
Instr.	კოცონ-ით	კოცონ-ებ-ით	–
Adv.	კოცონ-ად	კოცონ-ებ-ად	–
Voc.	კოცონ-ო	კოცონ-ებ-ო	კოცონ-ნ-ო

4.3.1.3 *Consonant-stem common nouns with irregular syncopation patterns*

As it was illustrated, the syncopation is expected when a stem has its final syllable with vowels ა /a/, ე /e/, or ო /o/, followed by the consonants ლ /l/, მ /m/, ნ /n/, or რ /r/. The stems with the final syllable -**ავ** may also syncopate **კარ-ავ** (tent) – **კარვის** and **ნაგ-ავ** (garbage) – **ნაგვის.** There are nouns in which the entire syllable -**ავ** is dropped, like in the noun ამბავ-**ი** (occurrence, happening, fact).

	Singular occurrence	*Plural occurrences*	*Archaic plural*
Nom.	ამბავ-ი	ამბ□□-ებ ი	ამბავ-ნ-ი
Erg.	ამბავ-მა	ამბ□□-ებ-მა	ამბავ-თა
Dat.	ამბავ-ს	ამბ□□-ებ-ს	ამბავ-თა
Gen.	ამბ□□-ის	ამბ□□-ებ-ის	ამბავ-თა
Instr.	ამბ□□-ით	ამბ□□-ებ-ით	–
Adv.	ამბ□□-ად	ამბ□□-ებ-ად	–
Voc.	ამბავ-ო	ამბ□□-ებ -ო	ამბავ-ნ-ო

Quite a few nouns with the stem syllable -ავ do not syncopate. For example: იგავ-ი (fable) იგავ-ის, იგავ-ით, იგავ-ად

ჭვავ-ი (rye) ჭვავ-ის, ჭვავ-ით, ჭვავ-ად
სვავ-ი (vulture) სვავ-ის, სვავ-ით, სვავ-ად

ჭილყვავ-ი (rook) ჭილყვავ-ის, ჭილყვავ-ით, ჭილყვავ-ად
ნაწნავ-ი (braid) ნაწნავ-ის, ნაწნავ-ით, ნაწნავ-ად

The noun *ღმერთ-ი* (God) also has an irregular declension; its stem in the genitive, instrumental, and adverbial may change into *ღვთ-*.

	Singular god	*Plural gods*	*Archaic plural*
Nom.	ღმერთ-ი	ღმერთ-ებ ი	ღმერთ-ნ-ი
Erg.	ღმერთ-მა	ღმერთ-ებ-მა	ღმერთ-თა
Dat.	ღმერთ-ს	ღმერთ-ებ-ს	ღმერთ-თა
Gen.	ღმერთ-ის // **ღვთ-ის**	ღმერთ-ებ-ის	ღმერთ-თა
Inst.	ღმერთ-ით // **ღვთ-ით**	ღმერთ-ებ-ით	–
Adv.	ღმერთ-ად // **ღვთ-ად**	ღმერთ-ებ-ად	–
Voc.	ღმერთ-ო	ღმერთ-ებ -ო	ღმერთ-ნ-ო

The meaning of some nouns depends on whether or not their stems are syncopated. When the noun *თვალ-ი* denotes the human organ *eye* or is used metaphorically, like *eye of the hurricane* or *eye of the sun*, its stem is not syncopated. However, the word *თვალი* may refer to a cartwheel or car tire, as well as to precious stones, like ruby and topaz. In the latter meanings it has a syncopating stem in singular forms of the genitive, instrumental, and adverbial cases, and the declension of its plural form is based on its syncopated stem.

თვალი – eye, human organ			
Nom.	თვალ-ი	თვალ-ებ-ი	თვალ-ნ-ი
Erg.	თვალ-მა	თვალ-ებ-მა	თვალ-თა
Dat.	თვალ-ს	თვალ-ებ-ს	თვალ-თა
Gen.	თვალ-ის	თვალ-ებ-ის	თვალ-თა
Instr.	თვალ-ით	თვალ-ებ-ით	–
Adv.	თვალ-ად	თვალ-ებ-ად	–
Voc.	თვალ-ო	თვალ-ებ -ო	თვალ-ნ-ო

თვალი – precious stone, wheel			
Nom.	თვალ-ი	თვ□ლ-ებ-ი	თვალ-ნ-ი
Erg.	თვალ-მა	თვ□ლ-ებ-მა	თვალ-თა
Dat.	თვალ-ს	თვ□ლ-ებ-ს	თვალ-თა
Gen.	თვ□ლ-ის	თვ□ლ-ებ-ის	თვალ-თა
Instr.	თვ□ლ-ით	თვ□ლ-ებ-ით	–
Adv.	თვ□ლ-ად	თვ□ლ-ებ-ად	–
Voc.	თვალ-ო	თვ□ლ-ებ -ო	თვალ-ნ-ო

The same applies to the word *კვალ-ი*. Its conjugation pattern depends on its meaning. *კვ□ლ-ის, კვ□ლ-ებ-ის* is a furrow made with a plough or tractor in the field; the same word without syncopating stem implies a trace or print left by an animate or inanimate being.

	Singular furrow	*Plural furrows*	*Archaic plural*
Nom.	კვალ-ი	კვ□ლ-ებ-ი	კვალ-ნ-ი
Erg.	კვალ-მა	კვ□ლ-ებ-მა	კვალ-თა
Dat.	კვალ-ს	კვ□ლ-ებ-ს	კვალ-თა
Gen.	კვ□ლ-ის	კვ□ლ-ებ-ის	კვალ-თა
Instr.	კვ□ლ-ით	კვ□ლ-ებ-ით	–
Adv.	კვ□ლ-ად	კვ□ლ-ებ-ად	–
Voc.	კვალ-ო	კვ□ლ-ებ -ო	კვალ-ნ-ო

Very small number of nouns ending with the syllable -ელ have syncopating stem when declined in their singular form but not in plural: ტანსაცმელი (clothing, garment), და ფეხსაცმელი (shoes, footwear).

	Singular	*Plural*
Nom.	ტანსაცმელ-ი	ტანსაცმელ-ებ ი
Erg.	ტანსაცმელ-მა	ტანსაცმელ-ებ-მა
Dat.	ტანსაცმელ-ს	ტანსაცმელ-ებ-ს
Gen.	**ტანსაცმ□ლ-ის**	**ტანსაცმელ-ებ-ის**
Instr.	**ტანსაცმ□ლ-ით**	**ტანსაცმელ-ებ-ით**
Adv.	**ტანსაცმ□ლ-ად**	**ტანსაცმელ-ებ-ად**
Voc.	ტანსაცმელ-ო	ტანსაცმელ-ებ -ო

There are several nouns that are in use with and without syncopation:

ლიმონ	ლიმონ-ის	ლიმონ-ით	ლიმონ-ად
lemon	// ლიმნ-ის	// ლიმნ-ით	// ლიმნ-ად
არჩევან	არჩევან-ის	არჩევან-ით	არჩევანად
choice	// არჩევნ-ის	// არჩევნ-ით	// არჩევნ-ად

The word **არჩევან-ი** in plural **არჩევნ-ებ-ი** means *elections* and is declined in a syncopated form.

*ეს **არჩევნები** ჩვენი ქვეყნისთვის ძალიან მნიშვნელოვანია.*
These elections are very important for our country.

	Singular *choice*	*Plural* *elections*
Nom.	არჩევან-ი	არჩევ□ნ-ებ-ი
Erg.	არჩევან-მა	არჩევ□ნ-ებ-მა
Dat.	არჩევან-ს	არჩევ□ნ-ებ-ს
Gen.	არჩევან-ის//არჩევ□**ნ-ის**	არჩევ□ნ-ებ-ის
Instr.	არჩევან-ით//არჩევ□**ნ-ით**	არჩევ□ნ-ებ-ით
Adv.	არჩევან-ად//არჩევ□**ნ-ად**	არჩევ□ნ-ებ-ად
Voc.	არჩევან-ო	არჩევ□ნ-ებ -ო

4.3.1.4 *Declension of vowel-stem common nouns*

The vowel-stem nouns are divided into three groups: non-truncating, truncating, and truncating with syncope.

4.3.1.5 *Declension of vowel-stem non-truncating common nouns*

The non-truncating nouns end with the vowels ი /i/, ო /o/, or უ /u/. These nouns do not have case ending in the nominative and their dative and genitive case forms are similar, or a replacement method which is used by the Georgian native speakers. For example, if we replace a non-truncating vowel-ending noun with one that truncates, it will help to establish its case:

წყარო-ს *მივუახლოვდით.*
We approached a spring (water).

მდინარე-ს მივუახლოვდით.
We approached a river.

In the second sentence, the word მდინარე-ს (river) is clearly in the dative case – i.e. წყარო-ს is in the dative case as well.

In the following sentence, წყარო is in the genitive case.

წყარო-ს წყალი დალია.
He drank spring water.
მდინარ-ის წყალი დალია.
He drank river water.

Another method for differentiating the dative and genitive case of the nouns ending with the vowels ო and უ is adding the extending vowel -ი to the case ending -ს:

წყარო-ს-ი ბუ-ს-ი
წყარო-თ-ი ბუ-თ-ი

Nouns (both a consonant or vowel stem) would require the extending vowel -ა:

სახლ-ის-ა ჩაი-ს-ა
სახლ-ით-ა ჩაი-თ-ა

Nouns ending with -ო:

დო (buttermilk), ეზო (yard), რტო (branch, bough), წერო (crane), ლოქო (catfish), ლობიო (beans), ოქრო (gold), etc.

	Singular		*Plural*	
	shelf	*brook*	*shelves*	*brooks*
Nom.	თარო	რუ	თარო-ებ-ი	რუ-ებ-ი
Erg.	თარო-მ	რუ-მ	თარო-ებ-მა	რუ-ებ-მა
Dat.	თარო-ს	რუ-ს	თარო-ებ-ს	რუ-ებ-ს
Gen.	თარო-ს (ი)	რუ-ს (ი)	თარო-ებ-ის	რუ-ებ-ის
Instr.	თარო-თ (ი)	რუ-თ(ი)	თარო-ებ-ით	რუ-ებ-ით
Adv.	თარო-დ	რუ-დ	თარო-ებ-ად	რუ-ებ-ად
Voc.	თარო-(ვ)	რუ	თარო-ებ -ო	რუ-ებ-ო

In Georgian there are no nouns of the native origin that have the vowel *ი*-ending stem. All common and personal *ი*-ending nouns are of foreign borrowings: ჩაი (tea), პაი (share), ტრამვაი (tram),

ტაქსი (taxi), ტატამი (tatami), სუში (sushi), ჰობი (hobby), ჰობოი (oboe). These nouns do not have case ending in the nominative, and their dative and genitive case forms are similar.

Nom. ჩაი დამისხი!
Pour me some tea.
Gen. ჩაი-ს სახლი
Tea house (lit. *house of tea*)
Nom. ტრამვაი მოვიდა.
The tram arrived.
Gen. ტრამვაი-ს გაჩერება
Tram stop

In order to establish the genitive case of such nouns, they should be replaced with any regular noun.

Gen. ყავ-ის სახლი – coffee house (lit. *house of coffee*)
= **Gen.** ჩაი-ს სახლი (house of tea)
Gen. ავტობუს-ის გაჩერება – bus stop (lit. *stop of bus*)
= **Gen.** ტრამვაი-ს გაჩერება tram stop (lit. *stop of tram*)

Stems ending with the vowel ი-remain unchanged in all cases in their singular forms. ჩაი (tea) and პაი (initial share) are never used in plural form. There have been a few cases when the word ტრამვაი was used in plural both in truncated and non-truncated forms: ტრამვაი-ებ-ი and ტრამვა-ებ-ი. ტაქსი and ტატამი are always truncated.

ტაქს□-ებ-ის გაჩერება
Taxi stop/parking place
ტატამ□-ებ-ის აღწერა
Description of tatamis

	Singular		*Plural*
	tea	*taxi*	*taxis*
Nom.	ჩაი	ტაქსი	ტაქს□-ებ-ი
Erg.	ჩაი-მ	ტაქსი-მ	ტაქს□-ებ-მა
Dat.	ჩაი-ს	ტაქსი-ს	ტაქს□-ებ-ს
Gen.	ჩაი-ს(ი)	ტაქსი-ს(ი)	ტაქს □-ებ-ის
Instr.	ჩაი-თ(ი)	ტაქსი -თ(ი)	ტაქს□-ებ-ით
Adv.	ჩაი-დ	ტაქსი-დ	ტაქს □-ებ-ად
Voc.	ჩაი	ტაქსი	ტაქს □-ებ-ო

The nouns borrowed from foreign languages ending with the vowel -ე never truncate. Such are the nouns: ატაშე (attache), ატელიე (studio), აუტოდაფე (auto-da-fe), ბე (advance payment) გალიფე (riding breeches), დოსიე (dossier), ვარიეტე (variety show), იუბილე (jubilee), კაფე (café), კაშნე (scarf), კლიშე (cliché), კომუნიკე (communique), კონფერანსიე (master of ceremonies), კორიფე (outstanding figure), კრუპიე (croupier), ტირე (dash), ჟელე (jelly), etc.

	Singular		Plural	
	studio	cafe	studios	cafes
Nom.	ატელიე	კაფე	ატელიე-ებ-ი	კაფე-ებ-ი
Erg.	ატელიე-მ	კაფე-მ	ატელიე-ებ-მა	კაფე-ებ-მა
Dat.	ატელიე-ს	კაფე -ს	ატელიე-ებ-ს	კაფე-ებ-ს
Gen.	ატელიე-ს(ი)	კაფე-ს(ი)	ატელიე-ებ-ის	კაფე-ებ-ის
Instr.	ატელიე-თ(ი)	კაფე-თ(ი)	ატელიე-ებ-ით	კაფე-ებ-ით
Adv.	ატელიე-დ	კაფე-დ	ატელიე-ებ-ად	კაფე-ებ-ად
Voc.	ატელიე-(ვ)	კაფე-(ვ)	ატელიე-ებ-ო	კაფე-ებ-ო

4.3.1.6 Declension of vowel-stem truncating common nouns

Generally, the vowel-stem nouns of the native Georgian origin ending with -ა and -ე are truncated in singular forms of the genitive and instrumental cases. In plural forms ა-ending nouns are truncated in every case, while ე-ending nouns never do. In the archaic plural, neither ა- nor ე-ending nouns are truncated.

	Singular mother	Plural mothers	Archaic plural mothers/nuns
Nom.	დედა	დედ□-ებ ი	დედა-ნ-ი
Erg.	დედა-მ	დედ□-ებ-მა	დედა-თა
Dat.	დედა-ს	დედ□-ებ-ს	დედა-თა
Gen.	დედ□-ის	დედ□-ებ-ის	დედა-თა
Instr.	დედ□-ით	დედ□-ებ-ით	–
Adv.	დედა-დ	დედ□-ებ-ად	–
Voc.	დედა-ø, დედა-ო//ვ	დედ□-ებ -ო	დედა-ნ-ო

	Singular *tree*	*Plural* *trees*	*Archaic* *plural*
Nom.	ხე	ხე-ებ-ი	ხე-ნ-ი
Erg.	ხე-მ	ხე-ებ-მა	ხე-თა
Dat.	ხე-ს	ხე-ებ-ს	ხე-თა
Gen.	ხ□-ის	ხე-ებ-ის	ხე-თა
Instr.	ხ□-ით	ხე-ებ-ით	–
Adv.	ხე-დ	ხე-ებ-ად	–
Voc.	ხე-ø, ხე-ო//ვ	ხე-ებ-ო	ხე-ნ-ო

The nouns ending with **-ა** do not truncate in any of the plural forms if their final vowel is of derivative nature. The common nouns of this type do not truncate in plural forms either. The vowel ა is a derivative suffix in the following nouns: ბიცოლა (aunt), *ბეკეკა* (baby goat), *ბოჩოლა* (calf), *კოდალა* (woodpecker), *ჭიანჭველა* (ant), *თოჯინა* (doll), *ენძელა* (snowdrop), *ტოროლა* (lark), etc.

	Singular *woodpecker*	*Plural* *woodpeckers*
Nom.	კოდალა	კოდალ□-ებ-ი
Erg.	კოდალა-მ	კოდალ□-ებ-მა
Dat.	კოდალა-ს	კოდალ□-ებ-ს
Gen.	კოდალა -ს(ი)	კოდალ□-ებ-ის
Instr.	კოდალა -თ(ი)	კოდალ□-ებ-ით
Adv.	კოდალა-დ	კოდალ□-ებ-ად
Voc.	კოდალა-(ვ)	კოდალ□-ებ-ო

The nouns with the ა-ending derivative suffixes are not truncated in singular forms but undergo truncation in all cases in their plural forms.

ა-ending derivative suffix are as follows:

– **ია:** ბიძ-ია (uncle), *ნაცარქექ-ია* (lazy-bone), *ნემსიყლაპ-ია* (dragonfly)

– **უნა // -უნია:** *ბიჭ-უნა // ბიჭ-უნია* (little boy), *დათ-უნა//დათ-უნია* (teddy bear), *თაგ-უნა //თაგ-უნია* (mousy), *მჟა-უნა* (sorrel)
– **ურა:***ხიდ-ურა, ნათ-ურა* (a light bulb), *კოშკ-ურა* (turret)

	Singular *girl*	*Plural* *girls*
Nom.	გოგონა	გოგონ□-ებ-ი
Erg.	გოგონა-მ	გოგონ□-ებ-მა
Dat.	გოგონა-ს	გოგონ□-ებ-ს
Gen.	გოგონა-ს(ი)	გოგონ□-ებ-ის
Instr.	გოგონა-თ(ი)	გოგონ□-ებ-ით
Adv.	გოგონა-დ	გოგონ□-ებ-ად
Voc.	გოგონა-(ვ)	გოგონ□-ებ-ო

	Singular *turret*	*Plural* *turrets*
Nom.	კოშკურა	კოშკურ□-ებ-ი
Erg.	კოშკურა-მ	კოშკურ□-ებ-მა
Dat.	კოშკურა -ს	კოშკურ □-ებ-ს
Gen.	კოშკურა -ს(ი)	კოშკურ□ -ებ-ის
Instr.	კოშკურა -თ(ი)	კოშკურ □-ებ-ით
Adv.	კოშკურა -დ	კოშკურ □ებ-ად
Voc.	კოშკურა -(ვ)	კოშკურ □ებ-ო

Nouns with the derivative ა-ending are declined either with their truncated or full form.

	ბახალა fledgling crow	
Gen.	ბახალა-ს(ი)	ბახალ□-ის(ა)
Inst.	ბახალა-თ(ი)	ბახალ□ -ით(ა)
	თოჯინა doll	
Gen.	თოჯინა-ს(ი)	თოჯინ□-ის(ა)
Instr.	თოჯინა-თ(ი)	თოჯინ□-ით(ა)

(Continued)

(Continued)

	მაწანწალა tramp	
Gen.	მაწანწალა-ს(ი)	მაწანწალ□-ის(ა)
Instr.	მაწანწალა-თ(ი)	მაწანწალ□ -ით(ა)
	ბაცილა bacillus	
Gen.	ბაცილა-ს(ი)	ბაცილ□-ის(ა)
Instr.	ბაცილა-თ(ი)	ბაცილ□-ით(ა)
	ჭიანჭველა ant	
Gen.	ჭიანჭველა-ს(ი)	ჭიანჭველ□-ის(ა)
Instr.	ჭიანჭველა-თ(ი)	ჭიანჭველ□-ით(ა)
	მაჩანჩალა dawdler	
Gen.	მაჩანჩალა-ს(ი)	მაჩანჩალ□-ის(ა)
Instr.	მაჩანჩალა-თ(ი)	მაჩანჩალ□-ით(ა)

All ა-ending nouns denoting a blood relation are truncated: მამა (father), დედა (mother), ბაბუა (grandfather), ბებია (grandmother), პაპა (grandfather), მამიდა (aunt), ბიძა (uncle). They follow the pattern of declension for the ა-ending nouns. However, if the speaker refers to his or her own relatives or those of the persons with whom he or she is speaking, these nouns are perceived as personal names and they do not truncate.

დედ-ის სიყვარულს ვერაფერი შეცვლის.
Nothing can replace a mother's love.
ეს დედა-ს საძინებელია.
This is (my, your) mother's bedroom.
პაპ-ის ხნის კაცია.
He is an old man (man of grandfatherly age)
ეს პაპა-ს ხელჯოხია.
This is (my, your) grandfather's walking sick.

Sometimes truncation of nouns is determined by the necessity to avoid confusing one word for another and hence misunderstanding of an intended message. Such are the words:

ლელვ-ა (name of a village) – ლელვ-ი (fig)
კუდ-ა (name given to a bull without a tail) – კუდი (tail)

4.3.1.7 *Vowel-stem common nouns with irregular declension patterns*

The nouns ending with the vowel **-ო** do not truncate except one, the word **ღვინო-**; it is truncated in singular forms of the genitive, instrumental, and adverbial cases. In the vocative case, the case marker *-ვ/v/* is preferable to avoid doubling of the final vowel.

	Singular *wine*	*Plural* *wines*	*Archaic plural*
Nom.	ღვინო	ღვინო-ებ-ი	ღვინო-ნ-ი
Erg.	ღვინო-მ	ღვინო-ებ-მა	ღვინო-თა
Dat.	ღვინო-ს	ღვინო-ებ-ს	ღვინო-თა
Gen.	ღვინ□-ის	ღვინო-ებ-ის	ღვინო-თა
Instr.	ღვინ□-ით	ღვინო-ებ-ით	–
Adv.	ღვინო -დ	ღვინო-ებ-ად	–
Voc.	ღვინო-(ვ)	ღვინო-ებ-ო	(ღვინო-ნ-ო)

Another **-ო** ending noun with an irregular declension pattern is **ხბო** (calf), which has two plural forms, ***ხბო-ებ-*** and ***ხბორ>-ებ-*** with the consonant **-რ** added to its stem. Both forms are acceptable in the standard Georgian.

	Singular *calf*	*Plural* *calves*	*Archaic plural*	
Nom.	ხბო	ხბო-ებ-ი	ხბორ-ებ-ი	ხბო-ნ-ი
Erg.	ხბო-მ	ხბო-ებ-მა	ხბორ-ებ-მა	ხბო-თა
Dat.	ხბო-ს	ხბო-ებ-ს	ხბორ-ებ-ს	ხბო-თა
Gen.	ხბო-ს(ი)	ხბო-ებ-ის	ხბორ-ებ-ის	ხბო-თა
Instr.	ხბო-თ(ი)	ხბო -ებ-ით	ხბორ-ებ-ით	–
Adv.	ხბო-დ	ხბო-ებ-ად	ხბორ-ებ-ად	–
Voc.	ხბო-ø, ხბო-ვ//ო	ხბო-ებ-ო	ხბორ-ებ-ო	ხბო-ნ-ო

The noun დრო (time) also has an irregular declension. It has two different forms in the genitive: დრო-ს and დრო-ის.

> *ახლა უკვე რაღა* ***დროსია!***
> Phraseological expression, meaning it's too late (for example, to improve something)

მიყვარს ძველი ***დროის*** *ამბები.*
I love the story of bygone years (lit. *of old times*).

4.3.1.8 Declension of vowel-stem truncating common nouns with syncope

There are only a few nouns that are both truncating and syncopating in three cases: the genitive, instrumental, and adverbial. They are **ქარხანა** (factory, plant), **ბეგარა** (tithe, levy), **პეპელა** (butterfly), **ტომარა** (sack), **ქვეყანა** (country), **ფანჯარა** (window), **მოყვარე** (relative, friend), and **მხარე** (region, part). Syncopation and truncation of these nouns occur in their singular as well as plural forms. Separate from these words, **პეპელა** should be distinguished, which shows two kinds of forms. On the one hand, it is syncopated and truncated: *პეპ□ლ□-ის ეფექტი* (the butterfly effect); on the other hand, it does not change the form at all: *პეპელა-ს ფრთები* (wings of butterfly).

	Singular *factory, plant*	*Plural* *factories, plants*	*Archaic plural*
Nom.	ქარხანა	ქარხ□ნ□-ებ ი	ქარხანა-ნ-ი
Erg.	ქარხანა-მ	ქარხ□ნ□-ებ-მა	ქარხანა-თა
Dat.	ქარხანა-ს	ქარხ□ნ□-ებ-ს	ქარხანა-თა
Gen.	ქარხ□ნ□-ის	ქარხ□ნ□-ებ-ის	ქარხანა-თა
Instr.	ქარხ□ნ□-ით	ქარხ□ნ□-ებ-ით	–
Adv.	ქარხ□ნა-დ	ქარხ□ნ□-ებ-ად	–
Voc.	ქარხანა-(ვ)	ქარხ□ნ□-ებ -ო	ქარხანა-ნ-ო

	Singular *relative, friend*	*Plural* *relatives, friends*	*Archaic plural*
Nom.	მოყვარე	მოყვ□რ □-ებ -ი	მოყვარე-ნ-ი
Erg.	მოყვარე-მ	მოყვ□რ □-ებ-მა	მოყვარე-თა
Dat.	მოყვარე-ს	მოყვ□რ □-ებ-ს	მოყვარე-თა
Gen.	მოყვ□რ □-ის	მოყვ□რ □-ებ-ის	მოყვარე-თა
Instr.	მოყვ□რ □-ით	მოყვ□რ □-ებ-ით	–
Adv.	მოყვ□რ □-ად	მოყვ□რ □-ებ-ად	–
Voc.	მოყვარე-(ვ)	მოყვ□რ □-ებ-ო	მოყვარე-ნ-ო

The exception to the mentioned rule is the word ***მხარე*** (side, area); it has truncation and syncopation in singular form but declines in plural without having its final vowel -ე truncated.

> *ამ სახლში უკანა **მხ□რ□**-იდან უნდა შეხვიდეთ.*
> You should enter this house from the back side.
> *დაპირისპირებული **მხარე**-ებ-ი შერიგდნენ.*
> The opposing sides (parties) reconciled.

	Singular *side, area*	*Plural* *sides, areas*
Nom.	მხარე	მხარე-ებ-ი
Erg.	მხარე-მ	მხარე-ებ-მა
Dat.	მხარე-ს	მხარე-ებ-ს
Gen.	მხ□რ□-ის	მხარე-ებ-ის
Instr.	მხ□რ-ით	მხარე -ებ-ით
Adv.	მხ□რ□-ად	მხარე-ებ-ად
Voc.	მხარე-ო, -ვ	მხარე-ებ-ო

4.4 Declension of proper names

Proper names include two subgroups: one is given and family names of persons and the other is geographic names. These two types of names have dissimilar declension patterns.

4.4.1 Declension of consonant-stem personal names

Given names of persons with consonant stems do not syncopate. Unless used figuratively or as generalized common names, they have neither the vocative case ending nor plural forms.

Family names ending with -შვილი never syncopate and have plural forms as well.

	Given name	
Nom.	გრიგოლ-ი	გურამ-ი
Erg.	გრიგოლ-მა	გურამ-მა

(Continued)

(Continued)

	Given name	
Dat.	გრიგოლ-ს	გურამ-ს
Gen.	გრიგოლ-ის	გურამ-ის
Instr.	გრიგოლ-ით	გურამ-ით
Adv.	გრიგოლ-ად	გურამ-ად
Voc.	გრიგოლ	გურამ

	Family name Singular	*Family name Plural*	*Archaic Plural*
Nom.	მჭედლიშვილ-ი	მჭედლიშვილ-ებ-ი	მჭედლიშვილ-ნ-ი
Erg.	მჭედლიშვილ-მა	მჭედლიშვილ-ებ-მა	მჭედლიშვილ-თა
Dat.	მჭედლიშვილ-ს	მჭედლიშვილ-ებ-ს	მჭედლიშვილ-თა
Gen.	მჭედლიშვილ-ის	მჭედლიშვილ-ებ-ის	მჭედლიშვილ-თა
Instr.	მჭედლიშვილ-ით	მჭედლიშვილ-ებ-ით	–
Adv.	მჭედლიშვილ-ად	მჭედლიშვილ-ებ-ად	–
Voc.	მჭედლიშვილ-ო	მჭედლიშვილ-ებ-ო	მჭედლიშვილ-ნ-ო

There are a few family names with syncopated stems in singular forms of the genitive, instrumental, and adverbial cases in singular forms and in all cases in their plural forms. Such names are *მაჩაბ-ელ-ი, წერეთ-ელ-ი, გომართ-ელ-ი, კორინთ-ელ-ი*. However, in their archaic plural forms, these names do not syncopate. The majority of family names with the same -ელ ending stems syncopate neither in their singular nor in plural forms – for example, ბარათ-ელ-ი, ცურტავ-ელ-ი, and ბარნავ-ელ-ი.

	Syncopating family names in singular	*Syncopating family names in plural*	
Nom.	წერეთელ-ი	წერეთ□ლ-ებ-ი	წერეთელ-ნ-ი
Erg.	წერეთელ-მა	წერეთ□ლ-ებ-მა	წერეთელ-თა
Dat.	წერეთელ-ს	წერეთ□ლ-ებ-ს	წერეთელ-თა
Gen.	წერეთ□ლ-ის	წერეთ□ლ-ებ-ის	წერეთელ-თა

	Syncopating family names in singular	*Syncopating family names in plural*	
Instr.	წერეთ□ლ-ით	წერეთ□ლ-ებ-ით	–
Adv.	წერეთ□ლ-ად	წერეთ□ლ-ებ-ად	–
Voc.	წერეთელ-ო	წერეთ□ლ-ებ-ო	წერეთელ-ნ-ო

4.4.2 Declension of consonant-stem geographic names

The declension of geographic names is similar to that of common names. Therefore, consonant-stem geographic names are syncopated just like consonant-stem common names. Their stem vowels ა, ე, and ო are dropped when followed by the consonants ლ, რ, მ, and ნ. Very seldom the vowel ო is changed to the consonant ვ as it happens in the consonant-stem common names: ***იორ-ი* > *ი-ვ-რ-ის*** (the river Iori). The following is a list of various geographic names of places, rivers, and regions.

- **– ალ:** ჩარგ-ალ-ი, ცხენისწყ-ალ-ი
- **– არ:** ალამბ-არ-ი, მტკვ-არ-ი, გუდამაყ-არ-ი, ნატახტ-არ-ი
- **– ამ:** ოკ-ამ-ი (It is not a syncopated geographic name.)
- **– ან:** ვარდისუბ-ან-ი, ვაშლოვ-ან-ი, ალაზ-ან, ფერეიდ-ან-ი (sometimes ფერეიდ-ან-ი is not syncopated), გუდამაყ-არ-ი, but ტიბაანი is non-syncopating
- **– ელ:** ყვარ-ელ-ი
- **– ერ:** ტეზ-ერ-ი
- **– ემ:** ჭერ-ემ-ი
- **– ენ:** ხოდაშ-ენ-ი
- **– ორ:** კოჯ-ორ-ი, but კოდ-ორ-ი is not a syncopated geographic name

In the geographical name ი-ორ-ი, the vowel **ო** may undergo reduction and change into the consonant -*ვ* in the genitive, instrumental, and adverbial cases: ივრ-ის, ივრ-ით, ივრ-ად.

- **-ომ:** დიღ-ომ-ი

Geographic names formed with ***-ის*** and ***-ეთ*** suffixes as well as ***სა-ეთ*** circumfix are not syncopated:

- **– ის:** თბილ-ის-ი, მანგლ-ის-ი, ტირძნ-ის-ი, თუხარ-ის-ი
- **– ეთ:** კახ-ეთ-ი, იმერ-ეთ-ი, სვან-ეთ-ი, ესპან-ეთ-ი, სომხ-ეთ-ი, ტაჯიკ-ეთ-ი

If the stem of a geographic name ends with the consonant *-მ*, it will be doubled in the ergative case: ოკამ-მა. Similarly, the stems ending with *-ს* will also have a double consonant in the dative case: თბილის-ს.

Unlike personal names, geographic names do not have plural forms.

Non-syncopating geographic names

Nom.	თბილის-ი	რუსთავ-ი	სოხუმ-ი
Erg.	თბილის-მა	რუსთავ-მა	სოხუ**მ-მ**ა
Dat.	თბილი**ს-ს**	რუსთავ-ს	სოხუმ-ს
Gen.	თბილის-ის	რუსთავ-ის	სოხუმ-ის
Instr.	თბილის-ით	რუსთავ-ით	სოხუმ-ით
Adv.	თბილის-ად	რუსთავ-ად	სოხუმ-ად
Voc.	თბილის-ო	რუსთავ-ო	სოხუმ-ო

Syncopating geographic names

	-არ	-ორ	
Nom.	მტკვარ-ი	კოჯორ-ი	იორ-ი
Erg.	მტკვარ-მა	კოჯორ-მა	იორ-მა
Dat.	მტკვარ-ს	კოჯორ-ს	იორ-ს
Gen.	მტკვ□**რ**-ის	კოჯ□რ-ის	ივრ-ის
Instr.	მტკვ□**რ**-ით	კოჯ□რ-ით	ივრ-ით
Adv.	მტკვ□**რ**-ად	კოჯ□რ-ად	ივრ-ად
Voc.	მტკვარ-ო	კოჯორ-ო	იორ-ო

There are a few cases when geographic names end with syllables containing the consonants *ლ*, *რ*, *მ*, and *ნ*, but nevertheless, they do not syncopate – for example, კოდ-ორ-ი, ბორჯ-ომ-ი (see the previous example).

4.4.3 *Declension of vowel-stem given names*

The vowel-stem given names do not syncopate and do not have the vocative case ending. To differentiate their dative and genitive cases from each other, they should be replaced with consonant-stem names.

	ა	ე	ი	ო	უ
Nom.	ნათია	ერეკლე	გივ-ი	ნინო	ნუნუ
Erg.	ნათია-მ	ერეკლე-მ	გივი-მ	ნინო-მ	ნუნუ-მ
Dat.	ნათია-ს	ერეკლე-ს	გივი-ს	ნინო-ს	ნუნუ-ს
Gen.	ნათია-ს(ი)	ერეკლე-ს(ი)	გივი-ს(ი)	ნინო-ს(ი)	ნუნუ-ს(ი)
Instr.	ნათია-თ(ი)	ერეკლე-თ(ი)	გივი-თ(ი)	ნინო-თ(ი)	ნუნუ-თ(ი)
Adv.	ნათია-დ	ერეკლე-დ	გივი-დ	ნინო-დ	ნუნუ-დ
Voc.	ნათია	ერეკლე	გივი	ნინო	ნუნუ

4.4.4 *Declension of vowel-stem family names*

ა-ending family names

The family names ending with -ა, both Georgian and non-Georgian, are not truncated when declined in singular forms. In the plural they are truncated in every case.

- **ია:** *თოდრია, ლორია, შონია, ცომაია*
- **ვა:** *ჩაჩავა, გალდავა, კანკავა, გვაზავა, ჯღარკავა*
- **ყვა:** *ინგოროყვა, ართილაყვა, როყვა*

	Singular	*Plural*
Nom.	გამსახურდია	გამსახურდი□-ებ-ი
Erg.	გამსახურდია-მ	გამსახურდი□-ებ-მა
Dat.	გამსახურდია-ს	გამსახურდი□-ებ-ს
Gen.	გამსახურდია-ს(ი)	გამსახურდი□-ებ-ის
Instr.	გამსახურდია-თ(ი)	გამსახურდი□-ებ-ით
Adv.	გამსახურდია-დ	გამსახურდი□-ებ-ად
Voc.	გამსახურდია-(ვ)	გამსახურდი□-ებ-ო

	Singular	*Plural*
Nom.	აგრბა	აგრბ□-ებ-ი
Erg.	აგრბა-მ	აგრბ□-ებ-მა
Dat.	აგრბა-ს	აგრბ□-ებ-ს
Gen.	აგრბა-ს(ი)	აგრბ□-ებ-ის

(*Continued*)

(Continued)

	Singular	Plural
Instr.	ავრზა-თ(ი)	ავრზ□-ებ-ით
Adv.	ავრზა-დ	ავრზ□-ებ-ად
Voc.	ავრზა-(ვ)	ავრზ□-ებ-ო

ე-ending family names

The family names ending with the syllable -ძე are declined as the ე-ending common names. Accordingly, they are truncated only in singular forms. They do not have the nominative case ending, while in the vocative, the case ending is optional, and the name may be with or without it. In plural forms the final -ე is doubled, one is the stem ending, and the other is the part of the plural suffix.

	Singular	Plural	Archaic plural
Nom.	კარანაძე	კარანაძე-ებ-ი	კარანაძე-ნ-ი
Erg.	კარანაძე-მ	კარანაძე-ებ-მა	კარანაძე-თა
Dat.	კარანაძე-ს	კარანაძე-ებ-ს	კარანაძე-თა
Gen.	კარანაძ□-ის	კარანაძე-ებ-ის	კარანაძე-თა
Instr.	კარანაძ□-ით	კარანაძე-ებ-ით	–
Adv.	კარანაძ-დ	კარანაძე-ებ-ად	–
Voc.	კარანაძე-(ვ)	კარანაძე-ებ-ო	კარანაძე-ნ-ო

Unlike ძე-ending family names other family names ending with -ე do not have a uniform declension pattern. For example, the name *მენაბდე* is truncated, while *გალოგრე* is not. *მენაბდე* truncates probably because it is originally a common noun.

	Singular	Plural	Archaic plural
Nom.	მენაბდე	მენაბდე-ებ-ი	მენაბდე-ნ-ი
Erg.	მენაბდე-მ	მენაბდე-ებ-ი	მენაბდე-თა
Dat.	მენაბდე-ს	მენაბდე-ებ-ს	მენაბდე-თა
Gen.	მენაბდ□-ის	მენაბდე-ებ-ის	მენაბდე-თა
Instr.	მენაბდ□-ით	მენაბდე-ებ-ით	–
Adv.	მენაბდე-დ	მენაბდე-ებ-ად	–
Voc.	მენაბდე-(ვ)	მენაბდე-ებ-ო	მენაბდე-ნ-ო

	Singular	*Plural*	*Archaic plural*
Nom.	გალოგრე	გალოგრე-ებ-ი	გალოგრე-ნ-ი
Erg.	გალოგრე-მ	გალოგრე-ებ-მა	გალოგრე-თა
Dat.	გალოგრე-ს	გალოგრე-ებ-ს	გალოგრე-თა
Gen.	გალოგრე-ს(ი)	გალოგრე-ებ-ის	გალოგრე-თა
Instr.	გალოგრე -თ(ი)	გალოგრე-ებ-ით	–
Adv.	გალოგრე-დ	გალოგრე-ებ-ად	–
Voc.	გალოგრე-(ვ)	გალოგრე-ებ-ო	გალოგრე-ნ-ო

None of the vowel-stem foreign family names are truncated either in their singular or plural forms unless they have -ა ending. Only exceptions are the names ending with -ი; they are truncated when declined in plural forms.

	Singular	*Plural*
Nom.	დანტე	დანტე-ებ-ი
Erg.	დანტე-მ	დანტე-ებ-მა
Dat.	დანტე-ს	დანტე-ებ-ს
Gen.	დანტე-ს(ი)	დანტე-ებ-ის
Inst.	დანტე-თ(ი)	დანტე-ებ-ით
Adv.	დანტე-დ	დანტე-ებ-ად
Voc.	დანტე-(ვ)	დანტე-ებ-ო

	Singular	*Plural*
Nom.	დიმიტრიადი	დიმიტრიად-ებ-ი
Erg.	დიმიტრიადი-მ	დიმიტრიად□-ებ-მ
Dat.	დიმიტრიადი-ს	დიმიტრიად□-ებ-ს
Gen.	დიმიტრიადი-ს(ი)	დიმიტრიად□-ებ-ის
Inst.	დიმიტრიადი-თ(ი)	დიმიტრიად□-ებ-ით
Adv.	დიმიტრიადი-დ	დიმიტრიად□-ებ-ად
Voc.	დიმიტრიადი	დიმიტრიად□-ებ-ო

	Singular	Plural	Singular	Plural
Nom.	დიდრო	დიდრო-ებ-ი	ორუ	ორუ-ებ-ი
Erg.	დიდრო-მ	დიდრო-ებ-მა	ორუ-მ	ორუ-ებ-მა
Dat.	დიდრო -ს	დიდრო -ებ-ს	ორუ-ს	ორუ-ებ-ს
Gen.	დიდრო -ს(ი)	დიდრო -ებ-ის	ორუ-ს(ი)	ორუ-ებ-ის
Instr.	დიდრო -თ(ი)	დიდრო ებ-ით	ორუ-თ(ი)	ორუ-ებ-ით
Adv.	დიდრო-დ	დიდრო-ებ-ად	ორუ-დ	ორუ-ებ-ად
Voc.	დიდრო	დიდრო-ებ-ო	ორუ	ორუ-ებ-ო

4.4.5 Declension of given and family names together

When the given and family names are declined together, only the stem of the former is used, and it remains unchanged in every case. However, a family name is declined in accordance with the rules referring to its ending. A family name is always in plural if it is preceded by two or more given names.

	Singular	Plural
Nom.	გალაკტიონ ტაბიძე	გალაკტიონ და ტიციან ტაბიძე-ებ-ი
Erg.	გალაკტიონ ტაბიძე-მ	გალაკტიონ და ტიციან ტაბიძე-ებ-მა
Dat.	გალაკტიონ ტაბიძე-ს	გალაკტიონ და ტიციან ტაბიძე-ებ-ს
Gen.	გალაკტიონ ტაბიძ -ის	გალაკტიონ და ტიციან ტაბიძე-ებ-ის
Instr.	გალაკტიონ ტაბიძ -ით	გალაკტიონ და ტიციან ტაბიძე-ებ-ით
Adv.	გალაკტიონ ტაბიძე -დ	გალაკტიონ და ტიციან ტაბიძე-ებ-ად
Voc.	გალაკტიონ ტაბიძე-(ვ)	გალაკტიონ და ტიციან ტაბიძე-ებ-ო

4.4.6 Vowel-stem geographic names

4.4.6.1 Non-truncating geographic names

The majority of geographic names ending with the vowels ი, ო, and უ are not truncated.

Geographic names with the ი-ending stems are not of Georgian origin, and they all decline without truncation:

> ტაიტი, ჰაიტი, ჯიბუტი, ფიჯი, ნიუ-ჯერსი, ბრუნეი, ურუგვაი, პარაგვაი, etc.

Geographic names ending with the vowel -ო could be both Georgian or foreign in origin:

> ნაგვაზაო, ონტოფო, სამიქაო, საზანო, სალხინო, ნახუნაო, წყალტუბო, თეთრიწყარო, კონგო, კოსოვო, სან-მარინო, ტოგო, ბურკინა-ფასო, მაროკო, მონაკო, მონტენეგრო, ფაკაოფო, etc.

Geographic names ending with the vowel -უ are as follows:

> ორულუ, ნაცატუ, კურზუ, ნაწულუკუ, პერუ, ბირაუ, ვინუატუ, ტოკელაუ, ტუვალუ, ატაფუ, ნუკუნონუ, etc.

Although geographic names decline just like common names, they have neither vocative case markers, nor plural forms.

	-ი *Tahiti*	-ო *Nagvazao*
Nom.	ტაიტი	ნაგვაზაო
Erg.	ტაიტი-მ	ნაგვაზაო-მ
Dat.	ტაიტი-ს	ნაგვაზაო-ს
Gen.	ტაიტი-ს(ი)	ნაგვაზაო-ს(ი)
Instr.	ტაიტი-თ(ი)	ნაგვაზაო-თ(ი)
Adv.	ტაიტი-დ	ნაგვაზაო-დ
Voc.	ტაიტი	ნაგვაზაო

	-ო *Morocco*	-უ *Kurzu*	-უ *Peru*
Nom.	მაროკო	კურზუ	პერუ
Erg.	მაროკო-მ	კურზუ-მ	პერუ-მ
Dat.	მაროკო-ს	კურზუ-ს	პერუ-ს
Gen.	მაროკო-ს(ი)	კურზუ-ს(ი)	პერუ-ს(ი)
Instr.	მაროკო-თ(ი)	კურზუ-თ(ი)	პერუ-თ(ი)
Adv.	მაროკო-დ	კურზუ-დ	პერუ-დ
Voc.	მაროკო	კურზუ	პერუ

4.4.6.2 *Truncating geographic names*

As was mentioned, the declension patterns of geographic names are mostly similar to those of common names. The vowel-stem names are truncated according the same rules as vowel-stem common names.

In the genitive and instrumental cases, both Georgian and foreign geographic names lose their final -ა:

> ა-ending truncating Georgian geographic names: მცხეთა, მლეთა, გავრა, ხურჩა, ოტობაია, ანაკლია, ჩხორია, etc.

ა-ending truncating foreign geographic names: ამერიკა (America), ინდიანა (Indiana), ჯორჯია (Georgia), ბარსელონა (Barcelona), ჰავანა (Havana), არგენტინა (Argentina), ანგოლა (Angola), გრენადა (Granada), შრი-ლანკა (Sri Lanka), კოსტა-რიკა (Costa Rica), ნიკარაგუა (Nicaragua), ლიეტუვა Lithuania), ლატვია (Latvia), ავსტრია(Austria), ბელგია (Belgium), დანია (Denmark), შვეიცარია (Switzerland), იტალია (Italy), პორტუგალია (Portugal), ბრაზილია (Brazil), ავსტრალია (Australia), ბოლივია (Bolivia), გერმანია (Germany), ეთიოპია (Ethiopia), იაპონია (Japan), იორდანია (Jordan), ბოსნია (Bosnia), etc. Geographic names of this type may have the vocative case ending.

	Singular			
Nom.	მცხეთა	გავრა	გენუა	პორტუგალია
Erg.	მცხეთა-მ	გავრა-მ	გენუა-მ	პორტუგალია-მ
Dat.	მცხეთა-ს	გავრა-ს	გენუა-ს	პორტუგალია-ს
Gen.	მცხეთ□-ის	გავრ□-ის	გენუ□-ის	პორტუგალი□-ის
Instr.	მცხეთ□-ით	გავრ□-ით	გენუ□-ით	პორტუგალი□-თ
Adv.	მცხეთა-დ	გავრა-დ	გენუა-დ	პორტუგალია-დ
Voc.	მცხეთა-(ვ)	გავრა-(ვ)	გენუა-(ვ)	პორტუგალია-(ვ)

Geographic names with the derivative -ა ending do not truncate: ნაქერალ-ა, შავნაბად-ა, წყალწითელ-ა, ხარისთვალ-ა, ხევხმელ-ა.

	-ა	-ა
Nom.	შავნაბადა	წყალწითელა
Erg.	შავნაბადა-მ	წყალწითელა-მ
Dat.	შავნაბადა-ს	წყალწითელა-ს
Gen.	შავნაბადა-ს(ი)	წყალწითელა-ს(ი)
Instr.	შავნაბადა-თ(ი)	წყალწითელა-თ(ი)
Adv.	შავნაბადა-დ	წყალწითელა-დ
Voc.	შავნაბადა-(ვ)	წყალწითელა-(ვ)

Not all Georgian geographic names ending with the vowel *-ე* are truncated. For example, the truncating names are as follows:

საირმე, *საჩხერე*, *ტყლაპოვაკე*, *ქვაციხე*, *ნახშირღელე*, *ოჩამჩირე*, *სკანდე*, *ლაშე*, etc.
The examples of names that do not truncate: *კვირიკე*, *ზვარე*, *ლეფოჩხუე*, *ლეძაძამე*, etc.

The same is with non-Georgian geographic names – for example, *ზიმბაბვე* (Zimbabwe), *სიერა-ლეონე* (Sierra Leone), *კაბო-ვერდე* (Cabo Verde), *ჩილე* (Chile), *დუშამბე* (Dushanbe), *ჰალე* (Halle), *კალე* (Calais), and *ლაგო-მაჯორე* (Lago Maggiore) are not truncated, but *ეგვიპტე* (Egypt), *კარლსრუე* (Carlsruhe), *ჰერნე* (Herne), *ტვენტე* (Twente) are truncated.

	ე-ending non-truncating Georgian geographic names	*ე-ending non-truncating foreign geographic names*
Nom.	ზვარე	ჰალე
Erg.	ზვარე-მ	ჰალე-მ
Dat.	ზვარე-ს	ჰალე-ს
Gen.	ზვარე-ს(ი)	ჰალე-ს(ი)
Instr.	ზვარე-თ(ი)	ჰალე-თ(ი)
Adv.	ზვარე-დ	ჰალე-დ
Voc.	ზვარე	ჰალე

	ე-ending truncating Georgian geographic names	*ე-ending truncating foreign geographic names*
Nom.	საირმე	ეგვიპტე
Erg.	საირმე-მ	ეგვიპტე-მ
Dat.	საირმე-ს	ეგვიპტე-ს
Gen.	საირმ□-ის	ეგვიპტ□-ის
Instr.	საირმ□-ით	ეგვიპტ□-ით
Adv.	საირმე-დ	ეგვიპტე-დ
Voc.	საირმე-(ვ)	ეგვიპტე-(ვ)

Chapter 5

Adjectives

5.1 Groups of adjectives

There are two groups of adjectives, the primary and derivative. The questions posed to adjectives are **როგორი** (what kind, what type), **რომელი** (which), **სადაური** (from where), and **როდინდელი** (from what time, what period).

The adjectives describe or refer to the character or features of a noun it precedes. In some specific contexts, one and the same adjective may answer to different questions:

მე მყავს ორი ძმა. ერთი **ზარმაცი** *და მეორე –* **ბეჯითი.**
I have two brothers, one lazy, the other diligent.
დღეს სტუმრად **ბეჯითი** *ძმა მეწვია.*
Today my diligent brother visited me.

When taken separately both these adjectives answer to the question **როგორი** (what kind). However, in the given context, the adjective in the second sentence answers to the question **რომელი** (which, which one). The answer will be – the diligent one.

In Georgian, an adjective can be composed by adding suffixes or circumfixes to various parts of speech, nouns, pronouns, etc. Thus, the adjective **ჩემ-იან-ი** (related to me, mine) derives from the possessive pronoun **ჩემ-ი** (my), **სადა-ურ-ი** (from where) is formed from **სად***(ა)*(interrogative pronoun *where*), **მზ-იან-ი** (sunny) is based on the noun **მზე** (sun), **უ-გულ-ო** (heartless), and **უ-ხელ-ო** (lacking a hand) are composed by means of the circumfix **უ-ო**.

DOI: 10.4324/9781315281131-8

5.1.1 Derivative adjectives

The derivative adjectives may be divided into several groups.

The meaning of derivative adjectives	*Suffixes and circumfixes*	*Examples*
Denoting possession of something or someone	– იან	შვილ-ი (child) > შვილ-იანი (with child)
	-იერ//-იელ	ნიჭ-ი (talent) > ნიჭ-იერ-ი (talented; with talent) ძალა (strength) > ძლ-იერ-ი (strong) (When the stem has the consonant **-რ-**, the same consonant in the suffix changes to **-ლ**.)
	-ოსან	მედალ-ი (medal) > მედალ-ოსან-ი (medalist)
	-ოვან	ფენა (layer) > ფენ-ოვან-ი (layered) ყვავილ-ი (flower) > ყვავილ-ოვან-ი (flowery, blooming)
	-ა	კუდ-ი (tail) > კუდ-ა (an animal **without a tail** or with **a shorter than normal tail**)
Denoting lack of certain quality or features	**უ-ო**	ეკალ-ი (thorn) > უ-ეკლ-ო (without thorn) კანონ-ი (law) > უ-კანონ-ო (lawless)
	უ-ურ//უ-ულ	გემო (taste) > უ-გემ-ურ-ი (tasteless) კაც-ი (man) > უ-კაც-ურ-ი (uninhabited) ფერ-ი (colour) > უ-ფერ-ულ-ი (colourless) (When the stem has the consonant **-რ-**, the same consonant in the suffix changes to **-ლ-**.)

The meaning of derivative adjectives	*Suffixes and circumfixes*	*Examples*
Denoting profession	მე-ე	ბაღი (garden) > მე-ბაღ-ე (gardener) პური (bread) > მე-პურ-ე (baker) კარ-ი (door) > მე-კარ-ე (doorman; goalkeeper)
	მე-ურ // მე-ულ	ბადე (grid) > მე-ბად-ურ-ი (fisherman) კლდე (rock) > მე-კლდე-ურ-ი (mountain climber) ბარგ- ი (luggage) > მე-ბარგ-ულ-ი (porter) (When the stem has the consonant **-რ-**, the same consonant in the suffix changes to **-ლ-**.)
Denoting purpose of something	სა-ო	სწავლა (studying) > სა-სწავლ-ო (educational, for study) რეცხვა (washing) > მრეცხავი > სა-მრეცხა-ო (laundromat; for washing) ჭედვა (forging) > მჭედელი > სა-მჭედლ-ო (blacksmith shop)
	სა-ე	ნაგავ-ი (garbage) > სა-ნაგვ-ე (garbage can, place for garbage) ფულ-ი (money) > სა-ფულ-ე (purse; for money) ყურ-ი (ear) > სა-ყურ-ე (earring)
	სა-ურ//ულ	თაგვ-ი (mouse) > სა-თაგ-ურ-ი mousetrap თავ-ი (head) > სა-თა-ურ-ი (title; to be put at the head) გარე (outside) > გარე-ულ-ი (wild)

(*Continued*)

(Continued)

The meaning of derivative adjectives	*Suffixes and circumfixes*	*Examples*
		(When the stem has the consonant **-რ-**, the same consonant in the suffix changes to **-ლ-**.)
	სა-არ	ომ-ი (war) > სა-ომ-არ-ი (military; for war) ჩუქება (to gift) > სა-ჩუქ-არ-ი gift, something to gift ფარ-ი (**shield**) > სა-ფარ-ი (shelter, place to hide)
Denoting the following: 1. Person's place of origin	**მ-ელ//-ელ** (origin of persons)	*ეგრ-ი (>ეგრ-ის-ი) (Egri) > მ-ეგრ-ელ-ი (person from Mingrelia) კახ-ი (Kakhi) > კახ-ელ-ი (person from Kakheti) კავკასია (Caucasus) > კავკასი-ელ-ი (Caucasian, from the Caucasus)
2. Origin of things	**-ურ//-ულ; მ-ურ//მ-ულ** (origin of things)	კახ-ი (Kakhi) > კახ-ურ-ი (from Kakheti; about inanimate nouns) კავკასია (Caucasus) > კავკასი-ურ-ი (Caucasian, from the Caucasus) *ეგრ-ი (>ეგრ-ის-ი) (Egri) > მ-ეგრ-ულ-ი Mingrelian რაჭა (Racha) > რაჭ-ულ-ი (something from the region of Racha) (When the stem has the consonant **-რ-**, the same consonant in the suffix changes to **-ლ-**.)

The meaning of derivative adjectives	*Suffixes and circumfixes*	*Examples*
3. Time or period something originated	-დელ (indicating the period)	შარშან (last year) > შარშან-დელ-ი last year's წელ-ი (year) > წლევან-დელ-ი (this year's) გუშინ (yesterday) > გუშინ-დელ-ი (yesterday's)
4. Relation to something or someone	-ეულ	ჩემ -ი (my) > ჩემ-ეულ-ი (related to me, my) თქვენ (you) > თქვენ-ეულ-ი (related to you, your) შორ-ი (far) > შორ-ეულ-ი (distant)
5. Attribution to something	-იურ	წელ-ი (year) > წლ-იურ-ი (annual) დღე (day) > დღ-იურ-ი (daily, diary) თვე (month) > თვ-იურ-ი (monthly)

5.2 Comparative and superlative adjectives

In Georgian all primary and some derivative adjectives can express various degrees of comparative quality. There are three degrees of comparison indicating the difference between various degrees of the features defined by adjectives.

The comparative and superlative meanings are denoted with the words **უფრო** (more) and **ყველაზე** (most) preceding the base form of adjectives.

1. **Primary adjectives**

გრძელი	უფრო გრძელი	ყველაზე//ძალიან გრძელი
long	longer	longest/very long

მოკლე	უფრო მოკლე	ყველაზე//ძალიან მოკლე
short	shorter	shortest/very short
ლამაზი	უფრო ლამაზი	ყველაზე//ძალიან//ძალზე ლამაზი
beautiful	more beautiful	most beautiful/very beautiful

2. **Derivative adjectives**

საინტერესო	უფრო საინტერესო	ყველაზე//ძალიან//ძალზე საინტერესო
interesting	more interesting	most/very interesting
პატიოსანი	უფრო პატიოსანი	ყველაზე//ძალიან პატიოსანი
honest	more honest	most/very honest
სამართლიანი	უფრო სამართლიანი	ყველაზე//ძალიან სამართლიანი
Just	more just	most/very just

The superlative adjectives are formed with the circumfix **უ-ეს.** Very often it may be replaced with the word **ძალიან** (very) preceding the base form of an adjective.

Positive	*Superlative/emphatic*
ძველ-ი old	უ-ძველ-ეს-ი, ძალიან ძველი oldest, very old
ლამაზ-ი beautiful	უ-ლამაზ-ეს-ი, ძალიან ლამაზი most beautiful, very beautiful
დიდ-ი great	უ-დიდ-ეს-ი, ძალიან დიდი greatest, outstanding

საქართველოში ქუთაისი **უძველესი** *ქალაქია.*
In Georgia, Kutaisi is the oldest city.
ჩვენ ჯგუფში თამარი **ულამაზესი** *ქალია.*
In our group, Tamar is the most beautiful woman.
რუსთაველი საქართველოს **უდიდესი** *პოეტია.*
Rustaveli is the greatest poet of Georgia.
ეს **უმოკლესი** *გზაა აქედან ბაზრამდე.*
This is the shortest road from here to the market.

Some adjectives of this type undergo a phonetic change in their superlative form:

Positive	*Superlative*	*Phonetic (and other) changes*
მწარ-ე bitter	უ-მწარ-ეს-ი bitterest, very bitter	The final stem vowel -*ე* is lost.
ტკბილ-ი sweet	უ-ტკბ-ეს-ი sweetest, very flat	The stem syllable-*ილ*- is lost.
გრძელ-ი long	უ-გრძ-ეს-ი longest, very long	The stem syllable -*ელ*- is lost.
ღრმა deep	უ-ღრმ-ეს-ი deepest, very deep	The final stem vowel -ა is lost.

Some superlative adjectives change the semantics of nouns they modify.

> **უმაღლესი** *სასწავლებელი* = **university** (lit. *the highest learning institution*; i.e. a type of institution)
> **უღრმესი** *მადლობა* = (my) most sincere (deepest) gratitude (i.e. a kind of gratitude)

A group of the primary adjectives referring mostly to colour, size, or taste may convey moderative quality they describe. The circumfix **მო–ო** is used to compose the adjectives of this type:

Positive	*Moderative degree*
თეთრ-ი white	მო-თეთრ-ო somewhat white, whitish
ლურჯ-ი blue	მო-ლურჯ-ო somewhat blue, bluish
დიდ-ი large, big	მო-დიდ-ო somewhat large, biggish
მაღალ-ი tall	მო-მაღლ-ო somewhat tall, tallish

The adjectives that undergo a phonetic or other change in their archaic superlative forms are subject to the same rule when they express moderative quality of some entity:

Positive	*Moderative degree*
მწარ-ე bitter	მო-მწარ-ო somewhat bitter, a bit bitter
ტკბილ-ი sweet	მო-ტკბ-ო somewhat sweet, sweetish
გრძელ-ი long	მო-გრძ-ო somewhat long, longish
მცირ-ე small, slight	მო-მცრ-ო somewhat small, smallish

The quality expressed by adjectives can be further modified by determinants like **ოდნავ** (slightly, a bit), **ძალიან//ძალზე** (exceedingly, very), **მეტად** (very), etc.:

> **მწარე** ((bitter) – **ოდნავ მწარე** (a bit bitter)
> **ცხელი** (hot) – **ძალზე ცხელი** (very hot)
> **ზრდილობიანი** (polite)– **მეტად ზრდილობიანი** (very polite)

Some adjectives have both regular and irregular comparative forms. It should be noticed that the circumfix **უ-ეს-ი** for both **კარგი** and **ცუდი** has comparative, not superlative, meaning. In the superlative form of **კარგი**, another circumfix **სა-ო** is added to **უ-ეს**.

Positive	*Comparative*	*Superlative*
კარგი good	უფრო კარგი უ-კეთ-ეს-ი better	ყველზე კარგი სა-უ-კეთ-ეს-ო best
ცუდი bad	უფრო ცუდი უ-არ-ეს-ი worse	ყველაზე ცუდი worst

5.3 Declension of adjectives

5.3.1 *Declension of adjectives without nouns*

All adjectives are declinable and have both singular and plural forms. They can be declined separately as well as together with nouns they precede.

The consonant- and vowel-stem adjectives follow the same declension rules as the corresponding types of nouns.

Declension of non-syncopating consonant-stem adjectives

	Singular *white*	*Plural* *whites*	*Archaic plural*
Nom.	თეთრ-ი	თეთრ-ებ ი	თეთრ-ნ-ი
Erg.	თეთრ-მა	თეთრ-ებ-მა	თეთრ-თა
Dat.	თეთრ-ს	თეთრ-ებ-ს	თეთრ-თა
Gen.	თეთრ-ის	თეთრ-ებ-ის	თეთრ-თა
Instr.	თეთრ-ით	თეთრ-ებ-ით	–
Adv.	თეთრ-ად	თეთრ-ებ-ად	–
Voc.	თეთრ-ო	თეთრ-ებ -ო	თეთრ-ნ-ო

Declension of consonant-stem syncopating adjectives

	Singular *red*	*Plural* *reds*	*Archaic plural*
Nom.	წითელ-ი	წით□ლ-ებ-ი	წითელ-ნ-ი
Erg.	წითელ-მა	წით□ლ-ებ-მა	წითელ-თა
Dat.	წითელ-ს	წით□ლ-ებ-ს	წითელ-თა
Gen.	წით□ლ-ის	წით□ლ-ებ-ის	წითელ-თა
Instr.	წით□ლ-ით	წით□ლ-ებ-ით	–
Adv.	წით□ლ-ად	წით□ლ-ებ-ად	–
Voc.	წითელ-ო	წით□ლ-ებ-ო	წითელ-ნ-ო

Some adjectives syncopate in the adverbial case but not in the dative and instrumental cases – for example, **სქელ-ი** (fat, thick).

Genitive	სქელ-ის
Instrumental	სქელ-ით
Adverbial	სქ□ლ-ად

Declension of vowel-stem truncating adjectives

	Singular *green*	*Plural* *greens*	*Archaic plural*
Nom.	მწვანე	მწვანე-ებ -ი	მწვანე-ნ-ი
Erg.	მწვანე -მ	მწვანე-ებ-მა	მწვანე-თა
Dat.	მწვანე -ს	მწვანე-ებ-ს	მწვანე-თა
Gen.	მწვან□-ის	მწვანე -ებ-ის	მწვანე-თა
Instr.	მწვან□-ით	მწვანე-ებ-ით	–
Adv.	მწვანე -დ	მწვანე-ებ-ად	–
Voc.	მწვანე-(ვ)	მწვანე -ებ-ო	მწვანე-ნ-ო

5.3.2 *Declension of adjectives preceding nouns*

5.3.2.1 *Declension of vowel-stem adjectives preceding nouns*

In the prepositional order, a vowel stem adjective preceding a noun does not decline and remain unchanged in all cases.

	Singular *muddy river*
Nom.	მღვრიე მდინარე
Erg.	მღვრიე მდინარე-მ
Dat.	მღვრიე მდინარე-ს
Gen.	მღვრიე მდინარ-ის
Instr.	მღვრიე მდინარ-ით
Adv.	მღვრიე მდინარე-დ
Voc.	მღვრიე მდინარე (-ვ)

	Plural *muddy rivers*	
Nom.	მღვრიე მდინარე-ებ-ი	მღვრიე მდინარე-ნ-ი
Erg.	მღვრიე მდინარე-ებ-მა	მღვრიე მდინარე-თა
Dat.	მღვრიე მდინარე-ებ-ს	მღვრიე მდინარე-თა
Gen.	მღვრიე მდინარე-ებ-ის	მღვრიე მდინარე-თა
Instr.	მღვრიე მდინარე-ებ-ით	–
Adv.	მღვრიე მდინარე-ებ-ად	–
Voc.	მღვრიე მდინარე-ებ-ო	მღვრიე მდინარე-ნ-ო

In the postpositional order, an adjective and a noun preceding it have all case endings. Their stems may change depending on their consonant or vowel endings.

	Singular *full satchel*	
Nom.	ჩანთა	სავსე
Erg.	ჩანთა-მ	სავსე-მ
Dat.	ჩანთა-ს	სავსე-ს
Gen.	ჩანთ□-ის	სავს□-ის
Instr.	ჩანთ□-ით	სავს□-ით
Adv.	ჩანთა-დ	სავსე-დ
Voc.	ჩანთა-ვ	სავსე-ვ

	Plural *full satchel*	*Archaic plural*	
Nom.	ჩანთ□-ებ-ი სავსე // სავსე-ებ-ი	ჩანთა-ნ-ი	სავსე-ნ-ი
Erg.	ჩანთ□-ებ-მა სავსე-მ // სავსე-ებ-ი	ჩანთა-თ	სავსე-თა
Dat.	ჩანთ□-ებ-ს სავსე-ს // სავსე-ებ-ს	ჩანთა-თა	სავსე-თა
Gen.	ჩანთ□-ებ-ის სავს□ -ის // სავსე-ებ-ის	ჩანთა-თა	სავსე-თა

(Continued)

(Continued)

	Plural *full satchel*	Archaic plural
Instr.	ჩანთ□-ებ-ით სავს□-ით // სავსე-ებ-ით	–
Adv.	ჩანთ□-ებ-ად სავსე-დ // სავსე-ებ-ად	–
Voc.	ჩანთ□-ებ-ო სავსე-ებ-ო	ჩანთა-ნ-ო სავსე-ნ-ო

In the previous chart, the noun ending with the vowel **-ა** and the adjective ending with -ე are both truncated in the genitive and instrumental cases in singular forms. In plural the **-ა** ending stem of the noun is truncated in all cases. In the archaic form, an adjective may agree with the preceding noun in case and number (**ჩანთ-ებ-მა სავსე-ებ-მა**) or only in case (**ჩანთ-ებ-მა სავსე-მ**).

In the inverted order, an adjective with a non-truncating stem may agree with the preceding noun in both case and number (**ჩანთ-ებ-ი სავსე-ებ-ი**), but not always in plural forms (**კედლ-ებ-ი ყრუ**). Basically, this is a matter of personal style of the speakers. In archaic plural forms, there is a full agreement in case and number.

	Singular *blind wall*
Nom.	კედელ-ი ყრუ
Erg.	კედელ-მა ყრუ-მ
Dat.	კედელ-ს ყრუ-ს
Gen.	კედ□ლ-ის ყრუ-ს-ი
Instr.	კედ□ლ-ით ყრუ-თ-ი
Adv.	კედ□ლ-ად ყრუ-დ
Voc.	კედელ-ო ყრუ (-ვ)

	Plural *blind walls*		Archaic plural	
Nom.	კედ□ლ-ებ-ი	ყრუ	კედელ-ნ-ი	ყრუ-ნ-ი
Erg.	კედ□ლ-ებ-მა	ყრუ -მ	კედელ-თა	ყრუ-თა

	Plural *blind walls*		*Archaic plural*	
Dat.	კედ□ლ-ებ-ს	ყრუ-ს	კედელ-თა	ყრუ-თა
Gen.	კედ□ლ-ებ-ის	ყრუ-ს-ი	კედელ-თა	ყრუ-თა
Instr.	კედ□ლ-ებ-ით	ყრუ-თ-ი	–	
Adv.	კედ□ლ-ებ-ად	ყრუ-დ	–	
Voc.	კედ□ლ-ებ-ო	ყრუ (-ვ)	კედელ-ნ-ო	ყრუ-ნ-ო

5.3.2.2 *Declension of consonant stem adjectives preceding nouns*

In the prepositional order, a consonant-stem adjective and a noun following it agree in case only partially. A noun has the full set of case endings, but an adjective has them only in three cases, the nominative, ergative, and vocative. The case endings are only partially present in the genitive and instrumental forms; in the dative and adverbial cases, an adjective is in its stem form. According to the norms of contemporary Georgian, adjectives should be used in their singular forms. However, for stylistic purposes, they may fully agree with nouns they precede both in case and number in their archaic forms.

	Singular *large village*
Nom.	დიდ-ი სოფელ-ი
Erg.	დიდ-მა სოფელ-მა
Dat.	დიდ-□ სოფელ-ს
Gen.	დიდ-ი□ სოფ□ლ-ის
Instr.	დიდ-ი□ სოფ□ლ-ით
Adv.	დიდ-□ სოფ□ლ-ად
Voc.	დიდ-ო სოფელ-ო

	Plural *large villages*	*Archaic plural*
Nom.	დიდ-ი სოფ□ ლ-ებ-ი	დიდ-ი //დიდ-ნ-ი სოფელ-ნ-ი
Erg.	დიდ-მა სოფ□ ლ-ებ-მა	დიდ-□ // დიდ-თა სოფელ-თა

(Continued)

(Continued)

	Plural *large villages*	Archaic plural
Dat.	დიდ-□ სოფ□ ლ-ებ-ს	დიდ-□ // დიდ-თა სოფელ-თა
Gen.	დიდ-ი□ სოფ□ ლ-ებ-ის	დიდ-□ // დიდ-თა სოფელ-თა
Instr.	დიდ-ი□ სოფ□ ლ-ებ-ით	–
Adv.	დიდ-□ სოფ□ ლ-ებ-ად	–
Voc.	დიდ-ო სოფ□ ლ-ებ-ო	დიდ-ო //დიდ-ნ-ო სოფელ-ნ-ო

	Singular *large village*	
Nom.	სოფელ-ი	დიდ-ი
Erg.	სოფელ-მა	დიდ-ი
Dat.	სოფელ-ს	დიდ-ს
Gen.	სოფ□ლ-ის	დიდ-ის
Instr.	სოფ□ლ-ით	დიდ-ით
Adv.	სოფ□ლ-ად	დიდ-ად
Voc.	სოფელ-ო	დიდ-ო

	Plural *large villages*	Archaic plural
Nom.	სოფ□ ლ-ებ-ი დიდ-ი//დიდ-ებ-ი	სოფელ-ნ-ი დიდ-ნ-ი
Erg.	სოფ□ ლ-ებ-მა დიდ-მა//დიდ-ებ-მა	სოფელ-თა დიდ-თა
Dat.	სოფ□ ლ-ებ-ს დიდ-ს//დიდ-ებ-ს	სოფელ-თა დიდ-თა
Gen.	სოფ□ ლ-ებ-ის დიდ-ის//დიდ-ებ-ის	სოფელ-თა დიდ-თა
Instr.	სოფ□ ლ-ებ-ით დიდ-ით//დიდ-ებ-ით	–
Adv.	სოფ□ ლ-ებ-ად დიდ-ად//დიდ-ებ-ად	–
Voc.	სოფ□ ლ-ებ-ო დიდ-ო//დიდ-ებ-ო	სოფელ-ნ-ო დიდ-ნ-ო

In the postpositional order, both a consonant stem adjective and a noun preceding it fully agree in case and number in their singular forms. In plural they may or may not fully agree, depending on the style of the text in which they are used. In archaic forms there is always full agreement in case and number.

Chapter 6

Numerals

6.1 Types of numerals

Numerals are divided into three groups: cardinal, ordinal, and fractional numerals. Cardinal numerals indicate quantity of things and can be denoted with Arabic numerals, such as **ორასი** (200) and **ათას ოცდახუთი** (1,025).

Quantifiers are words referring to indefinite quantity and cannot be denoted with numerals: **ბევრი** (many), **მრავალი** (a lot), **უთვალავი** (countless), **უამრავი** (numerous), **აურებელი** (multitude), **აურაცხელი** (untold number), **ურიცხვი** (numberless), **ცოტა** (few).

Numerals may have basic and complex structures. The basic numerals include the numbers from one to ten, twenty, a hundred, and the borrowed numerals: million, billion, trillion, quadrillion, and some others.

The complex numerals are as follows:

1. Two stems of numerals joined by the conjunction **და** (and): ოცდახუთ-ი (25), ოცდაჩვიდმეტი (37), სამოცდასამი (63), ოთხმოცდაოთხი (84).
2. Numerals with two stems joined without conjunction: **ორმოცი** (40), **ოთხმოცი** (80), **შვიდასი** (700), **ცხრაასი** (900).
3. Combined numerals formed by joining several separate numerals. Among them are those from 11 to 19. They consist of three stems of separate numerals:

Initial stem combination	*Phonetic transformation process*	*Present form of the numerals*
ათ-სამ-მეტი (=ათზე სამით მეტი) (three more than ten) 13	**ათ-სამ-მეტი** > **თ-სამ-მეტი** **>**	ცამეტი

(Continued)

DOI: 10.4324/9781315281131-9

(Continued)

Initial stem combination		*Phonetic transformation process*		*Present form of the numerals*
ათ-ოთხ-მეტი	14	**ათ-**ოთხ-მეტი	>	თოთხმეტი
ათ-ხუთ-მეტი	15	**ათ-**ხუთ-მეტი	>	თხუთმეტი
ათ-ექვს-მეტი	16	**ათ-**ექვს-მეტი	>	თექვსმეტი
ათ-შვიდ-მეტი	17	**ათ-**შვიდ-მეტი	>	
		თ-შვიდ-მეტი	>	ჩვიდ-მეტი
ათ-რვა-მეტი	18	ათ-რვა-მეტი	>	თ**ვრ**ამეტი
ათ-ცხრა-მეტი	19	ათ-ცხრა-მეტი	>	ცხრამეტი

Nouns preceded by numerals and quantifiers are always in singular form: *ათი სტუდენტი* (10 students), *თორმეტი მოციქული* (12 apostles), *ბევრი მეგობარი* (many friends), *უთვალავი ვარსკვლავი* (countless stars), etc.

6.1.1 Cardinal numerals

Georgian numerals are based on bi-decimal numeration – i.e. 20, 40, 60, and 80 – are the basic units to which the numbers from 1 to 19 are added. However, the round numbers from a hundred to a thousand are based on decimals: **ასი** (100), **სამასი** (300), **ხუთასი** (500), etc. Similarly, round numbers from a hundred thousand up to a million are based on decimals – **ორასი ათასი** (200,000), **შვიდასი ათასი** (700,000), **ცხრაასი ათასი** (900,000), after which comes მილიონი (a million). This pattern continues with round numbers with nine, twelve, and so on digits, *ad infinitum*.

Bi-decimal numeration from 20 to 100	
ოცი	20
ორ-მ-ოცი	2 × 20 = 40
სამ-ოცი	3 × 20 = 60
ოთხ-მ-ოცი	4 × 20 = 80
ოც და ხუთი	20 + 5 = 25
ოც და ათი	20 + 10 = 30
ოც და ცამეტი	20 + 13 = 33

Bi-decimal numeration from 20 to 100

ორ-მ-ოც და ექვსი	(2 × 20) + 6 = 46
ორ-მ-ოც და ჩვიდმეტი	(2 × 20) + 17 = 57
სამ-ოც და ექვსი	(3 × 20) + 6 = 66
სამ-ოც და თვრამეტი	(3 × 20) + 18 = 78
ოთხ-მ-ოც და შვიდი	(4 × 20) + 7 = 87
ოთხ-მ-ოც და ცხრამეტი	(4 × 20) + 19 = 99

In the previous chart, the numerals სამოცდათვრამეტი (78) may be presented with a mathematical formula (7 × 10) + 8 based on decimals. However, in Georgian it is counted as (3 × 20) + 18 – i.e. it is based on bi-decimal numerals.

In the numerals **ორმოცი** (40) და **ოთხმოცი** (80) -მ- is a remaining part of the affix მე-: **ორ-მე-ოცი > ორმოცი, სამ-მე-ოცი > სამოცი, ოთხ-მე-ოცი > ოთხმოცი.**

Numerals with four digits or more are combination of two- and three-digit numerals in the following order:

ორმოცდახუთი ათას ოცდასამი (45,023)
ცხრაას ოთხმოცდაოთხი მილიონ რვაას ორმოცდათორმეტი ათას შვიდას ოცდაათი (984,852,730)

6.1.2 Spelling of cardinal numerals

1. The numerals from one to one hundred and round numbers in hundreds are spelled together:
   ათი (10), **ოცდარვა** (28), ასი (100), **ექვსასი** (600), **რვაასი** (800), **ათასი** (1,000)
2. In complex numerals, thousands, hundreds, and numbers from 1 to 99 are spelled separately: **ათას ცხრაას სამოცდაექვსი** (1,966), **ორი ათას თორმეტი** (2,012).

   მეფე ვახტანგი გამეფდა 438 **(ოთხას ოცდათვრამეტ)** *წელს.*
   King Vakhtang was crowned in the year 438.

   დავით აღმაშენებელმა დიდგორის ბრძოლაში 1121 **(ათას ას ოცდაერთ)** *წელს გაიმარჯვა.*

   David the builder won the Didgori battle in the year 1121.

ბაგრატ მესამე 963 (**ცხრაას სამოცდასამ**) *წელს გამეფდა, 36 (ოცდათექვსმეტი) წელი იმეფა და აღესრულა 1014* (**ათას თოთხმეტ**) *წელს.*

Bagrat III was crowned in the year 963, ruled for 36 years, and died in the year 1014.

6.2 Ordinal and fractional numerals

Ordinal and fractional numerals are derived from the stem of cardinal numerals. An ordinal numeral is formed by adding the circumfix მე-ე to the stem of a cardinal numeral. The only exception is პირველ-*ი* (first) which is not derived from the stem of ერთ-*ი* (one), but from the noun პირ-*ი* (face or person).

In ordinal numerals the circumfix მე-ე is added:	
1. To the stem of two or more digit round numerals	ორ-ი/მე-ორ-ე (2nd) ას-ი/მე-ას-ე (100th) სამოც-ი/მე-სამოც-ე (60th) ხუთასი/მე-ხუთას-ე (500th) ათას-ი/მე-ათას-ე (1,000th)
2. To the stem of the numeral following the conjunction და in two-digit numerals	სამოც-და-ათი/სამოც-და-მე-ათ-ე (70th) ოც-და-ჩვიდმეტ-ი/ოც-და-მე-ჩვიდმეტ-ე (37th) სამოც-და-მე-თვრამეტ-ე (78th) ოთხმოც-და-მე-თხუთმეტ-ე (95th)
3. To the stem of the last numeral or the numeral after The conjunction და in the three-digit non-round and four-or-more-digit complex numerals	ას-მე-ერთ-ე (101st) ათას ოც-და-მე-ხუთ-ე (1,025th) ხუთი მილიონ რვაას ორმოც-და-მე-ცხრამეტ-ე (5,000,859th)

When ordinal numerals are written in Arabic numbers, the prefix მე- is added to the numerals that follow the rule 1 in the previous chart: მე-6, მე-12, მე-100. The only exception is ***1*-ელი(პირველი)**. All other ordinal numerals have -ე added after an Arabic number: ***55*-ე, *107*-ე, *1966*-ე**.

> დავითი **მეექვსე//მე-*6*// *VI*** კლასშია.
> David is in the 6th grade.
> **მეთორმეტე//მე-*12*//*XII*** საუკუნე საქართველოს ოქროს ხანა იყო.
> The 12th century was the golden age of Georgia.
> ლექცია **ასმეშვიდე// *107*-ე** აუდიტორიაში ტარდება.
> The lecture is in the 107th auditorium.

Ordinal numerals ending with the adverbial case marker -**დ** denote frequency: *მეორე*-**დ** (the second time), *მეხუთე*-**დ** (the fifth time,) *მეათე*-**დ** (the tenth time), etc. Fractional numerals are based on the stem of ordinal numerals in the adverbial case:

Numerals

Cardinal	ათ-ი 10	ცხრამეტ-ი 19
Ordinal	მე-ათ-ე 10th	მე-ცხრამეტ-ე 19th
Adv. of ordinals	მე-ათ-ე-დ 10th time	მე-ცხრამეტ-ე-დ 19th time
Fractional	მე-ათ-ე-დ-ი 1/10	მე-ცხრამეტე-დ-ი 1/19

Numerals

Cardinal	ხუთას ერთ-ი 501	მილიონ-ი 1,000,000
Ordinal	ხუთას მე-ერთ-ე 501st	მე-მილიონ-ე 1,000,000th
Adv. of ordinals	ხუთას მე-ერთ-ე -დ 501st time	მე-მილიონ-ე-დ 1,000,000th time
Fractional	ხუთას მე-ერთ-ე-დ-ი 1/501	მე-მილიონ-ე-დ-ი 1/1,000,000

ასის **მეათედი** ათია.
One-tenth of a hundred is ten.
ამ წიგნის მხოლოდ **მესამედი** წავიკითხე.
I read only one-third of this book
ზოგიერთი რადიოაქტიური ელემენტის დაშლა წამის **მემილიონედ** ნაწილში ხდება.
Some radioactive elements disintegrate in one-millionth of a second.

6.3 Declension of numerals

The declension of numerals, like that of nouns and adjectives, depends on their stem ending. The consonant-stem non-syncopating numerals are as follows:

1. all numerals except რვა (8), ცხრა (9), and the complex numerals ending with the vowel-stem numerals: ას რვა (108), ხუთას ცხრა (509), etc.
2. quantifiers denoting unspecified quantity: აურაცხელ-ი (untold number)
3. ordinal numeral პირველი (the 1st)
4. all fractional numerals: მეხუთედ-ი (1/5), მეცხრედ-ი (1/9), ოცდამერვედ-ი (1/28)

The consonant-stem syncopating numerals are as follows:

1. The consonant-stem quantifier მრავალი (a lot): მრავლ-ის, მრავლ-ად
2. The fractional quantifier ნახევარი (1/2, half): ნახევრ-ის

The vowel-stem numerals are as follows:

1. truncating cardinal numerals რვა (8), ცხრა (9), and all complex numerals ending with these two: ას რვა (108), ხუთას ცხრა (509)
2. non-truncating quantifiers: ცოტა (a few), მცირე (a little), etc., and all ordinal numerals except პირველი (the first): მეორე, მესამე, etc.

6.3.1 Declension of consonant-stem cardinal numerals

6.3.1.1 Declension of consonant-stem cardinal numerals

A consonant-stem cardinal numeral not followed by a noun is declined like a similar stem noun and is not syncopated. A numeral can have the plural only if it functions as a noun.

	Singular five	*Plural fives*	*Archaic plural*
Nom.	ხუთ-ი	ხუთ-ებ-ი	ხუთ-ნ-ი
Erg.	ხუთ-მა	ხუთ-ებ-მა	ხუთ-თა
Dat.	ხუთ-ს	ხუთ-ებ-ს	ხუთ-თა
Gen.	ხუთ-ის	ხუთ-ებ-ის	ხუთ-თა
Instr.	ხუთ -ით	ხუთ-ებ-ით	–
Adv.	ხუთ-ად	ხუთ-ებ-ად	–
Voc.	ხუთ -ო	ხუთ-ებ -ო	ხუთ-ნ-ო

	Singular billion	*Plural billions*	*Archaic plural*
Nom.	მილიარდ-ი	მილიარდ-ებ-ი	მილიარდ-ნ-ი
Erg.	მილიარდ-მა	მილიარდ-ებ-მა	მილიარდ-თა
Dat.	მილიარდ-ს	მილიარდ-ებ-ს	მილიარდ-თა
Gen.	მილიარდ-ის	მილიარდ-ებ-ის	მილიარდ-თა
Instr.	მილიარდ-ით	მილიარდ-ებ-ით	–
Adv.	მილიარდ-ად	მილიარდ-ებ-ად	–
Voc.	მილიარდ-ო	მილიარდ-ებ-ო	მილიარდ-ნ-ო

Declension of complex consonant-stem cardinal numerals

	Complex cardinal numerals 815; 5,000; 3,000,000		
Nom.	რვაას თხუთმეტ-ი	ხუთ-ი ათას-ი	სამ-ი მილიონ-ი
Erg.	რვაას თხუთმეტ-მა	ხუთ-ი ათას-მა	სამ-მა მილიონ-მა
Dat.	რვაას თხუთმეტ-ს	ხუთ-ი ათას-ს	სამ მილიონ-ს
Gen.	რვაას თხუთმეტ-ის	ხუთ-ი ათას-ის	სამ-ი მილიონ-ის

(Continued)

(Continued)

	Complex cardinal numerals 815; 5,000; 3,000,000		
Instr.	რვაას თხუთმეტ-ით	ხუთ-ი ათას-ით	სამ-ი მილიონ-ით
Adv.	რვაას თხუთმეტ-ად	ხუთ-ი ათას-ად	სამ მილიონ-ად
Voc.	რვაას თხუთმეტ-ო	ხუთ-ი ათას-ო	სამ-ო მილიონ-ო

Declension of consonant-stem ordinal numerals

Among ordinal numerals, only **პირველი** (the first) has consonant-ending stem. It is not syncopated, and when used as a noun, it has both types of plural forms, modern and archaic.

	Plural	*Singular*	*Archaic plural*
Nom.	პირველ-ი	პირველ-ებ-ი	პირველ-ნ-ი
Erg.	პირველ-მა	პირველ-ებ-მა	პირველ-თა
Dat.	პირველ-ს	პირველ-ებ-ს	პირველ-თა
Gen.	პირველ-ის	პირველ-ებ-ის	პირველ-თა
Instr.	პირველ-ით	პირველ-ებ-ით	–
Adv.	პირველ-ად	პირველ-ებ-ად	–
Voc.	პირველ-ო	პირველ-ებ-ო	პირველ-ნ-ო

პირველი *იანვარი ახალი წლის დღეა.*
The first of January is the New Year's day.
ჩვენ **პირველებმა** *გავიგეთ ეს ამბავი.*
We were the first to find out about this event.

Declension of consonant-stem fractional numerals

	Plural	*Singular*	*Archaic plural*
Nom.	მეხუთედ-ი	მეხუთედ-ებ ი	მეხუთდ-ნ-ი
Erg.	მეხუთედ-მა	მეხუთედ-ებ-მა	მეხუთედ-თა

	Plural	*Singular*	*Archaic plural*
Dat.	მეხუთედ-ს	მეხუთედ-ებ-ს	მეხუთედ-თა
Gen.	მეხუთედ-ის	მეხუთედ-ებ-ის	მეხუთედ-თა
Instr.	მეხუთედ-ით	მეხუთედ-ებ-ით	–
Adv.	მეხუთედ-ად	მეხუთედ-ებ-ად	–
Voc.	მეხუთედ -ო	მეხუთედ-ებ -ო	მეხუთედ-ნ-ო

6.3.1.2 *Declension of consonant-stem quantifiers*

	Non-syncopating countless	*Syncopating*		
		Declension separately		*Declension with other numerals*
		many	*half*	*eight and a half*
Nom.	აურაცხელ-ი	მრავალ-ი	ნახევარ-ი	რვა-ნახევარ-ი
Erg.	აურაცხელ-მა	მრავალ-მა	ნახევარ-მა	რვა-ნახევარ-მა
Dat.	აურაცხელ-ს	მრავალ-ს	ნახევარ-ს	რვა-ნახევარ-ს
Gen.	აურაცხელ-ის	მრავ□ლ-ის	ნახევ□რ-ის-ა	რვა-ნახევ□რ-ის
Instr.	აურაცხელ-ით	მრავ□ლ-ით	ნახევ□რ-ით-ა	რვა-ნახევ□რ-ით
Adv.	აურაცხელ-ად	მრავ□ლ-ად	ნახევ□რ-ად	რვა-ნახევ□რ-ად
Voc.	აურაცხელ-ო	მრავალ-ო	ნახევარ-ო	რვა-ნახევარ-ო

მრავალი is the only quantifier with syncopating stem in the genitive, instrumental, and adverbial cases. The word **ნახევარი** denoting the fractional numeral 1/2 (**ერთი მეორედი**, one-half) is syncopated whether used independently or as a part of composite numerals.

ხუთის **ნახევრის** *შემდეგ სახლში ვიქნები.*
After four thirty (half past four) I will be at home.
ეს კაცი **ნახევრად** *ქართველია.*
This man is half-Georgian.

6.3.2 Declension of vowel-stem numerals

6.3.2.1 Declension of vowel-stem cardinal numerals

All vowel-stem numerals – *რვა* (8), *ცხრა* (9), *ორმოცდაცხრა* (49), *სამას რვა* (308), etc.; see section 6.3 – are truncated in two cases: the genitive and instrumental. If these numerals are used as nouns, they decline in plural form as well. Consequently, their stem ends with the suffix -ებ causing truncation in all cases.

Declension of one-word vowel-stem cardinal numerals

	Singular 8	*Plural* 8s	*Archaic plural*
Nom.	რვა	რვ□-ებ-ი	რვა-ნ-ი
Erg.	რვა-მ	რვ□-ებ-მა	რვა-თა
Dat.	რვა-ს	რვ□-ებ-ს	რვა-თა
Gen.	რვ□-ის	რვ□-ებ-ის	რვა-თა
Instr.	რვ□-ით	რვ□-ებ-ით	–
Adv.	რვა-დ	რვ□-ებ-ად	–
Voc.	რვა-(ვ)	რვ□-ებ-ო	რვა-ნ-ო

	Singular 709	*Plural* 709s	*Archaic plural* 709s
Nom.	შვიდას ცხრა	შვიდას ცხრ-ებ-ი	შვიდას ცხრა-ნ-ი
Erg.	შვიდას ცხრა-მ	შვიდას ცხრ-ებ-მა	შვიდას ცხრა-თა
Dat.	შვიდას ცხრა-ს	შვიდას ცხრ-ებ-ს	შვიდას ცხრა-თა

	Singular 709	*Plural* 709s	*Archaic plural* 709s
Gen.	შვიდას ცხრ□-ის	შვიდას ცხრ-ებ-ის	შვიდას ცხრა-თა
Instr.	შვიდას ცხრ□-ით	შვიდას ცხრ-ებ-ით	–
Adv.	შვიდას ცხრა-დ	შვიდას ცხრ-ებ-ად	–
Voc.	შვიდას ცხრა-(ვ)	შვიდას ცხრ-ებ-ო	შვიდას ცხრა-ნ-ო

6.3.2.2 Declension of vowel-stem quantifiers

The quantifier *ცოტა* (a few, a little) does not truncate; *მცირე* (a small, a little) does.

	Non-truncating	*Truncating*
Nom.	ცოტა	მცირე
Erg.	ცოტა-მ	მცირე-მ
Dat.	ცოტა-ს	მცირე-ს
Gen.	ცოტა-ს-ი	მცირ□-ის
Instr.	ცოტა-თ-ი	მცირ□-ით
Adv.	ცოტა-დ	მცირე-დ
Voc.	ცოტა-(ვ)	მცირე- (ვ)

ცოტა ფული *მინდა ვისესხო და მანქანა ვიყიდო.*
I want to borrow a little money and buy a car.
ამ ფაქტების მხოლოდ **მცირე ნაწილია** *დაზუსტებული.*
Only a small part of these facts is confirmed.

6.3.2.3 Declension of vowel stem ordinal numerals

All ordinal numerals except *პირველი* (the first) have vowel-ending stem. When used as nouns, these numerals have plural forms as well. Since all ordinal numerals have a *-ე*-ending stem, the vowel is doubled when the *-ებ* suffix is added to it.

	Singular *fifth*	*Plural* *fifths*	*Archaic plural*
Nom.	მეხუთე	მეხუთე-ებ ი	მეხუთე-ნ-ი
Erg.	მეხუთე-მ	მეხუთე-ებ-მა	მეხუთე-თა
Dat.	მეხუთე-ს	მეხუთე-ებ-ს	მეხუთე-თა
Gen.	მეხუთ□-ის	მეხუთე-ებ-ის	მეხუთე-თა
Instr.	მეხუთ□ -ით	მეხუთე-ებ-ით	–
Adv.	მეხუთე-დ	მეხუთე-ებ-ად	–
Voc.	მეხუთე-(ო/ვ)	მეხუთე-ებ -ო	მეხუთე-ნ-ო

	Singular *21st*	*Plural* *21sts*	*Archaic plural*
Nom.	ოცდამეერთე	ოცდამეერთე-ებ-ი	ოცდამეერთე-ნ-ი
Erg.	ოცდამეერთე -მ	ოცდამეერთე-ებ-მა	ოცდამეერთე-თა
Dat.	ოცდამეერთე-ს	ოცდამეერთე-ებ-ს	ოცდამეერთე-თა
Gen.	ოცდამეერთ□-ის	ოცდამეერთე-ებ-ის	ოცდამეერთე-თა
Instr.	ოცდამეერთ□-ით	ოცდამეერთე-ებ-ით	–
Adv.	ოცდამეერთე-დ	ოცდამეერთე-ებ-დ	–
Voc.	ოცდამეერთე-(ვ)	ოცდამეერთე-ებ-ო	ოცდამეერთე-ნ-ო

უკვე **მეხუთედ** *გთხოვ, დამიბრუნო ჩემი წიგნი.*
Already for the fifth time, I am asking you to return my book.
ოცდამეერთე საუკუნემ *ახალი გლობალური პრობლემები წარმოქმნა.*
The 21st century created new global problems.

6.3.3 Declension of cardinal numerals extended by particles

Cardinal numerals may be extended by adding the particles -*ვე*, -*ოდე*, and -*ც* to their nominative form: *ორი-ვე* (both), *ხუთი-ვე* (all five of them), *ათი-ვე* (all ten of them), etc. The particle **-ოდე** can be translated as *about*, *approximately*, or *only* – *სამი-ოდე* (about or only three), *ექვსი-ოდე* (about or only six), *ასი-ოდე* (about or only a hundred). The particle -ც indicates inclusiveness or addition – *შვიდი-ც* (seven too, seven also, seven more), *თორმეტი-ც* (twelve too, twelve as well, twelve more), *ოცი-ც* (twenty too, twenty more)

Numerals with the particles -*ვე* and -*ოდე* become vowel-stem words and are declined without truncation. The particle -*ც* is placed at the end of a numeral after extended case endings: *სამ-ს-ა-ც*. Numerals with extended stems do not have the vocative case.

Extended one-word cardinal numerals
all five, about five, five too

Nom.	ხუთი-ვე	ხუთი-ოდე	ხუთ-ი-ც
Erg.	ხუთი-ვე-მ	ხუთი-ოდე-მ	ხუთ-მა-ც
Dat.	ხუთი-ვე-ს	ხუთი-ოდე-ს	ხუთ-ს-ა-ც
Gen.	ხუთი-ვე-ს(ი)	ხუთი-ოდე-ს(ი)	ხუთ-ის-ა-ც
Instr.	ხუთი-ვე-თ(ი)	ხუთი-ოდე-თ(ი)	ხუთ-ით-ა-ც
Adv.	ხუთი-ვე-დ	ხუთი-ოდე-დ	ხუთ-ად-ა-ც
Voc.	–	–	–

Extended complex cardinal numerals

	all 815		about 815	
Nom.	რვაას	თხუთმეტი-ვე	რვაას	თხუთმეტი-ოდე
Erg.	რვაას	თხუთმეტი-ვე-მ	რვაას	თხუთმეტი-ოდე-მ
Dat.	რვაას	თხუთმეტი-ვე--ს	რვაას	თხუთმეტი-ოდე-ს
Gen.	რვაას	თხუთმეტი-ვე-ს(ი)	რვაას	თხუთმეტი-ოდე-ს(ი)

(Continued)

(Continued)

	Extended complex cardinal numerals	
Instr.	რვაას თხუთმეტი-ვე-თ(ი)	რვაას თხუთმეტი-ოდე-თ(ი)
Adv.	რვაას თხუთმეტი-ვე-დ	რვაას თხუთმეტი-ოდე-დ
Voc.	–	–

	815 too
Nom.	რვაას თხუთმეტი-ც
Erg.	რვაას თხუთმეტ-მა-ც
Dat.	რვაას თხუთმეტ-ს-ა-ც
Gen.	რვაას თხუთმეტ-ის-ა-ც
Instr.	რვაას თხუთმეტ-ით-ა-ც
Adv.	რვაას თხუთმეტ-ად-ა-ც
Voc.	–

Declension of ordinal numerals with particle -ც

	sixth too	*nineteenth too*
Nom.	მეექვსე-ც	მეცხრამეტე-ც
Erg.	მეექვსე-მა-ც	მეცხრამეტე-მა-ც
Dat.	მეექვსე-ს-ა-ც	მეცხრამეტე-სა-ც
Gen.	მეექვს□-ის-ა-ც	მეცხრამეტ□-ის-ა-ც
Instr.	მეექვს□-ით-ა-ც	მეცხრამეტ□-ით-ა-ც
Adv.	მეექვსე-დ-ა-ც	მეცხრამეტე-დ-ა-ც

	815 too
Nom.	რვაას მეთხუთმეტე-ც
Erg.	რვაას მეთხუთმეტე-მა-ც

	815 too	
Dat.	რვაას	მეთხუთმეტე-ს-ა-ც
Gen.	რვაას	მეთხუთმეტ□-ის-ა-ც
Instr.	რვაას	მეთხუთმეტ□-ით-ა-ც
Adv.	რვაას	მეთხუთმეტე-და-ც

თქვენთან ***ორიოდე*** *კითხვა მაქვს.*
I have a couple of questions for you.
ეზოში ***ათიოდე*** *ბიჭი ფეხბურთს თამაშობდა.*
In the yard, about ten boys were playing football.
წელს ჩვენმა ***სამივე*** *დოქტორანტმა დაიცვა დისერტაცია.*
This year, all three of our doctoral students defended their dissertations.
ორას ოცივე *ჯარისკაცი მედლებით დააჯილდოვეს.*
All the 220 soldiers were awarded medals.
ორივე *აუდიტორია,* ***მეოთხეც*** *და* ***მეხუთეც*** *სავსეა სტუდენტებით.*
Both auditoriums, the fourth and the fifth, are filled with students.

Declension of ordinal numerals in their plural form with the particle-ც

	sixth ones too	*nineteenth ones too*
Nom.	მეექვსე-ებ-ი-ც	მეცხრამეტე-ებ-ი-ც
Erg.	მეექვსე-ებ--მა-ც	მეცხრამეტე-ებ-მა-ც
Dat.	მეექვსე-ებ-ს-ა-ც	მეცხრამეტე-ებ-ს-ა-ც
Gen.	მეექვსე-ებ-ის-ა-ც	მეცხრამეტე-ებ-ის-ა-ც
Instr.	მეექვსე-ებ-ით-ა-ც	მეცხრამეტე-ებ-ით-ა-ც
Adv.	მეექვსე-ებ-ად-ა-ც	მეცხრამეტე-ებ-ად-ა-ც
Voc.	–	–

	815th ones too	
Nom.	რვაას	მეთხუთმეტე-ებ-ი-ც
Erg.	რვაას	მეთხუთმეტე-ებ-მა-ც
Dat.	რვაას	მეთხუთმეტე-ებ-ს-ც

(Continued)

(Continued)

	815th ones too	
Gen.	რვაას	მეთხუთმეტე-ებ-ის-ა-ც
Instr.	რვაას	მეთხუთმეტე-ებ-ით-ა-ც
Adv.	რვაას	მეთხუთმეტე-ებ-ად-ა-ც
Voc.		–

Declension of fractional numerals with the particle -ც

	Singular *0.21 too*	*Plural* *0.21s too*
Nom.	ოცდამეერთედ-ი-ც	ოცდამეერთედ-ებ-ი-ც
Erg.	ოცდამეერთედ -მა-ც	ოცდამეერთედ -ებ-მა-ც
Dat.	ოცდამეერთედ -ს-ა-ც	ოცდამეერთედ-ებ-ს-ა-ც
Gen.	ოცდამეერთედ-ის-ა-ც	ოცდამეერთედ -ებ-ის-ა-ც
Instr.	ოცდამეერთედ-ით-ა-ც	ოცდამეერთედ-ებ-ით-ა-ც
Adv.	ოცდამეერთედ -ად-ა-ც	ოცდამეერთედ-ებ-ად-ა-ც
Voc.	–	–

დისერტაციის ***მეათედიც*** *კი არა აქვს დამთავრებული.*
He has not finished even one-tenth of his dissertation.
ამ საწამლავის ***ორმოცდამეათედიც*** *კი საკმარისია, რომ ცხენი მოკლას.*
Even one-fiftieth of this poison is enough to kill a horse.

6.3.4 Declension of numerals followed by nouns

6.3.4.1 Declension of vowel-stem numerals followed by nouns

Vowel-stem numerals preceding a noun remain in their stem form in all cases.

	Numerals preceding nouns			
	nine boys		*third shelf*	
Nom.	ცხრა	ბიჭი	მესამე	თარო
Erg.	ცხრა	ბიჭ-მა	მესამე	თარო-მ

	Numerals preceding nouns			
	nine boys		*third shelf*	
Dat.	ცხრა	ბიჭ-ს	მესამე	თარო-ს
Gen.	ცხრა	ბიჭ-ის	მესამე	თარო-ს-ი
Instr.	ცხრა	ბიჭ-ით	მესამე	თარო-თი
Adv.	ცხრა	ბიჭ-ად	მესამე	თარო-დ
Voc.	ცხრა	ბიჭ-ო	მესამე	თარო(-ვ)

	Numerals preceding nouns	*Quantifiers with nouns*	
	115th question	*a little sugar*	
Nom.	ასმეთხუთმეტე შეკითხვა	ცოტა	შაქარ-ი
Erg.	ასმეთხუთმეტე შეკითხვა-მ	ცოტა	შაქარ-მა
Dat.	ასმეთხუთმეტე შეკითხვა-ს	ცოტა	შაქარ-ს
Gen.	ასმეთხუთმეტე შეკითხვ□-ის	ცოტა	შაქ□რ-ის
Instr.	ასმეთხუთმეტე შეკითხვ□ით	ცოტა	შაქ□რ-ით
Adv.	ასმეთხუთმეტე შეკითხვა-დ	ცოტა	შაქ□რ-ად
Voc.	ასმეთხუთმეტე შეკითხვა-ვ	ცოტა	შაქარ-ო

Consonant-stem ordinal numerals added to the numerals borrowed from foreign languages (million, billion, etc.) drop the suffix -ე in all cases.

	Singular	*Plurals*	
	six millionth tourist	*second billionth tree*	
Nom.	მეექვსმილიონე ტურისტ-ი	მეორმილიარდე	ხე
Erg.	მეექვსმილიონე ტურისტ-მა	მეორმილიარდე	ხე-მ
Dat.	მეექვსმილიონე ტურისტ-ს	მეორმილიარდე	ხე-ს

(*Continued*)

(Continued)

	Singular	Plurals
	six millionth tourist	*second billionth tree*
Gen.	მეექვსმილიონე ტურისტ-ის	მეორმილიარდე ხ□-ის
Instr.	მეექვსმილიონე ტურისტ-ით	მეორმილიარდე ხ□-ით
Adv.	მეექვსმილიონე ტურისტ-ად	მეორმილიარდე ხე-დ
Voc.	მეექვსმილიონე ტურისტ-ო	მეორმილიარდე ხე-ვ(//ხე)

The particles **-ვე** and **-ოდე** added to the stem of numerals form vowel-stem numerals and are declined as such when preceding a noun. According to the norms of the literary Georgian, nouns qualified by any numeral must be in singular form.

	Singular	Plural
	all ten children	*about five sparrows*
Nom.	ათივე ბავშვ-ი	ხუთიოდე ბეღურა
Erg.	ათივე ბავშვ-მა	ხუთიოდე ბეღურა-მ
Dat.	ათივე ბავშვ-ს	ხუთიოდე ბეღურა-ს
Gen.	ათივე ბავშვ-ის	ხუთიოდე ბეღურ□-ის
Instr.	ათივე ბავშვ-ით	ხუთიოდე ბეღურ□-ით
Adv.	ათივე ბავშვ-ად	ხუთიოდე ბეღურა-დ
Voc.	ათივე ბავშვ-ო	ხუთიოდე ბეღურა-ვ(//ბეღურა)

6.3.4.2 *Declension of consonant-stem cardinal numerals followed by nouns*

Consonant-stem numerals followed by nouns are declined as consonant-stem adjectives preceding nouns. In the prepositional order, a noun following a consonant-stem numeral declines in all seven cases, while the numeral has the case endings only in the nominative, ergative, and vocative. The case endings are only partially present in the genitive and instrumental. In the dative and adverbial, numerals are present in their stem form. In the archaic forms, numerals and nouns agree with each other both in case and number.

	Singular *five books*	*Archaic plural* *five books*
Nom.	ხუთ-ი წიგნ-ი	ხუთ-ნ-ი წიგნ-ნ-ი
Erg.	ხუთ-მა წიგნ-მა	ხუთ-თა წიგნ-თა
Dat.	ხუთ-□ წიგნ-ს	ხუთ-თა წიგნ-თა
Gen.	ხუთ-ი□ წიგნ-ის	ხუთ-თა წიგნ-თა
Instr.	ხუთ -ი□ წიგნ-ით	–
Adv.	ხუთ- □ წიგნ-ად	–
Voc.	ხუთ -ო წიგნ-ო	ხუთ-ნ-ო წიგნ-ნ-ო

Declension of complex consonant-stem cardinal numerals followed by nouns

	815 persons		
Nom.	რვაას	თხუთმეტ-ი	ადამიან-ი
Erg.	რვაას	თხუთმეტ-მა	ადამიან-მა
Dat.	რვაას	თხუთმეტ-□	ადამიან-ს
Gen.	რვაას	თხუთმეტ-ი□	ადამიან-ის
Instr.	რვაას	თხუთმეტ-ი□	ადამიან-ით
Adv.	რვაას	თხუთმეტ-□	ადამიან-ად
Voc.	რვაას	თხუთმეტ-ო	ადამიან-ო

	seven thousand trees, three million					
Nom.	შვიდ-ი	ათას-ი	ხე	სამ-ი	მილიონ-ი	ხე
Erg.	შვიდ-ი	ათას-მა	ხე-მ	სამ-მა	მილიონ-მა	ხე-მ
Dat.	შვიდ-ი	ათას-□	ხე-ს	სამ	მილიონ-□	ხე-ს

(Continued)

(Continued)

	seven	*thousand*	*trees,*	*three*	*million*	
Gen.	შვიდ-ი	ათას-ი□	ხ□-ის	სამ-ი	მილიონ-ი□	ხ□-ის
Instr.	შვიდ-ი	ათას-ი□	ხ□-ით	სამ-ი	მილიონ-ი□	ხ□-ით
Adv.	შვიდ-ი	ათას-□	ხე-დ	სამ	მილიონ-□	ხე-დ
Voc.	შვიდ-ი	ათას-ო	ხე-ვ(//ხე)	სამ-ო	მილიონ-ო	ხე-ვ (//ხე)

	1,578 kg			
Nom.	ათას	ხუთას	სამოცდათვრამეტ-ი	კილო
Erg.	ათას	ხუთას	სამოცდათვრამეტ-მა	კილო-მ
Dat.	ათას	ხუთას	სამოცდათვრამეტ-□	კილო-ს
Gen.	ათას	ხუთას	სამოცდათვრამეტ-ი□	კილო-ს-ი
Instr.	ათას	ხუთას	სამოცდათვრამეტ-ი□	კილო-თ-ი
Adv.	ათას	ხუთას	სამოცდათვრამეტ-□	კილო-დ
Voc.	ათას	ხუთას	სამოცდათვრამეტ-ო	კილო-(ვ)

	52%	
Nom.	ორმოცდათორმეტ-ი	პროცენტ-ი
Erg.	ორმოცდათორმეტ-მა	პროცენტ-მა
Dat.	ორმოცდათორმეტ-□	პროცენტ-ს
Gen.	ორმოცდათორმეტ-ი□	პროცენტ-ის
Instr.	ორმოცდათორმეტ-ი□	პროცენტ-ით
Adv.	ორმოცდათორმეტ-□	პროცენტ-ად
Voc.	ორმოცდათორმეტ-ო	პროცენტ-ო

Declension of consonant-stem fractional numerals

	Singular *1/5 part*	
Nom.	მეხუთედ-ი	ნაწილ-ი
Erg.	მეხუთედ-მა	ნაწილ-მა
Dat.	მეხუთედ-□	ნაწილ-ს
Gen.	მეხუთედ-ი	ნაწილ-ის
Instr.	მეხუთედ-ი	ნაწილ-ით
Adv.	მეხუთედ-□	ნაწილ-ად
Voc.	მეხუთედ-ო	ნაწილ-ო

	Plural *1/5 parts*		*Archaic plural*	
Nom.	მეხუთედ-ი	ნაწილ-ებ-ი	მეხუთდ-ნ-ი	ნაწილ-ნ-ი
Erg.	მეხუთედ-მა	ნაწილ-ებ-მა	მეხუთედ-თა	ნაწილ-თა
Dat.	მეხუთედ-□	ნაწილ-ებ-ს	მეხუთედ-თა	ნაწილ-თა
Gen.	მეხუთედ-ი□	ნაწილ-ებ-ის	მეხუთედ-თა	ნაწილ-თა
Instr.	მეხუთედ-ი□	ნაწილ-ებ-ით	–	
Adv.	მეხუთედ-□	ნაწილ-ებ-ად	–	
Voc.	მეხუთედ-ო	ნაწილ-ებ-ო	მეხუთედ-ნ-ო	ნაწილ-ნ-ო

Fractional numerals derived from the foreign languages (million, billion, etc.) decline according to the rules explained previously – i.e. like any consonant-stem numeral, they precede nouns in their stem form in the dative and adverbial cases, but in the genitive and instrumental, the case endings are only partially present, and both the numeral and the noun have the corresponding case endings in the nominative and ergative.

	Singular *zero, one-trillionth part*	
Nom.	მეტრილიონედ-ი	ნაწილ-ი
Erg.	მეტრილიონედ-მა	ნაწილ-მა
Dat.	მეტრილიონედ-□	ნაწილ-ს
Gen.	მეტრილიონედ-ი□	ნაწილ-ის
Instr.	მეტრილიონედ-ი□	ნაწილ-ით
Adv.	მეტრილიონედ-□	ნაწილ-ად
Voc.	მეტრილიონედ-ო	ნაწილ-ო

	Plural *zero, two-billionth segments*	
Nom.	მეორმილიარდედ-ი	მონაკვეთ-ი
Erg.	მეორმილიარდედ-მა	მონაკვეთ-მა
Dat.	მეორმილიარდედ-□	მონაკვეთ-ს
Gen.	მეორმილიარდედ-ი□	მონაკვეთ-ის
Instr.	მეორმილიარდედ-ი□	მონაკვეთ-ით
Adv.	მეორმილიარდედ-□	მონაკვეთ-ად
Voc.	მეორმილიარდედ-ო	მონაკვეთ-ო

6.3.5 *Declension of numerals followed by numerals*

A consonant-stem numeral preceding another numeral decline in the same manner as one preceding a noun. It has case endings only in the nominative, ergative, and vocative. In the genitive and instrumental, the case endings are only partially present; in the dative and adverbial, they are in their stem form. The numeral following the prepositional numeral has all case endings. A vowel-stem numeral preceding another numeral does not have any case ending; the numeral following the prepositional numeral has all case endings.

	Singular 1/10		Plural 9/27	
Nom.	ერთ-ი	მეათედი	ცხრა	ოცდამეშვიდედ-ი
Erg.	ერთ-მა	მეათედ-მა	ცხრა	ოცდამეშვიდედ-მა
Dat.	ერთ-□	მეათედ-ს	ცხრა	ოცდამეშვიდედ-ს
Gen.	ერთ-ი□	მეათედ-ის	ცხრა	ოცდამეშვიდედ-ის
Instr.	ერთ-ი□	მეათედ-ით	ცხრა	ოცდამეშვიდედ-ით
Adv.	ერთ-□	მეათედ-ად	ცხრა	ოცდამეშვიდედ-ად
Voc.	ერთ-ო	მეათედ-ო	ცხრა	ოცდამეშვიდედ-ო

Even if a noun is inserted between numerals, the declension rule does not change and follows the previously mentioned pattern.

		1.2		
Nom.	ერთ-ი	მთელ-ი	ორ-ი	მეათედ-ი
Erg.	ერთ-მა	მთელ-მა	ორ-მა	მეათედ-მა
Dat.	ერთ-□	მთელ-□	ორ-□	მეათედ-ს
Gen.	ერთ-ი□	მთელ-ი□	ორ-ი□	მეათედ-ის
Instr.	ერთ-ი□	მთელ-ი□	ორ-ი□	მეათედ-ით
Adv.	ერთ-□	მთელ-□	ორ-□	მეათედ-ად
Voc.	ერთ-ო	მთელ-ო	ორ-ო	მეათედ-ო

		0.17		
Nom.	ნულ-ი	მთელ-ი	ჩვიდმეტ-ი	მეასედ-ი
Erg.	ნულ-მა	მთელ-მა	ჩვიდმეტ-მა	მეასედ-მა
Dat.	ნულ-□	მთელ-□	ჩვიდმეტ-□	მეასედ-ს
Gen.	ნულ-ი□	მთელ-ი□	ჩვიდმეტ-ი□	მეასედ-ის
Instr.	ნულ-ი□	მთელ-ი□	ჩვიდმეტ-ი□	მეასედ-ით
Adv.	ნულ-□	მთელ-□	ჩვიდმეტ-□	მეასედ-ად
Voc.	ნულ-ო	მთელ-ო	ჩვიდმეტ-ო	მეასედ-ო

			8.914		
Nom.	რვა	მთელ-ი	ცხრას	თოთხმეტ-ი	მეათასედ-ი
Erg.	რვა	მთელ-მა	ცხრას	თოთხმეტ-მა	მეათასედ-მა
Dat.	რვა	მთელ-□	ცხრას	თოთხმეტ-□	მეათასედ-ს
Gen.	რვა	მთელ-ი□	ცხრას	თოთხმეტ-ი□	მეათასედ-ის
Instr.	რვა	მთელ-ი□	ცხრას	თოთხმეტ-ი□	მეათასედ-ით
Adv.	რვა	მთელ-□	ცხრას	თოთხმეტ-□	მეათასედ-ად
Voc.	რვა	მთელ-ო	ცხრას	თოთხმეტ-ო	მეათასედ-ო

Chapter 7

Pronouns

7.1 Personal pronouns and their declension

Georgian language has first-, second-, and third-person pronouns with their corresponding plural forms. None of them denote a gender.

Person	*Singular*	*Plural*
I	მე	ჩვენ
II	შენ	თქვენ
III	ის, იგი, ეს, ეგ	ისინი, ესენი, ეგენი

First- and second-person pronouns, both singular and plural, do not have a full set of cases. Both these pronouns are used in the genitive case only together with a postposition. The first-person singular pronoun changes its stem in the genitive case. Only second-person pronouns have the vocative case.

	1st p. s.	*2nd p. s.*	*1st p. pl.*	*2nd p. pl.*
Nom.	მე	შენ	ჩვენ	თქვენ
Erg.	მე	შენ	ჩვენ	თქვენ
Dat.	მე, ჩემ-postposition	შენ, შენ-postposition	ჩვენ, ჩვენ-postposition	თქვენ, თქვენ-postposition
Gen.	ჩემ-postposition	შენ-postposition	ჩვენ-postposition	თქვენ-postposition
Instr.	–	–	–	–
Adv.	–	–	–	–
Voc.	–	შენ, შე	–	თქვენ, თქვე

DOI: 10.4324/9781315281131-10

Since personal pronouns do not have case endings, their function is determined by the verb and the syntactic structure of a sentence.

> *მე* ***შენ*** *საჩუქარი გიყიდე. = მე (ადამიან-მა* Erg.*) შენ (ადამიან-ს* Dat.) *საჩუქარი გიყიდე.*
> I (a man) bought a gift for you (a woman).
> ***შენ მე*** *რა კარგი საჩუქარი მიყიდე! = შენ (ადამიან-მა* Erg.*) მე (ადამიან-ს* Dat.) *რა კარგი საჩუქარი მიყიდე!*
> What a nice gift you (a man) bought for me (a woman).

If in the dative case a postposition is added to the personal pronouns, the case ending ***-ს*** will be dropped: ამას **ჩემ-ზე** (< ჩემ-ს-ზე) ამბობ? (Do you speak about me?) If the stems ***ჩემ-***, ***ჩვენ-***, ***შენ-***, and ***თქვენ-***with postposition (***ჩემ-ზე***, ***ჩემ-ში***, ***ჩემ-თან***, ***ჩვენ-ზე***, ***ჩვენ-ში***, ***ჩვენ-თან***, ***შენ-ზე***, ***შენ-ში***, ***შენ-თან***, ***თქვენ-ზე***, ***თქვენ-ში***, ***თქვენ-თან***) are used in the dative case, they cannot be person of a verb.

The same form is presented with the function of the genitive case:

> *ეს წიგნი* ***შენ-თვის*** *(=კაც-ის-თვის) მინდა.*
> I wanted this book for you (for a person).
> *წერილი* ***შენ-გან*** *(=მეგობრის-გან) მივიღე.*
> I received this letter from you (from a friend).

The second-person plural pronoun ***თქვენ*** is used in polite forms when addressing someone:

> *თქვენ ხვალ აქ იქნებით, ქალბატონო ანა?*
> Will you be here tomorrow, Ms. Ana?

The first-person pronoun ***ჩვენ*** may refer to the first and second person both, as well as to the first and third person; it may also imply all three – the first, second, and third persons.

> *ხვალ* ***ჩვენ*** *თეატრში მივდივართ.*
> We are going to the theatre tomorrow.

In this sentence the pronoun ***ჩვენ*** (we) may imply any of the following combinations: *you and I* (sing. or pl.); *he/she and I*; *they and I*; *you (sing. or pl.), he/she, and I*; *you (sing. or pl.)*; *they and I.*

Georgian has four third-person singular pronouns – ***ეს***, ***ეგ***, ***ის***, and ***იგი*** – and four corresponding pronouns in plural. None of them identify gender and all singular pronouns correspond to English: *he*, *she*, *it*. All four, especially the first three (ეს, ეგ, ის, იგი), function as demonstrative pronouns as well: ***ეს***, ***ეგ***–*this* and ***ის***, ***იგი***

–*that*. As personal pronouns, they are coordinated with verbs; as demonstrative determiners, they precede nouns:

> ***ის*** ქართულად ლაპარაკობს.
> He speaks Georgian.
> ***ის კაცი*** ქართულად ლაპარაკობს.
> That man speaks Georgian.

The choice of the pronouns *ეს*, *ეგ*, or *ის* depends on the spatial position of the speaker and interlocutor vis-à-vis the person or object to which they refer (see more detailed explanation on 7.4., "Demonstrative pronouns"). Third-person pronouns have two stems, one for the nominative and another for the rest of the cases. The non-nominative stem of third-person pronouns – ***იმა-***, ***ამა-***, ***მაგა***–are truncated in the instrumental and adverbial cases. In the ergative, they have the Old Georgian ergative marker -ნ.

	3rd p. s.	*3rd p. s.*	*3rd p. s.*
Nom.	ის, იგი	ეს	ეგ
Erg.	(ი)მა-ნ	(ა)მა-ნ	მაგა-ნ
Dat.	(ი)მა-ს (ი)მა- postposition	(ა)მა-ს (ა)მა- postposition	მაგა-ს მაგა- postposition
Gen.	(ი)მ□-ის- postposition	(ა)მ□-ის- postposition	მაგ□-ის- postposition
Instr.	(ი)მ□-ით	(ა)მ□-ით	მაგ-ით
Adv.	(ი)მა-დ	(ა)მა-დ	მაგა-დ
Voc.	–	–	–

The plural form of third-person pronouns is marked with the suffix -***ნ***: ***ისი-ნ-ი***, ***ესე-ნ-ი***, ***ეგე-ნ-ი***. There is also a rather rarely used third-person pronoun ***იგი-ნ-ი***.

	3rd p. pl.	*3rd p. pl.*	*3rd p. pl.*
Nom.	ისი-ნ-ი	ესენ-ი	ეგენ-ი
Erg.	მა-თ	(ა/ი)მა-თ	მაგა-თ
Dat.	მა-თ, მა-თ- postposition	(ა/ი)მა-თ, (ა/ი)მა-თ- postposition	მაგა-თ, (ა/ი)მა-თ- postposition

(Continued)

(Continued)

	3rd p. pl.	*3rd p. pl.*	*3rd p. pl.*
Gen.	მა-თ- postposition	(ა/ი)მა-თ- postposition	მაგა-თ- postposition
Instr.	მა-თ-ით	(ა/ი)მა-თ-ით	მაგა-თ-ით
Adv.	მა-თ-ად	(ა/ი)მა-თ-ად	მაგა-თ-ად
Voc.	–	–	–

If in the dative case postposition ***-ზე*** or ***-ში*** is added to the third-person singular pronouns, the case ending ***-ს*** will be dropped (compare with first- and second-person pronouns): ***ი/ამა-ზე*** < *ი/ამა-ს-ზე) ამბობ?* (Do you speak about him/her?), ***ამაში*** *ჩააწყვე!* (Put in this!), but *ამა-ზე ამბობ?* If the forms ***ი/ამა-თ-, მაგა-თ*** are used with postposition-***თან*** in the dative case, two *თ* will be in the word: ***ი/ამა-თ-თან, მაგა-თ-თან სტუმარი მოვიდა,*** but ***მა-თ-თან სტუმარი მოვიდა.*** (A guest visited them.) All third-person pronouns with postpositions in the dative case they cannot be person of a verb.

Third-person singular pronouns have a vowel-ending stem in all but the nominative and, therefore, are always truncated in the genitive and instrumental cases. Like first- and second-person pronouns, they may have suffixes in the dative and genitive cases:

Dative:

> *მა-ს-ზე დიდი ხანია წერენ გაზეთებში.*
> They have been writing about him in newspapers for a long time.
> ***მას-თან*** *მისვლა ყოველთვის მიხარია.*
> I am always happy to visit him.

Genitive:

> *ეს ჩანთა ჩემი* ***და-ის-თვის*** *ვიყიდე.*
> I bought this bag for my sister.
> ***მათ-გან*** *ამას არ ველოდი.*
> I did not expect this from them.

7.2 Reflexive pronouns

The word ***თავი*** (head, self) may function either as a noun or as a reflexive pronoun depending on the context. In the sentence ***მან***

თავი დაიბანა (he washed his head/hair), it functions as a noun referring to a part of a human body. However, in a different context – for example, **მან თავი გადაარჩინა.** (he saved himself), the word **თავი** functions as a reflexive pronoun – i.e. it indicates an action directed towards oneself.

> *თავი მოიკლა.*
> He killed himself.
> *თავი დაიმდაბლა.*
> He belittled himself.
> *მათ თავი დადეს თავისი ქვეყნისთვის.*
> They gave their lives for their country.

თავი has the same declension pattern as a consonant stem non-syncopating noun whether it functions as a noun or pronoun. It serves as a base for a number of pronouns, such as the possessive pronoun **თავისი** (his/her own), **თვით** (by oneself), **თავად** (by oneself), and **თვითონ** (by oneself).

7.3 Possessive pronouns and their declension

Possessive pronouns denote possession or ownership, as well as relationships between persons.

Person	*Singular*	*Plural*
I	ჩემ-ი my	ჩვენ-ი our
II	შენ-ი your	თქვენ-ი your
III	მის-ი (ა)მის-ი (ი)მის-ი მაგის-ი his, her his/hers	მათ-ი (ა)მათ-ი (ი)მათ-ი მაგათ-ი their

The first-person possessive pronoun ჩემი (my) is derived from the genitive case form of the personal pronoun მე. The genitive case of the second- and third-person possessive pronouns serve as the stems of the second- and third-person personal pronouns. Since the stem of the third-person personal pronoun varies, it is reflected in the forms of the corresponding possessive pronouns.

Third-person personal pronouns in the genitive case	*Third-person possessive pronouns in the nominative case*
მ-ის	მის-ი
ამ-ის	ამის-ი
იმ-ის	იმის-ი
მაგ-ის	მაგის-ი
მათ	მათ-ი
ამათ	ამათ-ი
იმათ	იმათ-ი
მაგათ	მაგათ-ი

As the chart shows, possessive pronouns are most probably derived from the personal pronouns. The ending of the pronouns *(ა)მ-ის-ი*,*(ი)მ-ის-ი*, and *მაგ-ის-ი* is derived from the genitive case ending in-**ის**. The ending **-თ** of the pronouns ***(ა)მა-თ-ი***,***(ი)მა-თ-ი***, and ***მაგა-თ-ი*** is their plural marker, while the final **-ი** is the nominative case marker. The pronouns ***თავ-ის-ი*** (one's own) and ***სხვ-ი-ს-ი*** (someone else's) are derived from the genitive case forms of the reflexive pronoun ***თავ–*** (self) and the pronoun ***სხვა*** (other, someone, or something else) by adding the nominative case marker **-ი**.

> *ჩემმა მასწავლებელმა* ***თავისი წიგნი*** *მაჩუქა.*
> My teacher presented me with her (own) book.
> *მეგობარმა* ***სხვისი წიგნი*** *მათხოვა.*
> A friend gave me someone else's book (a book that belongs to someone else).
> *ეს* ***ჩემი წიგნი*** *არ არის, ეს* ***სხვისი წიგნია.***
> This is not my book, it is someone else's (it belongs to someone else).
> ***მისი ძმა თქვენი კლასელი*** *არ არის?*
> Isn't his/her brother your classmate?
> ***მათი და შენი მეზობელია? (=შენი მეზობელი არის?).***
> Is their sister you neighbour?

Possessive pronouns are declined separately and together with nouns following them.

Declension of possessive pronouns without nouns

	Singular	*Plural*	
Nom.	ჩემ-ი	ჩემ-ებ-ი	ჩემ-ნ-ი
Erg.	ჩემ-მა	ჩემ-ებ-მა	ჩემ-თა
Dat.	ჩემ-ს	ჩემ-ებ-ს	ჩემ-თა
Gen.	ჩემ-ი(ს)	ჩემ-ებ-ის	ჩემ-თა
Instr.	ჩემ-ით	ჩემ-ებ-ით	–
Adv.	ჩემ-ად	ჩემ-ებ-ად	–
Voc.	ჩემ-ო	ჩემ-ებ-ო	ჩემ-ნ-ი

The possessive pronoun *თქვენი* may refer to a single person when used as a polite form of address:

> *ეს **თქვენი** წიგნია, ქალბატონო/ბატონო?*
> Is this *your* book, madam/sir?

7.3.1 Declension of possessive pronouns with nouns

Possessive pronouns, when declined together with nouns, follow the pattern of the adjective declension. The exceptions are the dative and adverbial case forms. In particular, adjectives in the dative and adverbial cases are present in their stem form while possessive pronouns acquire the ending ***-ს*** in both of these cases.

	Adjective preceding noun		*Possessive pronoun preceding noun*	
Dat.	კარგ-□	მეგობარ-ს	*ჩემ-ს*	მეგობარ-ს
Adv.	კარგ-□	მეგობ□რ-ად	*ჩემ-ს*	მეგობ□რ-ად

The following is a complete paradigm of the declension of possessive pronouns with nouns:

	Singular	
Nom.	ჩემ-ი	მეგობარ-ი
Erg.	ჩემ-მა	მეგობარ-მა

(*Continued*)

(Continued)

	Singular	
Dat.	ჩემ-ს	მეგობარ-ს
Gen.	ჩემ-ი□	მეგობ□რ-ის
Instr.	ჩემ-ი □	მეგობ□რ-ით
Adv.	ჩემ-ს	მეგობ□რ-ად
Voc.	ჩემ-ო	მეგობარ-ო

	Plural			
Nom.	ჩემ-ი	მეგობ□რ-ებ-ი	ჩემ-ი	მეგობარ-ნ-ი
Erg.	ჩემ-მა	მეგობ□რ-ებ-მა	ჩემ-თა	მეგობარ-თა
Dat.	ჩემ-ს	მეგობ□რ-ებ-ს	ჩემ-თა	მეგობარ-თა
Gen.	ჩემ-ი□	მეგობ□რ-ებ-ის	ჩემ-თა	მეგობარ-თა
Instr.	ჩემ-ი □	მეგობ□რ-ებ-ით		–
Adv.	ჩემ-ს	მეგობ□რ-ებ--ად		–
Voc.	ჩემ-ო	მეგობ□რ-ებ--ო	ჩემ-ნ-ო	მეგობარ-ნ-ო

The possessive pronoun ***თავისი*** refers to a single person and ***თავიანთი*** to more than one.

> *მარიამი თავის ლექსებს კითხულობს.*
> Mariam is reading her own poems.

In this sentence, თავისი refers to a single person, Mariam.

> *სტუდენტები თავიანთ ლექსებს კითხულობენ.*
> Students are reading their own poems.

In this sentence, the pronoun თავიანთი refers to more than one person.

There is an important difference between თავისი and მისი; the former means *his/her own*, and the latter refers to someone else's.

> *გიორგიმ **თავისი** რვეული მაჩვენა.*
> George showed me his notebook (the notebook belongs to George).
> *გიორგიმ **მისი** რვეული მაჩვენა.*
> George showed me his/her notebook (the notebook belongs not to George but to someone else).

*ნიკომ **თავისი** მოთხრობა წამიკითხა.*
Niko read me his story (Niko read me *his own* story, the one he wrote himself).
*მე ძალიან მომეწონა **მისი** მოთხრობა.*
I liked his story very much (I liked *his* story, the one he wrote).

	Singular	
Nom.	თავის-ი	მეგობარ-ი // მეგობ□რ-ებ-ი
Erg.	თავის-მა	მეგობარ-მა // მეგობ□რ-ებ-მა
Dat.	თავის	მეგობარ-ს // მეგობ□რ-ებ-ს
Gen.	თავის-ი□	მეგობ□რ-ის // მეგობ□რ-ებ-ის
Instr.	თავის-ი□	მეგობ□რ-ით // მეგობ□რ-ებ-ით
Adv.	თავის	მეგობ□რ-ად // მეგობ□რ-ებ-ად
Voc.	–	

	Plural	
Nom.	თავიანთ-ი	მეგობარ-ი // მეგობ□რ-ებ-ი
Erg.	თავიანთ-მა	მეგობარ-მა // მეგობ□რ-ებ-მა
Dat.	თავიანთ	მეგობარ-ს // მეგობ□რ-ებ-ს
Gen.	თავიანთ-ი□	მეგობ□რ-ის // მეგობ□რ-ებ-ის
Instr.	თავიანთ-ი□	მეგობ□რ-ით // მეგობ□რ-ებ-ით
Adv.	თავიანთ	მეგობ□რ-ად // მეგობ□რ-ებ-ად
Voc.	–	

The pronoun ***სხვისი*** (someone else's) refers to something in possession of a third person:

*ეს წიგნები **ჩემია**.*
These books are mine.
*ის წიგნები **თქვენია**.*
Those books are yours.
*ეგ წიგნები **სხვისია** (არც ჩემია და არც თქვენია).*
Those books are someone else's (neither mine nor yours).
The pronoun ***სხვისი*** has the same declension pattern as ***თავისი***.

7.4 Demonstrative pronouns

There are two types of the demonstrative pronouns, the primary and derivative. The primary demonstrative pronouns point at something or someone specifying its distance from the speaker. The demonstrative pronouns for the third-person singular are identical with the corresponding personal pronouns. Thus, the basic demonstrative pronouns are *ეს*, *ის*, *ეგ*, and *იგი*. The pronouns *ის* and *იგი* are synonymous but come from the different dialect areas. The latter was in use mostly in old Georgian. In modern Georgian *იგი* is often used with or without the particle -*ვე*, which is never added to the demonstrative pronouns: *ეს* and *ის* in the nominative case. Sometimes particle -ვე is added to *ეგ//ეგე>ეგევე*. Both იგივე and ეგევე means *the same* or *that very one*.

The demonstrative pronouns *ეს* (*this*) and *ის* (*that*) always precede a noun. It is important to distinguish them from the corresponding personal pronouns:

1. **Demonstrative pronoun ის with a noun**
   ის კაცი აქ არ ცხოვრობს.
   That man does not live here.

2. **Personal pronoun ის**
   ის ახლა ამერიკაშია.
   He is in America now.

The pronoun *ეს* is used to point at someone or something near the speaker, *ის* at something or someone further from the speaker, while ეგ refers to someone or something in the proximity of the second person. For example, *ეს სახლი* (this house) refers to a house near the person speaking. *ის სახლი* (that house) implies a house near the third person from the point of view of the speaker. *ეგ სახლი* (that house) indicates the house that is near the second person.

The demonstrative pronouns *ეს*, *ეგ*, and *ის* may be followed by nouns in plural forms and should be translated as *these* (ეს, ეგ) and *those* (ის), respectively.

ეს წიგნი ჩემია, *ის წიგნი* სხვისია.
This book is mine. That book is someone else's.
ეს წიგნები მაგიდაზე აწყვია. *ის წიგნები* სად არის?
These books are on the table. Where are those books?

There is a group of the derivative demonstrative pronouns referring to features of someone or something. The most of them are synonymous with a slight difference in meaning, which depends on the region they are in use, personal style of speech, or the distance from the person or object the speaker has in mind: *ასეთი//ესეთი* (this kind), *აგეთი//ეგეთი* (this kind that you have or is close to you), *ისეთი//იგეთი* (that kind), *ამგვარი* (this type), *მაგგვარი* (that type that you have or is close to you), *იმგვარი* (that type).

Some demonstrative pronouns may imply certain character of someone, or unspecified quantity of something: *ამნაირი* (this kind), *იმნაირი* (that kind), *მაგნაირი* (that kind – refers to the second person), *ამისთანა* (this kind), *მაგისთანა* (that kind – refers to the second person), *იმისთანა* (that kind), *ამდენი* (this much/many), *მაგდენი* (that much/many – refers to the second person), *იმდენი* (that much/many), etc.

The primary demonstrative pronouns *ეს* (one that is here), *ეგ* (one that is over there), and *ის//იგი* (one that is out there) are the bases for all the derivative pronouns:

ასეთი	ეგეთი	ისეთი
ამდენი	მაგდენი	იმდენი
ამგვარი	მაგგვარი	იმგვარი
ამნაირი	მაგნაირი	იმნაირი
ამისთანა	მაგისთანა	იმისთანა

Demonstrative pronouns may or may not precede nouns. The phonetic process that takes place in their stems during declension, depending on whether they have consonant or vowel endings in the nominative case.

7.4.1 Declension of demonstrative pronouns

Consonant-stem demonstrative pronouns

	Singular this kind	*Archaic plural these kinds*	
Nom.	ა/ისეთ-ი	ა/ისეთ-ებ-ი	ა/ისეთ-ნ-ი
Erg.	ა/ისეთ-მა	ა/ისეთ-ებ-მა	ა/ისეთ-თა
Dat.	ა/ისეთ-ს	ა/ისეთ-ებ-ს	ა/ისეთ-თა
Gen.	ა/ისეთ-ის	ა/ისეთ-ებ-ის	ა/ისეთ-თა
Instr.	ა/ისეთ-ით	ა/ისეთ-ებ-ით	–
Adv.	ა/ისეთ-ად	ა/ისეთ-ებ-ად	–
Voc.	ა/ისეთ-ო	ა/ისეთ-ებ-ო	ა/ისეთ-ნ-ო

	Singular this kind	*Plural these kinds*
Nom.	ა/იმნაირ-ი	ა/იმნაირ-ებ-ი
Erg.	ა/იმნაირ-მა	ა/იმნაირ-ებ-მა
Dat.	ა/იმნაირ-ს	ა/იმნაირ-ებ-ს
Gen.	ა/იმნაირ-ის	ა/იმნაირ-ებ-ის
Instr.	ა/იმნაირ-ით	ა/იმნაირ-ებ-ით
Adv.	ა/იმნაირ-ად	ა/იმნაირ-ებ-ად
Voc.	ა/იმნაირ-ო	ა/იმნაირ-ებ-ო

Demonstrative pronouns ***ამისთანა*** (this kind) and ***იმისთანა*** (that kind) are not truncated when declined in singular form; in plural, the truncation occurs before the ending -***ებ***.

	Singular this kind	*Plural these kinds*
Nom.	ა/იმისთანა	ა/იმისთან□-ებ-ი
Erg.	ა/იმისთანა-მ	ა/იმისთან□-ებ-მა
Dat.	ა/იმისთანა-ს	ა/იმისთან□-ებ-ს
Gen.	ა/იმისთანა-ს(ი)	ა/იმისთან□-ებ-ის
Instr.	ა/იმისთანა-თ(ი)	ა/იმისთან□-ებ-ით
Adv.	ა/იმისთანა-დ	ა/იმისთან□-ებ-ად
Voc.	ა/იმისთანა-ვ	ა/იმისთან□-ებ-ო

7.4.2 Declension of demonstrative pronouns preceding nouns

Third-person personal pronouns functioning as demonstrative pronouns have two stems and no case endings when declined together with nouns. They do not change when preceding a noun in plural form.

	Consonant-stem demonstrative pronouns			
		Singular		
Nom.	ეს/ის	კაცი	ეგ	კაცი
Erg.	ამ/იმ	კაც-მა	მაგ	კაც-მა
Dat.	ამ/იმ	კაც-ს	მაგ	კაც-ს
Gen.	ამ/იმ	კაც-ის	მაგ	კაც-ის
Instr.	ამ/იმ	კაც-ით	მაგ	კაც-ით
Adv.	ამ/იმ	კაც-ად	მაგ	კაც-ად
Voc.		–		–
		Plural		
Nom.	ეს/ის	კაც-ებ-ი	ეგ	კაც-ებ-ი
Erg.	ამ/იმ	კაც-ებ-მა	მაგ	კაც-ებ-მა
Dat.	ამ /იმ	კაც-ებ-ს	მაგ	კაც-ებ-ს
Gen.	ამ/იმ	კაც-ებ-ის	მაგ	კაც-ებ-ის
Instr.	ამ/იმ	კაც-ებ-ით	მაგ	კაც-ებ-ით
Adv.	ამ/იმ	კაც-ებ-ად	მაგ	კაც-ებ-ად
Voc.		–		

When demonstrative pronouns precede nouns, they are declined as adjectives with corresponding stem type – i.e. they are present in their stem form in the dative and adverbial cases, while in the genitive and instrumental, the case endings are only partially present. The nouns following them decline as usual.

	Consonant-stem demonstrative pronouns					
	Singular		*Plural*			
Nom.	ასეთ-ი	კაც-ი	ასეთ-ი	კაც-ებ-ი	ასეთ-ნ-ი	კაც-ნ-ი
Erg.	ასეთ-მა	კაც-მა	ასეთ-მა	კაც-ებ-მა	ასეთ – □	კაც-თა
Dat.	ასეთ – □	კაც-ს	ასეთ – □	კაც-ებ-ს	ასეთ – □	კაც-თა
Gen.	ასეთ-ი□	კაც-ის	ასეთ-ი□	კაც-ებ-ის	ასეთ – □	კაც-თა
Instr.	ასეთ-ი□	კაც-ით	ასეთ-ი □	კაც-ებ-ით	–	
Adv.	ასეთ-□	კაც-ად	ასეთ – □	კაც-ებ-ად	–	
Voc.	ასეთ-ო	კაც-ო	ასეთ-ო	კაც-ებ-ო	ასეთ-ნ-ო	კაც-ნ-ო

The vowel-stem demonstrative pronouns preceding nouns do not have case endings; they are present in their stem form.

	Vowel-stem demonstrative pronouns with noun			
	Singular		*Plural*	
Nom.	ა/იმისთანა	კაბა	ა/იმისთანა	კაბ□-ებ-ი
Erg.	ა/იმისთანა	კაბა-მ	ა/იმისთანა	კაბ□-ებ-მა
Dat.	ა/იმისთანა	კაბა-ს	ა/იმისთანა	კაბ□-ებ -ს
Gen.	ა/იმისთანა	კაბ□-ის	ა/იმისთანა	კაბ□-ებ-ის
Instr.	ა/იმისთანა	კაბ□-ით	ა/იმისთანა	კაბ□-ებ-ით
Adv.	ა/იმისთანა	კაბა-დ	ა/იმისთანა	კაბ□-ებ-ად
Voc.	ა/იმისთანა	კაბ□-ო	ა/იმისთანა	კაბ□-ებ-ო

7.4.3 Declension of demonstrative pronouns with added particles separately and with nouns

The pronoun *იგივე* (the same) has the case endings added to the particle *-ვე*. Both parts of the pronoun *ერთი და იგივე* (one and the same) have all case endings except the vocative. *ერთი* is declined as a consonant stem numeral, while *იგივე* has two stems: in the nominative *იგივე* and in all other cases *იმავე*, to which the case suffixes are added.

	Pronouns with added particles			
Nom.	იგივე	ერთ-ი	და	იგივე
Erg.	იმავე-მ	ერთ-მა	და	იმავე-მ
Dat.	იმავე-ს	ერთ-სა	და	იმავე-ს
Gen.	იმავე-ს(ი)	ერთ-ი	და	იმავე-ს(ი)
Instr.	იმავე-თ(ი)	ერთ-ი	და	იმავე-თ(ი)
Adv.	იმავე-დ	ერთ-სა	და	იმავე-დ
Voc.	–		–	

These pronouns preceding a noun or nouns change their stem in all cases after the nominative, but the case endings are added only to the nouns following them. The pronoun *ერთი* in the compound pronoun *ერთი და იგივე* (one-and-the-same) has the case endings in the ergative and dative.

	Pronouns with added particles		Pronouns with added particles followed by a noun			
Nom.	იგივე	ისარ-ი	ერთ-ი	და	იგივე	გზა
Erg.	იმავე	ისარ-მა	ერთ-**მა**	და	იმავე	გზა-მ
Dat.	იმავე	ისარ-ს	ერთ-**სა**	და	იმავე	გზა-ს//
			ერთ-**ი**	და	იმავე	გზა-ს
Gen.	იმავე	ის□რ-ის	ერთ-ი	და	იმავე	გზ□-ის
Instr.	იმავე	ის□რ-ით	ერთ-ი	და	იმავე	გზ□-ით
Adv.	იმავე	ის□რ-ად	ერთ-სა	და	იმავე	გზა-დ
Voc.		–			–	

7.5 Interrogative pronouns and their declension

The primary interrogative pronouns in Georgian are ***ვინ*** (who) and ***რა*** (what). The interrogative pronoun ***ვინ*** refers to a person, ***რა*** to other animate and inanimate objects.

- *ვინ მოვიდა?*
  Who has come?
- ***მეზობელი*** მოვიდა. (***ვინ*** refers to a person.)
  The neighbour has come.
- *ეს **რა** არის?* (***რა*** refers to an animal; i.e., an animate object.)
  What is it?
- ეს არის ***ძაღლი.***
  It is a dog.
- *ეს **რა** არის?*
  What is it?
- *ეს არის **ნამცხვარი.*** (***რა*** refers to the inanimate object.)
  It is a cake.

ვინ (who) may be used only in singular form; ***რა(what)*** both in singular and plural. Although რა has a vowel stem, only its singular form is truncated in three cases, but not in its plural form.

Interrogative pronouns				
Nom.	ვი-ნ	რა	რა-ებ-ი	რა-ნ-ი
Erg.	ვი-ნ	რა-მ	რა-ებ-მა	–
Dat.	ვი-ს	რა-ს	რა-ებ-ს	–
Gen.	ვი-ს	რ□-ის	რა-ებ-ის	–
Instr.	–	რ□-ით	რა-ებ-ით	–
Adv.	–	რა-დ	რა-ებ-ად	–
Voc.	–	–	–	–

The case of *ვინ* or *ვის* is determined by the case of the noun for which it stands in the affirmative sentence.

– *ვინ* რეკავს?
Who is calling?
– *მეგობარ-ი* რეკავს.
A friend is calling.

Since ***მეგობარ-ი*** is in the nominative case, the pronoun *ვინ* is assumed to be in the nominative.

– ***ვინ*** დაწერა ეს სტატია?
Who wrote this article?
– ***მეგობარ-მა*** დაწერა.
A friend wrote it.

The ergative case of ***მეგობარ-მა*** indicates that ***ვინ*** in the interrogative sentence is also in the ergative.

The interrogative *ვინ*, although never used in the plural form, may refer to more than one person.

– ***ვინ*** ამბობს ამას?
Who is saying this?
– *მეზობლები* ამბობენ.
The neighbours are saying.

There are several derivative interrogative pronouns in Georgian: ***რომელი*** (which, what) ***როგორი*** (what kind, what), ***რანაირი*** (what kind/sort), ***რამდენი*** (how much/many), ***როდინდელი*** (of what period, how old), ***რა და რა*** (what and what), ***ვინ და ვინ***

(who and who). It is quite obvious that the majority of them are derived from the interrogative pronoun **რა**.

რომელი is probably formed by adding the particle *-ელ* to **რა-მე**:

> **რომელი** *საათია?*
> What (lit. *which*) time is it?
> *რომელი გირჩევნია?*
> Which (one) do you prefer?

რამდენი has the particle **-ოდენ** added to **რა**; the pronoun **რაოდენი** is formed similarly, the particle **-ოდენ** added to **რა**. The pronoun **რაზომი** is synonymous with **რამდენი** and **რაოდენი**:

> **რამდენი** *ძმა გყავს?*
> How many brothers do you have?
> **რამდენი** *დრო გვაქვს?*
> How much time do we have?

როგორი is the combination of **რო***(რა)* and the noun **გვარი/გორი** (kind, type). The primary meaning of *გვარი/გორი* is "clan/surname." Thus, in modern Georgian *რა გვარი ხარ* means "what is your surname." However, in the mountainous regions of East Georgia, *რა გორისა ხარ?* could imply also question about one's origin, the area, or one's clan:

> **როგორი** *ჩაი გიყვარს, მწვანე თუ შავი?*
> What kind of tea do you like, green or black?
> This pronoun may express also admiration or surprise:
> **როგორი** *კარგი ამინდია!* – What nice weather!
> **როგორი** *სიცივეა!* – How cold it is!

The pronouns **რარიგი** and **რაერთი** are synonymous with **როგორი** and are formed by adding the noun **რიგი** (kind, type) and numeral **ერთი** (one) to the interrogative pronoun **რა**. These pronouns were commonly used in East Georgia but are presently obsolete.

რა და რა (what and what) is pronoun **რა** joined with the conjunction **და**. This construction refers to more than one thing.

– **რა და რა** *მოიტანა?* – What did he bring? (lit. *What and what did he bring?*)
– *პური და ხორცი მოიტანა.* – He brought some bread and meat.

ვინ და ვინ (who and who) is similar to **რა და რა**. Double **ვინ** joined with **და** refers to more than one person but the verb following it may be in the singular or plural form:

- ***ვინ და ვინ*** *წავიდა ბაზარში?*
  Who (and who) went to the market?
- ***დედა და დეიდა*** *წავიდნენ.*
  Mother and Aunt went away.
- ***ვინ და ვინ*** *მოიტანა ხილი ბაზრიდან?*
  Who (and who) brought the fruit from the market?
- ***დედამ და დეიდამ*** *მოიტანეს.*
  Mother and Aunt brought it.
- ***ვინ და ვინ*** *წერდით წერილს?*
  Who (and who) were writing the letter?
- *მე და ჩემი კლასელი ვწერდით წერილს.*
  I and my classmate were writing the letter.
- *ვინ და ვინ იყავით გუშინ გაკვეთილზე?*
  Who (and who) were present in the class yesterday?

1. The answer to a question that starts with **ვინ და ვინ** may include two subjects joined with the conjunction **და**, thus repeating the structure of the interrogative pronoun itself:

   - ***ვინ და ვინ*** *შემოვიდა?*
     Who (and who) came in?
   - ***გოგო და ბიჭი*** (nom.) *შემოვიდნენ.*
     A girl and a boy came in.

2. The answer may have only one subject in singular form:

   - ***ვინ და ვინ*** *შემოვიდა?*
     Who (and who) came in?
   - ***(მარტო)ერთი გოგო*** *შემოვიდა.*
     (Only) a girl came in.

3. The subject answering to the question **ვინ და ვინ** may be preceded by a numeral:

   - ***ვინ და ვინ*** *დაწერა?*
     Who (and who) wrote it?
   - ***ორმა მოსწავლემ*** *დაწერა.*
     Two students wrote it.
   - ***გოგომ და ბიჭმა დაწერეს.***
     A girl and a boy wrote (it).

The interrogative pronouns *რა* and *ვინ* connected with the conjunction და are used in other cases as well.

Dative: ვის და ვის დავურეკოთ?
Whom (and whom) should we call?
– დედას და მამას დავურეკოთ.
Let's call Mom and Dad.
– რას და რას ჩამოგიტანს?
What (and what) will he bring you?
– კაბას და ფეხსაცმელს ჩამომიტანს.
He will bring me a dress and shoes.

Genitive: ვისი და ვისი ნახვა გინდა?
Whom (and whom) do you want to see (visit)?
– მეგობრების და ნათესავების ნახვა მინდა.
I want to see (visit) friends and relatives.
– რისა და რის ნახვა გინდა?
What (and what) do you want to see (visit)?
– თბილისისა და ქუთაისის ნახვა მინდა.
I want to see (visit) Tbilisi and Kutaisi.

7.5.1 *Declension of interrogative pronouns preceding nouns*

The declension pattern of interrogative pronouns preceding nouns depends on their stem type. Vowel-stem interrogative pronouns are ordinarily present in the form of their stem in every case while nouns are declined as usual. *(რა წიგნ-ის, რა წიგნ-ით.)* Consonant-stem interrogative pronouns decline only partially.

	Consonant-stem interrogative pronouns followed by noun			
	Singular			
	what kind of pencil		*what kind of problem*	
Nom.	როგორ-ი	ფანქარ-ი	რომელ-ი	საკითხ-ი
Erg.	როგორ-მა	ფანქარ-მა	რომელ-მა	საკითხ-მა
Dat.	როგორ-□	ფანქარ-ს	რომელ-□	საკითხ-ს
Gen.	როგორ-ი□	ფანქ□რ-ის	რომელ-ი□	საკითხ-ის
Instr.	როგორ-ი□	ფანქ□რ-ით	რომელ-ი□	საკითხ-ით
Adv.	როგორ-□	ფანქ□რ-ად	რომელ-□	საკითხ-ად
Voc.	–		–	

	Consonant-stem interrogative pronouns with noun in plural			
Nom.	როგორ-ი	ფანჯ□რ-ებ-ი	რომელ-ი	საკითხ-ებ-ი
Erg.	როგორ-მა	ფანჯ□რ-ებ-მა	რომელ-მა	საკითხ-ებ-მა
Dat.	როგორ-□	ფანჯ□რ-ებ-ს	რომელ-□	საკითხ-ებ-ს
Gen.	როგორ-ი□	ფანჯ□რ-ებ-ის	რომელ-ი□	საკითხ-ებ-ის
Instr.	როგორ-ი□	ფანჯ□რ-ებ-ით	რომელ-ი□	საკითხ-ებ-ით
Adv.	როგორ-□	ფანჯ□რ-ებ-ად	რომელ-□	საკითხ-ებ-ად
Voc.	–		–	

7.6 Possessive-interrogative pronouns and their declension

There are only two possessive-interrogative pronouns – *ვისი* (*whose*) and *რისი/რისა* (*of what, belonging to what*). They are derived from the genitive case forms of the interrogative pronouns *ვინ* (who) and *რა* (what). They may be declined separately as well as with nouns following them, but they have no plural forms and lack two cases: the genitive and vocative. In some of the cases, the euphonic *ა* is inserted in front of the case endings. In Georgian, it is often used as an extension vowel to separate two consonants.

Declension of possessive-interrogative pronouns independently

	Possessive-interrogative pronouns	
Nom.	ვის-ი	რის-ი
Erg.	ვის-მა	რის-ა-მ
Dat.	ვის-ა-ს	რის-ა-ს
Gen.	–	–
Instr.	ვის-ით	რის-ით
Adv.	ვის-ად	რის-ად
Voc.	–	–

7.6.1 *Declension of possessive-interrogative pronouns preceding nouns*

The declension pattern of possessive-interrogative pronouns remains the same whether they precede nouns in singular or plural forms.

	Possessive-interrogative pronouns with noun			
Nom.	ვის-ი	წიგნ-ი	/	წიგნ-ებ-ი
Erg.	ვის-მა	წიგნ-მა	/	წიგნ-ებ-მა
Dat.	ვის –	წიგნ-ს	/	წიგნ-ებ-ს
Gen.	ვის-ი	წიგნ-ის	/	წიგნ-ებ-ის
Instr.	ვის-ი	წიგნ-ით	/	წიგნ-ებ-ით
Adv.	ვის-	წიგნ-ად	/	წიგნ-ებ-ად
Voc.			–	
Nom.	რის-ი	ნაწილ-ი	/	ნაწილ-ებ-ი
Erg.	რის-მა	ნაწილ-მა	/	ნაწილ-ებ-მა
Dat.	რის –	ნაწილ-ს	/	ნაწილ-ებ-ს
Gen.	რის-ი	ნაწილ-ის	/	ნაწილ-ებ-ის
Instr.	რის-ი	ნაწილ-ით	/	ნაწილ-ებ-ით
Adv.	რის –	ნაწილ-ად	/	ნაწილ-ებ-ად
Voc.			–	

7.7 Negative pronouns and their declension

Negative pronouns negate persons or objects. They are formed by adding negative particles to the interrogative pronouns *ვინ* and *რა*: **არა +ვინ, ვერა +ვინ, ნურა +ვინ, აღარა +ვინ, ვეღარა +ვინ.** All these pronouns may be translated as *nobody*, but each has its own nuanced meaning and is usually coupled with a corresponding negative particle, **არ**, **ვერ**, or **ნუ**, preceding a verb:

დღეს ჩემთან ***არავინ არ*** *მოვიდა.//****არავინ*** *მოვიდა.*
Nobody came over to me (my house) today.
დღეს ჩემთან ***ვერავინ ვერ*** *მოვიდა.//****ვერავინ*** *მოვიდა.*
Nobody was able to come over to me today.
დღეს ჩემთან ***ნურავინ ნუ*** *მოვა.//****ნურავინ//ნურვინ*** *მოვა.*
Nobody should come to me today.

The first sentence is a simple statement of the fact – for whatever reason nobody visited me. The second sentence implies inability of potential visitors to come over – increment weather, illness, or some other obstacle. The negative particle *ნუ* and all its derivations are always used in Imperative mode and, therefore, the third sentence express a wish or request not to come.

აღარა-ვინ,ვეღარა-ვინ,ნუღარა-ვინ – in these negative pronouns the negative particles emphasize semantics of negation to their general denominator – *nobody*: They may be coupled with negative particle ***არ, ვერ, ნუ***, or ***აღარ, ვეღარ, ნუღარ:***

დღეს ჩემთან ***აღარავინ არ*** *მოვიდა.*
Today nobody came to me (i.e. although we had a precious agreement that they would come).
აღარავინ აღარ მოვიდა.
Nobody came anymore.
დღეს ჩემთან ***ვეღარავინ ვერ//ვეღარ*** *მოვიდა.*
Today nobody was able to come to me (i.e. although they intended to come over but changed their plans for some reason)
დღეს ჩემთან ***ნუღარავინ ნუ*** *მოვა.*
Nobody should come to me today (i.e. I changed my mind, or my plans changed and I cannot see anybody today).

Some negative pronouns are formed by adding negative particles to the words: *ფერი* and *ერთი*: ***არა+ფერი,ვერა+ფერი,ნურა+ფერი,აღარა+ფერი,ვეღარა+ფერი,ნუღარა+ფერი.*** All these pronouns are synonymous and may be translated as *nothing*.

დღეს ***არაფერი არ*** გავაკეთე.
Today I did not do anything (not intended to do).
დღეს ***ვერაფერი ვერ*** გავაკეთე.
Today I was not able to do anything.
დღეს ***ნურაფერს ნუ*** გააკეთებ.
Today, do not do anything.
აღარაფერი აღარ ახარებს.
Nothing makes him happy anymore.
ვეღარაფრით ვერ დავეხმარე ჩემს მეგობარს.
I could not help my friend with anything anymore.
ნუღარავის ნუღარაფერს ეტყვი ამის შესახებ.
Don't tell anyone about that anymore.

არც ერთი, ვერც ერთი, and ***ნურც ერთი*** are formed by adding the negative particles to the word *ერთი* and means *not even one*. In these pronouns, the word *ერთი* indicates an undetermined, unspecified number of persons or inanimate objects. All three negative pronouns have their own distribution demonstrated in the following examples:

არც ერთი არ *მოვიდეს!*
Nobody *must* come!

ვერც ერთი ვერ *მოვა!*
Nobody *can* come!
ნურც ერთი ნუ *მოვა!*
Nobody *may* come!

Negative pronouns		
nobody	*nothing*	*nothing*
არავინ	არარა	არაფერი
ვერავინ	ვერარა	ვერაფერი
ნურავინ	ნურარა	ნურაფერი
აღარავინ	Pronouns in this	აღარაფერი
ვეღარავინ	section are rarely	ვეღარაფერი
ნუღარავინ	used.	ნუღარაფერი

Negative pronouns	
no kind	*none*
არავითარი	არც ერთი
ვერავითარი	ვერც ერთი
ნურავითარი	ნურც ერთი
აღარავითარი	აღარც ერთი
ვეღარავითარი	ვეღარც ერთი
ნუღარავითარი	ნუღარც ერთი

Negative pronouns including **ვინ** and **რა** in their structure do not have all cases. The pronouns that end with **ფერი** have the syncopating stem.

Declension of negative pronouns			
	nobody	*nothing*	*none*
Nom.	არავინ	ნურაფერ-ი	ნურც ერთ-ი
Erg.	არავინ	ნურაფერ-მა	ნურც ერთ-მა
Dat.	არავი-ს	ნურაფერ-ს	ნურც ერთ-ს
Gen.	არავი-ს	ნურაფ□რ-ის	ნურც ერთ-ის
Instr.	–	ნურაფ□რ-ით	ნურც ერთ-ით
Adv.	–	ნურაფ□რ-ად	ნურც ერთ-ად
Voc.	–	–	–

7.8 Definite pronouns and their declension

The definite pronouns are **თითოეული** (each, each and every one), **ყველა** (all, everyone, everything), **ყოველი** (each), **ყველაფერი** (everything), **სხვა** (someone or something else, another, different).

The pronouns **თვით**, **თვითონ და**, and **თავად** do not decline. The declinable definite pronouns have some deviations from the norm. Not all definite pronouns have plural forms, or they lack some declension forms.

The pronouns **თვით** and **თავად** are derived from the instrumental and adverbial case forms of the noun **თავ-ი: თ(ა)ვ-ით** and **თავ-ად**. The pronoun **თვითონ** is derived from **თვით მან** *(he herself.* **თვით-მან > თვით -ან > თვით-ონ**). These pronouns indicate that a person is acting independently without outside help or is himself an object of an action. When used as a pronoun, it identifies a specific person or object, differentiated from the others.

> **თვითონ** *მისი ძმა წავიდა პოლიციაში.*
> His brother *himself* went to the police (i.e. nobody else but his brother went there).
> *მისი ძმა* **თვითონ** *წავიდა პოლიციაში.*
> His brother went to the police *himself* (i.e. he was not asked or forced to do so).

The pronoun **ყველა** has a generalizing, inclusive meaning and refers to some unified quantity. It implies everything or everyone without exception. The pronouns **ყოველი** (every) and **თითოეული** (each) have similarly inclusive meaning. The base for the definite pronoun *თითოეული* (each, each and every one) is a noun – **თითი** (finger).

> **ყველა სტუდენტი** *აუდიტორიაშია.*
> All students are in the auditorium.
> **ყოველი სტუდენტი** *ვალდებულია ეს გამოცდა ჩააბაროს.*
> Every student must pass this exam.
> **თითოეული წიგნი** *ამ კატალოგშია აღრიცხული.*
> Each book is listed in this catalogue.

The pronoun **სხვა** refers to a person or object other than the one familiar to the speaker.

> *მე* **სხვა წიგნი** *მინდა.*
> I want another book (i.e. not this one).
> **სხვა ვინ** *არის ამ პარტიის წევრი?*
> Who else is a member of this party?

Declension of non-syncopating definite pronouns

	each
Nom.	თითოეულ-ი
Erg.	თითოეულ-მა
Dat.	თითოეულ-ს
Gen.	თითოეულ-ის
Instr.	თითოეულ-ით
Adv.	თითოეულ-ად
Voc.	(თითოეულ-ო)

Syncopating definite pronouns

	Singular		*Plural*
	everything	*every*	
Nom.	ყველაფერ-ი	ყოველ-ი	ყოველ-ნ-ი
Erg.	ყველაფერ-მა	ყოველ-მა	ყოველ-თა
Dat.	ყველაფერ-ს	ყოველ-ს	ყოველ-თა
Gen.	ყველაფ□რ-ის	ყოვ□ლ-ის	ყოველ-თა
Instr.	ყველაფ□რ-ით	ყოვ□ლ-ით	–
Adv.	ყველაფ□რ-ად	ყოვ□ლ-ად	–
Voc.	(ყველაფერ-ო)	(ყოველ-ო)	–

Non-truncating definite pronouns

	Singular *all*	*Plural*
Nom.	ყველა	ყველა-ნ-ი
Erg.	ყველა-მ	–
Dat.	ყველა-ს	–
Gen.	ყველა-ს(ი)	–
Instr.	ყველა-თ(ი)	–
Adv.	ყველა-დ	–
Voc.	ყველა-(ვ)	–

Declension of truncating definite pronouns

Truncating definite pronouns decline as corresponding vowel-stem nouns. They are truncated in the instrumental and adverbial cases and in all cases when declined in plural form.

	Singular *other*	*Plural* *others*	
Nom.	სხვა	სხვ□-ებ-ი	სხვა-ნ-ი
Erg.	სხვა-მ	სხვ□ა-ებ-მა	სხვა-თა
Dat.	სხვა-ს	სხვ□-ებ-ს	სხვა-თა
Gen.	სხვ□ -ის	სხვ□ -ებ-ის	სხვა-თა
Instr.	სხვ□-ით	სხვ□-ებ-ით	–
Adv.	სხვა-დ	სხვ□-ებ-ად	–
Voc.	(სხვა-ო)	(სხვ□-ებ-ო)	(სხვა-ნ-ო)

7.8.1 *Declension of definite pronouns preceding nouns*

The declension pattern of definite pronouns preceding nouns depends on their stem type. The vowel-stem definite pronouns do not change, while a noun following them is declined as usual.

	Singular	
Nom.	სხვა	მოსწავლე
Erg.	სხვა	მოსწავლე-მ
Dat.	სხვა	მოსწავლე-ს
Gen.	სხვა	მოსწავლ□-ის
Instr.	სხვა	მოსწავლ□-ით
Adv.	სხვა	მოსწავლე-დ
Voc.	სხვა	მოსწავლე-ვ

	Plural			
Nom.	სხვა	მოსწავლე-ებ-ი	სხვა	მოსწავლე-ნ-ი
Erg.	სხვა	მოსწავლე-ებ-მა	სხვა	მოსწავლე-თა

	Plural	
Dat.	სხვა მოსწავლე-ებ-ს	სხვა მოსწავლე-თა
Gen.	სხვა მოსწავლე-ებ -ის	სხვა მოსწავლე-თა
Instr.	სხვა მოსწავლე-ებ -ით	–
Adv.	სხვა მოსწავლე-ებ-ად	–
Voc.	სხვა მოსწავლე-ებ-ო	(სხვა-ნ-ო მოსწავლე-ნ-ო)

Consonant-stem definite pronouns preceding a noun decline only partially, while the noun following them has all case endings.

	Definite pronouns with noun	
Nom.	თითოეულ-ი	მოსწავლე
Erg.	თითოეულ-მა	მოსწავლე-მ
Dat.	თითოეულ-□	მოსწავლე-ს
Gen.	თითოეულ-ი□	მოსწავ□ლ-ის
Instr.	თითოეულ-ი□	მოსწავ□ლ-ით
Adv.	თითოეულ-□	მოსწავლე-დ
Voc.	–	

	Definite pronouns with noun	
Nom.	ყოველ-ი	მასწავლებელ-ი
Erg.	ყოველ-მა	მასწავლებელ-მა
Dat.	ყოველ – □	მასწავლებელ-ს
Gen.	ყოველ-ი□	მასწავლებლ-ის
Instr.	ყოველ-ი□	მასწავლებლ-ით
Adv.	ყოველ-□	მასწავლებლ-ად
Voc.	–	

7.9 Indefinite pronouns and their declension

Indefinite pronouns refer to one or more persons or objects. They may imply a stranger or strangers, their number, or some other features.

– *ვინმე შემოვიდა?*
Did anyone come in?
– *ვიღაც კაცი შემოვიდა.*
Someone came in (lit. *some man*).

Indefinite pronouns are formed with the suffixes *-მე* and *-ღაც* added to interrogative pronouns:

– მე	*Meaning*	– ღაც	*Meaning*
ვინმე	anyone, someone	ვიღაც	someone
რამე	any, anything, something	რაღაც	something
რომელიმე	any, anyone, someone	რომელიღაც	any, anyone, someone/ something out of a certain number
რამდენიმე	several, few	რამდენიღაც	unspecified quantity

A few more indefinite pronouns are **ზოგი** (some) and **ზოგიერთი** (some). The nouns **კაცი** (man) and **მავანი** (undefined, unspecified person) and the numeral **ერთი** (one) may also function as indefinite pronouns.

The pronouns **ვინმე**, **ვიღაც** and **მავანი** refer only to persons.

– **ვინმე** მოვა დღეს?
Will anyone come over today?
– დიახ, **ჩვენი ნათესავი** მოვა.
Yes, our relative will come over.
– **ვიღაც** მოვიდა?
Did someone come over?
– დიახ, ჩვენი **მეზობელი** მოვიდა.
Yes, our neighbour came over.
მორბის **კაცი** *და ყვირის.*
Someone (lit. *a man*) is running and shouting.
მორბის **მავანი** *და ყვირის.*
Someone is running and shouting.

The pronouns *კაცი* and *მავანი* used in the previous sentences may be replaced by the pronoun **ვიღაც** (someone), but if it precedes the noun *კაცი*, these two words together *ვიღაც კაცი* (a man, some man) will specify that it's a man running and not a woman or a child.

მორბის ***ვიღაც*** *და ყვირის.*
Someone is running and shouting.
მორბის ***ვიღაც კაცი*** *და ყვირის.*
Some man is running and shouting.

The indefinite pronouns ***რამე*** and ***რაღაც*** refer only to inanimate objects and animals.

– *ჭამე* ***რამე!*** *არ გშია?*
Have (eat) something. Aren't you hungry?
– ***ჩაის*** *დავლევ.*
I'll have tea.
– *ვხედავ,* ***რაღაც*** *მოგიტანია!*
I see you have brought something.
– ***შენი წიგნები*** *მოვიტანე.*
I brought your books.

Indefinite pronouns ***რამდენიმე*** and ***რადენიღაც(ა)***(several, some) and ***რომელიღაც(ა)***(someone, some kind of) may refer to persons as well as inanimate objects of unspecified quantity.

სახლის წინ ***რამდენიმე მეზობელი*** *შეიკრიბა.*
Several (some) neighbours gathered in front of the house.
რამდენიმე სახლი *ძალიან ლამაზია ამ ქუჩაზე.*
Several houses are very beautiful on this street.
რომელიღაც წიგნი *გადმოვიღე თაროდან.*
I took some (kind of a) book from the shelf.
რომელიღაც მეზობელი *მირეკავს.*
Some (one of the) neighbour is calling me.
ამ წიგნებიდან ***რამდენიღაც(წიგნი)*** *წაკითხული მაქვს.*
Out of these books I have read some (books).

Declension of vowel-stem indefinite pronouns referring to persons

	Singular *someone*	
Nom.	ვინმე	ვიღაც(ა)
Erg.	ვინმე-მ	ვიღაცა-მ

(Continued)

(Continued)

	Singular *someone*	
Dat.	ვინმე-ს	ვიღაცა-ს
Gen.	ვინმე-ს(ი)	ვიღაც□-ის
Instr.	ვინმე-თ(ი)	ვიღაც□-ით
Adv.	ვინმე-დ	ვიღაცა-დ
Voc.	–	–

Declension of vowel-stem indefinite pronouns referring to persons

	Plural *some individuals*	
Nom.	ვიღაც-ებ-ი	ვიღაც-ვიღაც-ებ-ი
Erg.	ვიღაც-ებ-მა	ვიღაც-ვიღაც-ებ-მა
Dat.	ვიღაც-ებ-ს	ვიღაც-ვიღაც-ებ-ს
Gen.	ვიღაც-ებ-ის	ვიღაც-ვიღაც-ებ-ის
Instr.	ვიღაც-ებ-ით	ვიღაც-ვიღაც-ებ-ით
Adv.	ვიღაც-ებ-ად	ვიღაც-ვიღაც-ებ-ად
Voc.	–	

Declension of consonant-stem indefinite pronouns referring to persons

	Singular *certain person*	*Plural* *certain persons*
Nom.	მავან-ი	მავან-ნ-ი
Erg.	მავან-მა	მავან-თა
Dat.	მავან-ს	მავან-თა
Gen.	მავან-ის	მავან-თა
Instr.	მავან-ით	–
Adv.	მავან-ად	–
Voc.	მავან-ო	მავან-ნ-ო

Declension of consonant-stem indefinite pronouns referring to inanimate objects

	Singular *something*	*anyone/* *anything*	*Plural* *somethings*
Nom.	რამე	რომელიმე	რამე-ებ-ი
Erg.	რამე-მ	რომელიმე-მ	რამე-ებ-მა
Dat.	რამე-ს	რომელიმე-ს	რამე-ებ-ს
Gen.	რამე-ს(ი) (რამ-ის)	რომელიმე-ს	რამე-ებ-ის
Instr.	რამე-თ(ი) (რამ-ით)	რომელიმე-თი	რამე-ებ-ით
Adv.	რამე-დ	რომელიმე-დ	რამე-ებ-ად
Voc.	–	–	–

	Singular *something*	*somethings*	*Plural* *all sort of things*
Nom.	რაღაცა	რაღაც-ებ-ი	რაღაც-რაღაც-ებ-ი
Erg.	რაღაცა-მ	რაღაც-ებ-მა	რაღაც-რაღაც-ებ-მა
Dat.	რაღაცა-ს	რაღაც-ებ-ს	რაღაც-რაღაც-ებ-ს
Gen.	რაღაც□-ის	რაღაც-ებ-ის	რაღაც-რაღაც-ებ-ის
Instr.	რაღაც□-ით	რაღაც-ებ-ით	რაღაც-რაღაც-ებ-ით
Adv.	რაღაცა-დ	რაღაც-ებ-ად	რაღაც-რაღაც-ებ-ად

Declension of indefinite pronouns referring to persons and inanimate objects

	Singular	
	a few	*some kind of, one of*
Nom.	რამდენიღაც(ა)	რომელიღაც(ა)
Erg.	რამდენიღაცა-მ	რომელიღაცა-მ
Dat.	რამდენიღაცა-ს	რომელიღაცა-ს
Gen.	რამდენიღაც-ის	რომელიღაც-ის
Instr.	რამდენიღაც-ით	რომელიღაც-ით
Adv.	რამდენიღაცა-დ	რომელიღაცა-დ

7.9.1 Declension of indefinite pronouns preceding nouns

As the following chart shows, an indefinite pronoun preceding a noun always remains in its stem form. If an indefinite pronoun indicates quantity the noun following it must be in singular form:

*ბიბლიოთეკიდან **რამდენიმე წიგნი** წამოვიღე.*
I brought with me a few books from the library.

	Singular *one of/any book/student*			
Nom.	რომელიმე	წიგნ-ი	/	მოსწავლე
Erg.	რომელიმე	წიგნ-მა	/	მოსწავლე-მ
Dat.	რომელიმე	წიგნ-ს	/	მოსწავლე-ს
Gen.	რომელიმე	წიგნ-ის	/	მოსწავლ-ის
Instr.	რომელიმე	წიგნ-ით	/	მოსწავლ-ით
Adv.	რომელიმე	წიგნ-ად	/	მოსწავლე-დ

	Singular *one of/any book/student*			
Nom.	რომელიღაც(ა)	წიგნ-ი	/	მოსწავლე
Erg.	რომელიღაც(ა)	წიგნ-მა	/	მოსწავლე-მ
Dat.	რომელიღაც(ა)	წიგნ-ს	/	მოსწავლე-ს
Gen.	რომელიღაც(ა)	წიგნ-ის	/	მოსწავლ-ის
Instr.	რომელიღაც(ა)	წიგნ-ით	/	მოსწავლ-ით
Adv.	რომელიღაც(ა)	წიგნ-ად	/	მოსწავლე-დ

*მომეცი **რომელიმე წიგნი!***
Give me a (any one of the books) book.
***რომელიღაც მოსწავლე** დაგვიანებით მოვიდა.*
One of the students came late.
***ვიღაც კაცი რაღაც საკითხს** არჩევდა.*
Some man was discussing some (kind of) problem.
***ვიღაც კაცები** იდგნენ მათი ეზოს წინ.*
Some men were standing in front of their yard.

მათ ***რაღაც წიგნები*** *მოიტანეს.*
They have brought some (kind of) books.

The indefinite pronouns ***ვიღაც*** (someone), ***რაღაც*** (something), and ***მავანი*** (someone) may precede nouns in singular as well as in plural form.

	Singular					
	some man		*certain man*		*some business*	
Nom.	ვიღაც(ა)	კაც-ი	მავანი	კაც-ი	რაღაც(ა)	საქმე
Erg.	ვიღაც(ა)	კაც-მა	მავან-მა	კაც-მა	რაღაც(ა)	საქმე-მ
Dat.	ვიღაც(ა)	კაც-ს	მავან -□	კაც-ს	რაღაც(ა)	საქმე-ს
Gen.	ვიღაც(ა)	კაც-ის	მავან-ი□	კაც-ის	რაღაც(ა)	საქმ□-ის
Instr.	ვიღაც(ა)	კაც-ით	მავან – ი□	კაც-ით	რაღაც(ა)	საქმ□-ით
Adv.	ვიღაც(ა)	კაც-ად	მავან -□	კაც-ად	რაღაც(ა)	საქმე-დ
Voc.	–		–		–	

	Plural	
	some men	
Nom.	ვიღაც(ა)	კაც-ებ-ი
Erg.	ვიღაც(ა)	კაც-ებ-მა
Dat.	ვიღაც(ა)	კაც-ებ-ს
Gen.	ვიღაც(ა)	კაც-ებ-ის
Instr.	ვიღაც(ა)	კაც-ებ-ით
Adv.	ვიღაც(ა)	კაც-ებ-ად
Voc.	–	

	Plural			
	certain men		*some businesses*	
Nom.	მავანი	კაც-ებ-ი	რაღაც(ა)	საქმე-ებ-ი
Erg.	მავან-მა	კაც-ებ-მა	რაღაც(ა)	საქმე-ებ-მა
Dat.	მავან -□	კაც-ებ-ს	რაღაც(ა)	საქმე-ებ-ს
Gen.	მავან-ი□	კაც-ებ-ის	რაღაც(ა)	საქმე-ებ-ის
Instr.	მავან-ი□	კაც-ებ-ით	რაღაც(ა)	საქმე-ებ-ით
Adv.	მავან-□	კაც-ებ-ად	რაღაც(ა)	საქმე-ებ-ად
Voc.	–		–	

7.10 Reciprocal pronouns and their declension

There are two synonymous reciprocal pronouns ***ერთმანეთი*** and ***ურთიერთი*** (each other) formed by doubling the numeral ***ერთ-ი*** (one). The first part of this pronoun is the cardinal numeral ***ერთ-*** in the ergative case: ***ერთ-მან*** (old form of the ergative case). In ***ურთიერთი*** the stem vowel ***ე*** is changed to ***უ***. The reciprocal pronoun ***ერთიმეორე*** (one another) consists of the cardinal numeral ***ერთი*** and the ordinal numeral ***მეორე***, both in their nominative case form. The ergative and adverbial cases of these pronouns are rarely used.

Nom.	ერთმანეთ-ი	ურთიერთ-ი
Erg.	ერთმანეთ-მა	ურთიერთ-მა
Dat.	ერთმანეთ-ს	ურთიერთ-ს
Gen.	ერთმანეთ-ის	ურთიერთ-ის
Instr.	ერთმანეთ-ით	ურთიერთ-ით
Adv.	ერთმანეთ-ად	ურთიერთ-ად
Voc.	–	–

Nom.	ერთურთ-ი	ერთიმეორე
Erg.	ერთურთ-მა	ერთიმეორე-მ
Dat.	ერთურთ-ს	ერთიმეორე-ს
Gen.	ერთურთ-ის	ერთიმეორ□-ის
Instr.	ერთურთ-ით	ერთიმეორ□-ით
Adv.	ერთურთ-ად	ერთიმეორე-დ
Voc.	–	–

*მათ **ერთმანეთი** ძალიან უყვართ.*
They love each other very much.
*მათ **ერთურთი** ძალიან უყვართ.*
They love each other very much.
*მათ **ერთიმეორე** ძალიან უყვართ.*
They love each other very much.

In modern Georgian the preferred form is ***ერთმანეთი***.

7.11 Relative pronouns and their declension

Relative pronouns are formed by adding the particle *ც(ა)* to interrogative pronouns.

Interrogative pronouns	*Relative pronouns*
ვინ? Who	ვინ-ც who(ever)
რა? What	რა-ც what(ever)
რომელი? Which	რომელი-ც whichever
როგორი? what type/kind	როგორი-ც which(ever) kind
რანაირი? what type/kind	რანაირი-ც which(ever) type/kind
რამდენი? how many	რამდენი-ც as many, whichever number
როდინდელი? how old	როდინდელი-ც however old

Relative pronouns are used in complex sentences in which they join a subordinate and the main clause. As a rule, relative pronouns introduce a subordinate clause, functioning as a conjunction and referring to one of the parts of the main clause:

ვინც *ჩვენთან არ არის,* ***ის*** *ჩვენი მტერია.*
Who (ever) is not with us, (he) is our enemy.
რაც *შენ გინდა, მეც* ***ის*** *მინდა.*
Whatever you want I want the same.
აიღე, ***რომელიც*** *გინდა.*
Take whichever you want.
როგორიც *შენ ხარ,* ***ისეთია*** *შენი ძმაც.*
Whatever (kind) you are, your brother is the same.
ამ მაღაზიაში არ არის ***ისეთი*** *კომპიუტერი,* ***რანაირიც*** *მე მინდა.*
In this store there is no computer of whichever kind I want.
ამ წელს ***იმდენი*** *სტუდენტი გვყავს,* ***რამდენიც*** *შარშან გვყავდა.*
This year we have the same number of students as (whichever number) we had last year.
როდინდელიც *უნდა იყოს ეს კაბა, მაინც ლამაზია.*
However old this dress is, it is still beautiful.

	Singular	
	whatever	*from whatever time*
Nom.	რა-ც	როდინდელ-ი
Erg.	რა-მა-ც	როდინდელ-მა-ც
Dat.	რა-ს-ა-ც	როდინდელ-ს-ა-ც
Gen.	რ□-ის-ა-ც	როდინდელ-ის-ა-ც
Instr.	რ□-ით-ა-ც	როდინდელ-ით-ა-ც
Adv.	რა-დ-ა-ც	როდინდელ-ად-ა-ც

As the declension pattern shows, the particle -ც is added after the case endings and is preceded by the euphonic -ა – which functions as a consonant divider.

Chapter 8

Compounds

There are two types of compounds in Georgian language, those made with two or more stems and those made with two or more separate words conjoined. Semantically they may have one or more meanings but function grammatically as a single word.

8.1 Semantics of compounds

The semantics of compounds with a single meaning does not derive from the combined meaning of their composite words. For example, the word ძვირფასი, meaning *dear*, *precious*, or *worthy*, is a combination of ძვირი (expensive) and ფასი (price). Similarly, the word ცისკარი (dawn) is made with ცა (sky) and კარი (door), დედამიწა (planet earth) consists of დედა (mother) and მიწა (earth), and ვერცხლისწყალი (mercury) is a combination of ვერცხლი (silver) and წყალი (water). Words combined in single meaning compounds are never connected with the conjunction და (and). They are always spelled together: ვერცხლისწყალი (mercury) გულთბილი (kind), თანამშრომელი (co-worker), ერთადერთი (single, only one).

The semantics of the compounds with two or more meanings derived from the meaning of their individual composite words are either hyphenated or connected with the conjunction და (and). Thus, და-ძმა (siblings, sister-brother), დედ-მამა (parents, mother-father), მამა-შვილი (father and child), სიძე-სიმამრი (son-in-law + father-in-law), რძალ-დედამთილი (daughter-in-law + mother-in-law), რძალ-მულ-დედამთილი (daughter-in-law + sister-in-law + mother-in-law), and ქართლ-კახეთ-იმერეთი (Kartli-Kakheti-Imereti, regions in Georgia)

8.2 Structure of compounds

The compounds may be composed of one reduplicated stem, two different stems, or two words.

DOI: 10.4324/9781315281131-11

8.2.1 *Compounds with reduplicated stems*

8.2.1.1. Compounds with reduplicated stems make a completely new meaning: **თავი** (head) – **თავთავი** (wheat/rye-ear); **წამი** (second, instant) – **წამწამი** (eyelash).

> ამ გოგონას გრძელი **წამწამები** აქვს.
> This girl has long eyelashes.
> მწიფე **თავთავი** ყოველთვის დაბლა იხრება.
> A ripe wheat-ear always bends down.

Some words in contemporary Georgian are originally compounds composed of reduplicated stems, but today they are not perceived as such: **ხუ(ლ)ხულა** (hovel), **ბე(რ)ბერი** (old), **პაწ(პ)აწინა** (tiny), **კო(რ)კორი** (bud), **ქუთ(ქ)უთო** (eyelid).

> ამ ვარდის ბუჩქს ბევრი **კოკორი** ჰქონდა.
> This rosebush had many buds.
> ეს **ხუხულა** უნდა დაინგრეს.
> This hovel should be torn down.
> ბავშვმა **პაწაწინა** კნუტი ხელში აიყვანა.
> The child picked up a tiny kitten.

8.2.1.2. Some compounds made from the same reduplicated stems are hyphenated and have a single semantic denotation. They are composed of various parts of speech and stress the meaning of their reduplicated components rather than creating a new one: **ტყე-ტყე** (through woods), **ხუთ-ხუთი** (by five), **ათ-ათი** (by ten), **ცხელ-ცხელი** (hot), **დიდ-დიდი** (big, large), **პატარ-პატარა** (little, small), **ჭრელ-ჭრელი** (multi-coloured). Some compounds of this type do not have a hyphen; instead, they may be connected with the conjunction და-: **ფეხდაფეხ** (by foot), **ცხენდაცხენ** (on horseback), **ხანდახან** (sometimes), and a few others.

> **ტყე-ტყე** გავუყევით გზას.
> We went through the woods.
> მონადირეები **ფეხდაფეხ** მისდევდნენ ნადირს.
> The hunters pursued the animal on foot.
> დედამ **დიდ-დიდი** ვაშლები ამოგვირჩია.
> Mother chose for us large apples.
> ეს მოთხრობა **პატარ-პატარა** თავებისგან შედგება.
> This story consists of short chapters.
> გოგონებს **ჭრელ-ჭრელი** ყელსახვევები უკეთიათ.
> The girls are wearing/have multicoloured scarves.

> *თითოეულ ჯგუფში* ***ხუთ-ხუთი*** *სტუდენტი იყო.*
> There were five students in each group.
> ***ერთ-ერთი*** *ჩვენგანი გააკეთებს განცხადებას.*
> One of us will make the statement.

8.2.1.3. Some compounds are formed by reduplication of a word. They change phonetically as a result of reduplication but are always spelled together. Such reduplication may be either rhyming or ablauting.

Rhyming reduplication: **არემარე** (surrounding, landscape)

Ablauting reduplication: **ბინდბუნდი** (dusk, twilight), **ბალახბულახი** (grass, weeds), **ნაყარნუყარი** (low quality, "throw-away"), **ქოხმახი** (hovel, shed)

> ***ბინდბუნდში*** *გზას ვერ ვხედავდით.*
> In the dusk we could not see the path.
> *ამ მაღაზიაში* ***ნაყარნუყარი*** *საქონელია.*
> In this store they have low quality goods.
> ***ახლომახლო*** *ბევრი* ***ქოხმახია.***
> Nearby there are many dilapidated hovels.

8.2.1.4. Some compounds are made of stems that do not have any meaning independently: **კაშკაში** (shine, glow), **ხარხარი** (laughter), **ნარნარი** (grace), **ციმციმი** (flicker), **ჭიკჭიკი** (chirp), **ლაქლაქი** (chatter, jabber), etc. Some compounds of this type have ablauting reduplication: **ჩხარაჩხური** (rattle), **წკაპაწკუპი** (ticktock), **ბაკაბუკი** (click-clack). If the final vowel *-ი* is replaced with the suffix *-ა* these compounds become adjectives: **კაშკაშა** (shiny), **ნარნარა** (graceful), **ლაქლაქა** (chatty).

> *უეცრად ქუსლების* ***ბაკაბუკი*** *მოგვესმა.*
> Suddenly we heard the clicking of heels.
> *შენი მეზობელი რა* ***ლაქლაქა*** (adjective) *ყოფილა!*
> What a babbler your neighbour is!
> *დაგვღალა ამდენი* ***ლაქლაქით*** (verbal noun).
> He tired us with his blabber.

As the examples indicate, these kinds of compounds are onomatopoeias and are always spelled as one word without a hyphen.

8.2.2 *Compounds with different stems*

8.2.2.1. Compounds made with semantically synonymous stems: **კვლევა-ძიება** (investigation, search + inquiry), **გზა-კვალი**

(direction, road + trace), ***ძალ-ღონე*** (strength, strength + vigor) ***სინდის-ნამუსი*** (conscience, conscience + scruples), ***ბედ-იღბალი*** (destiny, fate + luck), etc.

> *სიბნელეში **გზა-კვალი** აგვერია.*
> In the darkness we lost the direction.
> *ამ საქმის **კვლევა-ძიება** ისევ გრძელდება.*
> The investigation of this case still continues.
> *ამ კაცს **სინდის-ნამუსი** არ ჰქონია.*
> This man has no conscience.

8.2.2.2. Some compounds consist of antonymous stems: ***მტერ-მოყვარე*** (everyone, foe + friend), ***უფროს-უმცროსი*** (everybody, old + young), ***მთა-ბარი*** (world around, landcape, mountain + valley), etc.

> **მტერ-მოყვარე** აღიარებს საქართველოს მთა-ბარის სილამაზეს.
> Friend or foe, everyone acknowledges the beauty of Georgia's landscape.

8.2.2.3. The compounds with thematically synonymous stems: ***ოქრო-ვერცხლი*** (treasure, gold + silver), ***თვალ-მარგალიტი*** (treasure, riches, gem + pearl), ***წვერ-ულვაში*** facial hair (moustaches + beard), ***წერა-კითხვა*** (literacy, writing + reading), ***თვალ-წარბი*** (countenance, eye + brow), etc. Composite geographic names also belong to this group of compounds: ***რაჭა-ლეჩხუმი*** (Racha-Lechkhumi), ***მესხეთ-ჯავახეთი*** (Meskhet-Javakheti), ***ტაო-კლარჯეთი*** (Tao-Klarjeti), etc.

> *ამ უძველეს სამარხებში ბევრი **ოქრო-ვერცხლი** აღმოაჩინეს.*
> They discovered lot of treasure in these ancient graves.
> *ჩემი ბიჭი უკვე **წვერ-ულვაშს** იპარსავს.*
> My son already shaves his facial hair.
> *ეს იყო **წერა-კითხვის** გამავრცელებელი საზოგადოება.*
> It was the Society for Spreading Literacy.
> ***რაჭა-ლეჩხუმი** და **მესხეთ-ჯავახეთი** საქართველოს მხარეებია.*
> Racha-Lechkhumi and Meskhet-Javakheti are the regions of Georgia.

8.2.2.4. Compounds made with reduplicated verb forms with antonymous preverbs: ***აიარ-ჩაიარა*** (he walked up and down), ***აირბინ-ჩაირბინა*** (he ran up and down), ***მიედ-მოედო*** (he bibble-babbled). The same compounds are composed of gerunds and participles with antonymous preverbs: ***ავლა-ჩავლა*** (up and down walk), ***ამვლელ-ჩამვლელი*** (up and down passers-by); ***მიწერ-მოწერა*** (correspondence, writing back and forth), ***მიწერილ-მოწერილი*** (two-sided/mutual correspondence), ***გავლა-გამოვლა*** (to and fro strolling), ***გამვლელ-გამომვლელი*** (to and fro strollers, passers-by). Compounds made with synonyms, antonyms, and nouns of the similar thematic meaning are hyphenated: ***სტუმარ-მასპინძელი*** (guest-and-host), ***წერა-კითხვა*** (writing + reading, literacy), ***გამვლელ-გამომვლელი*** (passers-by), etc.

> ***გამვლელ-გამომვლელს*** *სადგურის გზას ვეკითხებოდი.*
> I asked passers-by the direction to the station.
> *ბევრი ილაპარაკა, ათას რამეს* ***მიედ-მოედო.***
> He talked a lot, bibble-babbled about a thousand things.
> *ძალიან საინტერესოა ჩერჩილისა და რუზველტის* ***მიწერ-მოწერა.***
> The correspondence between Churchill and Roosevelt is very interesting.
> *ამ კაცმა ჩვენი სახლის წინ რამდენჯერმე* ***აიარ-ჩაიარა.***
> This man walked up and down in front of our house several times.

8.2.2.5.

8.2.2.5.1. In some compound nouns the first component has attributive function defining the second component of the unit. Since Georgian does not have the grammatical category of gender, this type of compounds identifies biological gender in a composite noun: ***ქალ(-)ბატონი*** – madam, missus, (woman + master); ***ვაჟ(-)კაცი*** – man (man + person); ***ვაჟი(-)შვილი*** – son (man + child); ***ქალი(-)შვილი*** – daughter (woman + child); ***დედა(-)კაცი*** – woman (mother + person); ***მამა(-კაცი)*** – man (father + person); ***ხარ (-)ირემი*** – buck (bull + deer); ***ფურ(-)ირემი*** – doe (cow + deer), etc.

> ***ქალბატონი*** *თამარი და მისი* ***ქალიშვილი*** *უკვე მობრძანდნენ.*
> Ms. Tamar and her daughter have already arrived.
> *ავტობუსის გაჩერებასთან რამდენიმე* ***მამაკაცი*** *იდგა.*
> Several men stood at the bus stop.
> *ეს* ***ახალგაზრდა*** *ჩემი დის* ***ვაჟიშვილია.***
> This young man is my sister's son.

There are quite a few compounds with attributive nouns as the first component: ***დედამიწა*** (დედა + მიწა) – planet earth (mother + earth); ***დედაქალაქი*** (დედა + ქალაქი) – capital city (mother + city); ***დედოფალი*** (დედა + უფალი) – queen (mother + ruler); ***დედაენა*** (დედა + ენა) – mother + tongue; ***დედააზრი*** (დედა +

აზრი) – main point, essence (mother + idea); **ლუკმაპური** (ლუკმა + პური) (piece of bread); **გლეხკაცი** (გლეხ-(ი) + კაც-ი) (peasant).

> *თბილისი საქართველოს* ***დედაქალაქია.***
> Tbilisi is the capital city of Georgia.
> *არ მესმის ამ სტატიის* ***დედააზრი.***
> I don't understand the main point of this article.

Similar compounds consist of attributive adjectives as their first component: **ახალგაზრდა** (= ახალი გაზრდილი) – young person (newly grown); **შუაღამე** (შუა ღამე) – midnight (middle of the night); **ზედაპირი** (ზედა პირი) – surface (upper layer); **გარეუბანი** (გარე-უბანი) – suburb (outer area); **წინამორბედი** (წინა+მორბედი) fore-runner (fore + runner).

> *ეს* ***ახლაგაზრდა*** *კაცი თბილისის* ***გარეუბანში*** *ცხოვრობს.*
> This young man lives in a Tbilisi suburb.
> *უკვე* ***შუაღამეა.***
> It is already midnight.
> *ამ მაგიდის* ***ზედაპირი*** *ბავშვმა დაკაწრა.*
> The child scratched the surface of this table.

8.2.2.5.2. Compounds may be made with a numeral and a noun: **ერთგული** (ერთი გული) – faithful (one heart); **ორგული** (ორი გული) – traitorous (two hearts); **ორღობე** (ორი ღობე) – village road (two fences); **ორპირი** (ორი პირი) – double-dealer (two mouths); **ცხრაპირი** (ცხრა პირი) – thick layer (nine layers). Some geographic names may also have similar structure: **ცხრაწყარო** (ცხრა წყარო) – Tskhratsqaro (nine springs), a name of a village in Georgia.

> *არ მიყვარს* ***ორპირი*** *ადამიანი.*
> I do not like a double-dealer person.
> ***ცხრაწყაროს*** *უღელტეხილი ერთმანეთთან აკავშირებს. ბორჯომისა და* ***ახალციხის*** *მუნიციპალიტეტებს.*
> Tskhratsqaro Pass connects the Borjomi and Akhaltsikhe municipalities.

8.2.2.5.3. Compounds made with a noun and an adjective or a participle: **გონებამახვილი** (გონება + მახვილი) – sharp-witted (reason + sharp); **გულმაგარი** (გული + მაგარი) – brave (heart + strong); **თავმდაბალი** (თავი + მდაბალი) – modest (head + low); ***თავდადებული (თავი +დადებული)*** (თავი + დადებული) – faithful, person ready to sacrifice himself for a cause (head + put down); **გულკეთილი** (გული + კეთილი) kind (heart + kind). Some compounds of this type may have two nouns preceding a participle:

თავგზააბნეული (თავი + გზა + აბნეული) – disconcerted, bewildered (head + path + confused); **თავპირჩამომტირალი** (თავი + პირი + ჩამომტირალი) mournful (head + face + crying); **წვერულვაშგათეთრებული** (წვერი + ულვაში + გათეთრებული) – greybeard (beard + moustache-whitened).

> *მამა **გულკეთილი** კაცი იყო.*
> My father was a kind man.
> *ეს **წვერულვაშგათეთრებული კაცი** ჩემი მეზობელია.*
> This white bearded (lit: with mustache-beard-whitened) man is my neighbour.
> *თქვენ მეტისმეტად **თავმდაბალი** ბრძანდებით.*
> You are exceedingly modest.

8.2.2.5.4. Compounds made with a noun and a possessive pronoun in the second place denote kinship: **დედაჩემი** (დედა + ჩემი) – my mother (mother + my); **მამაშენი** (მამა + შენი) – your father (father + your); **პაპამისი** (პაპა + მისი) – his/her grandfather (grandfather + his/her); **ბიძაჩემი** (ბიძა + ჩემი) – my uncle (uncle + my); **ბიცოლაშენი** (ბიცოლა + შენი) – your aunt = wife of father's brother (uncle + wife + your); **დეიდამისი** (დეიდა + მისი) – his/her aunt = mother's sister (mother + sister + his/her); **მამიდამისი** (მამიდა + მისი) – his/her aunt = father's sister (father + sister + his/her).

> ***პაპაჩემი** გუშინ ჩამოვიდა თბილისში.*
> My grandfather arrived at Tbilisi yesterday.
> ***დეიდაშენი** კინოში შემხვდა.*
> I ran into your aunt in the movie theatre.
> ***მამათქვენი** როგორ ბრძანდება?*
> How is your father?

8.2.2.5.5. Compounds made with a noun in the genitive without the case marker **-ის** and a verbal stem with the derivative particle ა-: **ხარიპარია** (ხარ-ის + პარია) – cattle thief (bull thief); *ქარიყლაპია* (ქარი + ყლაპია) – wind swallower (wind + swallower); **ბელტიყლაპია** (ბელტ-ის + ყლაპია) – clod swallower (clod + swallower); **კაციჭამია** (კაც-ის + ჭამია) – man-eater.

> ***ბელტიყლაპია** ქართული ზღაპრის გმირია.*
> The clod-swallower is a personage in a Georgian folk tale.
> *ამ ადამიანს **კაციჭამია** დევს შევადარებდი.*
> I would compare this person to a man-eating monster.

8.2.2.5.6. Compounds made with the nouns, adjectives, numerals, or pronouns with a derivative affix/affixes: **ცოლქმრობა** (ცოლ-ქმარ-ობა) – family relationship, or literally, wife-husbandry (wife + husband + derivative suffix -ობა); **უკარფანჯრო** (უ-კარ-ფანჯარა-ო) – without a door and window (the prefix -უ + door + window + the suffix -ო), **დაძმური** (და-ძმა-ურ-ი) – literally, brother-sisterly (sister + brother + derivative suffix -ურ). Such compounds are spelt together, without a hyphen.

8.2.3 *Closed compounds*

8.2.3.1. The closed compounds most often consist of two independent nouns with the first of them in genitive case: **ვერცხლისწყალი** (ვერცხლ-ის + წყალი) – mercury (silver's + water); **თავისუფალი** (თავ-ის + უფალი) free (self + master). Many names of geographic locations also belong to this group: **კისისხევი** (კის-ის + ხევი) (Kisi + ravine); **ხიდისთავი** (ხიდ-ის + თავი) (bridge's + head); **უფლისციხე** (უფლ-ის + ციხე) (God's + fortress); **ცხენისწყალი** (ცხენ-ის + წყალი) (horse's + water).

მდინარე ***ცხენისწყალი*** *არ არის ძალიან ღრმა.*
The river Tskhenistsqali is not very deep.
არჩევნები ***თავისუფალი*** *უნდა იყოს.*
The elections must be free.
უფლისციხე *უძველესი არქეოლოგიური ძეგლია.*
Uplistsikhe is an ancient archaeological site.

8.2.3.2. Compounds consisting of an attributive word, usually a noun with or without truncated Genitive case ending followed by another noun: **ძმიშვილი** (ძმ-ის + შვილი) nephew/niece (brother's + child); **დისშვილი** (დ-ის + შვილი) nephew/niece (sister's + child); **დედინაცვალი** (დედ-ი(ს) + ნაცვალი) (mother's + replacement, stepmother); **წუთისოფელი** (წუთ-ი(ს) + სოფელი) (transient) life (trice's + world); **შვილიშვილი** (შვილ-ი(ს)+ შვილი) grandchild (child's + child); **კაციშვილი** (კაც-ი(ს) + შვილი) human being, person (man's + child). Georgian last names ending with -ძე and -შვილი: **ჭავჭავაძე** (ჭავჭავა-(ს) + ძე) Chavchavadze; **ჯავახიშვილი** (ჯავახ-ი(ს) + შვილი) Javakhishvili; **ბარათაშვილი** (ბარათა-(ს)+შვილი) Baratashvili; etc.

ეს ლამაზი გოგონა ჩემი ***ძმიშვილია.***
This pretty girl is my brother's daughter.
წუთისოფელი *სავსეა მოულოდნელობებით.*
Life is full of unexpected (happenings).
მისი ***შვილიშვილი*** *უკვე სტუდენტია.*
Her grandchild is already a student.
აუდიტორიაში ***კაციშვილი*** *არ იყო.*
There was not a single person in the auditorium.

8.2.3.3. Base words of compounds may be in a variety of cases as well:

Ergative: ***ერთმანეთი*** (ერთმან + ე(რ)თი) each other

Dative: ***თავმჯდომარე*** (თავ(ს) + მჯდომარე) – chair(man) (at the head sitting); ***თავსხმა*** (თავ(ს) + სხმა) – downpour (on head pouring),

თავგადასავალი (თავ(ს) + გადასავალი) – adventure/life story (over one's head happening)

Instrumental: ***ქვითკირი*** (ქვით + კირი) – limestone (stone + lime)

Adverbial: ***ყურადღება*** (ყურად + ღება) attention (lit. *to ear taking*); ***ერთადერთი*** (ერთად + ერთი) single, one and only (by one + one); ***ავადმყოფი*** (ავად + მყოფი) sick person (sick being)

ჩვენ უნდა გვიყვარდეს ***ერთმანეთი.***
We should love each other.
დანიელ დეფომ დაწერა „რობინზონ კრუზოს ***თავგადასავალი.***"
Daniel Defoe wrote "The Adventures of Robinson Crusoe."
თავმჯდომარემ *სხდომის პროგრამა წაიკითხა.*
The chairman read the agenda of the meeting.
ყურადღება! *მატარებელი ხუთ წუთში გავა!*
Attention! The train leaves in five minutes.
ჩვენ ***ერთადერთი*** *გზა გვაქვს მიზნის მისაღწევად.*
We have the only way to achieve (our) goal.

Compounds consisting of two nouns, the first of which has the archaic genitive case plural marker -**თა** in full or truncated form: ***გულთამხილავი*** (გულთა + მხილავი) omniscient (hearts' + seer); ***მზეთამზე*** (მზეთა + მზე) Mzetamze, the name of a village in Georgia (suns' + sun); ***ხუროთმოძღვარი*** (ხუროთ + მოძღვარი) architect (carpenters' + leader). In some of such compounds the particle -**თა** may be truncated: ***კაცთმოძულე*** (კაცთ + მოძულე) misanthrope (men's + hater); ***კაცთმოყვარე*** (კაცთ + მოყვარე) philanthrope, kind person (men's +lover).

შენ ნამდვილი ***გულთამხილავი*** *ხარ.*
You are (a) truly omniscient (person).
არსაკიძე მე-12 საუკუნის ქართველი ***ხუროთმოძღვარი*** *იყო.*
Arsakidze was a 12th-century Georgian architect.
ამ ***კაცთმოყვარე*** *ადამიანს ყველა პატივს სცემს.*
Everybody respects this kind man.

8.2.3.4. Compounds with adverbs or postpositions as their base word: ***ზედამხედველი*** (ზედა + მხედველი) overseer (over

+ seer); **წინდებული** (წინ+ დებული) preposition (fore + placed); **თანდებული** (თან+დებული) postposition (next + placed); **თანამშრომელი** (თანა + მშრომელი) co-worker (with + worker).

ქართულ ენაში ***წინდებულები*** *არ არის.*
There are no prepositions in the Georgian language.
ეს ქალბატონი ჩვენი ***თანამშრომელია.***
This lady is our co-worker.

8.2.3.5. Compounds of the same type are numerals connected with the conjunctive **და** (and). These are numerals from 21 to 99 inclusive, with the exception of **ორმოცი** (ორ-მ-ოცი) 40 (2 + 20); **სამოცი** (სამ-(მ)-ოცი) 60 (3 + 20); **ოთხმოცი** (ოთხ-მ-ოცი) 80 (4 + 20); **ოცდაათი** (ოც + და + ათი) 30 (20 and 10); **ორმოცდაორი** (ორმოც + და + ორი) 42 (40 and 2); and so on (see sections 6.1.–6.2. on numerals).

ჩვენს ჯგუფში ***ოცდათხუთმეტი*** *სტუდენტია.*
There are 35 students in our group.
დედაჩემი ***ოთხმოცდათორმეტი*** *წლისაა.*
My mother is 92 years old.

Chapter 9

Verbs

In the Georgian language, the verb is a very complex phenomenon. Unlike the noun, which has only two categories (case and number), the verb has morphological and derivative categories. There are four conjugation types and eleven tenses that are divided into three series. Each of them will be dealt with individually in the following chapters.

Conjugation groups and tense system of verbs

Conjugation groups

I conjugation	Active voice verbs
II conjugation	Dynamic-passive voice verbs
III conjugation	Medio-active verbs
IV conjugation	Static-passive and medio-passive verbs

The tense system of the Georgian verb

I series			
Present subseries	Present	Imperfect	Present subjunctive
Future subseries	Future	Conditional	Future subjunctive
II series	Aorist		Optative
III series	Perfect	Pluperfect	Perfect subjunctive

9.1 Person and number of the verb

9.1.1 *Persons and actants*

Georgian verbs can modify persons and actants. Person is a morphological content of the verb and therefore, the person value of the verb is determined by the number of person markers in it. For

DOI: 10.4324/9781315281131-12

example, *ზი-ს ის* (S_3) (he sits) is a monopersonal verb and its person marker is the suffix *-ს*.

Actants are the nouns to which the verb refers and modifies their forms. In the sentence *ზი-ს ის* (S_3), the verb refers to one actant and determines its case (nom.); the actant *ის* (*he*) is denoted in the verb with the third-person marker *-ს*.

Usually not all actants are marked in a verb, but their number determines its valency. The person value and valency may or may not coincide. Thus:

> იგი (ბიჭი – S_3) მას (წერილს – O_3) წერ-ს.
> He (boy – S_3) writes it (a letter – O_3).

წერ-ს is a one-person value verb since it has one person marker (S_3), denoted with the suffix *-ს*, but it is a bivalent verb since it refers to two actants: the subject (*boy*) and the direct object (*letter*).

The Georgian verb is polypersonal, but its morphological hierarchy allows only two person markers. As the following charts show, the markers are placed before and after the stem, but in each case only a single person marker is present.

> იგი (ბიჭი – S) მას (მეგობარს – O_{ind}) მას (წერილს O_d) ს-წერ-ს.
> He (boy – S) writes it (letter – O_d) to him (friend – O_{ind}).

In this sentence, the verb denotes the subject with the suffix *-ს* and the indirect object with prefix *ს-*. It is a bipersonal, but trivalent verb because it refers to and modifies three nouns: *boy*, *friend*, and *letter*. In addition, the verb in Georgian may modify more actants in various case forms, with or without postpositions.

> *ბიჭი მეგობარს **ფანქრით** წერილს სწერს.*
> The boy is writing a letter to a friend with a pencil.
> *პოეტი **მეუღლითურთ** მიიწვიეს შეხვედრაზე.*
> The poet was invited to the meeting together with his wife.
> *იგი **მეგობრებზე** ფიქრობდა.*
> He thought about his friends.

In these sentences the words ***ფანქრით*** (with a pencil) and ***მეუღლითურთ*** (with his wife) are actants (not persons) modified by the verb.

Number of persons		*Valency*	
Zeropersonal	წვიმ-ს (it rains) თოვ-ს (it snows) (These verbs have person markers, but they do not refer to any person.)	**Zerovalent**	წვიმს (it rains) თოვს (it snows) (The person markers do not refer to any actant.)
Monopersonal	ზი-ს (sits) წევ-ს (lies) დგა-ს (stands) წერ-ს (writes) ხატავ-ს (paints)	**Monovalent**	ზი-ს ის (he sits) წევ-ს ის (he lies) დგა-ს ის (he stands)
Bipersonal	ს-წერ-ს ს-თხოვ-ს	**Bivalent**	წერ-ს ის მას (he writes it to him) ვ-ხატავ მე მას (I paint him)
		Trivalent	ს-წერ-ს ის მას მას (he writes it to him) ს-თხოვ-ს ის მას მას (he asks him it)
		Quadrivalent	მ-იჭმიე შენ მე მას ის (you feed it to him for me) მ-ისმიე შენ მე მას ის (you give drink to him for me)

In addition to person indicators, the verb may have additional markers referring to actants it may modify. They will be discussed in the following chapters.

9.1.2 *Subject and number markers*

First- and second-person subjects are marked with prefixes; third-person, with suffixes. Only the first- and second-person forms have a distinct marker for plural forms; the third person and its plural forms are denoted with the same markers.

Subject markers			
Singular		*Plural*	
I	ვ –	I	ვ – -თ
II	(ხ-), Ø	II	(ხ-), Ø – -თ
III	– -ს, -ა, -ო	III	– -ნ, -ან, -ენ, -ნენ, -ეს

Conjugation of the verb ყოფნა (to be)

Singular		*Plural*	
I	ვ-არ (I am)	I	ვ-არ-თ (we are)
II	ხ-არ (you are)	II	ხ-არ-თ (you are)
III	არ-ი-ს (he[1] is)	III	არ-ი-ან (they are)

The first- and second-person markers are preceded only by preverbs:

Singular		*Plural*	
I	და-ვ-წერ (I will write)	I	და-ვ-წერ-თ (we will write)
II	და – წერ (you will write)	II	და – წერ-თ (you will write)
III	და – წერ-ს (he will write)	III	და – წერ-ენ (they will write)

[1] To simplify conjugation charts, the only singular third-person pronoun used throughout the book for ის/იგი is he. However, in Georgian ის/იგი may refer to she, he, or it, depending on the context.

The first-person marker *ვ-* will be doubled if the stem of the verb starts with the same consonant: *ვ-ვარცხნი* (I comb him), *ვ-ვარდები* (I fall), *ვ-ვარაუდ-ობ* (I suppose), etc.

In the spoken language the consonant *ვ-* is often dropped when followed with the vowel *-უ-*; however, the norms of literary Georgian require its use in written forms: *ვ-ურეკავ* (I call him), *ვ-უთხარი* (I told him), *ვ-უთვლი* (I send to him), and so on.

The second-person subject does not have any marker in contemporary Georgian. Its archaic marker *ნ-* is present only in two verbs: *to be* – **ნ**-არ (see the previous chart), and in two forms of the verb *to come* – მო-**ნ**-ვალ (you will come) and მო-**ნ**-ვედი (you came). In the verb ***მო-მ-ი-ნვალ*** (for example, *ნვალ წარმატებული მომინვალ = დამიბრუნდები.* – Tomorrow you will come to me [= you will return to me] victorious). **ნ-** cannot be separated as a subject prefix. It is a part of the stem.

Singular		*Plural*		*Singular*		*Plural*	
I	მო-ვალ (I will come)	I	მო-ვალ-თ (we will come)	I	მო-ვედი	I	მო-ვედი-თ
II	მო-**ნ**-ვალ (you will come)	II	მო-**ნ**-ვალ-თ	II	მო-**ნ**-ვედი	II	მო-**ნ**-ვედი-თ
III	მო-ვ-ა (He will come)	III	მო-ვლ-ენ	III	მო-ვიდა	III	მო-ვიდ-ნენ

The first- and second-person verb forms in plural are marked with the suffix *-თ*. The third-person plural may be marked with one of the suffixes: *-ნ*, *-ან*, *-ენ*, *-ნენ*, *-ეს*. They are used in various tenses and their distribution is clearly determined; they are not interchangeable.

ის წერ-ს – He writes — ისინი წერ-ენ They write

მან წერ-ა – He wrote — მათ წერ-ეს They wrote

მათ დაწერო-ნ Let them write

ის იყ-ო – He was — ისინი იყვ-ნენ They were

ისინი ყოფილ-ან They apparently have been

As was mentioned, the subject is always marked in the verb whether transitive or intransitive.

> *ქალ – ი* (S_3 Nom) *ზი-ს.*
> A woman sits/is sitting.
> *ბავშვ-ი* (S_3 nom.) *ეთამაშებ-ა მეგობარ-ს* (O_{ind}).
> The child is playing with a friend.

The subject marker is absent in different situations:

1. Monopersonal verbs:
   მოვალ (I will come) and *მოვედი* (I came)
2. If the verb combines the first- and second-person subject and object:

   > მე შენ **გ**-ხატავ.
   > I paint you.

   In this sentence only the object-person is denoted with the prefix **გ**- since in contemporary Georgian the verb does not have markers for both first- or second-person subject and first- or second-person object simultaneously. Placing the object marker *გ*- after the subject marker *ვ*- is not permissible; in such cases the preference is given to the object-person, while the first person is not denoted.

3. If the verb combines the second- and third-person subject and object:

   > **ის თქვენ** **გ**-იზი-თ.
   > He sits/is sitting (for example, in your lap).

Verbs requiring the auxiliary verb *to be* have dual markers for the first subject-person. In the verb form **ვ**-ზი-**ვ**-არ (I sit/am sitting), the base verb has its subject marker (**ვ**-ზი), to which the auxiliary verb with its subject marker (**ვ**-არ) is added. Such doubling of subject marker happens in intransitive verbs:

> ვ-დგა-ვ-არ
> I stand/am standing
> ვ-ყოფილ-ვ-არ
> I have been
> მო-ვ-სულ-ვ-არ
> I have come

9.1.3 *Direct/indirect object and number markers*

In Georgian verbs, both direct and indirect objects are denoted with prefixes. The first and second persons have the same markers for direct and indirect objects. In first-person object forms, the singular and plural object markers are different from each other. The plurality of the direct or indirect second-person object is marked with the suffix -*თ*, which also marks the plurality of the first- and second-person subject. In the third person, the indirect object is denoted with prefixes *ჰ*-, *ს*-, or *Ø*-, but the direct object has no marker. In the third person, the plural of objects usually is not marked.

Direct object markers			
Singular		*Plural*	
I	მ-	I	გვ –
II	გ-	II	გ – (-თ)
III	Ø	III	Ø

In combination with a first- or second-person object, the first- or second-person subjects are not marked with prefixes, while the third-person subject is marked with suffixes.

შენ მე მ(O_{1d})-ახარებ
მე შენ გ(O_{2d})-ახარებ
ის შენ გ(O_{2d})-ახარებ-ს(S_3)
ის მათ Ø(O_{2d})-ახარებ-ს(S_3)

-*ს* may also not appear as in *ის თქვენ გ-ახარებ-თ* (he makes you happy).

Distribution of the person and number markers in the bivalent object-oriented paradigm of the verb *ხატვა* (to paint)

O	*Stem*	*S*	*O*	*Stem*	*S*
მ me	ხატავ	ს he	გვ us	ხატავ	ს he
გ you	ხატავ	ს he	გ you	ხატავ	თ you
him	ხატავ	ს he	them	ხატავ	ს he

Since the first- and second-person verb forms have the same affixes for direct and indirect object, in both cases the morpho-phonological process develops similarly. If the verb stem starts with the consonant მ-, it will be doubled in its first-person singular form. The literary norms of the Georgian language require that both these consonants are retained in writing. The orthographically correct forms are as follows:

(9a) მ-მალავს ის მე (he hides me)
(9b) მ-მართებს ის მე (I am obliged to it)

Similarly, the consonant cluster გვგვ in the first-person plural forms should not be shortened in writing even though pronouncing the cluster may be somewhat difficult. Correct forms are გვ-გვრის (he gives us), მო-გვ-გვარა (he presented it to us), and და-გვ-გვიანებია (apparently, we have been late). If a verb starts with the consonant გ-, the object marker will double in the second-person plural. As in the previous cases, the correct written forms are გ-გუდავს (he strangles you), გ-გლეჯს (he tears you), გ-გონია (it seems to you), გ-გზავნის (he sends you), etc.

Indirect object markers			
Singular		*Plural*	
I	მ –	I	გვ –
II	გ –	II	გ – (-თ)
III	ჰ-, ს-, Ø –	III	ჰ-, ს-, Ø- – (თ)

Distribution of the third-person indirect object markers ჰ- and ს- depends on phonetic factors. ჰ- may precede the consonants – ბ, ფ, პ, გ, ქ, კ, ყ – while ს- is placed before დ, თ, ტ, ძ, ც, წ, ჯ, ჩ, and ჭ.

For example, in the verb ჰ-კითხ-ა (მან მას ის) (he asked him about it), the indirect object is marked with the prefix ჰ- preceding the stem consonant კ. In the verbs მი-ს-წერ-ა (he wrote it to him) and ს-თხოვ-ს (he asks it to him), ს- is placed before the consonant წ and თ.

Some verbs do not modify any indirect object-person, but they nevertheless have an indirect object marker: გა-ს-ტანს (it will last), *გამო-ს-ცემს* (it emits sound or he will publish a book), *გა-ს-ცემს* (he betrays), *გა-ს-წევს* (he will pull away), *ა-ს-წევს* (he will lift up), *ს-ჩადის* (he commits), *და-ს-ძენს* (he adds), *და-ჰ-ყო* (he spent).

In the following sentences, the verbs modify direct objects, but they have indirect object markers:

(S_3)	(O_{3i}) (S_3)	**(O_{3d})**
|	| |	|
იგი	**ა-ს-წევ-ს**	ტვირთს.
He	will pick up	the baggage.

(S_3)	**(O_{3i}) (S_3)**	**(O_{3d})**
|	| |	|
მან	**ა-ს-წი-ა**	ტვირთ-ი.
He	picked up	the baggage.

(S_3)	**(O_{3i})** (S_3)	**(O_{3d})**
|	| |	|
იგი	**ს-ჩადი-ს**	დანაშაულს.
He	commits	a crime.

(S_3)	(S_3)	**(O_{3d})**
|	|	|
მან	ჩაიდინ-ა	დანაშაულ-ი.
He	committed	a crime.

9.1.4 ***Subject and object cases***

Transitive and intransitive verbs may have their subjects in different cases, depending on the tense in which they are used. The subject of an intransitive verb never changes its case; it is always in the nominative case. The only exception is the subject of medio-active verbs, which are intransitive, and some III conjugation verbs do have a direct object:

მან (S_3) *ფეხბურთი* (O_{3d}) *ითამაშა* (he played football)
მან (S_3) *სიმღერა* (O_{3d}) *იმღერა* (he sang a song)
მან (S_3) *ტანგო* (O_{3d}) *იცეკვა* (he danced tango)

Declension of the intransitive verb subject

	Subject	*Verb*
I series	ბავშვ-ი nom. the child	თბებ-ა gets warmed up
II series	ბავშვ-ი **nom.** the child	გა-თბ-ა got warmed up
III series	ბავშვ-ი **nom.** the child	გა-მთბარ-ა has warmed up

Declension of the transitive verb subject

	Subject	*Verb*	*Object*
I series	ბავშვ-ი **nom.** the child	წერ-ს writes	წერილ-ს a letter
II series	ბავშვ-მა **erg.** the child	და-წერ-ა wrote	წერილ-ი a letter
III series	ბავშვ-ს **dat.** the child	და-უ-წერი-ა has written	წერილ-ი a letter

Not only the subject but the direct objects of transitive verbs change their case. In I series tenses they are in the dative case, in II and III series, they are in the nominative. Indirect objects never change the case; in I and II series tenses they are in the dative, and in III series, they become actants with postpositions.

Subject and object cases

Series	*Subject*	*Verb*	*Direct object*	*Indirect object*
I series	ბავშვ-ი Nom. the child	ს-წერ-ს writes	წერილ-ს Dat. a letter	მეგობარ-ს Dat. to a friend
II series	ბავშვ-მა Erg. the child	მი-ს-წერ-ა wrote	წერილ-ი Nom. a letter	მეგობარ-ს Dat. to a friend
III series	ბავშვ-ს Dat. the child	მი-უ-წერი-ა has written	წერილ-ი Nom. a letter	მეგობრ-ის-თვის to a friend (postpositional)
I series	ბავშვ-ი Nom. the child	წერ-ს writes	წერილ-ს Dat. a letter	
II series	ბავშვ-მა Erg. the child	და-წერ-ა wrote	წერილ-ი Nom. a letter	
III series	ბავშვ-ს Dat. the child	და-უ-წერი-ა has written	წერილ-ი Nom. a letter	

9.1.5 *Inversion of subject and object markers*

The subject marker refers to the subject (S→S), and the object marker to the object (O→O), but in some cases their function may be reversed – the subject marker denotes the object (S→O), and the object marker the subject (O→S). This happens in I and III conjugation verbs in III series tenses, where subject-object markers are inverted. The third-person direct object is marked by the subject marker (suffix) and the subject marker is replaced with the indirect object marker.

	(S_1) (O_{3d})
S→S:	მე ვ-წერ წერილ-ს
	I write a letter
	(S_1) **(O_1)** **(S_3)** (O_{3d})
O→S, S→O:	მე და-მ-იწერ-ი-ა წერილ-ი
	I have written a letter

	(S_1)
S→S:	მე ვ-ბეჭდავ ნაშრომ-ს
	I publish a work
	(O_1) **(S_3)** (O_{3d})
O→S, S→O:	და-მ-იბეჭდავს-ს ნაშრომ-ი
	I have published a work
	(O_1) **(S_3)** **(S_3)** **(O_1)**
O→ O, S→S:	მ-ვარცხნი-ს ის მე
	He is combing me
	(S_3) **(O_1)**
	მას და-ვ-უვარცხნი-ვ-არ მე
	He has combed me

In the verb *და-ვ-უვარცხნი-ვ-არ*, O_1 is marked twice with the prefix *ვ-*, the first at the beginning and the second in the first-person singular form of the auxiliary verb *to be*.

9.1.6 *Grammatical and actual verb persons*

There is a group of verbs that stands apart because of their reversed subject-object markers: *მაქვს* (I have something), *მყავს* (I have someone), *მქვია* (my name is), *მწყურია* (I am thirsty), *მშია* (I am hungry), *მიყვარს* (I love), *მძულს* (I hate), and so on.

მე მაქვს სახლი	(I have a house)
მე მყავს და	(I have a sister)

მე მიყვარს მუსიკა (I love music)
მე მძულს ქარი (I hate wind)

The verb *მიყვარს* (I love) is intransitive, which means its subject should be in the nominative and object in the dative in every series. But in the sentence *მე (ადამიან-ს) მიყვარს ის (ადამიან-ი)* (I (a person) love him (a person)) this rule does not apply. The real subject (RS) and real object (RO), on the one hand, and the grammatical subject (GS) and grammatical object (GO), on the other, do not coincide. The real subject (RS) of this verb, the first person, is in the dative, and real object (RO), the third person, in the nominative case. These are not inverted forms, which are characteristic of the I and III conjugation verbs only in III series; their grammatical subject (GS) is in the dative and their grammatical object is in the nominative.

RS = GS; RO=GO	*RS ≠ GR; RO ≠ GO*
ს(O_{3i})-წერ-ს**(S_3)** He writes something to someone იგი (S_3) (ბავშვ-ი) სწერს მას (O^d_3) (წერილ-ს) მას (O_{3i}) (მეგობარ-ს) He (a child) writes it (a letter) to him (a friend)	მ(GO_{1i})-აქვ-ს (GS_3) I have something მე RS(ადამიან-ს) მაქვს ის RO (სახლ-ი) I (a person) have it (a house)
ჰ(O_{3i})-კითხ-ა**(S_3)** She asked him something მან (ქალ-მა) ჰკითხა მას (ბავშვ-ს) ის (ამბავ-ი) She (a woman) asked him (a child) about it (a story).	მ(GO_{1i})-იყვარ-ს (GS_3) I love someone/something მე RS(ადამიან-ს) მიყვარს ის RO(ადამიან-ი) I (a person) love him (a person)

In all the verbs of this group, the grammatical subject (GS) and grammatical object (GO) markers are inverted. But they are intransitive and are not considered as inversive verbs.

9.2 Preverbs

9.2.1 *Structure of preverbs*

Georgian preverbs are added to the verb in front of all its other constituent parts, person markers, or any other prefixes. Preverbs may have a simple or complex structure; complex preverbs consist of two parts – a simple preverb followed by the preverb *მო-*, which always expresses speaker-oriented action: ჩა – ჩამო-, გა – გამო, შე – შემო, etc.

Simple preverbs	*Complex preverbs*
ა – up ქალი კიბეზე ა-დის. A woman is going up the stairs.	ამო – up ქალი კიბეზე ამო-დის. A woman is coming up the stairs.
გა – from inside to outside კაცი ოთახიდან გა-ვიდა. A man went out of the room.	გამო – from inside to outside კაცი ოთახიდან გამო-ვიდა. A man came out of the room.
და – down, downwards ტემპერატურა მინუს ათ გრადუსამდე და-ვიდა. The temperature went down to minus ten.	დამო – down and around This preverb is added to a single word, *დამო-კიდებულება* (attitude), which is not a verb but a noun.
მი – away from speaker ჩიტი მი-ფრინავს. A bird is flying away.	მიმო – back and forth, around, this way and that way მან თვალი მიმო-ავლო გარემოს. He looked around the area. ინფორმაციის მიმო-ცვლა აუცილებელია. It is necessary to exchange information.
მო – towards/to speaker or addressee ჩიტი მო-ფრინავს. A bird is flying (towards us).	მო-preverb in itself indicates the movement towards the speaker or the addressee.
შე – from outside to inside ჩიტი შე-ფრინდა გალიაში. A bird flew into the cage.	შემო – from outside to inside; around დედა ჩემს ოთახში შემო-ვიდა Mother came into (entered) my room. ბიჭმა ხეს შემოუარა. A boy walked around the tree.

(*Continued*)

(Continued)

Simple preverbs	*Complex preverbs*
ჩა- down (into) ბავშვი კიბეზე ჩა-ვიდა. A child went down the stairs.	**ჩამო-** down (into) towards the speaker ბავშვი კიბეზე ჩამო-ვიდა. The child came down (towards the speaker) the stairs.
წა- away/from something/ somebody ჩემი მეგობარი საზღვარგარეთ წა-ვიდა. My friend went abroad.	**წამო-** away/from something/ somebody towards the speaker მე სახლში წამო-ვედი. I came home.
გადა- go over to, go across იგი სხვა ბინაში გადა-ვიდა. He moved over to another apartment.	**გადმო-** come over, come across იგი ჩვენს ბინაში გადმო-ვიდა He moved over to our apartment.

However, not all preverbs have this property. In verbs like *ა-ასრულა* (fulfilled, realised), ***გა***-*ოცდა* (was surprised), ***შე***-*ისწავლა* (studied), or ***წა***-*იკითხა* (read), the preverbs indicate not direction but completion of an action.

Verbs with stems starting with vowel *ა*- or *ე*- will have the vowel doubled in their second- and third-person forms when preverbs ending with the same vowel are added to them: ***და***-*აფასე* (you valued), ***ჩა***-*აშენა* (he built in), ***შე***-*ეხვეწე* (you implored), ***შე***-*ევედრა* (he beseeched).

Georgian preverbs can be divided into archaic and modern. All archaic preverbs have their modern counterparts. In some cases, they may be replaced with their modern forms, but some are not interchangeable. These preverbs have different applications and sometimes different meanings as well. Archaic preverbs are encountered mostly in abstract, generalized, or even metaphoric statements and are preferred in an elevated style of speech or writing, while their modern counterparts add more concrete meaning to the verbs to which they are attached. Such are the preverbs: *აღ*- versus *ა*-, *გარდა*- versus *გადა*-, *გან*- versus *გა*-.

აღ-დგა (was restored), **გან**-ახლდა (was renewed), **აღ**-ორძინდა (flourished anew):

რკინიგზა აღ-დგა.
The railway was restored.

ა-დგა (got up), ა-ვიდა (went up):

სტუდენტი ა-დგა.
The student got up.

გარდა-ტეხს (changes something fundamentally):

არჩევნები გარდატეხს პოლიტიკურ ვითარებას.
The elections will change (fundamentally) the political situation.

გადა-ტეხს (break, break into two):

მეფემ ისრები ორად გადატეხა.
The king broke the arrows into two.

გან-იწმინდა (got purified spiritually, cleansed):

იგი განიწმინდა ცოდვებისაგან.
He cleansed himself from his sins.

გა-იწმინდა (cleaned something from dirt):

მან ფეხსაცმელები გაიწმინდა.
He cleaned his shoes.

Some archaic preverbs add a concrete lexical meaning to a small group of verbs: ***აღ***-*ფრთოვანდა* (got excited), ***აღმო***-*ჩნდა* (turned out), ***წარ***-*იხოცა* (got wiped out), ***გარდა***-*იცვალა* (passed away), ***აღ***-*იქვა* (perceived), ***წარმო***-*იშვა* (originated).

The following chart shows both the archaic and modern proverbs that may or may not be interchangeable depending on their specific meaning or stylistic overtones.

Archaic preverbs	*Modern preverbs*
აღ- ძველი ქალაქი **აღ**-ადგინეს. They restored (resurrected) the old town. მან **აღ**-ასრულა ჩვენი მიზანი. He attained our goal. ჩვენ უნდა **აღ**-ვასრულოთ ჩვენი ვალი სამშობლოს წინაშე. We should pay our debt (carry out our duty) to the motherland. ჯარისკაცებმა დროშა **აღ**-მართეს. The soldiers raised the flag. მასწავლებელმა ყველა მოსწავლე **აღ**-ნუსხა. The teacher verified (went over the list) every student's name.	**ა-** მან **ა**-ისრულა თვისი ნატვრა. He fulfilled his aspirations.

(Continued)

(Continued)

Archaic preverbs	*Modern preverbs*
მომხსენებელმა არაერთხელ **აღ-**ნიშნა ეს ფაქტი. The speaker mentioned this fact several times. მან **აღ-**წერა სიტუაცია ფრონტის ხაზზე. He described the situation on the frontline.	
აღმო- მეცნიერებმა ახალი პლანეტა აღმო-აჩინეს. The scientists discovered a new planet.	**ამო-**
გან- ექიმმა ავადმყოფი გან-კურნა. The doctor cured a patient. მომხსენებელმა ძველი და ახალი პრობლემები **გან-**აცალკევა. The speaker differentiated the old and new problems. მათ მოქმედების გეგმა **გან-**საზღვრეს. They delineated the plan of action. ლექტორმა **გან-**მარტა ტერმინის მნიშვნელობა. The lecturer explained the meaning of the term. იგი ვალდებულებისგან **გან-**თავისუფლდა. He was freed from his responsibilities. მიწისძვრა რამდენჯერმე **გან-**მეორდა. The earthquake happened several times.	**გა-** მან ძველი და ახალი ფეხსაცმელები **გა-**აცალკევა. He separated his old shoes from the new ones. იგი საზრუნავისგან **გა-**თავისუფლდა. He was liberated from his worries. მიწისძვრა რამდენჯერმე **გა-**მეორდა. The earthquake happened several times.
გარდა- ძველი საავადმყოფო ახალ კლინიკად გარდა-იქმნა. The old hospital was transformed into a new clinic. მღვდელმა ხალხს პირჯვარი გარდა-სახა. The priest made the sign of the cross over the crowd. იგი მოულოდნელად გარდა-იცვალა. He passed away unexpectedly.	**გადა-** ძველი საავადმყოფო ახალ კლინიკად გადა-იქცა. The old hospital became a new clinic.

Archaic preverbs	*Modern preverbs*
შთა- წიგნის კითხვის სიყვარული დედამ შთა-მინერგა. Mother instilled in me a love of reading. ამ სიყვარულის ისტორიამ მას ახალი ლექსი შთა-აგონა. This love story inspired him to write a new poem.	**ჩა-** წიგნის კითხვის სიყვარული დედამ **ჩა**-მინერგა. Mother instilled in me a love of reading.
წარ- რექტორმა ახალი დეკანი წარ-ადგინა. The rector introduced the new dean. რამდენიმე სტუდენტი ყრილობაზე წარ-გზავნეს. Several students were delegated to the convention.	**წა-**
წარმო- მან მგზნებარე სიტყვა წარმო-თქვა. He delivered an inspiring speech.	**წამო-**

As mentioned, if a verb has a preverb, it precedes its subject marker and prefix vowel. The only exception is the verb *ვ-ალ-იარებ* (I admit) in which the subject marker *ვ-* precedes the preverb **-ალ**. In modern usage, it is no longer a preverb. III series forms such as *მ-ი-ლიარებია* (I have admitted) and *უ-ლიარებია* (she/he has admitted) indicate that it has been reanalyzed as a neutral version marker and as a part of the stem (see the following sections on version and conjugation see). In all other cases, the subject marker must be placed after the preverb, not before or in the middle of it. In colloquial speech, the first-person subject marker *ვ-* sometimes occurs in the middle of the archaic preverb, after *ა* or *გა*, though such forms are considered non-standard. The correct forms are *ალ-ვ-ზარდე* (I brought up), not *ა-ვ-ლ-ზარდე*; *გან-ვ-არისხე* (I angered), not *გა-ვ-ან-რისხე*; *გან-ვ-აგრძე* (I proceeded), not *გა-ვ-ნ-აგრძე*. It is incorrect to drop the consonant *ვ* in the preverb *გან-*. The following chart shows the proper form of verbs with this preverb.

9.2.2 Functions of preverbs

Georgian preverbs have inflectional and derivational functions in modifying the meanings of verbs and creating new lexemes. They also display two types of spatial content: direction in space and orientation towards the speaker or addressee.

Correct form in high style	*Incorrect form*	*Correct form in contemporary literary usage*
გან-ახორციელებს– realizes	**ან**-ხორციელებს	ახორციელებს
გან-ასახიერებს – impersonates	ან-სახიერებს	ასახიერებს
გან-ასხვავებს – differentiates	**ან**-სხვავებს	ასხვავებს
გან-აზოგადებს – generalizes	**ან**-ზოგადებს	აზოგადებს

Preverbs modify the tense and aspect of verbs. Preverbs added to verbs in the present series make corresponding forms of the future subseries; preverbs added to verbs in the past indefinite tense denote the perfective aspect.

Present	*Future*
ვბრუნდები I come/am coming back	**და**-ვბრუნდები I will come back
იკრიბება They get/are getting together	**შე**-იკრიბება They will get together
ზრდის He is bringing up [a child]	**გა**-ზრდის He will bring up

ფილმი რომელ საათზე იწყება?
What time does the movie start?
წელს სწავლა ათ სექტემბერს დაიწყება.
This year classes will start on the tenth of September.
აქტივისტები იკრიბებიან ქალაქის ცენტრში.
Activists are gathering in the city centre.
ხვალ სად შეიკრიბებით?
Where will you gather tomorrow?
სადილს დღეს მე ვაკეთებ, მაგრამ ხვალ ვინ გააკეთებს?
I make dinner today, but who will make it tomorrow?

Past tense

Imperfective aspect	*Perfective aspect*
ღება paint/was painting	შე-ღება painted
არჩია choose/was choosing	ა-არჩია chose
ხერხა saw/was sawing	და-ხერხა sawed off
ჭრა cut/was cutting	გამო-ჭრა cut out
ატრიალა turn/was turning	გადმო-ატრიალა turned over

*ჩემმა მეზობელმა ღობე დიდხანს **ღება** და ბოლოს დღეს **შეღება**.*
My neighbour kept painting his fence for a long time and finally painted (finished painting) it today.
*მან საჩუქარი მთელი დღე **არჩია** და საუკეთესო ნახატი **აარჩია**.*
He was choosing a gift the entire day and chose an excellent painting.

Some preverbs when added to verbs of motion in the present series denote not completion but only spatial orientation of the movement when directed to the speaker or addressee.

მი-რბის	runs away	**მი**-ფრინავს	flies away
მო-რბის	runs here	**მო**-ფრინავს	flies here
და-რბის	runs around	**და**-ფრინავს	flies around
მი-ხოხავს	crawls away	**მი**-ძუნძულებს	trots away
მო-ხოხავს	crawls here	**მო**-ძუნძულებს	trot here
და-ხოხავს	crawls around	**და**-ძუნძულებს	trots around
მი-ცურავს	swims away	**მი**-სრიალებს	glides away
მო-ცურავს	swims here	**მო**-სრიალებს	glides here
და-ცურავს	swims around	**და**-სრიალებს	glides around
გა-დის	goes out	**მი**-ედინება	flows away
გამო-დის	comes out	**მო**-ედინება	flows here
და-დის	walks around	**გა**-ედინება	flows through
		ჩა-ედინება	flows into

მდინარე მტკვარი შუა ქალაქში ***მიედინება/მოედინება.***
The river Mtkvari flows towards/flows from the centre of the city.
აქ ***გაედინება*** *მდინარე მტკვარი.*
The river Mtkvari flows through here.
მდინარე მტკვარი კასპიის ზღვაში ***ჩაედინება.***
The river Mtkvari flows into the Caspian Sea.

Georgian verbs, except those denoting movement and verbs, such **აღ**-ნიშნავს (notes), **წარმო**-ადგენს (represents), and **მო**-სწონს (likes), do not have preverbs in the present tense. For many of them, it is the context that specifies their meaning. In the future tense, preverbs clarify their semantics.

(i) 1. მამა ახალ სახლს **აგებს.**
Father is building a new house.
მამამ ახალი სახლი **ა-აგო.**
Father built a new house.

2. ეს გუნდი თამაშს **აგებს.**
This team is losing the game.
ამ გუნდმა თამაში **წა-აგო.**
This team lost the game.

3. ჩემი და ლოგინს **აგებს.**
My sister is making the bed.
ჩემმა დამ ლოგინი **და-აგო.**
My sister made the bed.

(ii) 1. ის შენ ნათქვამს ვერ **იგებს.**
He does not understand your words.
მან შენი ნათქვამი ვერ **გა-იგო.**
He did not understand your words.

2. მეფე ომს **იგებს.**
The king is winning the war.
მეფემ ომი **მო-იგო.**
The king won the war.

3. ჩვენი ძროხა ყოველ წელს ხბოს **იგებს.**
Our cow has a (new) calf every year.
ჩვენმა ძროხამ ხბო **მო-იგო.**
Our cow had (gave birth to) a (new) calf.

(iii) 1. ეს ბიჭი ცუდად **იქცევა**.
This boy behaves reprehensibly.
ეს ბიჭი ცუდად **მო-იქცა**.

This boy behaved reprehensibly.

2. ის ხე **იქცევა**.
That tree is falling down.
ის ხე **წა-იქცა**.

That tree fell down.

3. ქვეყანა **იქცევა**.
The world falls apart.
ქვეყანა **და-იქცა**.

The world fell apart.

The concrete semantics of verbs have a core importance in each case, but preverbs may add new nuances. For example, the preverb **და-** conveys the meaning of plurality of a direct object in some verbs:

ქალ-მა (S) პურ-ი (O_d singular) გამო-აცხო.
The woman baked a loaf of bread.
ქალ-მა (S) პურ-ებ-ი (O_d plural) და-აცხო.
The woman baked several loaves of bread.

Preverbs have an object-modifying function and object role-shifting effect, such as changing the verbal valency semantically, and coding this change at the morphological level of the language.

Bivalent verb

კაც-მა (S)	ა-აშენ-ა	სახლ-ი (O_d)
The man	built	a house.

Trivalent verb

კაც-მა (S)	მი-აშენ-ა	სახლ-ს(O_{ind})	ოთახ-ი(O_d).
The man	built (at the side of)	the house	a room.

(= The man added a new room onto the house.)

Trivalent verb

კაც-მა	და-აშენ-ა	სახლ-ს (O_{ind})	სართულ-ი (O_d).
The man	built on (top of)	the house	(another) floor.

(= The man added another floor to the house.)

As the examples show, the preverbs *მი*-and *და*-increased the verbal valency in the base sentence. They also marked a new actant in the sentence, thus shifting the role of the direct and indirect objects.

Archaic preverbs carry a lexeme derivative function:

ახალი new (adjective)	გან-აახლა (he) renewed
მტკიცე firm, strong (adjective)	გან-ამტკიცა (he) affirmed, strengthened
მარტო alone (adjective)	გან-მარტოვდა (he) secluded himself
სავსე full (adjective)	აღ-ავსო (he) filled
ნუსხა roster (noun)	აღ-ნუსხა (he) marked (something in a roster)
ბეჭედი seal (noun)	აღ-ბეჭდა (he) imprinted, impressed

მათ ***განაახლეს*** *მოლაპარაკება ტყვეების გაცვლის შესახებ.*
They renewed talks on the prisoner exchange.
ამ ხელშეკრულებამ ***განამტკიცა*** *ჩვენი ქვეყნების სტრატეგიული პარტნიორობა.*
This treaty strengthened the strategic partnership of our countries.
დედოფალი კოშკში ***განმარტოვდა.***
The queen secluded herself in the tower.

9.3 Voice and transitivity of verbs

9.3.1 *Active voice*

There are three types of verbs expressing voice in Georgian: active, passive, and medial. The active voice verbs do not have a morphological marker, but they are identified by other parameters.

1. The subject of an active voice verb changes its case. This particular property defines the verb conjugation system in the Georgian language. In both subseries of I series, the subject is in the nominative case, in II series it is in the ergative, and in III series it is in the dative.
2. The active voice verbs are always transitive – i.e. they have a direct object in the dative case in I series, and in the nominative in II and III series.
3. Their indirect object is always in the dative case in I and II series.

4. They may be bi- or trivalent verbs. A bivalent verb modifies a subject and a direct object; a trivalent verb modifies a subject, a direct object, and a indirect object. There are some exceptions: bivalent verbs may have the subject and indirect object (and no direct object) – for example, *შეხედავს* (he will look), *მიაგნებს* (he will find), and *უყურებს* (he will watch).
5. A tripersonal verb becomes bipersonal when its dative case indirect object has a postposition in III series.
6. The active voice verbs have inverted subject-object markers in III series.

Active voice tripersonal verb				
Series	*Subject*	*Verb*	*Direct object*	*Indirect object*
I series	ბიჭ-ი Nom. A boy	ს-წერ-ს writes	წერილ-ს Dat. a letter	მეგობარ-ს Dat. to a friend
II series	ბიჭ-მა Erg. A boy	მი-ს-წერ-ა wrote	წერილ-ი Nom. a letter	მეგობარ-ს Dat. to a friend
III series	ბიჭ-ს Dat. A boy	მი-უ-წერი-ა has written	წერილ-ი Nom. a letter	~~მეგობრ-ის-თვის~~ to a friend Prepositional object/adjunct object

Active voice bipersonal verbs				
Series	*Subject*	*Verb*	*Direct object*	*Indirect object*
I series	მხატვარ-ი Nom. A painter	ხატავ-ს paints	სახლ-ს Dat. a house	–
II series	მხატვარ-მა Erg. A painter	და-ხატ-ა painted	სახლ-ი Nom. a house	–
III series	მხატვარ-ს Dat. A painter	და-უ-ხატავ-ს has painted	სახლ-ი Nom. a house	–

9.3.2 *Passive voice*

The majority of passive voice verbs are derived from active voice verbs. It happens when the following changes take place:

1. The subject is eliminated, and the number of persons modified by the verb is diminished.
2. The direct object becomes the subject of the verb.
3. The indirect object may maintain its function.

Tripersonal verbs become bipersonal as a result of conversion:

Active voice verb	*S*	O_d	Oi_d
უ-ხატავ-ს paints Tripersonal verbs	ის (მხატვარ-ი) he (a painter)	მას (ნახატ-ს) it (a picture)	მას (მეგობარ-ს) for him (a friend)
Passive voice verb	*S*		Oi_d
ე-ხატ-ებ-ა is (being) painted Bipersonal verb	ის (ნახატ-ი) it (a picture)		მას (მეგობარ-ს) for him (a friend)

Active voice verb	*S*	O_d	Oi_d
მ-ი-გზავნი-ს sends (is sending) Tripersonal verbs	ის (მეგობარ-ი) he (a friend)	მას (ფულ-ს) it (money)	მე (მეგობარ-ს) to me (a friend)
Passive voice verb	*S*		Oi_d
მ-ე-გზავნებ-ა is (being) sent Bipersonal verb	ის (ფულ-ი) it (money)		მე (მეგობარ-ს) to me

Biperson active voice verbs become monopersonal passive voice verbs after conversion:

Active voice verb	*S*	O_d
ხატავ-ს paints (is drawing) Bipersonal verb	ის (მხატვარ-ი) he (a painter)	მას (ნახატ-ს) it (a picture)
Passive voice verb	***S***	
ი-ხატებ-ა is (being) painted Monopersonal verb	ის (ნახატ-ი) it (a picture)	
Active voice verb	***S***	O_d
ააშენა built Bipersonal verb	მან (კაც-მა) he (a man)	ის (სახლი) it (house)
Passive voice verb	***S***	
ა-შენ-დ-ა is built Monopersonal verb	ის (სახლი) it (house)	

9.3.2.1 *Suffixal passive voice verbs*

Passive voice verbs may have suffixes, prefixes, or no markers of the passive voice. Suffixal passive voice verbs form their stem with the suffix -დ added to their root. The root may be of a nominal, adjectival, or verbal origin, and the meaning of the suffixal passive verb stem is generally inchoative: "to become X" or "to start X-ing." When suffixal passive voice verbs are derived from active voice verbs by conversion, they convey the meaning of "to start X-ing." There is a large number of passive voice verbs with the suffix -დ.

Noun	*Active voice verbs derived from nouns*	*Passive voice verbs with suffix - დ "to become X"*
კაც-ი Man	აკაცებ-ს ის მას He makes a man of him	კაც-დ-ებ-ა ის He becomes a man (he matures)

(*Continued*)

(Continued)

Noun	*Active voice verbs derived from nouns*	*Passive voice verbs with suffix - დ "to become X"*
მხეც-ი Beast	ამხეცებ-ს ის მას He makes a beast of him	მხეც-დ-ებ-ა ის He becomes a beast
ძველ-ი Old	აძველებ-ს ის მას He makes it old	ძველ-დ-ებ-ა ის It becomes old/ages
მწვანე Green	ამწვანებ-ს ის მას He makes it green	მწვან-დ-ებ-ა ის It becomes green
მაღალი Tall	ამაღლებ-ს ის მას He makes it tall	მაღლ-დ-ებ-ა ის It becomes tall
სხვისი Somebody else's	ასხვისებს ის მას He alienates it	სხვის-დ-ებ-ა ის It becomes alienated

ღვინოს მუხის კასრებში ***აძველებენ*** (active voice).
(They) age wine in oak barrels.
ღვინო მუხის კასრებში ***ძველდება*** (passive voice).
Wine is aged in oak barrels.
ქუსლებიანი ფეხსაცმელი ამ ქალს ***ამაღლებს*** (active voice).
High-heeled shoes make this woman taller.
ქუსლებიან ფეხსაცმელებში ეს ქალი ***მაღლდება*** (passive voice).
In high-heeled shoes this woman becomes taller.
წვიმა ბალახს ***ამწვანებს*** (active voice).
Rain makes grass green.
ბალახი ***მწვანდება*** (passive voice).
Grass becomes green.

9.3.2.2 *Prefixal passive voice verbs*

There are two types of prefixal passive voice verbs.

Passive voice verbs with the prefix ი-are monopersonal and are derived mostly from active voice bipersonal verbs.

Bipersonal active voice verbs	*Monopersonal passive voice verbs*
ასხამს ის მას He pours it	ი-სხმება ის It is poured

Bipersonal active voice verbs	*Monopersonal passive voice verbs*
წერს ის მას He writes it	ი-წერება ის It is written
ბეჭდავს ის მას He types it	ი-ბეჭდება ის It is typed
სვამს ის მას He drinks it	ი-სმევა ის It is drunk (it is drinkable)

Passive voice verbs with the prefix *ე*-are bipersonal and are derived from tripersonal active voice verbs.

Tripersonal active voice verbs	*Bipersonal passive voice verbs*
მიუძღვნის ის მას მას He will dedicate it to him	მი-ე-ძღვნება ის მას It will be dedicated to him
გადააფარებს ის მას მას He will cover it over it	გადა-ე-ფარება ის მას It will be spread over it
მიაწერს ის მას მას He will write it on it	მი-ე-წერება ის მას It will be written on it
დაახატავს ის მას მას He will draw it on it	და-ე-ხატება ის მას It will be drawn on it

პოეტი ლექსს ქვეყნის გმირებს ***მი-უ-ძღვნი-ს*** (active voice).
The poet will dedicate a poem to the country's heroes.
ეს ლექსი ქვეყნის გმირებს ***მი-ე-ძღვნებ-ა*** (passive voice).
This poem will be dedicated to the country's heroes.
მხატვარი ამ კედელს დიდ ფრესკას ***და-ა-ხატავ-ს*** (active voice).
The painter will paint a large fresco on this wall.
ამ კედელს დიდი ფრესკა ***და-ე-ხატებ-ა*** (passive voice).
On the wall a large fresco will be painted.

Passive voice verbs may sometimes express a variety of semantic connotations as shown in the following examples.

1. **Possibility**

Verbs denote the possibility of carrying out the action expressed by them. Usually, it refers to the quality of an object to which the action is directed: *იჭმევა/იჭმება* (it is edible), *ისმევა/ისმება* (it is drinkable), *გაისვლება* (it is possible to go out), *დაედგომება* (it is possible for him to stay), etc.

> *ეს პური* ***ი-ჭმევ-ა*** *თუ ძალიან ძველია?*
> Is this bread *edible (can it be eaten)*, or is too old?
> *ეს ღვინო უკვე არ* ***ი-სმევ-ა//ი-სმებ-ა.***
> This wine is not *drinkable* anymore.
> *ისეთი სიცივეა, გარეთ არ* ***გა-ი-სვლებ-ა.***
> It is so cold, it's *impossible to go out*.
> *მან თავი ისე შეირცხვინა, აქ აღარ* ***და-ე-დგომებ-ა*** (monopersonal passive).
> He behaved so shamefully that he *cannot stay* here anymore

2. **Feeling**

Verbs denote the attitude of the grammatical object to the grammatical subject: *მებევრება* (seems too much to me), *მეცოტავება* (seems too little to me), *მემძიმება* (feels heavy to me), *მემწარება* (feels bitter to me), *მეტკბილება* (feels sweet to me)

> *ამდენი მაგარი სასმელი* ***მ-ე-ბევრებ-ა.***
> So much hard liquor seems too much to me.
> *ასეთი ხელფასი* ***მ-ე-ცოტავებ-ა.***
> Such salary seems too little to me.
> *ჩანთა ძალიან* ***ე-მძიმ-ა.***
> The bag felt too heavy to him.
> *გუშინ ეს ვაშლი* ***გ-ე-ტკბილ-ა.***
> Yesterday this apple felt sweet to you.

3. **Disposition, mood**

Verbs can denote that an indirect object is disposed to carry out the action expressed by them: *მ-ე-ცინებ-ა* (I feel like laughing), *მ-ე-ტირებ-ა* (I feel like crying), *მ-ე-მღერებ-ა* (I feel like singing), *მ-ე-ცეკვებ-ა* (I feel like dancing), and so forth. When the indirect object is not inclined to carry out the action expressed with the verb, the negative particle **არ** should be used.

> ახლა სულ არ *მ-ე-მღერებ-ა.*
> I don't feel like singing at all right now.
> რა *გ-ე-ცეკვებ-ა*, საქმე არა გაქვს?
> What makes you dance; don't you have things to do?
> მის დანახვაზე სულ *მ-ე-ცინებ-ა.*
> Whenever I see him, I feel like laughing.

Verbs expressing mood or inclination of the indirect object to do something can be formed using the same pattern:

> რა *მ-ე-სტუმრებ-ა*, თავი მტკივა.
> I don't feel like (having) guest(s), I have a headache.
> იმდენი საქმე მაქვს, რა *მ-ე-თეატრებ-ა*.
> I have so much work, I am in no mood for (going to) the theatre.
> ძალიან ბევრი საქმე მაქვს, რა *მ-ე-ლასვეგასებ-ა*.
> I have a lot of work to do, I have no time (I am in no mood) for (going to) Las Vegas.

9.3.2.3 *Root passive voice verbs*

Root passive verbs can be derived from both transitive and intransitive verbs. Such verbs do not have passive voice markers, but they are easily recognizable, especially if they are converted from active voice verbs

> ათბობს (he warms it up) – თბება (it gets warmed up)
> აშრობს (he dries it up) – შრება (it gets dried up)
> ახმობს (he dehydrates it) – ხმება (it gets dehydrated)
> ატკბობს (he sweetens it) – ტკბება (it gets sweetened)

In contemporary Georgian there are rather few passive voice verbs without markers.

It is important to differentiate between the *dynamic* and *static* passive voice verbs with different conjugation patterns. The dynamic passive verbs denote the process or continuity of an action, while static verbs indicate the result of an action. This semantic difference is reflected in their conjugation pattern.

Passive voice verbs

Dynamic	*Static*
აკლდება ის მას It gets lost for him	აკლია ის მას It is missing (for him)
ეფინება ის მას It gets spread on it	აფენია ის მას It is spread on it
ეცხება ის მას It gets smeared on it	აცხია ის მას It is smeared on it

(Continued)

(Continued)

Passive voice verbs

Dynamic	*Static*
აკლდება ის მას It gets lost for him	აკლია ის მას It is missing (for him)
ეფინება ის მას It gets spread on it	აფენია ის მას It is spread on it
ეფარება ის მას It gets covered on it	აფარია ის მას It is covered on it
ეხატება ის მას It gets painted on it	ახატია ის მას It is painted on it
ეხურება ის მას It gets put on it	ახურავს ის მას It is put on it
ევალება ის მას It gets charged to him	ავალია ის მას It is charged to him
ლაგდება ის It gets arranged	ალაგია ის It is arranged
ინთება ის It gets lit up	ანთია ის It is lit up

ეს მალამო ღია ჭრილობას ***ე-ცხება.***
This ointment gets smeared (put) on an open wound.
ეს მალამო მის ღია ჭრილობას ***ა-ცხია.***
This ointment is smeared (put) on his open wound.
ეს ფანარი ყოველ საღამოს ***ი-ნთება.***
This streetlamp gets lit every evening.
ეს ფანარი უკვე ***ა-ნთია.***
This streetlamp is already lit.

Sometimes dynamic and static voice verbs may have different formal derivation, but they do not specify semantic difference between the process of an action and its end result:

მას საბუთების შემოწმება ***ე-ვალება.***
He is charged with verifying the documents.
მას საბუთების შემოწმება ***ა-ვალია.***
His duty is to verify documents.

9.3.3 Medial verbs

There are two groups of medial verbs, medio-active and medio-passive. Medio-active verbs use the forms of active voice verbs for the missing forms in their overall conjugation pattern, while medio-passive verbs use passive voice verbs for missing forms.

9.3.3.1 Medio-active verbs

Like active verbs, medio-actives have a case-changing subject, but they do not modify direct objects. In the following chart the missing forms of the medio-active verbs are replaced with the active voice verbs in the aorist tense.

ნადირობ-ს ის (მონადირე) He (hunter) hunts it	ინადირა მან (მონადირე-მ) He hunted
ცხოვრობს ის (კაც-ი) He (man) lives	იცხოვრა მან (კაც-მა) He (man) lived
მეფობს ის (მეფე) He (king) rules	იმეფა მან (მეფე-მ) He (king) ruled
ტირის ის (ბავშვ-ი) He (child) cries	იტირა მან (ბავშვ-მა) He (child) cried
იცინის ის (კაც-ი) He (man) laughs	იცინა მან (კაც-მა) He (man) laughed
ცურავს ის (მოცურავე) He (swimmer) swims	იცურა მან (მოცურავე-მ) He (swimmer) swam
ჩქარობს ის (მგზავრი) He (traveller) hurries	იჩქარა მან (მგზავრ-მა) He (traveller) hurried
წუხს ის (დედა) She (mother) worries	იწუხა მან (დედა-მ) She (mother) worried

In III series tenses, medio-active verbs have inverted subject markers as do the active voice verbs.

მ-იცხოვრია – I have lived
მ-იტირია – I have cried
მ-იცინია – I have laughed
→ S_1 is marked with the O_1 marker

Some active verbs are derived from the medio-active verbs, which are the initial for the derivation of the passive verbs by conversion. These verbs in the following chart are exceptional because active voice verbs are derived by transforming medio-active verbs, but the corresponding passive voice verbs are formed according to the rules discussed previously (see 9.3.2.).

Medio-active	*Active*	*Passive*
დუღს ის It boils (is boiling)	ადუღებს ის მას He boils it	დუღდება ის It starts boiling
უდუღს ის მას It boils (is boiling) for him	უდუღებს ის მას მას He boils it for him	უდუღდება ის მას It starts boiling for him
გორავს ის It is rolling	აგორებს ის მას He rolls it	გორდება ის It starts rolling
უგორავს ის მას It rolls (is rolling) for him	უგორებს ის მას მას He rolls it for him	უგორდება ის მას It starts rolling for him
წუხს ის He is bothered	აწუხებს ის მას He bothers him	წუხდება ის He gets bothered
უწუხს ის მას Someone/ something belonging to him is bothered	უწუხებს ის მას მას He bothers someone/ something belonging to him	უწუხდება ის მას Someone/ something belonging to him gets bothered
ცურავს// ცურაობს ის He swims (is swimming)	აცურავებს ის მას He makes/helps him swim	ცურდება ის He slides
ჭიდაობს ის He wrestles (is wrestling)	აჭიდავებს ის მას He makes/helps him wrestle	–
ბანაობს ის He bathes (is bathing)	აბანავებს ის მას He gives a bath to him	–
თევზაობს ის He is fishing	ათევზავებს ის მას He helps him to fish	–

წყალი ***დუღს*** (medio-passive voice).
The water is boiling.
ჩემი და წყალს ***ადუღებს*** (active voice).
My sister is boiling the water.

წყალი **დუღდება** (passive voice).
The water is starting to boil.
ბავშვი **ცურავს** (medio-passive).
The child is swimming.
დედა ბავშვს **აცურავებს** (active voice).
Mother is making (helping) a child to swim.

The translating verbs like უდუღდება and უგორდება into English represents a particular difficulty. The sentence დედას წყალი უდუღდება means "The water that mother wanted to boil is beginning to boil."

ბავშვს ბურთი **უგორდება.**
The child's ball (the child was holding) is rolling down.

9.3.3.2 *Medio-passive verbs*

Medial verbs that fill the incomplete tense forms of passive voice verbs are medio-passive. They are correlated with active voice verbs in the same manner as passive voice verbs converted from them.

Active verbs	*Passive verbs*	*Medio-passive verbs*
დგამს ის მას He puts it down	იდგმება ის It gets put down	დგას ის It is standing
აწვენს ის მას He makes him lie down	წვება ის He lies down	წევს ის He is lying down
აძულებს ის მას მას He makes him hate it	სძულდება ის მას He starts to hate it	სძულს ის მას He hates it
აყვარებს ის მას მას He makes him love it	უყვარდება ის მას He begins to love it	უყვარს ის მას He loves it
აწყურებს ის მას მას He makes him thirst for it	სწყურდება ის მას He begins to thirst for it	სწყურია ის მას He thirsts for it

The difference between ***დგამს*** and ***აწვენს*** is that the former means to put something down in an upright position, and the latter means to make someone or something lie down or put someone in bed.

> მე სკამს ფანჯარასთან *ვდგამ* (active voice).
> I put the chair by the window.
> სკამი ფანჯარასთან *დგას* (medio-passive voice).
> The chair is (standing) at the window.
> დედა შვილს ლოგინში *აწვენს* (active voice).
> Mother puts the child into bed.
> შვილი ლოგინში *წევს* (medio-passive).
> The child is (lying) in bed.
> მარილიანი საჭმელი წყალს *მაწყურებს* (active voice).
> Salty food makes me thirsty (to thirst for water).
> წყალი *მწყურია* (medio-passive verb).
> I am thirsty (thirst for water).

There is a separate group of verbs expressing feelings or impressions; they are called affective verbs: *მიყვარს* (I love), *მიკვირს* (I am surprised), *მიმძიმს* (it saddens for me), *მიჭირს* (I am in difficulty), *მომწონს* (I like), *მწამს* (I have faith in), *მწყინს* (I am hurt), *მძულს* (I hate), *მნებავს* (I desire), *მეზიზღება* (I despise), and some others. The grammatical and actual subject and object of these verbs do not coincide (see the grammatical and actual persons), and therefore, grammatical persons modified by them are defined according to their case.

> მო-მ-წონ-ს **ის** S_3 (ქალ-ი, nom.) **მე** O_{1i} (კაც-ს, dat.)
> I (a man, dat.) like her (a woman, nom.)

In this sentence, the verb *მო-მ-წონ-ს* is intransitive. The grammatical subject is determined by its case. In I series the subject of both transitive and intransitive verbs is in the nominative case, while direct and indirect objects are in the dative. According to this rule, in the verb *მო-მ-წონ-ს*, the noun *woman* (ქალ-ი) is the grammatical subject (GS) since it is in the nominative, and the noun *a man* (კაც-ს), here represented with the pronoun *I*, is the grammatical object (GO) because it is in the dative case.

There are about 40 such verbs in the Georgian language. Their conjugation patterns are similar to that of medio-passive verbs and will be discussed in the following chapters.

9.4 Version

As was shown in previous chapters, Georgian verbs are polypersonal; they may modify several nouns simultaneously and have subject and direct or indirect object markers. In addition, Georgian verbs may indicate goal-specific direction of the action from the subject to object(s) or between objects. The following sentences illustrate the case:

1. ვ-ა-შენებ მე (ადამიან-ი S_1) სახლს (O_d)
2. I (a person S_1) built a house (O_d).
   ა-ვ-ა-შენე მე (ადამიან-მა S_1) სახლ-ი (O_d)
   I (a person S_1) built a house (O_d).
3. ვ-ი-შენებ მე (ადამიან-ი S_1) სახლს (O_d)
4. I (a person S_1) build a house (O_d) for myself.
   ა-ვ-ი-შენე მე (ადამიან-მა S_1) სახლ-ი (O_d)
   I (a person S_1) built a house (O_d) for myself.
5. ვ-უ-შენებ მე (ადამიან-ი S_1) მას (ვაჟ-ს Oi_d) სახლს (O_d)
6. I (a person S_1) build a house (O_d) for my son.
   ა-ვ-უ-შენე მე (ადამიან-მა S_1) მას (ვაჟ-ს Oi_d) სახლ-ი (O_d)
   I (a person S_1) built a house (O_d) for my son.

The verb in all three sentences has the same root and modifies two or three actants of which only the subject (S_1) is indicated with the first-person marker *ვ-*, but it shows different relation between the subject and the object(s), or between objects.

In the first example, the verb *ვ-ა-შენ-ებ* does not indicate goal-specific action – i.e. it does not specify for whom the house, the direct object, is built.

აქ საავადმყოფოს ა-შენებენ.
Here they build (are building) a hospital.

The preverb **ა**-is followed by the version marker **ა**-.

აქ საავადმყოფოს ა-ა-შენებენ.
Here they will build a hospital.

In the second example, the verb *ვ-ი-შენებ* points at the goal-specific action – the house, the direct object, is built for the subject, the builder himself. Self-orientation of the action is marked with the *ი*-vowel.

In the third example, the verb *ვ-უ-შენებ* points at the goal-specific action too but indicates that the result of the subject's action (a direct object, house) is intended to belong to an indirect object (son).

Thus, the version markers *ი*-and *უ*-follow the preverb and/or the subject marker if these formants are present in the verb form. The version marker always precedes the stem.

9.4.1 *Neutral and locative versions*

A verb that does not indicate for whom the result of an action denoted by it is intended has neutral version forms. They may be marked with the prefix ა-or have no version marker at all.

Neutral version of bipersonal verbs with no marker

ვ-წერ-(თ) მე/ჩვენ მას/მათ I/we write it/them	ვ-ჭამ-(თ) მე/ჩვენ მას/მათ I/we eat it/them	ვ-ჭრ-ი-(თ) მე/ჩვენ მას/მათ I/we cut it/them
წერ-(თ) შენ/თქვენ მას/მათ You/you write it/them	ჭამ-(თ) შენ/თქვენ მას/მათ You/you eat it/them	ჭრ-ი-(თ) შენ/თქვენ მას/მათ You/you cut it/them
წერ-ს ის მას/მათ He writes it/them	ჭამ-ს ის მას/მათ He eats it/them	ჭრ-ი-ს ის მას/მათ He cuts it/them
წერ-ენ ისინი მას/მათ They write it/them	ჭამ-ენ ისინი მას/მათ They eat it/them	ჭრ-ი-ან ისინი მას/მათ They cut it/them

Neutral version forms of bipersonal transitive verbs with prefix -ა-

ვ-ა-კეთებ-(თ) მე/ჩვენ მას/მათ I/we make it/them	ვ-ა-შრობ-(თ) მე/ჩვენ მას/მათ I/we dry it/them
ა-კეთებ-(თ) შენ/თქვენ მას/მათ You/you make it/them	ა-შრობ-(თ) შენ/თქვენ მას/მათ You/you dry it/them
ა-კეთებ-ს ის მას/მათ He makes it/them	ა-შრობ-ს ის მას/მათ He dries it/them
ა-კეთებ-ენ ისინი მას/მათ They make it/them	ა-შრობ-ენ ისინი მას/მათ They dry it/them

The neutral version forms of tripersonal transitive verbs do not have any marker, with the exception of a few with the ა-prefix:

> შვილ-მა (S_3, erg.) დედა-ს (O_{3i}, dat.) ცრემლ-ი (O_{3d}, nom.) *შე-ა-შრო.*
> The child dried mother's tears (on her face).

Monopersonal verbs always denote a neutral version:

> *კვდება* ის (ცხენი).
> It (a horse) dies.

ა-ბია ის/ისინი (ცხენი/ცხენები).
It/they (horse/horses) is/are tied.
ა-წყვია ის/ისინი (ბარგი/ჩანთები)
It/they (luggage/bags) is/are arranged.

These monopersonal verbs do not modify an object and therefore denote neutral action, but they may convey subjective action if proprietary relation between the subject and the object is indicated. English translation of such verbs will require the use of possessive pronouns:

მას ცხენი ***უ****-კვდება.*
His horse is dying.
*თქვენ ცხენი ხეზე გ-****ი****-ბიათ.*
Your horse is tied to the tree.
*მე წიგნები თაროზე მ-****ი****-წყვია.*
My books are arranged on a shelf.

Prefix ა-can express not only neutral but a locative version, too. A locative version indicates that the action was performed in some spatial relation to the indirect object. The spatial relation is usually "onto":

ავტორი წიგნს გვარს ***ა-წერს.***
The author signs his name *on* the book.
კაბას ქინძისთავს ***ვ-ა-ბნევ.***
I fasten a brooch *on* the dress.
შენ ქვაბს თავსახური ***და-ა-ფარე.***
You put the lid *on* the pot.
ბავშვი კედელს რაღაცას ***ა-ხატავს.***
The child is painting something *on* the wall.

Compare with the neutral version:

ბავშვი რაღაცას ***Ø-ხატავს.***
The child is painting something.

The locative version is used seldom in Georgian.

9.4.2 *Subjective version*

Subjective version forms indicate that the direct object belongs to the subject or is intended for it. It is marked with the ი-prefix.

The subjective version is typical only for transitive verbs that clearly denote destination or goal-orientation of the action.

Subjective version forms are most frequently used in the following cases:

1. The subject, intentionally or unintentionally, acts upon itself: თავი და-ი-ბანა (washed his head/hair), ფრჩხილები და-ი-ჭრა (cut his fingernails), მუხლი ი-ტკინა (hurt his knee), გული და-ი-მშვიდა (calmed himself down), ტანსაცმელი ჩა-ი-ცვა (put his clothes on), ქამარი შემო-ი-რტყა (girded himself with his belt), ქუდი და-ი-ხურა (put on his hat)

   ჩემი მეგობარი წაიქცა და მუხლი ***იტკინა.***
   My friend fell down and hurt his knee.
   დღეს თავი დავიბანე და ფრჩხილები ***დავიჭერი.***
   Today I washed my hair (head) and cut my fingernails.
   დღეს ციოდა და მამაჩემის თბილი პალტო ***ჩავიცვი.***
   It was cold today and I put on my father's warm coat.
   ქუდი ***დაიხურე****, თორემ გაცივდები.*
   Put on your hat or you catch cold.

2. The direct object of a verb is intended for the subject: *ფული ი-სესხა* (borrowed money), *სახელი ი-კითხა* (asked the name), *დოკუმენტი მო-ი-პარა* (stole a document), *პური ი-თხოვა* (asked for bread).

   ჩემმა მეზობელმა მანქანის საყიდლად ფული ***ისესხა.***
   My neighbour borrowed money to buy a car.
   ვიღაცამ ჩემი საწვიმარი ***მოიპარა.***
   Someone stole my raincoat.

Intransitive verbs do not have a subjective version.

The subjective version forms of bipersonal verbs

ვ-**ი**-შენებ-(თ) მე/ჩვენ მას/მათ I/we build it/them for me/us	ვ-**ი**-კერავ-(თ) მე/ჩვენ მას/მათ I/we sew it/them for me/us
ი-შენებ-(თ) შენ/თქვენ მას/მათ You/you build it/them for you/you	**ი**-კერავ-(თ) შენ/თქვენ მას/მათ You/you sew it/them for you/you
ი-შენებ-ს/-ენ ის მას/მათ He/they builds/build it/them for himself/themself	**ი**-კერავ-ს/-ენ ის მას/მათ He/they sews/sew it/them for himself/themself

9.4.3 *Objective version*

Verbs in objective version forms denote an intended destination of an action or possessive correlation between objects. They indicate that the subject acts upon a direct object for the benefit or detriment of an indirect object or that the direct object belongs to the indirect object. Mostly objective version forms are tripersonal transitive verbs indicating that a subject acts for the benefit of someone who may be the first, second, or third person or persons.

The objective version markers are the prefixes *ი*-and *უ*-. The prefix *ი*-is used when an indirect object is the first or second person. It follows the first- or second-person indirect object markers.

> დედა (S_3) მე ($O_{id\text{-}1}$) კაბას ($O_{d\text{-}3}$) *მ-ი-კერავ-ს.*
> (My) mother sews a dress for me.

The objective version marker *ი*-shows, that the subject (*დედა*/ mother, indicated by suffix -*ს* in the verb) acts upon a direct object (*კაბას*/dress) for the benefit of the first-person indirect object (მე/ for me, indicated by prefix *მ*-in the verb). The objective version marker *ი*- shows that $O_{d\text{-}3}$ (i.e. direct object – *კაბა*) of the action expressed with the verb belongs to the indirect object – *მე* ($O_{id\text{-}1}$).

The same rule applies to the following examples:

> დედა (S_3) *ჩვენ* ($O_{id\text{-}1pl}$) კაბებს ($O_{d\text{-}3}$) *გვ-ი-კერავ-ს.*
> Mother sews the dresses for us.
> დედა (S_3) *შენ* ($O_{id\text{-}2}$) კაბას ($O_{d\text{-}3}$) *გ-ი-კერავ-ს.*
> Mother sews a dress for you.

The objective version marker *უ*-is not preceded by a third-person marker.

დედა (S_3) *მას* ($O_{id\text{-}3}$) კაბას ($O_{d\text{-}3}$) *უ-კერავ-ს.* (Mother sews a dress for her.)

The objective version marker *უ*-shows, that the subject (*დედა*/ mother, indicated by suffix -*ს* in the verb) acts upon a direct object (*კაბას*/dress) for the benefit of the third-person indirect object (*მას*/ for her; it is not indicated by person marker in the verb).

The objective version forms of the tripersonal verb წერ

მ-ი-წერ-(თ) შენ/თქვენ (S_2) მე ($O_{id\text{-}1}$) დავალებას($O_{d\text{-}3}$).
You/you write an assignment for me.

გვ-ი-წერ-(თ) შენ/თქვენ (S_2) ჩვენ (O_{id-1}) დავალებას(O_{d-3}).
You/you write an assignment for us.
მ-ი-წერ-ს ის (S_3) მე (O_{id-1}) დავალებას(O_{d-3}).
He writes an assignment for me.
მ-ი-წერ-ენ ისინი (S_3) მე (O_{id-1}) დავალებას(O_{d-3}).
They write an assignment for me.
გვ-ი-წერ-ს ის (S_3) ჩვენ (O_{id-1}) დავალებას(O_{d-3}).
He writes an assignment for us.
გვ-ი-წერ-ენ ისინი (S_3) ჩვენ (O_{id-1}) დავალებას(O_{d-3}).
They write an assignment for us.

გ-ი-წერ-(თ) მე/ჩვენ (S_1) შენ/თქვენ (O_{id-2}) დავალებას (O_{d-3}).
I/we write an assignment for you/you.
გ-ი-წერ-ს ის (S_3) შენ (O_{id-2}) დავალებას (O_{d-3}).
He writes an assignment for you.
გ-ი-წერ-ენ ისინი (S_3) შენ/თქვენ (O_{id-2}) დავალებას (O_{d-3}).
They write an assignment for you/you.

ვ-უ-წერ-(თ) მე/ჩვენ (S_1) მას/მათ (O_{id-3}) დავალებას(O_{d-3}).
I/we write an assignment for him/them.
უ-წერ-(თ) შენ/თქვენ (S_2) მას/მათ (O_{id-3}) დავალებას (O_{d-3}).
You/you write an assignment for him/them.
უ-წერ-ს ის (S_3) მას/მათ (O_{id-3}) დავალებას (O_{d-3}).
He writes an assignment for him/them.
უ-წერ-ენ ისინი (S_3) მას/მათ (O_{id-2}) დავალებას (O_{d-3}).
They write an assignment for him/them.

შენებ-

მ-ი-შენებ-(თ) შენ/თქვენ (S_2) მე (O_{id-1}) სახლს(O_{d-3}).
You/you build a house for me.
გვ-ი-შენებ-(თ) შენ/თქვენ (S_2) ჩვენ (O_{id-1}) სახლს(O_{d-3}).
You/you build a house for us.
მ-ი-შენებ-ს ის (S_3) მე (O_{id-1}) სახლს(O_{d-3}).
He builds a house for me.
მ-ი-შენებ-ენ ისინი (S_3) მე (O_{id-1}) სახლს(O_{d-3}).
They build a house for me.
გვ-ი-შენებ-ს ის (S_3) ჩვენ (O_{id-1}) სახლს(O_{d-3}).
He builds a house for us.
გვ-ი-შენებ-ენ ისინი (S_3) ჩვენ (O_{id-1}) სახლს(O_{d-3}).
They build a house for us.

გ-ი-შენებ-(თ) მე/ჩვენ (S_1) შენ (O_{id-2}) სახლს (O_{d-3}).
I/we build a house for you.

გ-ი-შენებ-ს ის (S_3) შენ (O_{id-2}) სახლს (O_{d-3}).
He builds a house for you.
გ-ი-შენებ-ენ ისინი (S_3) შენ (O_{id-2}) სახლს (O_{d-3}).
They build a house for you.

ვ-უ-შენებ-(თ) მე/ჩვენ (S_1) მას/მათ (O_{id-3}) სახლს(O_{d-3}).
I/we build a house for him/them.
უ-შენებ-(თ) შენ/თქვენ (S_1) მას/მათ (O_{id-3}) სახლს (O_{d-3}).
You/you build a house for him/them.
უ-შენებ-ს ის (S_3) მას (O_{id-3}) სახლს (O_{d-3}).
He builds a house for him.
უ-შენებ-ენ ისინი (S_3) მას/მათ (O_{id-3}) სახლს (O_{d-3}).
They build a house for him/them.

These examples show the following:

1. If the subject of an objective version verb is in the first person, the direct object may be intended for the second or the third person(s).

მე გ-ი-წერ *შენ* მას.	მე ვ-უ-შენებ *მას* მას.
I write it for *you*.	I build it for *him*.

2. If the subject is in the second person, the direct object is intended for the first or third person(s):

შენ მ-ი-წერ მას *მე*.	შენ უ-შენებ მას *მას/მათ*.
You write it for *me*.	You write it for *him/them*.

3. If the subject is in the third person, the direct object may be intended for any of the three persons, first, second, or third:

მ-ი-წერ-ს ის *მე მას*.	He writes it for *me*.
გ-ი-წერ-ს ის *შენ* მას.	He writes it for you.
უ-წერ-ს ის *მას* მას.	He writes it for *him*.

Since the prefix ი- marks either the subjective or objective version, it is important to differentiate one form from the other:

1. One indicator is the number of actants modified by a verb; bipersonal verbs have subjective version forms, while tripersonal verbs have objective version forms.

   მე (S_1) სახლი (O_{d-3}) ა-ვ-ი-შენე (bipersonal verb).
   I built a house for myself.

   მან (S_3) მე(O_{id-1}) სახლი (O_{d-3}) ა-მ-ი-შენ-ა (tripersonal verb).
   He built a house for me.

2. Changing the indirect object from the first or second person to the third person would require the objective version prefix *უ-*:

   მან (S3) მე (Oid-1) სახლი (Od-3) ა-მ-ი-შენ-ა.
   He built a house for me.
   მე (S1) მას (Oid-3) სახლი (Od-3) ა-ვ-უ-შენ-ე.
   I built a house for him.

3. Bipersonal intransitive verbs may convey the meaning of the objective version (object-oriented action). In such cases the English translation would require use of the possessive marker.

   ცხენი (S3) მო-უ-კვდ-ა კაცს (Od-3).
   The man's horse died.
   საჭმელი (S3) უ-მზადდება-ა ბავშვს (Od-3).
   The child's food is getting ready.
   იარა (S3) და-უ-ცხრებ-ა ავადმყოფს (Od-3).
   The sick person's wound will heal.

4. If a monopersonal verb is changed into a bipersonal, it will require the objective version form:

   ხმება ხე (S_3).
   A tree is dying (gets dry).
   უ-ხმებ-ა ხეები (S_{3pl}) მას(O_{d-3}) ეზოში.
   The trees (in his yard) are dying (getting dry)
   თავდებ-ა სემესტრი (S_3).
   The semester is ending.
   უ-თავდებ-ა სემესტრი (S_3) მას(O_{d-3}).
   His semester is ending.
   ბრწყინავ-ს ვარსკვლავი (S_3).
   The star is sparkling.
   უ-ბრწყინავ-ს თვალები (S_{3pl}) მას (O_{d-3}).
   Her eyes are sparkling.

9.5 Tense and its subcategories

Georgian verbs, according to their grammatical and structural categories, are grouped in tenses.[2] Each tense is manifested by specific forms of verbs that represent a synthesis of three grammatical categories: time, mood, and aspect.

[2] TMA is often used to identify the synthesis of the verbal categories of tense, mood, and aspect. Some scholars use a transcription of the Georgian term screeve (მწკრივი) introduced by Akaki Shanidze. In this book, the traditional term tense is used, which is more familiar for English-speaking readers.

9.5.1 Mood

Grammatical mood is the property of verbs that clarifies intended meaning of the speaker's statement. It is one of the categories of any verb with person markers and determines not the action expressed by the verb, but the attitude of the speaker towards it. If an action is presented as real, actually happening in the present, happened in the past, or will happen in the future, the verb is in the *indicative mood*:

ბიჭები ფეხბურთს თამაშობენ (Present).
Boys are playing football.
ბიჭები ფეხბურთს ითამაშებენ (Future).
The boys will play football.
ბიჭებმა ფეხბურთი ითამაშეს (Past).
The boys played football.

If the verb denotes a possible or desirable action in the present, past, or future, it is in the *subjunctive mood*:

ნეტავ დისერტაციას ***ვ-წერდე*** (present subjunctive mood)
Were I writing the dissertation
ნეტავ დისერტაცია დროულად ***და-მ-ეწერ-ა*** (past subjunctive mood).
It would have been good if I had written the dissertation on time.
დისერტაცია მალე ***და-მ-ეწერო-ს*** (perfect subjunctive mood).
(May it happen that) I write the dissertation soon.

Verbs in the subjunctive mood are often preceded with the auxiliary words: **ნეტავ** (may, I wish) or **ოღონდაც** (if only). They could also be placed in a subordinate clause with the conjunction **რომ** or follow the verb **შეიძლება** (may, it's possible) in its modal sense:

Verbs in the *imperative mood* denote an action that must be carried out. An order directed to the second person, singular or plural, is expressed with verbs in the aorist tense with the corresponding person and plural markers:

დაწერე-(თ)! (Write!) ***წაიკითხე-(თ)!*** (Read!) ***ისწავლე-(თ)!*** (Study!)

In addition, an order, suggestion, or instruction directed to the second person(s) is expressed with verbs in the optative form preceded by the modal verb **უნდა** (should):

უნდა დაწერო-(თ)! *უნდა წაიკითხო-(თ)!* *უნდა ისწავლო-(თ)!*
You/you should write! You/you should read! You/you should study!

Verbs expressing an order directed to the first or third person(s) are in the optative form:

დავწეროთ!	*დაწეროს/ნ!*
Let's write!	Let him/them write!
წავიკითხოთ!	*წაიკითხოს/ნ!*
Let's read!	Let him/them read!
ვისწავლოთ!	*ისწავლოს/ნ!*
Let's study!	Let him/them study!

The indicative and imperative mood of verbs like *დაწერე-(თ)* (you/you wrote), *დავწერო-(თ)* (I/we should write), *დაწეროს* (he should write), and *დაწერონ* (they should write) are differentiated from each other by intonation in speech and by corresponding punctuation marks in writing.

Depending on the contexts, the subjunctive and imperative moods may be expressed with verbs in the same tense forms.

Subjunctive mood	*Imperative mood*
ნეტავ დაწეროს. I wish he would write.	დაწეროს! He should/must write!
ოღონდაც დარეკოს. If only he would phone.	დარეკოს! He should/must phone!
რომ გააკეთოს. If he would only do it.	გააკეთოს! He should/must do!
შეიძლება გაჭრას. He may cut.	გაჭრას! He should/must cut!

In the negative imperative mood verbs are preceded with particles **ნუ** or **არ**. The former is used with verbs expressing an order or request in the present/future tense and addressing the first, second, or third person when an action is in progress.

Indicative mood	*Negative imperative mood*
ვწერთ I am writing.	ნუ ვწერთ! We should (must) stop writing!
წერ(თ) You are writing.	ნუ წერ(თ)! Stop writing!
წერს He is writing	ნუ წერს He should (must) stop writing!

Either the particle **არ** or **ნუ** is used with verbs addressing the second or third person and expressing an order or request not to do something in the future, the former with verbs in the subjunctive mood and the latter with verbs in the Future tense. The particle **ნუ** is preferred in requests rather than in orders:

Imperative		
Affirmative	*Negative*	
დაწერე-(თ)! (You, you all) write!	არ დაწერო-(თ) (You, you all) don't write!	ნუ დაწერ-(თ) (Please) don't write!
დაწერ-ო-ს/ნ! He/they should write!	არ დაწერ-ო-ს/ნ! He/they should/ must not write!	ნუ დაწერ-ს/ენ (Please) they should not write!
გააკეთ-ო-ს/ნ! He/they should do it!	არ გააკეთ-ო-ს/ნ! He/they should/ must not do it!	ნუ გააკეთებ-ს/ენ! (Please) he/they should not do it!
ააშენ-ო-ს/ნ! He/they should build it!	არ ააშენ-ო-ს/ნ! He should/ not build it!	ნუ ააშენებ-ს/ენ! (Please) they should/ must not build it!

The previous examples demonstrate that the same verb forms may denote different moods depending on the context:

წერ (indicative mood)
You write.

ნუ წერ! (negative imperative mood)
Stop writing!

დაწერე (indicative mood)
You wrote.

დაწერე! (imperative mood)
Write!

ნეტავ დაწერო (subjunctive mood)
May (I wish) you would write.

არ დაწერო! (imperative mood)
Do not write!

9.5.2 *Aspect*

In modern Georgian verbs may have a perfective or imperfective aspect, the former denoting a completed and the latter an incomplete action. These two forms are differentiated by the presence or absence of preverbs (see 9.2.2.). Verbs in the perfective aspect have preverbs whether they refer to the present, past, or future time. Thus, the verb *წერს* (he writes) indicates the imperfective aspect not only because the action is not completed but because it does not have a preverb. The verbs *დაწერა* (he wrote) and *დაწერს* (he will write) both denote the perfective aspect in spite of the fact that *დაწერს* refers to an action in the future, but it is the presence of a preverb that determines its aspect. The verbs *წერა* (he wrote/kept writing) and *და-წერა* (he wrote) both denote an action that happened in the past, but the former indicates the imperfective, and the latter the perfective aspect.

Future	
Imperfective aspect	*Perfective aspect*
იმღერებს (he) will sing	წა-იმღერებს (he) will sing a little
ისუნთქავს (he) will breathe	შე-ისუნთქავს (he) will take a breath
იჭრიალებს (it) will screech	გა-იჭრიალებს (it) will make a screeching sound
იფრენს (it) will fly	გადა-იფრენს (it) will fly over

მომღერალი ამ სიმღერას ***იმღერებს.***
The singer will sing this song.
მამაჩემი ხანდახან ***წაიმღერებს.***
My father sometimes sings a little.
ეს კარი სულ ***იჭრიალებს.***
This door will always screech.
ეს კარი ხანდახან ***გაიჭრიალებს.***
This door will screech sometimes.
ჩიტი ნელ-ნელა ***იფრენს.***
The bird will fly slowly.
ჩიტი ამ მთას ***გადაიფრენს.***
The bird will fly across this mountain.

There are verbs that never have a preverb: *არის* (is), *მეფობს* (he reigns), *უყვარს* (he loves), *ზის* (he sits), *ცდილობს* (he tries), *წერია* (it is written), *ახატია* (it is painted on), etc. On the other hand, there are verbs that may have a preverb but do not denote the perfective aspect (see 9.2.2.).

მი-ქრის
მო-ქრის
და-ქრის
rushes there, rushes here, rushes around

მი-ხოხავს
მო-ხოხავს
და-ხოხავს
crawls there, crawls here, crawls around

მი-ცურავს
მო-ცურავს
და-ცურავს
swims there, swims here, swims around

გა-დის
გამო-დის
და-დის
goes out, comes across, walks around

მი-ფრინავს
მო-ფრინავს
და-ფრინავს
flies there, flies here, flies around

მი-ძუნძულებს
მო-ძუნძულებს
და-ძუნძულებს
trots there, trots here, trots around

მი-სრიალებს
მო-სრიალებს
და-სრიალებს
glides there, glides here, glides around

მი-ედინება
მო-ედინება
გა-ედინება,
ჩა-ედინება
flows here, flows there, flows out, flows into

The both types of verbs mentioned in the previous paragraphs, as well as those in this chart, do not denote aspect. They are aspectless verbs.

9.6 Conjugation of verbs

9.6.1 *I series*

9.6.1.1 *Present subseries*

9.6.1.2.1 Present

Verbs in the present tense determine conjugation patterns for the present and future subseries, as well as for other series. Depending on the context, the present tense in Georgian functions as the English present imperfect or the present continuous tenses. It indicates an action that happens regularly, usually, or often or is happening right now. The present tense expresses the indicative mood and the imperfective aspect.

ლექსებს ვწერ. – The action takes place often, in general.
I write poems.
წერილს ვწერ. – The action is happening right now.
I am writing a letter.

Verbs in the present subseries do not have preverbs other than those indicating direction. In the following examples, the preverbs only point at the direction or frequency of an action, not at its perfective aspect or future tense:

მი-ფრინავს	მო-ფრინავს	და-ფრინავს
flies away	flies toward me or us or you	flies around

However, there are verbs that may have a preverb even in the present. Sometimes the time of the action indicated by the verb is determined by the context:

– სად არის ბიჭი?	– ბიჭი აუზში **ცურავს.**
Where is the boy?	The boy ***is swimming*** in the pool.

The verb **ცურავს** is in the present since the action coincides with the moment of speaking, but it may denote different meaning of time depending on a context:

თევზი **ცურავ-ს/და-ცურავ-ს.**
A fish ***swims/swims around*** (swimming is what fish does).

In this sentence, the verb, both with and without the preverb, does not convey any specific time. The verb without any preverb (***ცურავ-ს***) does not denote specifically the present; neither does it refer to the future when it has the preverb (***და-ცურავ-ს***).

ჩიტი ***და-ფრინავ-ს.***
A bird flies around (flying is what birds do).
ჩემი უმცროსი შვილი ბაღში ***და-დის.***
My youngest child goes to the kindergarten.

და-ცურავს, *და-ფრინავს*, and *და-დის* are verbs of the same type. They often do not denote any specific time but refer to an action carried out frequently or regularly, or it is an action peculiar to the subject.

In the following chart, some preverbs denote the time, while some of them do not.

Present tense or no tense marking	*Future tense*
მი-ცურავს is swimming away	შე-ცურავს will swim in(to)
მო-ცურავს is swimming (towards us)	გა-ცურავს will swim over
და-ცურავს swims/ is swimming around	გადა-ცურავს will swim across

მყვინთავი ჩვენკენ ***მო-ცურავს.***
The diver is swimming towards us (the present)
ეს გემი ბათუმსა და ფოთს შორის ***და-ცურავს.***
This ship cruises (swims) between Batumi and Poti.
ჩვენი გემი მალე ატლანტის ოკეანეში ***შე-ცურავს.***
Our ship will soon sail (swim) into the Atlantic Ocean.

I conjugation verbs in the present

I conjugation consists of transitive indicative mood verbs of two types: the **one-stem and two-stem verbs.**

1. **One-stem verbs**

These transitive indicative mood verbs have the same stem in all series. For example, ***ვწერ*** (write, with the stem ***წერ***) and ***ვთხოვ*** (ask/request, with the stem ***თხოვ***) are one-stem verbs because they do not change the stem in any series.

I series	ვ-**წერ** I write	ვ-**თხოვ** I ask
II series	ვ-**წერ**-ე I wrote	ვ-**თხოვ**-ე I asked
III series	მ-ი-**წერ**-ი-ა I have written	მ-ი-**თხოვ**-ი-ა I have asked

Present tense of one-stem verbs

ვ-წერ-(თ) მე/ჩვენ მას/მათ I/we write it/them	ვ-თხოვ-(თ) მე/ჩვენ მას მას/მათ I/we ask him for it/them
წერ-(თ) შენ/თქვენ მას/მათ You/you write it/them	ს-თხოვ-(თ) შენ/თქვენ მას მას/მათ You/you ask him for it/them
წერ-ს ის მას/მათ He writes it/them	თხოვ-ს ის მას/მათ He asks him for it/them
წერ-ენ ისინი მას/მათ They write it/them	თხოვ-ენ ისინი მას მას/მათ They ask him for it/them

2. **Two-stem verbs**

Two-stem transitive indicative mood verbs are marked with a *present/future stem formant* (P/FSF), which defines conjugation forms of the first and second subseries. These verbs are defined as *two-stem verbs* because their base to which person markers are added lose their P/FSF in the II series. Thus, in I series the stem of the verb ***ვ-აშენებ*** (I build) is ***აშენ-ებ***, in II series we have ***-აშენ*** - without P/FSF ***-ებ*** (*ავ-აშენ-ე* – I built).

I series	ვ-აშენ-ებ I build	ვ-კერ-ავ I sew
II series	ვ-აშენ-ე I built, I was building	ვ-კერ-ე I sewed, I was sewing

3. **One-stem verbs** do not have P/FSF in the present tense (see the conjugation of the verbs *წერ* and *თხოვ* previously).

Present tense of two-stem verbs

ვ-აშენ-ებ-(თ) მე/ჩვენ მას/მათ I/we build it/them	ვ-აღვიძ-ებ-(თ) მე/ჩვენ მას/მათ I/we wake him/them up
აშენ-ებ-(თ) შენ/თქვენ მას/მათ You/you build it/them	აღვიძ-ებ-(თ) შენ/თქვენ მას/მათ You/you wake him/them up
აშენ-ებ-ს ის მას/მათ He builds it/them	აღვიძ-ებ-ს ის მას/მათ He wakes him/them up
აშენ-ებ-ენ ისინი მას/მათ They build it/them	აღვიძ-ებ-ენ ისინი მას/მათ They wake him/them up

4. **Two-stem verbs** in the present tense may have several different P/FSF:

-ი

ვ-შლ-ი-(თ) მე/ჩვენ მას/მათ I/we erase it/them	ვ-თლ-ი-(თ) მე/ჩვენ/მას/მათ I/we carve it/them
შლ-ი-(თ) შენ/თქვენ/ მას/მათ You/you erase it/them	თლ-ი-(თ) შენ/თქვენ მას/მათ You/you carve it/them
შლ-ი-ს ის მას/მათ He erases it/them	თლ-ი-ს ის მას/მათ He carves it/them
შლ-ი-ან ისინი მას/მათ They erase it/them	თლ-ი-ან ისინი მას/მათ They carve it/them

-ავ

ვ-ხატ-ავ-(თ) მე/ჩვენ მას/მათ
I/we paint it/them
ხატ-ავ-(თ) შენ/თქვენ მას/მათ
You/you paint it/them
ხატ-ავ-ს ის მას/მათ
He paints it/them
ხატ-ავ-ენ ისინი მას/მათ
They paint it/them

-ამ

ვ-სვ-ამ-(თ) მე/ჩვენ მას
I/we drink it
სვ-ამ-(თ) შენ/თქვენ მას
You/you drink it
სვ-ამ-ს ის მას
He drinks it
სვ-ამ-ენ ისინი მას
They drink it

ებ

The conjugation chart of verbs with P/FSF *-ებ* is shown previously (*ვ-ა-შენ-ებ*, *ა-შენ-ებ*, etc.).

ემ

In contemporary Georgian there is only one verb of this kind – ***ვცემ*** (I beat, I publish). ***ვცემ*** (I beat) is considered to have a single stem, although originally it was a two-stem verb with P/FSF ***-ემ***, but ***ვცემ*** (I publish) is an active two-stem verb with P/FSF ***-ემ***.

ვ-ც-ემ-(თ) მე/ჩვენ მას/მათ
I/we publish it/them
ც-ემ-(თ) შენ/თქვენ მას/მათ
You/you publish it/them
ც-ემ-ს ის მას/მათ
He publishes it/them
ც-ემ-ენ ისინი მას/მათ
They publish it/them

ობ

ვ-გმ-ობ-(თ) მე/ჩვენ მას/მათ
I/we condemn it/him/them
გმ-ობ-(თ) შენ/თქვენ მას/მათ
You condemn it/him/them
გმ-ობ-ს ის მას/მათ
He condemns it/him/them
გმ-ობ-ენ ისინი მას/მათ
They condemn it/him/them

ვ-ატკბ-ობ-(თ) მე/ჩვენ მას/მათ
I/we sweeten/delight it/him/them
ატკბ-ობ-(თ) შენ/თქვენ მას/მათ
You sweeten/delight it/him/them
ატკბობ-ს ის მას/მათ
He sweeten/delight it/him/them
ატკბ-ობ-ენ ისინი მას/მათ
They sweeten it/him/them

-ოფ

P/FSF **-ოფ** is added only to a single verb -ყოფ (divide). However, the verb may have a variety of preverbs, each of them giving it different meanings: გა-ყოფ-ს (he will divide), ჩა-ყოფ-ს (he will stick into), გადა-ყოფ-ს (he will put over, stretch over), შე-ყოფ-ს (he will put into), etc. Preverbs are added to this verb in the future tense, as well as in I and II series forms.

ვ-ყ-ოფ-(თ) მე/ჩვენ მას/მათ
I/we divide it/them
ყ-ოფ-(თ) შენ/თქვენ მას/მათ
You/you divide it/them
ყ-ოფ-ს ის მას/მათ
He divides it/them
ყ-ოფ-ენ ისინი მას/მათ
They divide it/them

As the previous conjugation charts show, I conjugation verbs have the subject marker *-ს* for the third-person singular and *-ენ* for the third-person plural: *წერ-ს – წერ-ენ; გრძნ-ობ-ს – გრძნ-ობ-ენ; ხატ-ავ-ს – ხატ-ავ-ენ.* The only exception are the verbs with *-ი* P/FSF which have -ან, in the third-person plural forms: *ზრდ-ი-ს – ზრდ-ი-**ან**; შლ-**ის** – შლ-ი-**ან**; თლ-ი-ს – თლ-ი-**ან**.*

Ablaut verbs

Ablaut verbs change their root vowel in some series, which differentiates their tense forms from one another. Thus, the I series stem of the verb ***გრეხ*** (twist) changes to ***გრიხ*** in II series; therefore, these verbs belong to the two-stem verb group. There are two types of ablaut verbs:

1. **Verbs changing their I series root vowel - *ე*- to - *ი*- in II series**

ვ-კრეფ-(თ) მ/ეჩვენ მას/მათ I/we pick it/them	ვ-ჩხვლეტ-(თ) მე/ჩვენ მას/მათ I/we prick it/them
კრეფ-(თ) შენ/თქვენ მას/მათ You/you pick it/them	ჩხვლეტ-(თ) შენ/თქვენ მას/მათ You/you prick it/them
კრეფ-ს ის მას/მათ He picks it/them	ჩხვლეტ-ს ის მას/მათ He pricks it/them
კრეფ -ენ ისინი მას/მათ They pick it/them	ჩხვლეტ -ენ ისინი მას/მათ They prick it/them

Verb stems ending with *ევ*	Verb stems ending with *ენ*
ვ-ა-მჩნევ-(თ) მე/ჩვენ მას მას/მათ I/we notice it in him/them	ვ-ა-დგენ-(თ) მე/ჩვენ მას I/we establish/ascertain it
ა-მჩნევ-(თ) შენ/თქვენ მას მას/მათ You/you notice it in him/them	ადგენ-(თ) შენ/თქვენ მას You/you establish/ascertain it
ა-მჩნევ-ს ის მას მას/მათ He notices it in him/them	ა-დგენ-ს ის მას He establishes/ascertains it
ა-მჩნევ-ენ ის მას მას/მათ They notice it in him/them	ადგენ-ენ ისინი მას They ascertain it

2. **Ablaut verbs with P/FSF - *ი* in I series**

Their root vowel -ა-is syncopated but restored in II series:

I series	ვ-შლ-ი I erase	ვ-თლ-ი I whittle
II series	წა-ვ-შალ -ე I erased	გა-ვ-თალ-ე I whittled

The same happens when other P/FSFs are added to their root in I series:

ვ-კლ-ავ	მო-ვ-კალ-ი	ვ-ხნ-ავ	მო-ვ-ხან-ი
I kill	I killed	I plough	I ploughed

II conjugation verbs in the present

II conjugation verbs are dynamic passive. The majority of verbs of this group with the **ი**-and **ე**-prefix, -**დ** suffix and those without any markers have P/FSF -**ებ** and the ending -**ი** for the first and second persons, and the ending -**ა** for the third person. There are some exceptions with a different P/FSF – for example, *ე-რთ-ობ-ა*, *ე-ყრდნ-ობ-ა*, and *ე-ცნ-ობ-ა*.

There are only a few passive voice verbs where the present tense indicator -*ი* is maintained in the third-person forms: *ი-სმ-ი-ს* (is heard), *ი-თქმ-ი-ს* (is said), *იძვრ-ი-ს* (moves), *ე-რწყმ-ი-ს* (blends with), *ე-ლტვ-ი-ს* (aspires), *ე-რჩ-ი-ს* (assails). In these verbs, the suffix -**ი** should not be considered as a P/FSF since it is dropped in the subseries of the future tense, thus changing their stem.

Dynamic passive voice verbs are formed from their active counterparts, and therefore, they may have any P/FSFs of the latter.

The exception is a group of active voice verbs with the P/FSF *-ავ*. When the required marker of passive voice verbs, P/FSF *-ებ* is added to them, P/FSF *-ავ* collapses or is contracted which in turn leads to metathesis of the consonant *ვ*.

ვ-ხატ-ავ I paint	ვ-ი-ხატ-ებ-ი I am being painted	ვ-ე-ხატ-ებ-ი I am being painted on
კლ-ავ-ს He kills	ი-კვლ-ებ-ა He is being killed	ე-კვლ-ებ-ა He is being killed for him

If an active verb does not have any P/FSF it will still have *-ებ* in its passive form (წერ-ს – he writes; ი-წერ-ებ-ა – it is being written, is spelled).

Passive voice verbs derived from active verbs with a changing root vowel have P/FSF *-ებ* and the *-ი* ending in the first- and second-person forms. The majority of them change their root vowel *ე* to *ი*: ვ-გრეხ (I twist) – ვ-იგრიხ-ებ-ი (I am twisting). Only a small number of active verbs of this type do not change the root vowel in their passive forms but have the regular *-ებ-ი* ending.

Active verbs		*Passive verbs*	
		Monovalent verbs	*Bivalent verbs*
No P/FSF	წერ-ს He writes it	ვ-ი-წერ-ებ-ი I am written, spelled	ვ-ე-წერ-ებ-ი I get enlisted/ written in
	ს-წერ-ს He writes it to him	ი-წერ-ებ-ა He is written, spelled	ე-წერ-ებ-ა He gets enlisted/ written in
	ცემ-ს He beats up	ვ-ი-ცემ-ებ-ი I get beaten up ი-ცემ-ებ-ა He gets beaten up	
-ი	ვ-ზრდ-ი I grow (something)	ვ-ი-ზრდ-ებ-ი I grow ი-ზრდ-ებ-ა He grows	ვ-ე-ზრდ-ებ-ი I grow (for someone) ე-ზრდ-ებ-ა He grows (for someone)

Active verbs		*Passive verbs*	
		Monovalent verbs	*Bivalent verbs*
-ამ	სვ-ამ-ს He drinks	ვ-ი-სმ-ებ-ი I am being drunk, am drinkable ი-ს-მ-ებ-ა It is being drunk, is drinkable	ვ-ე-სმ-ებ-ი I am being drunk (for someone) ე-სმ-ებ-ა It is being drunk (for someone)
-ავ	ვ-ხატ-ავ I paint	ვ-ი-ხატ-ებ-ი I get painted ი-ხატ-ებ-ა He gets painted (P/FSF -ავ is dropped.)	ვ-ე-ხატ-ებ-ი I get painted (for someone) ე-ხატ-ებ-ა He gets painted (for someone)
-ებ	ვ-აწითლ-ებ I make someone blush/red	ვ-წითლ-დ-ებ-ი I blush წითლ-დ-ებ-ა He blushes	
-ობ	ვ-გრძნ-ობ I feel გრძნ-ობ-ს I feel	ვ-ი-გრძნ-ობ-ი I am felt ი-გრძნ-ობ-ა It is felt	
-ოფ	ვ-ყ-ოფ I divide	ვ-ი-ყ-ოფ-ი I get divided ი-ყ-ოფ-ა It gets divided	
Root vowel-changing verbs	ვ-გრეხ I twist გრეხს He twists ვ-ჭყლეტ I squash ვ-ჭვრეტ (I foresee) ვ-სხლეტ (I pull a trigger)	ვ-ი-გრიხ-ებ-ი I get twisted ი-გრიხ-ებ-ა He gets twisted ვ-ი-ჭყლიტ-ებ-ი I get squashed ი-ჭყლიტ-ებ-ა He gets squashed ვ-ი-ჭვრიტ-ებ-ი I look through ი-ჭვრიტ-ებ-ა He looks through	

(Continued)

(Continued)

Active verbs	*Passive verbs*	
	Monovalent verbs	*Bivalent verbs*
	-ე, typical for I series passive voice verbs with a changing vowel, is replaced with -ი- typical for II series. ვ-უ-სხლ□ტ-ებ-ი (I slip away from someone) Some vowel-changing verbs lose their root vowel. A small number of verbs do not change their root vowel in the passive, but get an -ებ-ი ending.	

Chart of II conjugation verb components

1. I grow; 2. I burn; 3. I blush.

Subject Marker		*Passive voice marker*	*Root*	*Passive voice marker*	*P/FSF*	*Tense ending*	*Subject marker*
1	ვ	ი	ზრდ	–	ებ	ი	
		ი	ზრდ	–	ებ	ი	
		ი	ზრდ	–	ებ	–	ა
2	ვ	ი	წვ	–	–	ი	
		ი	წვ	–	–	ი	
		ი	წვ	–	–	ი	ს
3	ვ	–	წითლ	დ	ებ	ი	
			წითლ	დ	ებ	ი	
			წითლ	დ	ებ	–	ა

Present tense of monopersonal verbs

ვ-ი-ვს-ებ-ი-(თ) მე/ჩვენ
I/we get filled up
ი-ვს-ებ-ი-(თ) შენ/თქვენ
You/you get filled up
ი-ვს-ებ-ა ის
He gets filled up
ი-ვს-ებ-ი-ან ისინი
They get filled up

(მი)-ვ-ი-პარ-ებ-ი-(თ) მე/ჩვენ
I/we sneak away
(მი)-ი-პარ-ებ-ი-(თ) შენ/თქვენ
You/you sneak away
(მი)-ი-პარ-ებ-ა ის
He sneaks away
(მი)-ი-პარ-ებ-ი-ან ისინი
They sneak away

ვ-ბერ-დ-ებ-ი-(თ) მე /ჩვენ
I/we get old
ბერ-დ-ებ-ი-(თ) შენ/თქვენ
You/you get old
ბერ-დ-ებ-ა ის
He gets old
ბერ-დ-ებ-ი-ან ისინი
They get old

ვ-ი-ჭყლიტ-ებ-ი-(თ) მე/ჩვენ
I/we get squashed
ი-ჭყლიტ-ებ-ი-(თ) შენ/თქვენ
You/you get squashed
ი-ჭყლიტ-ებ-ა ის
He gets squashed
ი-ჭყლიტ-ებ-ი-ან ისინი
They get squashed

ვ-სხლტ-ებ-ი-(თ) მე /ჩვენ
I/we slip away
სხლტ-ებ-ი-(თ) მე/თქვენ
You/you slip away
სხლტ-ებ-ა ის
He slips away
სხლტ-ებ-ი-ან ისინი
They slip away

Present tense of bipersonal verbs

ვ-ე-ცეკვ-ებ-ი მე მას/მათ
I dance with him/them
ე-ცეკვ-ებ-ი შენ მას/მათ
You dance with him/them
ე-ცეკვ-ებ-ა ის მას/მათ
He dances with him/them

ვ-ე-ცეკვ-ებ-ი-თ ჩვენ მას/მათ
We dance with him/them
ე-ცეკვ-ებ-ი-თ თქვენ მას/მათ
You dance with him/them
ე-ცეკვ-ებ-ი-ან ისინი მას/მათ
They dance with him/them

მ-ე-რჩ-ი-ს ის მე
He assails me

გვ-ე-რჩ-ი-ს ის ჩვენ
He assails us
მ-ე-რჩ-ი-ან ისინი მე
They assail me

გ-ე-რჩ-ი-ს ის შენ He assails you	გ-ე-რჩ-ი-თ ის თქვენ He assails you გ-ე-რჩ-ი-ან ისინი თქვენ They assail you
ე-რჩ-ი-ს ის მას/მათ He assails him/them	ე-რჩ-ი-ან ისინი მას/ მათ They assail him/them

III conjugation verbs in the present

III conjugation consists of medio-active verbs with or without P/FSFs; their subject, like that of the active voice verbs, may be in three different cases – the nominative in I series, the ergative in II, and the dative in III series. However, they do not have direct objects.

Without P/FSF	ქუხს (thunders), თრთის (trembles)
P/FSF -ი	ბარდნ-ი-ს (snows), სჯობნ-ი-ს (excels)
P/FSF -ავ	გორ-ავ-ს (rolls around), ცურ-ავ-ს (swims), ბრუნ-ავ-ს (rotates), გრგვინ-ავ-ს (thunders), ელ-ავ-ს (blazes), ზრუნ-ავ-ს (cares) A few verbs may appear with or without P/FSF: ფეთქ-**ავ**-ს//ფეთქ-ს (pulsates) ფრინ-**ავ**-ს//ფრენ-ს (flies)
P/FSF -ებ	აგვიან-ებ-ს (he is late), ბრიალ-ებ-ს (flames), ბრდღვიალ-ებ-ს (shines), ნეტარ-ებ-ს (enjoys) Reduplicating verbs: ჭიკჭიკ-ებ-ს (chirps), წიკწიკ-ებ-ს (ticks); ტიკტიკ-ებ-ს (bubbles)
P/FSF -ობ	ბავშვ-ობ-ს (behaves like a child), დარაჯ-ობ-ს (guards) მდებარე-ობ-ს (is situated), ქანა-ობ-ს (swings)
Verbs with root vowel alteration	უსტვენ-ს (whistles), სწყენ-ს (is harmed) ჰგვრემ-ს (is pained)

Conjugation of medio-active verbs

ვ-ცურ-ავ-(თ) მე/ჩვენ I/we swim	ვ-ფრინ-ავ-(თ) ვ-ფრენ-(თ) მე/ჩვენ I/we fly
ცურ-ავ-(თ) შენ/თქვენ You/you swim	ფრინ-ავ-(თ) შენ (თქვენ) ფრენ-(თ) შენ (თქვენ) You/you fly

ცურ-ავ-ს ის
He swims
ცურ-ავ-ენ ისინი
They swim

ფრინ-ავ-ს ის
ფრენ-ს ის
He flies
ფრინ-ავ-ენ ისინი
ფრენ-ენ ისინი
They fly

ვ-ჭიჭიკ-ებ-(თ) მე/ჩვენ
I/we chirp
ჭიკჭიკ-ებ-(თ) შენ/თქვენ
You/you chirp
ჭიკჭიკ-ებ-ს ის
He chirps
ჭიკჭიკ-ებ-ენ ისინი
They chirp

ვ-მეგობრ-ობ-(თ) მე/ჩვენ
I am/we are friends with
მეგობრ-ობ-(თ) შენ/თქვენ
You/you are friends with
მეგობრ-ობ-ს ის
He is friends with
მეგობრ-ობ-ენ ისინი
They are friends with

ვ-დარაჯ-ობ-(თ)
მე/ჩვენ მას/მათ
I/we guard him/them
დარაჯ-ობ-(თ)
შენ/თქვენ მას/მათ
You/you guard him/them
დარაჯ-ობ-ს ის მას/მათ
He guards him/them
დარაჯ-ობ-ენ ისინი მას/მათ
They guard him/them

ვ-ხელმძღვანელ-ობ-(თ)
მე/ჩვენ მას/მათ
I/we lead/advise him/them
ხელმძღვანელ-ობ-(თ) შენ/თქვენ
მას/მათ
You/you lead/advise him/them
ხელმძღვანელ-ობ-ს ის მას/მათ
He leads/advises him/them
ხელმძღვანელ-ობ-ენ
ისინი მას/მათ
They lead/advise him/them

Medio-active verbs without P/FSF generally do not have the present tense markers. However, some of these verbs have the tense marker *-ი*: *ვ-ყვირ-ი* (I scream), *ვკვნეს-ი* (I groan), *ვ-ტირ-ი* (I cry), *ვ-ყვირ-ი* (I shout).

ვ-ტირ-ი(თ) მე/ჩვენ
I/we cry
ტირ-ი შენ/თქვენ
You/you cry
ტირ-ი-ს ის
He cries
ტირ-ი-ან ისინი
They cry

ვ-თრთ-ი(თ) მე/ჩვენ
I tremble
თრთ-ი(თ) შენ/თქვენ
You/you tremble
თრთ-ი-ს ის
He trembles
თრთ-ი-ან ისინი
They tremble

When -ი is P/FSF, it appears only in the present tense subseries.

მ-ჯობნ-ი-ს ის მე He surpasses me	გვ-ჯობნ-ი-ს ის ჩვენ He surpasses us	გვ-ჯობნ-ი-ან ისინი ჩვენ They surpass us
გ-ჯობ ნ-ი-ს ის შენ He surpasses you	გ-ჯობნ-ი-თ ის თქვენ He surpasses you	გ-ჯობნ-ი-ან ისინი თქვენ They surpass you
ს-ჯობნ-ი-ს ის მას He surpasses him	ს-ჯობნ-ი-ს ის მათ He surpasses them	ს-ჯობნ-ი-ან ისინი მათ They surpass them

IV conjugation verbs in the present tense

IV conjugation verbs include intransitive static-passive and medio-passive verbs. Static-passive verbs appear only in the present tense but not in the other tenses of its subseries and are replaced with a variety of verbs in other tenses. There are a few such examples among medio-passive verbs as well: *დგას* (stands), *ზის* (sits), *წევს* (lies). The majority of medio-passive verbs appear in all subseries of the present tense.

Static-passive voice verbs may be monopersonal and bipersonal. Verbs of both groups have the -ა ending for the third-person singular forms but differ from each other in the first- and second-person forms in which monopersonal verbs require the auxiliary verb *to be*. Bipersonal verbs have an object-oriented structure – i.e. subject and object markers are inverted, such as *მ-ავალი-ა* (I am obliged) or *გვ-ავალი-ა* (we are obliged); these verbs have *მ-* and *გვ-* object markers that refer to their corresponding real subjects. But they, too, have the -ა ending in the third-person singular form.

Present tense of monopersonal verbs

ვ-ხატ-ი-ვ-არ-(თ) მე/ჩვენ I am/we are painted	ვ-წერ-ი-ვ-არ-(თ) მე/ჩვენ I am/we are written in, enrolled
ხატ-ი-ხ-არ-(თ) შენ/თქვენ You/you are painted	წერ-ი-ხ-არ-(თ) შენ/თქვენ You/you are written in, enrolled
ხატ-ი-ა ის He is painted	წერ-ი-ა ის He is written in, enrolled
ხატ-ი-ან ისინი They are painted	წერ-ი-ან ისინი They are written in, enrolled

The following verbs are conjugated similarly: *ვაწვენივარ* (I recline), *ვაგდივარ* (I lie on), *ვაფარივარ* (I am spread on), *ვასხივარ* (I am poured in), *ვაყრივარ* (I am scattered on), etc. The first-person forms are given here because both monopersonal and bipersonal verbs of IV conjugation have the same ending in the third-person singular forms – for example, აყრია (is/are scattered on it) and ყრია (is/are scattered around). The difference is marked by the prefix vowel **ა**-which changes the number of actants governed by the verb.

აყრია ის მას (ქვები) (Stones) are thrown on it (verb modifies two actants)

ყრია ის (ქვები) (Stones) are scattered around (verb modifies one actant)

The static medio-passive verbs require the auxiliary verb *to be* for the first and second person; for the third person, they have -*ს* ending, which differentiates them from static-passive voice verbs.

ვ-დგა-ვ-არ-(თ) მე/ჩვენ I/we are standing	ვ-წევ-არ-(თ) მე/ჩვენ I/we lie
დგა-ხ-არ-(თ) შენ/თქვენ You/you are standing	წევ-ხ-არ(თ) შენ (თქვენ) You/you lie
დგა-ს ის He is standing	წევ-ს ის He lies
დგა-ნან ისინი They are standing	წვა-ნან ისინი They lie

Static-passive monopersonal and medio-passive monopersonal verbs both have the auxiliary verb in the first- and second-person forms. They differ in the third-person forms, static-passive verbs have the -**ი-ა** ending, while medio-passive verbs end with the third-person marker -*ს*.

As in some other cases, if IV conjugation verbs have a preverb in the present tense, it only indicates the direction of the movement and not its aspect or tense.

(მო)-ვ-ჩან-ვ-არ მე I am seen	(მო)-ვ-ჩან-ვ-არ-თ ჩვენ We are seen
(მო)-ჩან-ხ-არ შენ You are seen	(მო)-ჩან-ხ-არ-თ თქვენ You are seen
(მო)-ჩან-ს ის He is seen	(მო)-ჩან-ან ისინი They are seen

Present tense of bipersonal verbs

მ-ა-ვალ-ი-ა ის მე I am charged with it	გვ-ა-ვალ-ი-ა ის ჩვენ We are charged with it

გ-ა-ვალ-ი-ა ის შენ You are charged with it	გ-ა-ვალ-ი-ა-თ ის თქვენ You are charged with it
ა-ვალ-ი-ა ის მას He is charged with it	ა-ვალ-ი-ა-თ ის მათ They are charged with it
მ-გონ-ი-ა ის მე It seems to me	გვ-გონ-ი-ა ის ჩვენ It seems to us
გ-გონ-ი-ა ის შენ It seems to you	გ-გონ-ი-ა-თ ის თქვენ It seems to you
ჰ-გონ-ი-ა ის მას It seems to him	ჰ-გონ-ი-ა-თ ის მათ It seems to them

The following verbs are conjugated similarly: *მკიდია* (it hangs on me), *მაფენია* (it is put over me), *მაფარია* (it is spread over me), *მაყრია* (it is thrown on me), *მაკერია* (it is sewn on me), *მახატია* (it is painted on me), *მარტყია* (it is wrapped around me), *მაწყვია* (it is placed on me), *მაცხია* (it is smeared on me).

9.6.1.2.2 Imperfect

In Georgian the imperfect combines the function of the simple past and past continuous tenses – i.e. a verb in the imperfect conveys an action that habitually happened or was happening continuously for certain period of time.

> *ჩემს მშობლებს წერილებს თითქმის ყოველდღე* ***ვწერდი.***
> I wrote letters to my parents almost daily (an action that happened often).
> *როცა დედა შემოვიდა ოთახში, მე წერილს* ***ვწერდი.***
> When Mother entered the room, I was writing a letter (an action that was happening at a certain moment).

The imperfect expresses the indicative mood and the imperfective aspect. Like in other forms of the present subseries, preverbs added to these verbs denote the direction of the action:

> *მიფრინავდა*
> flew/was flying away
> *მოფრინავდა*
> flew/was flying towards us
> *დაფრინავდა*
> flew/was flying around

Verbs in the imperfect are based on the verb forms of the present tense and are extended with suffixes -დ or -ოდ. They are extending markers:

1. -დ is added to I and III conjugation verbs, that is, to active and medio-active voice verbs, and to IV conjugation medio-passive voice verbs.
2. -ოდ is added to II conjugation dynamic-passive voice verbs and to a subgroup of medio-actives: ი-ცინი-ს (he laughs) – ი-ცინ-ოდ-ა (he was laughing).
3. Either -დ or and -ოდ is added to the two-stem verbs.
4. IV conjugation static-passive voice verbs do not have the imperfect.

Verbs in the first- and second-person forms, both singular and plural, end with the vowel -ი in the imperfect; third-person verbs end with the third-person marker.

ვ-თხოვ-დ-ი-(თ)
I/we asked/was/were asking
თხოვ-დ-ი-(თ)
You/you asked/were asking
თხოვ-დ-ა
He asked/was asking
თხოვ-დ-ნენ
They asked/were asking

Verb structure in the imperfect

Preverb	*Person marker*	*Passive voice marker*	*Root*	*Passive voice marker*	*P/FSF*	*Extending marker*	*Tense marker*	*Person and number marker*
–	ვ		წერ	–	–	დ	ი	თ
–			წერ			დ		ა
	გვ		თხოვ			დ	ი	თ
	გვ		თხოვ			დ		ნენ
	ვ		სვ		ამ	დ	ი	
			სვ		ამ	დ		ა
და/მი/მო	ვ		ფრინ		ავ	დ	ი	

(Continued)

(Continued)

Preverb	*Person marker*	*Passive voice marker*	*Root*	*Passive voice marker*	*P/FSF*	*Extending marker*	*Tense marker*	*Person and number marker*
და/ მი/მო			ფრინ		ავ	დ		ა
	ვ/გვ		გრეხ			დ	ი	
			გრეხ			დ		ა
	ვ	ი	ზრდ		ებ	ოდ	ი	
		ი	ზრდ		ებ	ოდ		ა
	ვ/გვ	ე	ცეკვ		ებ	ოდ	ი	
		ე	ცეკვ		ებ	ოდ		ა
	მ/გვ	ე	რჩ			ოდ		ა
	მ	ი	დუღ			დ		ა
	გ	ი	დუღ			დ	ი	
და	მ		ტრიალ		ებ	დ	ი	
და	მ		ტრიალ		ებ	დ		ა

I conjugation verbs in the imperfect

Without P/FSF

ვ-წერ-დ-ი-(თ) მე/ჩვენ მას/მათ
I was/we were writing

წერ-დ-ი-(თ) შენ/თქვენ მას/მათ
You/you were writing

წერ-დ-ა ის მას/მათ
He was writing

წერ-დ-ნენ ისინი მას/მათ
They were writing

ვ-თხოვ-დ-ი-(თ) მე/ჩვენ მას/მათ
I was/we were asking

თხოვ-დ-ი-(თ) შენ/თქვენ მას/მათ
You/you were asking

თხოვ-დ-ა ის მას/მათ
He was asking

თხოვ-დ-ნენ ისინი მას/მათ
They were asking

With P/FSF

ვ-ხატ-ავ-დ-ი-(თ)
მე/ჩვენ მას/მათ
I was/we were painting

ვ-სვ-ამ-დ-ი-(თ)
მე/ჩვენ მას/მათ
I was/we were drinking

ხატ-ავ-დ-ი-(თ)
შენ/თქვენ მას/მათ
You/you were painting

ხატ-ავ-დ-ა ის მას/მათ
He was painting

ხატ-ავ-დ-ნენ ისინი მას/მათ
They were painting

ვ-გრძნ-ობ-დ-ი-(თ)
მე/ჩვენ მას/მათ
I was/we were feeling it

გრძნ-ობ-დ-ი-(თ)
შენ/თქვენ მას/მათ
You/you were feeling it

გრძნ-ობ-დ-ა
ის მას/მათ
He was feeling it

გრძნ-ობ-დ-ნენ
ისინი მას/მათ
They were feeling it

ვ-კრეფ-დ-ი-(თ) მე/ჩვენ
I was/we were picking

კრეფ-დ-ი-(თ) შენ/თქვენ
You/you were picking

კრეფ-დ-ა ის
He was picking

კრეფ-დ-ნენ ისინი
They were picking

სვ-ამ-დ-ი -(თ)
შენ/თქვენ მას/მათ
You/you were drinking

სვ-ამ-დ-ა ის მას/მათ
He was drinking

სვ-ამ-დ-ნენ ისინი მას/მათ
They were drinking

ვ-ყ-ოფ-დ-ი-(თ)
მე/ჩვენ მას/მათ
I was/we were dividing

ყ-ოფ-დ-ი-(თ)
შენ/თქვენ მას/მათ
You were dividing

ყ-ოფ-დ-ა
ის მას/მათ
He was dividing

ყ-ოფ-დ-ა (ნენ)
ის/ისინი მას/მათ
They were dividing

ვ-ჩხვლეტ-დ-ი-(თ) მე/ჩვენ
I was/we were pricking

ჩხვლეტ-დ-ი-(თ) მე/თქვენ
You/you were pricking

ჩხვლეტ-დ-ა ის
He was picking

ჩხვლეტ-დ-ნენ ისინი
They were picking

II conjugation verbs in the imperfect

Monopersonal verbs

-ი- passive voice marker

ვ-ი-ვს-ებ-ოდ-ი-(თ) მე/ჩვენ
I was/we were filled

ი-ვს-ებ-ოდ-ი-(თ) შენ/თქვენ
You/you were filled

ი-ვს-ებ-ოდ-ა ის
He was filled

ი-ვს-ებ-ოდ-ნენ ისინი
They were filled

-დ- passive voice marker

ვ-ბერ-დ-ებ-ოდ-ი-თ მე/ჩვენ
I was/we were growing old

ბერ-დ-ებ-ოდ-ი-თ შენ/თქვენ
You/you were growing old

ბერ-დ-ებ-ოდ-ა ის
He was growing old

ბერ-დ-ებ-ოდ-ნენ ისინი
They were growing old

Bipersonal verbs

ე- passive voice marker

ვ-ე-ლაპარაკ-ებ-ოდ-ი-(თ)
მე/ჩვენ მას/მათ
I was/we were speaking to him/them

ვ-ე-ხმარ-ებ-ოდ-ი-(თ)
მე/ჩვენ მას/მათ
I was/we were helping him/them

ე-ლაპარაკ-ებ-ოდ-ი-(თ)
შენ/თქვენ მას/მათ
You/you were speaking to him/them

ე-ხმარ-ებ-ოდ-ი-(თ)
შენ/თქვენ მას/მათ
You/you were helping him/them

ე-ლაპარაკ-ებ-ოდ-ა
ის მას/მათ
He was speaking to him/them

ე-ხმარ-ებ-ოდ-ა
ის მას/მათ
He was helping him/them

ე-ლაპარაკ-ებ-ოდ-ნენ
ისინი მას/მათ
They were speaking to him/them

ე-ხმარ-ებ-ოდ-ნენ
ისინი მას/მათ
They were helping him/them

III conjugation verbs in the imperfect

Without P/FSF

ვ-ქუხ-დ-ი-(თ) მე/ჩვენ
I was/we were thundering

ვ-წუხ-დ-ი-(თ) მე/ჩვენ
I was/we were worried

ქუხ-დ-ი-(თ) შენ/თქვენ
You/you were thundering

წუხ-დ-ი-(თ) შენ/თქვენ
You/you were worried

ქუხ-დ-ა ის
He was thundering

წუხ-დ-ა ის
He was worried

ქუხ-დ-ნენ ისინი
They were thundering

წუხ-დ-ნენ ისინი
They were worried

With P/FSF

ვ-ჭიკჭიკ-ებ-დ-ი-(თ) მე/ჩვენ
I was/we were chirping

ვ-გრძნ-ობ-დ-ი-(თ) მე/ჩვენ
I was/we were feeling

ჭიკჭიკ-ებ-დ-ი-(თ) შენ/თქვენ
You/you were chirping

გრძნ-ობ-დ-ი-თ მე/თქვენ
You/you were feeling

ჭიკჭიკ-ებ-დ-ა ის
He was chirping

გრძნ-ობ-დ-ა ის
He was feeling

ჭიკჭიკ-ებ-დ-ნენ ისინი
They were chirping

გრძნ-ობ-დ-ნენ ისინი
They were feeling

Object-oriented paradigm with P/FSF

მ-ჯობნ-ი-დ-ა ის მე He was surpassing me	გვ-ჯობნ-ი-დ-ა ის ჩვენ He was surpassing us	გვ-ჯობნ-ი-დ-ნენ ისინი ჩვენ They were surpassing us
გ-ჯობნ-ი-დ-ა ის შენ He was surpassing you	გ-ჯობნ-ი-დ-ა-თ ის თქვენ He was surpassing you	გ-ჯობნ-ი-დ-ნენ ისინი თქვენ They were surpassing you
ს-ჯობნ-ი-დ-ა ის მას He was surpassing him	ს-ჯობნ-ი-დ-ა ის მათ He was surpassing them	ს-ჯობნ-ი-დ-ნენ ისინი მათ They were surpassing them

Vowel-changing medio-active verbs

ვ-უსტვენ-დ-ი-(თ) მე/ჩვენ მას/მათ I was/we were whistling at him/them	მ-წყენ-დ-ა ის მე It was harming me	
უსტვენ-დ-ი-(თ) შენ/თქვენ მას/მათ You/you were whistling at him/them	გვ-წყენ-დ-ა ის ჩვენ It was harming us	
უსტვენ-დ-ა-(ნენ) ის/ისინი მას/მათ He was/they were whistling at him/them	გ – წყენ-დ-ა ის შენ It was harming you	ს-წყენ-დ-ა/თ ის მას /მათ It was harming him/them

IV conjugation verbs in the imperfect

IV conjugation static-passive verbs form the imperfect only if they have the present subseries forms. In that case, the extending particle **-დ** or **-ოდ** will be added to their stem in the imperfect.

(მო)-ვ-ჩან-დ-ი-(თ) მე/ჩვენ I was/we were seen	(და)-მ-ტრიალ-ებ-დ-ა ის მე He was fussing over me	(და)-გვ-ტრიალ-ებ-დ-ა ის ჩვენ He was fussing over us
(მო)-ჩან-დ-ი-(თ) შენ/თქვენ You/you were seen	(და)-გ-ტრიალ-ებ-დ-ა ის შენ He was fussing over you	(და)-გ-ტრიალ-ებ-დ-ა-თ ის თქვენ He was fussing over you

(მო)-ჩან-დ-ა-(ნენ) ის/ისინი He was/they were seen	(და)-ტრიალ-ებ-დ-ა ის მას He was fussing over him	(და)-ტრიალ-ებ-დ-ა ის მათ He was fussing over them

9.6.1.2.3 Present subjunctive

Verbs in the present subjunctive are based on the present tense stem with the extending marker **-დ** or **-ოდ** followed by the tense marker *-ე* in the first- and second-person forms. In the third-person forms, the tense marker is followed by the person markers.

The present subjunctive denotes the subjunctive mood and the imperfective aspect. It expresses desirable or hypothetical action at present or in some unspecified time.

> *ნეტავ აქ* ***ვ-მუშა-ობ-დ-ე.*** – a desirable action in general.
> I wish I worked here.
> *ნეტავ ახლა აქ* ***ვ-მუშა-ობ-დ-ე.*** – a desirable action right now, at this very moment.
> I wish I am working here now

Like in other forms of the present subseries, preverbs added to these verbs indicate direction of the action, not its completion: *მი-ფრინავდეს* (that it fly there), *მო-ფრინავდეს* (that it fly here), *და-ფრინავდეს* (that it fly around).

Imperfect	*Present subjunctive*
ვ-თხოვ-დ-ი მე მას მას I asked	ვ-თხოვ-დ-ე მე მას მას If I ask
თხოვ-დ-ა ის მას მას He asked	თხოვ-დ-ე-ს ის მას მას If he asks
ვ-დარაჯ-ობ-დ-ი მე მას I guarded	ვ-დარაჯ-ობ-დ-ე მე მას If I guard
დარაჯ-ობ-დ-ა ის მას He guarded	დარაჯ-ობ-დ-ე-ს ის მას If he guards

The present subjunctive marker *-ე* is added to verbs in all forms except in the third-person plural.

Third-person forms	
Singular	*Plural*
ზრდ-ი-დ-ე-ს ის მას/მათ If he brings up	ზრდ-ი-დ-□-ნენ ისინი მას/მათ If they bring up
უსტვენ-დ-ე-ს ის მას/მათ If he whistles	უსტვენ-დ-□-ნენ ისინი მას/მათ If they whistle
წუხ-დ-ე-ს ის If he worries	წუხ-დ-□-ნენ ისინი If they worry

I conjugation verbs in the present subjunctive

Without P/FSF

ვ-წერ-დ-ე-თ მე/ჩვენ მას/მათ If I/we write to him/them	ვ-თხოვ-დ-ე-(თ) მე/ჩვენ მას/მათ If I/we ask him/them
წერ-დ-ე შენ/თქვენ მას/მათ If you/you write to him/them	თხოვ-დ-ე-(თ) შენ/თქვენ მას/მათ If you/you ask him/them
წერ-დ-ე-ს ის მას/მათ If he writes to him/them	თხოვ-დ-ე-ს ის მას/მათ If he asks him/them
წერ-დ-ნენ ისინი მას/მათ If they write to him/them	თხოვ-დ-ნენ ისინი მას/მათ If they ask him/them

With P/FSF

ვ-ხატ-ავ-დ-ე-(თ) მე/ჩვენ მას/მათ If I/we paint	ვ-ყ-ოფ-დ-ე-(თ) მე/ჩვენ მას/მათ If I/we divide
ხატ-ავ-დ-ე-(თ) შენ/თქვენ მას/მათ If you/you paint	ყ-ოფ-დ-ე -(თ) შენ/თქვენ მას/მათ If you/you divide
ხატ-ავ-დ-ე-ს ის მას/მათ If he paints	ყ-ოფ-დ-ე-ს ის მას/მათ If he divides
ხატ-ავ-დ-ნენ ისინი მას/მათ If they paint	ყ-ოფ-დ-ნენ ისინი მას/მათ If they divide

Conjugation of ablaut verbs in the present subjunctive

ვ-კრეფ-დ-ე-(თ)
მე/ჩვენ მას/მათ
If I/we pick

კრეფ-დ-ე-(თ)
შენ/თქვენ მას/მათ
You/you pick

კრეფ-დ-ე-ს
ის მას/მათ
If he picks

კრეფ-დ-ნენ
ისინი მას/მათ
If they pick

ვ-ჩხვლეტ-დ-ე-(თ)
მე/ჩვენ მას/მათ
If I/we prick

ჩხვლეტ-დ-ე-(თ)
შენ/თქვენ მას/მათ
If you/you prick

ჩხვლეტ-დ-ე-ს
ის მას/მათ
If he pricks

ჩხვლეტ-დ-ნენ
ისინი მას/მათ
If they prick

II conjugation verbs in the present subjunctive

Monopersonal verbs

ი- passive voice marker

ვ-ი-ვს-ებ-ოდ-ე-(თ) მე/ჩვენ
If I/we get filled

ი-ვს-ებ-ოდ-ე-(თ) შენ/თქვენ
If you/you get filled

ი-ვს-ებ-ოდ-ე-ს ის
If he gets filled

ი-ვს-ებ-ოდ-ნენ ისინი
If they get filled

-დ passive voice marker

ვ-ბერ-დ-ებ-ოდ-ე-თ მე /ჩვენ
If we grow old

ბერ-დ-ებ-ოდ-ე-თ შენ/თქვენ
If you/you grow old

ბერ-დ-ებ-ოდ-ე-ს ის
If he grows old

ბერ-დ-ებ-ოდ-ნენ ისინი
If they grow old

Bipersonal verbs

ე- passive voice marker

ვ-ე-ლაპარაკ-ებ-ოდ-ე-(თ)
მე/ჩვენ მას/მათ
If I/we talk with him/them

ე-ლაპარაკ-ებ-ოდ-ე-(თ)
შენ/თქვენ მას/მათ
If you/you talk with him/them

ე-ლაპარაკ-ებ-ოდ-ე-ს
ის მას/მათ
If he talks with him/them

ე-ლაპარაკ-ებ-ოდ-ნენ
ისინი მას/მათ
If they talk with him/them

ვ-ე-ხმარ-ებ-ოდ-ე-(თ)
მე/ჩვენ მას/მათ
If I/we help him/them

ე-ხმარ-ებ-ოდ-ე-(თ)
შენ/თქვენ მას/მათ
If you/you help him/them

ე-ხმარ-ებ-ოდ-ე-ს
ის მათ/მას
If he helps him/them

ე-ხმარ-ებ-ოდ-ნენ
ისინი მას/მათ
If they help him/them

III conjugation verbs in the present subjunctive

Without P/FSF

ვ-ქუხ-დ-ე-(თ) მე/ჩვენ If I/we thunder	ვ-წუხ-დ-ე-(თ) მე/ ჩვენ If I/we worry
ქუხ-დ-ე-(თ) შენ/თქვენ If you/you thunder	წუხ-დ-ე-(თ) შენ /თქვენ If you/you worry
ქუხ-დ-ე-ს ის If he thunders	წუხ-დ-ე-ს ის If he worries
ქუხ-დ-ნენ ისინი If they thunder	წუხ-დ-ნენ ისინი If they worry

With P/FSF

ვ-ჭიკჭიკ-ებ-დ-ე-(თ) მე/ჩვენ If I/we chirp	ვ-გრძნ-ობ-დ-ე-(თ) მე /ჩვენ If I/we feel
ჭიკჭიკ-ებ-დ-ე-(თ) შენ/თქვენ If you/you chirp	გრძნ-ობ-დ-ე-თ შენ/თქვენ If you/you feel
ჭიკჭიკ-ებ-დ-ე-ს ის If he chirps	გრძნ-ობ-დ-ე-ს ის If he feels
ჭიკჭიკ-ებ-დ ნენ ისინი If they chirp	გრძნ-ობ-დ-ნენ ისინი If they feel

With P/FSF

მ-ჯობნ-ი-დ-ე-ს ის მე If he surpasses me	გვ-ჯობნ-ი-დ-ე-ს ის ჩვენ If he surpasses us	გვ-ჯობნ-ი-დ-ნენ ისინი ჩვენ If they surpass us
გ-ჯობნ-ი-დ-ე-ს ის შენ If he surpasses you	გ-ჯობნ-ი-დ-ე-თ ის თქვენ If he surpasses you	გ-ჯობნ-ი-დ-ნენ ისინი თქვენ If they surpass you
ს-ჯობნ-ი-დ-ეს ის მას If he surpasses him	ს-ჯობნ-ი-დ-ე-ს ის მათ If he surpasses them	ს-ჯობნ-ი-დ-ნენ ისინი მათ If they surpass them

Vowel-changing verbs in the present subjunctive

ვ-უსტვენ-დ-ე-(თ) მე/ჩვენ მას If I/we whistle at him	მ-წყენ-დ-ე-ს ის მე If it harms me

უსტვენ-დ-ე-(თ) შენ/თქვენ მას If you/you whistle at him	გვ-წყენ-დ-ე-ს ის ჩვენ If it harms us	
უსტვენ-დ-ე-ს ის მას If he whistles at him	გ-წყენ-დ-ე-ს/თ ის შენ/თქვენ If it harms you/you	
უსტვენ-დ-ნენ ისინი მას If they whistle at him/her	ს-წყენ-დ-ე-ს ის მას If it harms him	ს-წყენ-დ-ე-თ ის მათ If it harms them

IV conjugation verbs in the present subjunctive

IV conjugation passive verbs form the present subjunctive only if they have the present subseries forms. In that case, the extending particle of the imperfect **-დ** or **-ოდ** is added to their stem followed by the present subjunctive marker *-ე*.

(მო)-ვ-ჩან-დ-ე-(თ) მე/ჩვენ If I/we be seen	(და)-მ-ტირ-ოდ-ე-ს ის მე If he cries over me	(და)-გვ-ტირ-ოდ-ე-ს ის ჩვენ If he cries over us
(მო)-ჩან-დ-ე-(თ) შენ/თქვენ If you/you be seen	(და)-გ-ტირ-ოდ-ე-ს ის შენ If he cries over you	(და)-გ-ტირ-ოდ-ე-თ ის თქვენ If he cries over you
(მო)-ჩან-დ-ე-ს ის If he be seen (მო)-ჩან-დ-ნენ ისინი	(და)-ტირ-ოდ-ე-ს ის მას If he cries over him	(და)-ტირ-ოდ-ნენ ისინი მათ If they cry over them

9.6.1.2 *Future subseries*

The future series includes three tenses: future, conditional, and future subjunctive. Each of these tenses are based on the corresponding present subseries.

Future tense

The future tense expresses an action that will happen in the future or will continue for some time. Verbs in the future tense have a preverb added to their present tense forms: *ვწერ* (I write/I am writing) – და-ვწერ (I will write/I will be writing).

> *ხვალ ამ წერილს* ***დავწერ.***
> Tomorrow I will write this letter.
> *ამ კვირაში საახალწლო ბარათებს* ***დავწერ.***
> This week I will be writing New Year postcards.

Conditional

The conditional conveys an action that could have happened in the past or might happen in the present under certain conditions. Verbs in the conditional have a preverb added to their imperfect form: *ვ-წერ-დ-ი* (I wrote, I was writing; imperfect) – **და-ვ-წერ-დ-ი** (conditional).

ამ წერილს დღესვე ***დავწერდი****, მაგრამ დრო არა მაქვს.*
I would write this letter today, but I don't have time.
ნინოსთან ***დავრეკავდით****, მაგრამ მისი ტელეფონის ნომერი არ ვიცით.*
We would call Nino, but we don't have her phone number.
ჩემი და ახალ მანქანას იყიდიდა, მაგრამ ფული არა აქვს.
My sister would buy a new car but does not have money.

Future subjunctive

The future subjunctive expresses a wished-for, tentatively assumed, or hypothetical action in the future. It is sometimes coupled with the conditional in the main clause. Verbs in the future subjunctive have a preverb added to their present subjunctive form: *ვ-ა-კეთ-ებ-დ-ე* (if I do, present subjunctive) – ***გა****-ვ-ა-კეთ-ებ-დ-ე* (if I were to do, future subjunctive). In complex sentences it may be coupled with the conditional.

რამდენს ვიცინებდი, ის რომ ამას ***დახატავდეს****.*
How I would laugh if he were to paint this.
ნეტავ უცბად ***გავმდიდრდებოდეთ****.*
I wish we suddenly became rich.
მათ რომ ეს ***დაევალებოდეთ****, უსათუოდ შეასრულებდნენ.*
If they were charged with this (duty) they would do this by all means.

The meaning of many verbs in the present tense is determined by the context in which they appear. In the future subseries, however, a preverb added to a verb determines its semantics:

შე-ვთხოვ (present) *ღმერთს თქვენს ჯანმრთელობას!*
I pray to God for your health.
მო-ვთხოვ (future) *მას პასუხს.*
I will demand an answer from him.
დღეს სადილს შენ ***გა-აკეთებ****?*
Will you make dinner today?
ამ სტატიას აუცილებლად ***გადა-ვაკეთებ****.*
I will rework/change this article by all means.

The meaning of some verbs remains constant in the present tense, the context notwithstanding, but their semantics may be modified by means of various preverbs in the future subseries:

Present	*Future*
ვ-წერ წერილს. I write a letter.	***და-ვ-წერ*** წერილს. I will write a letter.
ვ-წერ თხოვნას. I write a request.	***ჩა-ვ-წერ*** მას სიაში. I will write (include) him in the roster.
ვ-წერ განცხადებას. I write an application.	***გადა-ვ-წერ*** ამას ხვალ I will rewrite this tomorrow.

I conjugation

Present	ვ-წერ I write	ვ-თხოვ I ask	ვ-ა-შენ-ებ I build
Future	და-ვ-წერ I will write	მო-ვ-თხოვ I will demand	ა-ვ-ა-შენ-ებ I will build
Imperfect	ვ-წერ-დ-ი I wrote/was writing	ვ-თხოვ-დ-ი I asked/ I was asking	ვ-ა-შენ-ებ-დ-ი I built/was building
Conditional	და-ვ-წერ-დ-ი I would write	მო-ვ-თხოვ-დ-ი I would request	ა-ვ-ა-შენ-ებ-დ-ი I would build
Present Subjunctive	ვ-წერ-დ-ე If I write	ვ-თხოვ-დ-ე If I ask	ვ-ა-შენ-ებ-დ-ე If I build
Future subjunctive	და-ვ-წერ-დ-ე If I should write	მო-ვ-თხოვ-დ-ე If I should demand	ა-ვ-ა-შენ-ებ-დ-ე If I were to build

I conjugation one-stem verbs in the future subseries

Future	*Conditional*	*Future subjunctive*
და-ვ-წერ-(თ) მე/ჩვენ მას/მათ I/we will write it/them	და-ვ-წერ-დ-ი-(თ) მე/ჩვენ მას/მათ I/we would write it/them	და-ვ-წერ-დ-ე-(თ) მე/ჩვენ მას/მათ If I/we were to write it/them

Future	*Conditional*	*Future subjunctive*
და-წერ-(თ) შენ/თქვენ მას/მათ You/you will write it/them	და-წერ-დ-ი-(თ) შენ/თქვენ მას/მათ You/you would write it/them	და-წერ-დ-ე-(თ) შენ/თქვენ მას/მათ If you/you were to write it/them
და-წერ-ს ის მას/მათ He will write it/them	და-წერ-დ-ა ის მას/მათ He would write it/them	და-წერ-დ-ე-ს ის მასმათ If he were to write it/them
და-წერ-ენ ისინი მას/მათ They will write it/them	და-წერ-დ-ნენ ისინი მას/მათ They would write it/them	და-წერ-დ-ნენ ისინი მას/მათ If they were to write it/them
მოვითხოვ(თ) მე/ჩვენ მას I/we demand it	მოვითხოვ-დ-ი-(თ) მე/ჩვენ მას I/we would demand it	მო-ვ-ი-თხოვ-დ-ე-(თ) მე/ჩვენ მას If I/we were to demand it
მო-ი-თხოვ-(თ) შენ/თქვენ მას You/you demand it	მოითხოვ-დ-ი-(თ) შენ/თქვენ მას You/you would demand it	მო-ი-თხოვ-დ-ე-(თ) შენ/თქვენ მას If you/you were to demand it
მო-ი-თხოვ-ს ის მას He demands it	მო-ი-თხოვ-დ-ა ის მას He would demand it	მო-ი-თხოვ-დ-ე-ს ის მას If he were to demand it
მო-ი-თხოვ-ენ ისინი მას They demand it	მო-ი-თხოვ-დ-ნენ ისინი მას They would demand it	მო-ი-თხოვ-დ-ნენ ისინი მას If they were to demand it

I conjugation two-stem verbs in the future subseries

Future	*Conditional*	*Future subjunctive*
და-ვ-ხატ-ავ-(თ) მე/ჩვენ მას/მათ I/we will paint him/them	და-ვ-ხატ-ავ-დ-ი(თ) მე/ჩვენ მას/მათ I/we would paint him/them	და-ვ-ხატ-ავ-დ-ე-(თ) მე/ჩვენ მას/მათ If I/we were to paint him/them

(*Continued*)

(Continued)

Future	*Conditional*	*Future subjunctive*
და-ხატ-ავ-(თ) შენ/თქვენ მას/მათ You/you will paint him/them	და-ხატ-ავ-დ-ი(თ) შენ/თქვენ მას/მათ You/you would paint him/them	და-ხატ-ავ-დ-ე-(თ) შენ/თქვენ მას/მათ If you/you were to paint him/them
და-ხატ-ავ-ს ის მას/მათ He will paint him/them	და-ხატ-ავ-დ-ა ის მას/მათ He would paint him/them	და-ხატ-ავ-დ-ე-ს ის მას/მათ If he were to paint him/them
და-ხატ-ავ-ენ ისინი მას/მათ They will paint him/them	და-ხატ-ავ-დ-ნენ ისინი მას/მათ They would paint him/them	და-ვ-ხატ-ავ-დ-ნენ ისინი მას/მათ If they were to paint him/them

-ემ

P/FSF -ემ is added to a single verb root -ც.

Present	ს-ც-ემ-ს ახლა He is publishing it now
Imperfect	ს-ც-ემ-დ-ა შარშან He published it last year
Present subjunctive	ს-ც-ემ-დ-ე-ს ახლა If he publish it now ს-ც-ემ-დ-ეს მომავალ წელს If he should publish it next year

Future	*Conditional*	*Future Subjunctive*
გამო-ვ-ც-ემ-(თ) მე/ჩვენ მას/მათ I/we will publish it/them	გამოვცემ-დ-ი(თ) მე/ჩვენ მას/მათ I/we would publish it/them	გამოვცემ-დ-ე(თ) მე/ჩვენ მას/მათ If I/we were to publish it/them
გამო-ს-ც-ემ-(თ) შენ/თქვენ მას/მათ You/you will publish it/them	გამოსცემ-დ-ი(თ) შენ/თქვენ მას/მათ You/you would publish him/them	გამოსცემ-დ-ე(თ) შენ/თქვენ მას/მათ If you/you were to publish it/them

Future	*Conditional*	*Future Subjunctive*
გამო-ს-ც-ემ-ს ის მას/მათ He will publish it/them	გამოსცემ-დ-ა ის მას/მათ He would publish it/them	გამოსცემ-დ-ე-ს ის მას/მათ If he were to publish it/them
გამო-ს-ც-ემ-ენ ისინი მას/მათ They will publish it/them	გამოსცემ-დ-ნენ ისინი მას/მათ They would publish it/them	გამოსცემ-დ-ნენ ისინი მას/მათ If they were to publish it/them

The meaning of this verb *ც-ემ* changes, depending on the preverb added to it in the future subseries:

გა-ვ-ც-ემ = I will betray; გამო-ვ-ც-ემ = I will publish.

> *ამ ნაშრომებს მალე* ***გამო-ს-ცემ-ენ.***
> They will publish these works soon.
> *ნეტავ ისინი მეგობრებს არ* ***გა-ს-ცემ-დ-ნენ.***
> I wish they would not betray their friends.

-ოფ

The P/FSF **-ოფ** is added to a single verb *ყოფ,* the meaning of which depends on the context in the present tense and on preverbs that may be added to it in the future subseries:

Present	**Future**
ყოფს ქონებას	***გა****-ყოფს ქონებას.* He will divide (his) property.
ყოფს ხელს ჩანთაში	***ჩა****-ყოფს ხელს ჩანთაში.* He will put his hand into (his) bag.
ყოფს ხელს კარადაში.	***შე****-ყოფს ხელს კარადაში.* He will slide his hand into the cupboard.
ყოფს ხელს სკამის უკან.	***გადა****-ყოფს ხელს სკამის უკან.* He will stretch his hand over a chair

Future	*Conditional*	*Future subjunctive*
გა-ვ-ყ-ოფ-(თ) მე/ჩვენ მას/მათ I/we will divide it/them	გა-ვ-ყ-ოფ-დ-ი(თ) მე/ჩვენ მას/მათ I/we would divide it/them	გა-ვ-ყ-ოფ-დ-ე-(თ) მე/ჩვენ მას/მათ If I/we were to divide it/them

(Continued)

(Continued)

Future	*Conditional*	*Future subjunctive*
გა-ყ-ოფ-(თ) შენ/თქვენ მას/მათ You/you will divide it/them	გა-ყ-ოფ-დ-ი-(თ) შენ/თქვენ მას/მათ You/you would divide it/them	გა-ყ-ოფ-დ-ე-(თ) შენ/თქვენ მას/მათ If you/you were to divide it/them
გა-ყ-ოფ-ს ის მას/მათ He will divide it/them	გა-ყ-ოფ-დ-ა ის მას/მათ He would divide it/them	გა-ყ-ოფ-დ-ე-ს ის მას/მათ If he were to divide it/them
გა-ყ-ოფ-ენ ისინი მას/მათ They will divide it/them	გა-ყ-ოფ-დ-ნენ ისინი მას/მათ They would divide it/them	გა-ყ-ოფ-დ-ნენ ისინი მას/მათ If they were to divide it/them

Ablaut verbs

Ablaut verbs have the root vowel *-ე* both in their present and future subseries.

Future	*Conditional*	*Future subjunctive*
და-ვ-კრეფ-(თ) მე/ჩვენ მას/მათ I/we will pick it/them	და-ვ-კრეფ-დ-ი(თ) მე/ჩვენ მას/მათ I/we would pick it/them	და-ვ-კრეფ-დ-ე-(თ) მე/ჩვენ მას/მათ If I/we were to pick it/them
და-კრეფ-(თ) შენ/თქვენ მას/მათ You/you pick it/them	და-კრეფ-დ-ი-(თ) შენ/თქვენ მას/მათ You/you would pick it/them	და-კრეფ-დ-ე-(თ) შენ/თქვენ მას/მათ If you/you were to pick it/them
და-კრეფ-ს ის მას/მათ He will pick it/them	და-კრეფ-დ-ა ის მას/მათ He would pick it/them	და-კრეფ-დ-ე-ს ის მას/მათ If he were to pick it/them
და-კრეფ-ენ ისინი მას/მათ They pick it/them	და-კრეფ-დ-ნენ ისინი მას/მათ They would pick it/them	და-კრეფ-დ-ნენ ისინი მას/მათ If they were to pick it/them

The verbs ending with -*ევ* and -*ენ* conjugate similarly and have vowel -*ე* in all the future subseries:

Future	შე-ვ-ა-მჩნევ I will notice	და-ვ-ა-დგენ I will ascertain
Conditional	შე-ვ-ა-მჩნევ-დ-ი I would notice	და-ვ-ა-დგენ-დ-ი I would ascertain
Future subjunctive	შე-ვ-ა-მჩნევ-დ-ე If I should notice	და-ვ-ა-დგენ-დ-ე If I were to ascertain

მე ამ ცვლილებებს ***შევამჩნევდი.***
I would notice these changes.
ნეტავ ექსპერტი ამ დოკუმენტების წყაროს ***დაადგენდეს.***
If an expert were to ascertain the source of these documents.

Verbs losing their root vowel in the present subseries because of P/FSF added to them have a syncopated root in the Future subseries as well. For example, the root -*შლ*- with P/FSF -*ი*: *შლ-ი-ს* (he erases), *შლ-ი-დ-ა* (he was erasing), *შლ-ი-დ-ე-ს* (if he were to erase). The root vowel is restored in aorist: *წა-შალ-ა* (he erased).

Future	*Conditional*	*Future subjunctive*
წა-ვ-შლ-ი-(თ) მე/ჩვენ მას/მათ I/we will erase it/them	წა-ვ-შლ-ი-დ-ი-(თ) მე/ჩვენ მას/მათ I/we would erase it/them	წა-ვ-შლ-ი-დ-ე-(თ) მე/ჩვენ მას/მათ If I/we were to erase it/them
წა-შლ-ი-(თ) შენ/თქვენ მას/მათ You/you will erase it/them	წა-შლ-ი-დ-ი-(თ) შენ/თქვენ მას/მათ You/you would erase it/them	წა-შლ-ი-დ-ე-(თ) შენ/თქვენ მას/მათ If you/you were to erase it/them
წა-შლ-ი-ს ის მას/მათ He will erase it/them	წა-შლ-ი-დ-ა ის მას/მათ He would erase it/them	წა-შლ-ი-დ-ე-ს ის მას/მათ If he were to erase it/them
წა-შლ-ი-ან ისინი მას/მათ They will erase it/them	წა-შლ-ი-დ-ნენ ისინი მას/მათ They would erase it them	წა-შლ-ი-დ-ნენ ისინი მას/მათ If they were to erase it/them

ამ შეცდომებს ***წავშლით/გადავშლით.***
We will erase/strike through these mistakes.
წიგნს მეხუთე გვერდზე ***გადავშლით.***
We will open the book on page five.
ამ ჯგუფს ***დავშლით.***
We will disband this group.

II conjugation verbs in the future subseries

II conjugation verbs, i.e. dynamic passive voice verbs, have the same stem in the present and future subseries. Therefore, all of them (with *ი*-and *ე*-prefixes, *-დ* suffix, and without any markers) have the ***-ებ-ი*** ending in the first and second person and ***-ებ-ა*** in the third-person forms. In the conditional and future subjunctive, they have ***-ოდ*** followed by the tense markers: ***-ი*** in the conditional and ***-ე*** in the present subjunctive.

Future	*Conditional*	*Future Subjunctive*
დავბერდები-(თ) მე/ჩვენ I/we will get old	დავბერდებ-ოდ-ი(თ) მე/ჩვენ I/we would get old	დავბერდებ-ოდ-ე-(თ) მე/ჩვენ If I/we were to get old
დაბერდები-(თ) You/you will get old	დაბერდებ-ოდ-ი-(თ) შენ/თქვენ You/you would get old	დაბერდებ-ოდ-ე-(თ) შენ/თქვენ If you/you were to get old
დაბერდებ-ა ის He will get old	დაბერდებ-ოდ-ა ის He would get old	დაბერბდებ-ოდ-ე-ს ის If he were to get old
დაბერდები-ან ისინი They will get old	დაბერდებ-ოდ-ნენ ისინი They would get old	დავბერდებ-ოდ-ნენ ისინი If they were to get old

Dynamic passive voice verbs maintain their P/FSF in the present and future subseries – for example, *ი-ძვრ-ებ-ა* (he moves), *ი-ძვრ-ებ-ოდ-ა* (he moved), *ი-ძვრ-ებ-ოდ-ე-ს* (if he moves).

Future	*Conditional*	*Future Subjunctive*
დავიძვრები-(თ) მე/ჩვენ I/we will move	დავიძვრებ-ოდ-ი-(თ) მე/ჩვენ I/we would move	დავიძვრებ-ოდ-ე-(თ) მე/ჩვენ If I/we were to move
დაიძვრები-(თ) შენ/თქვენ You/you will move	დაიძვრებ-ოდ-ი-(თ) შენ/თქვენ You/you would move	დაიძვრებ-ოდ-ე-(თ) შენ/თქვენ If you/you were to move
დაიძვრებ-ა ის He will move	დაიძვრებ-ოდ-ა ის He would move	დაიძვრებ-ოდ-ე-ს ის If he should move
დაიძვრები-ან ისინი They will move	დაიძვრებ-ოდ-ნენ ისინი They would move	დაიძვრებ-ოდ-ნენ ისინი If they were to move

Conjugation of bipersonal dynamic verbs in the future subseries

Future	*Conditional*	*Future Subjunctive*
(გა)ვეთამაშები-(თ) მე/ჩვენ მას/მათ I/we will play with him/them	(გა)ვეთამაშებ-ოდ-ი-(თ) მე/ჩვენ მას/მათ I/we would play with him/them	(გა)ვეთამაშებ-ოდ-ე-(თ) მე/ჩვენ მას/მათ If I/we were to play with him/them
(გა)ეთამაშები-(თ) შენ/თქვენ მას/მათ You/you will play with him/them	(გა)ეთამაშებ-ოდ-ი-(თ) შენ/თქვენ მას/მათ You/you would play with him/them	(გა)ეთამაშებ-ოდ-ე-(თ) შენ/თქვენ მას/მათ If you/you were to play with him/them
(გა)ეთამაშებ-ა ის მას/მათ He will play with him/them	(გა)ეთამაშებ-ოდ-ა ის მას/მათ He would play with him/them	(გა)ეთამაშებ-ოდ-ე-ს ის მას/მათ If he were to play with him/them
(გა)ეთამაშებ-ი-ან ისინი მას/მათ They will play with him/them	(გა)ეთამაშებ-ოდ-ნენ ისინი მას/მათ They would play with him/them	(გა)ეთამაშებ-ოდ-ნენ ისინი მას/მათ If they were to play with him/them

III conjugation verbs in the future subseries

III conjugation verbs, i.e. medio-active verbs, cannot form the future subseries independently, they take some borrowed forms. They also have a version prefix *-ი* or *-უ*. In this regard the following cases should be differentiated from each other:

1. Medio-active verbs with the same stem in present and future subseries. They differ from each other when the version markers *-ი-* or *-უ-* appear in the future subseries.

ვ-ბუზღუნ-ებ	(I grumble)	*ვ-**ი**-ბუზღუნ-ებ*	(I will grumble)
ვ-შველ-ი	(I help him)	*ვ-**უ**-შველ-ი*	(I will help him)

Future	*Conditional*	*Future subjunctive*
ვ-უ-შველ-ი-(თ) მე/ჩვენ მას/მათ I/we will help him/them	ვ-უ-შველ-ი-დ-ი-(თ) მე/ჩვენ მას/მათ I/we would help him/them	ვ-უ-შველ-ი-დ-ე-(თ) მე/ჩვენ მას/მათ If I/we were to help him/them
უ-შველ-ი-(თ) შენ/თქვენ მას/მათ You/you will help him/them	უ-შველ-ი-დ-ი-(თ) შენ/თქვენ მას/მათ You/you would help him/them	უ-შველ-ი-დ-ე-(თ) შენ/თქვენ მას/მათ If you/you were to help him/them
უ-შველ-ი-ს ის მას/მათ He will help him/them	უ-შველ-ი-დ-ა ის მას/მათ He would help him/them	უ-შველ-ი-დ-ე-ს ის მას/მათ If he were to help him/them
უ-შველ-ი-ან ისინი მას/მათ They will help him/them	უ-შველ-ი-დ-ნენ ისინი მას/მათ They would help him/them	უ-შველ-ი-დ-ნენ ისინი მას/მათ If they were to help him/them

2. Medio-active verbs, both monopersonal and bipersonal, with different P/FSF in present and future subseries:

ვ-სადილ-**ობ**	ვ-ისადილ-**ებ**	(I dine, I will dine)
ვ-ნადირ-**ობ**	ვ-ინადირ-**ებ**	(I hunt, I will hunt)
ვ-მეფ-**ობ**	ვ-იმეფ-**ებ**	(I reign, I will reign)

A small number of medio-active verbs with P/SFS **-ობ** change not only P/FSF in the future subseries but also phonetic changes occur in the verb stem: *ქანა-ობ-ს* (he swings), *-ი-ქანა-ვ-ებ-ს* (he will swing), *ი-ქანა-ვ-ებ-დ-ა* (he would swing), *ი-ქან-ა-ვ-ებ-დ-ე-ს* (if he should swing) (see the conjugation of medio-active voice two-stem verbs in the perfect tense in 9.6.3.1.).

3. The medio-active verbs with P/FSF **-ი** in the present subseries change P/FSF in the future subseries, which causes the emergence of an affix that was absent in their forms of the present subseries:

   *იბრძვ-**ი**-ს* (he fights) – *იბრძ-**ოლ**-ებ-ს* (he will fight)
   *თრთ-**ი**-ს* (he trembles) – **ითრთ-ოლ-ებ-ს** (he will tremble
   *ქრ-**ი**-ს* (it blows) – *ი-ქრ-**ოლ**-ებ-ს* (it will blow)

Conjugation of monopersonal medio-active verbs

Future	*Conditional*	*Future Subjunctive*
ვიცხოვრებ-(თ) მე/ჩვენ I/we will live	ვიცხოვრებ-დ-ი-(თ) მე/ჩვენ I/we would live	ვიცხოვრებ-დ-ე-(თ) მე/ჩვენ If I/we were to live
იცხოვრებ-(თ) შენ/თქვენ You/you will live	იცხოვრებ-დ-ი-(თ) შენ/თქვენ You/you would live	იცხოვრებ-დ-ე-(თ) შენ/თქვენ If you/you were to live
იცხოვრებ-ს ის He will live	იცხოვრებ-დ-ა ის He would live	იცხოვრებ-დ-ე-ს ის If he were to live
იცხოვრებ-ენ ისინი They will live	იცხოვრებ-დ-ნენ ისინი They would live	იცხოვრებ-დ-ნენ ისინი If they were to live
ვითევზავებ-(თ) მე/ჩვენ I/we will fish	ვითევზავებ-დ-ი-(თ) მე/ჩვენ I/we would fish	ვითევზავებ-დ-ე-(თ) მე/ჩვენ If I/we were to fish
ითევზავებ-(თ) შენ/თქვენ You/you will fish	ითევზავებ-დ-ი-(თ) შენ/თქვენ You/you would fish	ითევზავებ-დ-ე-(თ) შენ/თქვენ If you/you were to fish
ითევზავებს ის He will fish	ითევზავებ-დ-ა ის He would fish	ი-თევზავ-ებ-დ-ე-ს If he were to fish
ითევზავებ-ენ ისინი They will fish	ითევზავებდ-ნენ ისინი They would fish	ითევზავებ-დ-ნენ ისინი If they were to fish

(*Continued*)

(Continued)

Future	*Conditional*	*Future Subjunctive*
ვიბრძ-ოლ-ებ-(თ) მე/ჩვენ I/we will fight	ვიბრძოლებ-დ-ი-(თ) მე/ჩვენ I/we would fight	ვიბრძოლებ-დ-ე-(თ) მე/ჩვენ If I/we were to fight
იბრძ-ოლ-ებ-(თ) შენ/თქვენ You/you will fight	იიბრძოლებ-დ-ი-(თ) შენ/თქვენ You/you would fight	იბრძოლებ-დ-ე-(თ) შენ/თქვენ If you/you were to fight
იბრძოლ-ებ-ს ის He will fight	იბრძოლებ-დ-ა ის He would fight	იბრძოლებ-დ-ე-ს If he were to fight
იბრძოლ-ებ-ენ მე/ჩვენ They will fight	იბრძოლებ-დ-ნენ ისინი They would fight	იბრძოლებ-დ-ნენ ისინი If they were to fight

Conjugation of bipersonal medio-active verbs

Future	*Conditional*	*Future subjunctive*
ვ-უ-პატრონ-ებ-(თ) მე/ჩვენ მას/მათ I/we will take care of him/them	ვ-უ-პატრონ-ებ-დ-ი-(თ) მე/ჩვენ მას/მათ I/we would take care of him/them	უ-პატრონ-ებ-დ-ე-(თ) მე/ჩვენ მას/მათ If I/we were to take care of him/them
უპატრონ-ებ-(თ) შენ/თქვენ მას/მათ You/you will take care of him/them	უპატრონ-ებ-დ-ი-(თ) შენ/თქვენ მას/მათ You/you would take care of him/them	უპატრონ-ებ-დ-ე-(თ) შენ/თქვენ მას/მათ If you/you were to take care of him/them
უპატრონ-ებ-ს ის მას/მათ He will take care of him/them	უპატრონ-ებ-დ-ა ის მას/მათ He would take care of him/them	უპატრონ-ებ-დ-ე-ს ის მას/მათ If he were to take care of him/them
უპატრონ-ებ-ენ ისინი მას/მათ They will take care of him/them	უპატრონ-ებ-დ-ნენ ისინი მას/მათ They would take care of him/them	უპატრონ-ებ-დ-ნენ ისინი მას/მათ If they were to take care of him/them

4. In the future subseries the affix *-(ი)ლ* is added to the stem of small number of verbs with P/FSF *-ი*. In this case, the consonant *-ვ*-emerges after the vowel *-უ*:

ბზუის	*იბზუვლებს*
It buzzes	It will buzz
ღმუის	*იღმუვლებს*
He roars	He will roar
შხუის	*იშხუვლებს*
It swishes	It will swish

Future	*Conditional*
(და)-ვ-ი-კივლ-ებ-(თ) მე/ჩვენ I/we will scream	(და)-ვ-ი-კივლ-ებ-დ-ი-(თ) მე/ჩვენ I/we would scream
(და)-ი-კივლ-ებ-(თ) შენ/თქვენ You/you will scream	(და)-ი-კივლ-ებ-დ-ი-(თ) შენ/თქვენ You/you would scream
(და)-ი-კივლ-ებ-ს ის He will scream	(და)-ი-კივლ-ებ-დ-ა ის He would scream
(და)-ი-კივლ-ებ-ენ ისინი They will scream	(და)-ი-კივლ-ებ-დ-ნენ ისინი They would scream

Future subjunctive
(და)-ვ-ი-კივლ-ებ-დ-ე-(თ) მე/ჩვენ If I/we were to scream
(და)-ი-კივლ-ებ-დ-ე-(თ) შენ/თქვენ If you/you were to scream
(და)-ი-კივლ-ებ-დ-ე-ს If he were to scream
(და)-ი-კივლ-ებ-დ-ნენ ისინი If they were to scream

5. Monopersonal medio-active verbs require an auxiliary verb in the present tense, but not in other tenses. However, in the future subseries, some changes happen in the stem of these verbs:

გა-ვ-**რბი**-ვ-არ (I run) – (გა)-ვ-ი-**რბენ** (I will run).

Future	Conditional
(გა)-ვ-ი-რბენ-თ მე/ჩვენ I/we will run	(გა)-ვ-ი-რბენ-დ-ი-(თ) მე/ჩვენ I/we would run
(გა)-ი-რბენ-თ შენ/თქვენ You/you will run	(გა)-ი-რბენ-დ-ი-(თ) შენ/თქვენ You/you would run
(გა)-ი-რბენ-ს ის He will run	(გა)-ი-რბენ-დ-ა ის He would run
(გა)-ი-რბენ-ენ ისინი They will run	(გა)-ი-რბენ-დ-ნენ ისინი They would run

Future subjunctive
(გა)-ვ-ი-რბენ-დ-ე-(თ) მე/ჩვენ If I/we were to run
(გა)-ი-რბენ-დ-ე-(თ) შენ/თქვენ You/you were to run
(გა)-ი-რბენ-დ-ე-ს If he were to run
(გა)-ი-რბენ-დ-ნენ ისინი If they were to run

6. The medio-active verbs with an alternating stem vowel maintain the same stem in the future subseries:

ს-**წყენ**-ს ის მას/მათ (it harms him/them) – ა-**წყენ**-ს ის მას/მათ (it will harm him/them)

Future	Conditional	Future subjunctive
მ-ა-წყენ-ს ის მე It harms me	მ-ა-წყენ-დ-ა ის მე It would harm me	მ-ა-წყენ-დ-ე-ს ის მე If it were to harm me
გვ-ა-წყენ-ს ის ჩვენ It harms us	გვ-ა-წყენ-დ-ა ის ჩვენ It would harm us	გვ-ა-წყენ-დ-ეს ის ჩვენ If it were to harm us
გ-ა-წყენ-ს ის შენ It harms you	გ-ა-წყენ-დ-ა ის შენ It would harm you	გ-ა-წყენ-დ-ე-ს ის შენ If it were to harm you
გ-ა-წყენ-თ ის თქვენ It harms you	გ-ა-წყენ-დ-ა-თ ის თქვენ It would harm you	გ-ა-წყენ-დ-ე-თ ის თქვენ If it were to harm you

Future	*Conditional*	*Future subjunctive*
ა-წყენ-ს ის მას/მათ It harms him/them	ა-წყენ-დ-ა ის მას/მათ It would harm him/them	ა-წყენ-დ-ე-ს ის მას/მათ If it were to harm him/them
ა-წყენ-ენ ისინი მას/მათ They harm him/them	ა-წყენ-დ-ნენ ისინი მას/მათ They would harm him/them	ა-წყენ-დ-ე-თ ისინი მას/მათ If it were to harm him/them

IV conjugation

All static-passive and medio-active verbs do not have P/FSF, whatever their forms may be in the present tense.

In monopersonal verbs, the auxiliary verb *to be* is replaced with P/FSF -ებ:

ვ-დგა-**ვარ**	(I am standing)	ვ-ი-დგ-ებ-ი	(I will be standing)
ვ-წე-**ვარ**	(I am lying)	ვ-ი-წვ-ებ-ი	(I will be lying)
ვ-წერ-ი-**ვარ**	(I am written in)	ვ-ე-წერ-ებ-ი	(I will be written in)

Future	*Conditional*	*Future Subjunctive*
ვიდგ-ებ-ი-(თ) მე/ჩვენ I/we will be standing	ვ-ი-დგ-ებ-ოდ-ი-(თ) მე/ჩვენ I/we would be standing	ვ-ი-დგ-ებ-ოდ-ე(თ) მე/ჩვენ If I/we were to stand
დავდგებ-ი-(თ) მე/ჩვენ I/we will stand	და-ვ-დგ-ებ-ოდ-ი-(თ) მე/ჩვენ I/we would stand	და-ვ-დგ-ებ-ოდ-ე-(თ) მე/ჩვენ If I/we were to stand
იდგ-ებ-ი-(თ) შენ/თქვენ You/you will be standing	იდგებ-ოდ-ი-(თ) შენ/თქვენ You/you would be standing	იდგებ-ოდ-ე(თ) შენ/თქვენ If you/you were to stand
დადგ-ებ-ი-(თ) შენ/თქვენ You/you will stand	დადგებ-ოდ-ი-(თ) შენ/თქვენ You/you would stand	დადგებ-ოდ-ე-(თ) შენ/თქვენ If you/you were to stand

(*Continued*)

(Continued)

Future	Conditional	Future Subjunctive
იდგ-ებ-ა ის He will be standing	იდგებ-ოდ-ა ის He would be standing	იდგებ-ოდ-ე-ს ის If he were to stand
იდგ-ებ-ი-ან ისინი They will be standing	იდგებ-ოდ-ნენ ისინი They would be standing	იდგებ-ოდ-ნენ ისინი If they were to stand
დადგ-ებ-ა ის He will stand	დადგებ-ოდ-ა ის He would stand	დადგებ-ოდ-ე-ს ის If he were to stand
დადგ-ებ-ი-ან ისინი They will stand	დადგებ-ოდ-ნენ ისინი They would stand	დადგებ-ოდ-ნენ ისინი If they were to stand

Bipersonal verbs have P/FSF *-ებ* and the prefix *-ე* as a passive voice marker.

Future	Conditional	Future Subjunctive
მ-ე-ყვარ-ებ-ა ის მე I will love him	მეყვარებ-ოდ-ა ის მე I would love him	მეყვარებ-ოდ-ე-ს ის მე If I were to love him
გვ-ე-ყვარ-ებ-ა ის ჩვენ We will love him	გვეყვარებ-ოდ-ა ის ჩვენ We would love him	გვეყვარებ-ოდ-ე-ს ის ჩვენ If we were to love him
გ-ე-ყვარ-ებ-ა-(თ) ის შენ/თქვენ You/you will love him	გეყვარებ-ოდ-ა-(თ) ის შენ/თქვენ You/you would love him	გეყვარებ-ოდ-ე-ს ის შენ If you were to love him
		გეყვარებ-ოდ-ე-თ ის თქვენ If you were to love him
ე-ყვარ-ებ-ა-(თ) ის მას/მათ He/they will love him	ეყვარებ-ოდ-ა-(თ) ის მას/მათ He/they would love him	ეყვარებ-ოდ-ა-(თ) ის მას/მათ He/they were to love him

Bipersonal verbs with an *-ია* ending in all three person forms in the present tense have P/FSF ***-ებ*** and the passive voice prefix ***ე***-in the future subseries.

Future	*Conditional*	*Future Subjunctive*
მ-ე-გონ-ებ-ა ის მე It will seem to me	მეგონებ-ოდ-ა ის მე It would seem to me	მეგონებ-ოდ-ე-ს ის მე If it were to seem to me
გვ-ე-გონ-ებ-ა ის ჩვენ It will seem to us	გვეგონებ-ოდ-ა ის ჩვენ It would seem to us	გვეგონებ-ოდ-ე-ს ის ჩვენ If it were to seem to us
გ-ე-გონ-ებ-ა-(თ) ის შენ/თქვენ It will seem to you/you	გეგონებ-ოდ-ა-(თ) ის შენ/თქვენ It would seem to you/you	გეგონებ-ოდ-ე-ს/თ ის შენ/თქვენ If it were to seem to you/you
ე-გონ-ებ-ა-(თ) ის მას/მათ It will seem to him/them	ეგონებ-ოდ-ა-(თ) ის მას/მათ It would seem to him/them	ეგონებ-ოდ-ა-(თ) ის მას/მათ If it were to seem to him/them

The following passive static verbs have the same conjugation forms: *მკიდია* (it hangs on me), *მაფენია* (it is spread over me), *მაფარია* (it covers me), *მაყრია* (it is dropped on me), *მაკერია* (it is sewn on me), *მახატია* (it is painted on me), *მარტყია* (it circles me), *მაცხია* (it is daubed/smeared on me), მავალია (it is my duty, I am charged with it).

Future	*Conditional*	*Future Subjunctive*
და-მ-ე-ვალ-ებ-ა ის მე It will be my duty	დამევალებ-ოდ-ა ის მე It would be my duty	დამევალებ-ოდ-ე-ს ის მე If it were to be my duty
და-გვ-ე-ვალ-ებ-ა ის ჩვენ It will be our duty	დაგვევალებ-ოდ-ი ის ჩვენ It would be our duty	დაგვევალებ-ოდ-ე-ს ის ჩვენ If it were to be our duty

(Continued)

(Continued)

Future	*Conditional*	*Future Subjunctive*
და-გ-ე-ვალ-ებ-ა-(თ) ის შენ/თქვენ It will be your/your duty	დაგევალებ-ოდ-ა-(თ) ის შენ/თქვენ It would be your/your duty	დაგევალებ-ოდ-ე-ს ის შენ If it were to be your duty დაგევალებ-ოდ-ე-თ ის თქვენ If it were to be your duty
და-ე-ვალ-ებ-ა-(თ) ის მას/მათ It will be his/their duty	დაევალებ-ოდ-ა-(თ) ის მას/მათ It would be his/their duty	დაევალებ-ოდ-ე-ს ის მას If it were to be his duty დაევალებ-ოდ-ე-თ ის მათ If it were to be their duty

In the future subseries IV, conjugation verbs are replaced with dynamic passive voice verbs. As a result, their P/FSF is changed: **-ავ** is replaced with– *ებ*:

მ-ნებ-ავ-ს	(I deign)	*მ-ე-ნებ-ებ-ა*	(I will deign)
მ-ძინ-ავ-ს	(I am asleep)	*(და)-მ-ე-ძინ-ებ-ა*	(I will fall asleep)
მ-ღვიძ-ავ-ს	(I will be awake)	*(გა)-მ-ე-ღვიძ-ებ-ა*	(I will wake up)

Future	*Conditional*	*Future Subjunctive*
მ-ე-ნებ-ებ-ა ის მე I will desire it	მენებებ-ოდ-ა ის მე I would desire it	მენებებ-ოდ-ე-ს ის მე If I were to desire it
გვ-ე-ნებ-ებ-ა ის ჩვენ We will desire it	გვენებებ-ოდ-ი ის ჩვენ We would desire it	გვენებებ-ოდ-ე-ს ის ჩვენ If we were to desire it

(Continued)

(Continued)

Future	*Conditional*	*Future subjunctive*
მ-ე-ნებ-ებ-ა-(თ) ის შენ/თქვენ You/you will desire it	გენებებ-ოდ-ა-(თ) ის შენ/თქვენ You/you would desire it	გენებებ-ოდ-ე-ს ის შენ If you were to desire it გენებებ-ოდ-ე-თ ის თქვენ If you were to desire it
ე-ნებ-ებ-ა-(თ) ის მას/მათ He/they will desire it	ე-ნებ-ებ-ოდ-ა-(თ) ის მას/მათ He/they would desire it	ე-ნებ-ებ-ოდ-ე-ს ის მას If he were to desire it ე-ნებ-ებ-ოდ-ე-თ ის მათ If they were to desire it
გამეღვიძებ-ა მე I will wake up	გამ(ე)ღვიძებ-ოდ-ა მე I would wake up	გამ(ე)ღვიძებ-ოდ-ე-ს მე If I were to wake up
გაგვეღვიძებ-ა ჩვენ We will wake up	გაგვ(ე)-ღვიძ-ებ-ოდ-ი ჩვენ We would wake up	გაგვ(ე)ღვიძებ-ოდ-ე-ს ჩვენ If we were to wake up
გაგეღვიძებ-ა-(თ) შენ/თქვენ You/you will wake up	გაგ(ე)ღვიძებ-ოდ-ა-(თ) შენ/თქვენ You/you would wake up	გაგ(ე-ღვიძ-ებ-ოდ-ე-ს შენ If you were to wake up გაგ(ე)ღვიძებ-ოდ-ე-თ თქვენ If you were to wake up
გაეღვიძებ-ა-(თ) მას/მათ He/they will wake up	გაგ(ე)ღვიძებ-ოდ-ა-(თ) მას/მათ He/they would wake up	გა(ე)ღვიძებ-ოდ-ე-ს/თ მას/მათ If he/they were to wake up

9.6.2 *II series*

9.6.2.1 *Aorist*

The aorist expresses an action in the past either completed or continuous depending on the presence or absence of a preverb.

გუშინ ეს წიგნი მთლიანად ***წავიკითხე*** (a completed action in past).
Yesterday I read (completed reading it) this entire book.

გუშინ ეს წიგნი მთელი დღე ***ვიკითხე*** (a continuous action in the past).

Yesterday I was reading (but did not finish reading it) this book entire day.

Many Georgian sayings and riddles employ the opposition of verbs in the aorist with and without preverbs:

ვკეცე, ვკეცე, ვერ დავკეცე (გზა).
I kept folding it up, folding it up (but) could not fold it up (road).
ვაშრე, ვაშრე, ვერ გავაშრე (ენა).
I kept drying it, drying it (but) could not dry it up (tongue).

The meaning of the verbs *ვკეცე* and *ვაშრე* convey the idea of continuous action, while *დავკეცე* and *გავაშრე* express completed action.

In some verbs, presence or absence of a preverb may change the meaning of the verb to which they are added. Thus, *ვ-თხოვ-ე* means *I asked*, while *მო-ვ-თხოვ-ე* is translated as *I demanded*.

Verbs in the aorist always express indicative mood if they are not used for imperative in the second-person forms. The difference is only in the intonation. Compare:

Aorist, indicative mood: [ვიცი, რომ] *ეს წერილი* ***დაწერე***.
[I know that] You wrote this letter.
Aorist, imperative mood: *ეს წერილი* ***დაწერე!***
Write this letter!

I conjugation verbs in the aorist

The majority of I conjugation verbs in the aorist are marked with the suffix -*ე*, which is replaced with the third-person markers -ა in its singular and -*ეს* in plural form.

1. The one-stem verbs have the same stem in I and II series forms:

Present/future:	**(და)-წერ-**თ შენ/თქვენ მას/მათ You/you (will) write
Aorist:	**(და)-წერ**-ე-თ შენ/თქვენ ის/ისინი You/you wrote
Present/future:	**(მო)**-ვ-თხოვ მე მას/მათ I ask/will ask it him/them
Aorist:	**(მო)**-ვ-თხოვ-ე მას/მათ ის/ისინი I asked it from him/them

(და)-წერ-ე-(თ) შენ/თქვენ ის/ისინი You/you were writing/ wrote it/them	ს-თხოვ-ე შენ მას/მათ ის (დახმარება) You asked him/them for it (for help) მო-ს-თხოვ-ე შენ მას/მათ ის (პასუხი) You demanded it (an answer) from him/them
(და)-წერ-ა მან ის/ისინი He was writing/wrote it/them	ს-თხოვ-ა მან მას/მათ ის (დახმარება) He asked him/them for it (for help) მო-ს-თხოვ-ა მან მას/მათ ის (პასუხი) He demanded it (an answer) from him/them
(და)-წერ-ეს მათ ის/ისინი They were writing wrote it/them	ს-თხოვ-ეს მათ მას/მათ ის (დახმარება) They asked him/them for it (for help) მო-ს-თხოვ-ეს მათ მას/მათ ის (პასუხი) They demanded it (an answer) from him/them

2. The two-stem verbs have their P/FSF in I series but not in II series:

Present/future:	The stem ***-ხატ-*** with P/FSF ***-ავ*** **(და)-ხატ-ავ-(თ)** შენ/თქვენ მას You/you (will) paint it
Aorist:	The stem ***-ხატ-*** without P/FSF **(და)-ხატ**-ე-(თ) შენ/თქვენ ის You/you were painting/painted it
Present/future:	The stem ***აშენ-*** with P/FSF ***-ებ*** **(ა)-შენ-ებ-**(თ) შენ/თქვენ მას You/you (will) build it
Aorist:	The stem ***აშენ-*** without P/FSF **(ა)-აშენ**-ე-(თ) შენ/თქვენ ის You/you (were building) built it

Conjugation of two-stem verbs in the aorist

(და)-ვ-ხატ-ე(თ) მე/ჩვენ ის/ისინი I/we (was/were painting) painted it/them	(ა)-ვ-აშენ-ე-(თ) მე ჩვენ ის/ისინი I was/we were building/built it/them
(და)-ხატ-ე-(თ) შენ/თქვენ ის/ისინი You/you were painting/painted it/them	(ა)-აშენ-ე(თ) შენ/თქვენ ის/ისინი You/you were building/built it/ them

(და)-ხატ-ა მან ის/ისინი
He was painting/painted it/them
(და)-ხატ-ეს მათ ის/ისინი
They were painting/painted it/them

(ა)-აშენ-ა მან ის/ისინი
He was building/built it/them
(ა)-აშენ-ეს მათ ის/ისინი
They were building/built it/them

(და)-ვ-ვარცხნ-ე(თ) მე/ჩვენ ის/ისინი
I was/we were combing/combed him/them

(და)-ვ-ატკბ-ე-(თ) მე/ჩვენ ის/ისინი
I was/we were delighting/delighted him/them

(და)-ვარცხნ-ე-(თ) შენ/თქვენ ის/ისინი
You/you were combing/combed him/them

(და)-ატკბ-ე(თ) შენ/თქვენ ის/ისინი
You/you were delighting/delighted him/them

(და)-ვარცხნ-ა მან ის/ისინი
He was combing/combed him/them
(და)-ვარცხნ-ეს მათ ის/ისინი
They were combing/combed him/them

(და)-ატკბ-ო მან ის/ისინი
He was delighting/delighted him/them
(და)-ატკბ-ეს მათ ის/ისინი
They were delighting/delighted him/them

Some verbs in the aorist have the suffix -**ი** instead of -**ე** in the first- and second-person forms. In the third-person singular forms, it is replaced with the ending -**ა** and with -**ეს** in the third-person plural forms.

(და)-ვ-წვ-**ი**-(თ) მე/ჩვენ ის/ისინი
I was/we were burning/burnt it/them

(გა)-ვ-უშვ-**ი**-(თ) მე/ჩვენ ის/ისინი
I was/we were letting/let him/them go

(და)-წვ-**ი**-(თ) შენ/თქვენ ის/ისინი
You/you were burning/burnt it/them

(გა)-უშვ-**ი**-(თ) შენ/თქვენ ის/ისინი
You/you were letting/let him/them go

(და)-წვ-ა მან ის/ისინი
He was burning/burnt it/them
(და)-წვ-ეს მათ ის/ისინი
They were burning/burnt it/them

(გა)-უშვ-ა მან ის/ისინი
He was letting/let him/them go
(გა)-უშვ-ეს მათ ის/ისინი
They were letting/let him/them go

The ablaut group includes verbs with no root vowel in I series, but the vowels **ა** or **ე** appear in II series. This happens especially in the verbs with P/FSF -**ი**. In II series P/FSF -**ი** is dropped and the root vowels **ა** or **ე** is restored.

Conjugation of ablaut verbs in the aorist

There are two groups of the ablaut verbs. Some verbs with the root vowel *ე* have it replaced with the vowel *ი* in II series:

ვკრეფ – ვკრიფე (I pick, I picked)
ვგრეხ – ვგრიხე (I twist, I twisted)
ვ-ჩხვლეტ – ვ-ჩხვლიტე (I prick, I pricked).

(და)-ვ-კრიფ-ე-(თ) მე/ჩვენ ის/ისინი I was/we were picking/picked it/them	(და)-ვ-ჩხვლიტ-ე-(თ) მე/ჩვენ ის/ისინი I was/we were stinging/stung him/them
(და)-კრიფ-ე-(თ) შენ/თქვენ ის/ისინი You/you were picking/picked it/them	(და)-ჩხვლიტ-ე-(თ) შენ/თქვენ ის/ისინი You/you were stinging/stung him/them
(და)-კრიფ-ა მან ის/ისინი He was picking/picked it/them	(და)-ჩხვლიტ-ა მან ის/ისინი He was stinging/stung him/them.
(და)-კრიფ-ეს მათ ის/ისინი They were picking/picked it/them	(და)-ჩხვლიტ-ეს მათ ის/ისინი They were stinging/stung him/them

Similarly, the stem of verbs ending with -*ევ* and -*ენ* changes in the I and II series.

Verbs ending with ევ *(Present: ვ- ა- მჩნევ)*	*Verbs ending with ენ* *(Present: ვ- ა- დგენ)*
(შე)-ვ-ა-მჩნი□-ე-(თ) მე/ჩვენ მას/მათ ის I was/we were noticing/noticed it in him/them	(და)-ვ-ა-დგინ-ე-(თ) მე/ჩვენ ის I was/we were deciding/decided it
(შე)-ა-მჩნი□-ე-(თ) შენ/თქვენ მას/მათ ის You/you were noticing/noticed it in him/them	(და)-ა-დგინ-ე-(თ) შენ/თქვენ ის You/you were deciding/decided it
(შე)-ა-მჩნი□-ა მან მას/მათ ის He was noticing/noticed it in him/her/them	(და)-ა-დგინ-ა მან ის He was deciding/decided it
(შე)-ა-მჩნი□-ეს მათ მას/მათ ის They were noticing/noticed it in him/them	(და)-ა-დგინ-ეს მათ ის They were deciding/decided it

P/FSF	*Present/future*	*Aorist*
-ავ	(მო)-ვ-კ□ლ-ავ I (will) kill	(მო)-ვ-კალ-ი I was killing/killed
	(შე)-ვ-კ□რ-ავ I (will) tie	(შე)-ვ-კარ-ი I was tying/tied
	(და)-ვ-ძ□რ-ავ I (will) move	(და)-ვ-ძარ-ი I was moving/moved
	(და)-ვ-წ□ნ-ავ I (will) weave	(და)-ვ-წან-ი I was weaving/weaved
-ებ	(და)-ვ-ასწ□რ-ებ I (will) get on time	(და)-ვ-ასწარ-ი I was getting/got on time
	(და)-ვ-აკ□ლ-ებ I (will) reduce	(და)-ვ-აკელ-ი I was reducing/reduced
	(გა)-ვ-ძ□ლ-ებ I (will) endure	(გა)-ვ-ძელ-ი I was enduring/endured
-ი	(გა)-ვ-შ□ლ-ი I (will) spread	(გა)-ვ-შალ-ე I was spreading/spread
	(გა)-ვ-თ□ლ-ი I (will) whittle	(გა)-ვ-თალ-ე I was whittling/whittled
	(მი)-ვ-უძღვ□ნ-ი I (will) dedicate	(მი)-ვ-უძღვენ-ი I was dedicating/dedicated
	(შე)-ვ-ქმ□ნ-ი I (will) create	(შე)-ვ-ქმენ-ი I was creating/created
	(გა)-ვ-ხს□ნ-ი I (will) open	(გა)-ვ-ხსენ-ი I was opening/opened
	(გა)-ვ-ც□რ-ი I (will) sift	(გა)-ვ-ცერ-ი I was sifting/sifted
-ობ	(შე)-ვ-იგრძ□ნ-ობ I (will) feel	(შე)-ვ-იგრძენ-ი I felt
	(მი)-ვ-არყდ□ნ-ობ I (will) lean	(მი)-ვ-აყრდენ-ი I leaned
	(და)-ვ-იპყ□რ-ობ I (will) conquer	(და)-ვ-იპყარ-ი I conquered
	(გა)-ვ-იც□ნ-ობ I (will) get acquainted	(გა)-ვ-იცან-ი I got acquainted
-ოფ	(და)-ვ-ყ□-ოფ I (will) divide	(და)-ვ-ყავ-ი I divided

The suffix *-ე* as an aorist marker occurs more frequently than any other. It is used with the one-stem and two-stem verbs. The verbs changing their root vowels belong to a subcategory of the one-stem verbs.

There are some exceptions like:

ვ-ხატ-ავ – (და)-ვ-ხატ-ე, but ვ-ფქვ-ავ – (და)-ვ-ფქ-ვ-ი.
Some verbs in the aorist have the suffix -ო instead of -ა as the marker of the third-person singular form: დარგ-ო (he planted), აგ-ო (he built), აქ-ო (he praised), აანთ-ო (he lit), აავს-ო (he filled), დაიწყ-ო (he started), გაათბ-ო (he warmed up), დააცხ-ო (he baked).

These verbs have a regular *-ეს* marker in the third-person plural forms:
აავს-ო – აავს-ეს (he filled – they filled)
დაიწყ-ო – დაიწყ-ეს (he started – they started)
გაათბ-ო – გაათბ-ეს (he warmed up – they warmed up)
დააცხ-ო – დააცხ-ეს (he baked – they baked)

და-ვ-რგ-ე-(თ) მე /ჩვენ ის/ისინი I/we planted it/them	(შე)-ვ-აქ-ე-(თ) მე/ჩვენ ის/ისინი I/we praised him/them
(და)-რგ-ე-(თ) შენ/თქვენ ის/ისინი You/you planted it/them	(შე)-აქ-ე-(თ) შენ/თქვენ ის/ისინი You/you praised him/them
(და)-რგ-ო მან ის/ისინი He planted it/them	(შე)-აქ-ო მან ის/ისინი He praised him/them
(და)-რგ-ეს მათ ის/ისინი They planted it/them	(შე)-აქ-ეს მათ ის/ისინი They praised him/them

II conjugation verbs in the aorist

II conjugation verbs, i.e. dynamic passive voice verbs, in II series tenses drop the P/FSF *-ებ* or *-ობ*, which they have in their I series forms. In some verbs it leads to restoration of their root vowel, truncated in I series:

ვ-ი-**შლ**-ებ-ი (present) – I am being expunged.
წა-ვ-ი-**შალ**-ე (aorist) – I got expunged.

-ი and *-ე* prefixal passive voice verbs have an aorist marker *-ე*. Verbs with the suffix *-დ* and those without any markers have an Aorist marker *-ი*. The tense marker *-ე* or *-ი* is added always to the first- and second-person forms, while in the third-person forms it has -ა or -ო in singular, and *-ნენ* in plural.

The passive voice verbs derived from active voice verbs with an alternating root vowel change the vowel in I series forms:

active voice *გრეხს* (twists) – passive *იგრიხება* (is twisted)
ჭყლეტს (he crushes) – *ჭყლიტა* (he crushed)

The stem with the restored vowel is used in II series.

The following chart shows all markers occurring in II conjugation verbs.

The passive voice verbs			
Monopersonal verbs Present/Future	*Monopersonal verbs Aorist*	*Bipersonal verbs Present/Future*	*Bipersonal verbs Aorist*
Passive verbs without markers			
(გა)-ვ-თბ-ებ-ი I (will) warm up	გა-ვ-თბ-ი I warmed up		
(გა)-თბ-ებ-ა He will warm/ warms up	გა-თბ-ა He warmed up		
Passive verbs with ი- prefix		**Passive verbs with ე- prefix**	
(ჩა)-ვ-ი-წერ-ებ-ი I (will) get written in	(ჩა)-ვ-ი-წერ-ე I got (myself) written in his roster	(ჩა)-ვ-ე-წერ-ებ-ი I (will) get enlisted	(ჩა)-ვ-ე-წერ-ე I got enlisted in (his roster)
(ჩა)-ი-წერ-ებ-ა He will get/gets written in	(ჩა)-ი-წერ-ა He got himself written in his roster	(ჩა)-ე-წერ-ებ-ა He will get/gets enlisted	(ჩა)-ე-წერ-ა ის მას He got enlisted in (his roster)
(გა)-ვ-ი-ზ□რდ-ებ-ი I (will) grow up	(გა)-ვ-ი-ზარდ-ე I grew up	(გა)-ვ-ე-ზ□რდ-ებ-ი I (will) grow up (for someone)	(გა)-ვ-ე-ზარდ-ე I grew up (for someone)
(გა)-ი-ზ□რდ-ებ-ა He will grow/ grows up	(გა)-ი-ზარდ-ა He grew up	(გა)-ე-ზ□რდ-ებ-ა He will grow/ grows up (for someone)	(გა)-ე-ზარდ-ა He grew up (for someone)
(და)-ვ-ი-ხატ-ებ-ი I (will) get painted	(და)-ვ-ი-ხატ-ე I got painted	(და)-ვ-ე-ხატ-ებ-ი I (will) get painted (on something)	(და)-ვ-ე-ხატ-ე I got painted (on something)
(და)-ი-ხატ-ებ-ა He will get/gets painted	(და)-ი-ხატ-ა He got painted	(და)-ე-ხატ-ებ-ა He will get/ gets painted (on something)	(და)-ე-ხატ-ა He got painted (on something)

The passive voice verbs			
Monopersonal verbs Present/Future	*Monopersonal verbs Aorist*	*Bipersonal verbs Present/Future*	*Bipersonal verbs Aorist*
(გა)-ვ-წითლ-დ-ები I (will) blush (გა)-წითლ-დ-ება He (will) blushes	გა-ვ-წ-ითლ-დ-ი I blushed გა-წითლ-დ-ა He blushed		
(გა)-ვ-ი-ყ□-ოფ-ი I get divided (გა)-ი-ყ-ოფ-ა He gets divided	გა-ვ-ი-ყავ-ი I got divided გა-ი-ყ-ო He got divided		
A small number of verbs do not change the root vowel in passive but get -ებ-ი ending. (და)-ვ-ი-გრიხ-ები I get twisted (და)-ი-გრიხ-ება He gets twisted (გა)-ვ-ი-ჭყლიტ-ები I get squashed (გა)-ი-ჭყლიტ-ება He gets squashed	და-ვ-ი-გრიხ-ე I got twisted და-ი-გრიხ-ა He got twisted გა-ვ-ი-ჭყლიტ-ე I got squashed გა-ი-ჭყლიტ-ა He got squashed		
Some vowel-changing verbs lose their root vowel; compare with active voice verb roots: სხლეტ-სხლიტ (გა)-ვ-სხლ□ტ-ები I (will) slip out (გა)-სხლ□ტ-ება He (will) slip out	(გა)-ვ-სხლ□ტ-ი I slipped out (გა)-სხლ□ტ-ა He slipped out		

The specific features of II conjugation verbs and morphemes constituting them can be presented in the following chart:

Preverb	*Subject marker*	*Passive voice marker*	*Root*	*Passive voice marker*	*Tense ending*	*Subject marker*
და	ვ		ტკბ		ი	
და			ტკბ			ა
და	ვ		სახლ	დ	ი	
და			სახლ	დ		ა
და	ვ	ი	გრიხ		ე	
და		ი	გრიხ			ა
გა	ვ	ე	ზარდ		ე	
გა		ე	ზარდ			ა

Aorist of II conjugation verbs

Monopersonal verbs	*Bipersonal verbs*
(და)-ვ-ი-ხატ-ე-(თ) მე/ჩვენ I/we got painted	(და)-ვ-ე-ხატ-ე-(თ) მე/ჩვენ მას I/we got painted (on something)
(და)-ი-ხატ-ე-(თ) შენ/ჩვენ You/you got painted	(და)-ე-ხატ-ე-(თ) შენ/ჩვენ მას You/you got painted (on something)
(და)-ი-ხატ-ა ის He got painted	(და)-ე-ხატ-ა ის მას He got painted (on something)
(და)-ი-ხატ-ნენ ისინი They got painted	(და)-ე-ხატ-ნენ ისინი მას They got painted (on something)

II conjugation verbs without P/FSF and those with suffix -დ

Monopersonal verbs		*Bipersonal verbs*
გა-ვ-თბ-ი-(თ) მე/ჩვენ I/we got warmed up	და-ვ-ბერ-დ-ი-(თ) მე/ჩვენ I/we got old	გა-ვ-უ-სხლტ-ი-(თ) მე/ჩვენ მას/მათ I/we slipped away from him/them

Monopersonal verbs		*Bipersonal verbs*
გა-თბი-(თ) შენ/თქვენ You/you got warmed up	და-ბერ-დ-ი-(თ) შენ/თქვენ You/you got old	გა-უ-სხლტ-ი-(თ) შენ/თქვენ მას/მათ You/you slipped away from them/them
გა-თბ-ა ის He got warmed up გა-თბ-ნენ ისინი They got warmed up	და-ბერ-დ-ა ის He got old და-ბერ-დ-ნენ ისინი They got old	გა-უ-სხლტ-ა ის მას/მათ He slipped away from him/them გა-უ-სხლტ-ნენ ისინი მას/მათ They slipped away from him/them

III conjugation verbs in the aorist

III conjugation verbs, i.e. medio-active verbs, have the suffix -ე in the aorist. All verbs lose their P/FSF and monopersonal medio-active verbs acquire the prefix -ი, indicating self-directed action.

Present		*Aorist*	
ქუხს	thunders	იქუხა	thundered
გორავს	rolls around	იგორა	rolled around
ფეთქავს	pulsates	იფეთქა	pulsated
მეგობრობს	is friendly with	იმეგობრა	was friendly with

Medio-active verbs with an alternating root vowel have the vowel -ე replaced with -ი in II series:

Present		*Aorist*	
სწყენს	harms him	აწყინა	harmed him
ფრენს	flies	იფრინა	flew
სტვენს	whistles	ისტვინა	whistled

Conjugation of medio-active verbs in the aorist

ვ-ი-ცურ-ე-(თ) მე/ჩვენ I/we swam	ვ-ი-მეგობრ-ე-(თ) მე/ჩვენ I was/we were a friend/friends
ი-ცურ-ე-(თ) შენ/თქვენ You/you swam	ი-მეგობრ-ე-(თ) შენ/თქვენ You/you were a friend/friends
ი-ცურ-ა მან He swam	ი-მეგობრ-ა მან He was a friend
ი-ცურ-ეს მათ They swam	ი-მეგობრ-ეს მათ They were friends

Conjugation of medio-active ablaut verbs

Present/future ვ-(ი)-ფრენ	Present/future მ-(ა)-წყენ-ს
ვ-ი-ფრინ-ე-(თ) მე/ჩვენ I/we flew around	მ-ა-წყინ-ა მან მე It harmed me
ი-ფრინ-ე-(თ) შენ/თქვენ You/you flew around	გ-ა-წყინ-ა მან შენ It harmed you
ი-ფრინ-ა მან He flew around	ა-წყინ-ა მან მას It harmed him
ი-ფრინ-ეს მათ They flew around	ა-წყინ-ეს მათ მას They harmed him

A few medio-active verbs get an additional consonant, or even a syllable preceding the Aorist marker. These additions are probably crossovers from their active mode forms:

Present	ვ-კივ-ი მე I scream	ვ -ქრ-ი მე I blow	ვ-თრთ-ი მე I tremble
Aorist	ვ-ი-კივლ-ე მე I screamed	ვ-ი-ქროლ-ე მე I blew	ვ-ი-თრთოლ-ე მე I trembled
Active mode	ა-კივლ-ა მან ის He made him scream	ა-ქროლ-ა მან ის He made him blow	ა-ათრთოლ-ა მან ის He made him tremble

Aorist

ვ-ი-კივლ-ე-(თ) მე/ჩვენ I/we screamed	ვ-ი-ქროლ-ე-(თ) მე/ჩვენ I/we blew	ვ-ი-თრთოლ-ე-(თ) მე/ჩვენ I/we trembled

ი-კივლ-ე-(თ) შენ/თქვენ You/you screamed	ი-ქროლ-ე-(თ) შენ/თქვენ You/you blew	ი-თრთოლ-ე-(თ) შენ/თქვენ You/you trembled
ი-კივლ-ა მან He screamed	ი-ქროლ-ა მან It blew	ი-თრთოლ-ა მან It trembled
ი-კივლ-ეს მათ They screamed	ი-ქროლ-ეს მათ They blew	ი-თრთოლ-ეს მათ They trembled

Bipersonal medio-active verbs in the aorist

Only a small group of bipersonal medio-active verbs have II series forms: *ვდარაჯობ* (I guard), *ვმტრობ* (I am an enemy of), *ვპატრონობ* (I take care of), *ვყარაულობ* (I guard), *ვხელმძღვანელობ* (I lead), *ვშველი* (I help). In II series forms they have the prefix -*უ*, indicating the action directed towards or for the benefit of others. They also have the suffix -*ე* as the tense marker in the first- and second-person forms. For the third-person singular and plural forms they have -*ა* and -*ეს* endings, respectively.

ვ-უ-დარაჯ-ე-(თ) მე /ჩვენ მას I/we guarded it	ვ-უ-ხელმძღვანელ-ე-(თ) მე/ჩვენ მას/მათ I/we led/organized it/them
უ-დარაჯ-ე-(თ) შენ/თქვენ მას You/you guard it	უ-ხელმძღვანელ-ე-(თ) შენ/თქვენ მას/მათ You/you led/organize it/them
უ-დარაჯ-ა მან მას He guarded it	უ-ხელმძღვანელ-ა მან მას/მათ He led/organized it/them
უ-დარაჯ-ეს მათ მას They guarded it	უ-ხელმძღვანელ-ეს მათ მას/მათ They led/organized it/them

მ-აჯობ-ა მან მე He bested me	მ-ა-ჯობ-ეს მათ მე They bested me
გვ-ა-ჯობ-ა მან ჩვენ He bested us	გვ-ა-ჯობ-ეს მათ ჩვენ They bested us
გ-ა-ჯობ-ა-(თ) მან შენ/თქვენ He bested you/you	გ-ა-ჯობ-ეს მათ თქვენ They bested you
ა-ჯობ-ა მან მას/მათ He bested him/them	ა-ჯობ-ეს მათ მას/მათ They bested him/them

IV conjugation verbs in the aorist

Passive voice static verbs are replaced with the passive voice verbs with the prefix *-ე* in II series forms:

Present	ვ-ხატი-ვ-არ I am painted on	ვ-წერ-ი-ვ-არ I am written in	ვ-გდ-ი-ვ-არ I am lying
Aorist	ვ-ე-ხატ-ე I was painted on	ვ-ე-წერ-ე I was written in	ვ-ე-გდ-ე I was lying

Conjugation of static verbs in aorist medio-passive verbs

ვ-ი-დექი-(თ) მე /ჩვენ I was/we were standing	ვ-ი-წექ-ი-(თ) მე/ჩვენ I was/we were lying down
და-ვ-დექ-ი-(თ) მე /ჩვენ I/we stood	და-ვ-წექ-ი-(თ) მე/ჩვენ I/we lay down
ი-დექი-(თ) შენ/თქვენ You/you were standing	წევ-ხ-არ(თ) შენ/თქვენ You//you are lying down
და-დექ-ი-(თ) შენ/თქვენ You/you stood	და-წექ-ი-(თ) შენ/თქვენ You/you lay down
ი-დგ-ა ის He was standing	ი-წვ-ა ის He was lying down
და-დგ-ა ის He stood	და-წვ-ა ის He lay down
ი-დგნ-ნენ ისინი They were standing	ი-წვ-ნენ ისინი They were lying down
და-დგ-ნენ ისინი They stood	და-წვ-ნენ ისინი They lay down

(მო)-ვ-ჩან-დ-ი მე I was seen	(მო)-ვ-ჩან-დ-ი-(თ) ჩვენ We were seen
(მო)-ჩან-დ-ი შენ You were seen	(მო)-ჩან-დ-ი-თ თქვენ You were seen
(მო)-ჩან-დ-ა ის He was seen	(მო)-ჩან-დ-ნენ ისინი They were seen

Aorist of bipersonal verbs

(და)-მ-ე-ვალ-ა ის მე I was charged with it (a task)	მ-ე-გონ-ა ის მე It seemed to me
(და)-გვ-ე-ვალ-ა ის ჩვენ We were charged with it	გვ-ე-გონ-ა ის ჩვენ It seemed to us

(და)-გ-ე-ვალ-ა ის შენ	გ-ე-გონ-ა ის შენ
You were charged with it	It seemed to you
(და)-გ-ე-ვალ-ა-თ ის თქვენ	გ-ე-გონ-ა-თ ის თქვენ
You were charged with it	It seemed to you
(და)-ე-ვალ-ა ის მას	ე-გონ-ა ის მას
He was charged with it	It seemed to him
(და)-ე-ვალ-ა-(თ) ის მათ	ე-გონ-ა-(თ) ის მათ
They were charged with it	It seemed to them

The following verbs are conjugated similarly: *მეკიდა* (it was hanging on me), *მეფინა* (it was spread over me), *მეფარა* (it was put over me), *მეყარა* (it was thrown on me), *მეკერა* (it was sewn on me), *მეხატა* (it was painted on me), *მერტყა* (it was tied around me), *მეცხო* (it was smeared on me), and so on.

9.6.2.2 *Optative*

The optative is defined as the II subjunctive, which points at its position in the subsystem of subjunctive tenses in the Georgian verb system. The tense and mood it implies belong to the II series group of verbs. The optative denotes a desired, necessary, possible, or intended action in the future. Verbs in the optative are often used together with words indicating modality *ნეტავ*, *უნდა*, *საჭიროა*, and *რომ*:

ეს სამუშაო **უნდა დავასრულო.**
I *have to finish* this work.
ეს სამუშაო **რომ დავასრულო,** ბევრი დრო მჭირდება.
To finish this work, I need a lot of time.
ნეტავ მალე **დავასრულო** ეს სამუშაო.
I wish I could/would finish this work soon.

While the present subjunctive denotes desired or intended action at some unspecified time or at this very moment, the optative refers to such action in the future:

ნეტავ ჩემს დისერტაციას უკვე ***ვ-ამთავრ-ებ-დ-ე*** (present subjunctive).
I wish I were already finishing my dissertation.
ნეტავ ჩემი დისერტაცია მალე ***დავამთავრ-ო*** (optative).
I wish to finish my dissertation soon.
ხილს ამ მაღაზიაში უნდა ***ყიდულ-ობ-დ-ე*** (present subjunctive).
You should buy fruit in this store.
ხვალ ხილი ამ მაღაზიაში უნდა ***იყ-ი-დ-ო*** (optative).
Tomorrow you should buy fruit in this store.

ბავშვი აქ არ უნდა ***თამაშ-ობ-დ-ე-ს*** (present subjunctive).
A child should not play/be playing here.
ბავშვმა აქ ***ითამაშ-ო-ს*** (optative)
Let the child play here.

Verbs in the optative are used to convey a request or order to the third person.

დღეს სადილი ნინომ ***გააკეთოს.***
Let Nino make the dinner today.
უთხარი შენ ძმას, ჩემი წიგნი ***დამიბრუნოს.***
Tell your brother to return my book/to give my book back.
დღეს არავინ ***დამირეკოს!***
Nobody should call me today!

Verbs in the optative may convey the perfective or imperfective aspect, depending on the presence or absence of the preverb. The optative is based on the aorist forms of verbs in accordance with their conjugation type.

I conjugation verbs in the optative

Aorist		*Optative*	
-ე	დავწერ-ე I wrote	-ო	დავწერ-ო I should write
-ი	გავუშვ-ი I released	-ა	გავუშვ-ა I should release
	დავძარ-ი I moved (a car)		დავძრ-ა I should move
-ი	დავასწარ-ი I got ahead (of someone)	-ო	დავასწრ-ო I should get ahead
	an exception		
-ი	მივეც-ი I gave	-ე	მივც-ე I should give

The verbs in the optative always have a tense marker unlike in the aorist where the tense marker is absent in the third-person forms:

დაწერ-ა – დაწერ-**ო**-ს (write); გაუშვ-ა – გაუშვ-**ა**-ს (let go)
დაძრ-ა – დაძრ-**ა**-ს (move); დაასწრ-ო – დაასწრ-**ო**-ს (outrun, get ahead of someone)

One-stem verbs in the optative

(და)-ვ-წერ-ო-(თ) მე/ჩვენ ის/ისინი
I/we should write it/them

ვ-თხოვ-ო მე მას ის (დახმარება)
I should ask him (for) it
(help)მო-ვ-თხოვ-ო მე მას ის (პასუხი)
I should demand it (an answer) from him

(და)-წერ-ო-(თ) შენ/თქვენ ის/ისინი
You/you should write it/them

ს-თხოვ-ო შენ მას ის (დახმარება)
You (should) ask him (for) it (help)
მო-ს-თხოვ-ო შენ მას ის (პასუხი)
You should demand it (an answer) (from) him

(და)-წერ-ო-ს მან ის/ისინი
He should write it/them
(და)-წერ-ო-ნ მათ ის/ისინი
They should write it/them

ს-თხოვ-ო-ს მან მას ის (დახმარება)
He should ask him (for) it (help)
მო-ს-თხოვ-ო-ს მან მას ის (პასუხი)
He should demand it (an answer) (from) him
ს-თხოვ-ო-ნ მათ მას ის (დახმარება)
They should ask him (for) it (help)
მო-ს-თხოვ-ო-ნ მან მას ის (პასუხი)
They should demand it (an answer) (from) him

Two-stem verbs in the optative

(და)-ვ-ხატ-ო-(თ)მე/ჩვენის/ისინი
I/we should paint it/them
(და)-ხატ-ო-(თ) შენ/თქვენ ის/ისინი
You/you should paint it/them
(და)-ხატ-ო-ს მან ის/ისინი
He should paint it/them
(და)-ხატ-ო-ნ მათ ის/ისინი
They should paint it/them

(ა)-ვ-აშენ-ო-(თ) მე/ჩვენ ის/ისინი
I/we should build it/them
(ა)-აშენ-ო- (თ) შენ/თქვენ ის/ისინი
You/you should build it/them
(ა)-აშენ-ო-ს მან ის/ისინი
He should build it/them
(ა)-აშენ-ო-ნ მათ ის/ისინი
They should build it/them

(და)-ვ-ვარცხნ-ო-(თ) მე/ჩვენ ის/ისინი I/we should comb him/them	(და)-ვ-ატკბ-ო-(თ) მე/ჩვენ ის/ისინი I/we should delight him/them
(და)-ვარცხნ-ო-(თ) შენ/თქვენ ის/ისინი You/you should comb him/them	(და)-ატკბ-ო-(თ) შენ/თქვენ ის/ისინი You/you should delight him/them
(და)-ვარცხნ-ო-ს მან ის/ისინი He should comb him/them	(და)-ატკბ-ო-ს მან ის/ისინი He should delight him/them
(და)-ვარცხნ-ო-ნ მათ ის/ისინი They should comb him/them	(და)-ატკბ-ო-ნ მათ ის/ისინი They should delight him/them

Ablaut verbs

Ablaut verbs include the following:

1. **Verbs with root vowel *-ე-* , which is replaced with *-ი-* in II series**

(Present: ვ- კრეფ)	*(Present: ვ- ჩხვლეტ)*
(და)-ვ-კრიფ-ო-(თ) მე/ჩვენ ის/ისინი I/we should pick it/them	(და)-ვ-ჩხვლიტ-ო-(თ) მე/ჩვენ ის/ისინი I/we should prick it/them
(და)-კრიფ-ო-(თ) შენ/თქვენ ის/ისინი You/you should pick it/them	(და)-ჩხვლიტ-ო-(თ) შენ/თქვენ ის/ისინი You/you should prick it/them
(და)-კრიფ--ო-ს მან ის/ისინი He should pick it/them	(და)-ჩხვლიტ-ო-ს მან ის/ისინი He should prick it/them
(და)-კრიფ-ო-ნ მათ ის/ისინი They should pick it/them	(და)-ჩხვლიტ-ო-ნ მათ ის/ისინი They should prick it/them

2. **Verbs ending with - *ევ*; verbs ending with - *ენ***

(Present: ვ- ამჩნევ)	*(Present: ვ- ადგენ)*
(შე)-ვ-ა-მჩნი□-ო-(თ) მე/ჩვენ მას ის I/we should notice it (in) him	(და)-ვ-ა-დგ-ინ-ო-(თ) მე/ჩვენ ის I/we should ascertain it

(Present: ვ- ამჩნევ)	(Present: ვ- ადგენ)
(შე)-ა-მჩნ-ი□-ო-(თ) შენ/თქვენ მას ის You/you should notice it (in) him	(და)-ა-დგ-ინ-ო-(თ) შენ/თქვენ ის You/you should ascertain it
(შე)-ა-მჩნ-ი□-ო-ს მან მას ის He should notice it (in) him	(და)-ა-დგ-ინ-ო-ს მან ის He should ascertain it
(შე)-ა-მჩნ-ი□-ო-ნ მათ მას ის They should notice it (in) him	(და)-ადგ-ინ-ო-ნ მათ ის They should ascertain it

3. **Verbs of the I conjugation with the - *ი* aorist marker**

These verbs have the suffix -ა in the optative:

(და)-ვ-წვ-ა-(თ) მე/ჩვენ ის/ისინი I/we should burn it/them	(გა)-ვ-უშვ-ა-(თ) მე/ჩვენ ის/ისინი I/we should release him
(და)-წვ-ა-(თ) შენ/თქვენ ის/ისინი You/you should burn it/them	(გა)-უშვ-ა-(თ) შენ/თქვენ ის/ისინი You/you should release him
(და)-წვ-ა-ს მან ის/ისინი He should burn it/them	(გა)-უშვ-ა-ს მან ის/ისინი He should release him
(და)-წვ-ა-ნ მათ ის/ისინი They should burn it/them	(გა)-უშვ-ა-ნ მათ ის/ისინი They should release him

Ablaut verbs with no root vowel in I series, have their root vowels -ა or -*ე* restored when their P/FSF is dropped in aorist. The majority of these verbs have no root vowel in the optative.

In the following chart, all verbs are in the first-person singular forms.

Present/future	*Aorist*	*Optative*
(მო)-ვ-კ□ლ-ავ I will kill	(მო)-ვ-კალ-ი I killed	(მო)-ვ-კ□ლ-ა I should kill
(შე)-ვ-კ□რ-ავ I will tie	(შე)-ვ-კარ-ი I tied	(შე)-ვ-კ□რ-ა I should ties
(და)-ვ-ძ□რ-ავ I will move	(და)-ვ-ძარ-ი I moved	(და)-ვ-ძ□რ-ა I should move
(და)-ვ-წ□ნ-ავ I will plait	(და)-ვ-წან-ი I plaited	(და)-ვ-წ□ნ-ა I should plait

(*Continued*)

(Continued)

Present/future	*Aorist*	*Optative*
(და)-ვ-ასწ□რ-ებ I will get ahead	(და)-ვ-ასწარ-**ი** I got ahead	(და)-ვ-ასწ□რ-**ო** I should get ahead
(და)-ვ-აკ□ლ-ებ I will lessen	(და)-ვ-აკელ-ი I lessened	(და)-ვ-აკ□ლ-ო I should lessen
(გა)-ვ-ძ□ლ-ებ I will endure	(გა)-ვ-ძელ-ი I endured	(გა)-ვ-ძ□ლ-ო I should endure
(გა)-ვ-შ□ლ-ი I will spread	(გა)-ვ-შალ-ე I spread	(გა)-ვ-შალ-ო I should spread
(გა)-ვ-თ□ლ-ი I will whittle	(გა)-ვ-თალ-ე I whittled	(გა)-ვ-თალ-ო I should whittle
(მი)-ვ-უძღვ□ნ-ი I will dedicate	(მი)-ვ-უძღვენ-ი I dedicated	(მი)-ვ-უძღვ□ნ-ა I should dedicate
(შე)-ვ-ქმ□ნ-ი I will create	(შე)-ვ-ქმენ-ი I created	(შე)-ვ-ქმ□ნ-ა I should create
(გა)-ვ-ხს□ნ-ი I will open	(გა)-ვ-ხსენ-ი I opened	(გა)-ვ-ხს□ნ-ა I should open
(გა)-ვ-ც□რ-ი I will sift	(გა)-ვ-ცერ-ი I sifted	(გა)-ვ-ც□რ-ა I should sift
(შე)-ვ-იგრძ□ნ-ობ I will feel	(შე)-ვ-იგრძენ-ი I felt	(შე)-ვ-იგრძ□ნ-ო I should feel
(მი)-ვ-არყდ□ნ-ობ I will lean	(მი)-ვ-აყრდენ-ი I leaned	(მი)-ვ-არყდ□ნ-ო I should lean
(და)-ვ-იპყ□რ-ობ I will conquer	(და)-ვ-იპყარ-ი I conquerred	(და)-ვ-იპყ□რ-ო I should conquer
(გა)-ვ-იც□ნ-ობ I will become acquainted with	(გა)-ვ-იცან-ი I became acquainted with	(გა)-ვ-იც□ნ-ო I should become acquainted with
(და)-ვ-ყ□-ოფ I will divide	(და)-ვ-ყავ-ი I divided	(და)-ვ-ყ□ – ო I should divide

As the chart shows, verbs with *Ø-ა/ე* root vowel may change in a number of ways in the optative. The majority of these verbs lose their root vowel, but there are a few that do not, like *თალ* (*გავ**თალ**ო*, should whittle) and *შალ* (*გავ**შალ**ო*, should erase). In addition, this type of ablaut verbs has the suffixes -**ო** or -**ა** as the optative markers. As a rule, I conjugation verbs with the suffix -*ე* in the aorist have the suffix -**ო** in the optative, those with the suffix -ი have suffix -**ა**.

(გა)-ვ-შალ-ო-(თ)
მე/ჩვენ ის
I/we should spread it
(გა)-შალ-ო-(თ)
მე/ჩვენ ის
You/you should
spread it
(გა)-შალ-ო-ს მან ის
He should spread it
(გა)-შალ-ო-ნ მათ ის
They should spread it

(და)-ვ-ყ-ო მე ის
I should divide it
(და)-ყ-ო(თ)
შენ/თქვენ ის
You/you should
divide it
(და)-ყ-ო-ს მან ის
He should divide it
(და)-ყ-ო-ნ მათ ის
They should divide it

(გა)-ვ-ხსნ-ა მე ის
I should untie it
(გა)-ხსნ-ა-(თ)
შენ/თქვენ ის
You/you should
untie it
(გა)-ხსნ-ა-ს მან ის
He should open it
(გა)-ხსნ-ა-ნ მათ ის
They should open it

II conjugation verbs in the optative

Aorist		*Optative*	
-ე	გავეზარდ-ე I grew up (for him)	-ო	გავეზარდ-ო I should grow up (for him)
-ი	გავძვერ-ი I slipped away	-ე	გავძვრ-ე I should slip away
-ი	დავიყავ-ი I got divided	-ო	დავიყ-ო I should get divided

II conjugation verbs, i.e. dynamic-passive verbs with P/FSF *-ებ* or *-ობ* in I series drop it in II series. In some verbs this change restores their root vowel.

The following chart shows all possible modifications of the II conjugation passive verbs in the optative:

Passive voice verbs			
Monopersonal verbs Aorist	*Monopersonal verbs Optative*	*Bipersonal verbs Aorist*	*Bipersonal verbs Optative*
Verbs without markers			
გა-ვ-თბ-ი I warmed up	გა-ვ-თბ-ე I should warm up		
გა-თბ-ა He warmed up	გა-თბ-ე-ს He should warm up		

(Continued)

(Continued)

Passive voice verbs			
Monopersonal verbs Aorist	*Monopersonal verbs Optative*	*Bipersonal verbs Aorist*	*Bipersonal verbs Optative*
Verbs with prefix - ი-		**Verbs with prefix ე-**	
(ჩა) -ვ-ი-წერ-ე მე (თავი) მის სიაში I got (myself) written in his roster (ჩა)-ი-წერ-ა ის მის სიაში He got (himself) written in his roster	(ჩა) -ვ-ი-წერ-ო მე (თავი) მის სიაში I (should get (myself) written in his roster (ჩა)-ი-წერ-ო-ს ის მის სიაში He should get (himself) written in his roster	(ჩა)-ვ-ე-წერ-ე მე მას I was written in (his roster) (ჩა)-ე-წერ-ა ის მას He was written in (his roster)	(ჩა)-ვ-ე-წერ-ო მე მას I should be written in (his roster) (ჩა)-ე-წერ-ო-ს ის მას He should be written in (his roster)
(გა)-ვ-ი-ზარდ-ე I grew up (გა)-ი-ზარდ-ა He grew up	(გა)-ვ-ი-ზარდ-ო I should grow up (გა)-ი-ზარდ-ო-ს He should grow up	(გა)-ვ-ე-ზარდ-ე I grew up (for him) (გა)-ე-ზარდ-ა He grew up (for him)	(გა)-ვ-ე-ზარდ-ო I should grow up (for him) (გა)-ე-ზარდ-ო-ს He should grow up (for him)
(და)-ვ-ი-ხატ-ე I got painted (და)-ი-ხატ-ა He got painted	(და)-ვ-ი-ხატ-ო I should get painted (და)-ი-ხატ-ო-ს He should get painted	(და)-ვ-ე-ხატ-ე I got painted (on him) (და)-ე-ხატ-ა He got painted (on him)	(და)-ვ-ე-ხატ-ო I should get painted (on him) (და)-ე-ხატ-ო-ს He should get painted (on him)
გა-ვ-წითლ-დ-ი I blushed გა-წითლ-დ-ა He blushed	გა-ვ-წითლ-დ-ე I (should) blush გა-წითლ-დ-ე-ს He should blush		
და-ვ-ი-ყავ-ი I got divided და-ი-ყ-ო He got divided	და-ვ-ი-ყ-ო I should get divided და-ი-ყ-ო-ს He should get divided		

Passive voice verbs			
Monopersonal verbs Aorist	*Monopersonal verbs Optative*	*Bipersonal verbs Aorist*	*Bipersonal verbs Optative*
დავიგრიხე I got twisted	დავიგრიხო I should get twisted	დავეგრიხე I got twisted to him	დავეგრიხო I should get twisted
დაიგრიხა He got twisted	დაიგრიხოს He should get twisted	დაეგრიხოს He got twisted to him	დაეგრიხოს He should get twisted
Compare its active voice forms: გრეხს (he) twists – II გრიხა/ twisted) გავიჭყლიტე I got squashed გაიჭყლიტა He got squashed	გავიჭყლიტო I should get squashed გაიჭყლიტოს He should get squashed	გავეჭყლიტე I got squashed გაეჭყლიტოს He got squashed	გავეჭყლიტო I should get squashed გაეჭყლიტოს He got squashed

Some vowel-changing verbs lose their root vowel (compare its active voice forms):

I series: სხლეტს/pulls
II series: მო-სხლიტა/pulled
გა-ვ-სხლ□ტ-ი
I slipped away

გა-ვ-სხლ□ტ-ე
I should slip away
და-სხლ□ტ-ე-ს
He should slip away

The alteration of the *ე-ი* vowels in the ablaut verbs does not always occur and the passive verb may have a truncated root in the optative as well:

გა-ვ-სხლ□ტ-ი
I slipped away
გა-ვ-უ-სხლ□ტ-ე
I should slip away from someone

In addition, passive verbs derived from active voice verbs with alternating root vowels have their root vowel changed already in I series:

Active voice: გრეხს (twists)
Passive voice: **იგრიხ**ება (is twisted)
Optative: და**იგრიხ**ოს (it should get twisted)

Conjugation of dynamic-passive voice verbs in the optative and conjugation of verbs with prefixes

Monopersonal verbs	*Bipersonal verbs*
(და)-ვ-ი-ხატ-ო-(თ) მე/ჩვენ I/we should get painted	(და)-ვ-ე-ხატ-ო-(თ) მე/ჩვენ მას I/we should get painted on it
(და)-ი-ხატ-ო-(თ) შენ/თქვენ You/you should get painted	(და)-ე-ხატ-ო-(თ) შენ/თქვენ მას You/you should get painted on it
(და)-ი-ხატ-ო-ს ის He should get painted	(და)-ე-ხატ-ო-ს ის მას He should be painted on it
(და)-ი-ხატ-ო-ნ ისინი They should get painted	(და)-ე-ხატ-ო-ნ ისინი მას They should be painted on it

Conjugation of passive voice verbs without markers and those with the suffix -დ

Monopersonal verbs		*Bipersonal verbs*
გა-ვ-თბ-ე-(თ) მე/ჩვენ) I/we should get warmed	და-ვ-ბერ-დ-ე-(თ) მე/ჩვენ I/we should grow old	გა-ვ-უ-სხლტ-ე-(თ) მე/ჩვენ მას/მათ I/we should slip away from him/them
გა-თბ-ე-(თ) შენ/თქვენ You/you should get warmed	და-ბერ-დ-ე-(თ) შენ/თქვენ You/you should grow old	გა-უ-სხლტ-ე-(თ) შენ/თქვენ მას/მათ You/you should slip away from him/them

Monopersonal verbs		*Bipersonal verbs*
გა-თბ-ე-ს ის He should get warmed	და-ბერ-დ-ე-ს ის He should grow old	გა-უ-სხლტ-ე-ს ის მას/მათ He should slip away from him/them
გა-თბ-ნენ ისინი They should get warmed	და-ბერ-დ-ნენ ისინი They should grow old	გა-უ-სხლტ-ნენ ისინი მას/მათ They should slip away from him/them

The third-person plural forms of II conjugation verbs in the aorist and optative coincide and their meaning can be determined by the context.

გათოშილი ლეკვები **გათბნენ.**
The freezing puppies *got warmed up*.
ნეტავ გათოშილი ლეკვები **გათბნენ.**
I wish the freezing puppies would *get warmed up*.
ჩვენი მშობლები **დაბერდნენ.**
Our parents *grew* old.
ნეტავ ჩვენი მშობლები ბედნიერად **დაბერდნენ.**
I wish my parents would *grow* old happily.

Prefixal passives have different forms in the third-person plural in the aorist and optative. For example:

ისინი ტყეში **დაიკარგ-ნენ**. (Aorist)
They got lost in the forest.
ღმერთმა ნუ ქნას, რომ ტყეში **დაიკარგ-ო-ნ**. (Optative)
God forbid getting lost in the forest.
ეს ბავშვები ამ ქალაქში **გაიზარდ-ნენ**. (Aorist)
These children grew up in this city.
ნეტავ მათი შვილებიც ამ ქალაქში **გაიზარდ-ო-ნ**. (Optative)
(May) I wish these children should grow in this town as well.

III conjugation verbs in the optative

III conjugation verbs, i.e. medio-active verbs, change their aorist suffix -ე to the tense marker -ო in the optative.

Monopersonal medio-active verbs have the prefix -ი indicating subjective version:

იქუხა (thundered) – იქუხოს (should thunder)
იფრინა (flew around) – იფრინოს (should fly around)
იგორა (rolled around) – იგოროს (should roll around)
იფეთქა (blew up) – იფეთქოს (should blow up)
იმეგობრა (became friends with) – იმეგობროს (should became friends with).

The rule of the vowel alteration applies to the optative. The verbs with the *ე-ი* vowel pattern have the root vowel **-ი-**:

აწყინა (harmed) – აწყინოს (should harm)
იფრინა (flew around) – იფრინოს (should fly around)
ისტვინა (whistled) – ისტვინოს (should whistle)

Conjugation of medio-active verbs

ვ-ი-ცურ-ო-(თ) მე/ჩვენ I/we should swim	ვ-ი-მეგობრ-ო-(თ) მე/ჩვენ I/we should be a friend/friends
ი-ცურ-ო-(თ) შენ/თქვენ You/you should swim	ი-მეგობრ-ო-(თ) შენ/თქვენ You/you should be a friend/friends
ი-ცურ-ო-ს მან He should swim	ი-მეგობრ-ო-ს მან He should be a friend
ი-ცურ-ო-ნ მათ They should swim	ი-მეგობრ-ო-ნ მათ They should be friends

Conjugation of root vowel alternating medio-active verbs

ვ-ი-ფრინ-ო-(თ) მე/ჩვენ I/we should fly around	მ-ა-წყინ-ო-ს მან მე It should harm me
ი-ფრინ-ო-(თ) შენ/თქვენ You/you should fly around	გ-ა-წყინ-ო-ს მან შენ It should harm you
ი-ფრინ-ო-ს მან He should fly around	ა-წყინ-ო-ს მან მას It should harm him
ი-ფრინ-ო-ნ მათ They should fly around	ა-წყინ-ო-ნ მათ მას They should harm him

A few medio-active verbs have their roots extended in the aorist and optative with a vowel or even a syllable in front of the tense marker:

ქრი-ს (it blows/glides)
იქრ-ოლ-ა (it blew/glided)
იქრ-ოლ-ო-ს (it should blow/glide)

Aorist	ვ-ი-კივლ-ე I screamed	ვ-ი-ქროლ-ე მე I glided around	ვ-ი-თრთოლ-ე მე I trembled
Optative	ვ-ი-კივლ-ო I should scream	ვ-ი-ქროლ-ო მე I should glide around	ვ-ი-თრთოლ-ო მე I should tremble
Active voice	ა-კივლ-ა He made him scream	ა-ქროლ-ა მან ის He made him glide around	ა-ა-თრთოლ-ა მან ის He made him tremble

Optative

ვ-ი-კივლ-ო-(თ) მე/ჩვენ I/we should scream	ვ-ი-ქროლ-ო-(თ) მე/ჩვენ I/we should glide around	ვ-ი-თრთოლ-ო-თ მე/ჩვენ) I/we should tremble
ი-კივლ-ო-(თ) შენ/თქვენ You/you should scream	ი-ქროლ-ო-(თ) შენ/თქვენ You/you should glide around	ი-თრთოლ-ო-(თ) შენ/თქვენ) You/you should tremble
ი-კივლ-ო-ს მან He should scream	ი-ქროლ-ო-ს მან He should glide around	ი-თრთოლ-ო-ს მან He should tremble
ი-კივლ-ო-ნ მათ They should scream	ი-ქროლ-ო-ნ მათ They should glide around	ი-თრთოლ-ო-ნ მათ They should tremble

Bipersonal medio-active verbs

ვ-უ-დარაჯ-ო-(თ) მე/ჩვენ მას/მათ I/we should guard him	ვ-უ-ხელმძღვანელ-ო-(თ) მე/ჩვენ მას/მათ I/we should lead him
უ-დარაჯ-ო-(თ) შენ/თქვენ მას/მათ You/you should guard him	უ-ხელმძღვანელ-ო-(თ) შენ/თქვენ მას/მათ You/you should lead him
უ-დარაჯ-ო-ს მან მას/მათ He should guard him	უ-ხელმძღვანელ-ო-ს მან მას/მათ He should lead him
უ-დარაჯ-ო-ნ მათ მას/მათ They should guard him	უ-ხელმძღვანელ-ო-ნ მათ მას/მათ They should lead him

მ-ა-ჯობ-ო-ს მან მე He (should) surpass me	მ-ა-ჯობ-ო-ნ მათ მე They should surpass me
გვ-ა-ჯობ-ო-ს მან ჩვენ He should surpass us	გვ-ა-ჯობ-ო-ნ მათ ჩვენ They should surpass us
გ-ა-ჯობ-ო-ს მან შენ He should surpass you	

გ-ა-ჯობ-ო-თ მათ შენ/თქვენ
He/they should surpass you/you

გ-ა-ჯობ-ო-ნ მათ შენ/თქვენ
They should surpass you/you

ა-ჯობ-ო-ს მან მას/მათ
He should surpass him/them

ა-ჯობ-ო-ნ მათ მას/მათ
They should surpass him/them

IV conjugation verbs in the optative

Static-passive voice verbs mostly are replaced with passive verbs with the prefix *ე-* in the II series and therefore in distribution of the optative as well, which can be seen in their tense markers.

Aorist		*Optative*	
-ე	(და)-ვ-ე-ხატ-ე I got painted on	-ო	(და)-ვ-ე-ხატ-ო I should get painted on
-ი	ვ-ი-დექ-ი I stood	-ე	ვ-ი-დგ-ე I should stand

Conjugation of static verbs

A group of medio-passive verbs have different roots in the present/future and aorist tenses. Their forms in the optative are based not on the aorist but on their I series roots.

დგ (present/future) – **დექ/დგ** (aorist)
წევ/წვ (present/future) – **წექ/წვ** (aorist)

ვ-ი-დგ-ე-(თ) მე/ჩვენ
I/we should be standing

და-ვ-დგ-ე-(თ) მე/ჩვენ
I/we should stand

ი-დგ-ე-(თ) შენ/თქვენ
You/you should be standing

და-დგ-ე-(თ) შენ/თქვენ
You/you should stand

ვ-ი-წვ-ე-(თ) მე/ჩვენ
I/we should be lying down

და-ვ-წვ-ე-(თ) მე/ჩვენ
I/we should lie down

ი-წვ-ე-(თ) შენ/თქვენ
You/you should be lying down

და-წვ-ე-(თ) შენ/თქვენ
You/you should lie down

ი-დგ-ე-ს ის He should be standing	ი-წვ-ე-ს ის He should be lying down
და-დგ-ე-ს ის He should stand	და-წვ-ე-ს ის He should lie down
ი-დგ-ნენ ისინი They should be standing	ი-წვ-ნენ ისინი They should be lying down
და-დგ-ნენ ისინი They should stand	და-წვ-ნენ ისინი They should lie down

Optative of bipersonal verbs

მ-ე-ვალ-ო-ს ის მე I should be charged with it (duty)	მ-ე-გონ-ო-ს ის მე It should seem to me
გვ-ე-ვალ-ო-ს ის ჩვენ We should be charged with it	გვ-ე-გონ-ო-ს ის ჩვენ It should seem to us
გ-ე-ვალ-ო-ს ის შენ You should be charged with it	გ-ე-გონ-ო-ს ის შენ It should seem to you
გ-ე-ვალ-ო-თ ის თქვენ You should be charged with it	გ-ე-გონ-ო-თ ის თქვენ It should seem to you
ე-ვალ-ო-ს ის მას He should be charged with it	ე-გონ-ო-ს ის მას It should seem to him
ე-ვალ-ო-თ ის მათ They should be charged with it	ე-გონ-ო-თ ის მათ It should seem to them

The following verbs are conjugated similarly: *მეკიდოს* (it should be hung on me), *მეფინოს* (it should be spread over me), *მეფაროს* (it should be covered over me), *მეყაროს* (it should be strewn on me), *მეკეროს* (it should be sewn on me), *მეხატოს* (it should be painted on me), *მერტყას* (it should be circled around me), *მეწყოს* (it should be placed on me), *მეცხოს* (it should be smeared on me), and so on.

9.6.3 *III series*

9.6.3.1 *Perfect*

Verbs in the perfect tense express the past tense and indicative mood. It often implies that the subject did not witness or was not aware of the action being completed. The very name of the tense in Georgian – ***თურმეობითი*** – stems from the word ***თურმე***, meaning *apparently* and *evidently*, thus indicating the evidential character of the described action.

> *ჩვენს მეზობელს ახალი მანქანა* ***უყიდია.***
> Our neighbour (apparently) has bought a new car.
> *გიორგი გუშინ ლონდონში* ***გაფრენილა.***
> George (apparently) has gone (lit. *flown*) to London.
> *ეს ეკლესია მეათე საუკუნეში* ***აუშენებიათ.***
> They (apparently) have built this church in the 10th century.
> *კრება ხვალისთვის* ***გადაუტანიათ.***
> They (apparently) postponed the meeting for tomorrow.

However, if verbs in the perfect tense are preceded with the negating particle არ, they may lose evidential inference and posit a simple negative statement:

1. – *ნახე ეს ფილმი?*	Did you see this film?
– *ჯერ არ მინახავს.*	I have not seen it yet.
2. – *ნახე ეს ფილმი?*	Did you see this film?
– *არ ვნახე.*	I didn't see it, did not want to see it.
3. – *ნახე ეს ფილმი?*	Did you see this film?
– *(დიახ,) ვნახე.*	Yes, I saw it.

In *dialogue 1* the verb in the perfect tense conveys a simple statement of the fact that has no evidential meaning. The statement implies that person has not seen the film for some reason – they didn't have time, tickets were sold out, etc.

In *dialogue 2* the verb in the aorist implies that the person intentionally refused to see the film for some reason – they don't like the film director, the film deals with an unpleasant subject matter, etc.

In *dialogue 3* the verb in the aorist states a simple fact that the person saw the film.

The aspect of the perfect tense forms depends on presence or absence of the preverb. A verb with a preverb denotes the perfective aspect and without it the imperfective aspect.

> *ვხედავ, ეს წიგნები დიდი ყურადღებით* ***გიგროვებია.***
> I see, you have (apparently) been collecting these books with great care.
> *მას ბევრი ძველი მარკა* ***შეუგროვებია.***
> He has (apparently) collected a lot of old stamps.

As in all other cases, the preverb in the perfect tense has an additional derivative function.

კითხვაზე სწორი პასუხი ***გა-მიცია.***
I have (apparently) given the correct answer to this question.
ეს წერილი ჯერ ადრესატისთვის არ ***გადა-***_მიცია._
I have not yet sent the letter to the addressee.
მთავრობას დეკრეტი ***გამო-უცია.***
The government (apparently) has issued a decree.

I conjugation verbs in the perfect tense

1. All I conjugation active voice transitive verbs have inverted person markers – i.e. the subject is denoted with the object marker and vice versa.

   ვ-წერ მე (ადამიან-**ი**) მას (წერილ-ს)
   I (a person) *write* it (a letter)
   და-ვ-წერ-ე მე (ადამიან-**მა**) ის (წერილ-ი)
   I (a person) *wrote* it a letter)
   და-მ-ი-წერ-ია მე (ადამიან-**ს**) ის (წერილ-ი)
   I (a person) *have written* (a letter)

2. The tripersonal (subject, direct object, indirect object) active voice verbs in the perfect tense become bipersonal verbs, thus losing one person, as a rule, the indirect object, which usually acquires the postposition -**თვის** and cannot be designated with any marker in the verb in the perfect.

	Subject		*Direct object*	*Indirect object*
I series Present	კაც-ი man	**უ-შენ-ებ-ს** builds	სახლ-ს house	შვილ-ს for (his) son
II series Aorist	კაც-მა	**ა-უ-შენ-ა** built	სახლ-ი	შვილ-ს
III series Perfect	კაც-ს	**ა-უ-შენ-ებ-ი-ა** has built	სახლ-ი	შვილ-**ის-თვის** Object with postposition/ adjunct object

3. Verbs in the perfect tense may have object-oriented forms, but they are devoid of the object-oriented meaning. An object marker indicates a subject. In the first- and second-person forms they have the prefix -**ი**, and in the third person, the prefix -**უ**. The version markers in this case cannot express the category of version.

და-მ-ი-წერ-ი-ა მე ის I have written it	(მო)-მ-ი-თხოვ-ი-ა მე ის (მისთვის) I have asked it (from him)
და-გვ-ი-წერ-ი-ა ჩვენ ის We have written it	(მო)-გვ-ი-თხოვ-ი-ა ჩვენ ი-ს (მისთვის) We have asked it (from him)
და-გ-ი-წერ-ი-ა-(თ) შენ/თქვენ ის You/you have written it	(მო)-გ-ი-თხოვ-ი-ა-(თ) შენ/თქვენ ის (მისთვის) You/you have asked it (from him)
და-უ-წერ-ი-ა-(თ) მას/მათ ის He/they has/have written it	(მო)-უ-თხოვ-ი-ა-(თ) მას/მათ ის (მისთვის) He/they has/have asked it (from him)

4. As the following chart shows, the structure of I conjugation verb forms in the perfect tense coincides with object-oriented verbs of the static-passive voice. However, active verbs have inverted person marking and a preverb, while the static-passive voice verbs have neither.

Static-passive voice verbs in the present tense	*Active voice verbs in the perfect tense*
მ-ი-წერ-ი-ა მე (სიაში) I have (it) written (in a roster)	და-მ-ი-წერ-ი-ა მე ის (მისთვის) I have written it (for him)
გვ-ი-წერ-ი-ა ჩვენ (სიაში) We have (it) written (in a roster)	და-გვ-ი-წერ-ი-ა ჩვენ ის (მისთვის) We have written it (for him)
გ-ი-წერ-ი-ა-(თ) შენ /თქვენ (სიაში) You/you have (it) written (in a roster)	და-გ-ი-წერ-ი-ა-(თ) შენ /თქვენ ის (მისთვის) You/you have it written (for him)
უ-წერ-ია-(თ) მას/მათ (სიაში) He/they has/have (it) written (in a roster)	და-უ-წერ-ი-ა-(თ) მას/მათ ის (მისთვის) He/they has/have written it (for him)

5. In the perfect tense forms, active verbs have a stem of either I or II series.
6. P/FSF of I series is used in the verb forms with following P/FSF:

-ი

Verbs with -ი P/FSF have their root vowel truncated, but it reappears in II series: *ვ-შლ-ი* (I erase) – *წა-ვ-შალ-ე* (I erased). In III series the root remains syncopated.

და-მ-ი-შლ-ი-ა მე ის
I have dispersed it
და-გვ-ი-შლ-ი-ა ჩვენ ის
We have dispersed it

და-გ-ი-შლ-ი-ა-(თ)
შენ /თქვენ ის
You/you have dispersed it

და-უ-შლ-ი-ა-(თ)
მას/მათ ის
He/they has/have dispersed it

(მო)-მ-ი-თხოვ-ი-ა მე ის
(მისთვის)
I have asked it (from him)
(მო)-გვ-ი-თხოვ-ი-ა ჩვენ ის
(მისთვის)
We have asked it (from him)

(მო)-მ-ი-თხოვ-ი-ა მე ის
(მისთვის)
I have asked it (from him)
(მო)-გვ-ი-თხოვ-ი-ა ჩვენ ის
(მისთვის)
We have asked it (from him)

(მო)-უ-თხოვ-ი-ა-(თ)
მას/მათ ის (მისთვის)
He/they has/have asked it (from him)

ავ

და-მ-ი-ხატ-ავ-ს მე ის
I have painted it
და-გვ-ი-ხატ-ავ-ს ჩვენ ის
We have painted it
და-გ-ი-ხატ-ავ-ს/თ
შენ /თქვენ ის
You/you have painted it
და-უ-ხატ-ავ-ს/თ მას/მათ ის
He/they has/have painted it

-ამ

შე-მ-ი-სვ-ამ-ს მე ის
I have drunk it
შე-გვ-ი-სვ-ამ-ს ჩვენ ის
We have drunk it
შე-გ-ი-სვ-ამ-ს/თ
შენ/თქვენ ის
You/you have drunk it
შე-უ-სვ-ამ-ს/თ მას/მათ ის
He/they has/have drunk it

The verbs with P/FSF *-ავ* and *-ამ* can be used with these formants in the perfect tense, but very often they are lost and replaced by the ending-*ია:დამიხატია* or *შემისვია.*

ა-მ-ი-შენ-ებ-ი-ა მე ის I have built it	გა-მ-ი-ღვიძ-ებ-ი-ა მე ის I have woken him up
ა-გვ-ი-შენ-ებ-ი-ა ჩვენ ის We have built it	გა-გვ-ი-ღვიძ-ებ-ი-ა ჩვენ ის We have woken him up
ა-გ-ი-შენ-ებ-ი-ა(თ) შენ /თქვენ ის You/you have built it	გა-გ-ი-ღვიძ-ებ-ი-ა(თ) შენ/თქვენ ის You/have woken him up
ა-უ-შენ-ებ-ი-ა(თ) მას/მათ ის He/they has/have built it	გა-უ-ღვიძ-ებ-ი-ა(თ) მას/მათ ის He/they has/have woken him up

As mentioned, some verbs in III series are based on their II series stem and consequently lose their P/FSF:

1. **The small group of verbs with - *ებ* P/FSF, especially those without the root vowel:**

   ვ-ა-ქ-ებ – მიქია
   ვ-ა-ღ-ებ – გამიღია
   ვ-ი-წყ-ებ – დამიწყია

მ-ი-ქ-ი-ა მე ის I have praised him	გა-მ-ი-ღ-ი-ა მეის I have opened it	და-მ-ი-წყ-ი-ა მე ის I have started it
გვ-ი-ქ-ი-ა ჩვენ ის We have praised it	გა-გვ-ი-ღ-ი-ა ჩვენ ის We have opened it	და-გვ-ი-წყ-ი-ა ჩვენ ის We have started it
გ-ი-ქ-ი-ა-(თ) შენ /თქვენ ის You/you have praised it	გა-გ-ი-ღ-ი-ა-(თ) შენ/თქვენ ის You/you have opened it	და-გ-ი-წყ-ი-ა-(თ) შენ/თქვენ ის You/you have started it
უ-ქ-ი-ა-(თ) მას/მათ ის He has/they have praised it	გა-უ-ღ-ი-ა-(თ) მას/მათ ის He has/they have opened it	და-უ-წყ-ი-ა-(თ) მას/მათ He has/they have started it

2. **P/FSF** - *ემ – გამო-ვ-ც-ემ, გა-ვ-ც-ემ*

P/FSF *-ემ* is added to a single stem *-ც* (*ვ-ცემ, ს-ცემ, ცემ-ს*, etc. to publish something). The same stem *-ცემ* may generate several different meanings in the future tense when various preverbs are added to it: *გამო-ვ-ც-ემ* (I will issue, publish it), *გა-ვ-ც-ემ* (I will give, distribute, betray it), *მი-ვ-ც-ემ* (I will give it to), *გადა-ვ-ც-ემ* (I will convey it to, give it to).

გამო-მ-ი-ც-ი-ა მე ის/ისინი.
I have published it/them.
ჩვენ გამო-გვ-ი-ც-ი-ა ჩვენ ის/ისინი.
We have published it/them.
გა-მ-ი-ც-ი-ა მე ის/ისინი.
I have distributed it/them.
ჩვენ გა-გვ-ი-ც-ი-ა ის/ისინი.
We have distributed it/them.
გამო-გ-ი-ც-ი-ა-(თ) შენ/თქვენ ის/ისინი.
You/you have published it/them.
გა-გ-ი-ც-ი-ა-(თ) შენ/თქვენ ის/ისინი.
You/you have distributed it/them.
გამო-უ-ც-ი-ა-(თ) მას/მათ ის/ისინი.
He has/they have published it/them.
გა-უ-ც-ი-ა-(თ) მას/მათ ის/ისინი.
He has/they have distributed it/them.

ჩემი წიგნი ჯერ არ გამომიცია.
I have not published my book yet.
მის ძმას უკვე ორი წიგნი გამოუცია.
His brother has already published two books.
პრიზები სამი ავტორისთვის გადაუციათ.
They have given prizes to three authors.
მას ამ კითხვაზე პასუხი არ გაუცია.
He hasn't given an answer to this question.

3. P/FSF - *ოფ – და-ვ-ყ-ოფ, ჩა-ვ-ყ-ოფ*

და-მ-ი-ყვ-ი-ა მე ის/ისინი I have divided it/them	ჩა-მ-ი-ყვ-ი-ა მე ის/ისინი I have put it/them in
და-გვ-ი-ყვ-ი-ა ჩვენ ის/ისინი We have divided it/them	ჩა-გვ-ი-ყვ-ი-ა ჩვენ ის/ისინი We have put it/them in
და-გ-ი-ყვ-ი-ა-(თ) შენ/თქვენ ის/ისინი You/you have divided it/them	ჩა-გ-ი-ყვ-ი-ა-(თ) შენ/თქვენ ის/ისინი You/you have put it/them
და-უ-ყვ-ი-ა-(თ) მას/მათ ის/ისინი He/they has/have divided it/them	ჩა-უ-ყვ-ი-ა-(თ) მას/მათ ის/ისინი He/they has/have divided it

ლექტორს სტუდენტები პატარა ჯგუფებად ***დაუყვია.***
The lecturer has divided the students into small groups.
ჩანთაში ხელი ***ჩამიყვია.***
I have put my hand into the satchel.
წრე ორ თანაბარ ნაწილად ***გამიყვია.***
I have divided the circle into two equal parts.

4. P/FSF - *ობ* – *ვ-გრძნ-ობ, და-ვ-ა-ტკბ-ობ*

მ-ი-გრძნ-ი-ა მე ის
I have felt it
გვ-ი-გრძნ-ი-ა ჩვენ ის
We have felt it
გ-ი-გრძნ-ი-ა-(თ) შენ/თქვენ ის
You/you have felt it
უ-გრძნ-ი-ა-(თ) მას/მათ ის
He has/they have felt it

და-მ-ი-ტკბ-ი-ა მე ის/ისინი
I have delighted/sweetened him/them
და-გვ-ი-ტკბ-ი-ა ჩვენ ის/ისინი
We have delighted him/them
(და)-გ-იტკბ-ი-ა-(თ) შენ/თქვენ ის/ისინი
You/you have delighted him/them
(და)-უ-ტკბ-ი-ა-(თ) მას (მათ) ის/ისინი
He has/they have delighted him/them

მას ტკივილი არ ***უგრძნია.***
He has not felt the pain.
ასეთი შიში არასოდეს ***მიგრძნია.***
I have never felt such fear.
თქვენ თქვენი სიმღერით მსმენელები ***დაგიტკბიათ.***
You have delighted the listeners with your singing.
ჩაი რატომ არ ***დაგიტკბია?***
Why did not you sweeten the tea?

Ablaut verbs

In the perfect tense the vowel -*ე* reappears in the ablaut verb roots.

(და)-მ-ი-კრეფ-ი-ა მე ის/ისინი
I have picked it/them
(და)-გვ-ი-კრეფ-ი-ა ჩვენ ის/ისინი
We have picked it/them
(და)-გ-ი-კრეფ-ი-ა-(თ) შენ/თქვენ ის/ისინი
You/you have picked it/them

(გა)-მ-ი-ხვრეტ-ი-ა მე ის/ისინი
I have pierced it/them
(გა)-გვ-ი-ხვრეტ-ი-ა ჩვენ ის/ისინი
We have pierced it/them
(გა)-გ-ი-ხვრეტ-ი-ა-(თ) შენ/თქვენ ის/ისინი
You/you pierced it/them

(და)-უ-კრეფ-ი-ა-(თ)	(გა)-უ-ხვრეტ-ი-ა-(თ)
მას/მათ ის/ისინი	მას/მათ ის/ისინი
He has/they have picked it/them	He has/they pierced it/them

ჩვენ აქ ყვავილები ხშირად ***დაგვიკრეფია.***
We have often picked flowers here.
ბავშვებს ტყეში მოცვი ***დაუკრეფიათ.***
The children have picked blueberries in the wood.
ტყვიას მისი გული ***გაუხვრეტია.***
The bullet pierced his heart.

The verbs ending with ***-ევ*** and ***-ენ*** in I series.

-ევ-ending verbs	*-ენ-ending verbs*
შე-მ-ი-მჩნ-ევ-ი-ა მე ის (მისთვის) I have noticed it (in him)	წარ-მ-ი-დგ-ენ-ი-ა მე ის (მისთვის) I have presented it (to him)
შე-გვ-ი-მჩნ-ევ-ი-ა ჩვენ ის (მისთვის) We have noticed it (in him)	წარ-გვ-ი-დგ-ენ-ი-ა ჩვენ ის (მისთვის) We have presented it (to him)
შე-გ-ი-მჩნ-ევ-ი-ა-(თ) შენ/თქვენ ის (მისთვის) You/you have noticed it (in him)	წარ-გ-ი-დგ-ენ-ი-ა-(თ) შენ/თქვენ ის (მისთვის) You/you have presented it (to him)
შე-უ-მჩნ-ევ-ი-ა-(თ) მას/მათ ის (მისთვის) He/they noticed it (in him)	წარ-უ-დგ-ენ-ი-ა-(თ) მას/მათ ის მისთვის He/they has/have presented it (to him)

Some ablaut verbs have the syncopated root when P/FSF ***-ი*** is added to them: *ვ-****თლ****-ი* – *და-მ-ი-****თლ****-ი-ა* (I cut, peel); *ვ-****შლ****-ი* – *წა-მ-ი-****შლ****-ი-ა* (I erase). Compare with aorist forms: *და-ვ-****თალ****-ე* and *წა-ვ-****შალ****-ე*.

However, syncopation occurs in the verbs with different P/FSF as well. For example, *ვ-კლ-ავ* (I kill) and *ვ-ხნ-ავ* (I plough) conjugate in the perfect tense like all other verbs with P/FSF ***-ავ***. It will be maintained in all singular and plural forms without the ending **-ი-ა** added to it:

მო-მ-ი-კლ-ავ-ს
I have killed
და-მ-ი-ხნ-ავ-ს
I have plowed

In the perfect tense the system of morphemes for all active voice verbs with one and two P/FSFs is shown in the following chart. An object marker indicates a subject and a version marker in this case cannot express the category of version:

1. You/you have written.
2. I have published.
3. We have built.
4. You have drunk.
5. They have painted.

	Preverb	*Object marker*	*Version marker*	*Root*	*P/FSF*	*Tense marker*	*Subject marker*	*Plural marker*
1	და	გ	ი	წერ		ი	ა	თ
2	გამო	მ	ი	ც		ი	ა	
3	ა	გვ	ი	შენ	ებ	ი	ა	
4	შე	გ	ი	სვ	ამ		ს	
5	და		უ	ხატ	ავ			თ

Object-oriented bipersonal verbs in the perfect tense have the auxiliary verb *to be* for the first- and second-person forms. As in the III series forms, the inversion is sustained – i.e. a subject is identified with the object marker and vice versa: გა-ვ-უ-ხარ-ებ-ი-ვ-არ მას მე (he has delighted me) – here the first-person subject marker -*ვ* refers to the first-person object.

გა-ვ-უ-ხარ-ებ-ი-ვ-არ-(თ)
მას/მათ მე/ჩვენ
He/they has/have delighted me/us

გა-უ-ხარ-ებ-ი-ხ-არ-(თ)
მას/მათ შენ/თქვენ
He/they has/have delighted you/you

გა-ვ-უ-მდიდრ-ებ-ი-ვ-არ-(თ)
მას/მათ მე/ჩვენ
He/they has/have enriched me/us

გა-უ-მდიდრ-ებ-ი-ხ-არ-(თ)
მას/მათ შენ/თქვენ
He/they has/have enriched you/you

გა-უ-ხარ-ებ-ი-ა-(თ)
მას /მათ ის/ისინი
He/they has/have delighted him/them

გა-უ-მდიდრ-ებ-ი-ა-(თ)
მას/მათ ის/ისინი
He/they has/have enriched him/them

Bipersonal ablaut verbs have similar structure with the auxiliary verb *to be*.

შე-ვ-უ-მჩნევ-ი-ვ-არ-(თ)
მას/მათ მე/ჩვენ
He/they has/have noticed me/us

წარ-ვ-უ-დგენ-ი-ვ-ა-რ-(თ)
მას/მათ მე/ჩვენ
He/they has/have presented me/us

შე-უ-მჩნევ-ი-ხ-არ-(თ)
მას/მათ შენ/თქვენ
He/they have noticed you/you

წარ-უ-დგენ-ი-ხ-არ-(თ)
მას/მათ შენ/თქვენ
He/they have presented you/you

შე-უ-მჩნევ-ი-ა-(თ)
მას (მათ) ის/ისინი
He/they has/have noticed him/them

წარ-უ-დგენ-ი-ა-(თ)
მას/მათ ის/ისინი
He/they have presented him/them

As the chart shows, the first- and second-person forms have a similar structure; in the first-person, form the preverb is followed not by an object marker but a subject marker (with different function). Thus, active voice verbs have two types of morpheme structure. The third-person forms have the same markings as the subject oriented verbs:

1. They have made (him) blush/encouraged him.
2. He/they has/have made us blush/encouraged you.

	Preverb	*Person marker*	*Version marker*	*Root*	*P/FSF*	*Tense marker*	*Person marker*	*Plural marker*
1	გა		უ	წითლ	ებ	ი	ა	თ
2	წა		უ	ხალის	ებ	ი	ა	თ

	Preverb	*Subject marker*	*Version marker*	*Root*	*P/FSF*	*Tense marker*	*Auxiliary verb: Subject marker*	*Auxiliary verb: Root*	*Auxiliary verb: Plural marker*
1	გა	ვ	უ	წითლ	ებ	ი	ვ	არ	თ
2	გა		უ	ხალის	ებ	ი	ხ	არ	თ

II conjugation

The perfect tense forms of monopersonal dynamic-passive verbs are based on their past participle to which the auxiliary verb *to be* is added in its present tense *-ვარ(თ)* to the first- and second-person forms. In the third-person forms, both in singular and plural, the auxiliary verb is present in its shortened form.

Perfect tense of monopersonal verbs

გა-ვ-მდიდრებულ-ვ-არ-(თ) მე/ჩვენ
I/we have become rich

გა-მდიდრებულ-ხ-არ-(თ) შენ/თქვენ
You/you have become rich

გა-მდიდრებულ-ა (<არს) ის
He has become rich

გა-მდიდრებულ-ან (<არიან) ისინი
They have become rich

გა-ვ-პარულ-ვ-არ-(თ) მე/ჩვენ
I/we have slipped away

გა-პარულ-ხ-არ-(თ) შენ/თქვენ
You/you have slipped away

გა-პარულ-ა-(ნ) ის/ისინი
He/they has/have slipped away

და-ვ-ბერებულ-ვარ-(თ) მე/ჩვენ
I/we have aged (become old)

და-ბერებულ-ხარ-(თ) შენ /თქვენ
You/you have aged

და-ბერებულ-ა-(ნ) ის/ისინი
He/they has/have aged

და-ვ-მალულ-ვ-არ-(თ) მე/ჩვენ
I/we have hidden (ourselves)

და-მალულ-ხ-არ-(თ) შენ/თქვენ
You/you have hidden

და-მალულ-ა-(ნ) ის/ისინი
He/they has/have hidden

The conjugation of ablaut verbs follows the same rule.

გა-ვ-ჭყლეტილ-ვ-არ-(თ) მე /ჩვენ
I/we have been crushed

გა-ჭყლეტილ-ხ-არ(თ)შენ/თქვენ
You/you have been crushed

გა-ჭყლეტილ-ა-(ნ) ის/ისინი
He/they have been crushed

და-ვ-გრეხილ-ვ-არ-(თ) მე /ჩვენ
I/we have been twisted

და-გრეხილ-ხ-არ-თ შენ /თქვენ
You/you have been twisted

და-გრეხილ-ა-(ნ) ის/ისინი
He has/they have been twisted

II conjugation of monopersonal verbs in the perfect tense

1. I/we have hidden myself/ourselves.
2. He/they has/have hidden himself/themselves.
3. You have aged.

4. I/we have blushed.
5. He/they has/have flown away.
6. I/we have been crushed.

	Preverb	*Person marker*	*Past passive participle*			*Auxiliary verb*		
			Root	*P/FSF*	*Past passive participle formant suffix*	*Person marker*	*Root*	*Person/ number marker*
1	და	ვ	მალ	–	ულ	ვ	არ	თ
2	და	–	მალ	–	ულ			ა//ან
3	და	–	ბერ	ებ	ულ	ხ	არ	თ
4	გა	ვ	წითლ	ებ	ულ	ვ	არ	თ
5	გა			ფრენ	ილ			ა//ან
6	გა	ვ	ჭყლეტ		ილ	ვ	არ	თ

Bipersonal verbs in the perfect tense

Bipersonal dynamic passive voice verbs are based on their gerund which is followed by the tense marker -**ი**.

შე-მ-ბმ-ი-ა/ან ის/ისინი მე
I have been attacked by him/them

შე-გვ-ბმ-ი-ა/ან ის/ისინი ჩვენ
We have been attacked by him/them

შე-გ-ბმ-ი-ა/ან ის/ისინი შენ
You/you have been attacked by him/them

შე-ბმ-ი-ა/ან ის/ისინი მას
He has been attacked by him/them

გა-მ-კეთ-ებ-ი-ა ის/ისინი მე
It/they has/have been done for me

გა-გვ-კეთ-ებ-ი-ა ის/ისინი ჩვენ
It/they has/have been done for us

გა-გ-კეთ-ებ-ი-ა-(თ) ის/ისინი შენ//თქვენ
It/they has/have been done for you/you

გა-ჰ-კეთ-ებ-ი-ა-(თ) ის/ისინი მას//მათ
It has/they have been done for im/them

ჩვენ მტერი ბევრჯერ ***შეგვბმია.***
We have often been attacked by the enemy.
მის ძმას ვეფხვი ***შებმია.***
His brother has been attacked by a tiger.

მის ძმას ყველა საქმე კარგად *გაჰკეთებია.*
All the problems have been done/solved well for his brother.

Perfect tense forms of the II conjugation bipersonal verbs

Preverb	*Object marker*	*Root*	*Tense marker*	*Person/number marker*
შე	მ	ბმ	ი	ა//ან
შე	გვ	ბმ	ი	ა

In Georgian, gerunds are derived from the stem of active voice I series verbs. Passive voice verbs do not have their own gerund. However, there are a few exceptions:

1. The verbs with only passive voice forms: *მორევა* (overpowering), *გაწყრომა* (scolding), *დადგომა* (standing), and others. They do not have the suffix -*ომ* in their active voice forms, but it appears in the passive voice forms.

მო-მ-კვდომ-ი-ა მე ის
I have lost him/them
(i.e. he/they died)
მო-გვ-კვდომ-ი-ა
ის/ისინი ჩვენ
We have lost him/them

გა-მ-წყრომ-ი-ა-(ნ) მე ის/ისინი
I have been scolded by him/them
გა-გვ-წყრომ-ი-ა-(ნ) ჩვენ
ის/ისინი
We have been scolded by him/them

მო-გ-კვდომ-ი-ა-(თ)
ის/ისინი შენ//თქვენ
You/you have lost him/them

გა-გ-წყრომ-ი-ა-(თ)
შენ//თქვენ ის/ისინი
You/you have been scolded by him/them

მო-ჰ-კვდომ-ი-ა-თ
ის/ისინი მას//მათ
He has lost him/them

გა-ს-წყრომ-ი-ა-(ნ)
მას//მათ ის/ისინი
He/they have been scolded by him/them

ჩემს მეგობარს მამა *მოჰკვდომია.*
My friend's father has died.
ჩემს შვილს მასწავლებელი *გასწყრომია.*
The teacher has scolded my child.

2. Verbs with different gerunds for the active and passive voice forms have different roots in perfect tense.

Active voice gerunds	*Passive voice gerunds*
ტეხვა breaking	ტყდომა getting broken
წვენა putting down	წოლა lying down
წაყვანა taking away	წაყოლა following someone

და-მ-წოლ-ი-ა-(ნ) ის//ისინი მე
It has/they have fallen upon me

და-გვ-წოლ-ი-ა-(ნ) ის/ისინი ჩვენ
It has/they have fallen upon us

და-გ-წოლ-ი-ა-(ნ) შენ/თქვენ ის//ისინი
It has/they have fallen upon you

და-ს-წოლ-ი-ა-(ნ) მას/მათ ის/ისინი
It has/they have fallen upon him/them

წა-მ-ყოლ-ი-ა-(ნ) მე ის/ისინი
He/they have followed me

წა-გვ-ყოლ-ი-ა-(ნ) ჩვენ ის/ისინი
He has/they have followed us

წა-გ-ყოლ-ი-ა-(თ) შენ/თქვენ ის/ისინი
He has/they have followed you/you

წა-ჰ-ყოლ-ი-ა-(ნ) მას/მათ ის/ისინი
He has/they have followed him/them

მხრებზე მძიმე ტვირთი **დამწოლია.**
A heavy burden has fallen upon my shoulders.
ჩემი ბიჭი მაღაზიაში **წაგყოლია.**
My boy has followed you to the store.

III conjugation

III conjugation verbs, i.e. the medio-active voice verbs, have a few similarities with active voice verbs:

1. They have a case-changing subject even though it does not modify a direct object.

   I Present **ვ-ზრუნავ** მე (ადამიან-ი)
   I (a person, nominative case) care
   II Aorist **ვ-ი-ზრუნ-ე** მე (ადამიან-მა)
   I (a person, ergative case) cared
   III Perfect **მ-იზრუნია** მე (ადამიან-ს)
   I (a person, dative case) have cared

2. In III series the medio-active voice verbs have inverted person markers. The verb *მ-იზრუნია* shown is a monopersonal verb but has the object marker *მ-*.

3. The medio-active voice verbs have a version marker *ი-/უ-*in III series, but it does not indicate the subject-object relation.

მ-ი-ცინ-ი-ა მე I have laughed	გვ-ი-ცინ-ი-ა ჩვენ We have laughed
გ-ი-ცინ-ი-ა შენ You have laughed	გ-ი-ცინ-ი-ა-თ თქვენ You have laughed
უ-ცინ-ი-ა მას He has laughed	უ-ცინ-ი-ა-თ მათ They have laughed

Some verbs without P/FSF have some suffixes in II and III series, which they did not have in I series. For example, the verb *თრთის* (it trembles) has the suffix **-ოლ**:

მ-ი-თრთ-ოლ-ი-ა მე
I have trembled
გვ-ი-თრთ-ოლ-ი-ა ჩვენ
We have trembled
გ-ი-თრთ-ოლ-ი-ა-(თ) შენ/თქვენ
You/you have trembled
უ-თრთ-ოლ-ი-ა-(თ) მას/მათ
He/they have trembled

4. As the charts of verbs with a single P/FSF show, medio-active verbs have the same **-ია** ending in III series as do active-voice verbs.
5. The medio-active voice verbs with P/FSF drop it in II and III series forms.

Conjugation of medio-active voice two-stem verbs in the perfect tense

მ-ი-ცურ-ი-ა მე I have swum	და-მ-ი-გვიან-ი-ა მე I have been late	მ-ი-ზრუნ-ი-ა მე I have taken care
გვ-ი-ცურ-ი-ა ჩვენ We have swum	და-გვ-ი-გვიან-ი-ა ჩვენ We have been late	გვ-ი-ზრუნ-ი-ა ჩვენ We have taken care
გ-ი-ცურ-ი-ა-(თ) შენ/თქვენ You/you have swum	და-გ-ი-გვიან-ი-ა-(თ) შენ/თქვენ You/you have been late	გ-ი-ზრუნ-ი-ა-(თ) თქვენ You/you have taken care
უ-ცურ-ი-ა-(თ) მას/მათ He has/they have Swum	და-უ-გვიან-ი-ა-(თ) მას/მათ He has/they have been late	უ-ზრუნ-ი-ა-(თ) მას/მათ He has/they have taken care

ჩვენ შავ ზღვაში ხშირად ***გვიცურია.***
We have often swum in the Black Sea.
შენ ლექციებზე ***დაგიგვიანია.***
You have been late to classes.
მას ამ საკითხზე უკვე ***უზრუნია.***
He has taken care of this problem.

The verbs with P/FSF -***ობ*** have the consonant ***ვ*** in the perfect tense, as well as in the future subseries (see 9.6.1.3.):

ქანაობს – უქანა***ვ***ია (swing – has swung)
თევზაობს – უთევზა***ვ***ია (is fishing – has fished)
ცურაობს – უცურა***ვ***ია (swims – has swum).

მ-ი-ქანავ-ი-ა მე I have swung	მ-ი-თევზავ-ი-ა მე I have fished	მ-ი-ცურავ-ი-ა მე I have swum
გვ-ი-ქანავ-ი-ა ჩვენ We have swung	გვ-ი-თევზავ-ი-ა ჩვენ We have fished	გვ-ი-ცურავ-ი-ა ჩვენ We have swum
გ-ი-ქანავ-ი-ა-(თ) შენ/თქვენ You/you have swung	გ-ი-თევზავ-ი-ა-(თ) შენ/თქვენ You/you have fished	გ-ი-ცურავ-ი-ა-(თ) მე/შენ You/you have swum
უ-ქანავ-ი-ა-(თ) მას/მათ He has/they have swung	უ-თევზავ-ი-ა-(თ) მას/მათ He has/they have fished	უ-ცურავ-ი-ა-(თ) მას/მათ He has/they have swum

The verbs with alternating vowels have the vowel ***ე*** in I series and in the perfect tense forms.

მ-ი-ფრენ-ი-ა მე
I have flown around
გვ-ი-ფრენ-ი-ა ჩვენ
We have flown around
გ-ი-ფრენ-ი-ა-(თ) შენ/თქვენ
You/you have flown around
უ-ფრენ-ი-ა-(თ) მას/მათ
He has/they have flown around

The medio-active voice bipersonal verbs lose their indirect object in III series; it acquires a postposition thus becoming an adjunct object.

I series (present)	II series (aorist)	III series (perfect)
ვ-ჯობნ-ი-(თ) მე/ ჩვენ მას/მათ I/we surpass him/ them	ვ-ა-ჯობ-ე-(თ) მე/ჩვენ მას/მათ I/we surpass him/ them	მ-ი-ჯობნ-ი-ა მე მისთვის/მათთვის I have surpassed him გვ-ი-ჯობნ-ი-ა ჩვენ მისთვის/მათთვის We have surpassed him/ them
ჯობნ-ი-(თ) შენ/თქვენმას/მათ You/you surpass him/them	ა-ჯობ-ე-(თ) შენ/თქვენ მას/მათ You/you surpassed him/them	გ-ი-ჯობნ-ი-ა-(თ) (თ) შენ/თქვენ მისთვის/მათთვის You/you have surpassed him/them
ჯობნ-ი-ს/ან ის/ისინი მას/მათ He/they surpass/ surpasses him/ them	ა-ჯობ-ა/ეს მან/მათ მას/მათ He/they surpassed/ surpassed him/ them	უ-ჯობნ-ი-ა-(თ) მას/მათ მისთვის/მათთვის He has/they have surpassed him/them

Since the indirect object turns into adjunct object all bipersonal medio-active voice verbs become monopersonal verbs in III series.

მ-ი-დარაჯ-ი-ა მე მისთვის I have guarded it	მ-ი-ხელმძღვანელ-ი-ა მე მისთვის I have supervised him
გვ-ი-დარაჯ-ი-ა ჩვენ We have guarded	გვ-ი-ხელმძღვანელ-ი-ა ჩვენ We have supervised
გ-ი-დარაჯ-ი-ა-(თ) შენ (თქვენ) You/you have guarded	გ-ი-ხელმძღვანელ-ი-ა-(თ) შენ/თქვენ You/you have supervised
უ-დარაჯ-ი-ა-(თ) მას (მათ) He/they have guarded	უ-ხელმძღვანელ-ი-ა-(თ) მას/მათ He/they has/have supervised

IV conjugation

IV conjugation consists of the static-passive and medio-passive voice verbs. Both types of these verbs have an auxiliary verb *to be* in III series forms. In the perfect tense static-passive voice verbs have the auxiliary verb in its present tense forms added to their passive participle.

1. I/we have been painted
2. He/they has/have been painted
3. It/they has/have been spread
4. You/you have fallen down

	Preverb	Person marker	Past passive participle			Auxiliary verb		
			Root	*P/FSF*	*Suffix forming passive participle*	*Person marker*	*Root*	*Person/ number marker*
1	და	ვ	ხატ	–	ულ	ვ	არ	თ
2	და	–	ხატ	–	ულ			ა/ან
3	და		გებ	–	ულ			ა/ან
4	და		ცემ		ულ	ხ	არ	თ

Conjugation of monopersonal static-passive voice verb

ვ-წერებულ-ვ-არ-(თ) მე/ჩვენ სიაში I/we have been written (included) (in the roster)	ვ-ხსენებულ-ვ-არ-(თ) მე /ჩვენ I/we have been mentioned
წერებულ-ხ-არ-(თ) შენ/თქვენ You/you have been written	ხსენებულ-ხ-არ-(თ) შენ/თქვენ You/you have been mentioned
წერებულ-ა (ან) ის/ისინი He has/they have been written	ხსენებულ-ა-(ნ) ის/ისინი He has/they have been mentioned

The medio-passive voice verbs are based on their gerund with P/FSF to which the auxiliary verb *to be* is added. (შე)ყვარება (loving) + corresponding forms of *to be* in the present tense:

ვ-ყვარები-ვ-არ-(თ) მე/ჩვენ მას/მათ I/we have been loved by him/them	მო-ვ-წონები-ვ-არ-(თ) მე /ჩვენ მას/მათ I/we have been liked by him/them
ჰ-ყვარები-ხ-არ-(თ) შენ/თქვენ მას/მათ You/you have been loved by him/them	მო-ს-წონები-ხ-არ-(თ) შენ/თქვენ მას/მათ You/you have been liked by him/them
ჰ-ყვარები-ა-(თ) ის/ისინი მას/მათ He has/they have been loved by him/them	მო-ს-წონები-ა-(თ) ის/ისინი მას/მათ He has/they have been liked by him/them

9.6.3.2 *Pluperfect*

The pluperfect, like the perfect tense, denotes a not-witnessed action in the past and implies evidentiality of the reported action. Its name in Georgian is derived from the word თურმე (as is the case with the perfect tense) – i.e. *evidently* and *apparently*. The pluperfect differs from the perfect in that it denotes an action preceding another event in the past.

> თურმე მას კონვერტზე მისამართი უკვე **დაეწერა.**
> Apparently, he had already written the address on the envelope.

An action – **დაეწერა** (had written) – precedes the action that happened in the past before it was seen.

The pluperfect has another function – namely, it denotes a desirable or necessary action in the past that did not happen. In such cases a verb in the pluperfect is often introduced with the word ნეტავ (I wish), modal verb უნდა (should, must), or *that*- or *if*-clause and is coupled with a verb in the conditional in the main clause.

> ნეტავ ეს წერილი ადრე **დამეწერა.**
> I wish I had written this letter earlier.
> ეს წერილი რომ ადრე **დამეწერა**, უკვე გავგზავნიდი.
> If I had written this letter earlier, I would have sent it already.
> წერილი უნდა **დამეწერა** და **გამეგზავნა** მისთვის.
> I should have written a letter and sent to him.
> აჯობებდა, რომ წერილი **დამეწერა** და **გამეგზავნა** მისთვის.
> It would have been better if I had written a letter and sent to him.

The aspect of a verb in the pluperfect depends on whether it has a preverb.

> გუშინ სახლი მთელი დღე რომ **მელაგებინა** (pluperfect), მაინც ვერ **დავალაგებდი** (conditional).
> Yesterday (even) if I had been tidying up the house the entire day, I still would not have finished doing it.
> შენი წიგნები სხვა თაროზე უნდა **დამელაგებინა.**
> I should have put/arranged your books on another shelf.
> მას რომ ეს სახლი მთელი წელი **ეშენებინა** (Pluperfect), ალბათ **ააშენებდა** (conditional).
> Had he been building this house for the entire year, he probably would have built (finished building) it.

ეს ეკლესია ქართველ ბერებს უნდა ***აეშენებინათ*** *მრავალი საუკუნის წინ.*
(Probably) Georgian monks must have built this church many centuries ago.

I conjugation

I conjugation verbs have the same stem in the pluperfect as in the aorist, but it has the pre-radical vowel *ე*, which comes from the static-passive voice forms. The aorist marker -*ე* is maintained in their first- and second-person forms.

Aorist	**(და)-ვ-ხატ-ე** (painted)
	მე (მხატვარ-მა S – erg., I, a painter)
	ის (სურათ-ი -O_{dr} – nom., that, a picture)
Pluperfect	**(და)-ვ-ე-ხატ-ე** (had painted)
	მას (მხატვარ-ს S – dat., he, a painter)
	მე (ადამიან-ი O_{dr} – nom., me, a person)

Apart from these formal similarities between the aorist and pluperfect, there are important differences as well:

1. The pluperfect forms of I conjugation verbs have inverted person markers; the object is marked with the subject marker while the subject with the object marker.
2. A tripersonal verb becomes a bipersonal verb since in the pluperfect it does not modify the indirect object.

ახალი მანქანა ვიყიდე და ნეტავ არ ***მეყიდა.***
I bought a new car and I wish I had not bought it.
მე მამაჩემს წერილს ხშირად ვუგზავნი, დღეს კი მისთვის ამანათი უნდა ***გამეგზავნა.***
I often send letters to my father, but today I should have sent him a parcel.

Pluperfect of the I conjugation one-stem verbs

და-მ-ე-წერ-ა მე ის I had written it	მ-ე-თხოვ-ა ის/ისინი (მისთვის) I had asked for it/them (from him)
და-გვ-ე-წერ-ა ჩვენ We had written it	გვ-ე-თხოვ-ა ის/ისინი We had asked for it/them
და-გ-ე-წერ-ა-(თ) შენ/თქვენ ის You/you had written it	გ-ე-თხოვ-ა-(თ) შენ/თქვენ ის/ისინი You/you had asked for it/them

და-ე-წერ-ა-(თ) მას/მათ ის/ისინი He/they had written it	ე-თხოვ-ა-(თ) მას/მათ ის/ისინი He/they had asked for it/them

> *ალბათ განცხადება უნდა **დაგვეწერა.***
> Probably we should have written an application.
> *უკეთესი იქნებოდა, რომ ეს წიგნი მისგან **გეთხოვათ.***
> It would have been better if you had asked this book from him// asked him for this book.

The I conjugation two-stem verbs generally do not have P/FSF in the pluperfect because pluperfect forms are based on the aorist forms.

და-მ-ე-ხატ-ა მე ის/ისინი I had painted it/them	და-ვ-ე-ხატ-ე მას მე He/they had painted me
და-გვ-ე-ხატ-ა ჩვენ ის/ისინი We had painted it/them	
და-გ-ე-ხატ-ა-(თ) შენ/თქვენ ის/ისინი You/you had painted it/them	და-ე-ხატ-ე-(თ) მას შენ/თქვენ He/they had painted you/you
და-ე-ხატ-ა-(თ) მას/მათ ის/ისინი They had painted it/them	და-ე-ხატ-ა-(თ)მას/მათ ის/ისინი They had painted it/them
მ-ე-ცემ-ა მე ის/ისინი I had beaten him/them	ვ-ე-ცემ-ე მას მე He had beaten me
გვ-ე-ცემ-ა ჩვენ ის/ისინი We had beaten him/them	ვ-ეცემ-ე-თ მას/მათ ჩვენ He/they had beaten us
გ-ე-ცემ-ა-(თ) შენ/თქვენ ის/ისინი You/you had beaten him/them	ე-ცემ-ე-(თ) მას/მათ შენ/თქვენ He/they had beaten you/you
ე-ცემ-ა-(თ) მას/მათ ის/ისინი He/they had beaten him/them	ე-ცემ-ა-(თ) მას/მათ ის/ისინი He/they had beaten him/them

> *ეს კარიკატურა რომ არ **დაგეხატა,** ის არ გაბრაზდებოდა.*
> If you had not painted this caricature, he would not have become angry.
> *მე დამაპატიმრებდნენ, ის კაცი რომ **მეცემა.***
> I would have been arrested if I had beaten that man.

გამო-მ-ე-ც-ა მე ის/ისინი I had published it/them	გა-ვ-ე-ც-ე-(თ) მას/მათ მე/ჩვენ He/they betrayed me/us

გამო-გვ-ე-ც-ა
ჩვენ ის/ისინი
We had published it/them

გამო-გ-ე-ც-ა-(თ)
შენ/თქვენ ის/ისინი
You/you had published it/them

გა-ე-ც-ე-(თ)
მას/მათ შენ/თქვენ
He/they had betrayed you/you

გამო-ე-ც-ა-(თ)
მას/მათ ის/ისინი
He/they had published it/them

გა-ე-ც-ა-თ
მას/მათ ის/ისინი
He/they had betrayed him/them

Some verbs with P/FSF ***-ებ*** retain it and have what looks like the causative particle ***-ინ*** but has no causative function.

ა-მ-ეშენ-ებ-**ინ**-ა მე ის/ისინი — I had built it/them
ა-გვ-ე-შენ-ებ-**ინ**-ა ჩვენ ის/ისინი — We had built it/them
ა-გ-ე-შენ-ებ-**ინ**-ა-(თ) შენ/თქვენ ის/ისინი — You/you had built it/them
ა-ე-შენ-ებ-**ინ**-ა-(თ) მას/მათ ის/ისინი — He/they had built it/them

Some verbs have both forms, with and without *-ინ*:

მო-მ-ე-პატიჟ-ა
მო-მ-ე-პატიჟ-ებ-**ინ**-ა
მე ის/ისინი
I had invited him/them

მო-გვ-ე-პატიჟ-ა
მო-გვ-ე-პატიჟ-ებ-**ინ**-ა
ჩვენ ის/ისინი
We had invited him/them

მო-გ-ე-პატიჟ-ა-(თ)
მო-გ-ე-პატიჟ-ებ-**ინ**-ა-(თ)
შენ/თქვენ ის/ისინი
You/you had invited him/them

მო-ე-პატიჟ-ა-(თ)
მო-ე-პატიჟ-ებ-**ინ**-ათ
მას/მათ ის/ისინი
He/they had invited him/them

> *ყველა მეზობელი უნდა* ***მომეპატიჟა.***
> *ყველა მეზობელი უნდა* ***მომეპატიჟებინა.***
> I should have invited all neighbours.

მ-ე-ბრძან-ა
მ-ე-ბრძან-ებ-**ინ**-ა მე ის/ისინი
I had ordered it/them

გვ-ე-ბრძან-ა
გვ-ე-ბრძან-ებ-**ინ**-ა ჩვენ ის/ისინი
We had ordered it/them

გ-ე-ბრძან-ა-(თ)
გ-ე-ბრძან-ებ-**ინ**-ა-(თ)
შენ/თქვენ ის/ისინი)

You/you have ordered it/them

ე-ბრძან-ა-(თ)
ე-ბრძან-ებ-**ინ**-ა-(თ)
მას/მათ ის/ისინი

He/they had ordered it/them

*მას **ებრძანა** მსახურისთვის ჩემი სასახლეში მიყვანა.*
*მას **ებრძანებინა** მსახურისთვის ჩემი სასახლეში მიყვანა.*
He had (apparently) ordered his servant to bring me to the palace.

გა-მ-ე-ღვიძ-ებ-ინ-ა
მე ის/ისინი
I had awakened him/them

გა-ვ-ე-ღვიძ-ებ-ინ-ე-(თ)
მას მე/ ჩვენ
He/they had awakened me/us

გა-გვ-ე-ღვიძ-ებ-ინ-ა
ჩვენ ის/ისინი
We had awakened him/them

გა-გ-ე-ღვიძ-ებ-ინ-ა-(თ)
შენ/თქვენ ის/ისინი
You/you had awakened him/them

გა-გ-ე-ღვიძ-ებ-ინ-ე-(თ)
შენ/თქვენ მე/ჩვენ
You/you had awakened me/us

გა-ე-ღვიძ-ებ-ინ-ა-(თ)
მას/მათ ის/ისინი
He/they had awakened him/them

გა-ე-ღვიძ-ებ-ინ-ა-(თ)
მას/მათ ის/ისინი
He/they had awakened him/them

The verbs losing their P/FSF *-ებ* in the perfect tense do not have the particle *-ინ* in the pluperfect:

ვ-ა-ქ-ებ – მ-ი-ქ-ი-ა (I praise – had praised)
ვ-ი-წყ-ებ – და-მ-ი-წყ-ი-ა (I start – had started)
ვ-ა-ღ-ებ – გა-მ-ი-ღ-ი-ა (I open – had opened)

მ-ე-ქ-ო მე ის/ისინი
I had praised him/them

ვ-ე-ქ-ე-(თ) მას/მათ მე/ჩვენ
He/they had praised me/us

გვ-ე-ქ-ო ჩვენ ის/ისინი
He had praised him/them

გ-ე-ქ-ო-(თ) შენ/თქვენ ის/ისინი
That you/you had praised him/them

გ-ე-ქ-ე-(თ) შენ/თქვენ მე/ჩვენ
You/you had praised me/us

ე-ქ-ო-(თ) მას/მათ ის/ისინი
He/they had praised him/them

ე-ქ-ე-(თ) მას/მათ შენ/თქვენ
He/they had praised you/you

Ablaut verbs

The verbs with syncopated root in I series because of P/FSF -**ი** added to it have their root vowel restored in the pluperfect:

ვ-შლ-ი – წა-მ-ე-შალ-ა (I erase – had erased)
ვ-თხრ-ი – გა-მ – ე-თხარ-ა (I dig – I had dug)
ვ-თლ-ი – გა-მ-ე-თხარ-ა (I peel – I had peeled)

წა-მ-ე-**შალ-**ა მე ის/ისინი I had erased it/them	წა-ვ-ე-**შალ-**ე(თ) მას/მათ მე/ჩვენ He/they had erased me/us
წა-გვ-ე-შალ-ა ჩვენ ის/ისინი We had erased it/them	
წა-გ-ე-შალ-ა-(თ) შენ/თქვენ ის/ისინი You/you had erased it/them	წა-ე-შალ-ე-(თ) მას/მათ შენ/თქვენ He/they had erased you/you
წა-ე-შალ-ა-(თ) მას/მათ ის/ისინი He/they had erased it/them	წა-ე-შალ-ა-(თ) მას/მათ ის/ისინი He/they had erased it/them

ეს აბზაცი არ უნდა ***წაგეშალათ.***
You should not have erased this paragraph.
მას რომ სიიდან არ ***წავეშალე****, მეც მოვიდოდი ამ კრებაზე.*
If he had not erased me from the list, I would have come to this meeting, too.

There are verbs with a syncopated root vowel in the pluperfect but not because of an added P/FSF, as happens in I series, but because they acquire the third-person marker: *ვ-კალ-ავ* > *ვ-კლ-ავ* (I kill) – the root vowel **ა** is syncopated because of P/FSF -***ავ*** is added to the stem. It re-emerges in II series where the P/FSF is removed: *მო-ვ-კალ-ი.*

მო-მ-ე-კლ-ა (I had killed) – here the root vowel is syncopated because the third-person marker -**ა** is added to it. It re-emerges in the object-oriented verbs: მო-ვ-ე-კალ-ი (he had killed me), მო-გ-ე-კალ-ი (you had killed me).

მო-მ-ე-**კლ-**ა მე ის/ისინი I had killed him/them	მო-გ-ე-**კალ-**ი(თ) შენ/თქვენ მე/ჩვენ You/you had killed me/us
მო-გვ-ე-**კლ-**ა ჩვენ ის/ისინი We had killed him/them	
მო-გ-ე-**კლ-**ა-(თ) შენ/თქვენ ის/ისინი You/you had killed him/them	მო-ე-**კალ-**ი-(თ) მას/მათ შენ/თქვენ He/they had killed you/you

მო-ე-კლ-ა-(თ) მას/მათ ის/ისინი He/they had killed him/them	მო-ე-კლ-ა-(თ) მას/მათ ის/ისინი He/they had killed him/them

The ablaut verbs with the *ე-ი* root vowel alteration have the vowel *ი* in pluperfect: *ვ-ჩხვლეტ* (I prick) – *და-მ-ე-ჩხვლიტ-ა* (I had pricked); *ვ-ხვრეტ* (I pierce) – *გა-მ-ე-ხვრიტ-ა* (I had pierced).

და-მ-ე-ჩხვლიტ-ა მე ის/ისინი I have prickled it/them	და-ვ-ე-ჩხვლიტ-ე(თ) მას/მათ მე/ჩვენ He/they had prickled me/us
და-გვ-ე-ჩხვლიტ-ა ჩვენ ის/ისინი We have prickled it/them	
და-გ-ე-ჩხვლიტ-ა-(თ) შენ/თქვენ ის/ისინი You/you have prickled it/them	და-ე-ჩხვლიტ-ე-(თ) მას/მათ შენ/თქვენ He/they had prickled you/you
და-ე-ჩხვლიტ-ა-(თ) მას/მათ ის/ისინი He/they prickled it/them	და-ე-ჩხვლიტ-ა-(თ) მას/მათ ის/ისინი He/they prickled it/them

The verbs ending with *-ევ* and *-ენ* have a similar conjugation. The roots of these verbs have the vowel *ე* replaced with *-ი*. The possible pluperfect forms could have been *ვ-ა-**მჩნ-ევ*** > შე-მ-ე-**მჩნ-ივ**-ა and *ვ-ა-**ღვ-ენ*** > *და-მ-ე-**ღვ-ინ**-ა*.

However, the consonant *ვ* is lost because of a phonetic change: შე-მ-ე-**მჩნი**-ა.

Verbs ending with *-ევ*

შე-მ-ე-მჩნი-ა მე ის (მისთვის) I had noticed it (in him)	შე-ვ-ე-მჩნი-ე-(თ) მას/მათ მე/ჩვენ He/they had noticed me/us
შე-გვ-ე-მჩნი-ა ჩვენ ის (მისთვის) We had noticed it (in him)	
შე-გ-ე-მჩნი-ა-(თ) შენ/თქვენ ის (მისთვის) You/you had noticed it (in him)	შე-ე-მჩნი-ე-(თ) მას/მათ შენ (თქვენ) He/they had noticed you/you
შე-ე-მჩნი-ა-(თ) მას/მათ ის (მისთვის) He/they had noticed it (in him)	შე-ე-მჩნი-ა-(თ) მას/მათ ის He/they had noticed it

Verbs ending with -ენ

და-მ-ე-დგინ-ა მე ის
I had ascertained/established it

და-გვ-ე-დგინ-ა ჩვენ ის
We had ascertained it

და-გ-ე-დგინ-ა-(თ) შენ/თქვენ ის
You/you had ascertained it

და-ე-დგინ-ა-(თ) მას/მათ ის
He/they had ascertained it

> *ნეტავ ეს ფაქტი ადრე* ***დაგვედგინა.***
> I wish we had ascertained this fact earlier.
> *ექიმს დიაგნოზი დროზე რომ არ* ***დაედგინა****, ავადმყოფი ვერ გადარჩებოდა.*
> If the doctor had not established the diagnosis in time, the patient would not have survived.

II conjugation

The pluperfect forms of the II conjugation, i.e. dynamic-passive voice verbs, depend on the number of persons they modify.

The pluperfect forms of monopersonal dynamic passive voice verbs are based on their past passive participle to which the aorist forms of the auxiliary verb *to be* are added.

The pluperfect of monopersonal verbs

გა-ვ-მდიდრებულ-იყავ-ი-(თ) მე/ჩვენ I/we had become rich	და-ვ-ბერებულ-იყავ-ი-(თ) მე /ჩვენ I/we have grown old
გა-მდიდრებულ-იყავ-ი-(თ) შენ/თქვენ You/you had become rich	და-ბერებულ-იყავ-ი-თ შენ/თქვენ You/you had grown old
გა-მდიდრებულ-ი-ყ-ო ის He had become rich	და-ბერებულ-იყ-ო ის He had grown old
გა-მდიდრებულ-იყვ-ნენ ისინი They had become rich	და-ბერებულ-იყვ-ნენ ისინი They had grown old

> *ჩვენ რომ* ***გავმდიდრებულიყავით****, ამ ქოხში არ ვიცხოვრებდით.*
> If we had become rich, we would not live in this hut.
> *ჩვენი საყვარელი მასწავლებელი ძალიან* ***დაბერებულიყო.***
> Our beloved teacher had grown very old.

Ablaut verbs

Monopersonal ablaut passive voice verbs follow the same rule. They have a past passive participle for their I series stem – *ჭყლეტ* (crush), *გრეხ* (twist), etc. – to which the aorist forms of the auxiliary verb *to be* are added. In the first and second person, the -ი suffix marks the tense.

გა-ვ-ჭყლეტილ-იყავ-ი-(თ) მე/ჩვენ I/we had been crushed	და-ვ-გრეხილ-იყავ-ი-(თ) მე /ჩვენ I/we had been twisted
გა-ჭყლეტილ-იყავ-ი-(თ)შენ/თქვენ You/you had been crushed	და-გრეხილ-იყავ-ი-თ შენ/თქვენ You/you had been twisted
გა-ჭყლეტილ-იყ-ო ის He had been crushed	და-გრეხილ-იყ-ო-ს ის He had been twisted
გა-ჭყლეტილ-იყვ-ნენ ისინი They had been crushed	და-გრეხილ-იყვ-ნენ ისინი They had been twisted

The pluperfect of the II conjugation monopersonal verbs

The pluperfect forms of II conjugation, i.e. dynamic-passive voice verbs, are based on their aorist forms extended with the particle -**ოდ** and have the suffix -ი as the tense marker. The morpheme distribution is shown in the following charts.

1. ვიმალები – დავმალულიყავი (I hide – had hidden myself)

Preverb	*Person marker*	*Past passive participle: root*	*P/FSF*	*Suffix of past passive participle*	*Aorist forms of the auxiliary verb to be*	*Tense marker*	*Person/ number marker*
და	ვ	მალ	–	ულ	იყავ	ი	თ
და	–	მალ	–	ულ	იყ	ო	
და	–	მალ	–	ულ	იყვ		ნენ

2. ვბერდები – დავბერებულიყავი (I grow old – had grown old)

Preverb	*Person marker*	*Past passive participle: root*	*P/FSF*	*Suffix of past passive participle*	*Aorist forms of the auxiliary verb to be*	*Tense marker*	*Person/ number marker*
და	ვ	ბერ	ებ	ულ	იყავ	ი	თ
და	–	ბერ	ებ	ულ	იყ	ო	
და	–	ბერ	ებ	ულ	იყვ		ნენ

II conjugation of bipersonal verbs

და-ვ-ლაპარაკ-ებ-ოდ-ი-(თ) მე/ჩვენ მას/მათ
I/we had spoken/talked with him/them

და-ვ-ხმარ-ებ-ოდ-ი-(თ) მე/ჩვენ მას/მათ
I/we had helped him/them

და-ლაპარაკ-ებ-ოდ-ი-(თ) შენ/თქვენ მას/მათ
You/you had spoken/talked with him/them

და-ხმარ-ებ-ოდ-ი-(თ) შენ/თქვენ მას/მათ
You/you had helped him/them

და-ლაპარაკ-ებ-ოდ-ა/ნენ ის/ისინი მას/მათ
He/they had spoken/talked to him/them

და-ხმარ-ებ-ოდ-ა/ნენ ის/ისინი მას/მათ
He/they had helped him/them

*ნეტავ დირექტორს **დავლაპარაკებოდი** და ეს საკითხი მშვიდობიანად **მომეგვარებინა**.*
I wish I had spoken with the manager and resolved this problem peacefully.
*უნდა **დალაპარაკებოდი** ჩემს ძმას და ის ყველაფერს აგიხსნიდა.*
You should have talked with my brother, and he would have explained everything to you.
*მას ვინმე რომ **დახმარებოდა**, ახლა გამოცდა ჩაბარებული ექნებოდა.*
If someone had helped him, he would have passed his exams by now.

Medio-active verbs without P/FSF

მ-ე-ცინ-ა მე
I had laughed

გვ-ე-ცინ-ა ჩვენ
We had laughed

გ-ე-ცინ-ა შენ
You had laughed

გ-ე-ცინ-ა-თ თქვენ
You had laughed

ე-ცინ-ა მას
He had laughed

ე-ცინ-ა-თ მათ
They had laughed

*ამდენი რომ **მეცინა**, მუცელი ამტკივდებოდა.*
If I had laughed so much, I would have had a belly ache.
*ამაზე კი არ უნდა **გეტირათ**, უნდა **გეცინათ**.*
You should not have cried but should have laughed at it.

The suffixes that appear in the perfect forms of medio-active verbs without P/FSF are present in their pluperfect forms as well. These suffixes were absent in their I series stem. For example, the suffix **-ოლ** is added to the verb *თრთის* (he trembles) both in the perfect (*მ-ი-თრთ-ოლ-ია*) and pluperfect forms.

მ-ე-თრთ-ოლ-ა მე
I had trembled
გვ-ე-თრთ-ოლ-ა ჩვენ
We had trembled
გ-ე-თრთ-ოლ-ა-(თ) შენ/თქვენ
You/you had trembled
ე-თრთ-ოლ-ა-(თ) მას/მათ
He/they trembled

Medio-active verbs with P/FSF

These verbs lose their P/FSF both in the perfect and pluperfect forms:

მ-ე-ცურ-ა მე I had swum	და-მ-ე-გვიან-ა მე I had been late	მ-ე-ზრუნ-ა მე I had taken care
გვ-ე-ცურ-ა ჩვენ We had swum	და-გვ-ე-გვიან-ა ჩვენ We had been late	გვ-ე-ზრუნ-ა ჩვენ We had taken care
გ-ე-ცურ-ა-(თ) შენ/თქვენ You/you had swum	და-გ-ე-გვიან-ა-(თ) შენ/თქვენ You/you had been late	გ-ე-ზრუნ-ა-(თ) შენ/თქვენ You/you had taken care
ე-ცურ-ა-(თ)მას/მათ He/they had swum	და-ე-გვიან-ა-(თ) მას/მათ He/they had been late	ე-ზრუნ-ა-(თ) მას/მათ He/they had taken care

*ეს მდინარე რომ **გადაგვეცურა**, იქიდან მზის ჩასვლას დავინახავდით.*
If we had crossed (swum across) this river, we would have seen the sunset from there.
*გამოცდაზე არ უნდა **დაგვეგვიანა**.*
You should not have been late for the exam.
*მას ამაზე ადრე რომ **ეზრუნა**, ახლა ეს პრობლემა არ ექნებოდა.*
If he had taken care of this earlier, he would not have this problem now.

Thus, I, II, and III series forms are as follows:

ვცურავ – I swim/am swimming
ვიცურე – I swam
მეცურა – I had swum

In some verbs P/FSF *-ობ* is lost in their perfect tense forms, and as a result of a phonetic change, the consonant *-ვ-* appears in their stem:

ქანაობს – უქანა**ვი**ა (he swings – had swung)
თევზაობს – უთევზა**ვი**ა (he is fishing – had fished)
ცურაობს – უცურა**ვი**ა (he swims – had swum)

The same phonetic change happens in the pluperfect as well:

მ-ე-ქანავ-ა მე I had swung	მ-ე-თევზავ-ა მე I had fished	მ-ე-ცურავ-ა მე I had swum
გვ-ე-ქანავ-ა ჩვენ We had swung	გვ-ე-თევზავ-ა ჩვენ We had fished	გვ-ე-ცურავ-ა ჩვენ We had swum
გ-ე-ქანავ-ა-(თ) შენ/თქვენ You/you had swung	გ-ე-თევზავ-ა-(თ) შენ/თქვენ You/you had fished	გ-ე-ცურავ-ა-(თ) შენ/თქვენ You/you had swum
ე-ქანავ-ა-(თ)მას/მათ He/they had sung	ე-თევზავ-ა-(თ)მას/მათ He/they had fished	ე-ცურავ-ა-(თ)მას/მათ He/they had swum

ამდენ ხანს არ უნდა ***გექანავა*** *და თავი არ* ***გეტკინებოდა.***
You should not have swung so long, and you would not have had a headache.
აქ რომ ***გვეთევზავა,*** *ბევრ თევზს დავიჭერდით.*
If we had been fishing here, we would have caught a lot of fish.

The verbs with the alternating root vowels have *ე* in the perfect tense and *ი* in the pluperfect. The same happens with the alternating syllables *ენ/ინ*; in the pluperfect the root will have ***ინ.***

მ-ე-ფრ**ინ**-ა მე I had flown around	მ-ე-სტვ**ინ**-ა მე I had whistled
გვ-ე-ფრ**ინ**-ა ჩვენ We had flown around	გვ-ე-სტვ**ინ**-ა ჩვენ We had whistled
გ-ე-ფრ**ინ**-ა-(თ) შენ/თქვენ You/you had flown around	გ-ე-სტვ**ინ**-ა-(თ) შენ/თქვენ You/you had whistled
ე-ფრ**ინ**-ა-(თ) მას/მათ He/they had flown around	ე-სტვ**ინ**-ა-(თ) მას/მათ He/they had whistled

Bipersonal medio-active verbs lose their indirect object in the pluperfect. It acquires a postposition.

მ-ე-ჯობნ-ა მე მისთვის I had surpassed him	გ-ე-ჯობნ-ა-(თ) შენ/თქვენ მისთვის You/you had surpassed him
გვ-ე-ჯობნ-ა ჩვენ მისთვის We had surpassed him	ე-ჯობნ-ა-(თ) მას/მათ მისთვის He/they had surpassed him

ნეტავ ჩვენს მოჭიდავეს მეტოქისათვის ***ეჯობნა****, მაშინ ჩვენს გუნდს სამი ოქროს მედალი ექნებოდა.*
I wish our wrestler had defeated (surpassed) his opponent, then we would have had three gold medals.
მას რომ ჩემთვის ***ეჯობნა****, ბევრს იტრაბახებდა.*
If he had surpassed me, he would have boasted a lot.

მ-ე-დარაჯ-ა მე მისთვის/მათთვის I had guarded/watched out for him/them	მ-ე-ხელმძღვანელ-ა მე მისთვის/მათთვის I had directed/advised him/them
გვ-ე-დარაჯ-ა ჩვენ მისთვის/მათთვის We had guarded/watched out him/them	გვ-ე-ხელმძღვანელ-ა ჩვენ მისთვის/მათთვის We had directed/advised him/them
გ-ე-დარაჯ-ა-(თ) შენ/თქვენ მისთვის/მათთვის You/you had guarded/watched out him/them	გ-ე-ხელმძღვანელ-ა-(თ) შენ/თქვენ მისთვის/მათთვის You/you had directed/advised
ე-დარაჯ-ა-(თ) მას/მათ მისთვის/მათთვის He/they had guarded	ე-ხელმძღვანელ-ა-(თ) მას/მათ მისთვის/მათთვის (If) he/they had directed/advised

In the pluperfect, just like in the perfect tense, all bipersonal medio-active verbs become monopersonal because an indirect object modified by them is transformed into an adjunct object.

მინდოდა ფოსტალიონისთვის ***მედარაჯა****, მაგრამ ჩამეძინა.*
I wanted to watch for the mailman, but I fell asleep.
ამ გუნდისთვის თქვენ უნდა ***გეხელმძღვანელათ****.*
You should have conducted this chorus.

IV conjugation verbs

Monopersonal IV conjugation verbs are based on their past participle forms to which the aorist forms of the auxiliary verb *to be* are added:

ვ-წერებულ-იყავ-ი(თ) მე/ჩვენ (სიაში) I/we had been written/included (in a list)	და-ვ-ხატულ-იყავ-ი-(თ) მე/ჩვენ I/we had been painted

წერებულ-იყავ-ი(თ) შენ/თქვენ (სიაში) You/you had been written/included (in a list)	და-ხატულ-იყავ-ი-(თ) შენ/თქვენ You/you had been painted
წერებულ-იყ-ო ის (სიაში) He had been written/included (in a list)	და-ხატულ-იყ-ო ის He had been painted
წერებულ-იყვ-ნენ ისინი(სიაში) They had been written/included (in a list)	დახატულ-იყვ-ნენ ისინი They had been painted

ნეტავ იმ სიაში ჩვენც ***ვწერებულიყავით.***
I wish we (our names) had been written in that list.
იმ სიაში ჩვენც უნდა ***ვწერებულიყავით.***
In that list we (our names), too, should have been written.

IV conjugation bipersonal verbs have the extending suffix **-ოდ** added to their stem in the pluperfect.

ვ-ყვარებ-ოდ-ი-(თ) მე/ჩვენ მას/მათ He/they had loved me/us	მო-ვ-წონებ-ოდ-ი-(თ) მე /ჩვენ მას/მათ He/they had liked me/us
ჰ-ყვარებ-ოდ-ი-(თ) შენ/თქვენ მას/მათ He/they had loved you/you	მო-ს-წონებ-ოდ-ი-(თ) შენ/თქვენ მას/მათ He/they had liked you/you
ჰ-ყვარებ-ოდ-ა-(თ) ის მას/მათ He/they had loved	მო-ს-წონებ-ოდ-ა-(თ) ის მას/მათ He/they had liked him
ჰ-ყვარებ-ოდ-ნენ ისინი მას/მათ He/they had loved them	მო-ს-წონებ-ოდ-ნენ ისინი მას/მათ He/they had liked them

9.6.3.3 *Perfect subjunctive*

The perfect subjunctive tense has largely fallen out of use in both written and spoken Georgian, and depending on the context, other tenses conveying subjunctive mood are used instead (the present and future subjunctives, the optative or pluperfect). Verbs in the perfect subjunctive tense refer to two diametrically opposed temporal fields; they either denote probable, but counterfactual action in the past, or a wished-for and desirable action in the future. In the former case, the statements referring to the past always imply denial that the action expressed in the perfect subjunctive could have taken place. In the latter case, the use of the perfect subjunctive is restricted mostly to curses, oaths, or toasts. Understandably, it presents a particular challenge to translate these verbs into English adequately. As an approximate equivalent to the Georgian perfect subjunctive, in the following charts, we use the English past perfect tense when referring to the past and the present subjunctive when referring to a wished-for action in the future.

1. Verbs in the perfect subjunctive referring to a counterfactual action in the past:

   არავის ახსოვს, მას რამე დანაშაული ***ჩაედინოს.***
   No one remembers his having committed any wrongdoing (i.e. he could not have done it).
   ისე ლაპარაკობს, თითქოს „ვეფხისტყაოსანი“ მას ***დაეწეროს.***
   He speaks as if he had written “The Knight in the Panther’s Skin” (i.e. of course, he did not write this famous poem).
   არა მგონია, მე ეს წიგნი სახლში ***წამეღოს.***
   I do not think I took (had taken) home this book (i.e. I most certainly did not).

2. Verbs in the perfect subjunctive referring to a wished-for and desirable action in the future:

   სულ კარგად და ბედნიერად ***გეცხოვროთ!***
   May you always live well and happily!
   ყველა ბრძოლაში ***გაემარჯვებინოს*** *ჩვენს ხალხს!*
   May our people be victorious in all battles!
   გისურვებთ წარმატებით ***დაგემთავრებინოთ*** *ეს სამუშაო!*
   May you complete this work successfully!

3. A wish or desire for something to happen may be expressed in four different ways depending on the context.

   ნეტავ ეს საქმე მალე ***დაამთავრო*** (Optative).
   May you finish this work soon.
   ნეტავ ამ საქმეს უკვე ***ამთავრებდე*** (Present Subjunctive).
   I wish you be (were) already finishing this works.
   ნეტავ ამ საქმეს მალე ***დაამთავრებდე*** (Future Subjunctive).
   I wish you were to finish this work soon.
   ნეტავ ეს საქმე წარმატებით ***დაგემთავრებინოს*** (Perfect Subjunctive).
   May (I wish) you finish this work soon.

In each of these sentences the verb refers either to the present subjunctive, future subjunctive, optative, and perfect subjunctive.

Because of the peculiar character of the perfect subjunctive, ordinarily a verb in the optative is preferable when referring to a desirable action in the future. The perfect subjunctive forms sound too affected.

I conjugation

The verbs in the perfect subjunctive are based on the pluperfect forms, in both tenses the root is preceded with the pre-radical vowel -*ე*, which usually marks the static-passive voice verbs. However, the tense markers in the perfect subjunctive forms are the same as in the optative for all three persons.

Optative:	მე (მხატვარ-მა S-erg.)	**(და)-ვ-ხატ-ო**
	I (an artist)	should paint
	ის (სურათ-ი Od-nom.)	
	it (a picture)	
Pluperfect:	მე (მხატვარ-ს S-dat.)	**(და)-მ-ე-ხატ-ა**
	(I wish) I (an artist)	have painted
	ის (სურათ-ი Od-nom.)	
	it (a picture)	
Perfect subjunctive:	მე (მხატვარ-ს S-Dat)	**(და)-მ-ე-ხატ-ო-ს**
	(May) I (an artist)	paint
	Or (If) I (an artist)	had painted
	ის (სურათ-ი Od-nom.)	
	it (a picture)	
	it (picture)	

The verbs in the perfect subjunctive have the same properties as in the perfect and pluperfect. The person markers of the active voice verb are inverted, the object is denoted with the person markers of the subject and vice versa. The tripersonal verbs in all these three tenses become bipersonal and the indirect object becomes an adjunct object.

Conjugation of one-stem active voice verbs in the perfect subjunctive

და-მ-ე-წერ-ო-ს მე ის/ისინი If I had written it/them	მ-ე-თხოვ-ო-ს მე ის/ისინი If I had asked it/them
დე-გვ-ე-წერ-ო-ს ჩვენ ის/ისინი If we had written it/them	გვ-ე-თხოვ-ო-ს ჩვენ ის/ისინი If we had asked it/them
და-გ-ე-წერ-ო-ს/თ შენ/თქვენ ის/ისინი If you/you had written it/them	გ-ე-თხოვ-ო-ს/თ შენ/თქვენ ის/ისინი If you/you had asked it/them

და-ე-წერ-ო-ს/თ
მას/მათ ის/ისინი
If he/they had written it/them

ე-თხოვ-ო-ს/თ
მას/მათ ის/ისინი
If he/they had asked it/them

მეგობარს წერილს ***ვწერ*** (present tense).
I write a letter to (my) friend.
მეგობარს წერილი უნდა ***მივწერო*** (optative).
I should write a letter to (my) friend.
მეგობრისთვის წერილი ***მიმიწერია*** (present perfect).
I have written a letter to (my) friend.
მეგობრისთვის წერილი უნდა ***მიმეწერა*** (pluperfect).
I should have written a letter to (my) friend.
მეგობრისთვის წერილი ხშირად ***მიმეწეროს*** (perfect subjunctive).
May (I wish) I often write a letter to my friend.

As these examples show, a tripersonal verb **წერ** (write) in the present and optative tenses becomes a bipersonal in the perfect, pluperfect, and perfect subjunctive because the indirect object ***მეგობარს*** (to a friend) acquires the postposition ***-თვის*** (***მეგობრისთვის***, for a friend) and is no longer modified by the verb.

Conjugation of two-stem active voice verbs in the perfect subjunctive

Since the perfect subjunctive verb forms are based on the optative, the majority of them do not have P/FSF.

და-მ-ე-ხატ-ო-ს მე ის/ისინი
If I had painted it/them

და-ვ-ე-ხატ-ო/თ მას მე/ჩვენ
If he/they had painted me/us

და-გვ-ე-ხატ-ო-ს ჩვენ ის/ისინი
If we had painted it/them

და-გ-ე-ხატ-ო-ს/თ
შენ/თქვენ ის/ისინი
If you/you had painted it/them

და-ე-ხატ-ო-(თ)
მას/მათ შენ/თქვენ
If he/they has/have painted you/you

და-ე-ხატ-ო-ს/თ
მას/მათ ის/ისინი
If he/they had painted it

და-ე-ხატ-ო-ს/თ
მას/მათ ის/ისინი
If he/they had painted him/them

მ-ე-ცემ-ო-ს მე ის/ისინი
If I had beaten him/them

ვ-ე-ცემ-ო/თ მას/მათ მე/ჩვენ
If he/they had beaten me/us

გვ-ე-ცემ-ო-ს ჩვენ ის/ისინი
If we had beaten him/them

გ-ე-ცემ-ო-ს/თ შენ/თქვენ ის/ისინი If you/you had beaten him/them	ე-ცემ-ო-ს/თ მას/მათ შენ/თქვენ If he/they had beaten you/you
ე-ცემ-ო-ს/თ მას/მათ ის/ისინი If he/they had beaten him/them	ე-ცემ-ო-ს/თ მას/მათ ის/ისინი If he/they had beaten him/them

არა მგონია, მას ეს პეიზაჟი ***დაეხატოს.***
I do not think he had painted this landscape (i.e. most probably he did not).
ვინ დაიჯერებს, ამ პატარა ბიჭებს ეს კაცი ***ეცემოთ?***
Who would believe these little boys had beaten up this man? (i.e. the boys are no match to this man).
ნეტავ მას ჩემი პორტრეტი ***დაეხატოს.***
I wish he paint my portrait.

The verbs with the tense marker -ა in the pluperfect, usually will have the -ო marker in the perfect subjunctive, as was already shown:

ჩაედინ-**ა**: ჩაედინ-**ო**-ს, მიმეწერ-ა: მიმეწერ-**ო**-ს;
დაეხატ-ა: დაეხატ-**ო**-ს; გეთხოვ-**ა**: გეთხოვ-**ო**-ს.
ეცემ-ა: ეცემ-**ო**-ს; დაგემთავრებინ-**ა**: დაგემთავრებინ-**ო**-ს;

Some verbs with the tense marker **-ა** in the pluperfect will have the **-ე** marker in the perfect subjunctive:

Aorist:	გამო-ვ-ე-ც-ი	I published
Pluperfect:	გამო-მ-ე-ც-**ა**	I had published
Perfect Subjunctive	გამო-მ-ე-ც-**ე**-ს	(if) I had published

გამო-მ-ე-ც-ე-ს მე ის/ისინი
(If) I had published it/them
გამო-გვ-ე-ც-ე-ს ჩვენ ის/ისინი
(If) we had published it/them
გამო-გ-ე-ც-ე-ს-(თ) შენ/თქვენ ის/ისინი
(If) you/you had published it/them
გამო-ე-ც-ე-ს მას ის/ისინი
(If) he had published it/them
გამო-ე-ც-ე-თ მათ ის/ისინი
(If) they had published it/them

Some verbs with the P/FSF **-ებ** have an additional marker **-ინ**, which is spelled as the causative particle **-ინ**, but it does not have a causative function.

ა-მ-ე-შენ-ებ-ინ-ო-ს მე ის/ისინი (If) I had built it/them	და-მ-ე-სრულ-ებ-ინ-ო-ს მე ის/ისინი (If) I had finished it/them
ა-გვ-ე-შენ-ებ-ინ-ო-ს ჩვენ ის/ისინი (If) we had built it/them	და-გვ-ე-სრულ-ებ-ინ-ო-ს ჩვენ ის/ისინი (If) we had finished it/them
ა-გ-ე-შენ-ებ-ინ-ო-ს/თ შენ/თქვენ ის/ისინი (If) you/you had built it/them	და-გ-ე-სრულ-ებ-ინ-ო-ს/თ შენ/თქვენ ის/ისინი (If) you/you had finish it/them
ა-ე-შენ-ებ-ინ-ო-ს/თ მას/მათ ის/ისინი (If) he/they had built it/them	და-ე-სრულ-ებ-ინ-ო-ს/თ მას/მათ ის/ისინი (If) he/they had finished it/them

მითხრეს, ვითომ მას წიგნი ***გამოეცეს****, მაგრამ არ მჯერა.*
I was told the supposedly he had published a book, but I do not believe it.
ვეჭვობ, მათ უკვე ***დაესრულებინოთ*** *ეს პროექტი.*
I doubt they had finished this project.
მალე ***ავვეშენებინოს*** *ჩვენი სახლი.*
May we build our house soon.

Like in the optative, some verbs in the perfect subjunctive have two synonymous forms, one with the *-**ინ*** after *-**ებ*** and the other without it:

მო-მ-ე-პატიჟ-ო-ს მო-მეპატიჟ-ებ-**ინ**-ო-ს მე ის /ისინი	(If) I had invited him/them
მო-გვ-ე-პატიჟ-ო-ს მო-გვ-ე-პატიჟ-ებ-**ინ**-ო-ს ჩვენ ის/ისინი	(If) we had invited him/them
მო-გ-ე-პატიჟ-ო-ს/თ მო-გ-ე-პატიჟ-ებ-**ინ**-ო-ს/თ შენ/თქვენ ის/ისინი	(If) you/you had invited him/them
მო-ე-პატიჟ-ო-ს/თ მო-ე-პატიჟ-ებ-**ინ**-ო-ს/თ მას/მათ ის/ისინი	(If) he/they had invited him/them

*მომავალ წელს ყველა ჩემი მეგობარი **მომეპატიჟოს** და მათთვის მემასპინძლოს.*
*მომავალ წელს ყველა ჩემი მეგობარი **მომეპატიჟებინოს** და მათთვის მემასპინძლოს.*
May I invite all my friends and host them next year.

მ-ე-ბრძან-ო-ს მ-ე-ბრძან-ებ-**ინ**-ო-ს მე ის/ისინი	(If) I had ordered it/them
გვ-ე-ბრძან-ო-ს გვ-ე-ბრძან-ებ-**ინ**-ო-ს ჩვენ ის/ისინი	(If) we had ordered it/them
გ-ე-ბრძან-ო-ს/თ გ-ე-ბრძან-ებ-**ინ**-ო-ს-/თ შენ ის/ისინი	(If) you had ordered it/them
ე-ბრძან-ო-ს/თ ე-ბრძან-ებ-**ინ**-ო-ს/თ მას ის/ისინი	(If) he had ordered it/them

*მას რა უფლება აქვს, ჩვენთვის **ებრძანოს** ამ ბინის დაცლა?!*
*მას რა უფლება აქვს, ჩვენთვის **ებრძანებინოს** ამ ბინის დაცლა?!*
What right does he have to order us to vacate this apartment?!

გა-მ-ე-ღვიძ-ებ-ინ-ო-ს მე ის/ისინი (If) I had awakened him/them	გა-ვ-ეღვიძ-ებ-ინ-ო-(თ) მას/მათ მე/ ჩვენ (If) he/they had awakened me/us
გა-გვ-ე-ღვიძ-ებ-ინ-ო-ს ჩვენ ის/ისინი (If) we had awakened him/them	
გა-გ-ე-ღვიძ-ებ-ინ-ო-ს/თ შენ/თქვენ ის/ისინი (If) you/you had awakened him/them	გა-გ-ე-ღვიძ-ებ-ინ-ო-ს/თ შენ/თქვენ ის/ისინი (If) you/you had awakened him/them
გა-ე-ღვიძ-ებ-ინ-ო-ს/თ მას/მათ ის/ისინი (If) he/they had awakened him/them	გა-ე-ღვიძ-ებ-ინ-ო-ს/თ მას/მათ ის/ისინი (If) he/they had awakened him/them

*ნეტავ ბავშვები უფრო ადრე **გაგეღვიძებინოს**.*
I wish you had awakened the children earlier.

The verbs dropping their P/FSF *-ებ* in the perfect and pluperfect do not have it in the perfect subjunctive.

მ-ე-ქ-ო-ს მე ის/ისინი (If) I had praised him/them	ვ-ე-ქ-ო-(თ) მას/მათ მე/ ჩვენ (If) he/they had praised me/us
გვ-ე-ქ-ო-ს ჩვენ ის/ისინი (If) we had praised him/them	
გ-ე-ქ-ო-ს/თ შენ/თქვენ ის/ისინი (If) you/you had praised him/them	გ-ე-ქ-ო-ს/თ შენ/თქვენ ის/ისინი (If) you/you had praised me/us
ე-ქ-ო-ს/თ მას/მათ ის/ისინი (If) he/they had praised him/them	ე-ქ-ო-ს/თ მას ის/ისინი (If) he/they had praised him/the

შენ ვინ გითხრა, თითქოს მას ჩემი სტატია ***ექოს****?*
Who told you as if he had praised my article?
მას არ სჯერა, რომ ჩვენ მისი თამაში ***გვექოს****.*
He does not believe we had praised his acting.
არ მახსოვს, მათ როდისმე ვინმე ***ექოთ****.*
I don't remember that they have ever praised anybody.

Ablaut verbs

Since ablaut verbs in the perfect subjunctive are based on the optative forms, their syncopated root vowel in I series will be restored in the perfect subjunctive.

Present	ვ-შ□ლ-ი-(თ)
Optative	წა-ვ-**შალ**-ო
Perfect Subjunctive	წა მ-ე-**შალ**-ო-ს

The verbs with syncopated stem in I series caused by the P/FSF -ი, have their root vowel restored in the perfect subjunctive (ვ-**შლ**-ი – წა-მ-ე-**შალ**-ოს).

წა-მ-ე-**შალ**-ო-ს მე ის/ისინი (If) I had erased it/them	წა-ვ-ე-**შალ**-ო-(თ) მას/მათ მე/ჩვენ (If) he/they had erased me/us
წა-გვ-ე-შალ-ო-ს ჩვენ ის/ისინი (If) we had erased it/them	
წა-გ-ე-შალ-ო-ს/თ შენ/თქვენ ის/ისინი (If) you/you had erased it/them	წა-ე-შალ-ო-(თ) მას/მათ შენ/თქვენ (If) he/they had erased you/you
წა-ე-შალ-ო-ს/თ მას/მათ ის/ისინი (If) he/they had erased it/them	წა-ე-შალ-ო-ს/თ მას/მათ ის/ისინი (If) he/they had erased him/them

However, there are a few verbs that have their stem syncopated not because of P/FSF, as it happens in I series, but because of the perfect subjunctive tense markers added to them.

მო-მ-ე-**კლ**-ა-ს მე ის/ისინი
(If) I had killed him/them

მო-ვ-ე-**კალ**-ი-(თ) მას/მათ მე/ჩვენ
(If) he/they had killed me/us

მო-გვ-ე-**კლ**-ა-ს
ჩვენ ის/ისინი
(If) we had killed him/them

მო-გ-ე-**კლ**-ა-ს/თ
შენ/თქვენ ის/ისინი
(If) you/you had killed him/them

მო-ე-**კალ**-ი-(თ) მას/მათშენ/თქვენ
(If) he/they had killed you/you

მო-ე-**კლ**-ა-ს/თ
მას/მათ ის/ისინი
(If) he/they had killed him/them

მო-ე-**კლ**-ა-ს/თ
მას/მათ ის/ისინი
(If) he/they had killed him/them

ვერ წარმომიდგენია, სიხარულს ვინმე ***მოეკლას.***
I can't imagine happiness ever had killed anyone.
ტყუილია, თითქოს მათ დათვი ***მოეკლათ.***
It's a lie that they had killed a bear.

The ablaut verbs with stem vowel *ე-ი* alteration have the vowel *ი* in the perfect subjunctive.

და-მ-ე-**ჩხვლიტ**-ო-ს
მე ის/ისინი
(If) I had pricked him/them

და-ვ-ე-**ჩხვლიტ**-ო-(თ)
მას/მათ მე/ჩვენ
(If) he/they had pricked me/us

და-გვ-ე-ჩხვლიტ-ო-ს
ჩვენ ის/ისინი
(If) we had pricked him/them

და-გ-ე-ჩხვლიტ-ო-ს/თ
შენ/თქვენ ის/ისინი
(If) you/you had pricked him/them

და-ე-ჩხვლიტ-ო-(თ)
მას/მათ შენ/თქვენ
(If) he/they had pricked you/you

და-ე-ჩხვლიტ-ო-ს/თ
მას/მათ ის/ისინი
(If) he/they had pricked him/them

და-ე-ჩხვლიტ-ო-ს/თ
მას/მათ ის/ისინი
(If) he/they had pricked him/them

The verbs ending with -*ევ* and -*ენ* conjugate similarly, the vowel *ე* is replaced with *ი*.

-ევ-ending verbs

შე-მ-ე-მჩნიო-ს მე ის/ისინი (მისთვის) (If) I had noticed it/them (in him)	შე-ვ-ე-მჩნი-ო-(თ) მას/მათ მე/ჩვენ (If) he/they had noticed me/us
შე-გვ-ე-მჩნი-ო-ს ჩვენ ის/ისინი (მისთვის) (If) we had noticed it/them (in him)	
შე-გ-ე-მჩნი-ო-ს/თ შენ ის/ისინი (მისთვის) (If) you/you had noticed it/them (in him)	შე-ე-მჩნი-ო-თ მას/მათ შენ/თქვენ (If) he/they had noticed you/you
შე-ე-მჩნი-ო-ს/თ მას ის/ისინი (მისთვის) (If) he/they had noticed it/them (in him)	შე-ე-მჩნი-ო-ს/თ მას ის/ისინი (მისთვის) (If) he/they had noticed it/them (in him)

-ენ ending verbs

და-მ-ე-დგინ-ო-ს მე ის (მისთვის) (If) I had established/proved it (to him) და-გვ-ე-დგინ-ო-ს ჩვენ ის (მისთვის) (If) we had established/proved it (to him)	და-მ-ე-წვინ-ო-ს მე ის/ისინი (If) I had put him/them (to bed) და-გვ-ე-წვინ-ო-ს ჩვენ ის/ისინი (If) we had put him/them (to bed)
და-გ-ე-დგინ-ო-ს/თ შენ/თქვენ ის (მისთვის) (If) you/you had established/ proved it (to him)	და-გ-ე-წვინ-ო-ს/თ შენ/თქვენ ის/ისინი (If) you/you had put him/them (to bed)
და-ე-დგინ-ო-ს/თ მას/მათ ის (მისთვის) (If) he/they had established/ proved it (to him)	და-ე-წვინ-ო-ს/თ მას/მათ ის/ისინი (If) he/they had put him/them (to bed)

ვერ ვიტყვი, მისი ცუდი ხასიათი ადრეც ***შეგვემჩნიოს.***
I cannot say we had noticed his bad temper before.
გისურვებთ, სიმართლე რაც შეიძლება მალე ***დაგედგინოთ.***
May (I wish) you prove the truth as soon as possible.

II conjugation

II conjugation verbs, i.e. the dynamic-passive voice verb forms, in the perfect subjunctive are determined by their person valency.

1. Monopersonal dynamic-passive verb forms in the perfect subjunctive are based on their past passive participles with the optative forms of the auxiliary verb *to be* added to them. The first and second persons have the suffix -ო as the tense marker followed by person and number markers.

The perfect subjunctive of monopersonal verbs

გა-ვ-მდიდრებულ-იყ-ო-(თ) მე/ჩვენ (If) I/we had become rich	და-ვ-ბერ-ებ-ულ-იყ-ო-(თ) მე/ჩვენ (If) I/we had become old
გა-მდიდრებულ-იყ-ო-(თ) შენ/თქვენ (If) you/you had become rich	და-ბერებულ-იყ-ო-(თ) შენ/თქვენ (If) you/you had become old
გა-მდიდრებულ-იყ-ო-ს ის (If) he had become rich	და-ბერებულ-იყ-ო-ს ის (If) he had become old
გა-მდიდრებულ-იყვ-ნენ ისინი (If) they had become rich	და-ბერებულ-იყვ-ნენ ისინი (If) they had become old

Monopersonal ablaut passive verbs follow the same rule. Their past passive participles are based on their I series stem: *ჭყლეტ* (crush), *გრეხ* (twist), and others to which the optative forms of the auxiliary verb *to be* are added.

გა-ვ-ჭყლეტილ-იყ-ო-(თ) მე/ჩვენ (If) I/we had been squashed	და-ვ-გრეხილ-იყ-ო-(თ) მე/ჩვენ (If) I/we had been twisted
გა-ჭყლეტილ-იყ-ო-(თ)შენ/თქვენ (If) you/you had been squashed	და-გრეხილ-იყ-ო-(თ)შენ/თქვენ (If) you/you had been twisted
გა-ჭყლეტილ-იყ-ო-ს ის (If) he had been squashed	და-გრეხილ-იყ-ო-ს ის (If) he had been twisted
გა-ჭყლეტილ-იყვ-ნენ ისინი (If) they had been squashed	და-გრეხილ-იყვ-ნენ ისინი (If) they had been twisted

2. II conjugation dynamic-passive verbs in the perfect subjunctive are based on their present subjunctive forms. Therefore, they have the extending marker -**ოდ**, and the tense marker -*ე*.

Bipersonal verbs

და-ვ-ლაპარაკ-ებ-ოდ-ე-(თ) მე/ჩვენ მას/მათ (If) I we had spoken with him/them	და-ვ-ხმარ-ებ-ოდ-ე-(თ) მე/ჩვენ მას/მათ (If) I/we had helped him/them
და-ლაპარაკ-ებ-ოდ-ე-(თ) შენ/თქვენ მას/მათ (If) you/you had spoken with him/them	და-ხმარ-ებ-ოდ-ე-(თ) შენ/თქვენ მას/მათ (If) you/you had helped him/them
და-ლაპარაკ-ებ-ოდ-ე-ს ის მას/მათ (If) he had spoken with him/them	და-ხმარ-ებ-ოდ-ე-ს ის მას/მათ (If) he had helped him/them
და-ლაპარაკ-ებ-ოდ-ნენ ისინი მას/მათ (If) they had spoken with him/them	და-ხმარ-ებ-ოდ-ნენ ისინი მას/მათ (If) they had helped him/them

არ მახსოვს, ის რომელიმე ჩვენგანს ***დალაპარაკებოდეს*** *ამაზე.*
I do not remember he had talked to any of us about it.
ღმერთი ***დახმარებოდეს*** *ყველა თქვენგანს!*
May God help everyone of you!
ყველა ლტოლვილს ***დავხმარებოდეთ!***
May we help all refugees.

III conjugation verbs

III conjugation verbs, i.e. the medio-active verbs, in the perfect subjunctive have all the properties of their forms in other tenses of III series:

1. The case-changing subject, even though they do not have a direct object
2. Inversion of person markers
3. The version marker does not indicate the category of version

The medio-active verbs in the perfect subjunctive are based, like active voice verbs, on their optative forms and have the pre-radical vowel -*ე*, which comes from the static-passive voice verb forms.

Medio-active verbs without P/FSF

მ-ე-ცინ-ო-ს მე (If) I had laughed	გვ-ე-ცინ-ო-ს ჩვენ (If) we had laughed
გ-ე-ცინ-ო-ს შენ (If) you had laughed	გ-ე-ცინ-ო-თ თქვენ (If) you had laughed

ე-ცინ-ო-ს მას (If) he had laughed	ე-ცინ-ო-თ მათ (If) they had laughed

The verbs without P/FSF that get additional suffixes in II series, maintain them in the perfect subjunctive as well. For example, the verb *თრთის* (he trembles) gets in the future subjunctive and optative the suffix -**ოლ**, which remains in its perfect subjunctive forms.

მ-ე-თრთ-ოლ-ო-ს მე
(If) I had trembled

გვ-ე-თრთ-ოლ-ო-ს ჩვენ
(If) we had trembled

გ-ე-თრთ-ოლ-ო-ს/-თ შენ/თქვენ/
(If) you/you had trembled

ე-თრთ-ოლ-ო-ს/-თ მას/მათ
((If) he/they had trembled

Medio-active verbs with P/FSF

These verbs lose their P/FSF in the perfect subjunctive.

Conjugation of two-stem medio-active verbs in the perfect subjunctive

მ-ე-ცურ-ო-ს მე (If) I had swum	და-მ-ე-გვიან-ო-ს მე (If) I had been late	მ-ე-ზრუნ-ო-ს მე (If) I have cared
გვ-ე-ცურ-ო-ს ჩვენ (If) we had swum)	და-გვ-ე-გვიან-ო-ს ჩვენ (If) we had been late	გვ-ე-ზრუნ-ო-ს ჩვენ (If) we had cared
გ-ე-ცურ-ო-ს/-თ შენ/თქვენ (If) you/you had swum	და-გ-ე-გვიან-ო-ს/-თ შენ/თქვენ (If) you/you had been late	გ-ე-ზრუნ-ო-ს/-თ შენ/თქვენ (If) you/you had cared
ე-ცურ-ო-ს/-თ მას/მათ (If) he/they had swum	და-ე-გვიან-ო-ს/-თ მას/მათ (If) he/they had been late	ე-ზრუნ-ო-ს/-თ მას/მათ (If) he/they had cared

In some verbs the consonant **ვ** appears as a result of a phonetic change caused by the dropping of their P/FSF -**ობ** in II series:

ქანაობს (He swings; he is swinging)	უქანავია ექანავა

თევზაობს (He fishes; he is fishing)	უთევზავია ეთევზავა
ცურაობს (He swims; he is swimming)	უცურავია ეცურავა

This change does not always take place in the perfect subjunctive.

მ-ე-ქანა-ო-ს მე (If) I had swung	მ-ე-თევზავ-ო-ს მე (If) I had been fishing	მ-ე-ცურავ-ო-ს მე (If) I had swum
გვ-ე-ქანა-ო-ს ჩვენ (If) we had swung	გვ-ე-თევზავ-ო-ს ჩვენ (If) we had been fishing	გვ-ე-ცურავ-ო-ს ჩვენ (If) we had swum
გ-ე-ქანა-ო-ს/თ შენ/თქვენ (If) you/you had swung	გ-ე-თევზავ-ო-ს/თ შენ/თქვენ (If) you/you had been fishing	გ-ე-ცურავ-ო-ს/თ შენ/თქვენ (If) you/you had swum
ე-ქანა-ო-ს/თ მას/მათ (If) he/they had swung	ე-თევზავ-ო-ს/თ მას/მათ (If) he/they had been fishing	ე-ცურავ-ო-ს/თ მას/მათ (If) he/they had swum

The verbs with the alternating root vowel have the vowel **ე** in I series but **ი** in II and III series. Similarly, verbs with the **-ენ/-ინ** alteration have the -**ინ**-ending stem in II and III series.

მ-ე-ფრ**ინ**-ო-ს მე (If) I had flown	მ-ე-სტვ**ინ**-ო-ს მე (If) I had whistled
გვ-ე-ფრ**ინ**-ო-ს ჩვენ (If) we had flown	გვ-ე-სტვ**ინ**-ო-ს ჩვენ (If) we had whistled
გ-ე-ფრ**ინ**-ო-ს/თ შენ/თქვენ (If) you/you had flown	გ-ე-სტვ**ინ**-ო-ს/თ შენ/თქვენ (If) you/you had whistle
ე-ფრ**ინ**-ო-ს/თ მას/მათ (If) he/they had flown	ე-სტვ**ინ**-ო-ს/თ მას/მათ (If) he/they had whistled

Bipersonal medio-active verbs lose their indirect object in the perfect subjunctive and a postposition is added to them.

მ-ე-ჯობნ-ო-ს მე მის**თვის**/მათ**თვის**
(If) I had surpassed him/them
გვ-ე-ჯობნ-ო-ს ჩვენ მის**თვის**/მათ**თვის**
(If) we had surpassed him/them

გ-ე-ჯობნ-ო-ს/თ შენ /თქვენ მისთვის/მათ**თვის**
(If) you/you had surpassed him/them

ე-ჯობნ-ო-ს/თ მას/მათ მისთვის/მათ**თვის**
(If) he they had surpassed him/them

All bipersonal medio-active verbs become monopersonal in the perfect subjunctive as happens in other III series tenses since their indirect object changes into an adjunct object.

მ-ე-დარაჯ-ო-ს მე (მისთვის/მათ**თვის**) (If) I had guarded (him/them)	მ-ე-ხელმძღვანელ-ო-ს მე (მისთვის/მათ**თვის**) (if) I had directed/guided (him/them)
გვ-ე-დარაჯ-ო-ს ჩვენ (მისთვის/მათ**თვის**) (If) we had guarded (him/them)	გვ-ე-ხელმძღვანელ-ო-ს ჩვენ (მისთვის/მათ**თვის**) (If) we had directed/guided (him/them)
გ-ე-დარაჯ-ო-ს/თ შენ/თქვენ (მისთვის/მათ**თვის**) (If) you/you had guarded (him/them)	გ-ე-ხელმძღვანელ-ო-ს/თ შენ/თქვენ (მისთვის/მათ**თვის**) (If) you/you had directed/guided(him/them)
ე-დარაჯ-ო-ს/თ მას/მათ (მისთვის/მათ**თვის**) (If) he/they had guarded (him/them)	ე-ხელმძღვანელ-ო-ს/თ მას/მათ (მისთვის/მათ**თვის**) (If) he/they had directed/guided (him/them)

IV conjugation

IV conjugation monopersonal verb forms are based on their past passive participle followed by the auxiliary verb *to be* in its optative forms.

ვ-წერებულ-იყ-ო-(თ) მე/ჩვენ (If) I/we had been written	და-ვ-ხატულ-იყ-ო-(თ) მე /ჩვენ (If) I/we had been painted
წერებულ-იყ-ო-(თ) შენ/თქვენ (If) you/you had been written	და-ხატულ-იყ-ო-(თ) შენ/თქვენ (If) you/you had been painted
წერებულ-იყ-ო-ს ის (If) he had been written	და-ხატულ-იყ-ო-ს ის (If) he had been painted
წერებულ-იყვ-ნენ ისინი (If) they had been written	დახატულ-იყვ-ნენ ისინი (If) they had been painted

Bipersonal verbs of IV conjugation have extending marker -**ოდ**, followed with the tense marker -*ე*.

მ-ყვარებ-ოდ-ე-ს მე ის/ისინი (If) I had loved him/them	მო-ვ-წონებ-ოდ-ე-(თ) მას/მათ მე /ჩვენ (If) he/they had liked me/us
გვ-ყვარ-ებ-ოდ-ე-ს ჩვენ ის/ისინი (If) we had loved him/them	
გ-ყვარებ-ოდ-ე-ს/თ შენ/თქვენ ის/ისინი (If) you/you had loved him/them	მო-ს-წონებ-ოდ-ე-(თ) მას/მათ შენ/თქვენ (If) he/they had liked you/you
ჰ-ყვარებ-ოდ-ე-ს/თ მას/მათ ის/ისინი (If) he/they had loved him/them	მო-ს-წონებ-ოდ-ე-ს/თ მას/მათ ის/ისინი (If) he/they had liked him/them

*გეფიცები, თუ შენს გარდა ვინმე **მყვარებოდეს**.*
I swear, if I had loved anybody but you.
*ნეტავ მათ ჩვენი პროექტი **მოსწონებოდეთ**!*
May (I wish) they like our project.

9.7 Irregular verbs

9.7.1 *Irregular verbs with changing stems in agreement with a plural subject*

A small group of verbs have different stems in their singular and plural forms.

1. ზი- სხედ, ჯექ/ჯედ/ჯდ –სხედ/სხდ – to sit, be seated

   ზი-is the root used only in singular forms of present tense and is replaced with *სხედ/სხდ*-in plural. They belong to IV conjugation – i.e. monopersonal static-passive voice verbs and therefore use an auxiliary verb ***to be*** in their first- and second-person forms.
   ზი-is changed in agreement with its tense as well. In future tense it is replaced with the root *ჯდ/ჯექ*.

   ჯდომა (sitting down) is a dynamic-passive voice verb and has P/FSF *-ებ* in the present tense. In the aorist it has the stem *ჯექ* (a phonetic variation of *ჯედ*)//*ჯდ*. In plural it changes to *სხედ/სხდ*.

Present	*Imperfect*	*Present subjunctive*
ვ-ზი-ვ-არ მე I sit (am sitting) ვ-სხედ-ვ-არ-თ ჩვენ We sit (are sitting)	–	–
ვ-ჯდებ-ი მე I sit (am sitting) down ვ-სხდ-ებ-ი-თ ჩვენ We sit (are sitting down)	ვ-ჯდ-ებ-ოდ-ი მე I was sitting down ვ-სხდ-ებ-ოდ-ი-თ ჩვენ We were sitting down	ვ-ჯდ-ებ-ოდ-ე მე If I were sitting ვ-სხდ-ებ-ოდ-ე-თ ჩვენ If we were sitting
ზი-ხ-არ შენ You sit (are sitting) სხედ-ხ-არ-თ თქვენ You sit (are sitting)	–	–
ჯდ-ებ-ი შენ You are sitting down სხდ-ებ-ი-თ თქვენ You are sitting down.	ჯდ-ებ-ოდ-ი შენ You were sitting down სხდ-ებ-ოდ-ი-თ თქვენ You were sitting down	ჯდ-ებ-ოდ-ე შენ If you were sitting სხდ-ებ-ოდ-ე-თ თქვენ If you were sitting
ზი-ს ის He sits (is sitting) სხედ-ან ისინი They sit (are sitting)	–	–
ჯდ-ებ-ა ის He is sitting down სხდ-ებ-ი-ან ისინი They are sitting down	ჯდ-ებ-ოდ-ა ის He was sitting down სხდ-ებ-ოდ-ნენ ისინი They were sitting down	ჯდ-ებ-ოდ-ე-ს ის If he were sitting down სხდ-ებ-ოდ-ნენ ისინი If they were sitting down

Future	*Conditional*	*Future subjunctive*
და-ვ-ჯდ-ებ-ი მე I will sit down და-ვ-სხდ-ებ-ი-თ ჩვენ We will sit down	დავჯდებ-ოდ-ი მე I would sit down დავსხდებ-ოდ-ით ჩვენ We would sit down	დავჯდებ-ოდ-ე მე If I were to sit დავსხდებ-ოდ-ე-თ ჩვენ If we were to sit

(*Continued*)

(Continued)

და-ჯდ-ებ-ი შენ You will sit down	დაჯდებ-ოდ-ი შენ You would sit down	დაჯდებ-ოდ-ე შენ If you were to sit
და-სხდ-ებ-ი-თ თქვენ You will sit down	დასხდებ-ოდ-ი-თ თქვენ You would sit down	დასხდებ-ოდ-ე-თ თქვენ If you were to sit
და-ჯდ-ებ-ა ის He will sit down	დაჯდებ-ოდ-ა ის He would sit down	დაჯდებ-ოდ-ე-ს ის If he were to sit
და-სხდ-ებ-ი-ან ისინი They will sit down	დასხდებ-ოდ-ნენ ისინი They would sit down	დასხდებ-ოდ-ნენ ისინი If they were to sit down
Aorist		*Optative*
ვ-ი-ჯექ-ი მე I was sitting down		ვ-ი-ჯდ-ე მე I should be sitting down
ვ-ი-სხედ-ი-თ ჩვენ We were sitting down		ვ-ი-სხდ-ე-თ ჩვენ We should be sitting down
და-ვ-ჯექ-ი მე I sat down		და-ვ-ჯდ-ე მე I should sit down
და-ვ -სხედ -ი-თ ჩვენ We sat down		და-ვ-სხდ-ე-თ ჩვენ We should sit down
ი-ჯექ-ი შენ You were sitting down		ი-ჯდ-ე შენ You should be sitting down
ი-სხედ-ი-თ თქვენ You were sitting down		ი-სხდ-ე-თ თქვენ You should be sitting down
და-ჯექ-ი შენ You sat down		და-ჯდ-ე შენ You should sit down
და-სხედ-ი-თ თქვენ You sat down		და-სხდ-ე-თ თქვენ You should sit down

ი-ჯდ-ა ის He was sitting down ი-სხდ-ნენ ისინი They were sitting down და-ჯდ-ა ის He sat down და-სხდ-ნენ ისინი They sat down		ი-ჯდ-ე-ს ის He should be sitting down ი-ჯდ-ნენ ისინი They should be sitting down და-ჯდ-ე-ს ის He should sit down და-სხდ-ნენ ისინი They should sit down

Perfect	*Pluperfect*	*Perfect subjunctive*
დავმჯდარ-ვარ მე I have sat down	დავმჯდარ-იყავი მე I had sat down	დავმჯდარ-იყო მე If I had sat down
დავმსხდარ-ვართ ჩვენ You have sat down	დავმსხდარ-იყავით თქვენ We had sat down	დავმსხდარ-იყოთ ჩვენ If we had sat down
დამჯდარ-ხარ შენ You have sat down	დამჯდარ-იყავი შენ You had sat down	დამჯდარ-იყო შენ If you had sat down
დამსხდარ-ხართ თქვენ You have sat down	დამსხდარ-იყავით თქვენ They had sat down	დამსხდარ-იყოთ თქვენ If you had sat down
დამჯდარ-ა ის He has sat down	დამჯდარ-იყო ის He had sat down	დამჯდარ-იყოს ის If he had sat down
დამსხდარ-ან ისინი They have sat down	დამასხდარ-იყვნენ ისინი They had sat down	დამსხდარ-იყვნენ ისინი If they had sat down

გუშინ ჩვენს აივანზე მტრედი ***იჯდა.***
Yesterday a dove was sitting on our balcony.
ბავშვები ეზოში ბალახზე ***ისხდნენ.***
The children were sitting on the grass in the yard.
მე და ჩემი მეგობარი პირველ რიგში ***ვსხედვართ.***
My friend and I are sitting in the front row.

ჩიტები ყოველთვის ***სხდებოდნენ*** *ჩვენი ფანჯრის რაფაზე, წელს კი ერთხელაც არ* ***დამსხდარან.***
Birds always sat on our windowsill, this year they have not sat even once.
ამდენი საქმე რომ არ მქონდეს, ***დავჯდებოდი*** *და ტელევიზორს ვუყურებდი.*
If I didn't have so much to do, I would sit down and watch television.
ნეტავ უფრო ახლოს ***დავსხმდარიყავით,*** *ყველაფერს უკეთესად დავინახავდით.*
I wish we had sat closer, we would have seen everything better.

2. **ვარდ- ცვივ-** *to fall*

The verbs based on these roots are dynamic-passive and therefore have ***-ებ-ი/***
– ებ-ა endings in the present tense series. The stem **ვარდ-**is used only in its singular forms, while ***ცვივ-***replaces it in the plural and with the animate/inanimate beings or collective nouns (CN). Both these roots may have preverbs whenever necessary. They change the meaning of the verb:

Present: მე ვვარდები/ჩვენ ვცვივდებით means "I/we fall" or "I/we rush."
Future: მე ჩამო-ვვარდები/ჩვენ ჩამო-ვცვივდებით – "I'll/we'll fall."
Future: მე შე-ვვარდები/ჩვენ შე-ვცვივდებით – "I'll/we'll rush into (something)."

Present	*Imperfect*	*Present Subjunctive*
ვ-ვარდ-ებ-ი მე I fall	ვ-ვარდ-ებ-ოდ-ი მე I fell/was falling	ვ-ვარდ-ებ-ოდ-ე მე If I fall/am falling
ვ-ცვივ-დ-ებ-ი-თ ჩვენ We fall	ვ-ცვივდ-ებ-ოდ-ი-თ ჩვენ We fell/were falling	ვ-ცვივდ-ებ-ოდ-ე-თ ჩვენ If we fall/are falling
ვარდ-ებ-ი შენ You fall	ვარდ-ებ-ოდ-ი შენ You fell/were falling	ვარდ-ებ-ოდ-ე შენ If you fall/are falling
ცვივ-დ-ებ-ი-თ თქვენ You fall	ცვივდ-ებ-ოდ-ი-თ თქვენ You fell/were falling	ცვივდ-ებ-ოდ-ე-თ თქვენ If they fall/are falling

ვარდ-ებ-ა ის He falls	ვარდ-ებ-ოდ-ა ის He fell/was falling	ვარდ-ებ-ოდ-ე-ს ის If he fall/is falling
ცვივ-დ-ებ-ა ის CN fall	ცვივდ-ებ-ოდ-ა ის CN fell/was falling	ცვივდ-ებ-ოდ-ე-ს ის CN fell/are falling
ცვივ-დ-ებ-ი-ან ისინი It falls/they fall	ცვივდ-ებ-ოდ-ნენ ისინი They fell/were falling	ცვივდ-ებ-ოდ-ნენ ისინი If they fall/are falling

Future	*Conditional*	*Future Subjunctive*
შე-ვ-ვარდ-ებ-ი მე I will rush into	შევვარდებ-ოდ-ი მე I would rush into	შევვარდებ-ოდ-ე მე If I were to rush into
შე-ვ-ცვივ-დ-ებ-ი-თ ჩვენ We will rush into	შევცვივდებ-ოდ-ი-თ ჩვენ We would rush into	შევცვივდებ-ოდ-ე-თ ჩვენ If we were to rush into
შე-ვარდ-ებ-ი შენ You will rush	ჩამოვარდებ-ოდ-ი შენ You would rush	შევარდებ-ოდ-ე შენ If you were to rush into
შე-ცვივ-დ-ებ-ი-თ თქვენ You will rush	შეცვივდებ-ოდ-ი-თ თქვენ You would rush into	შეცვივდებ-ოდ-ე-თ თქვენ If you were to rush into
შე-ვარდ-ებ-ა ის He will rush into	შევარდებ-ოდ-ა ის He would rush into	შევარდებ-ოდ-ე-ს ის If he were to rush into
შე-ცვივ-დ-ებ-ა ის CN will rush into	შეცვივდებ-ოდ-ა ის CN will rush into	შეცვივდებ-ოდ-ე-ს ის CN will were to into
შე-ცვივ-დ-ებ-ი-ან ისინი They will rush into	შეცვივდებ-ოდ-ნენ ისინი They would rush into	შე-ცვივ-დ-ებ-ოდ-ნენ ისინი If they were to rush into

Aorist		*Optative*
შე-ვ-ვარდ-ი მე I rushed into		შე-ვ-ვარდ-ე მე I should rush into
შე-ვ-ცვივ-დ-ი-თ ჩვენ We fell into		შე-ვ-ცვივ-დ-ე-თ ჩვენ We should rush

(*Continued*)

(Continued)

შე-ვარდ-ი შენ You rushed into		შე-ვარდ-ე შენ You should rush into
შე-ცვივ-დ-ი-თ თქვენ You rushed into		შე-ცვივ-დ-ე-თ თქვენ They should rush into
შე-ვარდ-ა ის He rushed into		შე-ვარდ-ე-ს ის He should rush into
შე-ცვივ-დ-ა ის CN rushed into		შე-ცვივ-დ-ე-ს ის CN should rush into
შე-ცვივ-დ-ნენ ისინი They rushed into		ჩამო-ცვივ-დ-ნენ ისინი They should rush into

Perfect	*Pluperfect*	*Perfect Subjunctive*
შევვარდნილ-ვარ მე I have rushed into	შევვარდნილ-იყავი მე I had rushed into	შევვარდნილ-იყო მე If I had rushed into
შევცვენილ-ვართ ჩვენ We have rushed into	შევცვენილ-იყავით ჩვენ We had rushed into	შე-ვ-ცვენილ-ი-ყ-ო-თ ჩვენ If we had rushed into
	შეცვენილ-ან ისინი They rushed into	
შევარდნილ-ხარ შენ You have rushed into	შევარდნილ-იყავი შენ You had rushed into	შევარდნილ-იყო შენ If you had rushed into
შეცვენილ-ხართ თქვენ You have rushed into	შეცვენილ-იყავით თქვენ You had rushed into	შეცვენილ-იყოთ თქვენ If you had rushed into
შევარდნილ-ა ის He has rushed into	შევარდნილ-იყო ის He had rushed into	შევარდნილ-იყოს ის If he rushed into
შე-ცვენილ-ა ის CN have rushed into	შეცვენილ-იყო ის CN had rushed into	შეცვენილ-იყოს ის If CN rushed into
შეცვენილ-ან ისინი They rushed into	შეცვენილ-იყვნენ They had rushed into	შეცვენილ-იყვნენ ისინი If they had fallen

ხიდან (ერთი) ვაშლი ***ჩამოვარდა.***
An apple fell from the tree.
ხიდან მწიფე ვაშლები ***ჩამოცვივდა.***
Ripe apples fell from the tree.
ეკონომიკური კრიზისის გამო ისინი მძიმე მდგომარეობაში ***ჩაცვივდნენ.***
Because of the economic crisis, they fell into hard times.
ეს ყუთი რომ არ ჩამომეღო, უსათუოდ ***ჩამოვარდებოდა.***
If I hadn't taken down this box, it would have fallen down for sure.
ბავშვები ხიდან რომ ***ჩამოცვვენილიყვნენ,*** *აუცილებლად რამეს იტკენდნენ.*
If the kids had fallen down from the tree, they would have definitely hurt themselves.
ხალხი ***შეცვივდა*** *შენობაში.*
People rushed into the building.
არ მახსოვს, რომ ხალხი ამ შენობაში ***შეცვენილიყოს.***
I don't remember people ever breaking into this building.

ცვივ- fall

The IV conjugation verb *ცვივ* denotes the action of falling of the animate/inanimate beings or collective nouns (CN) in third-person singular or first-, second-, or third-person plural.

Present	*Imperfect*	*Present subjunctive*
ვ-ცვივ-ი-თ We fall/(CN) fall	ვ-ცვი-ოდ-ი-თ We were falling	ვ-ცვი-ოდ-ე-თ If we fall
ცვივ-ი-თ You fall/(CN) fall	ცვი-ოდ-ი-თ You were falling	ცვი-ოდ-ე-თ If you fall
ცვივ-ა It falls/(CN) fall	ცვი-ოდ-ა It/(CN) was falling	ცვი-ოდ-ე-ს If it/(CN) falls
It is/they are falling	ცვი-ოდ-ნენ They were falling	ცვი-ოდ-ნენ If they fall

(Continued)

(Continued)

Future	*Conditional*	*Future Subjunctive*
–	–	–
Aorist		*Optative*
და-ვ-ცვივ-დ-ი-თ We/(CN) fallen down		და-ვ-ცვივ-დ-ე-თ If we/(CN) were fallen
და-ცვივ-დ-ი-(თ) You/(CN) fallen down		და-ცვივ-დ-ე-(თ) If you/(CN) were fallen
და-ცვივ-დ-ა It/(CN) fallen down		და-ცვივ-დ-ე-ს If it/(CN) were fallen
და-ცვივ-დ-ნენ They fallen down		და-ცვივ-დ-ნენ If they were fallen
Perfect	*Pluperfect*	*Perfect subjunctive*
დავცვენილ-ვართ We have fallen	დავცვენილ-იყავით We had fallen	დავცვენილ-იყოთ May we fall
დაცვენილ-ხარ(თ) We have fallen	დაცვენილ-იყავით You had fallen	დაცვენილ-იყო(თ) May you fall
დაცვენილ-ა/ნ It/(CN)/they has fallen	დაცვენილ-იყო It/(CN) had fallen	დაცვენილ-იყოს May It//(CN) fall
	დაცვენილ-იყნენ They had fallen	დაცვენილ-იყვნენ May they fall

ფოთოლი (CN)//ფოთლები ***ცვივა.***
Leaf falls/leaves fall.
Leaf is/leaves are falling.
ნეტავ ფოთოლი(CN)//ფოთლები მალე ***დაცვივდეს.***
The leaf/leaves were fallen soon.
ფოთოლი(CN)//ფოთლები მთელ ეზოში ***დაცვენილა.***
The leaf/leaves has/have fallen all over the yard.

3. **გდ- ყრ- – to lie, be scattered around**

გდია-ყრია: both are IV conjugation static-passive voice verbs.

The verbs *გდია-ყრია* imply that something does not just lie but is thrown down or scattered around; when referring to a person, it means someone has fallen/is plopped/dropped down.

Present	*Imperfect*	*Present Subjunctive*
ვ-გდ-ი-ვ-არ მე I am lying ვ-ყრ-ი-ვ-არ-თ ჩვენ We are lying გ-დ-ი-ხ-არ შენ You are lying ყრ-ი-ხ-არ-თ თქვენ You are lying გდ-ი-ა ის He is lying ყრ-ი-ან ისინი They are lying	–	–
Future	*Conditional*	*Future Subjunctive*
და-ვ-ე-გდ-ებ-ი მე I will lie	დავეგდებ-ოდ-ი მე I would lie	დავეგდებ-ოდ-ე მე If I were to lie
და-ვ-ი/ე-ყრ-ებ-ი-თ ჩვენ We will lie	დავი/ეყრებ-ოდ-ი-თ ჩვენ (მას) We would lie	დავი/ე-ყრებ-ოდ-ე-თ ჩვენ (მას) If we were to lie
და-ე-გდ-ებ-ი შენ You will lie	დაეგდებ-ოდ-ი შენ You would lie	დაეგდებ-ოდ-ე შენ If you were to lie
და-ი/ე-ყრ-ებ-ი-თ თქვენ You will lie	დაიყრებ-ოდ-ი-თ თქვენ (მას) You would lie	დაი/ეყრებ-ოდ-ე-თ თქვენ (მას) If we were to lie
და-ე-გდ-ებ-ა ის He will lie	დაეგდებ-ოდ-ა ის He would lie	დაეგდებ-ოდ-ე-ს ის If he were to lie
და-ი/ე-ყრ-ებ-ა ის CN will lie	დაი/ეყრებ-ოდ-ა ის CN would lie	დაი/ეყრებ-ოდ-ე-ს ის If CN were to lie
და-ი/ე-ყრ-ებ-ი-ან ისინი They will lie	დაი/ეყრებ-ოდ-ნენ ისინი (მას) They would lie	დაი/ეყრებ-ოდ-ნენ ისინი (მას) If they were to lie

(Continued)

(Continued)

Aorist	*Optative*
და-ვ-ე-გდ-ე მე I lay	(და)-ვ-ე-გდ-ო მე I should lie
და-ვ-ე-ყარ-ე-თ ჩვენ We lay	(და)-ვ-ე-ყარ-ო-თ ჩვენ We should lie
და-ე-გდ-ე შენ You lay	(და)-ე-გდ-ო შენ You should lie
(და)-ე-ყარ-ე-თ თქვენ You lay	(და)-ე-ყარ-ო-თ თქვენ You should lie
(და)-ე-გდ-ო ის He lay	(და)-ე-გდ-ო-ს ის He should lie
(და)-ე-ყარ-ნენ ისინი They lay	(და)-ე-ყარ-ო-ნ ისინი They should lie

Perfect	*Pluperfect*	*Perfect subjunctive*
დავგდებულ-ვარ მე I have lain	დავგდებულ-იყავი მე I had lain	დავგდებულ-იყო მე If I had lain
დავყრილ-ვართ ჩვენ We have lain	დავყრილ-იყავით ჩვენ We had lain	დაყრილ-იყოთ ჩვენ If we had lain
დაგდებულ-ხარ შენ You have lain	დაგდებულ-იყავი შენ You had lain	დაგდებულ-იყავი შენ If you had lain
დაყრილ-ხართ თქვენ You have lain	დაყრილ-იყავით თქვენ You had lain	დაყრილ-იყოთ თქვენ If you had lain
დაგდებულ-ა ის He has lain	დაგდებულ-იყო ის He had lain	დაგდებულ-იყოს ის If he had lain
დაყრილ-ან ისინი They have lain	დაყრილ-იყვნენ ისინი They had lain	დაყრილ-იყვნენ ისინი If they had lain

დაჭრილი მეომარი მინდორში ***გდია.***
The fallen warrior is lying in the field.
დაჭრილი მეომრები მინდორში ***ყრიან.***
(The bodies of) fallen warriors are scattered around in the field.
დღეს სახლში დაღლილი მოვედი და საწოლზე ***დავეგდე.***
Today I came home tired and plopped down on (my) bed.
ნეტავ ქუჩაში არ ***დავყრილიყავით.***
I wish we hadn't thrown down on the street.

4. დევ- წყვ- – to lie, be put/placed/arranged

These are roots of the static-passive voice verbs and belong to the IV conjugation. As a rule, these verbs are used exclusively with inanimate nouns and their meaning is determined by the context of the sentence in which they appear. In the following chart, the first- and second-person forms of these verbs are mostly hypothetical.

Present	*Imperfect*	*Present subjunctive*
ვ-დევ-არ მე I am placed ვ-ა-წყვ-ი-ვ-არ-თ ჩვენ We are placed	–	–
დევ-ხ-არ შენ You are placed ა-წყვ-ი-ხ-არ-თ თქვენ You are placed	–	–
დევ-ს ის It is placed ა-წყვ-ი-ა ისინი They are placed	–	–
Future	*Conditional*	*Future subjunctive*
ვ-ი-დ-ებ-ი მე I will be placed ვ-ე-წყ-ობ-ი-თ ჩვენ We will be placed	ვ-იდებოდი მე I would be placed ვ-ეწყობოდი-თ ჩვენ We would be placed	ვ-ი-დ-ებ-ოდ-ე მე If I were to be placed ვ-ეწყობოდ-ე-თ ჩვენ If we were to be placed

(Continued)

(Continued)

ი-დ-ებ-ი შენ You will be placed ე-წყ-ობ-ი-თ თქვენ You will be placed	ი-დ-ებ-ოდ-ი შენ You would be placed ე-წყ-ობ-ოდ-ი-თ თქვენ They would be placed	ი-დ-ებ-ოდ-ე შენ If you were to be placed ე-წყ-ობ-ოდ-ე-თ თქვენ If you were to be placed
ი-დ-ებ-ა ის It will be placed ე-წყ-ობ-ი-ან ისინი They will be placed	ი-დ-ებ-ოდ-ა ის It would be placed ე-წყ-ობ-ოდ-ნენ ისინი They would be placed	ი-დ-ებ-ოდ-ე-ს ის If it were to be placed ე-წყ-ობ-ოდ-ნენ ისინი If they were to be placed
Aorist		*Optative*
ვ-ი-დ-ე მე I was placed ვ-ე-წყვ-ე-თ ჩვენ We were placed		ვ-ი-დ-ო მე I were to be placed ვ-ე-წყ-ო-თ ჩვენ We were to be placed
ი-დ-ე შენ You were placed ე-წყვ-ე-თ თქვენ You were placed		ი-დ-ო შენ You were to be placed ე-წყ-ო-თ თქვენ You were to be placed
ი-დ-ო ის It was placed ე-წყ-ო ისინი They were placed		ი-დ-ო-ს ის It were to be placed ე-წყ-ო-ნ ისინი They were to be placed
Perfect	*Pluperfect*	*Perfect subjunctive*
ვდებულ-ვარ მე I have been placed (და)ვწყობილ-ვართ ჩვენ We have been placed	ვდებულ-იყავი მე I had been placed (და)ვწყობილ-იყავით ჩვენ We had been placed	ვდებულ-იყო მე If I had been placed (და)ვწყობილ-იყოთ ჩვენ If we had been placed

(Continued)

Perfect	Pluperfect	Perfect subjunctive
დებულ-ხარ შენ You have been placed	დებულ-იყავი შენ You had been placed	დებულ-იყო შენ If you had been placed
(და)წყობილ-ხართ თქვენ You have been placed	(და)წყობილ-იყავით თქვენ You had been placed	(და)წყობილ-იყოთ თქვენ If you had been placed
დებულ-ა ის It has been placed	დებულ-იყო ის It had been placed	დებულ-იყოს ის If it had been placed
(და)წყობილ-ან ისინი They have been placed	(და)წყობილ-იყვნენ ისინი They had been placed	(და)წყობილ-იყვნენ ისინი If they had been placed

*წიგნი თაროზე **დევს**.*
The book is put (placed) on the shelf.
*წიგნები თაროზე **აწყვია**.*
Books are placed (arranged) on the shelf
*ნეტავ ეს საბუთი უკვე ჩემს მაგიდაზე **იდოს**.*
I wish this document were already on my table.
*ნეტავ ეს საბუთები უკვე ჩემს მაგიდაზე **ეწყოს**.*
I wish these documents were already on my table.
*ეს წიგნი აქ უნდა **დებულიყო**.*
This book should have been put/placed here.
*ეს წიგნები აქ უნდა **დაწყობილიყო**.*
These books should have been placed here.

5. **კვდ- ხოც-** to die

The verbs derived from these roots are dynamic-passive and belong to II conjugation.

Present	Imperfect	Present subjunctive
ვ-კვდ-ებ-ი მე I die/am dying	ვ-კვდ-ებ-ოდ-ი მე I was dying	ვ-კვდ-ებ-ოდ-ე მე If I die
ვ-ი-ხოც-ებ-ი-თ ჩვენ We die/are dying	ვ-ი-ხოც-ებ-ოდ-ი-თ ჩვენ We were dying	ვ-ი-ხოც-ებ-ოდ-ე-თ ჩვენ If we die

(Continued)

(Continued)

კვდ-ებ-ი შენ You die/are dying	კვდ-ებ-ოდ-ი შენ You were dying	კვდ-ებ-ოდ-ე შენ If you die
ი-ხოც-ებ-ი-თ თქვენ You die/are dying	ი-ხოც-ებ-ოდ-ი-თ თქვენ They were dying	ი-ხოც-ებ-ოდ-ე-თ თქვენ If you die
კვდ-ებ-ა ის He dies/is dying	კვდ-ებ-ოდ-ა ის He was dying	კვდ-ებ-ოდ-ე-ს ის If he dies
ი-ხოც-ებ-ი-ან ისინი They die/are dying	ი-ხოცებ-ოდ-ნენ ისინი They were dying	ი-ხოც-ებ-ოდ-ნენ ისინი If they die
Future	*Conditional*	*Future subjunctive*
მო-ვ-კვდ-ებ-ი მე I will die	მოვკვდებ-ოდ-ი მე I would die	მოვკვდებ-ოდ-ე მე If I were to die
და-ვ-ი-ხოც-ებ-ი-თ ჩვენ We will die	დავიხოცებ-ოდ-ი-თ ჩვენ We would die	დავიხოცებ-ოდ-ე-თ ჩვენ If we were to die
მო-კვდ-ები შენ You will die	მოკვდებ-ოდ-ი შენ You would die	მოკვდებ-ოდ-ე შენ If you should die
და-ი-ხოც-ებ-ი-თ თქვენ You will die	დაიხოცებ-ოდ-ი-თ თქვენ You would die	დაიხოცებ-ოდ-ე-თ თქვენ If you were to die
მო-კვდ-ებ-ა ის He will die	მოკვდებ-ოდ-ა ის He would die	მოკვდებ-ოდ-ე-ს If he were to die
და-ი-ხოც-ებ-ი-ან ისინი They will die	დაიხოცებ-ოდ-ნენ ისინი They would die	და-ი-ხოც-ებ-ოდ-ნენ ისინი If they were to die
Aorist		*Optative*
მო-ვ-კვდ-ი მე I died		მო-ვ-კვდ-ე მე I should die
და-ვ-ი-ხოც-ე-თ ჩვენ We died		და-ვ-ი-ხოც-ო-თ ჩვენ We should die
		მო-კვდ-ე შენ

მო-კვდ-ი შენ You died		You should die
და-ი-ხოც-ე-თ თქვენ You died		და-ი-ხოც-ო-თ თქვენ You should die
მო-კვდ-ა ის He died		მო-კვდ-ე-ს ის He should die
და-ი-ხოც-ნენ ისინი They died		

Perfect	*Pluperfect*	*Perfect subjunctive*
მოვმკვდარ-ვარ მე I have died	მოვმკვდარ-იყავი მე I had died	მოვმკვდარ-იყო მე If I had died
დავხოცილ-ვართ ჩვენ We have died	დავხოცილ-იყავით ჩვენ We had died	და-ვხოცილ-იყოთ ჩვენ If we had died
მომკვდარ-ხარ შენ You have died	მომკვდარ-იყავი შენ You had died	მომკვდარ-იყო შენ If you had died
დახოცილ-ხართ თქვენ You have died	დახოცილ-იყავით თქვენ You had died	დახოცილ-იყოთ თქვენ If you had died
მომკვდარ-ა ის He has died	მომკვდარ-იყო ის He had died	მომკვდარ-იყოს ის If he had died
დახოცილ-ან ისინი They have died	დახოცილ-იყვნენ ისინი They have died	დახოცილ-იყვნენ ისინი If they had died

ამ ომში ჩემი მეზობელი ***მოკვდა.***
In this war my neighbour died.
ამ ომში ჩვენი თანამემამულეები ***დაიხოცნენ.***
In this war our countrymen died.
დაშავებული არ ***მომკვდარა****, საავადმყოფოში გადაიყვანეს.*
The injured person did not die; he was taken to the hospital.

დაშავებულები არ ***დახოცილან,*** *საავადმყოფოში გადაიყვანეს.*
The injured persons did not die, they were taken to the hospital.
ნეტავ არ ***მომკვდარიყო,*** *ქვეყნისთვის ბევრ კარგ საქმეს გააკეთებდა.*
I wish he hadn't died; he would have done a lot of good things for the country.
ნეტავ არ ***დახოცილიყვნენ,*** *ქვეყნისთვის ბევრ კარგ საქმეს გააკეთებდნენ.*
I wish they hadn't died; they would have done a lot of good things for the country.

9.7.2 Irregular verbs with changing stems in agreement with a plural direct object

1. გდ- ყრ- – to throw, to drop

The verbs derived from the stems *გდ-* and *ყრ-* are interchangeable in agreement with the number of objects they modify. All these verbs are transitive and belong to I conjugation.

Present	*Imperfect*	*Present subjunctive*
ვ-ა-გდ-ებ-(თ) მე/ჩვენ მას I/we drop it ვ-ყრ-ი-(თ) მე/ჩვენ მათ I/we drop them	ვ-ა-გდ-ებ-დ-ი-(თ) მე/ჩვენ მას I was/we were dropping it ვ-ყრ-ი-დ-ი-(თ) მე/ჩვენ მათ I was/we were dropping them	ვ-ა-გდ-ებ-დ-ე-(თ) მე/ჩვენ მას If I/we drop it ვ-ყრ-ი-დ-ე-(თ) მე/ჩვენ მათ If I/we drop them
Present	*Imperfect*	*Present subjunctive*
ა-გდ-ებ-(თ) შენ/თქვენ მას You/you drop it ყრ-ი-(თ) შენ/თქვენ მათ You/you drop them	ა-გდ-ებ-დ-ი-(თ) შენ/თქვენ მას You/you were dropping it ყრ-ი-დ-ი-(თ) შენ/თქვენ მათ You/you were dropping them	ა-გდ-ებ-დ-ე-(თ) შენ/თქვენ მას If you/you drop it ყრ-ი-დ-ე-(თ) შენ/თქვენ მათ If you/you drop them

ა-გდ-ებ-ს ის მას He drops it	ა-გდ-ებ-დ-ა ის მას He was dropping it	ა-გდ-ებ-დ-ე-ს ის მას If he drops it
ყრ-ი-ს ის მათ He drops them	ყრ-ი-დ-ა ის მათ He was dropping them	ყრ-ი-დ-ე-ს ის მათ If he drops them
ყრ-ი-ან ისინი მათ They drop them	ყრ-ი-დ-ნენ ისინი მათ They were dropping them	ყრ-ი-დ-ნენ ისინი მათ If they drop them
Future	*Conditional*	*Future subjunctive*
ჩა-ვ-ა-გდ-ებ-(თ) მე/ჩვენ მას I/we will drop it	ჩავაგდებ-დ-ი-(თ) მე/ჩვენ მას I/we would drop it	ჩავაგდებ-დ-ე-(თ) მე/ჩვენ მას If I/we were to drop it
ჩა-ვ-ყრ-ი-თ მე/ჩვენ მათ I/we will drop them	ჩავყრი-დ-ი-თ მე/ჩვენ მათ I/we would drop them	ჩავყრი-დ-ე-თ მე/ჩვენ მათ If I/we were to drop them
ჩა-ა-გდ-ებ-(თ) შენ/თქვენ მას You/you will drop it	ჩააგდ-ბ-დ-ი-(თ) შენ/თქვენ მას You/you would drop it	ჩააგდებ-დ-ე-(თ) შენ/თქვენ მას If you/you were to drop it
ჩა-ყრ-ი-(თ) შენ/თქვენ მათ You/you will drop them	ჩაყრი-დ-ი-(თ) შენ/თქვენ მათ You/you would drop them	ჩაყრი-დ-ე-(თ) შენ/თქვენ მათ If you/you were to drop them
ჩა-ა-გდ-ებ-ს ის მას He will drop it	ჩააგდებ-დ-ა ის მას He would drop it	ჩააგდებ-დ-ე-ს ის მას If he were to drop it
ჩა-ყრ-ი-ს ის მათ He will drop them	ჩაყრი-დ-ა ის მათ He would drop them	ჩაყრი-დ-ე-ს ის მათ If he were to drop them
ჩა-ყრ-ი-ან ისინი მათ They will drop it	ჩაყრი-დ-ნენ ისინი მათ They would drop them	ჩაყრი-დ-ნენ ისინი მათ If they were to drop them

(*Continued*)

(Continued)

Aorist	*Optative*
ჩა-ვ-ა-გდ-ე-(თ) მე/ჩვენ ის I/we dropped it	ჩა-ვ-ა-გდ-ო-(თ) მე/ჩვენ ის I/we should drop it
ჩა-ვ-ყარ-ე-(თ) მე/ჩვენ ისინი I/we dropped them	ჩა-ვ-ყარ-ო-(თ) მე/ჩვენ ისინი I/we should drop them
ჩა-ა-გდ-ე-(თ) შენ/თქვენ ის You/you dropped it	ჩა-ა-გდ-ო-(თ) შენ/თქვენ ის You/you should drop it
ჩა-ყარ-ე-(თ) შენ/თქვენ ისინი You/you dropped them	ჩა-ყარ-ო-(თ) შენ/თქვენ ისინი You/you should drop them
ჩა-ა-გდ-ო/ეს მან/მათ ის He/they dropped it	ჩა-ა-გდ-ო-ს/ნ მან/მათ ის He/they should drop it
ჩა-ყარ-/ეს მან/მათ ისინი He/they dropped them	ჩა-ყარ-ო-ს/ნ მან/მათ ისინი He/they should drop them

Perfect	*Pluperfect*	*Perfect subjunctive*
ჩა-მ-ი-გდ-ი-ა მე ის I have dropped it	ჩა-მ-ე-გდ-ო მე ის I had dropped it	ჩა-მ-ე-გდ-ო-ს მე ის If I had dropped it
ჩა-გვ-ი-გდ-ი-ა ჩვენ ის We have dropped it	ჩა-გვ-ე-გდ-ო ჩვენ ის We had dropped it	ჩა-გვ-ე-გდ-ო-ს ჩვენ ის If we had dropped it
ჩა-მ-ი-ყრ-ი-ა მე ისინი I have drop them	ჩა-მ-ე-ყარ-ა მე ისინი I had dropped them	ჩა-მ-ე-ყარ-ო-ს მე ისინი If I had dropped them
ჩა-გვ-ი-ყრ-ი-ა ჩვენ ისინი We have dropped them	ჩა-გვ-ე-ყარ-ა ჩვენ ისინი We had dropped them	ჩა-გვ-ე-ყარ-ო-ს ჩვენ ისინი If we had dropped them

ჩა-გ-ი-გდ-ი-ა-(თ) შენ /თქვენ ის You/you have dropped it	ჩა-გ-ე-გდ-ო-(თ) შენ/თქვენ ის You/you had dropped it	ჩა-გ-ე-გდ-ო-ს/თ შენ/თქვენ ის If you had dropped it
ჩა-გ-ი-ყრ-ი-ა-(თ) შენ/თქვენ ისინი You/you have dropped them	ჩა-გ-ე-ყარ-ა-(თ) შენ/თქვენ ისინი You/you had dropped them	ჩა-გ-ე-ყარ-ო-ს/თ შენ/თქვენ ისინი If you/you had dropped them
ჩა-უ-გდ-ი-ა-(თ) მას /მათ ის He has/they have dropped it	ჩა-ე-გდ-ო-(თ) მას/მათ ის He/they had dropped it	ჩა-ე-გდ-ო-ს/თ მას/მათ ის If he/they had dropped it
ჩა-უ-ყრ-ი-ა-(თ) მას/მათ ისინი He has/they have dropped	ჩა-ე-ყარ-ა-(თ) მას/მათ ისინი They had dropped them	ჩა-ე-ყარ-ო-ს/თ მას/მათ ისინი If he/they had dropped them

ბავშვმა წყალში კენჭ-ი (Od Sin.) ***ჩააგდო.***
A child threw a pebble in the water.
ბავშვმა წყალში კენჭ-ებ-ი (Od Pl.) ***ჩაყარა.***
A child threw pebbles in the water.
ბიჭი კალათში ბურთ-ს (Od Sin.) ***ჩააგდებს.***
The boy will throw a ball into the basket.
ბიჭი კალათში ბურთ-ებ-ს(Od Pl.) ***ჩაყრის.***
The boy will throw the balls into the basket.
მსაჯმა სპორტსმენ-ი (Od Sin.) ***გააგდო*** *საფეხბურთო მოედნიდან.*
The referee removed (threw out) a sportsman from the playing field.
მსაჯმა სპორტსმენ-ებ-ი (Od Pl.) ***გაყარა*** *საფეხბურთო მოედნიდან.*
The referee removed (threw out) the sportsmen from the playing field.

2. დ-ებ – წყ-ობ/ლაგ-ებ to put/place down, arrange

All three verbs *დ-ებ-ს* (he puts/puts down), *აწყ-ობ-ს*, and *ალაგ-ებ-ს* (he puts/puts down) are transitive verbs and belong to the I conjugation. The following tables will show the conjugation of two pairs: *დ-ებ-ს – აწყ-ობ-ს.*

Present	*Imperfect*	*Present subjunctive*
ვ-დ-ებ-(თ) მე/ჩვენ მას I/we put it down ვ-ა-წყ-ობ-(თ) მე/ჩვენ მათ I/we put them down	ვ-დ-ებ-დ-ი-(თ) მე/ჩვენ მას I/we was putting it down ვ-ა-წყ-ობ-დ-ი-(თ) მე/ჩვენ მათ I was/we were putting them down	ვ-დ-ებ-დ-ე-(თ) მე/ჩვენ მას If I/we put it down ვ-ა-წყ-ობ-დ-ე-(თ) მე/ჩვენ მათ If I/we put them down
დ-ებ-(თ) შენ/თქვენ მას You/you put it down ა-წყ-ობ-(თ) შენ/თქვენ მათ You/you put them down	დ-ებ-დ-ი-(თ) შენ/თქვენ მას You/you were putting it down ა-წყ-ობ-დ-ი-(თ) შენ/თქვენ მათ You/you were putting them down	დ-ებ-დ-ე-(თ) შენ/თქვენ მას If you/you put it down ა-წყ-ობ-დ-ე-(თ) შენ/თქვენ მათ If you/you put it down
დ-ებ-ს/ენ ის/ისინი მას/მათ He puts/they put it/them down ა-წყ-ობ-ს/ენ ის/ისინი მას/მათ He puts/they put it/them down	დ-ებ-დ-ა/ნენ ის/ისინი მას/მათ He was/they were putting it/them down ა-წყ-ობ-დ-ა/ნენ ის/ისინი მას/მათ He was/they put putting it/them down	დ-ებ-დ-ე-ს/ნენ ის/ისინი მას/მათ If he/they put it/ them down ა-წყ-ობ-დ-ე-ს/ნენ ის/ისინი მას/მათ If he/they put it/ them down

Future	*Conditional*	*Future subjunctive*
და-ვ-დ-ებ-(თ) მე/ჩვენ მას I/we will put it down და-ვ-ა-წყ-ობ-(თ) მე/ჩვენ მათ I/we will put them down	დავდებ-დ-ი-(თ) მე/ჩვენ მას I/we would put it down დავაწყობ-დ-ი-(თ) მე/ჩვენ მათ I/we would put it/ them down	დავდებ-დ-ე-(თ) მე/ჩვენ მას If I/we were to put it down დავაწყობ-დ-ე-(თ) მე/ჩვენ მათ If I/we were to put them down

და-დ-ებ-(თ) შენ/თქვენ მას You/you will put it down	დადებ-დ-ი-(თ) შენ/თქვენ მას You/you would put it down	დადებ-დ-ე-(თ) შენ/თქვენ მას If you/you were to put it down
და-ა-წყ-ობ-(თ) შენ/თქვენ მათ You/you will put them down	დააწყობ-დ-ი-(თ) შენ/თქვენ მათ You/you would put them down	დააწყობ-დ-ე-(თ) შენ/თქვენ მათ If you/you were to put them down
და-დ-ებ-ს/ენ ის/ისინი მას He/they will put it down	დადებ-დ-ა/ნენ ის/ისინი მას He/they would put it down	დადებ-დ-ე-ს/ნენ ის/ისინი მას If he/they were to put it down
და-ა-წყ-ობ-ს/ენ ის/ისინი მათ He/they will put them down	დააწყობ-დ-ა/ნენ ის/ისინი მათ He/they would put them down	დააწყობ-დ-ე-ს/ნენ ის/ისინი მათ If he/they were to put them down

Aorist	*Optative*
და-ვ-დ-ე-(თ) მე/ჩვენ ის I/we put it down	და-ვ-დ-ო-(თ) მე/ჩვენ ის I/we should put it down
და-ვ-ა-წყვ-ე-(თ) მე/ჩვენ ისინი I/we put them down	და-ვ-ა-წყ-ო-(თ) მე/ჩვენ ისინი I/we should put them down
და-დ-ე-(თ) შენ/თქვენ ის You/you put it down	და-დ-ო-(თ) შენ/თქვენ ის You/you should put it down
და-ა-წყვ-ე-(თ) შენ/თქვენ ისინი You/you put them down	და-ა-წყ-ო-(თ) შენ/თქვენ ისინი You/you should put them down
და-დ-ო/ეს მან/მათ ის He/they put it down	და-დ-ო-ს/ნ მან/მათ ის/ისინი He should put it down
და-ა-წყ-ო მან ისინი He put them down	და-ა-წყ-ო-ს/ნ მან/მათ ის/ისინი He/they should put them down
და-ა-წყვ-ეს მათ ისინი They put them down	

(*Continued*)

(Continued)

Perfect	*Pluperfect*	*Perfect subjunctive*
და-მ-ი-დ-ი-ა მე ის I have put it down	და-მ-ე-დ-ო მე ის I had put it down	და-მ-ე-დ-ო-ს მე ის If I had put it down
და-გვ-ი-დ-ი-ა ჩვენ ის We have put it down	და-გვ-ე-დ-ო ჩვენ ის We had put it down	და-გვ-ე-დ-ო-ს ჩვენ ის If we had put it down
და-მ-ი-წყვ-ი-ა მე ისინი I have put them down	და-მ-ე-წყ-ო მე ისინი I had put them down	და-მ-ე-წყ-ო-ს მე ისინი If I had put them down
და-გვ-ი-წყვ-ი-ა ჩვენ ისინი We have put them down	და-გვ-ე-წყ-ო ჩვენ ისინი We had put them down	და-გვ-ე-წყ-ო-ს ჩვენ ისინი If we had put them down
და-გ-ი-დ-ი-ა-(თ) შენ/თქვენ ის You/you have put it down	და-გ-ე-დ-ო-(თ) შენ/თქვენ ის You/you had put it down	და-გ-ე-დ-ო-(თ) შენ/თქვენ ის If you/you had put it down
და-გ-ი-წყვ-ი-ა-(თ) შენ/თქვენ ისინი You/you have put them down	და-გ-ე-წყ-ო-(თ) შენ/თქვენ ისინი You had put them down	და-გ-ე-წყ-ო-ს/თ შენ/თქვენ ისინი If you/you had put them down
და-უ-დ-ი-ა-(თ) მას/მათ ის He/they have put it down	და-ე-დ-ო-(თ) მას/მათ ის He/they had put it down	და-ე-დ-ო-ს/თ მას/მათ ის If he/they had put it down
და-უ-წყვ-ი-ა-(თ) მას/მათ ისინი He has/they have put it down	და-ე-წყ-ო-(თ) მას/მათ ისინი He/they had put them down	და-ე-წყ-ო-ს/თ მას/მათ ისინი If he/they had put them down

*მე **ვდებ** თეფშს მაგიდაზე.*
I put a plate on the table.
*მე **ვაწყობ//ვალაგებ** თეფშებს მაგიდაზე.*
I put plates on the table.
*მან წიგნი **დადო** თაროზე.*
He put a book on the shelf.
*მან წიგნები **დააწყო//დაალაგა** თაროზე.*
He put/arranged books on the shelf.

The verb დალაგება may be used independently without being coordinated with the direct object number. In that case it means *to put in order* or *to tidy up*.

> *ბავშვი თავის სათამაშოებს* ***ალაგებს.***
> The child is putting his toys in order.
> *დედამ სახლი* ***დაალაგა.***
> Mother cleaned up (tidied up) the house.

These verbs are interchangeable their passive voice forms as well.

> *ნეტავ ეს წიგნი თავის ადგილას* ***იდოს.***
> I wish this book were put in its place.
> *ნეტავ ეს წიგნები თავის ადგილას* ***ელაგოს//ეწყოს.***
> I wish these books were in their place.

3. ტეხ- მტვრ- to break, smash

The verbs derived from these stems are transitive and belong to the I conjugation. The stem ***მტვრევ***, like all verbs ending with *-ევ*, have *-ივ* in II series, as well as in the pluperfect and perfect subjunctive forms in which it loses the *ვ* consonant.

Present	*Imperfect*	*Present subjunctive*
ვ-ტეხ-(თ) მე/ჩვენ მას I/we break it ვ-ა-მტვრევ-(თ) მე/ჩვენ მათ I/we break them ტეხ-(თ) შენ/თქვენ მას You/you break it	ვ-ტეხ-დ-ი-(თ) მე/ჩვენ მას I was/we were breaking it ვ-ა-მტვრევ-დ-ი-(თ) მე/ჩვენ მათ I was/we were breaking them ტეხ-დ-ი-(თ) შენ/თქვენ მას You/you were breaking it	ვ-ტეხ-დ-ე-(თ) მე/ჩვენ მას If I/we break it ვ-ა-მტვრევ-დ-ე-(თ) მე/ჩვენ მათ If I/we break them ტეხ-დ-ე-(თ) შენ/თქვენ მას If you/you break it
ა-მტვრევ-(თ) შენ/თქვენ მათ You/you break them	ა-მტვრევ-დ-ი-(თ) შენ/თქვენ მათ You/you were breaking them	ა-მტვრევ-დ-ე-(თ) შენ/თქვენ მათ If you/you break them

(Continued)

(Continued)

Present	*Imperfect*	*Present subjunctive*
ტეხ-ს/ენ ის/ისინი მას He/they breaks it	ტეხ-დ-ა/ნენ ის/ისინი მას He was/they were breaking it	ტეხ-დ-ე-ს/ნენ ის/ისინი მას If he breaks/they break it
ა-მტვრევ-ს/ენ ის/ისინი მათ He/they break/s them	ა-მტვრევ-დ-ა/ნენ ის/ისინი მათ He/they was/were breaking them	ა-მტვრევ-დ-ე-ს/ნენ ის/ისინი მათ If he/they break/s them
Future	*Conditional*	*Future subjunctive*
გა/და-ვ-ტეხ-(თ) მე/ჩვენ მას I/we will break it	გა/დავტეხ-დ-ი-(თ) მე/ჩვენ მას I/we would break it	გა/დავტეხ-დ-ე-(თ) მე/ჩვენ მას If I/we were to break it
და-ვ-ამტვრევ-(თ) მე/ჩვენ მათ I/we will break them	დავამტვრევ-დ-ი-(თ) მე/ჩვენ მათ I/we would break them	დავამტვრევ-დ-ე-(თ) მე/ჩვენ მათ If I/we were to break them
გა/და-ტეხ-(თ) შენ/თქვენ მას You/you will break it	გა/და-ტეხ-დ-ი-(თ) შენ/თქვენ მას You/you would break it	გა/დატეხ-დ-ე-(თ) შენ/თქვენ მას If you/you were to break it
და-ა-მტვრევ-(თ) შენ/თქვენ მათ You/you will break them	დაამტვრევ-დ-ი-(თ) შენ/თქვენ მათ You/you would break them	დაამტვრევ-დ-ე-(თ) შენ/თქვენ მათ If you/you were to break them
გა/და-ტეხ-ს/ენ ის/ისინი მას/მათ He will break it	გა/დატეხ-დ-ა/ნენ ის/ისინი მას He/they would break it	გა/დატეხ-დ-ე-ს/ნენ ის/ისინი მას If he/they were to break it
და-ა-მტვრევ-ს/ენ ის/ისინი მათ He/they will break them	დაამტვრევ-დ-ა/ნენ ის/ისინი მათ He/they would break them	დაამტვრევ-დ-ე-ს/ნენ ის/ისინი მათ If he/they were to break it

Aorist	*Optative*
გა/და-ვ-ტეხ-ე-(თ) მე/ჩვენ ის I/we broke it	გა/და-ვ-ტეხ-ო-(თ) მე/ჩვენ ის I/we should break it
და-ვ-ა-მტვრი-ე-(თ) მე/ჩვენ ისინი I/we broke them	და-ვ-ა-მტვრი-ო-(თ) მე/ჩვენ ისინი I/we should break them
გა/და-ტეხ-ე-(თ) შენ/თქვენ ის You/you broke it	გა/და-ტეხ-ო-(თ) შენ/თქვენ ის You/you should break it
და-ა-მტვრი-ე-(თ) შენ/თქვენ ისინი You/you broke them	და-ა-მტვრი-ო-(თ) შენ/თქვენ ისინი You/you should break them
გა/და-ტეხ-ა/ეს მან/მათ ის He/they broke it	გა/და-ტეხ-ო-ს/ნ მან/მათ ის He/they should break it
და-ა-მტვრი-ა/ეს მან/მათ ისინი He/they broke them	და-ა-მტვრი-ო-ს/ნ მან/მათ ისინი He/they should break them

Perfect	*Pluperfect*	*Perfect subjunctive*
გა/და-მ-ი-ტეხ-ი-ა მე ის I have broken it	გა/და-მ-ე-ტეხ-ა მე ის I had broken it	გა/და-მ-ე-ტეხ-ო-ს მე ის If I had broken it
გა/და-გვ-ი-ტეხ-ი-ა ჩვენ ის We have broken it	გა/და-გვ-ე-ტეხ-ა ჩვენ ის We had broken it	გა/და-გვ-ე-ტეხ-ო-ს ჩვენ ის If we had broken it
და-მ-ი-მტვრევ-ი-ა მე ისინი I have broken them	და-მ-ე-მტვრ-ი-ა მე ისინი I had broken them	და-მ-ე-მტვრ-ი-ო-ს მე ისინი If I had broken them
და-გვ-ი-მტვრევ-ი-ა ჩვენ ისინი We have broken them	და-გვ-ე-მტვრ-ი-ა ჩვენ ისინი We had broken them	და-გვ-ე-მტვრ-ი-ო-ს ჩვენ ისინი If we had broken them

(*Continued*)

(Continued)

გა/და-გ-ი-ტეხ-ი-ა-(თ) შენ/თქვენ ის You/you have broken it	გა/და-გ-ე-ტეხ-ა-(თ) შენ/თქვენ ის You/you had broken it	გა/და-გ-ე-ტეხ-ო-ს/თ შენ/თქვენ ის If you/you had broken it
და-გ-ი-მტვრევ-ი-ა-(თ) შენ/თქვენ ისინი You/you have broken them	და-გ-ე-მტვრ-ი-ა-(თ) შენ/თქვენ ისინი You/you had broken them	და-გ-ე-მტვრ-ი-ო-ს/თ შენ/თქვენ ისინი If you/you had broken them
გა/და-უ-ტეხ-ი-ა-(თ) მას/მათ ის He/they have broken it	გა/და-ე-ტეხ-ა-(თ) მას/მათ ის He/they had broken it	გა/და/-ე-ტეხ-ა-(თ) მას/მათ ის If he/they had broken it
და-უ-მტვრევ-ი-ა-(თ) მას/მათ ისინი He has/they have broken them	და-ე-მტვრ-ი-ა-(თ) მას/მათ ისინი He/they had broken them	და-ე-მტვრ-ი-ა-(თ) მას/მათ ისინი If he/they had broken them

ბავშვი სათამაშოს ***ტეხს.***
The child is breaking (his) toy.
ბავშვი სათამაშოებს ***ამტვრევს.***
The child breaks (his) toys.
ბავშვმა სათამაშოები ***დაამტვრია.***
The child broke (his) toys.
ჩემი მეზობელი ისე მიყურებს, თითქოს მე ***გამეტეხოს*** *მისი ფანჯარა.*
My neighbour is looking at me as if I had broken his window.
ეს ხეები გუშინ ქარს ***დაუმტვრევია.***
The wind broke these trees yesterday.

4. ბ- სხ- to tie on, put on

The verbs derived from these roots ***იბამს*** and ***ისხამს*** refer to the ability of a tree or trees to "produce" or "sprout" fruit. Like other verbs discussed previously, they mark the change of a direct object number from singular to plural form.

In the following chart all forms with the exception of those referring to the third person, either singular or plural, are purely hypothetical.

Present	*Imperfect*	*Present subjunctive*
ვ-ი-ბ-ამ-(თ) მე/ჩვენ მას I/we sprout it	ვ-ი-ბ-ამ-დ-ი-(თ) მე/ჩვენ მას I was/we were sprouting it	ვ-ი-ბ-ამ-დ-ე-(თ) მე/ჩვენ მას If I/we sprout it
ვ-ი-სხ-ამ-(თ) მე/ჩვენ მათ I/we sprout them	ვ-ი-სხ-ამ-დ-ი-(თ) მე/ჩვენ მათ I was/we were sprouting them	ვ-ი-სხ-ამ-დ-ე-(თ) მე/ჩვენ მათ If I/we sprout them
ი-ბ-ამ-(თ) შენ/თქვენ მას You/you sprout it	ი-ბ-ამ-დ-ი-(თ) შენ/თქვენ მას You/you were sprouting it	ი-ბ-ამ-დ-ე-(თ) შენ/თქვენ მას If you/sprout it
ი-სხ-ამ-(თ) შენ/თქვენ მათ You/you sprout them	ი-სხ-ამ-დ-ი-(თ) შენ/თქვენ მათ You/you were sprouting them	ი-სხ-ამ-დ-ე-(თ) შენ/თქვენ მათ If you/you sprout them
ი-ბ-ამ-ს ის/ისინი მას It sprouts/they sprout it	ი-ბ-ამ-დ-ა ის/ისინი მას It/they were sprouting it	ი-ბ-ამ-დ-ე-ს ის/ისინი მას If it/they sprout it
ი-სხ-ამ-ენ ისინი მათ It/they sprout them	ი-სხ-ამ-დ-ა/ნენ ის/ისინი მათ It/they were sprouting them	ი-სხ-ამ-დ-ე-ს/ნენ ის/ისინი მათ If it/they sprouted them
Future	*Conditional*	*Future subjunctive*
მო-ვ-ი-ბ-ამ-(თ) მე/ჩვენ მას I/we will sprout it/them	მოვიბამ-დ-ი-(თ) მე/ჩვენ მას I/we would sprout it/them	მოვიბამ-დ-ე-(თ) მე/ჩვენ მას If I/we were to sprout them
მო-ვ-ი-სხ-ამ-(თ) მე/ჩვენ მათ We will sprout them	მოვისხამ-დ-ი-(თ) მე/ჩვენ მას მათ I/we would sprout them	მოვისხამ-დ-ე-(თ) მე/ჩვენ მათ If I/we were to sprout them
მო-ი-ბ-ამ-(თ) შენ/თქვენ მას You/you will sprout them	მოიბამ-დ-ი-(თ) შენ/თქვენ მას You/you would sprout them	მოიბამ-დ-ე-(თ) შენ/თქვენ მას If you/you were to sprout them

(*Continued*)

(Continued)

Future	*Conditional*	*Future subjunctive*
მო-ი-სხ-ამ-(თ) შენ/თქვენ მათ You/you will sprout them	მოისხამ-დ-ი-(თ) შენ/თქვენ მათ You/you would sprout them	მოისხამ-დ-ე-(თ) შენ/თქვენ მათ If you/you were to sprout them
მო-ი-ბ-ამ-ს/ენ ის/ისინი მას It/they will sprout it მო-ი-სხ-ამ-ს/ენ ის/ისინი მათ It/they will sprout them	მოიბამ-დ-ა/ნენ ის/ისინი მას It/they would sprout it/them მოისხამ-დ-ა/ნენ ის/ისინი მათ It/they would sprout them	მოიბამ-დ-ე-ს/ნენ ის/ისინი მას If it/they were to sprout it/them მოისხამ-დ-ე-ს/ნენ ის/ისინი მათ If it/they were to sprout them

Aorist		*Optative*
მო-ვ-ი-ბ-ი-(თ) მე/ჩვენ ის I/we sprouted it/them		მო-ვ-ი-ბ-ა-(თ) მე/ჩვენ ის I/we should sprout it/them
მო-ვ-ი-სხ-ი-(თ) მე/ჩვენ ისინი I/we sprouted them		მო-ვ-ი-სხ-ა-(თ) მე/ჩვენ ისინი I/we should sprout them
მო-ი-ბ-ი-(თ) შენ/ თქვენ ის You/you sprouted it მო-ი-სხ-ი-(თ) შენ/თქვენ ისინი You/you sprouted them		მო-ი-ბ-ა-(თ) შენ/თქვენ ის You/you should sprout it მო-ი-სხ-ა-(თ) შენ/ თქვენ ისინი You/you should sprout them
მო-ი-ბ-ა/ეს მან/მათ ის It/they spouted it მო-ი-სხ-ა/ეს მან/მათ ისინი It/they sprouted them		მო-ი-ბ-ა-ს/ან მან/მათ ის It/they should sprout it მო-ი-სხ-ა-ს/ან მან/მათ ის ისინი It/they should sprout them

Perfect	*Pluperfect*	*Perfect subjunctive*
მო-მ-ი-ბ-ამ-ს მე ის I have sprouted it მო-გვ-ი-ბ-ამ-ს ჩვენ ის We have sprouted it მო-მ-ი-სხ-ამ-ს მე ისინი I have sprouted them მო-გვ-ი-სხ-ამ-ს ჩვენ ისინი We have sprouted them	მო-მ-ე-ბ-ა მე ის I had sprouted it მო-გვ-ე-ბ-ა ჩვენ ის We had spouted it მო-მ-ე-სხ-ა მე ისინი I had sprouted them მო-გვ-ე-სხ-ა ჩვენ ისინი We had sprouted them	მო-მ-ე-ბ-ა-ს მე ის If I had sprouted it მო-გვ-ე-ბ-ა-ს ჩვენ ის/ისინი If we had sprouted it/them მო-მ-ე-სხ-ა-ს მე ის If I had sprouted it მო-გვ-ე-სხ-ა-ს ჩვენ ისინი If we had sprouted them
მო-გ-ი-ბ-ამ-ს/თ შენ/თქვენ ის You/you have sprouted it მო-გ-ი-სხ-ამ-ს/თ შენ/თქვენ ისინი You/you have sprouted them	მო-გ-ე-ბ-ა-(თ) შენ/თქვენ ის You/you had sprouted it მო-გ-ე-სხ-ა-(თ) შენ/თქვენ ისინი You/you had sprouted them	მო-გ-ე-ბ-ა-ს/თ შენ/თქვენ ის If you/you had sprouted it მო-გ-ე-სხ-ა-ს/თ შენ/თქვენ ისინი If you/you had sprouted them
მო-უ-ბ-ამ-ს/თ მას/მათ ის It/they has sprouted it მო-უ-სხ-ამ-ს/თ მას/მათ ისინი It has/they have sprouted them	მო-ე-ბ-ა-(თ) მას/მათ ის It/they had sprouted it მო-ე-სხ-ა-(თ) მას/მათ ისინი It/they had sprouted them	მო-ე-ბ-ა-(თ) მას/მათ ის If it/they had sprouted it მო-ე-სხ-ა-(თ) მას/მათ ისინი If it/they had sprouted them

წელს ჩემმა ხემ მხოლოდ ერთი ვაშლი ***მოიბა.***
This year my tree sprouted only one apple.
შარშან ჩემმა ხემ ბევრი ვაშლი ***მოისხა.***
Last year my tree sprouted many apples.

The roots **ბ-** and **სხ-** may independently generate verbs that do not denote plurality of their direct objects:

კაცმა ხეს ***თოკი*** *მოაბა.*
A man tied a rope to the tree.

*კაცმა ხეს **თოკები მოაბა.***
A man tied ropes to the tree.
დაისხი ღვინო!
Pour yourself the wine.
*დედამ ჩაიდანში **წყალი ჩაასხა.***
Mother poured the water into the tea-cattle.

5. კლ- – ხოც- to kill/slaughter

The verbs with these roots are transitive and belong to the I conjugation. As a rule, the stem *კლ-* is used with the preverb ***მო-*** and the stem ***ხოც-*** with ***და-***.

Present	*Imperfect*	*Present subjunctive*
ვ-კლ-ავ-(თ) მე/ჩვენ მას I/we kill him	ვ-კლ-ავ-დ-ი-(თ) მე/ჩვენ მას I was/we were killing him	ვ-კლ-ავ-დ-ე-(თ) მე/ჩვენ მას If I/we kill him
ვ-ხოც-ავ-(თ) მე/ჩვენ მათ I/we kill them	ვ-ხოც-ავ-დ-ი-(თ) მე/ჩვენ მათ I was/we were killing them	ვ-ხოც-ავ-დ-ე-(თ) მე/ჩვენ მათ If I/we kill them
კლ-ავ-(თ) შენ/თქვენ მას You/you kill him	კლ-ავ-დ-ი-(თ) შენ/თქვენ მას You/you were killing him	კლ-ავ-დ-ე-(თ) შენ/თქვენ მას If you/you kill him
ხოც-ავ-(თ) შენ/ თქვენ მათ I/we kill them	ხოც-ავ-დ-ი-(თ) შენ/თქვენ მას You/you were killing them	ხოც-ავ-დ-ე-(თ) შენ/თქვენ მათ If you/you kill them
კლ-ავ-ს ის მას He kills him	კლ-ავ-დ-ა ის მას He was killing him	კლ-ავ-დ-ე-ს ის მას If he kill him
კლ-ავ-ენ ისინი მას They kill him	კლ-ავ-დ-ნენ ისინი მას They were killing him	კლ-ავ-დ-ნენ ისინი მას If they kill him
ხოც-ავ-ს ის მათ He kills them	ხოც-ავ-დ-ა ის მათ He was killing them	ხოც-ავ-დ-ე-ს ის მათ If he kill them
ხოც-ავ-ენ ისინი მათ They kill them	ხოც-ავ-დ-ნენ ისინი მათ They were killing them	ხოც-ავ-დ-ნენ ისინი მათ If they kill them

Future	*Conditional*	*Future subjunctive*
მო-ვ-კლ-ავ-(თ) მე/ჩვენ მას I/we will kill him	მო-ვ-კლ-ავ-დ-ი-(თ) მე/ჩვენ მას I/we would kill him	მო-ვ-კლ-ავ-დ-ე-(თ) მე/ჩვენ მას If I/we were to kill him
და-ვ-ხოც-ავ-(თ) მე/ჩვენ მათ I/we will kill them	და-ვ-ხოც-ავ-დ-ი-(თ) მე/ჩვენ მათ I/we would kill them	და-ვ-ხოც-ავ-დ-ე-(თ) მე/ჩვენ მათ If I/we were to kill them
მო-კლ-ავ-(თ) შენ/თქვენ მას You/you will kill him	მო-კლ-ავ-დ-ი-(თ) შენ/თქვენ მას You/you would kill him	მო-კლ-ავ-დ-ე-(თ) შენ/თქვენ მას If you/you were to kill him
და-ხოც-ავ-(თ) შენ/თქვენ მათ You/you will kill them	და-ხოც-ავ-დ-ი-(თ) შენ/თქვენ მათ You/you would kill them	და-ხოც-ავ-დ-ე-(თ) შენ/თქვენ მათ If you/you were to kill them
მო-კლ-ავ-ს/ენ ის/ისინი მას He/they will kill him	მო-კლ-ავ-დ-ა/ნენ ის/ისინი მას He/they would kill him	მო-კლ-ავ-დ-ე-ს/ნენ ის/ისინი მას If he/they were to kill him
და-ხოც-ავ-ს/ენ ის/ისინი მას He/they will kill them	და-ხოც-ავ-დ-ა/ნენ ის/ისინი მათ He/they would kill them	და-ხოც-ავ-დ-ე-ს/ნენ ის/ისინი მათ If he/they were to kill them

Aorist		*Optative*
მო-ვ-კალ-ი-(თ) მე/ჩვენ ის I/we killed him		მო-ვ-კლ-ა-(თ) მე/ჩვენ ის I/we should kill him
და-ვ-ხოც-ე-(თ) ჩვენ ის/ისინი I/we killed them		და-ვ-ხოც-ო-(თ) მე/ჩვენ ის/ისინი I/we should kill them
მო-კალ-ი-(თ) შენ/ თქვენ ის You/you killed him		მო-კლ-ა-(თ) შენ/ თქვენ ის You/you should kill him
და-ხოც-ე-თ თქვენ ის/ისინი You/you killed them		და-ხოც-ო-თ თქვენ ის/ისინი You/you should kill them

(*Continued*)

(Continued)

მო-კლ-ა/ეს მან/მათ ის He/they killed him		მო-კლ-ა-ს/ან მან/მათ ის He/they should kill him
და-ხოც-ა/ეს მან/მათ ისინი He/they killed them		და-ხოც-ო-ს/ნ მან ისინი He/they should kill them
Perfect	*Pluperfect*	*Perfect subjunctive*
მო-მ-ი-კლ-ავ-ს მე ის I have killed him	მო-მ-ე-კლ-ა მე ის I had killed him	მო-მ-ე-კლ-ა-ს მე ის If I had killed him
მო-გვ-ი-კლ-ავ-ს ჩვენ ის We have killed him	მო-გვ-ე-კლ-ა ჩვენ ის We had killed him	მო-გვ-ე-კლ-ა-ს ჩვენ ის If we had killed him
და-მ-ი-ხოც-ავ-ს მე ისინი I have killed them	და-მ-ე-ხოც-ა მე ისინი I had killed them	და-მ-ე-ხოც-ო-ს მე ის If I had killed them
და-გვ-ი-ხოც-ავ-ს ჩვენ ისინი We have killed them	და-გვ-ე-ხოც-ა ჩვენ ისინი We had killed them	და-გვ-ე-ხოც-ო-ს ჩვენ ის If we had killed them
მო-გ-ი-კლ-ავ-ს/თ შენ/თქვენ ის You/you have killed him	მო-გ-ე-კლ-ა-(თ) შენ/თქვენ ის You/you had killed him	მო-გ-ე-კლ-ა-ს/თ შენ/თქვენ ის If you/you had killed him
და-გ-ი-ხოც-ავ-ს/თ შენ/თქვენ ისინი You/you have killed them	და-გ-ე-ხოც-ა-(თ) შენ/თქვენ ისინი You/you had killed them	და-გ-ე-ხოც-ო-ს/თ შენ/თქვენ ისინი If you/you had killed them
მო-უ-კლ-ავ-ს/თ მას/მათ ის He has/they have killed him	მო-ე-კლ-ა-(თ) მას/მათ ის He/they had killed him	მო-ე-კლ-ა-ს/თ მას/მათ ის If he/they had killed him
და-უ-ხოც-ავ-ს/თ მას/მათ ისინი He/they has killed them	და-ე-ხოც-ა-(თ) მას/მათ ისინი He/they had killed them	და-ე-ხოც-ო-ს/თ მას/მათ ისინი If he/they had killed them

მეფემ ომში მტერი ***მოკლა.***
The king killed (his) enemy in the battle.
მეფემ ომში მტრები ***დახოცა.***
The king killed (his) enemies in the battle.
ჩვენს კატას თაგვი ***მოუკლავს.***
Our cat has killed a mouse.
მგელს ჩვენი ცხვრები ***დაუხოცავს.***
A wolf has killed our sheep.

9.7.3 Honorific verbs of polite conversation

In Georgian there is a set of conventional rules of polite conversation that require the use of honorific verbs expressing deference of the speaker to the person addressed or referred to. All these honorific verbs are derived from the stems ***ბრძან-***, ***რთმ-***, and ***ხლ-***. The meaning of these verbs is determined by the context in which they replace the regular verbs used in ordinary conversations.

The honorific verbs referring to the second or third person are always in plural form whether it refers to one or more persons.

1. The honorific verbs derived from the stem ***ბრძან*** are used in reference to the second and third persons in polite conversation.

ყოფნა	to be	ბრძანება
ხარ	You are	ბრძანდები(თ)
არის	He is	ბრძანდება
არიან	They are	ბრძანდებიან

დაჯდომა	**to sit**	**დაბრძანება**
დაჯექი	You sat down	დაბრძანდი(თ)
დაჯდა	He sat down	დაბრძანდა
დასხდნენ	They sat down	დაბრძანდნენ
დაჯდე	You should sit down	დაბრძანდე(თ)
დაჯდეს	He should sit down	დაბრძანდეს
დასხდნენ	They should sit down	დაბრძანდნენ
დამჯდარხარ	You have sat down	დაბრძანებულხართ
დამჯდარა	He has sat down	დაბრძანებულა
დამჯდარიყავი	You had sat down	დაბრძანებულიყავით
დამჯდარიყო	He had sat down	დაბრძანებულიყო
დამსხდარიყვნენ	He had sat down	დაბრძანებულიყვნენ

წასვლა	**to go/leave**	**წაბრძანება**
წ/მოხვედი	You went	წა/მობრძანდი(თ)
წა/მოვიდა	He went	წა/მობრძანდა
წა/მოსულხარ	You have gone	წა/მობრძანებულხართ
წა/მოსულა	He has gone	წა/მობრძანებულა
წა/მოსულიყავი	You had gone	წა/მობრძანებულიყავით
წა/მოსულიყო	He had gone	წაბ/მორძანებულიყო
წასულიყვნენ	They had gone	წა/მობრძანებულიყვნენ

მი/მოსვლა	**to go, to come**	**მი/მობრძანება**
მი/მოდიხარ	You go/come	მი/მობრძანდებით
მი/მოდის	He goes/comes	მი/მობრძანდება
მი/მოდიან	They go/come	მი/მობრძანდებიან
მი/მოხვედი	You came	მი/მობრძანდით
მი/მოვიდა	He came	მი/მობრძანდა
მი/მოსულხარ	You have come	მი/მობრძანებულხართ
მი/მოსულა	He has come	მი/მობრძანებულა
მი/მოსულა	They have come	მი/მობრძანებულან

– ***დაბრძანდით***, *ქალბატონო ნინო!*
Sit down, please, Ms. Nino.
– *როდის* ***ჩამობრძანდით*** *ლონდონიდან?*
When have you arrived from London?
– *იმედია კარგად* ***ბრძანდებით.***
I hope you are well.
– *უკან როდის* ***წაბრძანდებით?***
When will you go back?
– *დირექტორი აქ არ* ***ბრძანდება?***
Isn't the manager here?
– *არა, ჯერ არ* ***მობრძანებულა.***
No, he has not come yet.
– *როდის* ***მობრძანდება?***
When will he come?
– *ცხრა საათისთვის უნდა* ***მობრძანებულიყო.***
He should have come by nine o'clock.

2. The verbs derived from the stem ***ბრძან*** may replace the verb *to say*.

მბობა to say	*ბრძანება*	*თქმა* to say	*ბრძანება*
ამბობ(თ) You/you say	ბრძანებ(თ)	თქვი(თ) You said	ბრძანე(თ)
ამბობს He says	ბრძანებს	თქვა He said	ბრძანა
ამბობენ They say	ბრძანებენ	თქვეს They said	ბრძანეს
იტყვი(თ) You will say	ბრძანებ(თ)	თქვა(თ) You should say	ბრძანო(თ)
იტყვის He will say	ბრძანებს	თქვას He should say	ბრძანოს
იტყვიან They will say	ბრძანებენ	თქვან They should say	ბრძანონ
		გითქვამს/თ You/you have said	გიბრძანებია(თ)
		უთქვამს/თ He/they has/have said	უბრძანებია
		თქმა to say	*ბრძანება*
		გეთქვას/თ If you/you should say	გებრძანოს/თ
		ეთქვას/თ If he/they should say	ებრძანოს/თ

– *ბატონო გიორგი, თქვენ* ***გიბრძანებიათ****, რომ ამ საბუთის ასლია საჭირო.*
Mr. George, you have (apparently) said that a copy of this document is required.
– *ქალბატონი მერი ამერიკაში* ***წაბრძანებულა****.*
Ms. Mary has gone to America.
– *რას* ***ბრძანებთ!*** *მართლა?*
You don't say! Really?

3. The honorific forms for the verbs *to be* and *to come* are used in reference to the first and third persons and should be in plural form. Its meaning could be approximated with the expression *to be/come at one's service*.

ყოფნა to be	*ხლება*	*მოსვლა*	to come	*ხლება*
ვარ I am	გახლავართ	მოვედი	I came	გეახელით
		მოვიდა	He came	გეახლათ
არის He is	გახლავთ	მოვიდნენ	They came	გეახლნენ
		მოვალ(თ)	I will come	გეახლებით
		მოვა	he will come	გეახლებათ
		მოვლენ		გეახლებიან
		მოვსულვარ	I have come	გხლებივართ
		მოსულა/ნ	He has come	გხლებიათ/ან
		მოვსულიყავი(თ) I should have come		გხლებოდით
		მოსულიყო He should have come		გხლებოდათ
		მოსულიყვნენ		გხლებოდნენ

– *ბატონი დავითი უკვე აქ* ***გახლავთ*** *და ხუთ წუთში* ***გეახლებათ.***
Mr. David is already here and will come over to you in five minutes.
– *მე თქვენი ძმის მეგობარი* ***გახლავართ*** *და დღეს ერთი თხოვნით* ***გეახელით.***
I am a friend of your brother and today I came over to you with a request.

4. The honorific verbs derived from the stem ***რთმევ*** may mean *to give*, *offer*, or *present* or *to eat*. The latter meaning applies only to the second person in plural and third person in singular and plural forms.

მიტანა to offer, to take to		*ჭამა* to eat	*მირთმევა*
მივუტან(თ) I/we will give/offer	მივართმევ(თ)	ვჭამ(თ) I/we eat	გეახლებით
მიუტან(თ) You will give/offer	მიართმევ(თ)	ჭამ(თ) You/you eat	მიირთმევთ
მიუტანს/ენ He/they will give/offer	მიართმევს/ენ	ჭამს/ენ He/they eats	მიირთმევს/ენ

მივუტანე I/we gave/offered	მივართვი(თ)	ვჭამე(თ) I/we ate	გეახელით
მიუტანე You gave/offered	მიართვი(თ)	ჭამე(თ) You/you ate	მიირთვით
მიუტანა he gave/offered	მიართვა	ჭამა/ეს He/they ate	მიირთვა/ეს
მიმიტანია I have given/ offered	მიმირთმევია	მიჭამია I have eaten	მიგირთმევია(თ)
მიგიტანია You have given/ offered	მიგირთმევია(თ)	გიჭამია(თ) You have eaten	მიურთმევიათ
მიუტანია He has given/ offered	მიურთმევია(თ)	უჭამია(თ) He has eaten	
მიმეტანა I should have given/offered	მიმერთმია	ჭამოს/ნ You/you should eat	მიირთვა(თ)
მიგვეტანა We should have given/offered	მიგვერთმია(თ)	ჭამოს/ნ He/they should eat	მიირთვას/ნ
მიგეტანა/თ You should have given/offered	მიგერთმია(თ)		
მიეტანა/თ He/they should have given/offered	მიერთმია(თ)		

გუშინ დამთავრდა სემესტრი და ჩვენს მასწავლებელს თაიგული ***მივართვით.***

Yesterday the semester was finished, and we presented our teacher with a bouquet of flowers.

– ***მიართვი*** *სტუმარს ღვინო!*

Offer the guest (some) wine.

– *ხაჭაპურს რატომ არ* ***მიირთმევთ? მიირთვით****! ძალიან გემრიელია.*

Why aren't you having the cheese-bread? Please, have some, it is delicious.

The verbs generated from the root **ხლ-** imply the action committed to serve or please someone – thus, in a polite conversation, the answer to the invitation.

– *მიირთვით ხილი!*
Have some fruit.
– *გმადლობთ,* ***გეახლებით.***
Thank you, I am having some.
In this sense this verb mostly used in the present and aorist tenses.
– *მიირთვით ნამცხვარი!*
Have (eat, try) the cake.
– *გმადლობთ, უკვე* ***გეახელით.***
Thank you, I already had (ate) a piece.

9.7.4 *Irregular verbs with changing stems by tense*

A group of Georgian verbs change their roots in accordance with tenses. However, there is a common denominator for each of them: verbs of the present subseries are based on their present tense stem and those of the future subseries are derived from the future tense stem. In III series these verbs have the same stem as in II series.

1. ***ყოფნა:არის-იქნება-იყო*** *– to be*

   The verbs **არის** (is), **იქნება** (will be), and **იყო** (was) are medio-passive. **არის** (is) has only the present tense forms in the present subseries. In all the three tenses of the future subseries the verb *to be* is based on the stem **იქნებ**, in II series on **იყო** and in III series on its past participle **ყოფილ-**.

Present	*Imperfect*	*Present subjunctive*
ვ-არ-(თ) I/we am/ar	–	–
ხ-არ-(თ) You/you are	–	–
არ-ი-ს He is	–	–
არ-ი-ან They are		

Future	*Conditional*	*Future subjunctive*
ვ-იქნ-ებ-ი-(თ) მე/ჩვენ I/we will be	ვ-ი-ქნ-ებ-ოდ-ი-(თ) მე/ჩვენ I/we would be	ვ-ი-ქნ-ებ-ოდ-ე-(თ) მე/ჩვენ If I/we were to be
ი-ქნ-ებ-ი-(თ) შენ/თქვენ You/you will be	ი-ქნ-ებ-ოდ-ი-(თ) შენ/თქვენ You/you would be	ი-ქნ-ებ-ოდ-ე-(თ) შენ/თქვენ If you/you were to be
ი-ქნ-ებ-ა ის He will be	ი-ქნ-ებ-ოდ-ა ის He would be	ი-ქნ-ებ-ოდ-ე-ს ის If he were to be
იქნ-ებ-ი-ან ისინი They will be	იქნ-ებ-ოდ-ნენ ისინი They would be	იქნ-ებ-ოდ-ნენ ისინი If they were to be

Aorist		*Optative*
ვ-ი-ყავ-ი-(თ) მე/ჩვენ I was/we were		ვ-ი-ყ-ო-(თ) მე/ჩვენ I/we should be
ი-ყავ-ი-(თ) შენ/თქვენ You/you were		ი-ყ-ო-(თ) შენ/თქვენ You/you should be
ი-ყ-ო ის He was		ი-ყ-ო-ს ის He should be
ი-ყვ-ნენ ისინი They were		იყვ-ნენ ისინი They should be

Perfect	*Pluperfect*	*Perfect subjunctive*
ვყოფილ-ვარ(თ) მე/ჩვენ I/we have been	ვყოფილ-იყავი(თ) მე/ჩვენ I/we had been	ვყოფილ-იყო(თ) მე/ჩვენ If I/we had been
ყოფილ-ხარ(თ) შენ/თქვენ You/you have been	ყოფილ-იყავი(თ) შენ/თქვენ You/you had been	ყოფილ-იყო(თ) შენ/თქვენ If you/you had been
ყოფილ-ა ის He has been	ყოფილ-იყო ის He had been	ყოფილ-იყოს ის If he had been
ყოფილ-ან ისინი They have been	ყოფილ-იყვნენ ისინი They had been	ყოფ-ილ-ი-ყვ-ნენ ისინი If they had been

მე ქართველი ***ვარ.***
I am Georgian.
ისინი ქართველები ***არიან.***
They are Georgian.
რომ შეეძლოთ, ისინი ახლა ჩვენთან ***იქნებოდნენ.***
If they could, they would have been with us now.
ნეტავ ახლა სტუდენტები ***ვიყოთ.***
I wish we were students now.
დღეს მაღაზიაში არ ***ყოფილხარ?***
Haven't you been at the store today?
ისინი რომ აქ ყოფილიყვნენ, მეცოდინებოდა.
If they had been here, I would have known.

2. სვლა: -ვალ -ველ/ვიდ -დი – *to go, come*

These stems are distributed in the following manner:
In all present subseries (the present, imperfect, and present subjunctive) the verb forms are based on the root -***დი***. As all monopersonal passive voice verbs, they require the auxiliary verb *to be* in the first- and second-person forms.

The future tense forms are based on the root -***ვალ***. The rest of the future subseries forms (the conditional, future subjunctive) and the optative are derived from the root -***ვიდ***.In the aorist the first- and second-person forms are based on the root -***ველ***; in the third-person forms we have again -***ვიდ***.Although the both stems -***ვალ*** and -***ველ*** start with consonant ***ვ***-; it is not doubled in the first-person forms: ***მო-ვალ*** (I will arrive, come), not ***მო-ვ-ვალ;მო-ველ-ი*** (I arrived, came), not ***მო-ვ-ველ-ი.***

Like all IV conjugation verbs their forms in III series are based on the past passive participle, in this case on ***მო-სულ-ი*** (come, arrived) plus the corresponding forms of the auxiliary verb *to be*.

Present	*Imperfect*	*Present subjunctive*
მო-ვ-დი-ვ-არ-(თ) მე/ჩვენ I/we come	მო-ვ-დი-ოდ-ი-(თ) მე/ჩვენ I was/we were coming	მო-ვ-დი-ოდ-ე-(თ) მე/ჩვენ If I/we come
მო-დი-ხ-არ-(თ) შენ/თქვენ You/you come	მო-დი-ოდ-ი-(თ) შენ/თქვენ You/you were coming	მო-დი-ოდ-ე-(თ) შენ/თქვენ If you/you come

მო-დი-ს ის He comes	მო-დი-ოდ-ა ის He was coming	მო-დი-ოდ-ე-ს ის If he come
მო-დი-ან ისინი They come	მო-დი-ოდ-ნენ ისინი They were coming	მო-დი-ოდ-ნენ ისინი If they come

Future	*Conditional*	*Future subjunctive*
მო-ვალ-(თ)მე/ჩვენ I/we will come	მო-ვიდ-ოდ-ი-(თ) მე/ჩვენ I/we would come	მო-ვიდ-ოდ-ე-(თ) მე/ჩვენ If I/we were to come
მო-ხ-ვალ-(თ) შენ/თქვენ You/you will come	მო-ხ-ვიდ-ოდ-ი-(თ) შენ/თქვენ You/you would come	მო-ხ-ვიდ-ოდ-ე-(თ) შენ/თქვენ If you/you were to come
მო-ვ-ა ის He will come	მო-ვიდ-ოდ-ა ის He would come	მო-ვიდ-ოდ-ე-ს ის If he were to come
მო-ვლ-ენ ისინი They will come	მო-ვიდ-ოდ-ნენ ისინი They would come	მო-ვიდ-ოდ-ნენ ისინი If they were to come

Aorist		*Optative*
მო-ვედ-ი-(თ) მე/ჩვენ I/we came		მო-ვიდ-ე-(თ) მე/ჩვენ I/we should come
მო-ხ-ვედ-ი-(თ) შენ/თქვენ You/you came		მო-ხ-ვიდ-ე-(თ) შენ/თქვენ You/you should come
მო-ვიდ-ა ის He came		მო-ვიდ-ე-ს ის He should come
მო-ვიდ-ნენ ისინი They came		მო-ვიდ-ნენ ისინი They should come

Perfect	*Pluperfect*	*Perfect subjunctive*
მო-ვ-სულ-ვ-არ-(თ) მე/ჩვენ I/we have come	მო-ვ-სულ-ი-ყავ-ი-(თ) მე/ჩვენ I/we had come	მო-ვ-სულ-ი-ყ-ო მე/ჩვენ If I/we had come
მო-სულ-ხ-არ-(თ) შენ/თქვენ You/you have come	მო-სულ-ი-ყავ-ი-(თ) შენ/თქვენ You/you had come	მო-სულ-ი-ყ-ო შენ/თქვენ If you/you had come
მო-სულ-ა ის He has come	მო-სულ-ი-ყ-ო ის He had come	მო-სულ-ი-ყ-ო-ს ის If he had come
მო-სულ-ან ისინი They have come	მო-სულ-ი-ყვ-ნენისინი They had come	მო-სულ-ი-ყვ-ნენისინი If they had come

In the present subseries these verbs may have variety of preverbs – *მო-, მი-, ა-, გა-, გადა-, გადმო-, ჩა(მო)-, შე(მო)-* – but they indicate only the direction of the movement, not perfective aspect. Depending on the context, the verbs with these preverbs may be translated as *to go*, *leave*, *enter*, *move/cross over*, *arrive*, etc.

> *მატარებელი 6 საათზე* ***გადის****.*
> The train *leaves* at 6 o'clock.
> *რომელ უნივერსიტეტში* ***შედიხარ****?*
> Which university are you *entering* (applying to)?
> *მასწავლებელი საკლასო ოთახში* ***შემოვიდა****.*
> The teacher *entered* the classroom.
> *მოხუცი კაცი ხიდზე ნელა* ***გადადის****.*
> An old man slowly crosses the bridge.
> *მომავალ წელს თბილისში* ***გადმოვდივართ****.*
> Next year we are moving to Tbilisi.
> *შენი და ბერლინში როდის* ***ჩამოდის****?*
> When is your sister arriving in Berlin?

In the future subseries the verb ***მივდივარ*** will be replaced either with ***მივალ*** or ***წავალ***, depending on the intended meaning. As a rule, ***მი***-implies a specific place or person known to the speaker, while ***წა***-is somewhat less precise. *მივალ* focuses on the arrival at the destination, while *წავალ* on the leaving:

> *სამ საათზე მივალ პარკში (=სამ საათზე ვიქნები პარკში).*
> I will go to the park at three o'clock (= I will be at the park at three o'clock).
> *სამ საათზე წავალ პარკში (=სამ საათზე გავდივარ პარკისკენ).*
> I will go to the park at three o'clock (= I will leave for the park at three o'clock).
> *ხვალ ექიმთან* ***მივდივარ****.*
> Tomorrow I am going to (see) a doctor.
> *მომავალ კვირას ისინი ვაშინგტონში* ***მიდიან****.*
> Next week they are going to Washington.
> *შენი ძმა სად* ***წავიდა****?*
> Where did your brother go?
> *მაღაზიაში* ***წასულა****.*
> (Apparently) he has gone to a store.
> *ჩემი ძმა აქ არის?*
> Is my brother here?
> *არა, უკვე* ***წავიდა****.*
> No, he already left.
> *აქ არავინ არის, ყველა* ***წასულა****.*
> Nobody is here, everybody has left.

The verbs **მოვდივარ**, **მოვალ**, and **წამოვალ** imply the movement towards the speaker or the person whom the speaker addresses.

> – *ჩვენთან როდის მოდიხარ?*
> When are you coming to our place?
> – *ხვალ საღამოს მოვალ.*
> I will come over tomorrow evening.
> – *თქვენ თუ ბაზარში მიდიხართ, ჩვენც წამოვალთ.*
> If you are going to the market we too, will come along.

The only exception to the mentioned rules is the preverb **და-**, which in the fure and perfect series has the stem -**ვლ** in the aorist and -**იარ** in the optative. Unlike the preverbs mentioned, **და-** indicates not the direction, but frequency or continuity of the action. Depending on a context, a verb with this preverb may be translated as *go*, *visit*, or *frequent (a place)*.

Present	*Imperfect*	*Present subjunctive*
და-ვ-დი-ვ-არ-(თ) მე/ჩვენ I/we walk/go to	და-ვ-დი-ოდ-ი-(თ) მე/ჩვენ I was/we were walking/going to	და-ვ-დი-ოდ-ე-(თ) მე/ჩვენ If I/we walk/go to
და-დი-ხ-არ-(თ) შენ/თქვენ You/you walk/go to	და-დი-ოდ-ი-(თ) შენ/თქვენ You/you were walking/going to	და-დი-ოდ-ე-(თ) შენ/თქვენ If you/you walk/go to
და-დი-ს/ან ის/ისინი He/they walk/s/go/es to	და-დი-ოდ-ა/ნენ ის/ისინი He/they was/were walking/going to	და-დი-ოდ-ე-ს/ნენ ის/ისინი If he/they walk/go to
Future	*Conditional*	*Future subjunctive*
ვ-ი-ვლ-ი-(თ) მე/ჩვენ I/we will walk/go to	ვ-ი-ვლ-ი-დ-ი-(თ) მე/ჩვენ I/we would walk/go to	ვ-ი-ვლ-ი-დ-ე-(თ) მე/ჩვენ If I/we were to walk/go to
ი-ვლ-ი-(თ) შენ/თქვენ You/you will walk/go to	ი-ვლ-ი-დ-ი-(თ) შენ/თქვენ You/you would walk/go to	ი-ვლ-ი-დ-ე-(თ) შენ/თქვენ If you/you were to walk/go to

(Continued)

(Continued)

ი-ვლ-ი-ს/ან ის/ ისინი H/theye will walk/ go to	ი-ვლ-ი-დ-ა/ნენ ის/ისინი He/they would walk/go to	ი-ვლ-ი-დ-ე-ს/ნენ ის/ისინი If he/they were to walk/go to
Aorist		*Optative*
(და)-ვ-ი-არ-ე-(თ) მე/ჩვენ I/we walked/ went to		(და)-ვ-ი-არ-ო-(თ) მე/ჩვენ I/we should walk/ go to
(და)-ი-არ-ე-(თ) შენ/თქვენ You/you walked/ went to		(და)-ი-არ-ო-(თ) შენ/თქვენ You/you should walk/go to
(და)-ი-არ-ა/ეს მან/მათ He/they walked/ went to		(და)-ი-არ-ო-ს/ნ მან/მათ He/they should walk/go to
Perfect	*Pluperfect*	*Perfect Subjunctive*
(და)მივლია მე I have walked/ gone to	(და)მევლ-ო მე I had walked/ gone to	(და)მევლ-ო-ს მე If I had walked/ gone to
(და)გვივლია ჩვენ We have walked/ gone to	(და)გვევლ-ო ჩვენ We had walked/ gone to	(და)გვევლ-ო-ს ჩვენ If we had walked/ gone to
(და)გივლია(თ) შენ/თქვენ You/you have walked/gone to	(და)გევლ-ო-(თ) შენ/თქვენ You/you had walked/gone to	(და)გევლ-ო-ს/თ შენ/თქვენ If you/you had walked/gone to
(და)უვლია(თ) მას/მათ He has/they have walked/gone to	(და)ევლ-ო-(თ) მას/მათ He/they had walked/gone to	(და)ევლ-ო-ს/თ მას/მათ If he/they had walked/gone to

*როცა აქ ვცხოვრობდი, ამ სკოლაში **დავდიოდი**.*
When I lived here, I went to this school.
*დღეს ყველა მაღაზია **დავიარე**, მაგრამ რაც მინდოდა, ვერ ვნახე.*
Today I went (walked over, visited) to every store but could not find what I wanted.

*ის ამ ბიბლიოთეკაში კვირაში ორჯერ **დადის.***
He goes to (visits) this library twice a week.
*საქართველოს ყველა რაიონი **დამივლია,** მაგრამ ასეთი ლამაზი ადგილი არ მინახავს.*
I have been (walked over, around) in every region of Georgia but have not seen such a beautiful place.
*დღეს მაღაზიებში **ვივლი,** მინდა ზამთრის პალტო ვიყიდო.*
Today I will walk around (visit) stores; I want to buy a winter coat.
*მომავალ წელს ჩემი ბიჭი სკოლაში **ივლის.***
Next year my son will go to school.

3. **შვრ-/ქენ-/იზამ-:** *to do*

This is the stem of a medio-active monopersonal verb with a case-changing subject. In the present series, it conjugates according to the passive voice verb conjugation pattern. However, in III series, their subject-object markers are inverted as it usually happens in medio-active verb forms.

The stems are distributed in the following manner:

Present subseries: ***შვრებ-***
Future subseries: ***იზამ-***
Aorist and perfect series: ***ქნ-/ქენ-***

Present	*Imperfect*	*Present subjunctive*
ვ-შვრ-ებ-ი-(თ) მე/ჩვენ I/we do	ვ-შვრ-ებ-ოდ-ი-(თ) მე/ჩვენ I was/we were doing	ვ-შვრ-ებ-ოდ-ე-(თ) მე/ჩვენ If I/we do
შვრ-ებ-ი-(თ) შენ/თქვენ You/you do	შვრ-ებ-ოდ-ი-(თ) შენ/თქვენ You/you were doing	შვრ-ებ-ოდ-ე-(თ) შენ/თქვენ If you/you do
შვრ-ებ-ა ის He does	შვრ-ებ-ოდ-ა ის He was doing	შვრ-ებ-ოდ-ე-ს ის If he does?
შვრ-ებ-ი-ან ისინი They do	შვრ-ებ-ოდ-ნენ ისინი They were doing	შვრ-ებ-ოდ-ნენ ისინი If they do

(Continued)

(Continued)

Future	*Conditional*	*Future subjunctive*
ვ-ი-ზამ-(თ) მე/ჩვენ I/we will do	ვ-ი-ზამ-დ-ი-(თ) მე/ჩვენ I/we would do	ვ-ი-ზამ-დ-ე-(თ) მე/ჩვენ If I/we were to do
ი-ზამ-(თ) შენ/თქვენ You/you will do	ი-ზამ-დ-ი-(თ) შენ/თქვენ You/you would do	ი-ზამ-დ-ე-(თ) შენ/თქვენ If you/you were to do
ი-ზამ-ს ის He will do	ი-ზამ-დ-ა ის He would do	ი-ზამ-დ-ე-ს ის If he were to do
ი-ზამ-ენ ისინი They will do?	ი-ზამ-დ-ნენ ისინი They would do	ი-ზამ-დ-ნენ ისინი If they were to do

Aorist		*Optative*
ვ-ქენ-ი-(თ) მე/ჩვენ I/we did		ვ-ქნ-ა-(თ) მე/ჩვენ I/we should do
ქენ-ი-(თ) შენ/თქვენ You/you did		ქნ-ა-(თ) შენ/თქვენ You/you should do
ქნ-ა მან He did		ქნ-ა-ს მან He should do
ქნ-ეს მათ They did		ქნ-ან მათ They should do

Perfect	*Pluperfect*	*Perfect subjunctive*
მ-ი-ქნ-ი-ა მე I have done	მ-ე-ქნ-ა მე I had done	მ-ე-ქნ-ა-ს მე If I had done
გვ-ი-ქნ-ი-ა ჩვენ We have done	გვ-ე-ქნ-ა ჩვენ We had done	გვ-ე-ქნ-ა-ს If we had done
გ-ი-ქნ-ი-ა-(თ) შენ/თქვენ You/you have done	გ-ე-ქნ-ა-(თ) შენ/თქვენ You/you had done	გ-ე-ქნ-ა-ს/თ შენ/თქვენ If you/you had done
უ-ქნ-ი-ა-(თ) მას/მათ He has/they have done	ე-ქნ-ა-(თ) მას/მათ He/they had done	ე-ქნ-ა-ს/თ მას/მათ If he/they had done

All these forms are used mostly in figurative sense and never refer to actually doing or making something.

*რა **ქენი**, იყავი ექიმთან?*
What did you do, did you see the doctor?
*ეხლა ვერაფერს **ვიზამთ**, ვნახოთ ხვალ რა იქნება!*
We cannot do anything now, let's see what happens tomorrow.
*ჩემი პასპორტი დავკარგე და რა **ვქნა**, არ ვიცი.*
I lost my passport and don't know what to do.
*რას **იზამ**? ასეთია ცხოვრება!*
What can you do? That's life!

4. *მბობა–თქმა:ამბობს–იტყვის–თქვა– to say*

These bipersonal verbs conjugate as active voice verbs of I conjugation. Accordingly, their subject and object change their case in III series.

The stem distribution pattern is the following:

Present subseries: **ამბობ**
Future subseries: ***იტყვი***
Aorist and Perfect series: *-თქვ*

Present	*Imperfect*	*Present subjunctive*
ვ-ამბ-ობ-(თ) მე/ჩვენ მას/მათ I/we say it/them	ვ-ამბ-ობ-დ-ი-(თ) მე/ჩვენ მას/მათ I was/we were saying it/them	ვ-ამბ-ობ-დ-ე-(თ) მე/ჩვენ მას/მათ If I/we say it/them
ამბ-ობ-(თ) შენ/თქვენ მას/მათ You/you say it/them	ამბ-ობ-დ-ი-(თ) შენ/თქვენ მას/მათ You/you were saying it/them	ამბ-ობ-დ-ე-(თ) შენ/თქვენ მას/მათ If you/you say it/them
ამბ-ობ-ს ის მას/მათ He says it/them	ამბ-ობ-დ-ა ის მას/მათ He was saying it/them	ამბ-ობ-დ-ე-ს ის მას/მათ If he says it/them
ამბ-ობ-ენ ისინი მას/მათ They say it/them	ამბ-ობ-დ-ნენ ისინი მას/მათ They were saying it/them	ამბ-ობ-დ-ნენ ისინი მას/მათ If they say it/them

(Continued)

(Continued)

Future	*Conditional*	*Future subjunctive*
ვ-ი-ტყვ-ი-(თ) მე/ჩვენ მას/მათ I we will say it/ them	ვ-ი-ტყ-ოდ-ი-(თ) მე/ჩვენ მას/მათ I/we would say it/ them	ვ-ი-ტყ-ოდ-ე-(თ) მე/ჩვენ მას/მათ If I/we were to say it/them
ი-ტყვ-ი-(თ) შენ/თქვენ მას/მათ You/you will say them	ი-ტყ-ოდ-ი-(თ) შენ/თქვენ მას/მათ You/you would say it/them	ი-ტყ-ოდ-ე-(თ) შენ/თქვენ მას/მათ If you/you were to say it/them
ი-ტყვ-ი-ს ის მას/მათ He will say it/ them	ი-ტყ-ოდ-ა ის მას/მათ He would say it/ them	ი-ტყ-ოდ-ე-(თ) მას/მათ If he were to say it/ them
ი-ტყვ-ი-ან ისინი მას/მათ They will say it/ them	ი-ტყ-ოდ-ნენ ისინი მას/მათ They would say it/ them	ი-ტყ-ოდ-ნენ ისინი მას/მათ If they were to say it/them

Aorist		*Optative*
ვ-თქვ-ი-(თ) მე/ჩვენ ის/ისინი I/we said it/ them		ვ-თქვ-ა-(თ) მე/ჩვენ ის/ისინი I/we should say it/ them
თქვ-ი-(თ) შენ/თქვენ ის/ისინი You/you sad it/ them		თქვ-ა-(თ) შენ/თქვენ ის/ისინი You/you should say it/them
თქვ-ა მან ის/ისინი He said it/them		თქვ-ა-ს მან ის/ისინი He should say it/them
თქვ-ეს მათ ის/ისინი They said it/them		თქვ-ან მათ ის/ისინი He should say it/them

Perfect	*Pluperfect*	*Perfect subjunctive*
მ-ი-თქვ-ამ-ს მე ის/ისინი I have said it/them	მ-ე-თქვ-ა მე ის/ისინი I had said it/them	მ-ე-თქვ-ა-ს მე ის/ისინი If I had said it/them
გვ-ი-თქვ-ამ-ს ჩვენ ის/ისინი We have said it/them	გვ-ე-თქვ-ა ჩვენ ის/ისინი We had said it/them	გვ-ე-თქვ-ა-ს ჩვენ ის/ისინი If you had said it/them

Perfect	*Pluperfect*	*Perfect subjunctive*
გ-ი-თქვ-ამ-ს შენ ის/ისინი You have said it/ them	გ-ე-თქვ-ა-(თ) შენ/თქვენ ის/ისინი You/you had said it/ them	გ-ე-თქვ-ა-ს შენ ის/ისინი If you had said it/ them
გ-ი-თქვ-ამ-თ თქვენ ის/ისინი You have said it, them		გ-ე-თქვ-ა-თ თქვენ ის/ისინი If you had said it/ them
უ-თქვ-ამ-ს მას ის/ისინი He has said it/them	ე-თქვ-ა-(თ) მას/მათ ის/ისინი He/they had said it/ them	ე-თქვ-ა-ს მას ის/ისინი If he had said it/them
უ-თქვ-ამ-თ მათ ის/ისინი They have said it/ them		ე-თქვ-ა-თ მათ ის/ისინი If they had said it/ them

კაც-ი (S. nom.) *ამბობს სიმართლე-ს* (O_d dat.).
The man says the truth.
კაც-ი (S. nom.) *იტყვის სიმართლე-ს* (O_d dat.).
The man will say the truth.
კაც-მა (S. erg.) *თქვა სიმართლე* – Ø (O_d nom.).
The man said the truth.
კაც-ს (S. dat.) *უთქვამს სიმართლე* – Ø (O_d nom.).
The man has said the truth.

5. **უბნობა, თხრობა: ეუბნება – ეტყვის – უთხრა:** ***to tell, say, narrate, recount***

Unlike the bipersonal ***ამბობს***, ***იტყვის***, and ***თქვა***, these are tripersonal verbs. The presence of an indirect object requires the forms ***ეუბნება***, ***ეტყვის***, and ***უთხრა***. III series forms are based on the ***თქვ***-stem and become bipersonal verbs.

Present	*Imperfect*	*Present subjunctive*
ვ-ე-უბნ-ებ-ი(თ) მე/ჩვენ მას/მათ მას/მათ I/we tell him/them it/them	ვეუბნებ-ოდ-ი-(თ) მე/ჩვენ მას/მათ მას/მათ I was/we were telling him/them it/them	ვეუბნებ-ოდ-ე-(თ) მე/ჩვენ მას/მათ მას/მათ If I/we tell him/them it/them

(*Continued*)

(Continued)

ე-უბნ-ებ-ი-(თ) შენ/თქვენ მას/მათ მას/მათ You/you tell him/them it/them	ეუბნებ-ოდ-ი-(თ) მე/ჩვენ მას/მათ მას/მათ You/you were telling him/them it/them	ეუბნებ-ოდ-ე-(თ) მე/ჩვენ მას/მათ მას/მათ If you/you tell him/them it/them
ე-უბნ-ებ-ა ის მას/მათ მას/მათ He tells him/them it/them	ეუბნებ-ოდ-ა მას/მათ მას/მათ He was telling him/them it/them	ეუბნებ-ოდ-ე-ს ის მას/მათ მას/მათ If he tell him/them it/them
ე-უბნ-ებ-ი-ან ისინი მას/მათ მას/მათ They tell him/them it/them	ეუბნებ-ოდ-ნენ ისინი მას/მათ მას/მათ They were telling him them it/them	ეუბნებ-ოდ-ნენ ისინი მას/მათ მას/მათ If they tell him/them it/them
Future	*Conditional*	*Future subjunctive*
ვ-ე-ტყვ-ი-(თ) მე/ჩვენ მას/მათ მას/მათ I/we will tell him/them it/them	ვ-ე-ტყ-ოდ-ი-(თ) მე/ჩვენ მას/მათ მას/მათ I/we would tell him/them it/them	ვ-ე-ტყ-ოდ-ე-(თ) მე/ჩვენ მას/მათ მას/მათ If I/we were to tell him/them it/them
ე-ტყვ-ი-(თ) შენ/თქვენ მას/მათ მას/მათ You/you will tell him/them it/them	ე-ტყ-ოდ-ი-(თ) შენ/თქვენ მას/მათ მას/მათ You/you would tell him/them it/them	ე-ტყ-ოდ-ე-(თ) შენ/თქვენ მას/მათ მას/მათ If you/you were to tell him/them it/them
ე-ტყვ-ი-ს ის მას/მათ მას/მათ He will tell him/them it/them	ე-ტყ-ოდ-ა ის მას/მათ მას/მათ He would tell him/them it/them	ე-ტყ-ოდ-ე-ს ის მას/მათ მას/მათ If he were to tell him/them it/them
ე-ტყვ-ი-ან ისინი მას/მათ მას/მათ They will tell him/them it/them	ე-ტყ-ოდ-ნენ ისინი მას/მათ მას/მათ They would tell him/them it/them	ე-ტყ-ოდ-ნენ ისინი მას/მათ მას/მათ If they were to tell him/them it/them

Aorist		*Optative*
ვ-უ-თხარ-ი-(თ) მე/ჩვენ მას/მათ მას/მათ I/we told him/ them it/them		ვ-უ-თხრ-ა-(თ) მე/ჩვენ მას/მათ მას/მათ I/we should tell him/them it/them
უ-თხარ-ი-(თ) შენ/თქვენ მას/მათ მას/მათ You/you told him/ them it/them		უ-თხრ-ა-(თ) შენ/თქვენ მას/მათ მას/მათ You/you should tell him/them it/them
უ-თხრ-ა მან მას/მათ მას/მათ He told him/them it/them		უ-თხრ-ა-ს მან მას/მათ მას/მათ He should tell him/ them it/them
უ-თხრ-ეს მათ მას/მათ მას/მათ They told him/ them it/them		უ-თხრ-ა-ნ მათ მას/მათ მას/მათ They should tell him/them it/them

Perfect	*Pluperfect*	*Perfect subjunctive*
მ-ი-თქვ-ამ-ს მე ის/ისინი I have told it/them	მ-ე-თქვ-ა მე ის/ისინი I had told it/them	მ-ე-თქვ-ა-ს მე ის/ისინი If I had told it/them
გვ-ი-თქვ-ამ-ს ჩვენ ის/ისინი We have told it/ them	გვ-ე-თქვ-ა ჩვენ ის/ისინი We had told it/ them	გვ-ე-თქვ-ა-ს ჩვენ ის/ისინი If we had said it/ them

Perfect	*Pluperfect*	*Perfect subjunctive*
გ-ი-თქვ-ამ-ს შენ ის/ისინი You have told it/ them	გ-ე-თქვ-ა-(თ) შენ/თქვენ ის/ისინი You/you had told it/them	გ-ე-თქვ-ა-ს შენ ის/ისინი If you had told it/ them
გ-ი-თქვ-ამ-თ თქვენ ის/ისინი They have told it/ them		გ-ე-თქვ-ა-თ თქვენ ის/ისინი If you had told it/ them

(*Continued*)

(Continued)

უ-თქვ-ამ-ს მას ის/ისინი He has told it/them	ე-თქვ-ა-(თ) მას/მათ ის/ისინი He/they had told it/them	ე-თქვ-ა-ს მას ის/ისინი If he had told it/them
უ-თქვ-ამ-თ მათ ის/ისინი They have told it/them		ე-თქვ-ა-თ მათ ის/ისინი If they had told it/them

– *ამას ვის* ***ეუბნები?!***
Who are you telling this?!
– *ეს ადრე უნდა* ***გეთქვა!***
You should have said it earlier.
– *ეს რატომ ადრე არ* ***მითხარი?***
Why didn't you tell me this earlier?
– ***გვითხარი,*** *რა ხდება.*
Tell us what's going on.

ვერ დავიჯერებ, რომ მას ასეთი სიტყვები ***ეთქვას.***
I cannot believe that he had said such words.
ბავშვმა დედას სიმართლე უნდა ***უთხრას.***
The child should tell (say) the truth to his mother.
უკეთესი იქნებოდა, სიმართლე რომ ***ეთქვა.***
It would have been better if he had told the truth.
მას ჩემთვის არაფერი ***უთქვამს.***
He has not said anything to me.

6. ***ხედვა–ნახვა, დანახვა; ხედავს–ნახავს, დაინახავს*** – to see, find, understand

These are the I conjugation bipersonal transitive verbs and have inverted subject-object markers in III series. In the present subseries the stem ***ხედავ*** is the base form, in the future subseries as well as II and III series – ***ნახავ.***

Present	*Imperfect*	*Present subjunctive*
ვ-ხედ-ავ-(თ) მე/ჩვენ მას/მათ	ვ-ხედ-ავ-დ-ი-(თ) მას/მათ მე/ჩვენ მას/მათ	ვ-ხედ-ავ-დ-ე-(თ) მე/ჩვენ მას/მათ
I/we see him/them	I was/we were seeing him/them	If I/we see him/them

ხედ-ავ-(თ) შენ/თქვენ მას/მათ You/you see him/ them	ხედ-ავ-დ-ი-(თ) შენ/თქვენ მას/მათ You/you were seeing him/them	ხედ-ავ-დ-ე-(თ) შენ/თქვენ მას/მათ If you/you see him/ them
Present	*Imperfect*	*Present subjunctive*
ხედ-ავ-ს ის მას/მათ He sees him/ them	ხედ-ავ-დ-ა ის მას/მათ He was seeing him/them	ხედ-ავ-დ-ე-ს ის მას/მათ If he see him/ them
ხედ-ავ-ენ ისინი მას/მათ They see him/ them	ხედ-ავ-დ-ნენ ისინი მას/მათ They were seeing him/them	ხედ-ავ-დ-ნენ ისინი მას/მათ If they see him/ them
Future	*Conditional*	*Future subjunctive*
ვ-ნახ-ავ-(თ) მე/ჩვენ მას/მათ და-ვ-ი-ნახ-ავ-(თ) მე/ჩვენ მას/მათ I/we will see him/ them	ვნახავ-დ-ი-(თ) მე/ჩვენ მას/მათ დავინახ-ავ-დ-ი-(თ) მე/ჩვენ მას/მათ I/we would see him/them	ვნახავ-დ-ე-(თ) მე/ჩვენ მას/მათ დავინახ-ავ-დ-ე-(თ) მე/ჩვენ მას/მათ If I/we were to see him/them
ნახავ-(თ) შენ/თქვენ მას/მათ და-ი-ნახ-ავ-თ შენ/თქვენ მას/მათ You/you will see him/them	ნახავ-დ-ი-(თ) შენ/თქვენ მას/მათ დაინახავ-დ-ი-თ შენ/თქვენ მას/მათ You/you would see him/them	ნახავ-დ-ე-(თ) შენ/თქვენ მას/მათ დაინახავ-დ-ე-თ შენ/თქვენ მას/მათ If you/you were to see him/them
ნახავ-ს ის მას/მათ და-ი-ნახ-ავ-ს ის მას/მათ He will see him/ them	ნახავ-დ-ა ის მას/მათ დაინახავ-და ის მას/მათ He would see him/ them	ნახავ-დ-ე-ს ის მას/მათ დაინახავ-დ-ე-ს ის მას/მათ If he were to see him/them
ნახ-ავ-ენ ისინი მას/მათ და-ი-ნახ-ავ-ენ ისინი მას/მათ They will see him/ them	ნახავ-დ-ნენ ისინი მას/მათ დაინახავ-დ-ნენ ისინი მას/მათ They would see him/them	ნახავ-დ-ნენ ისინი მას/მათ დაინახავ-დ-ნენ ისინი მას/მათ If they were to see him/them

(*Continued*)

(Continued)

Aorist		*Optative*
ვ-ნახ-ე-(თ) მე/ჩვენ ის/ისინი და-ვ-ი-ნახ-ე-(თ) მე/ჩვენ ის/ისინი I/we saw him/ them		ვ-ნახ-ო-(თ) მე/ჩვენ ის/ისინი და-ვ-ი-ნახ-ო-(თ) მე/ ჩვენ ის/ისინი I/we should see him/ them
ნახ-ე-(თ) შენ/თქვენ ის/ისინი და-ი-ნახ-ე-(თ) შენ/თქვენ ის/ისინი You/you saw him/ them		ნახ-ო-(თ) შენ/თქვენ ის/ისინი და-ი-ნახ-ო-(თ) შენ/თქვენ ის/ისინი You/you should see him/them
ნახ-ა მან ის/ისინი და-ი-ნახ-ა მან ის/ისინი He saw him/ them		ნახ-ო-ს მან ის/ისინი და-ი-ნახ-ო-ს მან ის/ისინი He should see him/ them
ნახ-ეს მათ ის/ისინი და-ი-ნახ-ეს მათ ის/ისინი They saw him/ them		ნახ-ო-ნ მათ ის/ისინი და-ი-ნახ-ონ მათ ის/ისინი They should see him/them

Perfect	*Pluperfect*	*Perfect subjunctive*
(და)-მ-ი-ნახ-ავ-ს მე ის/ისინი I have seen him/them	(და)-მ-ე-ნახ-ა მე ის/ისინი I had seen him/them	(და)-მ-ე-ნახ-ო-ს მე ის/ისინი If I had seen him/them
(და)-გვ-ი-ნახ-ავ-ს ჩვენ ის/ისინი We have seen him/ them	(და)-გვ-ე-ნახ-ა ჩვენ ის/ისინი We had seen him/ them	(და)-გვ-ე-ნახ-ო-ს ჩვენ ის/ისინი If we had seen him/ them
(და)-გ-ი-ნახავ-ს შენ ის/ისინი You have seen him/ them	(და)-გ-ე-ნახ-ა(თ) შენ/თქვენ You/you had seen him/them	(და)-გ-ე-ნახ-ო-ს შენ ის/ისინი If you had seen him/ them
(და)-გ-ი-ნახ-ავ-თ თქვენ ის/ისინი You have seen him/ them		(და)-გ-ე-ნახ-ო-თ თქვენ ის/ისინი If you had seen him/ them

(და)-უ-ნახ-ავ-ს მას ის/ისინი He has seen him/them	(და)-ე-ნახ-ა-(თ) მას/მათ ის/ისინი He/they had seen him/them	(და)-ე-ნახ-ო-ს მას ის/ისინი If he had seen him/them
(და)-უ-ნახ-ავ-(თ) მათ ის/ისინი They have seen him/them		(და)-ე-ნახ-ო-თ მათ ის/ისინი If they had seen him/them

The verb forms based on the stem **ნახავ-** denote both their figurative meaning, as well as physical ability of seeing something.

ასეთ სილამაზეს სად ***ნახავ****?!*
Where could you see/find such beauty!
ყველა მაღაზია დავიარე, მაგრამ რაც მინდოდა, ვერ ***ვნახე****.*
I went into (walked all over) every store but did not find what I wanted.
ვნახოთ*, დირექტორი რას იტყვის.*
Let's see what the manager will say.
დღეს ერთი საინტერესო ფილმი ***ვნახე****. შენც უსათუოდ უნდა* ***ნახო****.*
I saw an interesting movie today. You, too, should see it.

These verbs may have the preverb **და-** in all but the present series and denote specifically physical ability *to see*, *catch a glimpse*, or *notice*.

აქედან ვერაფერს ***დავინახავთ****, ცოტა ახლო მივიდეთ.*
We won't be able to see anything from here, let's move a little closer.
დაინახე*, ჩემმა ძმამ რა ზუსტად ჩააგდო ბურთი კალათში?*
Did you see (catch a glimpse) how precisely my brother threw the ball into the basket?
ასეთ სიბნელეში რას ***დაინახავ****?*
What can one see in this darkness?

7. ***აქვს–ექნება–ჰქონია–*** has – will have – has had (referring to an inanimate object)
8. ***ჰყავს –ეყოლება –ჰყოლია–*** has – will have – has had (referring to persons)

Both these verbs are bipersonal medio-passive and change stems in accordance to tenses. Like some other verbs discussed earlier, actual and grammatical subject and object persons should be differentiated. A grammatical subject is determined according to its case, and since both verbs are intransitive, their indirect objects are in the dative case in all three series.

> მ-ყავ-ს ის S_1 (მამა, nom.) მე O_1^{id} (ადამიან-ს, dat.)
> I O_1^{id} (person, dat.) have him S_1 (father, nom).
> მ-აქვ-ს ის S_1 (ბილეთი, nom.) მე O_1^{id} (ადამიან-ს, dat.)
> I O_1^{id} (person, dat.) have it S_1 (ticket, nom.)

The opposition of the verbs *აქვს* and *ჰყავს* is an exception in the Georgian verb system. The subject of the verb *აქვს* may be only an inanimate object, while the subject of the verb *ჰყავს* is always animate.

> მე მაქვს წიგნ(ებ)ი, ფანქარი/ფანქრები, დრო, იდეა
> I have a book(s), pencil(s), time, an idea, etc.
> მე მყავს დედა, მამა, ერთი ძმა და ორი და.
> I have mother, father, one brother, and two sisters.
> მე ლამაზი კატა მყავს.
> I have a beautiful cat.

The only exception to this rule is the words for *vehicle* (*car*, *bicycle*, *boat*, etc.), which require the verb *მ-ყავ-ს*, not *მ-აქვ-ს*.

> *მე ძველი მანქანა* ***მყავს.***
> I have an old car.
> *შენ* ***გყავს*** *მანქანა?*
> Do you have a car?
> *ნეტავ ახლა ჩემი მანქანა* ***მყოლოდა.***
> I wish I had my car now.

Present	*Imperfect*	*Present subjunctive*
მ-ყავ-ს ის/ ისინი მე I have him/them	მ-ყავ-დ-ა ის/ისინი მე I had him/them	მ-ყავ-დ-ე-ს ის/ისინი მე If I have him/them
გვ-ყავ-ს ის/ისინი ჩვენ We have him/them	გვ-ყავ-დ-ა ის/ისინი ჩვენ We had him/them	გვ-ყავ-დ-ე-ს ის/ისინი ჩვენ If we have him/them
გ-ყავ-ს ის/ისინი შენ You have him/them	გ-ყავ-დ-ა-(თ) ის/ისინი შენ/თქვენ You/you had him/ them	გ-ყავ-დ-ე-ს ის/ისინი შენ If you have him/them
გ-ყავ-თ ის/ისინი თქვენ You have him/them		გ-ყავ-დ-ე-თ ის/ისინი თქვენ If you have him/them

ჰ-ყავ-ს ის/ისინი მას He has him/them ჰ-ყავ-თ ის/ისინი მათ They have him/them	ჰ-ყავ-დ-ა-(თ) ის/ისინი მას/მათ He/they had him/them	ჰ-ყავ-დ-ე-ს ის მას/მათ If he have him/them ჰ-ყავ-დ-ე-თ ისინი მას/მათ If they have him/them

Future	*Conditional*	*Future Subjunctive*
მ-ე-ყოლ-ებ-ა ის/ისინი მე I will have him	მეყოლებ-ოდ-ა ის/ისინი მე I would have him/them მეყოლებ-ოდ-ნენ ისინი მე I would have them	მეყოლებ-ოდ-ე-ს ის მე If I were to have him მ-ე-ყოლ-ებ-ოდ-ნენ ისინი მე If I were to have them
გვ-ე-ყოლ-ება ის/ისინი ჩვენ We will have him/them	გვეყოლებ-ოდ-ა ის/ისინი ჩვენ We would have him/them გვეყოლებ-ოდ-ნენ ისინი ჩვენ We would have them	გვეყოლებ-ოდ-ე-ს ის/ისინი ჩვენ If we were to have him/them გვყოლებ-ოდ-ნენ ისინი ჩვენ If we were to have them
გ-ე-ყოლ-ებ-ა-(თ) ის/ისინი შენ/თქვენ You/you will have him/them?	გეყოლებ-ოდ-ა-(თ) ის/ისინი შენ/თქვენ You/you would have him/them გეყოლებ-ოდ-ნენ ისინი შენ/თქვენ You/you would have them	გეყოლებ-ოდ-ე-ს/თ ის/ისინი შენ/თქვენ If you/you were to have him/them გეყოლებ-ოდ-ნენ ისინი შენ/თქვენ If you/you were to have them
ე-ყოლ-ებ-ა-(თ) ის/ისინი მას/მათ He will have him/them	ეყოლებ-ოდ-ა-(თ) ის/ისინი მას/მათ He/they would have him/them ეყოლებ-ოდ-ნენ ისინი მათ They would have them	ეყოლებ-ოდ-ე-ს/თ ის/ისინი მას/მათ If he/they were to have him/them ეყოლებ-ოდ-ნენ ისინი მას/მათ If he/they were to have them

(*Continued*)

(Continued)

Aorist		*Optative*
მ-ე-ყოლ-ა ის /ისინი მე I had him/ them		მ-ე-ყოლ-ო-ს ის/ისინი მე I should have him/ them
გვ-ე-ყოლ-ა ის/ისინი ჩვენ We had him/them		გვ-ე-ყოლ-ო-ს ის/ისინი ჩვენ We should have him/them
გ-ე-ყოლ-ა-(თ) ის/ისინი შენ/თქვენ You/you have had him/them		გ-ე-ყოლ-ო-ს/თ ის/ისინი შენ/თქვენ You/you should have him/them
ე-ყოლ-ა-(თ) ის/ისინი მას/მათ He has/they have him/them		ე-ყოლ-ო-ს/თ ის/ისინი მას/მათ He/they should have him/them
მ-ყოლ-ი-ა ის/ისინი მე I have had him/ them	მ-ყოლ-ოდ-ა ის/ისინი მე I had had it/them	მ-ყოლ-ოდ-ე-ს ის/ისინი მე If I had had him/ them
გვ-ყოლ-ი-ა ის/ისინი ჩვენ We have had him/ them	გვ-ყოლ-ოდ-ა ის/ისინი ჩვენ We had had him/ them	გვ-ყოლ-ოდ-ე-ს ის/ისინი ჩვენ If we had had him/ them
გ-ყოლ-ი-ა-(თ) ის/ისინი შენ/თქვენ You/you have had him/them	გ-ყოლ-ოდ-ა-(თ) ის/ისინი შენ/თქვენ You/you had had him/them	გ-ყოლ-ოდ-ე-ს/თ ის/ისინი შენ/ თქვენ If you had had him/ them
ჰ-ყოლ-ი-ა-(თ) ის/ისინი მას/მათ He has/they have him/them	ჰ-ყოლ-ოდ-ა-(თ) ის/ისინი მას/მათ He/they had had him/them	ჰ-ყოლ-ოდ-ე-ს/თ ის/ისინი მას/მათ If he had had him/ them

მალე მას შვილი ***ეყოლება.***
Soon she will have a baby.
მათ უკვე სამი შვილი ***ჰყოლიათ.***
They (apparently) have three children already.
ბედნიერი იქნებოდა, შვილი რომ ***ჰყოლოდა.***
She would be happy if she had a child.
შვილები რომ არ ***მყავდეს,*** *წავიდოდი ამ ქალაქიდან.*
If I didn't have my children, I would leave (go away from) this city.

Present	*Imperfect*	*Present subjunctive*
მ-აქვ-ს ის/ისინი მე I have it/them	მ-ქონ-დ-ა ის/ისინი მე I had it/them	მ-ქონ-დ-ე-ს ის/ისინი მე If I have it/them
გვ-აქვ-ს ის/ისინი ჩვენ We have it/them	გვ-ქონ-დ-ა ის/ისინი ჩვენ We had it/them	გვ-ქონ-დ-ე-ს ის/ისინი ჩვენ If we have it/them
გ-აქვ-ს ის/ისინი შენ You have it/them გ-აქვ-თ ის/ისინი თქვენ You have it/them	გ-ქონ-დ-ა-(თ) ის/ისინი შენ/თქვენ You/you had it/them	გ-ქონ-დ-ე-ს ის/ისინი შენ If you have it/them გ-ქონ-დ-ე-თ ის/ისინი თქვენ If you have it/them
აქვ-ს ის/ისინი მას He has it/them აქვ-თ ის/ისინი მათ They have it/them	ჰ-ქონ-დ-ა-(თ) ის/ისინი მას/მათ He/they had it/them	ჰ-ქონ-დ-ე-ს ის/ისინი მას If he have it/them ჰ-ქონ-დ-ე-თ ის/ისინი მათ If they have it/them
მ-ე-ქნ-ებ-ა ის/ისინი მე I will have it/them	მ-ე-ქნ-ებ-ოდ-ა ის /ისინი მე I would have it/them	მ-ე-ქნ-ებ-ოდ-ე-ს ის/ისინი მე If I were to have it/them
გვ-ე-ქნ-ებ-ა ის/ისინი ჩვენ We will have it/them	გვ-ე-ქნ-ებ-ოდ-ა ის/ისინი ჩვენ We would have it/them	გვ-ე-ქნ-ებ-ოდ-ე-ს ის/ისინი ჩვენ If we were to have it/them

(*Continued*)

(Continued)

Future	*Conditional*	*Future subjunctive*
გ-ე-ქნ-ებ-ა-(თ) ის/ისინი შენ/თქვენ You/you will have it/them	გ-ე-ქნ-ებ-ოდ-ა-(თ) ის/ისინი შენ/თქვენ You/you would have it/them	გ-ე-ქნ-ებ-ოდ-ე-ს/თ ის/ისინი შენ/ თქვენ If you/you were to have it/them
ე-ქნ-ებ-ა-(თ) ის/ისინი მას/მათ He/they will have it/them	ე-ქნ-ებ-ოდ-ა-(თ) ის/ისინი მას/მათ He/they would have it/them	ე-ქნ-ებ-ოდ-ე-ს/თ ის/ისინი მას/მათ If you/you were to have it/them
Aorist		*Optative*
–		–

Perfect	*Pluperfect*	*Perfect subjunctive*
მ-ქონ-ი-ა ის/ისინი მე I have had it/them	მ-ქონ-ოდ-ა ის/ისინი მე I had had it/them	მ-ქონ-ოდ-ე-ს ის/ისინი მე If I had had it/them
გვ-ქონ-ი-ა ის/ისინი ჩვენ We have had it/the	გვ-ქონ-ოდ-ა ის/ისინი ჩვენ We had had it/ them	გვ-ქონ-ოდ-ე-ს ის/ისინი ჩვენ If we had had it/ them
გ-ქონ-ი-ა-(თ) ის/ისინი შენ/თქვენ You/you have had it/them	გ-ქონ-ოდ-ა-(თ) ის/ისინი შენ/თქვენ You/you had had it/them	გ-ქონ-ოდ-ე-ს/თ ის/ისინი შენ/ თქვენ If you/you had had it/ them
ჰ-ქონ-ი-ა-(თ) ის/ისინი მას/მათ He has/they have it/them	ჰ-ქონ-ოდ-ა-(თ) ის/ისინი მას/მათ He/they had had it/them	ჰ-ქონ-ოდ-ე-ს/თ ის/ისინი მას/მათ If he/they had had it/the

__გაქვთ__ ჩემი მისამართი?
Do you have my address?
შენს ძმას საინტერესო ინფორმაცია __ჰქონია.__
(Apparently) your brother has had interesting information.

*ფული რომ **მქონდეს**, ევროპაში ვიმოგზაურებდი.*
If I had money, I would travel in Europe.
*მას რომ დრო **ჰქონოდა**, გვესტუმრებოდა.*
If he had had time, he would have visited us.
*ეს წიგნი შენ **გქონდეს**, მე არ მჭირდება.*
Have (keep) this book, I don't need it.

9. ***მიაქვს–მიიტანს–მიიტანა** take/carry/take to*
10. ***მიაქვს–წაიღებს–წაიღო** take/carry/take away*

The verbs **მი-აქვს** (he carries) and **მი-იტანს** (he will take to) may have any of a number of preverbs – **ა-**, **მო-**, **მი-**, **გა-**, **და-**, **შე-**, **ჩა-**, **გადა-**, **გადმო**, **შემო**, etc. – which indicate only direction of the movement but neither the future tense nor perfective aspect of the action.

The preverb **მო-** and its composites like **გამო-**, **შემო-**, **ჩამო**, and **გადმო-** denote the movement towards the speaker(s) (the first and second persons), and **მი-**away from him or them.

As with the verb **და-ვ-დი-ვარ** and the like, the preverb **და-**conveys the frequency not the direction of the action.

*ჩანთა მეორე სართულზე **ამაქვს**.*
I carry (am carrying) the bag up to the second floor.
*ნაგავი ყოველდღე გარეთ **გაგვაქვს**.*
We take the garbage out every day.
*ბავშვს სახლში სიხარული **შემოაქვს**.*
The child brings joy into the (our) house.
*ეს წიგნი ყველგან **დამაქვს**.*
I always carry around this book.

მი-მ-აქვ-ს (I take/carry to) and all other forms based on the root **აქვ-** are object oriented intransitive verbs. In all but the present subseries, they are replaced with bipersonal transitive verbs **მი-ვ-იტან** (I will take to) and **წა-ვ-იღებ** (I will take away) with a case-changing subject. The verbs **წა-ვ-იღებ** and **მი-ვ-იტან** may be used in tandem, the former indicating the initial point of the movement and the latter denoting its destination.

*ამ წიგნებს **წავიღებ** და ბიბლიოთეკაში **მივიტან**.*
I will take (from here) these books and take them to the library.
*ეს ფული **წაიღე** და ბანკში **მიიტანე**.*
Take this money (from here) and take it to the bank.

The stem -ღებ- may generate a number of verbs with variety of meanings if the preverb წა- is replaced with other preverbs:

მი-იღებ-ს
He will receive
გადმო-იღებს
He will bring down/will copy
გადა-იღებ-ს
He will photograph
შემო-იღებ-ს
He will introduce
ჩამო-იღებ-ს
He will take/bring down

Present	*Imperfect*	*Present subjunctive*
მი-მ-აქვ-ს ის მე I take it/them მი-გვ-აქვ-ს ისინი ჩვენ We take it/them	მი-მ-ქონ-დ-ა ის მე I was taking it/them მი-გვ-ქონ-დ-ა ისინი ჩვენ We were taking it/them	მი-მ-ქონ-დ-ე-ს ის მე If I take it/them მი-გვ-ქონ-დ-ე-ს ისინი ჩვენ If we take it/them
მი-გ-აქვ-ს/თ შენ/თქვენ ის/ისინი You/you take it/them	მი-გ-ქონ-დ-ა-(თ) შენ/თქვენ ის/ისინი You/you were taking it/them	მი-გ-ქონ-დ-ე-ს/თ შენ/თქვენ ის/ისინი If you take it/them
მი-აქვ-ს/თ მას/მათ ის/ისინი He/they take/s it/them	მი-ჰ-ქონ-დ-ა-(თ) მას/მათ ის/ისინი He was/they were taking it/them	მი-ჰ-ქონ-დ-ე-ს/თ მას/მათ ის/ისინი If he/they takes it/them
Future	*Conditional*	*Future subjunctive*
მი-ვ-ი-ტან-(თ) მე/ჩვენ მას/მათ I/we will take it/them in	მი-ვ-ი-ტან-დ-ი-(თ) მე/ჩვენ მას/მათ I/we would take it/them	მი-ვ-ი-ტან-დ-ე-(თ) მე/ჩვენ მას/მათ If I/we were to take it/them
წა-ვ-ი-ღ-ებ-(თ) მე/ჩვენ მას/მათ I/we will take it/them	წა-ვ-ი-ღ-ებ-დ-ი-(თ) მე/ჩვენ მას/მათ I/we would take it/them	წა-ვ-ი-ღ-ებ-დ-ე-(თ) მე/ჩვენ მას/მათ If I/we were to take it/them

მი-ი-ტან-(თ) შენ/თქვენ მას/მათ You/you will take it/them	მი-ი-ტან-დ-ი-(თ) შენ/თქვენ მას/მათ You/you would take it/them	მი-ი-ტან-დ-ე-(თ) შენ/თქვენ მას/მათ If you/you were to take it/them
წა-ი-ღ-ებ-(თ) შენ/თქვენ მას/მათ You/you will take it/them	წა-ი-ღ-ებ-დ-ი-(თ) შენ/თქვენ მას/მათ You/you would take it/them	წა-ი-ღ-ებ-დ-ე-(თ) შენ/თქვენ მას/მათ If you/you were to take it/them
მი-ი-ტან-ს/ენ ის/ისინი მას/მათ He/they will take it/them	მი-ი-ტან-დ-ა/ნენ ის/ისინი მას/მათ He/they would take it/them	მი-ი-ტან-დ-ე-ს/ნენ ის/ისინი მას/მათ If he/they were to take it/them
წა-ი-ღ-ებ-ს/ენ ის/ისინი მას/მათ He/they will take it/them	წა-ი-ღ-ებ-დ-ა/ნენ ის/ისინი მას/მათ He/they would take it/them	წა-ი-ღ-ებ-დ-ე-ს/ნენ ის/ისინი მას/მათ If he/they were to take it/them
Aorist		*Optative*
მი-ვ-ი-ტან-ე-(თ) მე/ჩვენ ის/ისინი I/we took it/them		მი-ვ-ი-ტან-ო-(თ) მე/ჩვენ ის/ისინი I/we should take it/them
წა-ვ-ი-ღ-ე-(თ) მე/ჩვენ ის/ისინი I/we took it/them		წა-ვ-ი-ღ-ო-(თ) მე/ჩვენ ის/ისინი I/we should take it/them
მი-ი-ტან-ე-(თ) შენ/თქვენ ის/ისინი You/you took it/them in		მი-ი-ტან-ო-(თ) შენ/თქვენ ის/ისინი You/you should take it/them in
წა-ი-ღ-ე-(თ) შენ/თქვენ ის/ისინი You/you took it/them		წა-ი-ღ-ო-(თ) შენ/თქვენ ის/ისინი You/you should take it/them
მი-ი-ტან-ა/ეს მან/მათ ის/ისინი He/they took it/them		მი-ი-ტან-ო-ს/ნ მან/მათ ის/ისინი He/they should take it/them
წა-ი-ღ-ო/ეს მან/მათ ის/ისინი He/they took it/them		წა-ი-ღ-ო-ს/ნ მან/მათ ის/ისინი He should take it/them

(*Continued*)

(Continued)

Perfect	*Pluperfect*	*Perfect subjunctive*
მი-მ-ი-ტან-ი-ა მე ის/ისინი I have taken it/them	მი-მ-ე-ტან-ა მე ის/ისინი I had taken it/them	მი-მ-ე-ტან-ო-ს მე ის/ისინი If I had taken it/them
მი-გვ-ი-ტან-ი-ა ჩვენ ის/ისინი We have taken it/ them	მი-გვ-ე-ტან-ა ჩვენ ის/ისინი We had taken it/ them in	მი-გვ-ე-ტან-ო-ს ჩვენ ის/ისინი If we had taken it/ them
წა-მ-ი-ღ-ი-ა მე ის/ისინი I have taken it/them	წა-მ-ე-ღ-ო მე ის/ისინი I had taken it/them	წა-მ-ე-ღ-ო-ს მე ის/ისინი If I had taken it/them
წა-გვ-ი-ღ-ი-ა ჩვენ ის/ისინი We have taken it/ them	წა-გვ-ე-ღ-ო ჩვენ ის/ისინი We had taken it/ them	წა-გვ-ე-ღ-ო-ს ჩვენ ის/ისინი If we had taken it/ them
მი-გ-ი-ტან-ი-ა-(თ) შენ/თქვენ ის/ისინი You/you have taken it/them in	მი-გ-ე-ტან-ა-(თ) შენ/თქვენ ის/ისინი You/you had taken it/them in	მი-გ-ე-ტან-ო-ს/თ შენ/თქვენ ის/ისინი If you/you had taken it/them in
წა-გ-ი-ღ-ი-ა-(თ) შენ/თქვენ ის/ისინი You/you have taken it/them	წა-გ-ე-ღ-ო-(თ) შენ/თქვენ ის/ისინი You/you had taken it/them	წა-გ-ე-ღ-ო-ს/თ შენ/თქვენ ის/ისინი If you/you had taken it/them
მი-უ-ტან-ი-ა-(თ) მას/მათ ის/ისინი He/they have taken it/them	მი-ე-ტან-ა-(თ) მას/მათ ის/ისინი He/they had taken it/them in	მი-ე-ტან-ო-ს/თ მას/მათ ის/ისინი If he/they had taken it/them
წა-უ-ღ-ი-ა-(თ) მას/მათ ის/ისინი He has/they have taken it/them	წა-ე-ღ-ო-(თ) მას/მათ ის/ისინი He/they had taken it/them	წა-ე-ღ-ო-ს/თ მას/მათ ის/ისინი If he/they had taken it/them

*სად **მიგაქვს** ეს ჩემოდანი?*
Where are you taking this suitcase?
*ეს ყვავილები ჩემთვის **მოგაქვს**?*
Are you bringing these flowers to me?
*საქართველოდან საზღვარგარეთ **გააქვთ** ღვინო და **შემოაქვთ** სამშენებლო მასალა.*
(They) export (take out) wine from Georgia and import (bring in) building materials.

ეს მძიმე ჩანთა ყოველდღე ***დამაქვს.***
I carry around this heavy bag every day.

The perfective aspect of this verb is expressed with the forms based on the stems **იტან-** and **იღებ-**.

ეს ყუთი გარეთ ***გაიტანე!***
Take this box out.
დღეს ბანკიდან ფული ***გამოვიტანე.***
Today I took out (some) money from the bank.
საელჩო ქალაქის სხვა რაიონში ***გადაუტანიათ.***
(They) have moved (took away) the embassy to another part of the city.
ვინ ***წაიღო*** *ჩემი კალამი?*
Who took (away) my pen?
დღეს ეს წიგნები ბიბლიოთეკაში არ უნდა ***წაგეღო?***
Shouldn't you have taken these books to the library today?

11. ც- ცოდნ- *to know something*

The verb **ვიცი** (I know) is derived from the root ც-, which is replaced with ცოდნ- in II and III series. It is unique in that in the present subseries its subject is in the ergative, not in the nominative case, and in the dative in the future subseries. It does not have II series forms since **ვიცი** is historically a II series form. In III series it is conjugated as an active voice verb with usual inversion, its subject is in the dative and direct object in the nominative case.

Present	*Imperfect*	*Present subjunctive*
ვ-ი-ც-ი-(თ) მე/ჩვენ ის/ისინი I/we know it/them	ვ-ი-ც-ოდ-ი-(თ) მე/ჩვენ ის/ისინი I/we knew it/them	ვ-ი-ც-ოდ-ე-(თ) მე/ჩვენ ის/ისინი If I/we know it/them
ი-ც-ი-(თ) შენ/თქვენ ის/ისინი You/you know it/them	ი-ც-ოდ-ი-(თ) შენ/თქვენ ის/ისინი You/you knew it/them	ი-ც-ოდ-ე-(თ) შენ/თქვენ ის/ისინი If you/you know it/them
ი-ც-ი-ს/ან მან/მათ ის/ისინი He/they knows it/them	ი-ც-ოდ-ა/ნენ მან/მათ ის/ისინი He/they knew it/them	ი-ც-ოდ-ე-ს/ნენ მან/მათ ის/ისინი If he/they knows it/them

(Continued)

(Continued)

Future	*Conditional*	*Future subjunctive*
მ-ე-ცოდინ-ებ-ა მე ის/ისინი I will know it/them	მეცოდინებ-ოდ-ა მე ის/ისინი I would know it/them	მეცოდინებ-ოდ-ე-ს მე ის/ისინი If I were to know it/them
გვ-ე-ცოდინ-ებ-ა ჩვენ ის/ისინი We will know it/them	გვეცოდინ-ებ-ოდ-ა ჩვენ ის/ისინი We would know it/them	გვეცოდინებ-ოდ-ე-ს ჩვენ ის/ისინი If we were to know it/them
გ-ე-ცოდინ-ებ-ა-(თ) შენ/თქვენ ის/ისინი You/you will know it/them	გეცოდინებ-ოდ-ა-(თ) შენ/თქვენ ის/ისინი You/you would know it/them	გეცოდინებ-ოდ-ე-ს/თ შენ/თქვენ ის/ისინი If you/you were to know it/them
ე-ცოდინ-ებ-ა-(თ) მას/მათ ის/ისინი He/they will know it/them	ეცოდინებ-ოდ-ა-(თ) მას/მათ ის/ისინი He/they would know it/them	ეცოდინებ-ოდ-ე-ს მას ის/ისინი If he were to know it/them ეცოდინებ-ოდ-ე-თ მათ ის/ისინი If they were to know it/them
Aorist –		*Optative* –

Perfect	*Pluperfect*	*Perfect subjunctive*
მ-ცოდნ-ი-ა მე ის/ისინი I have known it	მ-ცოდნ-ოდ-ა მე ის/ისინი I had known it/them	მ-ცოდნ-ოდ-ე-ს მე ის/ისინი If I had known it/them
გვ-ცოდნ-ი-ა ჩვენ ის/ისინი You have known it	გვ-ცოდნ-ოდ-ა ჩვენ ის/ისინი We had known it/them	გვ-ცოდნ-ოდ-ე-ს ჩვენ ის/ისინი If we had known it/them

გ-ცოდნ-ი-ა-(თ) შენ/თქვენ ის/ისინი You/you have known it	გ-ცოდნ-ოდ-ა-(თ) შენ/თქვენ ის/ისინი You had known it/ them	გ-ცოდნ-ოდ-ე-ს/თ შენ ის/ისინი If you/you had known it/them
ს-ცოდნ-ი-ა-(თ) მას/მათ ის/ისინი He has/they have known it/them	ს-ცოდნ-ოდ-ა-(თ) მას/მათ ის/ისინი He/they had known it/them	ს-ცოდნ-ოდ-ე-ს/თ მას/მათ ის/ისინი If he/they had known it/them

*ვინ **იცის**, ხვალ რა მოხდება!*
Who knows what will happen tomorrow!
*რომ **იცოდე**, როგორ მინდა შენი ნახვა.*
If you knew how I wish to see you.
*ჩანს, მათ ეს ამბავი არ **სცოდნიათ**.*
Looks like they have not known (about) this event.
*მე რომ ეს **მცოდნოდა**, უსათუოდ გეტყოდი.*
If I had known this, I would have told you for sure.
*ამ კაცის სახელი ყველამ უნდა **იცოდეს**.*
Everyone should know the name of this man.

9.7.5 *Irregular verbs with changing stems by aspect*

1. სმ- ლევ-

   სმა (შესმა) – დალევა – to drink

The verb *(შე)სმა* belongs to the I conjugation and has a full set of the tense forms. However, it is usually replaced in all but the Present subseries with the verb **დალევა**, which has no forms without preverbs and therefore always denotes perfective aspect and is not used in the present tense.

Present	*Imperfect*	*Present subjunctive*
ვ-სვამ-(თ) მე/ჩვენ მას/მათ I/we drink it/ them	ვ-სვამ-დ-ი-(თ) მე/ჩვენ მას/მათ I was/we were drinking it/them	ვ-სვამ-დ-ე-(თ) მე/ჩვენ მას/მათ If I/we drink it/ them

(Continued)

(Continued)

სვამ-(თ) შენ/თქვენ მას/მათ You/you drink it/them	სვამ-დ-ი-(თ) შენ/თქვენ მას/მათ You/you were drinking it/them	სვამ-დ-ე-(თ) შენ/თქვენ მას/მათ If you/you drink it/them
სვამ-ს/ენ ის/ისინი მას/მათ He/they drinks it/ them	სვამ-დ-ა/ნენ ის/ისინი მას/მათ He/they was drinking it/them	სვამ-დ-ე-ს/ნენ ის/ისინი მას/მათ If he/they drinks it/them
Future	*Conditional*	*Future subjunctive*
შე-ვ-სვამ-(თ) მე/ჩვენ მას/ მათ და-ვ-ლევ-(თ) მე/ჩვენ მას/ მათ I/we will drink it/ them	შე-ვ-სვამ-დ-ი-(თ) ჩვენ მას/ მათ და-ვ-ლევ-დ-ი-(თ) ჩვენ მას/ მათ I/we would drink it/them	შე-ვ-სვამ-დ-ე-(თ) ჩვენ მას/ მათ და-ვ-ლევ-დ-ე-(თ) მე/ჩვენ მას/ მათ If I/we were to drink it/them
შე-სვამ-(თ) შენ/თქვენ მას/მათ და-ლევ-(თ) შენ/თქვენ მას/მათ You/you will drink it/them	შე-სვამ-დ-ი-(თ) შენ/თქვენ მას/მათ და-ლევ-დ-ი-(თ) შენ/თქვენ მას/მათ You/you would drink it/them	შე-სვამ-დ-ე-(თ) შენ/თქვენ მას/მათ და-ლევ-დ-ე-(თ) შენ/თქვენ მას/მათ If you/you were to drink it/them
შე-სვამ-ს/ნენ ის/ისინი მას/ მათ და-ლევ-ს/ნენ ის/ისინი მათ/ მათ He/they will drink it/them	შე-სვამ-დ-ა/ნენ ის/ისინი მას/ მათ და-ლევ-დ-ა/ნენ ის/ისინი მას/ მათ He/they would drink it/them	შე-სვამ-დე-ს/ნენ ის/ისინი/მას/ მათ და-ლევ-დ-ე-ს/ნენ ის/ისინი მას/ მათ If he/they were to drink it/them

Aorist	*Optative*
(შე)-ვ-სვ-ი-(თ) მე/ჩვენ ის/ისინი და-ვლი-ე-(თ) მე/ჩვენ ის/ისინი I/we drank it/them	(შე)-ვ-სვ-ა-(თ) მე/ჩვენ ის/ისინი და-ვ-ლი-ო-(თ) მე/ჩვენ ის/ისინი I/we should drink it/them
(შე)-სვ-ი-(თ) შენ/თქვენ ის/ისინი და-ლი-ე-(თ) შენ/თქვენ ის/ისინი You/you drank it/them	(შე)-სვ-ა-(თ) შენ/თქვენ ის/ისინი და-ლი-ო-(თ) შენ/თქვენ ის/ისინი You/you should drink it/them
(შე)-სვ-ა/ეს მან/მათ ის/ისინი და-ლი-ა/ეს მან/მათ ის/ისინი He/they drank it/them	(შე)-სვ-ა-ს/ნ მან/მათ ის/ისინი და-ლი-ო-ს/ნ მან/მათ ის/ისინი He/they should drink it/them

Perfect	*Pluperfect*	*Perfect subjunctive*
(შე)-მ-ი-სვ-ამ-ს მე ის/ისინი და-მ-ი-ლევია მე ის/ისინი I have drunk it/them	(შე)-მ-ე-სვ-ა მე ის/ისინი და-მ-ე-ლი-ა მე ის/ისინი I had drunk it/them	(შე)-მ-ე-სვ-ა-ს მე ის/ისინი და-მ-ე-ლი-ო-ს მე ის/ისინი If I had drunk it/them
(შე)-გვ-ი-სვ-ამ-ს ჩვენ ის/ისინი და-გვ-ი-ლევ-ია ჩვენ ის/ისინი We have drunk it/them	(შე)-გვ-ე-სვ-ა ჩვენ ის/ისინი და-გვ-ე-ლი-ა ჩვენ ის/ისინი We had drunk it/them	(შე)-გვ-ე-სვ-ა-ს ჩვენ ის/ისინი და-გვ-ე-ლი-ო-ს ჩვენ ის/ისინი If we had drunk it/them
(შე)-გ-ი-სვამ-ს/თ შენ ის/ისინი და-გ-ი-ლევ-ია/თ შენ ის/ისინი You/you have drunk it/them	(შე)-გ-ე-სვ-ა(თ) შენ ის/ისინი და-გ-ე-ლი-ა(თ) შენ ის/ისინი You/you had drunk it/them	(შე)-გ-ე-სვ-ა-ს/თ შენ ის/ისინი და-გ-ე-ლი-ო-ს/თ შენ ის/ისინი If you had drunk it/them

(Continued)

(Continued)

Perfect	*Pluperfect*	*Perfect subjunctive*
(შე)-უ-სვამ-ს/თ მას/მათ ის/ისინი და-უ-ლევ-ია/თ მას/მათ ის/ისინი He/they has drunk it/them	(შე)-ე-სვ-ა(თ) მას/მათ ის/ისინი და-ე-ლი-ა(თ) მას/მათ ის/ისინი He/they had drunk it/them	(შე)-ე-სვ-ა-ს/თ მას/მათ ის/ისინი და-ე-ლი-ო-ს/თ მას/მათ ის/ისინი If he/they had drunk it/them

In contemporary Georgian, the forms based on ***შესვ-*** are used exclusively in the present series. In all other forms, they sound too mannered and are used solely at ceremonious functions, like a celebratory dinner or some such events. The forms based on ***ლევ-*** can be used in both formal and informal cases but never in the present tense.

მე ყოველ დილით ორ ჭიქა ჩაის ***ვსვამ.***
Every morning I drink two cups of tea.
ჩემი და ყავას არასოდეს არ ***სვამდა,*** *ეხლა* ***სვამს.***
My sister never drank coffee, now she drinks it.
წამალი ***დალიე?***
Did you take (your) medication?
შევსვათ/დავლიოთ *ჩვენი სტუმრის სადღეგრძელო!*
Let's drink a toast to our guest.

2. ძლევ- ცემ- to give

The verb ***აძლევს*** conjugates in all three series, but if a preverb is added to it, its meaning will change significantly from the one it has in the present subseries. The following examples illustrate the difference:

მეგობარს ფულს ***ვაძლევ.***
I give money to (my) friend.
მეგობარს ფული ***შევაძლიე.***
I offered money to (my) friend.

In the second sentence the verb ***შე-ვაძლიე*** implies that the subject (*I*) tried to give the direct object (money) to the indirect object (friend), but the latter refused to take it. In order to denote the completion of the action (i.e. perfective aspect) mentioned in the first sentence the verb ***მივეცი*** should be used.

Present	*Imperfect*	*Present subjunctive*
ვ-ა-ძლევ-(თ) მე/ჩვენ მას /მათ მას/მათ I/we give him/them it/them	ვ-ა-ძლევ-დ-ი-(თ) მე/ჩვენ მას /მათ მას/მათ I was/we were giving him/them it/them	ვ-ა-ძლევ-დ-ე-(თ) მე/ჩვენ მას /მათ მას/მათ If I/we give him/ them it/them
ა-ძლევ-(თ) შენ/თქვენ მას მას You/you give him/ them it/them	ა-ძლევ-დ-ი-(თ) შენ/თქვენ მას მას You/you were giving him/them it/them	ა-ძლევ-დ-ე-(თ) შენ/თქვენ მას მას If you/you give him/ them it/them
ა-ძლევ-ს/ენ ის/ ისინი მას მას/მათ He/they give/s him/ them it/them	ა-ძლევ-დ-ა/ნენ ის/ისინი მას მას He/they was/were giving him/them it/ them	ა-ძლევ-დ-ე-ს/ნენ ის/ისინი მას მას If he/they give/s him/ them it/them
Future	*Conditional*	*Future subjunctive*
მი-ვ-ცემ-(თ) მე/ჩვენ მას /მათ მას/მათ I/we will give him/ them it/them	მი-ვ-ცემ-დ-ი-(თ) მე/ჩვენ მას /მათ მას/მათ I/we would give him/them it/ them	მი-ვ-ცემ-დ-ე-(თ) მე/ჩვენ მას /მათ მას/მათ If I/we were to give him/them it/them
მი-ს-ცემ-(თ) შენ/თქვენ მას/მათ მას/მათ You/you will give him/them it/ them	მი-ს-ცემ-დ-ი-(თ) შენ/თქვენ მას მას You/you would give him/them it/them	მი-ს-ცემ-დ-ე-(თ) შენ/თქვენ მას/მათ მას/მათ If you/you were to give him/them it/ them
მი-ს-ცემ-ს/ენ ის/ისინი მას/მათ მას/მათ He/they will give him them it/them	მი-ს-ცემ-დ-ა/ნენ ის/ისინი მას/მათ მას/მათ He/they would give him/them it/them	მი-ს-ცემ-დ-ე-ს/ნენ ის/ისინი მას/მათ მას/მათ If he/they were to give him/them it/ them

(*Continued*)

(Continued)

Aorist		*Optative*
მი-ვ-ეც-ი-(თ) მე/ჩვენ მას /მათ ის/ისინი I/we gave him/them it/them		მი-ვ-ც-ე-(თ) მე/ჩვენ მას /მათ ის/ისინი I/we should give him/them it/them
მი-ეც-ი-(თ) შენ/თქვენ მას/მათ ის/ისინი You/you gave him/ them it/them		მი-ს-ც-ე-(თ) შენ/თქვენ მას /მათ ის/ისინი You/you should give him/them it/them
მი-ს-ც-ა/ეს მან/მათ მას/მათ ის/ისინი He/they gave him/ them it/them		მი-ს-ც-ე-ს/ენ მან/მათ მას/მათ ის/ისინი He/they should give him/them it/them

Perfect	*Pluperfect*	*Perfect subjunctive*
მი-მ-ი-ც-ი-ა მე ის/ისინი (მისთვის/მათთვის) I have given it/them (to him/them)	მი-მ-ე-ც-ა მე ის/ისინი (მისთვის/მათთვის) I had given it/them (to him/them)	მი-მ-ე-ც-ე-ს მე ის/ისინი (მისთვის/მათთვის) If I had given it/them (to him/them
მი-გვ-ი-ც-ი-ა ჩვენ ის/ისინი (მისთვის/მათთვის) We have given it/ them (to him/them)	მი-გვ-ე-ც-ა ჩვენ ის/ისინი (მისთვის/მათთვის) We had given it/ them (to him/them)	მი-გვ-ე-ც-ე-ს ჩვენ ის/ისინი (მისთვის/მათთვის) If we had given it/ them (to him/them)
მი-გ-ი-ც-ი-ა-(თ) შენ/თქვენ ის/ისინი (მისთვის/მათთვის) You/you have given it/ them (to him/them)	მი-გ-ე-ც-ა-(თ) შენ/თქვენ ის/ისინი (მისთვის/მათთვის) You/you had given it/ them (to him/them)	მი-გ-ე-ც-ე-ს/თ შენ/თქვენ ის/ისინი (მისთვის/მათთვის) If you/you had given it/them (to him/them)

Perfect	*Pluperfect*	*Perfect subjunctive*
მი-უ-ც-ი-ა-(თ) მას/მათ ის/ისინი (მისთვის/მათთვის) He has/they have given it/them (to him/them)	მი-ე-ც-ა-(თ) მას/მათ ის/ისინი (მისთვის/მათთვის) He/they had given it/them (to him/ them)	მი-ე-ც-ე-ს/თ მას/მათ ის/ისინი (მისთვის/მათთვის) If he/they had given it/them (to him/ them)

ბავშვს ამ წამალს რატომ **აძლევ**?
Why are you giving the child this medication?
ბავშვს ამ წამალს ნუ **მისცემ!**
Don't give the child this medication.
მომეცი ჩემი კალამი!
Give me my pen.
მეგობარმა **მომცა** ეს წიგნი.
A friend gave me this book.
კატას ძვალს ნუ **აძლევ**!
Don't give the cat a bone.
ახლა რომ ხმას **აძლევდე**, ვის მისცემდი?
If you were voting (giving your vote) now, who would you vote (give it) for?
ეს რჩევა მისთვის მის ძმას **მიუცია.**
(Apparently) his brother gave him this advice.

The active voice tripersonal verbs **აძლევს** and **მისცა** may be converted to bipersonal passive voice verbs **ეძლევა** *and* **მიეცა** in corresponding tenses.

ეს ფირმა (S_3 nom.) იმიგრანტებს (O_3 ^{id} dat.) სამუშაოს (O_3 ^{id} dat.) **ა-ძლ-ევ-ს.**
This firm gives work to immigrants.
სამუშაო (O_3 ^{id} nom.) ლეგალურ იმიგრანტებს (S_3 dat.) **ეძლევა.**
Work is given to legal immigrants.
ამ ფირმამ (S_3 erg.) იმიგრანტებს (O_3 ^{id} dat.) სამუშაო (O_3 ^{id} nom.) **მი-ს-ც-ა.**
This firm gave work to immigrants.
იმიგრანტებს (O_3 ^{id} dat.) სამუშაო (S_3 nom.) **მიეცა.**
Immigrants were given work.

9.8 Verbal nouns

Gerunds and participles have properties of verbs as well as nouns. They decline and have the same function in a sentence as nouns; however, they should be considered as verbal forms since they share their lexical meaning and derivational inflections with verbs.

9.8.1 *Gerund and its derivation*

In Georgian, gerunds are derived from the active form of verbs, but they do not have person markers and are conjugated like nouns. With the exception of a few, they do not have a plural form. Their verbal properties are orientation and aspect since they may have preverbs. Besides, they can express causative and very seldom they can distinguish category of voice. The active and passive voice verbs have the same gerunds with the exception of a few that are shown in the following chart.

The gerunds are derived from the stem of verbs in the present or future tense forms to which the suffix -ა is added. For example, *ვ-ა-შენ-ებ/ა-ვ-ა-შენ-ებ* (I build/will build) is the present/future forms of an active voice verb in I series. Its stem is*(ა)შენებ* from which the gerund *(ა)შენებ-ა* is derived. If a verb has a preverb in the Future subseries, it remains in its gerund form.

The suffix -ა sometimes causes phonetic changes:

P/FSF - ი is truncated:

ხსნ-ი-ს → ხსნ-ა (unties – untying)
ჭრ-ი-ს → ჭრ-ა (cuts – cutting)
თხრ-ი-ს → თხრ-ა (digs – digging)

P/FSF - ავ and -ამ are syncopated:

(და)-ხურ-ავ-ს → (და)-ხურვ-ა (will) shut – shutting)
ცურ-ავ-ს → ცურვ-ა (swims – swimming)
წურ-ავ-ს → წურვ-ა (squeezes – squeezing)
ასხამს → სხმ-ა (pours – pouring)
(და)-აბამს →(და)-ბმ-ა (will) tie down – tying down)

P/FSF - ავ is syncopated when it preceded by the consonants ნ, რ, and ლ, and the latter consonants, in turn, are preceded by another consonant, the remaining consonant -ვ- is metathesized and becomes a part of the stem:

(და)ხნ-ავ-ს → ხვნ-ა (will) plow – plowing)
(მო)კლ-ავ-ს → (მო)კვლ-ა (will) kill – killing
(მო)სრ-ავ-ს → მოსვრ-ა//მოსრ-ვ-ა (will) wipe out – wiping out

Other P/FSFs do not undergo any changes:

–ებ: (გა)-ა-წითლ-ებ-ს → გაწითლებ-ა; (will) redden – reddening)
(გა)ა-ღვიძ-ებ-ს → გაღვიძება (will) wake up – waking up)
– ობ: გრძნ-ობ-ს → გრძნობა (feels – feeling)
(და)ატკბ-ობ-ს → (და)ტკბ-ობ-ა (will) sweeten – sweetening)
– ოფ: (გა)ყ-ოფ-ს → (გა)ყ-ოფ-ა (will) divide – dividing)

Verbs in the present or future tense with the alternating stem vowel (ე – ი) always have the vowel -*ე*- in their gerund forms:

(და)ჭყლეტ-ს → (და)ჭყლეტა (will) crush – crushing)
(და)გრეხ-ს → გრეხ-ა (twists – twisting)
(გა)გლეჯ-ს → (გა)გლეჯ-ა (will) tear – tearing)

Some verbs have the infixes -*ოლ* and -*ომ* inserted before the gerund formant suffix -ა. Other gerund formants are the archaic suffix -*ილ* and circumfixes: *სი-ილ*, *სი-ულ*, and *ს-ა*, rather seldom used in contemporary Georgian.

Gerund formants

-ა	წერ-ა (writing), მატ-ებ-ა (increasing), კითხვ-ა (reading), კვნეტ-ა (biting)
-ნ-ა	თხოვ-ნ-ა (asking, request), ხსოვ-ნ-ა (remembering, remembrance), ვარდ-ნ-ა (falling), ძებ-ნ-ა (seeking), შოვ-ნ-ა (finding) Several verbs derived from nouns have the consonant -ნ- not only in their gerunds but also in finite forms: თოხ-ნ-ა (hoeing, derived from the noun თოხი – hoe) – თოხ-ნ-ის კოც-ნ-ა (kissing, kiss) – კოც-ნ-ის ვარცხ-ნ-ა (combing) – ვარცხ-ნ-ი-ს ჩიჩქ-ნ-ა (picking) – ვჩიჩქ-ნ-ი-ს ტკეპ-ნ-ა (flattening) – ტკეპ-ნ-ი-ს
-ოლ-ა	სრ-ოლ-ა (shooting), თრთ-ოლა (trembling), (ვა)ძღ-ოლ-ა (leading), ძრწ-ოლ-ა (shuddering), ბრძ-ოლ-ა (fighting), წ-ოლ-ა (lying down)
-ომ-ა	დგ-ომ-ა (standing), კრთ-ომ-ა (startling), ხტ-ომ-ა (jumping), ჯდ-ომ-ა (sitting down), შრ-ომ-ა (labouring), კვდ-ომ-ა (dying), (შე)ცდ-ომ-ა (being mistaken, mistake), წვდ-ომ-ა (perceiving), ხტ-ომ-ა (jumping) The gerunds derived from passive voice verbs have the infix **-*ომ*** preceding the suffix **-ა**.

Active voice gerunds	*Passive voice gerunds*
ტეხ-ა (breaking)	ტყდ-ომ-ა (being broken)
წყვეტ-ა (snapping)	წყდ-ომ-ა (being wiped out)
ხეთქა (crushing)	სკდ-ომ-ა (bursting)

-ილ	დუმ-ილ-ი (being silent, silence), ქუხ-ილ-ი (thundering), დუღ-ილ-ი (boiling), წუხ-ილ-ი (worrying), ტყუ-ილ-ი (lying, lie), ტკივ-ილ-ი (feeling pin, pain), კივ-ილ-ი (screaming), ყვირ-ილ-ი (shouting), ბღავ-ილ-ი (bellowing), კნავ-ილ-ი (mewing), ყმუ-ილ-ი (howling)
სი--ილ	სი-ც-ილ-ი<სი-ცინ-ილ-ი (laughing, laughter), სირბ-ილ-ი (running, run), სი-ძულვ-ილ-ი (hating, hatred), სი-რცხვ-ილ-ი (being ashamed, shame), შიმშილი<სი-მშ-ილ-ი (being hungry, hunger)

(Continued)

(Continued)

Gerund formants	
სი--ულ	სი-ხარ-ულ-ი (rejoicing, joy), სი-ყვარ-ულ-ი (loving, love), სი-ნან-ულ-ი (regretting, regret), სი-არ-ულ-ი (walking, walk), სი-ბრალ-ულ-ი (pitying, pity)
ს--ა	ს-ვლ-ა (walk, walking), შე-ს-ყიდვ-ა (purchasing, buying), გამო-ს-ყიდვ-ა (redeeming) When the stem *ყიდვ* does not have a preverb or have the preverb *გა-*, the gerund derived from it will not have the prefix *ს-*: *ყიდვ-ა* (buying), *გა-ყიდვა* (selling, sale).

წერა-კითხვა *ადრე ვისწავლე.*
I learned writing and reading early.
ერთი ***თხოვნა*** *მაქვს.*
I have one request.
დამნაშავის ***ძებნა*** *გრძელდება.*
The search for the perpetrator continues.
წინ ბევრი ***ბრძოლა*** *გველის.*
We have many fights ahead (of us).
აქ ***დგომა*** *აკრძალულია.*
Standing here is forbidden (it is forbidden to stand here)
ახლა ***დუმილი*** *სჯობს.*
Now silence is preferable.
შორიდან ***ყმუილი*** *მოგვესმა.*
From afar we heard howling.
ათასობით ადამიანი ***შიმშილით*** *დაიხოცა.*
Thousands died of hunger.
ახალი მანქანის ***ყიდვა*** *მინდა.*
I want to buy a new car.

Gerunds have the morphological category of causative:

*კეთება – კეთებ***ინ***ება* (doing – making do)
*ყიდვა – ყიდვ***ინ***ება* (buying – making buy)
*ძებნა – ძებნ***ინ***ება* (searching – making search)
However, these forms are too artificial and are seldom used.

Gerunds of some verbs are the nouns from which these verbs are derived:

ლაპარაკი – ლაპარაკობს (speech – speaks)
საუბარი – საუბრობს (conversation – converses

ჩხუბი – ჩხუბობს (quarrel – quarrels)
ზანზარი – ზანზარებს (shake – shakes)
ღიღინი – ღიღინებს (hum -hums)
ღრიალი – ღრიალებს (bellow – bellows)

Only substantivized gerunds have plural forms:

სხდომა – სხდომ-ებ-ი (meeting – meetings)
კითხვა – კითხვ-ებ-ი (asking – questions)
სვლა – სვლ-ებ-ი (move – moves)
ჩვენს ინსტიტუტში ***სხდომები*** *ხშირად ტარდება.*
Meetings are often scheduled in our institute.
ეს ***კითხვები*** *არ მესმის.*
I don't understand these questions.
მოჭადრაკე საინტერესო ***სვლებს*** *აკეთებდა.*
The chess player made interesting moves.

9.8.2 Participles

Unlike gerunds, participles have the category of voice in addition to orientation, aspect, and causation. They are declinable and have the same functions as nouns in a sentence; they have singular and plural forms as well. The causative participles, like causative gerunds, are artificial forms and seldom used in contemporary Georgian.

9.8.2.1 *Active voice participles*

The active voice participles are declinable words formed with the prefix **მ-** and a number of suffixes shown in the following chart. They are mostly substantivized and answer the questions: **ვინ** (who) and **რა** (what); they have both singular or plural forms and function as either a subject or an object in a sentence.

The basis of active voice participles is the stem of I series verbs; therefore, if a verb has a preverb and/or P/FSF, they remain in the participle derived from it. The participle formant **მ-** or the first syllable of a circumfix follow the preverb, and the final syllable of the circumfix is placed after its P/FSF. For example, ***ა-შენ-ებ-ს*** (he builds) is an active voice verb with the preverb **ა**-and P/FSF ***ებ-***, the participle derived from it with the circumfix ***მ–ელ*** is ***ა-მ-შენებ-ელ-ი***, a person who builds.

P/FSF ***-ი*** is usually truncated: ***თლ-ი-ს→მ-თლ-ელ-ი*** (he carves – carver), ***(გა)ზრდ-ი-ს→(გა)მ-ზრდ-ელ-ი*** (he (will) educate – educator).

P/FSFs ***-ავ*** and ***-ამ*** remain in participles if they are formed only with the prefix ***მ-***: ***კერ-ავ-ს–მ-კერ-ავ-ი*** (tailor, seamstress), ***ყვინთ-ავ-ს–მ-ყვინთ-ავ-ი*** (diver).

However, there are some synonymous participle couples in which these P/FSFs may be syncopated:

> *ხატ-ავ-ს—და-მ-ხატ-ავ-ი//და-მ-ხატ-ვ-ელ-ი* (painter)
> *ქარგ-ავ-ს – (და)მ-ქარგ-ავ-ი//(და)მ-ქარგ-ვ-ელ-ი* (embroider)
> Similar parallel forms are derived from verbs with other P/FSFs:
> *ადნ-ობს–(და)-მ-დნ-ობ-ი//მ-დნ-ობ-ელ-ი* (melter)
> *ყოფ-ს – (გა)მ-ყ-ოფ-ი//(გა)-მ-ყ-ოფ-ელ-ი* (divider)
> **მ-ელ** and ***მა-ელ*** circumfixes are interchangeable:
> *ალ-ა-სრულ-ებ-ს—ალ-მ-სრულ-ებ-ელ-ი/ალ-მა-სრულ-ებ-ელ-ი* (executor)
> *შე-ა-წუხ-ებ-ს—შე-მ-წუხ-ებ-ელ-ი/შე-მა-წუხ-ებ-ელ-ი* (nuisance)
> *წა-ა-ხალის-ებ-ს—წა-მ-ხალის-ებ-ელ-ი//წა-მა-ხალის-ებ-ელ-ი* (one who encourages)

Active voice participle formants

მ-	მ-ლესავ-ი (grinder), მ-ბეჭდავ-ი (printer), მ-კერავ-ი (tailor), მ-პარავ-ი (thief), მ-ღებ-ავ-ი (painter), მ-რეცხავ-ი (laundress), მ-ყვინთავ-ი (diver), მ-კითხავ-ი (fortune-teller)
მ-ელ **მა-ელ**	მ-კითხვ-ელ-ი (reader), მ-ქადაგ-ებ-ელ-ი (preacher), მ-კვლ-ელ-ი (killer), მ-სმენ-ელ-ი (listener), და-მა-არს-ებ-ელ-ი (founder), და-მ-მარცხ-ებ-ელ-ი (defeater), (გა)-მა-ნადგურ-ებ-ელ-ი (destroyer), შე-მა-დგენ-ელ-ი (component), და-მა-მტკიცებ-ელ-ი (conforming), მ-ატარ-ებ-ელ-ი (carrier, train)
მე-ელ	მე-ტყვ-ელ-ი (expressive), მე-წვ-ელ-ი (milking (cow), მე-შვ-ელ-ი (auxiliary)
მ-არ **(მ-ალ)**	მ-ხატვ-არ-ი (painter) მ-ტარვ-ალ-ი (adversary), მ-წერ-ალ-ი მ-(writer), მ-კურნ-ალ-ი (healer)

მყვინთავებმა ჩაძირული გემი აღმოაჩინეს.
The divers discovered a sunken ship.
*ამ ჯარის **დამმარცხებელი** არავინ არ არის.*
There is no one who can defeat (a defeater of) this army.
*ამ ფერმას კარგი **მეწველი** ძროხები ჰყავს.*
This farm has good milk cows.
__მწერალი მკითხველებს__ შეხვდა.
The writer met the readers.

მქადაგებელმა **მსმენელებს** *მიმართა.*
The preacher addressed the listeners.
პოლიციამ **მკვლელი** *დააპატიმრა.*
Police arrested the killer.

If active voice participles precede a noun, they become adjectives and function as attributes in a sentence.

ჩვენს მეზობლად **მკერავი ქალი** *ცხოვრობს.*
A seamstress lives in our neighbourhood.
ხვალ ჩვენი **მკურნალი ექიმი** *მოვა.*
Tomorrow our family (healer) doctor will visit us.
დამამტკიცებელი საბუთები *გვჭირდება.*
We need confirming documents.

9.8.2.2 *Passive voice participles*

Passive voice participles are declinable words denoting an action carried out by the subject of a passive voice verb. The gerund ***მ-შენებ-ელ-ი*** (builder), derived from the active voice verb ***ა-შენ-ებ-ს*** (builds), indicates the subject who carries out the action denoted by this verb. Its direct object will be expressed with a passive voice participle: ***ასაშენებელი*** (something to be built), ***აშენებული*** (something built), or ***აუშენებელი*** (something not yet built). Conversion of an active voice verb changes its direct object to the subject of a passive voice verb.

Passive voice participles have affirmative and negative forms that differ from one another. Only affirmative passive participles have the category of tense, and its past and future forms are dissimilar.

9.8.2.2.1 Past passive participles

Past passive participles denote an action carried out by the subject of a passive voice verb and are derived mostly from passive verbs of I series by means of various formants. If a verb has a preverb, it is followed by the prefix of any circumfix forming these participles, while the suffix is placed after P/FSF. ***იხატება*** (is being painted) is a passive voice verb; the passive participle derived from it denotes the action that happened in the past: ***ნახატი*** (something painted, a picture).

The suffix ***ნა-*** is added to I series verbs with or without P/FSF:

წერ-ს–ნა-წერ-ი (written), ***ი-ძენ-ს–შე-ნა-ძენ-ი*** (acquisition, something acquired), ***ყოფ-ს–გა-ნა-ყოფ-ი*** (something divided), ***კაწრ-ავ-ს–გა-ნა-კაწრ-ი*** (a scratch, scar).

The suffix **-ილ** is used in participles derived from:

1. **single-stem verbs:** *და-წერ-ილ-ი* (written), *მო-ტან-ილ-ი* (brought), *და-ბან-ილ-ი* (washed);
2. **vowel-changing verbs:** *და-გრეხ-ილ-ი* (twisted), *და-დგენ-ილ-ი* (established), *შე-კრებ-ილ-ი* (collected, gathered)
3. **two-stem verbs with P/FSFs:**

– **ი:** *გა-თლ-**ილ**-ი* (sharpened, whittled)
one exception: *გაყიდ-**ულ**-ი* (sold)

– **ოფ:** *და-ყ-ოფ-**ილ**-ი* (divided, broken up), *გა-ყ-ოფ-**ილ**-ი* (divided)

– **ობ:** *გა-პ-ობ-**ილ**-ი* (split), *და-მხ-ობ-**ილ**-ი* (overthrown)

– **ავ** P/FSF is usually dropped: *შე-ფერ-**ილ**-ი* (coloured), *და-ნომრ-**ილ**-ი* (numbered), *შემო-ღობ-**ილ**-ი* (fenced), *გა-ბერ-**ილ**-ი* (blown, swollen)

The suffix **-ულ** is used with the two-stem verbs:

– **ებ:** *ა-გ-ებ-**ულ**-ი* (built), *გა-მწვან-ებ-**ულ**-ი* [made green (with trees, shrubs)], *ა-შენ-ებ-**ულ**-ი* (built)

– **ავ:** P/FSF is usually dropped: *მო-ხატ-**ულ**-ი* (coverd with drawings), *და-კარგ-**ულ**-ი* (lost), *დამალ-**ულ**-ი* (hidden), *მო-პარ-**ულ**-ი* (stolen)

– **ამ:** the vowel **-ა** of this P/FSF is syncopated: *და-დგ-მ-**ულ**-ი* (put on, staged), *ჩა-ც-მ-**ულ**-ი* (dressed)

– **ევ** and **-ემ** – ending verbs: *და-ბნე-**ულ**-ი* (bewildered), *და-რღვე-**ულ**-ი* (annulled), *მი-ცემ-**ულ**-ი* (given), *გა-ცემ-**ულ**-ი* (issued)

ნა- -ილ circumfix and the suffix **-ულ** may be used with the same stems; the resulting participles are synonymous:

ნა-ხატ-ი – და-ხატ-ულ-ი (painted)
მო-ნა-გებ-ი – მო-გებ-ულ-ი (gained)
ნა-ნახ-ი – ნახ-ულ-ი (seen)
მო-ნა-ტანი – მო-ტან-ილ-ი (brought)
წა-ნა-ღებ-ი – წა-ღებ-ულ-ი (taken away)
ნა-შენ(ებ)-ი – ა-შენებ-ულ-ი (built)
ნა-ბეჭდ-ი – და-ბეჭდ-ილ-ი (printed)
ნა-თქვამი – თქმ-ულ-ი (said)
ნა-კეთებ-ი – გა-კეთებ-ულ-ი (made)

In the composite words *ნაკეთები* is shortened to *ნაკეთი*: ***ხელნაკეთი** ნივთი* (a handmade object).

მ-არ (dissimilated **მ-ალ**) circumfix forms passive participles from verbs without any P/FSF:

მ-არ: და-მ-დნ-არ-ი (melted), და-მ-ჯდ-არ-ი (sat down), გა-მ-თბ-არ-ი (warmed up), გა-მსკდ-არ-ი (burst), და-მჭკნარი (withered), გა-მხმარი (dried)
მ-ალ: გა-მ-შრ-ალ-ი (dried), და-მ-თვრ-ალ-ი (drunk), და-მ-ტკბ-არ-ი (sweetened), გამქრალი (extinguished, disappeared)

Past passive participle formants

ნა-	ნა-ხატ-ი (painted, a picture), ნა-წერ-ი (written), ნა-ზარდ-ი (grown), ნა-ყიდ-ი (bought)
-ილ	და-წერ-ილ-ი (written), გა-ზრდ-ილ-ი (grown), შე-კერ-ილ-ი (sewn)
-ულ	და-ხატ-ულ-ი (painted), და-ხურ-ულ-ი (closed), გა-ღებ-ულ-ი (opened), გა-სუქებ-ულ-ი (fattened), გა-ყიდ-ულ-ი (sold), ა-შენებ-ულ-ი (built)
მ-არ (მ-ალ)	გა-მ-ხმ-არ-ი (dried), გა-მ-დნ-არ-ი (melted), გა-მ-თბ-არ-ი (dried), და-მ-ფრთხ-ალ-ი (scared)

ფანქრით ***ნაწერი*** *განცხადება მიუღებელია.*
A pencil written application is unacceptable.
ეს ჩემი ***შეკერილი*** *კაბაა.*
This is a dress sewn by me.
დღეს ბანკი ***დახურულია.***
Today the bank is closed.
ეზო ***გამხმარი*** *ფოთლებით არის მოფენილი.*
The yard is covered with dried leaves.

9.8.2.2.2 Future passive participles

The future passive participles denote not only an action carried out by the subject of a passive voice verb in the future but can also imply the tool with which the action is carried out.

სა-წერ-ი *დავალება* (an assignment to be written) – in this phrase, the future passive participle indicates an action that should be done in the future.
სა-წერ-ი *კალამი* (writing pen) – here the future passive participle denotes the tool with which the action (writing) is carried out.
სახატავი *ქაღალდი* (paper for painting/drawing), ***სახატავი*** *ფუნჯი* (painting brush), ***საკერავი*** *კაბები* (dresses to be sewn), ***საკერავი*** *მანქანა* (sewing machine)

When participles are formed with the circumfix სა-ელ, P/FSFs -ი is dropped and -ავ is syncopated. The სა- and სა-ელ may be used to form synonymous future past passive participles დასაკრავი – დასაკვრელი (something to be played/to play on).

Future passive participles formants	
სა-	წა-სა-ღებ-ი (something to be taking away), სა-წერ-ი (something to be written/to write with), სა-ხარშ-ი (something to be boiled/to boil in)
სა-ელ	გა-სა-კეთებ-ელ-ი (something to be made/to make with), და-სა-ჭრ-ელ-ი/სა-ჭრ-ელ-ი (something to be cut/to cut with)

ეს ფოსტაში ***წასაღები*** *წერილებია.*
These letters are to be taken to the post office.
ეს პურის (და) ***საჭრელი*** *დანაა.*
This is a knife for cutting bread.
დღეს ბევრი საქმე მაქვს ***გასაკეთებელი****.*
I have a lot of things to do today.

9.8.2.2.3 Negative passive participles

The negative passive participles are formed with the circumfix **უ-ელ**. As with other types of participles, if the base verb has a preverb, the vowel უ – is placed after the preverb, the syllable **-ელ** follows P/FSF and precedes conjugation markers: *და-უ-წერ-ელ-ი* (unwritten), *ამო-უ-ლევ-ელ-ი* (inexhaustible), *გა-უ-კეთებ-ელი* (undone, not done). The P/FSF **-ავ** is syncopated and the remaining consonant **-ვ** is metathesized: *და-უ-ხვნ-ელ-ი* (not ploughed), *შე-უ-კვრ-ელ-ი* (not tied).

The participles formed with the circumfixes **მ-არ//მ-ალ** have only the prefix **უ**-to form negative passive participles: *და-უ-მ-დნ-არ-ი* (not melted), *გა-უ-მ-თბ-არ-ი* (not warmed up). The prefix **უ**-and the circumfix **უ-ელ** are interchangeable: *და-უ-ხატ-ავ-ი – და-უ-ხატ-ვ-ელ-ი* (not painted), *(და)-უ-ლევ-ი* (not drunk), *ამო-უ-ლევ-ელ-ი* (inexhaustible).

Negative passive participle formants	
უ-	გა-უ-მ-თბ-არ-ი (not warmed up, unheated), და-უ-ხატ-ავ-ი (not painted), გა-უ-თიბ-ავ-ი (not mowed), უ-ნახ-ავ-ი (unseen, not yet seen)
უ-ელ	და-უ-წერ-ელ-ი (unwritten), და-უ-ხატ-ვ-ელ-ი (not painted), გა-უ-ზრდ-ელ-ი (not grown, rude), და-უ-მთავრ-ებ-ელ-ი (unfinished)

რატომ ჭამ ***გაუმთბარ*** *წვნიანს?*
Why are you eating the unheated soup.
ეს ***დაუწერელი*** *კანონია.*
This is an unwritten law.
ამ მწერალს რამდენიმე ***დაუმთავრებელი*** *რომანი აქვს.*
This writer has several unfinished novels.

9.8.2.3 *Medial voice participles*

There are two types of medial voice participles, the medial-active and medial passive. The participles cannot be derived from some medial-active voice verbs like *ვმეფობ* (I rule), *ვცოცხლობ* (I live), *ვხუმრობ* (I joke), *ვმეგობრობ* (I am friends with), and a few others.

The verbs with P/FSF **-ავ** form their participles with the suffix ***მ-*** or circumfixes ***მ-არე//მ-ალე***. When the latter are used the P/FSF **-ავ** is syncopated:

მ-ღელ-ვ-არე (touching, agitating)
ბრწყინ-ვ-ალე, მ-ბრწყინავ-ი (shining, brilliant)

The circumfix **მო-ე** forms participles from reduplicated verbs:

მო-ჭიკჭიკ-ე (chirping)
მო-ხითხით-ე (giggling)
მო-ლაქლაქ-ე (chatterer, pratler)
მო-ბაჯბაჯ-ე (stamping)

The same circumfix may form participles from some other verbs as well: *მო-ცურავ-ე* (swimmer), *მო-ჭიდავ-ე* (wrestler), *მო-ძალად-ე* (oppressor).

The circumfixes ***მ-არ//მ-ალ*** and ***მ-არე//მ-ალე*** are used to form participles from the one-stem verbs:

მ-ტირ-ალ-ი (one who weeps/sheds tears)
მ-ქუხ-არე (thundering)
მ-წუხ-არე (mournful)
მ-დუმ-არე (silent)

Participles derived from medio-passive verbs are based on their gerunds and formed with the circumfix ***მ-არ***:

დგომა (standing) → ***მ-***დგომ***-არე*** (stood)
ჯდომა (sitting) → ***მ-***ჯდომ***-არე*** (sat)
წოლა (lying down) → ***მ-***წოლ***-არე*** (lied down)
დება (putting down) → ***მ-***დებ***-არე*** (put down, located)

Only one medio-passive verb has participles referring to all three tenses, the present, past and future. Its root is **ვალ-**. The present and future participles are derived from this root with the prefixes

მა-and *სა*-: *მო-მა-ვალ-ი* (future, coming), *მო-სა-ვალ-ი* (one who is to come/arrive, harvest).

Past participles are based on its gerund: *მო-ს-ულ-ი* (who has come/arrived).

Some synonymous participles are also based on the gerund *მო-მ-სვლ-ელ-ი* (one coming, arriving), *მო-სა-სვლ-ელ-ი* (one who is to come, arrive), *მო-უ-სვლ-ელ-ი* (one who has not come/arrived).

Medial voice participle formants

მ-	მ-ცურ-ავ-ი (swimmer, swimming/floating), მ-ხოხ-ავ-ი (crawling), მ-გმინ-ავ-ი (groaning)
მო-ე	მო-ჭიკჭიკ-ე (chirping), მო-ჭიდავ-ე (wrestling, wrestler), მო-ახლ-ე (accompanying, servant), მო-სისხლ-ე (deadly enemy)
მ-არ (მ-ალ)	მ-დნ-არ-ი (melting), მ-ტკნ-არ-ი (fresh) მ-ძინ-არ-ი (sleeping), მ-ცინ-არ-ი (laughing), მ-ყვირ-ალ-ი (shouting), მ-ყრ-ალ-ი (stinking)
მო-არ მ-არე (მ-ალე) -ალე	მო-(მ)-ღიმ-არ-ი (smiling), მო-ტირ-ლ-ი (lamenting) მ-ჭმუნვ-არე (grieving, sad), მ-ქუხ-არე (thundering), მ-დუღ-არე (boiling), მ-დუმ-არე (silent), მ-დინ-არე (flowing, river), გა-მ-ჭვირვ-ალე (transparent), ბრწყინვ-ალე (shining, brilliant)

მგმინავი *ავადმყოფი საოპერაციო ოთახში შეიყვანეს.*
The groaning patient was taken to the operation room.
შეჯიბრში ქართველმა ***მოჭიდავეებმა*** *გაიმარჯვეს.*
The Georgian wrestlers won the competition.
ამ ტბაში ***მტკნარი*** *წყალია.*
This is a freshwater lake (in this lake water is fresh).
მიხარია, რომ ***მომღიმარი*** *გნახე.*
I am glad, I saw you smiling.
ეს სპორტსმენი ჩვენი გუნდის ***ბრწყინვალე*** *ვარსკვლავია.*
This sportsman is a shining star of our team.

Chapter 10

Adverbs

An adverb is a part of speech that modifies:

1. A verb

   *სტუმარი **გვიან** მოვიდა.*
   The guest arrived late.

2. A gerund or a participle

   *სტუმარმა **გვიან** მოსვლა მოიბოდიშა.*
   The guest apologized for late arrival.
   ***გვიან მოსული** სტუმარი ჩვენი მეზობელია.*
   The late-arrived guest is our neighbour.

3. An adjective

   *ეს **ძალიან** ღრმა მდინარეა.*
   This is a very deep river.

4. Another adverb

   *ის **ძალიან** კარგად ლაპარაკობს ქართულად.*
   He speaks Georgian very well.

Adverb does not decline and has no person or tense markers.

10.1 Primary and derivative adverbs

In Georgian, very few adverbs are primary; the majority of them are derivative. The primary adverbs that are not derived from any other parts of speech are *აქ* (here), *იქ* (there), *წინ* (in front of), *უკან* (behind), *გარე(თ)* (outside), *შინ* (inside, at home), *ახლა* (now), and some others.

The significant number of adverbs are nouns with the case markers that have lost the case function. It is the context of a sentence that differentiates a declinable noun from an adverb:

DOI: 10.4324/9781315281131-13

ღამე ***დღეს*** *მოსდევს.* (The night follows the day.) ***დღეს*** is the noun ***დღე*** in the dative case and functions as the indirect object of the verb.

დღეს *თბილა.* (Today is warm.) ***დღეს*** is an adverb derived from the noun in the dative case; it does not function either as the subject or object of the verb.

The adverbs most frequently consist of adjectives and participles with the adverbial case ending: *კარგ-ად* (well), *ცუდ-ად* (poorly), *მშვიდ-ად* (calmly), *ფართო-დ* (widely), *ღია-დ* (openly), *მკურნალ-ად* (as healer).

The following chart shows adverbs formed with and without case endings and postpositions.

Cases	*Adverbs*
Bare stem	დღე (day), ღამე (night), ძალიან (very), ძლიერ (strongly, very)
Reduplicated base stem	მთა-მთა (along mountains), სოფელ-სოფელ (village-by-village), ქუჩა-ქუჩა (street-by-street), ნაკუწ-ნაკუწ (bit-by-bit), ლუკმა-ლუკმა (piece-by-piece)
Dative	ძირ-ს (down), ახლო-ს (near), შორ-ს (far), შორიახლო-ს (nearby), საღამო-ს (in the evening), დილა-ს (in the morning), დღე-ს (today), წელ-ს (this year), დიდხან-ს (for a long time), ოდე-ს (when; this is an archaic form and seldom used in contemporary Georgian)
Dative with postposition	**-ში**: თავ-ში (at the start), შუაშ-ი (in the middle), ბოლო-ში (at the end), კარ-ში (outdoors) **-ზე**: შუა-ზე (in the middle), გან-ზე (aside), გვერდ-ზე (at the side)
Genitive	**-გზ-ის**: ორგზის (twice), ხუთგზის (five times) **-წინ**: გუშინწინ (<გუშინ-ის-წინ) (the day before yesterday), დღე-ის სწორს (this day next week), ხვალ-ის სწორს (a week after tomorrow)
Genitive with postposition	**-თვის:** ამ-ის-თვის (for this), იმ-ის-თვის (for that, because)
Genitive + dative	დაწყებ-ის-ა-ს (at the beginning), დასრულებ-ის-ა-ს (at the end), მისვლ-ის-ა-ს (at the time of arriving)

Cases	*Adverbs*
Instrumental	**Derived from nouns:** გვერდ-ით (by side, nearby), შორ-ით (from afar), ღამ-ით (at night), ძალ-ით (by force), ფეხ-ით (on foot), ღამ-ით (by night) **Derived from adverbs:** წინა-თ (earlier, in the past), გარე-თ (outside), შიგნ-ით (inside), ზემო-თ (at the top), ქვევ-ით (down), აქეთ (this way), იქით (that way)
Genitive + instrumental	დღ-ის-ით (by day, by daytime)
Instrumental with postposition	**-კენ**: საით-კენ (where to) **-დან(<ით-გან):** შიგნ-ი-დან (from inside), უკნ-ი-დან (from behind), ზევ-ი-დან (from above), ქვევ-ი-დან (from below), შუ-ი-დან (from the middle), მაღლ-ი-დან (from above), დაბლ-ი-დან (from below), სა-ი-დან (from where), თავ-ი-დან (from the beginning), ბოლო-დან (from the end)
Adverbial	ალმაცერ-ად (askance, obliquely), ძველ-ად (in the past, long ago), უცბ-ად (suddenly), ყოვლ-ად (completely, absolutely), ამჟამ-ად (at present time, now, today), სრულ-ად (fully), ამ-ად (for this), იმ-ად (for that) **with partly truncated case endings:** ჩქარა (< ჩქარ-ად (fast)), ნელა (< ნელ-ად) (slowly), ნელ-ნელა (leisurely), მაღლა (< მაღლ-ად) (high up, upward), დაბლა (< დაბლ-ად) (down, at the bottom), მართლა (< მართლად) (really) **adjectives and participles in adverbial case have adverbial function**: კარგ-ად (well), დინჯ-ად (calmly, slowly), გაბედულ-ად (with confidence, boldly), დაცულ-ად (safely) **nouns in adverbial case have adverbial function**: სოფლ-ად (in countryside), ქალაქ-ად (in urban place), ბარ-ად (in flatlands), ველ-ად (in fields, steppes)

*მთელი **ღამე** არ ეძინა.*
He did not sleep the entire night.
***ღამღამობით** ლექსებს წერს.*
During nights he writes poems.
*წერილი **ნაკუნ-ნაკუწ** დავხიე.*
I tore the letter into small pieces (ripped piece-by-piece).
***ქუჩა-ქუჩა** ნუ დადიხარ.*
Don't wander around in the streets (walk street-by-street).
*ბაზარში **ფეხით** წავედი.*
I went to the market on foot.
*ზეიმი **დიდხანს** გავრძელდა.*
The festivities lasted for a long time.
***გუშინწინ** ბიძაჩემმა დამირეკა.*
The day before yesterday, my uncle called me.
*იგი **ხუთჯერ/ხუთგზის** გახდა მსოფლიო ჩემპიონი ჭადრაკში.*
He became the chess world champion five times.
***დღისით** მძინავს, **ღამით** ვმუშაობ.*
I sleep during the day, work at night.
***ძველად** აქ სოფელი იყო, მაგრამ **ამჟამად** არავინ ცხოვრობს.*
Long time ago there was a village here, but now nobody lives (here).
*გვიამბე შენი ამბავი **თავიდან.***
Tell us your story from the beginning.
*ნუ ღელავ, ილაპარაკე **მშვიდად** და **გაბედულად.***
Don't be nervous, speak calmly and with confidence.
*მოხუცი ქალი **ნელ-ნელა** ამოდიოდა კიბეზე.*
An old woman was slowly walking up the stairs.
*ამ სურათში **აქეთ** მე ვზივარ, **გვერდით** დედაჩემია, **შუაში** ჩემი ცოლი, **უკან** კი ჩემი ძმა დგას.*
In this picture, I sit on this side, by (my) side is my mother, in the middle is my wife, and behind (us) my brother is standing.

In addition to the cases, adverbs can be formed by means of various suffixes:

-ივ: მხრ-ივ (> მხარე – side; ერთი მხრივ – on the one side/hand) ჩვეულებრივ (usually) (> ჩვეულება – habit), თვალნათლივ (clearly, obviously), (> თვალნათელი, with light eyes). Such derivation has ირგვლ-ივ (around), but restoring the starting form is difficult.
-ხელ is used only with the numeral **ერთი** (one): ერთ-ხელ (once)
-ჯერ may be used with any numeral except **ერთი** (one): ხუთ-ჯერ (five times), ას-ჯერ (hundred times), შვიდას ოცდახუთ-ჯერ (seven hundred twenty-five times), etc.

-მა: აღ-მა (uphill), დაღ-მა (downhill), გაღ-მა (on the opposite bank), გამოღ-მა (on this bank), წაღ-მა (right side), უკუღ-მა (wrong side)

There is a separate group of composite adverbs formed according to the rule of compound of formation (see 8.2.).

10.2 Semantic groups of adverbs

The adverbs provide information about place, time, frequency, degree, intention, level of certainty, or other circumstances of the action denoted by verbs.

Every adverb responds to this or that question, which in itself may be an adverb. The interrogative adverbs with the particle **-ც** at the end may serve as conjunctions in compound sentences joining the main and subordinate clause. For example, in the interrogative sentence ***საიდან** ჩამოხვედი?* (where did you come from?), the word **საიდან** (from where) is an interrogative adverb. In the sentence *იქ დაბრუნდი, **საიდანაც** ჩამოხვედი* (go back where you came from) the adverb **საიდანაც** (from where) functions as a conjunction. It is formed by adding the particle **-ც** to **საიდან**. The euphonic **-ა-** is inserted between the adverb and particle **-ც**.

The meaning and function of an adverb depends on the context which it is used. An adverb following a noun function as a postposition. ***უკან** როდის ბრუნდები?* (When are you coming back?) – in the sentence the word **უკან** (back, behind) is an adverb indicating place and expresses the direction of the action denoted by the verb. In the sentence *სახლის **უკან** პატარა ბაღი გვაქვს* (behind the house we have a little garden), the word **უკან** follows a noun in the genitive case and has the function of a postposition. The composite adverb **წინდაწინ** (beforehand, early) may denote the time when an action took place: *ბილეთები **წინდაწინ** ჰქონდა ნაყიდი* (he had bought the tickets beforehand). If this composite is spelled separately, it functions as an adverb with a different semantics: *სულ **წინ და წინ** გევლოთ!* (May you always move forward/progress!).

– *სადამდე უნდა მდიო?*
How far do you intend to follow me?

– *სახლამდე.*
To the house

– ***სანამდე** უნდა მდიო?*
How far do you intend to follow me?

– *დილამდე.*
Till morning

The answer to the question specifies that the word **სადამდე** is an adverb indicating place **სახლამდე** (to the house). An answer to the question **სანამდე** is an adverb expressing time **დილამდე** (till morning).

სადილი **უცბად** შეჭამა (he ate dinner fast) – here **უცბად** is an adverb denoting the manner of the action and answers the question **როგორ** (how). In the sentence **უცბად** დაბრუნდა (he returned soon/right away), the meaning of **უცბად** is synonymous with **მალე**, an adverb indicating time of the action and answers the question **როდის** (when).

The following chart shows the type of adverbs and the questions they answer.

Groups of adverbs		
	Questions	*Adverbs*
Adverbs of place	სად (where) საიდან (from where, whence) სადამდე (till where) საითკენ (which way)	**Primary:** აქ (here), იქ (there), წინ (ahead), უკან (behind, back), მაღლა (above, up), დაბლა (below) **With case endings:** ძირ-ს (down), ახლო-ს (near), შორ-ს (far), ბოლო-ს (at the end, finally), გვერდ-ით, (at the side, nearby), ქვემო-თ (down, below), გარე-თ (outside) **With postpositions:** აქე-დან (from here), აქა-მდე (till here), თავ-ში (at the head), შუა-ში (in the middle), ბოლო-ში (at the end), ბოლო-ს-კენ (towards the end) **With preverb:** აღმა (uphill), დაღმა (downhill), გამოღმა (on this bank) **Composites:** აქა-იქ (here-and-there), ზევით-ქვევით (up-and-down), აღმა-დაღმა (uphill-downhill), გაღმა-გამოღმა (on that bank-and-this bank)

Groups of adverbs

	Questions	*Adverbs*
Adverbs of time	როდის (when) რა დროიდან (from what time) რა დრომდე (till what time) რამდენ ხანს (how long)	ახლა (now), წელან (recently), გუშინ (yesterday), ხვალ (tomorrow), ზეგ (the day after tomorrow), ჯერ (so far, yet), მერე (later), მალე (soon) **With the ablative case ending**: იშვიათ-ად (seldom) **Other case endings:** მისვლ-ის-ას, დღ-ის-ით, ღამ-ით, გაის-ად. **With postpositions:** დილი-დან (from morning), საღამო-მდე (till evening), წინდაწინ (beforehand) აქა-მდე (till now/this place), იქა-მდე (till there/then), მანა-მდე (earlier, before) **With particles:** მაშინ-ღა (only then), ოდეს-მე (sometime), ოდეს-ღაც (long ago) **Composites:** ამაღამ (tonight), შარშანწინ (the year before last), ხანდახან (sometimes, once in a while), გუშინწინ (the day before yesterday), ერთბაშად (suddenly, all of a sudden), ნელ-ნელა (slowly)
Adverbs of manner or circumstance	როგორ (how) რა ვითარებაში (under what circumstances) რანაირად (how, in what manner)	ძალიან (very), ძლიერ (forcefully, very) **With adverbial case endings:** მშვიდ-ად (calmly), ძალ-ად (by force), ფრი-ად (rather), უცბ-ად (suddenly), ერთბაშ-ად (suddenly, all of a sudden), მაგრ-ად (forcefully, very), ამგვარ-ად (thus), ხშირ-ად (often), იშვიათ-ად (seldom)

(Continued)

(Continued)

Groups of adverbs

	Questions	*Adverbs*
		Derived from pronouns: ასე (this way), ისე (that way), ეგრე (this way), მაგრე (that way) **Composites:** თანდათან (by and by, gradually), ნელ-ნელა (slowly), ჩქარ-ჩქარა (quickly), ერთმხრივ (on the one hand), ყოველმხრივ (in every way), ყოველნაირად (in every manner), ალმაცერად (askance), პირქვე (prone), თავქვე (downhill)
Adverbs of cause	რატომ (why)	ამიტომ (because of this, therefore), იმიტომ (because of that, therefore), მაგიტომ (that's why), ასე (this way), ისე (that way)
Adverbs of purpose	რატომ (why) რისთვის (for what) რად (for what)	**With case ending:** ამა-დ (for this) **With postpositions:** ამ-ის-თვის (for this), იმ-ის-თვის (for that)
Adverbs of quantity and measure	რამდენად (for how much, to what degree) რამდენჯერ (how many times) რა ოდენობით (in what quantity რა ზომით (by what measure)	ნაკლებ (less), სულ (altogether) **With case endings:** სრულებ-ით (absolutely, completely), ამდენ-ად (for this much, thus), იმდენ-ად (thus), ნაკლება-ად (seldom, less), მთლ-ად (entirely), ცოტ-ად (less), მეტ-ად (very, too much) **With -ჯერ particle:** შვიდ-ჯერ (seven times), ათას-ჯერ (thousand times) **With-გზის particle:** შვიდ-გზის (sevenfold), მრავალ-გზის (manyfold)

Groups of adverbs		
	Questions	*Adverbs*
		Composites: ერთიორად (twofold), ერთიასად (hundredfold), ცოტ-ცოტა (a little)
Interrogative adverbs		**Primary:** სად (where), რატომ (why), როგორ (how)
		With particle: რამდენ-ჯერ (how many times)
		With case endings: როდ-ის (when), რამდენ ხან-ს (for how long), რა-დ (for what), რანაირ-ად (how, in what manner)
		With postpositions: სა-ი-დან (from where),
		სა-ით-კენ (to where), სად-ა-მდე (till where)
		რა დროი-დან (from what time), როდე-მდე (till what time), რის-თვის (for what)
Relative adverbs		სადა-ც (wherever), საიდანა-ც (from wherever), საითკენა-ც (toward whichever direction), სადამდე-ც (till wherever), როდესა-ც (whenever), რა დროიდანა-ც (from whatever period), რამდენ ხანსა-ც (for whowever long), როდემდე-ც (till whenever), როგორ-ც (as, whatever way), რამდენჯერა-ც (as often as), რატომა-ც (for whatever), რადა-ც (no matter what), რისთვისა-ც (for whatever reason), რანაირადა-ც (in whatever manner)

მაღლა მთებში უკვე თოვს.
Up in the mountains it is already snowing.
ჩემი სახლი **აქედან** შორს არის.
My house is far from here.
გარეთ ცივა.
It's cold outside.
ეს **აქედან აქამდე** ზეპირად უნდა იცოდე.
You should learn this by heart from here to here.
აქამდე სად იყავი?
Where were you till now?
მდინარის **გაღმა** ჩვენი სოფელია.
On the other side of the river is our village.
გუშინ წვიმდა, **დღეს** ისევ მზეა.
Yesterday it was raining, today is sunny again.
მე მათ **იშვიათად** ვხედავ.
I seldom see them.
ის **ყოველმხრივ** შესანიშნავი ადამიანია.
He is a remarkable person in every way.
გაისად იტალიაში მივდივარ.
Next year I am going to Italy.
ის **დილიდან საღამომდე** ბიბლიოთეკაშია.
He is in the library from morning till evening.
ჩემმა დამ **შარშან** დაიცვა დისერტაცია.
My sister defended (her) dissertation last year.
ადრე ხშირად ვმოგზაურობდი.
Before I travelled often.
აქ **ამისთვის** მოხვედი?
Did you come here for this?
მას **სრულებით** არ აინტერესებს პოლიტიკა.
He is completely uninterested in politics.
ეს წიგნი **სამჯერ** მაქვს წაკითხული.
I have read this book three times.
სადაც ჩვენ ვცხოვრობთ, იქ კარგი ქართული რესტორანია.
Where we live there is a good Georgian restaurant.

Chapter 11

Postpositions

There are several types of postpositions in Georgian. Some of them are added to a noun as a clitic. A case ending of the noun with a postposition may be either retained, truncated, changed phonetically, or dropped altogether. Postpositions may affect the case ending of a noun but does not change its stem. All possible phonetic changes of a stem, syncopation, truncation, or both remain intact. Some postpositions are not attached to a noun but follow them as separate words. Each postposition affects the meaning of the noun to which it is attached.

Postpositions are added to nouns in all cases except ergative and vocative.

Case	*Postposition*	*Function*	*Example*
Nom.	-ვით like	Added only to consonant stem nouns after the case ending and denotes similarity with something.	მტრედ-ი-ვით, like a dove
Dat.	-ვით like	Added to both consonant and vowel stem nouns after the case anding and extending vowel; denotes similarity; mostly added to vowel stem nouns.	მზე-ს-ა-ვით, like sun მტერ-ს-ა-ვით, like enemy (Such forms are becoming obsolescent.)

(*Continued*)

DOI: 10.4324/9781315281131-14

(Continued)

Case	Postposition	Function	Example
	-თან at, near	Denotes proximity, togetherness. The case ending is dropped when added to consonant stem nouns but retained with vowel stem nouns. If a stem ends with the consonant *-თ-*, it will be doubled.	მეგობარ-**თან**, with a friend დედა-**ს-თან**, with mother ყუთ-**თან**, at the box
	-ზე on, at, about	Denotes position or place of a noun and time when added to numerals. Case ending *-ს* is lost. If a stem ends with the consonant, -**ზ**-it will be doubled.	სახლ-**ზე**, on (top) of a house, about a house კონცერტ-ზე, at the concert, about the concert კოვ**ზ**-ზე, on a spoon ორ-ზე, at two (o'clock) რვა-ზე, at eight (o'clock)
Dat.	**-ში** in/inside, to	Denotes position or place of a noun. The case ending-*ს* is dropped. Stems ending with the consonant *-შ*-will have it doubled.	სახლ-**ში**, at home, in a house მივდივარ თბილის-**ში**, I am going to Tbilisi კომ**შ**-**ში**, inside a quince ქო**შ**-**ში**, in a slipper
	შუა between/in between	Stands separately at the end of a noun phrase and denotes a place or position. All but the last noun in singular or plural form preceding it may have the case ending extended with the euphonic *-ა*.	სახლ-**ს-ა და** გზა-**ს** **შუა**, between the house and the road სახლ-ებ-**ს-ა** და გზ-ებ-**ს** **შუა**, between houses and the roads ორ ზღვა-**ს** **შუა**, between two seas

Case	*Postposition*	*Function*	*Example*
	შორის between/ among/amid	Stands separately and denotes a position or place. All but the last noun in singular or plural form preceding it may have their case ending extended with the extending vowel **-ა**.	თბილის**-ს-ა და** ქუთაის**-ს შორის**, between Tbilisi and Kutaisi საქართველო**-ს-ა და** საფრანგეთ**-ს შორის**, between Georgia and France
Gen.	**-გან** from, out of, with	Added to both consonant and vowel stem nouns. Denotes person (from whom), material (out of what), or cause (why) of an action. The case ending may be extended with the euphonic **-ა**.	ამხანაგ**-ის-გან**, from a friend ხ**-ის-გან**, (made) of wood/wooden ხმაურ**-ის-(ა)-გან**, because of noise
	-კენ to/towards	Denotes direction of an action and may be added to nouns with or without an extending vowel **-ა**.	სახლ**-ის-(ა)-კენ**, towards home წყლ**-ის-(ა)-კენ**, towards water მზ**-ის-(ა)-კენ**, towards sun თინა**-ს-(ა)-კენ**, to Tina
	-თვის for	Denotes a function (for what) and is added to nouns with or without an extending vowel **-ა**.	ბინ**-ის-(ა)-თვის**, for apartment მეგობრ**-ის-(ა)-თვის**, for friend ქვეყნ**-ის-(ა)-თვის**, for the country
	-ებრ like	Denotes similarity and is added to nouns after case ending or to their stem.	ლომ**-ის-(ა)-ებრ**, like lion

(Continued)

(Continued)

Case	Postposition	Function	Example
	-თანავე immediately (after)	Denotes time of action and is added mostly to verbal nouns (gerunds)	ჩაცმ**-ის-თანავე**, as soon as getting dressed ადგომ**-ის-თანავე**, as soon as getting up მოსვლ**-ის-თანავე**, immediately after arriving გახსნ**-ის-თანავე**, immediately after opening
Gen.	**გამო** because of	Stands separately. Denotes cause or reason of action.	დაგვიანებ**-ის გამო**, because of tardiness ავადმყოფობ**-ის გამო**, because of illness
	მიმართ/ მომართ towards	Stand separately. Denote direction. In contemporary Georgian mostly მიმართ is used.	ადამიან-ის მიმართ, towards a person/ human being
	გარდა except/ besides	Stands separately.	ზამთრ**-ის გარდა**, except winter ლაპარაკ **-ის გარდა**, except/besides speaking
	გარეშე without	Stands separately.	მეგობრ**-ის გარეშე**, without a friend
	შესახებ about	Stands separately.	ექიმ**-ის შესახებ**, about a doctor გზ**-ის შესახებ**, about a way
	მიერ by	Stands separately.	კაც**-ის მიერ**, by a man ბავშვ**-ის მიერ**, by a child
Inst.	**-ურთ** together with	Is added to a noun after case ending.	მეუღლ**-ით-ურთ**, together with spouse

Case	*Postposition*	*Function*	*Example*
	-დან < -გან from	When the postposition *-გან* is added to a noun in the instrumental case, both the case ending and the postposition are phonetically changed წიგნ-**ით-**გან > წიგნ-**ი-დან**. It denotes the starting point in time (from what time) or places (from where).	ქალაქ-**ი-დან**, from city ხუთი საათ-**ი-დან**, from five o'clock (on)
Adv.	-მდე/-მდის up to/as far as/till, until	In contemporary Georgian frequently used form is **-*მდე*;** It denotes the final point of an action in time or place and approximate quantity of something. When added to a consonant stem noun, the consonant **-დ** of the case ending is dropped: სახლ-**ად-მდე** > სახლ-**ა-მდე**. When added to vowel stem nouns the case ending is dropped.	ქალაქ-**ა-მდე**, up to city კარ-**ა-მდე**, up to door ცა-**მდე**, up to the sky ტყე-**მდე**, up to the woods ათ-ა-მდე, till ten (o'clock) or nearly ten; about ten (boys) ცხრა-მდე, till nine (o'clock) or about nine ას-ა-მდე ადამიანი, up to hundred persons

When more than two nouns in either dative or genitive case are joined with the conjunctions **და** (and) or *თუ* (if), between the last two nouns only the second noun has a postposition while the first is in its extended form: *სოფელში*, *ქალაქში*, and *მთა-***სა და** *ბარ-***ში** (in villages, towns, mountains and plains). In spoken language *მთა-***ში** *და ბარ-***ში** are used, but it is considered a substandard form.

Case	*With postposition*	*With postposition*	*With postposition*	*With postposition*
Nom.	ბაღ-ი-ვით, like garden	–	–	–
Erg.	–	–	–	–
Dat.	ბაღ-ში, in garden თამაშ-ში, in play ბაღ-ზე, on/ about garden ხაზ-ზე, online	კლდე-ს-ა-ვით, like a cliff	ბაღ-თან, near garden ყუთ-თან, near a box კლდე-ს-თან, near cliff	–
Gen.	ცემენტ-ის-გან, with/from cement ქვ□-ის-გან, with/from/of stone	ბაღ-ის-კენ, towards garden სოფ□ლ-ის-კენ, towards village	ბაღ-ის-თვის, for garden სოფ□ლ-ის-თვის, for village	ჩაცმ□-ის-თანავე, as soon as getting dressed ადგომ□-ის-თანავე, as soon as getting up
	ბაღ-ის გამო, because of garden აშენებ□-ის გამო, because of building კაც-ის მიერ, by man მგ□ლ-ის მიერ, by wolf წყარო-ს მიერ, by rivulet ელენე-ს მიერ, by Hellen ც□-ის მიერ, by the sky მოყვ□რ□-ის მიერ, by friend	ბაღ-ის გარდა, besides garden ფუტკ□რ-ის გარდა, besides bee მთ□-ის გარდა, besides/ except mountain ტომ□რ-ის გარდა, except sack	ბაღ-ის მიმართ, towards garden სტუმ□რ-ის მიმართ, towards guest ც□-ის მიმართ, towards the sky მოქალაქ□-ის მიმართ, towards citizen ელენე-ს მიმართ, towards Hellen მოყვ□რ□-ის მიმართ, towards fellow man	ბაღ-ის გარეშე, without garden სტუმ□რ-ის გარეშე, without guest მოქალაქ□-ის გარეშე, without citizen მოყვ□რ□-ის გარეშე, without fellow man

Case	*With postposition*	*With postposition*	*With postposition*	*With postposition*
Instr.	მეგობ□რ-ით-ურთ, together with friend	ქალაქ-ი-დან, from city სოფ□ლ-ი-დან, from village	–	–
Adv.	ქალაქ-ა-მდე, up to the city სოფლ-ა-მდე, up to the village რუ-მდე, up to the rivulet ტყე-მდე, up to the woods	–	–	–

-ვით

მგელ-ი-ვით მშია.
I am hungry like a wolf.

-თან

დღეს ავადმყოფ ***მეგობარ-თან*** *მივდივარ.*
I am going to a sick friend.

-ზე

ბავშვი სახლის ***სახურავ-ზე*** *აძვრა.*
A child climbed to the roof of the house.
სტადიონ-ზე *უამრავი ხალხი შეგროვდა.*
A lot of people gathered at the stadium.
დილის ცხრა ***საათ-ზე*** *აქ უნდა ვიყო.*
I should be here at nine o'clock in the morning.

-ში

ლექტორი ***აუდიტორია-ში*** *შემოვიდა.*
The lecturer came into the auditorium.
მე ორ ***საათ-ში*** *დავბრუნდები.*
I will be in two hours.

შუა

ორ ქვის ***სახლს შუა*** *პატარა ბაღია.*
Between the two stone houses, there is a small garden.

ტყესა და მდინარეს ***შუა*** *სოფელია.*
Between the woods and the river, there is a village.

შორის

ამ ორ ***ავტორს შორის*** *რომელი მოგწონს?*
Between these two authors, which one do you like?
1941 წელს ომი დაიწყო ***გერმანიასა და საბჭოთა კავშირს შორის.***
In 1941 war broke out between Germany and the Soviet Union.

-გან

ჩემმა ძმამ ***ხ-ის-გან*** *კატა გამოთალა.*
My brother carved out a cat from (a piece of) wood.

-კენ

ბიბლიოთეკ-ის-კენ *მიდიხარ?*
Are you going to the library?
მაღაზი-ის-კენ *მივდივარ.*
I am going towards the store.

-თვის

დედამ ***ბავშვებ-ის-თვის*** *საჩუქრები იყიდა.*
Mother bought gifts for the children.

-ებრ

ამ ***მსახიობ-ის-ებრ*** *ლამაზი არავინ მინახავს.*
I have not seen anyone as beautiful as this actress.

-თანავე

კრების ***დამთავრებ-ის-თანავე*** *სახლში წავედით.*
As soon as the meeting was over, we went home.

მიმართ

დიდი პატივისცემის გრძნობა მაქვს ამ ***ადამიან-ის მიმართ.***
I have great respect for this man.

გარდა

ზაფხულ-ის გარდა *ყველა სეზონი მიყვარს.*
I love all seasons except summer.
ჩემი ***მეზობლ-ის გარდა*** *აქ არავის ვიცნობ.*
I don't know anyone here except my neighbour.

გარეშე

ამ პრობლემის ***გადაწყვეტ-ის გარეშე*** *წინ ვერ წავალთ.*
We cannot move ahead without solving this problem.

შესახებ

არაფერია ცნობილი ამ ***ექსპედიცი-ის შესახებ.***
Nothing is known about this expedition.

მიერ

ჩვენ ***მამაჩემ-ის მიერ*** *აშენებულ სახლში ვცხოვრობთ.*
We live in the house built by my father.

-ურთ

პრეზიდენტი ***მეუღლ-ით-ურთ*** *დაესწრო შეხვედრას.*
The president attended the meeting together with his spouse.

-დან

*მაღაზი-****ი-დან*** *მოდიხარ?*
Are you coming from the shop?
ბანკ-ი-დან *მოვდივარ.*
I am coming from the bank.
ბავშვები ***ბაღ-ი-დან*** *ქუჩაში გამოვიდნენ.*
Children came out of the garden into the street.

-მდე/მდის

თბილისიდან ***ქუთაის-ა-მდე*** *ორას ოცდათხუთმეტი კილომეტრია.*
There are two hundred and thirty-five kilometres from Tbilisi to Kutaisi.

Chapter 12

Conjunctions

In modern Georgian, there are two types of conjunctions, the basic and complex. The number of the *basic conjunctions* is relatively small: და (and), ან (or), თუ (if, and, or), კი (while, but), რომ (that), ხოლო (while), რათა (so that), მაგრამ (but), რადგან (since, because). The number of the *complex conjunctions* – for example, ვეღარც-ვეღარც (neither . . . nor anymore), ხან–ხან კიდევ (sometimes . . . sometimes), როგორც . . . ისე (as . . . as) and many others – is larger and will be discussed in the following subchapters.

With regard to their function, conjunctions are divided into two large groups: coordinating and subordinating. The coordinating conjunctions include several subgroups: coordinating, contrastive, separating, and equating conjunctions.

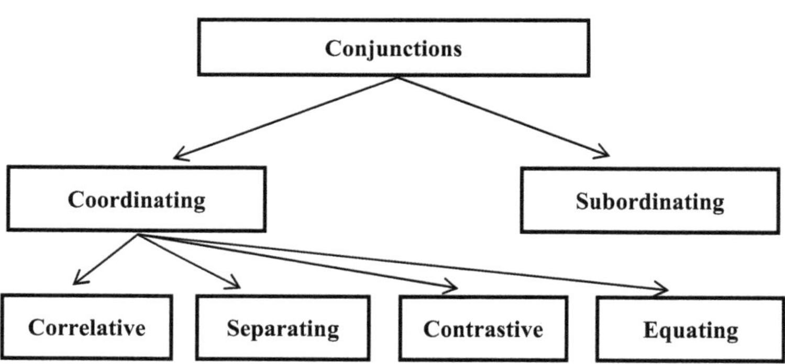

12.1 Coordinating conjunctions

12.1.1 *Correlative conjunctions*

Coordinating conjunctions join two or more elements of the same grammatical category: nouns, verbs, adjectives, pronouns, phrases, or two syntactically co-equal sentences with compound clauses.

DOI: 10.4324/9781315281131-15

The oldest and most frequently used correlative conjunction is **და** (and).

> *ჩემმა დამ ბაზარში ყურძენი* **და** *ატამი იყიდა.*
> My sister bought grapes and peaches at the market.
> *ბიბლიოთეკაში წავედი* **და** *რამდენიმე წიგნი გამოვიტანე.*
> I went to the library and took out several books.

When several similar grammatical elements are connected, the conjunction და is placed before the last of them.

> მე მყავს ბებია, პაპა, დედა, მამა, ორი ძმა **და** ერთი და.
> I have Grandmother, Grandfather, Mother, Father, two brothers and a sister.
> ჩემი და მთელი დღე წერდა, კითხულობდა, მეგობრებს ურეკავდა **და** ტელევიზორს უყურებდა.
> My sister was writing, reading, calling her friends, and watching television the entire day.
> დედაჩემს დაბადების დღისთვის ვარდები ვუყიდე: წითელი, ყვითელი, თეთრი **და** ვარდისფერი.
> I bought for Mother's birthday roses: red, yellow, white, and pink.

Another correlative conjunction **თუ** may serve the same purpose, thus adopting the semantics of the conjunction **და**:

> კაცი **თუ** ქალი, გოგო **თუ** ბიჭი – ყველა ზეიმობდა ჩვენი ფეხბურთელების გამარჯვებას.
> Men and/or women, girls and/or boys, and everybody celebrated the victory of our football team.
> ყველანაირი ქართული ღვინო მიყვარს, თეთრი **თუ** წითელი, მშრალი **თუ** ტკბილი.
> I love all kinds of Georgian wine, white and/or red, dry and/or sweet.
> ჩემი მეგობარი წერს **თუ** ხატავს, ყველაფერს ძალიან კარგად აკეთებს.
> Whether she writes or paints, my friend does everything very well.

In the examples, the conjunction **თუ** can be replaced with the **და** without changing the structure of the sentences they join together.

The particle **-ც** may also function as the conjunction **და**:

> ყველამ მოგვილოცა: მეგობრებმა**ც**, მეზობლებმა**ც**, ნათესავებმა**ც**.
> We were congratulated by everybody, our friends, neighbours, (as well as) relatives.

The same is with the conjunction *კიდეც* with or without *და* preceding it:

> **კიდეც** ვიმღერებ (და) **კიდეც** ვიცეკვებ.
> I will (both) sing and dance.

In the *negative sentences*, the following paired particles function as correlative conjunctions: ***არც–არც***, ***ვერც–ვერც***, ***ნურც–ნურც*** (neither . . . nor), ***აღარც–აღარც***, ***ვეღარც-ვეღარც*** (neither . . . nor anymore). They may be used with or without the conjunction **და**:

> *__არც__ მშია (და) __არც__ მწყურია.*
> I am neither hungry (and) nor thirsty.
> *__ვერც__ ბანკში წავედი (და) __ვერც__ მაღაზიაში.*
> I could go neither to the bank (and) nor to the store.
> *__ნურც__ თქვენ წუხართ (და) __ნურც__ მე მაწუხებთ.*
> Neither trouble yourself (and) nor trouble me.
> *ისე დაიღალა, __აღარც__ ჭამა უნდა (და) __აღარც__ ახალი ამბების ყურება.*
> He is so tired, wants neither to eat nor to watch the news (anymore).

If the parts of a sentence or two independent clauses are joined with these correlatives without the conjunctions **და**, they will be separated with a comma.

> ისე დაიღალა, **აღარც** ჭამა უნდა, **აღარც** ახალი ამბების ყურება.
> He is so tired, he wants neither to eat, nor to watch the news.

12.1.2 Separating conjunctions

There are single and paired separating conjunctions. The former are *თუ*, *ან*, and *ანდა* (if, or) and *თუნდა(ც)*and *გინდ(აც)* (even if); they may be coupled: **ან–ან, ან–ანდა, ან–ან *კიდევ*** (either . . . or); ***გინდ–გინდ, თუნდ–თუნდ*** (even if); **ხან–ხან, ხან– –ხანაც, ხან–ხან *კიდევ*** (sometimes . . . sometimes). These conjunctions separate or oppose two or more parts of a sentence or two or more clauses. As a rule, they stress the possibility of a choice between two entities.

> „**ან** თავისუფლება მომეცი **ან** – სიკვდილი."
> "Give me liberty, or give me death."

ან შავი ფანქრით დაწერე **ან** ლურჯით.
Write either with a black pen, or with a blue one.
ან დაგვირეკოს, **ან კიდევ** მოგვწეროს.
(Let him) either call or write to us.
ხან ტირის, **ხან კი** იცინის.
(He) sometimes cries, sometimes laughs.
ხან მე შემომხედავდა, **ხან** – დედამისს.
(He) sometimes looked at me, sometimes at his mother.
რა უცნაური ამინდია – **ხან** მზეა, **ხანაც** წვიმს.
What a strange weather, sometimes it's sunny, sometimes it rains
ხან ადრე მოდის, **ხან კიდევ** ძალიან იგვიანებს.
Sometimes he comes over early, sometimes very late.

The conjunction ***თუ*** replaces ***ან*** and ***ან–ან*** in interrogative sentences.

რას მიირთმევთ – ჩაის **თუ** ყავას?
What would you have, tea or coffee?

ან ჩაი მოგვიტანე **ან** ყავა!
Bring us either tea or coffee!

The conjunctions ***გინდ/გინდაც*** and ***თუნდ/თუნდაც*** have synonymous meanings and are mutually replaceable.

მე ამ წიგნს ხვალამდე ვერ დავამთავრებ, **თუნდ/თუნდაც/გინდ / გინდაც** მთელი ღამე ვიკითხო.
I will not be able to finish this book even if I read through the night.

The conjunctions ***გინდ-გინდ*** are derived from the second-person form of the verb *to want/wish*, *-გინდა(თ)*, and in some cases it may be replaced with the first-person forms of the same verb -***მინდა*** (I want) in singular, or ***გვინდა*** (we want) in plural.

გინდა *წადი,* ***გინდა*** *დარჩი.*
Do whatever you want, either go, or stay.
მინდა *დავწერ,* ***მინდა*** *არ დავწერ.*
I'll do whatever I wish, either will write, or won't write.
მინდა *დავწერ,* ***მინდა*** *– არა.*
I'll do whatever I wish, either write, or not.
გვინდა *ვითამაშებთ,* ***გვინდა*** *არ ვითამაშებთ.*
We'll do whatever we want, either will play or won't play.
გვინდა *ვითამაშებთ,* ***გვინდა*** *– არა.*
We'll do whatever we wish, either will play, or not.

12.1.3 Contrastive conjunctions

Contrastive conjunctions could be used singly or in pairs. The singles are **მაგრამ** (but), **კი** (and/while, but), **ხოლო** (while, and), **ოღონდ** (but, only), and **თუნდაც** (even if, even though). The paired conjunctions introduce independent clauses and join them structurally. Most of them are synonymous with various degree of intensity and could be translated as *not . . . but* or *not only . . . but*: **არა . . . არამედ, ნუ . . . არამედ, არა მარტო . . . არამედ, კი არ . . . არამედ, არამცთუ . . . არამედ**, and **როგორც . . . ისე** (as . . . as).

ბევრს ვეცადე, ***მაგრამ*** *ვერ დავითანხმე.*
I tried hard but couldn't make him agree.
თუნდაც *იწვიმოს, ჩვენ მაინც წავალთ.*
Even if it rains, we will go anyway.
მე ქართველი ვარ, ის ***კი*** *– გერმანელი.*
I am Georgian and he is German.
მე გასართობად ***კი არ*** *მოვედი აქ,* ***არამედ*** *სამუშაოდ.*
I come here not for fun, but for work.
ის ***არა მარტო*** *ფრანგულად ლაპარაკობს,* ***არამედ*** *ესპანურიც იცის.*
He speaks not only French but knows Spanish as well.

The contrastive adjectives may clarify an opposing clause:

ითამაშეთ, ***ოღონდ*** *ჩუმად!*
Play but quietly!
კი არ *სთხოვო,* ***არამედ*** *მოითხოვე.*
Do not beg but demand.
ისინი კონცერტზე წავიდნენ, ***ხოლო*** *ჩვენ სახლში დავბრუნდით.*
They went to a concert, while we returned home.

The conjunction **კი** replaces **ხოლო**, and therefore, they cannot be used in the same sentence together; the former is placed after the contrasting word, while the latter at the start of the sentence:

შენ გიტარაზე დაუკარი, შენ ***კი*** *იმღერე!*
You play guitar, and you sing.
შენ გიტარაზე დაუკარი, ***ხოლო*** *შენ იმღერე.*
You play guitar, while you sing.
მე წერილს დავწერ, მან ***კი*** *გააგზავნოს.*
I will write a letter, and he should send it.
მე წერილს დავწერ, ***ხოლო*** *მან გააგზავნოს.*
I will write a letter, while he should send it.

12.1.4 *Equating conjunctions*

There are only two equating conjunctions in Georgian: **ანუ** (that is) and **ესე იგი** (that is, hence, therefore). Both imply similarity or sameness of words or phrases they connect. **ესე იგი** is often abbreviated as **ე.ი.**

> *ჩვენ, **ანუ** მე და მთელი ჩემი ოჯახი, ამ ზაფხულს ბათუმში მივდივართ.*
> We, that is, I and my entire family go to Batumi this summer.
> *საქართველოს ყოველ მოქალაქეს, **ანუ** ქართული პასპორტის მქონე პირს, აქვს არჩევნებში მონაწილეობის უფლება.*
> Every citizen of Georgia, that is, a person owing Georgian passport, has the right to vote.
> *„ვაზროვნებ, **ესე იგი** ვარსებობ."*
> "I think, therefore I exist."
> *ევროკავშირი, **ესე იგი** ევროპის სახელმწიფოთა კავშირი შეიქმნა 1993 წელს.*
> The European Union, i.e. the Union of the European States, was founded in the year 1993.

The conjunction **ესე იგი** may be placed at the start of a sentence in response to a statement or information presented to the speaker. In such cases it corresponds to the English *it means that* or any phrase of similar meaning. The sentence starting with **ესე იგი** may be either affirmative or interrogative.

> *მათ იციან ჩვენი ტელეფონის ნომერი.*
> They know our phone number.
> ***ესე იგი** დღეს დაგვირეკავენ.*
> It means that they will call us today.
> *ჩემი და ავად არის.*
> My sister is sick.
> ***ესე იგი** ხვალ ჩვენთან ვერ მოვა?*
> Does it mean she won't be able to come to our place tomorrow?

12.2 Subordinating conjunctions

The subordinating conjunctions are used in complex sentences to join the main and subordinate clauses. Their function is specified by the type of subordinate sentences they join to the main clause. A few coordinating conjunctions may function as subordinate conjunctions as well. There are three of them: **თუ**, **ოლონდ**, and **რომ**.

თუ may serve as a subordinating conjunction in conditional sentences: *კარგი იქნება,* ***თუ*** *ამ წერილს დღეს გავგზავნით* (it will be good if we send this letter today).

ოღონდ is a contrastive conjunction when it qualifies the action expressed with the verb in the sentence it introduces: *დაწერე,* ***ოღონდ*** *მალე დაასრულე* (write, but finish it soon).

ოღონდ functions as a subordinating conjunction in conditional clauses: *ითამაშე,* ***ოღონდ*** *ჩუმად* (play, but quietly).

The most polyfunctional is the correlative conjunction ***რომ***, which is used in various types of subordinate clauses as an adverbial clauses:

> *ადრე უნდა მივიდეთ,* ***რომ*** *წინა რიგში დავსხდეთ.*
> We should go early so that we can sit in the front row (modifier of the purpose).
> *ადრე* ***რომ*** მოსულიყავი, არ დავიგვიანებდით.
> If you had come earlier, we wouldn't have been late (conditional clause).
> *დარწმუნებული ვარ,* ***რომ*** *მაპატიებ.*
> I am sure, you will forgive me (simple object modifier).
> *ორი საათი* ***რომ*** *გახდება, აქ ვიქნები.*
> When it's two o'clock, I'll be here (modifier of time).
> *ამ ქუჩაზე* ***რომ*** *მაღაზიაა, იქ შევხვდეთ.*
> Where the store is on this street, let's meet there (modifier of place).

Subordinating conjunctions may lead various types of adverbial clauses:

1. **Space:** სადაც (where), საიდანაც (from where), საითკენაც (to where), რომ (that)

   სადაც *შენ ხარ, ისიც იქ არის.*
   Where you are, he is there, too.

   საითკენაც *გაიხედავ, ყველგან ყვავილებია.*
   Wherever you look, there are flowers everywhere.

2. **Time:** რომ (that), როდესაც, როცა, როს, ოდეს (when), რაჟამს, რაწამს, რაწამსაც, თუ არა (as soon as), ვითარცა (like), რაკი (since), სანამ, როგორც, როგორც, ვიდრე – ვიდრემდის, მანამდის, მანამ-სანამ (until, till, before)

   როცა *ახალგაზრდა ვიყავი, ფეხბურთს ვთამაშობდი.*
   When I was young, I was playing football.

__სანამ__ ფეხსაცმელებს იყიდი, მოიზომე.
Before you buy shoes, try them on.

სახლში დაბრუნდები __თუ არა,__ დამირეკე.
As soon as you return home, call me.

3. **Cause:** რომ (so), რამეთუ, რადგან, რადგანაც, რაკი (since), ვინაიდან, იმიტომ რომ, ამიტომ რომ (because)

   __რადგან__ არ მიდიხარ, ამ წინადადების გადათარგმნაში მომეხმარე.
   Since you are not leaving, help me translate this sentence.

   ჩემი ძმა ლონდონში ვერ წავა, __იმიტომ რომ__ ძალიან დაკავებულია.
   My brother won't be able to go to London because he is very busy.

4. **Purpose:** რათა, რომ, იმისთვის რომ (so that, in order to)

   ისინი უკვე წავიდნენ __რათა__ კრებაზე დროულად მისულიყვნენ.
   They already left (in order) to get to the meeting on time.

5. **Condition:** თუ, თუკი, უკეთუ (if), ოღონდ (but), რომ (that)

   __თუკი__ დამეხმარები, ძალიან მადლობელი ვიქნები.
   If you help me, I'll be most grateful.

6. **Cause-and-consequence:** თუარა, თორემ (or, otherwise)

   დამიჯერე, __თორემ__ ინანებ!
   Listen to me, or you'll be regret.

7. **Oppositional:** თუმცა (however), თუნდაც, თუნდა, გინდ, გინდაც, რომ, რაგინდ (even if, no matter), როგორც – ისე (as – it).

   თქვენს აზრს პატივს ვცემ, __თუმცა__ ვერ დაგეთანხმებით.
   I respect your opinion, however, I can't agree with you.

   __რაგინდ__ ძლიერი ან მდიდარი იყო, სიკვდილს ვერ გაექცევი.
   No matter how strong or rich you are, you won't be able to run away from death.

The opposing clauses may be expressed either in negative or affirmative forms:

__როგორც__ ველოდით, __ისე__ მოხდა.
It happened as we expected.
__როგორც__ ველოდით, __ისე__ __არ__ მოხდა.
It didn't happen as we expected.
__როგორც__ გინდა, __ისე__ გააკეთებს.
He will do as you want.

როგორც *გინდა,* ***ისე ვერ*** *გააკეთებს.*
He cannot do as you want.
როგორც *გინდა,* ***ისე არ*** *გააკეთებს.*
He will not do as you want.
როგორც *იყო,* ***ისე*** *იქნება.*
It will be as it was.
როგორც *იყო,* ***ისე აღარ*** *იქნება.*
It will not be anymore as it was.

8. **Conclusion:** ასე რომ, ისე რომ (thus), რომ (that)

   ასე რომ, *ამით არაფერი შეიცვლება.*
   Thus, nothing can be changed by this.

9. **Comparative:** როგორც (as), ვითარცა, ვით (how), რარიგადაც (whatever way)

   როგორც იცი, ეს დიდი ხნის წინ მოხდა.
   As you know, this happened a long time ago.

10. **Agreement:** თუმცა (however), გინდ, თუნდ, გინდაც, თუნდაც (even if)

    მოვიდეს, ***თუნდაც*** *დაგვიანებით.*
    Let him come over, even if late.

Chapter 13

Particles

A particle is a part of speech that may be added to words or sentences. Particles added to a word either change or modify its meaning. They do not have any syntactic function but can add a semantic nuance to the sentence in which they are used.

There are two types of particles: the simple and complex. The former are undividable units like **აჰა, აი, ჰო, კი, ხომ, აბა**, etc., while the latter can be divided into their component parts. The majority of simple particles do not have their own lexical definition but impart a new meaning to the word to which they are added. Some of them may consist of a single letter, like ა or -ც:

დედაც ჩვენთან ერთად იყო (-ც is added to a noun).
Mother, too, was with us.
ეს ორიც მოგვეცით (-ც is added to a numeral).
Give us these two as well.
მეც იქ ვიყავი (-ც is added to a pronoun).
I, too, was there.

There is a group of simple particles the meaning of which is derived from the various words with independent lexical definition. Thus, the particles უნდა (should), ლამის (just about), ეგება (maybe), and თქვა (he said) are derived from verbs. ერთი (a, one), ეს (this), and რა (what) come from numerals and pronouns. Some are derived from adverbs: როდი (when), ოდეს (ever), აგერ (here), მერე (then).

Complex particles are composites combining various parts of speech: ხოლმე (used to), კინაღამ (almost), მეთქი (I said), თითქოს (as if, supposedly), აკი (didn't/you say), თითქმის (almost), ვაითუ (what if), დიახ (yes), ვითომ (as if), თურმე (apparently), etc.

In Georgian, particles have variety of functions. Some of them have a similar meaning and form a group of synonymous units.

DOI: 10.4324/9781315281131-16

It is impossible to translate adequately each particle into English; their meaning is clarified in a context:

ისე დავიღალე, ***ლამის*** *დამეძინოს.*
I am so tired, I am almost falling asleep.
ეგება *ხვალ არ იწვიმოს.*
Maybe it will not rain tomorrow.
ერთი *მითხარი, ეს რისთვის გინდა.*
Tell me, what do you want this for?
მე ამ პარკში ხშირად მოვდიოდი ***ხოლმე.***
I used to come to this park often.
კინაღამ *ხელი დავიწვი.*
I almost burnt my hand.
თითქოს *უნდა დაერეკა, მაგრამ არ დარეკა.*
He was supposed to call but didn't call.
აკი *მითხარი, რომ გამოივლიდი.*
Didn't you tell me you would come over?
ეს კაცი ***თურმე*** *მილიონერი ყოფილა.*
This man is apparently a millionaire.

13.1 Interrogative particles

The interrogative particles are **ხომ**, **განა**, **ნუთუ**, and **თუ**. They are used in interrogative sentences, but each of them may have a slightly different meaning. Thus, **ხომ** and **განა** clarify or stress the statement expressed in a sentence; **ნუთუ** implies surprise.

ხომ *არ წასულა?*
He has not left, has he?
წავიდა, ***ხომ?***
He left, didn't he?
ხომ *გითხარი?!*
Didn't I tell you?!
ჭკვიანია, არ ეტყობა ***თუ?***
He is clever, doesn't it show?
განა *ესმოდა, რასაც აკეთებდა?*
He did not understand what he was doing, did he?
ნუთუ *არ იცოდი?*
Is it possible that you didn't know?
ნუთუ *უკვე სამი საათია?*
Could it be (that) it is three o'clock already?

13.2 Limiting particles

The limiting particles are *-მე*, *-ღა*, *-ღა(ცა)*, and *-ვე*. They are simple particles and are added to various nouns, pronouns, and numerals sometimes forming derivative meanings.

რამდენიმე მეგობარი შევიკრიბეთ.
A few of us, friends, got together.
რამდენიმე წუთის შემდეგ ტელეფონმა ისევ დარეკა.
After a few minutes, the phone rang again.

In these sentences, ***-მე*** is added to the nominative form of the interrogative pronoun *რამდენი* (how many). The derivative form *რამდენი-**მე*** (a few) may be further extended with the particle *-ღა*, thus stressing its limiting meaning *რამდენი**მე-ღა*** (only a few):

*რამდენი**მეღა** დარჩა ცოცხალი.*
Only a few are still alive.

The particle *-ღაც(ა)* consisting of two parts *-ღა* and *ც(ა)* may be added to an interrogative pronoun denoting uncertainty or indefiniteness: ***რამდენი*** (how many) – ***რამდენი-ღაცა*** (a certain amount), ***რომელი*** (which) – ***რომელი-ღაცა*** (one of, certain):

*ეს ამბავი **რომელიღაც** გაზეთში ეწერა, მაგრამ არ მახსოვს რომელში.*
This story was printed in one of the newspapers, but I don't remember which one.
***რომელიღაც** თქვენგანს დაურეკავს პოლიციაში.*
One of you has (apparently) called the police.
*ახალ წლამდე ორი კვირა**ღა** დარჩა.*
There are about (only) two weeks left till the New Year.
*დღეს ვის**ღა** ახსოვს მისი სახელი.*
Today who remembers his name?
*ათი სტუდენტიდან ოთხი**ღა** დადის ლექციებზე.*
Out of ten students only four attend classes.

The particle ***-ვე*** may be added to nouns, numerals, adjectives, and adverbs stressing their meaning:

მამაჩემი ამ სახლში დაიბადა და ამ სახლში***ვე*** გარდაიცვალა.
My father was born in this house and died in this same house.
მე აქ***ვე*** ვცხოვრობ.
I live right here.
ეს ხუთი***ვე*** წიგნი ჩემია.
All these five books are mine.

The numerals with the particle -*ვე* decline as -*ე*-ending nouns and may have case endings and postpositions added to them:

> ორი**ვემ** უარი თქვა კინოში წასვლაზე (erg. case).
> Both declined to go to the movies,
> სამი**ვესთან** კარგი ურთიერთობა მაქვს (the dative case with the postposition -**თან**).
> I have good relationship with all three of them.

13.3 Negation particles

The negative particles are **არ**, **არა**, **ვერ**, **ნუ**, **არც**, **ვერც**, **ნურც**, **აღარ**, **ვეღარ**, **ნუღარ**, **აღარც**,**ვეღარც**, **ნუღარც**, and **როდი**. The basic negative particles are არ, ვერ, and ნუ, and they differ from each other semantically.

არ expresses categorical negation of a statement:

> დღეს **არ** დაურეკავს.
> Today he has not called.

ვერ indicates the inability of a person to carry out the action expressed with a verb:

> დღეს ვერ დარეკავს.
> Today he will not be able to call.

ნუ and **არ** are both used to denote negative imperative, **ნუ** preceding verbs in present or future tenses, **არ** preceding verbs in the optative. **არ** adds more urgency and force to the verb it precedes; **ნუ** conveys a request rather than an order.

> **ნუ** ცეკვავთ! (Present tense) = **არ** იცეკვოთ! (Optative)
> Do not dance!
> **ნუ** იხმაურებთ! (Future tense) = **არ** იხმაუროთ! (Optative)
> Do not make noise!
> **ნუ** წახვალთ! (Future tense) = **არ** წახვიდეთ! (Optative)
> Don't leave!

In a dialogue, a negative sentence with the particle **არ** may be replaced with the negation **არა**:

> ლექცია დაიწყო?
> Has the lecture started?
> **არა.**
> No.
> ლექცია **არ** დაწყებულა.
> The lecture has not started.

არ and **არა** may replace each other, especially when forming words with negative meaning in the same manner as does the prefix *უ*-:

უცოდინარი – **არ**მცოდნე – ignorant (one who does not know, clueless)

უთქმელი – **არ**თქმული – unsaid

არაკაცი – villain (lit. *not man*, *not human*)

არასანდო – untrustworthy

არასერიოზული – not serious

არ particle may express surprise:

> *მეც* **არ** *გამიკვირდა!*
> Wasn't I surprised, too! (It did surprise me!)
> *თურმე გამოცდაზე* **არ** *ჩაჭრილა!*
> Apparently, he did not fail the exam!

არ, **ვერ**, and **ნუ** particles may be extended with the particles **-ღა** and **-ც** or even both of them together: **არც**, **ვერც**, **ნურც**, **აღარ(ც)**, **ვეღარ(ც)**, **ნუღარ(ც)**. The particles **არც**, **ვერც**, and **ნურც** are most frequently used in pairs and correspond to English *either . . . or* and *neither . . . nor*.

> **არც** მისი მისამართი ვიცი და **არც** ტელეფონის ნომერი.
> I know neither his address, nor phone number.
> *დღეს* **ვერც** *მაღაზიაში წავედი და* **ვერც** *ბაზარში.*
> Today I was not able to go either to the store or to the market.
> **ნურც** *დაურეკავ და* **ნურც** *წერილს გაუგზავნი. //***არც** დაურეკო და **არც** წერილი გაუგზავნო.
> Do not call (him) and neither send (him) a letter.

The particles **აღარ(ც)**, **ვეღარ(ც)**, and **ნუღარ(ც)** imply change of intention expressed with the verb they precede. With the particle **-ც**, they are used in pairs as well.

> **აღარ** *მინდა მასთან შეხვედრა.*
> I don't want to meet him anymore (i.e. I intended to meet him but changed my mind).
> *წვიმა დაიწყო და მაღაზიაში* **აღარ** *წავედი.*
> It started raining and I didn't go to the store (i.e. I intended to do so but changed my mind).
> **აღარც** *მშია,* **აღარც** *მწყურია.*
> I am neither hungry nor thirsty.
> *ბოდიში, რომ* **ვერ** *გნახე, როცა თბილისში ვიყავი.*
> Sorry, I couldn't (was not able) to see you when I was in Tbilisi.

ვერც მე და *ვერც* შენ ამ ადამიანს ვერ ვუშველით.
Neither I nor you can help this person.
ნუღარ ილაპარაკებ ამ თემაზე.
Do not speak on this topic anymore.
ნუღარც წერ და **ნუღარც** კითხულობ, წადი, გაისეირნე.
Do not write and do not read either, go out for a stroll.

The particle **როდი**, seldom used in spoken Georgian, has the same function as **არ**:

ვაფრთხილებ, მაგრამ **როდი** მისმენენ. ვაფრთხილებ, მაგრამ **არ** მისმენენ.
I warn (keep warning) them, but they do not listen.

13.4 Affirmative particles

The affirmative particles are დიახ and ჰო, კი; the former is requited in polite forms of speech. They are most frequently used in dialogues and may replace an entire sentence; the former is a polite form of the latter:

წავიდა?
Did (he) leave?
დიახ./ჰო./კი.
Yes, sir/madam/Yes.
მოიტანე ყვავილები?
Have you brought the flowers?
დიახ/ჰო/კი, მოვიტანე ყვავილები.
Yes, sir/madam/Yes, I have brought the flowers.

13.5 Reported speech particles

The indirect speech particles are -მეთქი, -თქო, and -ო. They usually convey the utterance of a speaker verbatim, but the words spoken by him or her are not put in quotation marks. The particle -მეთქი is derived from the phrase **მე ვთქვი** (I said) and, therefore, is used by a speaker repeating his own words to someone or to himself.

თქვენ აქ ცხოვრობთ-**მეთქი** – ვკითხე უცნობს.
I asked the stranger: Do you live here?
რატომ არ მოდის-**მეთქი**, გავიფიქრე.
Why isn't he coming over, I thought (said to myself).

However, when more than one speaker's words are repeated, the particle -ო is used:

> *რატომ არ მოდის**ო**, ვიკითხეთ.*
> We asked (thought/said to ourselves): why isn't he coming over?

The particle -**თქო** is derived from **თქვა** (he said) and is used when a speaker asks someone to convey his/her words to the third party. The verb forms of such sentences refer to the third person(s) in agreement with the semantics of -**თქო**.

> *ნინო, ბატონ მერაბ-ს უთხარი, ახლა დრო არა აქვს* **-თქო.**
> Nino, tell Mr. Merab, I don't have time right now (lit. *He does not have time, he said*).
> *შინ მალე დაბრუნდება-**თქო**, დაამშვიდე დედაჩემი.*
> I will return home soon, calm Mother down (lit. *He will return home soon, he said*).

The particle **-ო** is used when the words of a second or third party is repeated or conveyed.

> *მოვალ**ო**, ხომ მითხარი?*
> I will come over, didn't you say? (The speaker is repeating the words of his/her interlocutor.)
> *მოვალ**ო**, შემპირდა იგი.*
> I will come over, he promised me. (The speaker is repeating the words of a third party.)
> *თქვენი სტატია მიღებულია**ო**, – გამახარა რედაქტორმა.*
> Your article is accepted, the editor made me happy. (The speaker is repeating the words of a third party.)

13.6 Approximating particles

The approximating particles are **ოდე**, **ლამის**, **კინაღამ**, and **თითქმის**. All these particles are synonymous and could be translated as *almost*, *about*, *just about*, or *nearly*. The particle **-ოდე** is added to numerals and may have various case endings. The other three precede nouns and verbs.

> *ორი**ოდე** გვერდი დამრჩა წასაკითხი.*
> I have about two pages left to read.
> ***თითქმის** დავამთავრე ჩემი სტატია.*
> I almost finished my article.

__კინაღამ__ დამავიწყდა შენი გაფრთხილება.
I almost forgot to warn you.
ლამის გული წამივიდეს.
I am close to fainting.
მისმა ვალმა **ლამის** ათი ათასს მიაღწია.
His debt reached nearly ten thousand.

13.7 Emphasizing particles

The emphasizing articles are *-ც/-ცა, -ცკი, კიდევ, კიდეც, მაინც*, and *უკვე*.

The particle *კიდევ* has two functions; it is an adverb meaning *more* or *again* and, as such, always precedes a verb, but in interrogative sentences it acts as a particle *else*. In spoken Georgian the final letter -*ვ* is often dropped.

__კიდე(ვ) მითხარი__, რა იცი ამის შესახებ.
Tell me more what you know about it.
__კიდე(ვ) მისწერე__ წერილი.
Write (him) a letter again.
__კიდე(ვ) წაიკითხე__ და ზეპირად ისწავლე.
Read (it) again and learn it by heart.
__კიდე(ვ)__ რა მოიტანა?
What else did he bring?
__კიდე(ვ)__ ვინ მოდის კინოში?
Who else is coming to the movies?
__კიდე(ვ)__ რას მეტყვი? What else will you tell me?

The particle **მაინც** refers to a verb and intensifies its meaning and often implies the need for clarification.

ბევრი ახალი ამბავი მოგვიყვა.
He told us a lot of news.
__მაინც__ რა თქვა?
What exactly/specifically did he say?

მაინც is sometimes doubled, forming a new particle, **მანც(ა)დამაინც**, with or without the euphonic -ა and intensifies the meaning of the word it precedes:

__მაინცადამაინც__ მე უნდა გამოგყვე?
Should I specifically (and nobody else) accompany you?
__მაინცადამაინც__ ეს კაცი რატომ დაასახელე?
Why did you name this particular person?
__მაინცდამაინც__ დღეს იწვიმა! – It just had to rain today!

The particle უკვე corresponds to English *already*:

> *უკვე დაასრულა სამუშაო.*
> (He) already finished the work.
> *უკვე ყველამ იცის მისი სახელი.*
> Already everyone knows his name.
> *უკვე ყველგან მღერიან ამ სიმღერას.*
> Already everywhere they sing this song.

13.8 Particles expressing wish or desire

ნეტავ*(ი)* and ნეტა particles expressing a wish are used with verbs in subjunctive tenses. In some cases, especially when placed at the end of a sentence, they may be translated as *I wonder*.

> ნეტავ*(ი)* *მალე დაასრულებდე ამ საქმეს.*
> I wish you should finish this business soon.
> ნეტავ*(ი)* *ჩემი ვაჟი მალე დაბრუნდებოდეს.*
> I wish my son should return soon.
> *რას ფიქრობს,* ნეტავ*(ი)?*
> What does (he) thinks, I wander (lit. *I wish I knew*).

Sometimes ნეტავი is placed at the end of a sentence in which a verb is in indicative mood. Without this particle it would be a regular interrogative sentence.

> **რას ფიქრობს, ნეტავი?**
> What does he think, I wonder?
> **რას ფიქრობს?**
> What does he think?
> **სად წავიდა, ნეტავი?**
> Where did he go, I wonder?
> **სად წავიდა?**
> Where did he go?

დაე and ვინძლო are particles denoting a wish or goodwill in someone's address. Their meaning may be approximated in English as *let/may it be* or *let/may it happen*. They sound somewhat affected and are seldom used in contemporary Georgian.

> დაე *აღსრულდეს უფლის ნება!*
> May the will of God be fulfilled!
> დაე *მუდამ ანათებდეს მზე!*
> Let the sun shine forever!

დაე ასრულდეს შენი ოცნება!
May your dream come true!
ვინძლო *მტერი არ გაახარო.*
May you do not let the enemy rejoice.

13.9 Selective particles

The selective particles are **-ღა**, ***მხოლოდ***, and ***მარტო***, meaning *only*; **-ღა** is added to any part of speech except verb; ***მხოლოდ*** and ***მარტო*** are independent words. As a rule, ***მარტო*** precedes a subject of a sentence, and ***მხოლოდ*** may be used with other parts of speech.

ახლა**ღა** გავიგე ეს ამბავი. = **მხოლოდ** ეხლა გავიგე ეს ამბავი.
Only now did I find out about it.
ერთი სტატია**ღა** დამრჩა წასაკითხი. = **მარტო/მხოლოდ** ერთი სტატია დამრჩა წასაკითხი.
I have only one article left to read.

13.10 Particles expressing possibility or supposition

იქნებ, ***ეგებ***, and ***სწორედ*** are the particles expressing possibility or supposition. The first two corresponding to English ***may be,perhaps*** are interchangeable. The particle ***სწორედ*** (***exactly, precisely***) is also used in same contexts but with the modal verb ***უნდა*** (should, must) preceding it.

იქნებ/ეგებ გვითხრას, რა აწუხებს.
Maybe he will tell us what bothers (him).
იქნებ/ეგებ მიხვდა *თავის შეცდომას.*
Maybe (he) understood (his) mistake.
სწორედ ჩვენ ***უნდა გვითხრას***, რა აწუხებს.
He should tell us precisely (not others) what's bothering (him).
სწორედ *ახლა* ***უნდა მიხვდეს*** *თავის შეცდომას.*
It's precisely now that (he) should understand (his) mistake.

13.11 Imitative particles

There are two imitative particles ***თითქოს*** (supposedly, looks like) and ***ვითომ*** (as if, supposedly). The particle ***თითქოს*** is always connected with a verb and indicates a doubt or error in judgment. ***ვითომ*** implies the falsity of a statement.

> ***თითქოს*** *უნდა ეწვიმა.*
> It looked like it was going to rain (but it did not).
> ***თითქოს*** *აპირებდა ჩვენთან მოსვლას.*
> He was supposedly coming to us (but he did not).

The particle ***თითქოს*** is often used with a verb in perfect subjunctive, thus repudiating or casting doubt on the action expressed by it.

> *ისე ტრაბახობს,* ***თითქოს*** *რამე სასარგებლო* ***გაეკეთებინოს.***
> He boasts so as if he had done something useful (i.e. he has not done anything useful).
> *ჩვენზეა გაბრაზებული,* ***თითქოს*** *ჩვენ არ გაგვეფრთხილებინოს.*
> He is angry at us as if we had not warned him about it (i.e. we did warn him).
> ***ვითომ*** *რამე იცოდეს, ისე ლაპარაკობს.*
> He speaks as if knows anything (i.e. it's doubtful he does).
> ***ვითომ*** *ვერ დამინახა, ისე ჩამიარა.*
> He walked past me as if he didn't see me (i.e. he probably saw me).
> ***ვითომ*** *დარეკავს?*
> (Do you think) he might call?

When the particle ***ვითომ*** precedes a noun, it indicates doubtfulness or even false quality: ***ვითომ*** *პოეტი* (supposed poet), ***ვითომ*** *გმირი* (supposedly a hero).

13.12 Indicative particles

აი, ***აჰა***, and ***ჰა*** are the indicative particles. All three are synonymous and correspond to English *here it is*, *here we are*, etc.

> ***აი,*** *ჩვენი სახლი.*
> Here is our house.
> ***აჰა,*** *მოვედით!*
> Here we are (we arrived).
> ***ჰა,*** *შენ ბურთი, წადი და ითამაშე.*
> Here is a ball for you, go and play.

13.13 Particle denoting frequency of action

The particle ***ხოლმე*** indicates frequency of an action. It is used exclusively with a verb preceding it and denotes repetitive character of an action.

ჩვენ ხშირად ვიკრიბებოდით ***ხოლმე*** *ჩემს ბინაში, ვყვებოდით* ***ხოლმე*** *გასართობ ამბებს და ვიცინოდით* ***ხოლმე.***
We would often gather in my apartment, (would) tell funny stories, and (would) laugh.

13.14 Particle denoting not witnessed action

The particle *თურმე* is used to denote an action that the speaker has not witnessed or does not remember. It is most often used with verbs in the perfect tense.

თურმე *წერილი მისთვის უკვე გამიგზავნია და არ მახსოვდა.*
Apparently, I have already sent him a letter but did not remember.
წუხელ ***თურმე*** *წვიმა მოსულა.*
Looks like/apparently it rained last night.
ჩემთვის ***თურმე*** *ფეხსაცმელები უყიდია.*
Apparently, (he) bought shoes for me.

13.15 Parts of speech functioning as particles

The cardinal numeral *ერთი* and verb *მოდი* are used as particles.

ერთი is a numeral, but when used in a sentence in the imperative mood, it softens the order, making it sound as a request. *მოდი* (come) is a verb but as a particle it is placed at the beginning of a sentence and corresponds to English *let's*.

ერთი *შენი ამბავი მოგვიყევი.*
Tell us your story (please).
ერთი *ეგ ჭიქა მომაწოდე.*
Pass me that glass (please).
მოდი, *კინოში წავიდეთ!*
Let's go to the movies.
მოდი, *გიორგის დავურეკოთ!*
Let's call George.

Chapter 14

Interjections

The interjection is a word, phrase, or sound grammatically unrelated to any other part of a sentence, expressing an emotion, feeling, or mood of the speaker.

In Georgian, most often used interjections are sounds consisting of the consonant *ჰ* together with various vowels: *აჰ, ეჰ, იჰ, ოჰ, უჰ, აჰა, ეჰე, ოჰო, უჰუ, ჰეი, ჰაუ, ჰოი*, etc. Less frequently other consonants are used as well: *ვაჰ/ვახ, ფუ, ფუი, იფ, ფუჰ, ვაი, ვუი, ჰერი, ჰერი*, etc.

Some interjections consist of vowels only: *ოი, ეი, აი, უი*, etc.

Joy/delight	***უჰ/ოჰ,*** *როგორ გამახარე!* Oh, you made me happy!
Sadness	***ოჰ/ოი,*** *რა ძნელია მარტოობა!* Oh, how difficult loneliness is.
Surprise	***ოჰო//ოჰ,*** *ეს ვინ მოსულა!* Oh, look who is here!
Disgust	***ფუ/ფუი,ფუჰ,*** *რა საზიზღარი სუნია!* Ugh, what a foul smell!
Regret	***ეჰ/ოჰ,*** *ამას არ მოველოდი!* Oh, I did not expect this! ***ოჰ/ეჰ,*** *როგორ შევრცხვით!* Ah, shame on us!
Remorse	***უი/ოი,*** *დაგვაგვიანდა!* Ooh, we are late!
Anger	***ვაჰ/ვახ,*** *რამდენჯერ უნდა გავიმეორო?!* Hey, how many times should I repeat this?!

(Continued)

DOI: 10.4324/9781315281131-17

(Continued)

Approval	*ჰოი, ჩემო მშვენიერო!* Oh, my beauty! *იფ, იფ, რა გემრიელია!* Mmm, it's delicious!
Pain	*ვაი/აჰ, როგორ მტკივა თავი!* Ah, this headache! *ვაი, თითი ვიტკინე!* Ouch, I hurt my finger!
Wish	*ოჰ, ნეტავ ჩემს შვილს მალე შევხვდებოდე!* Oh, how I wish to see my son soon!
Ridicule	*ოჰ, რადგან შენ იტყვი!* Well, if you say so!
Offer	*ჰა/აჰა შენ ფული და ნაყინი იყიდე!* Here, take this money and buy yourself an ice cream.
Surprise	*ვაა, ეს არ ვიცოდი.* Gee, I didn't know that!
Suggestion/ invitation to go somewhere	*მეგობრებო, ბათუმისკენ* ***ჰერი, ჰერი!*** Friends, let's go to Batumi.

As these examples show, often one and the same interjection may express various emotions or feelings.

The interjection may be a word or phrase:

ბიჭოს is derived from the word ***ბიჭი*** (boy) in the vocative case, *ბიჭ-ო*, which in its turn is used as a new stem in the dative, *ბიჭო-ს!* Usually, it expresses surprise or less frequently irritation:

ბიჭოს*, მოუგია თამაში!*
Look at that, he won the game!
სანამდე უნდა მალოდინო?! ***ბიჭოს!***
How long should I wait for you?! For God's sake!

ბიჭო, the vocative form of ***ბიჭი***, may be used as an interjection expressing surprise or excitement:

ბიჭო, ბიჭო! *ნახე, რა ხდება!*
Boy, oh boy! Look what's happening!

აფსუს expresses regret: ***აფსუს!*** *რა ლამაზი სურა გავტეხე.*
Ah, what a beautiful vase I broke.

ბარაქალა indicates approval:

ბარაქალა! *საამაყო ქალი ხარ!*
Bravo! You can be proud of yourself!

გლახ/ვაგლახ: გლახ is a shortened form of the word **გლახ-აკ-ი** (beggar, wretch); **ვაგლახ** is a combination of two interjections **ვა** and **გლახ.** They both express sorrow, grief, or regret:

ვაგლახ, *ჩემო თავო, როგორ დავუძლურდი!*
Woe to me, how enfeebled I have become.
ვაგლახ, *იმ გმირებიდან არავინ არის ცოცხალი!*
Alas, not one of those heroes is alive!

ვაშა expresses excitement:

ვაშა! *გავიმარჯვეთ!* ***ვაშა!***
Hurrah! We won!

ყოჩაღ is derived from an adjective **ყოჩაღ-ი** (energetic, sprightly) and is used as an interjection in its stem form expressing approval:

ყოჩაღ, *გოგოებო! კარგი საქმე გაგიკეთებიათ!*
Well done, girls! You did a good job!

The two interjections – **აბა** and ***მაშ*** – are used in response to someone's statement and express concurrence, joy, or agreement with the speaker's statement. Sometimes they are interchangeable and, depending on a context, may have several different meanings, like *indeed*, *here*, *then*, *does it mean*, *you can say so*, *yup*, etc.

ეს რა კარგი ხაჭაპური გამოგიცხვია!
What a great cheese-bread you have baked!
მაშ! *ვიცი როგორ გამოვაცხო.*
Yup! I know how to bake.
ხვალ ლექციები არა მაქვს.
I don't have classes tomorrow.
მაშ /აბა *მოდიხარ ჩვენთან?*
Does it mean you are coming with us?
ხელი ვიტკინე.
I hurt my hand.
აბა *მაჩვენე.*
Here, show it to me.
ეს შენი წიგნი არ არის, ჩემია.
This is not your book, it's mine.

აბა/მაშ *ჩემი სად არის?*
Then, where is mine?
ასეთი საშინელი სიცხე თბილისში არ მახსოვს.
I don't remember such terrible heat in Tbilisi.
აბა!
Indeed!

Some words are used as interjections in their shortened forms:

ჩუ is a shortened form of the adjective **ჩუმ-ი** (quiet, silent) or its adverbial case form **ჩუმად** (quietly, silently)

ჩუ! ჩუ! მოვუსმინოთ ახალ ამბებს!
Shush! Shush! Let's listen to the news!
ჩუ! არ ისმის!
Shush! Impossible to hear!

სუ is synonymous with **ჩუმად** and expresses a demand to be quiet:

სუ! მომასმენინეთ რას ამბობს!
Shush! Let me hear what he is saying!
სუ! ნუ ტირით!
Hush! Don't cry!

აგე is the shortened form of the adverbial of place **აგერ** (here) and is used to point at something or someone and corresponds to English *here* or *there*, depending on a context:

აგე, სტუმრებიც მოვიდნენ!
Here, our guests have arrived!
აგე, გოლიც გაიტანეს!
There, they scored a goal!

In Georgian language there are interjections that are used specifically for animals or birds to shoo them away or urge them to move faster:

ჰაუ (for birds):	*ჰაუ, ჰაუ, ჩიტებო, ნუ შემიჭამეთ ბალი!* Shoo, shoo away, birds, don't eat my cherries.
აცხა (for cats):	*აცხა, კატა! წადი აქედან!* Shoo away, cat! Go away from here!
აქშა/აქში/ქშა/ქში (mostly for chickens):	*აქშა, აქშა, ქათმებო! ყვავილები არ დამიკენკოთ!* Shoo, shoo away, chicken! Don't peck on my flowers.

აცე (for donkeys):	*აცე, ვირო! ნაბიჯს მოუჩქარე!* Hey, donkey, move faster!
აჩუ (for horses):	**აჩუ, აჩუ, ცხენო!** Giddy-up, giddy-up horse!
ჰაიტ (to scare animals, or sometimes people):	**ჰაიტ!** *აქ რას აკეთებთ?!* Hey, what are you doing here?!
ოჰოჰოო (for oxen):	*ოჰოჰოო, აქეთ გამოდით! ამ გზაზე იარეთ!* Hey, move this way!

Sometimes, when interjections are used as nouns, they can be declinable:

> **ვაი-ს** (interjection **ვაი** in the dative case) *გავეყარე და* **უი-ს/უი-ს** (interjection **ვუი/უი** in the dative case) *შევეყარე.*
> I ran away from one woe and got into another.
> **ვაშა-ს** (interjection **ვაშა** in the genitive case). *ძახილი ქვეყანას ვერ ააშენებს.*
> Shouting hurrah won't do much good (lit. *will not build the country*).

In a sentence with an interjection, the predicate is often absent. In the following examples, interjections function as the subject of these sentences.

> **ფუი** *შენს კაცობას!*
> Shame on you!
> **ვაი** *ჩემს თავს!*
> Woe to me!
> **ვაშა** *თქვენს გამარჯვებას!*
> Hurrah to your victory!
> **ბარაქალა** *ჩვენს შრომას!*
> Bravo to our deeds!

Syntactic structures

Chapter 15

Noun phrase

15.1 Noun/subject

The subject is the main part of a sentence. It answers the questions **ვინ** (who) or **რა** (what) and is most frequently denoted with a noun but may be denoted by a pronoun, adjective, verbal noun, numeral, and participle.

> ***მატარებელი*** (noun) *სადგურიდან გავიდა.*
> The train left the station.
> ***მწვანე*** (adjective) *ჩემი საყვარელი ფერია.*
> Green is my favourite colour.
> ***მაღალი*** (adjective) *გაოცებული იყურებოდა.*
> The tall one looked bewildered.
> ***ერთი*** (numeral) *გაიქცა.*
> One ran away.
> ***მეორეს*** (numeral) *გაქცევა არ უნდოდა.*
> The second one did not want to run away.
> ***იგი*** (pronoun) *ცნობილი მომღერალია.*
> He is a famous singer.
> ***ჩვენ*** (pronoun) მალე დავბრუნდებით.
> We will return soon.
> თქვენი **ნახვა** (verbal noun) ძალზე სასიამოვნოა.
> It's very nice to see you.

The case of the subject is always determined by the verb denoting the predicate. If the predicate is a I or III conjugation verb, its subject will change its case in all three series; if it is a II and IV conjugation verb, its subject remains unchanged. In most cases, the sentence begins with the subject, but its place depends on the speaker, provided that the chosen word order does not obscure the meaning.

In the sentence -***მატარებელი*** (noun) *სადგურიდან გავიდა* – the subject may be shifted around: *სადგურიდან* ***მატარებელი*** *გავიდა;*

DOI: 10.4324/9781315281131-19

გავიდა სადგურიდან ***მატარებელი;*** or *გავიდა* ***მატარებელი*** *სადგურიდან*. The structure of the sentence in all these variations remains the same, but each word order reflects the speaker's attitude to the reported fact, and therefore, its different components are stressed.

In some cases, changing the word order, especially shifting the subject, may make the information ambiguous. This happens if the subject is an adjective. Thus, in the sentence ***მაღალი*** *გაოცებული იყურებოდა* (the tall one looked bewildered), changing the word order into *გაოცებული* ***მაღალი*** *იყურებოდა* (the bewildered tall one was looking) will change the function of the adjective ***გაოცებული***. However, changing the place of a subject denoted with an adjective does not always obscure the meaning. In the sentence ***მწვანე*** *ჩემი საყვარელი ფერია* (green is my favourite colour), shifting the subject will not change the meaning: *ჩემი საყვარელი ფერია* ***მწვანე;*** *ჩემი საყვარელი* ***მწვანე*** *ფერია*.

15.2 Noun/direct and indirect objects

In Georgian, both the direct and indirect objects are main parts of sentence. Their presence in a sentence depends on the verb denoting predicate. Monopersonal verbs do not have objects. A predicate denoted with a bipersonal transitive verb indicates the presence of a subject and a direct object; if a bipersonal verb is intransitive, the sentence will have a subject and indirect object; a predicate denoted with tripersonal verb implies the presence of both a direct and indirect object. If a trivalent verb is in one of the III series forms, the sentence will have a subject and direct object.

The predicate is a monopersonal verb:

> *გოგონა* (subject) *ხის ჩრდილში ზის* (predicate).
> The girl sits in the shade of the tree.

The predicate is a bipersonal transitive verb:

> *მასწავლებელმა* (S) *ფანქრები* (Od) *დაარიგა* (P).
> The teacher *distributed pencils.*

The predicate is a tripersonal transitive verb:

> *მასწავლებელმა* (S) *ბავშვებს* (Oid) *ფანქრები* (Od) *დაათლევინა*.
> The teacher made (helped) the children sharpen the pencils.

The predicate is a tripersonal verb in a III series form:

მასწავლებელს (S) *ბავშვებისთვის* (Opostposition) *ფანქრები* (Od) *დაუთლევინებია.*
The teacher has made (helped) the children sharpen the pencils.

The case of the subject as well as the direct and indirect objects is determined by the verb denoting predicate. The indirect object is always in the dative. The direct object is in the dative case when the verb denoting predicate is in a I series form; it is in the nominative if the verb is in a II or III series form. The direct and indirect objects are both in the dative case if the predicate is denoted with a transitive verb in I series, but they are differentiated from each other when the verb denoting predicate is shifted to another series:

გამყიდველ-ი (S) ***ქალ-ს*** (dative case object) ***ხურდა-ს*** (dative case object) *უბრუნებს.*
The seller returns the change to the woman.

In order to differentiate the direct and indirect object from each other, the predicate should be put in any of the II series verb form:

გამყიდველ-მა (S) ***ქალ-ს*** (dative case indirect object) ***ხურდ-ა*** (nominative case direct object) *დაუბრუნა.*
The seller returned the change to the woman.

Like the subject, both the direct and indirect objects may be denoted with any noun, pronoun, adjective, numeral, verbal noun, participle, or even particles.

ერთმა (S, numeral) *მეორეს* (Od, numeral) *ყურში რაღაც* (Od, pronoun) *ჩასჩურჩულა.*
One (person) whispered into the other's ear.
მე (S, pronoun) *შენ* (Oid, pronoun) *ის* (Od, pronoun) *შარშან მოგეცი.*
I gave it to you last year.
მე (Oid, pronoun) *მწვანე* (S, adjective) *წითელს* (Od, adjective) *მირჩევნია.*
I prefer the green (colour) to the red.
მე ***არას*** (Od, negative particle) *არ ვიღებ,* ***არა*** *არ მითხრა.*
I don't accept a *no*, don't tell me *no*.

A sentence may lack any of its main parts, a subject or object, but the verb denoting the predicate implies the relevant pronouns. In the sentence ***ის შარშან მოგეცი*** (gave it last year), the person markers of the predicate ***მოგეცი*** points at the missing subject and indirect object: *მე შენ ის შარშან მოგეცი* – *I* gave it to *you* last year. Like a subject, a direct and indirect object may be shifted around as long as the chosen word order does not obscure the meaning of the sentence: *ის შარშან* ***მე შენ*** *მოგეცი; შარშან* ***მე*** *ის* ***შენ*** *მოგეცი;* ***შენ*** *მოგეცი ის* ***მე*** *შარშან etc.*

15.3 Adjectives

The adjectives can modify the subjects, direct objects, and indirect objects. They can also be used without a modified noun. There are two kinds of adjectives: the attributive adjective and genitive modifier. The attributive adjective describes or qualifies a noun or pronoun and is denoted with a primary or derivative adjective and an attributive modifier. It answers the questions: ***რომელი*** (which), ***როგორი*** (what kind), ***რამდენი*** (how many/much), ***მერამდენე*** (which one), ***სადაური*** (from where), and ***როდინდელი*** (how old, of what time). A genitive modifier is a noun or a word semantically equal to noun and denotes not quality or quantity of something but refers to the word it modifies. It answers the questions ***ვისი*** (whose) and ***რისი*** (of what).

15.3.1 Attributive adjectives

An attributive modifier may be a noun, adjective, numeral, or pronoun. An attributive adjective whose stem ends with a consonant agrees with the modified noun in case. If the adjective ends with vowel, it does not agree with the modified noun in case.

ბატონი (a noun) ***დავითი*** *მობრძანდა.*
Mr. David arrived.
ექიმ (a noun) ***გიორგაძეს*** *ვეძებთ.*
We are looking for Doctor Giorgadze.
გუშინდელი (adjective) ***პური*** *დავჭერით.*
We cut yesterday's bread.
ბევრ (numeral) ***შეკითხვას*** *სვამდა.*
He asked a lot of questions.
პირველ (numeral) ***რიგს*** *სტუმრებისთვის ინახავდნენ.*
The first row was reserved for the guests.
რექტორთან შეხვედრაზე ***ხუთასამდე*** (numeral) ***სტუდენტი*** *შეიკრიბა.*
About five hundred students gathered to meet the rector.
ეს (demonstrative pronoun) ***სკოლა*** *დავამთავრე.*
I graduated from this school.
ჩემს (possessive pronoun) ***ვაჟს*** *მსახიობობა უნდა.*

My son wants to be an actor.
რამდენი (interrogative pronoun) **სტუდენტია კლასში?**
How many students are in the class?
ვიღაც (indefinite pronoun) **უცნობი** მოგვიახლოვდა.
Some stranger approached us.
ერთი (indefinite pronoun) **სტუდენტი** განსაკუთრებით აქტიურობდა.
One student was particularly active.
მწვანე (adjective) **კაბას** გიყიდი.
I will buy you a green dress.
ყველა (definite pronoun) **სახლი** შეიღება.
All houses got painted.

An attributive adjective is always a part of the noun phrase and is attached either to the subject, direct and indirect object, another adjective, or an adverb. In the sentence ჩემი ძმა **მორიდებული ადამიანია** (my brother is a timid person), there are two modified nouns: **ჩემი ძმა** (my brother), which is the noun phrase of the sentence, and **მორიდებული ადამიანია** (=ადამიანი არის, is a timid person), which is a predicate. The attributive adjective **მორიდებული** (timid) modifies the noun part of the predicate.

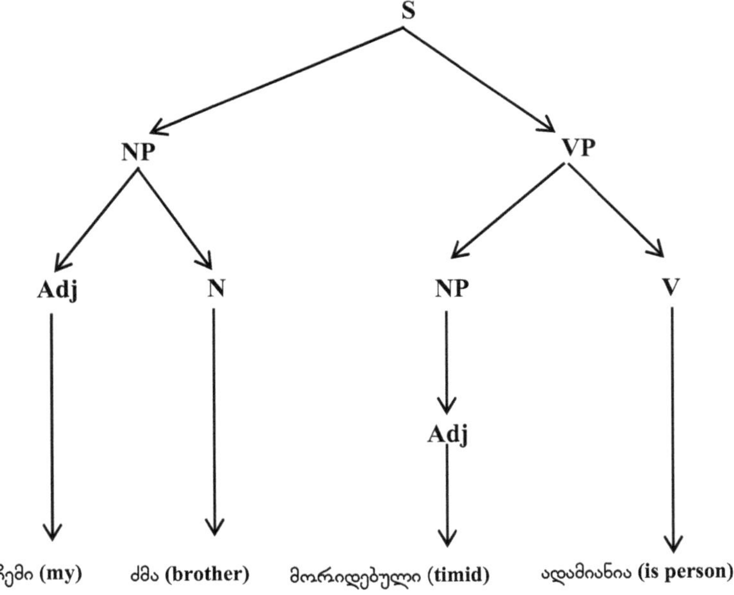

The attributive adjective either precedes or follows the word it modifies or is separated from it by other parts of the sentence. The

agreement of such syntactic couples in case and number determines their unity even when they are distanced from each other. The type of their agreement in case and number depends on the stem of an adjective and its place in a sentence. If an attributive adjective has a vowel-ending stem, it remains unchanged in a prepositional order: *მივადექით* ***ფართო მინდორს*** (we approached a wide field). In a postpositional order an adjective agrees with the modified noun in case: *მივადექით* ***მინდორს ფართოს***. If a modified noun is in plural form an adjective may or may not agree with it both in case and number in postpositional order (***ჩანთ-ებ-ი სავსე-ებ-ი***, full satchels; ***კედლ-ებ-ი ყრუ***, windowless walls). In prepositional order an adjective with a consonant-ending stem may be in full or partial agreement in case with the modified word:

> *ბევრი* ***ლამაზი სოფელი*** *გავიარეთ მანქანით.*
> We passed through many beautiful villages by car.
> ***ლამაზ სოფლებს*** *ჩავუარეთ მანქანით.*
> We passed by beautiful villages by car.

In postpositional order there is full agreement in singular forms, but in plural forms, agreement is only partial. Both types of agreements are permissible: ***სოფლებს ლამაზს*** (beautiful village) and ***სოფლებს ლამაზებს*** (beautiful villages). It is the matter of a stylistic choice and depends on the character of the text in which such pairs are used. In archaic plural forms, the agreement is always complete:

> ***მაღალნი მთანი // მთანი მაღალნი*** დაგვყურებდნენ თავზე.
> High mountains looked down upon us.

15.3.2 Genitive modifier

As mentioned earlier, a genitive modifier is denoted by a noun or a word of equal grammatical properties. It designates:

1. Ownership: ***მწერლ-ის ნაწარმოებ-ი*** – works of the writer (the modified noun is the property of the modifier)
2. ***წიგნ-ის ავტორ-ი*** – the author of the book (the modified noun belongs to the modifier)
3. Material: ***აგურ-ის სახლ-ი*** – a brick house (house of brick, brick house)
4. Function: ***ჩაი-ს ჭიქა*** – a teacup (a cup for tea)

There are two kinds of syntactic relationships between a genitive modifier and the word it modifies: subordination and coordination.

In a prepositional order the modified word requires a modifier in genitive case. This is subordination:

> ***ტელეფონი-ის ზარ-მა*** *გამაღვიძა.*
> The phone call woke me up.
> *სტუდენტები* ***წიგნ-ის ავტორ-ს*** *შეხვდნენ.*
> The students met the author of the book.
> ჩემი მშობლები ***აგურ-ის სახლ-ში*** *ცხოვრობენ.*
> My parents live in a brick house.
> *რძე* ***ჩაის ჭიქ-ით*** *დალია.*
> He drank milk from a teacup.

Postpositional order is rarely used. Usually, such pairs are both subordinate and coordinated. The pair is subordinate because the modified word requires a modifier in the genitive case, but there is also coordination between the members of the pair since the genitive modifier is also coordinated with the case of the modified word:

> ზარ-**მა** (erg.) *ტელეფონ-**ის-ა-მ*** (gen. + erg.) გამომაღვიძა.
> The phone call (call of the phone) woke me up.
> *ნაწარმოებ-**ს*** (dat.) *(ამ) მწერლ-**ის-ა-ს*** (gen. + dat.) სიამოვნებით ვკითხულობ.
> I read with pleasure the works of this writer.

Chapter 16

Verb phrase

16.1 Predicate

A predicate always includes a verb in a finite form with person markers. There are two types of predicates, simple and compound. A simple predicate may be denoted with a verb in any tense form; a complex predicate consists of two parts, a declinable word and an auxiliary verb.

16.1.1 Simple predicate

A simple predicate contains either a simple or complex verb. The following sentences have predicates denoted with simple verbs:

> მან **გადაცურა** მდინარე.
> He crossed the river.
> შენ საინტერესო სტატია **დაგიწერია.**
> You have written an interesting article.
> წვიმა **მოდის.**
> It is raining.

In modern Georgian there is a group of verbs derived from complex predicates: **თბილა** (it's warm), **ცხელა** (it's hot), **ცივა** (it's cold), **გრილა** (it's cool), **ბნელა** (it's dark), **კმარა** (enough).

> ამ ოთახში ძალიან **ცხელა.**
> It is very hot in this room.
> **კმარა** ამდენი სიცილი!
> Enough laughing!
> აქ **გრილა.**
> It is cool here.
> უკვე **ბნელა.**
> It is already dark.

A simple predicate may be denoted with a complex verb: ცხადყო (made it clear, proved), შეურაცხყო (insulted, offended), უზრუნველყო (provided), უგულებელყო (ignored).

DOI: 10.4324/9781315281131-20

გამოძიებამ ***ცხადყო*** *ეჭვმიტანილის დანაშაული.*
The investigation proved the guilt of the suspect.
ამ სიტყვებმა ჩემი მეგობარი ***შეურაცხყო.***
These words offended my friend.
მთავრობამ უსახლკარო ოჯახი საცხოვრებელი ადგილით ***უზრუნველყო.***
The government provided the homeless family with a shelter.
უსაფრთხოების ზომებს ნუ ***უგულებელყოფთ!***
Do not ignore the security rules!

A simple predicate may be preceded with a modal verb **უნდა** (should, must), which does not conjugate. It should not be confused with the verb **ნდომა** (to wish), which conjugates in all tenses and has person and number markers *(მინდა, გინდა, უნდა,* etc.). **მინდა** and **უნდა** have different meanings:

მე ***მინდა დავალაგო*** *ეს ოთახი.*	*მე* ***უნდა დავალაგო*** *ეს ოთახი.*
I want to tidy up this room.	I should (must) tidy up this room.

უნდა + verb is a simple predicate consisting of two parts. The verb following **უნდა** can be in optative, pluperfect, or present subjunctive tenses and conveys various degrees of necessity or obligation:

უნდა + optative: ***უნდა დაალაგოს***
He should tidy up (responsibility).
უნდა + pluperfect: ***უნდა ჩამოსულიყო***
He should have arrived (necessity/expectation).
უნდა + present subjunctive*:* ***უნდა გვახსოვდეს***
We should remember (obligation).

16.1.2 Compound predicate and its structure

A compound predicate consists of an auxiliary verb and a declinable word, noun or pronoun either in singular, or in plural form and mostly in the Nominative case.

ჩვენი სტუმარი ***ენამახვილი კაცი გამოდგა.***
Our guest turned out to be a witty man.
ჩვენ ***მწერლები ვართ,*** *ისინი კი* ***მხატვრები არიან.***
We are writers, and they are painters.
მე ***ისა ვარ,*** *გუშინ რომ შეგხვდით.*
I am the one who met you yesterday.
ეს ჩანთა ***მისია//მისი არის.***
This suitcase is his.

When the nominal component of a compound predicate is dropped, an attributive part of the omitted noun becomes a component part of the predicate.

*ჩვენი მეზობელი ოცი წლის **ბიჭი იყო.***
Our neighbour was a twenty-year-old young man.

In this sentence the compound predicate is ***ბიჭი იყო***. If the word ***ბიჭი*** is dropped, the predicate will be the attribute of its omitted part – ***ოცი წლის*** (twenty years old):

*ჩვენი მეზობელი **ოცი წლის(ა)იყო.***
Our neighbour was twenty years old.

In the majority of cases, the verbal part of a compound predicate is the verb ***ყოფნა*** (to be) in various tenses. When the subject is in third-person singular form, often only the enclitic vowel -**ა** will be present attached to the nominal part of the predicate. If the word to which it is attached ends with a consonant, the vowel **ა** will be doubled.

*ჩემი და **ექიმია** = **ექიმი არის.***
My sister is a doctor.
*ეს წიგნი **ჩემია** = **ჩემი არის.***
This book is mine.
ჩემი წიგნი ***ესაა*** = ჩემი წიგნი ***ეს არის.***
My book is this (one).
მამა ***ავადაა*** = მამა ***ავად არის.***
Father is sick.

In polite conversations, ***გახლავართ***, ***ბრძანდებით***, or ***ბრძანდება*** replaces ***ყოფნა*** and becomes the auxiliary part of a compound predicate (for more details, see 9.7.3.):

*მე **მხატვარი გახლავართ.***
I am a painter, (sir).
*თქვენ **რექტორი ბრძანდებით?***
Are you the rector, (sir)?
*ის **ექიმი ბრძანდება.***
He is a doctor.

In addition to ***ყოფნა*** (to be), a number of other verbs are used as the auxiliary part of a compound predicate: ***გახდა*** (became), ***დარჩა*** (remained), ***გამოვა*** (will become, will happen), ***გამოდგა*** (it turned out), ***აღმოჩნდა*** (it turned out), ***ჩანს*** (looks like), ***ჰგონია*** (he thinks):

ჩემი ვაჟი **სტუდენტი გახდა.**
My son became a student.
დირექტორი შედეგებით **კმაყოფილი დარჩა.**
The manager was satisfied with the results.
თქვენი ეჭვი **უსაფუძვლო გამოდგა.**
Your suspicion turned out to be groundless.
ეს ინფორმაცია **არასწორი აღმოჩნდა.**
This information turned out to be wrong.
ეს ახალგაზრდა **ნიჭიერი ჩანს.**
This young man seems talented.
მას თავი უკვე **პრეზიდენტი ჰგონია.**
He thinks he is already the president.

The sequence of nominal and verbal parts of a compound predicate is not strictly determined and may be shifted around:

სტუდენტი გახდა = გახდა სტუდენტი (became a student)
კმაყოფილი დარჩა = დარჩა კმაყოფილი (remained satisfied)
უსაფუძვლო გამოდგა = გამოდგა უსაფუძვლო (turned out to be groundless)
არასწორი აღმოჩნდა = აღმოჩნდა არასწორი (turned out to be wrong)
ნიჭიერი ჩანს = ჩანს ნიჭიერი (seems talented)
პრეზიდენტი ჰგონია = ჰგონია პრეზიდენტი (thinks he is the president)

In addition, nominal and verbal parts of a compound predicate may be separated by other parts of a sentence:

მე შენ **მშიშარა** ხომ არ **გგონივარ?**
You don't think I am a coward, do you?
ინჟინერი მე კი არა **ვარ,** ჩემი ძმაა.
I am not an engineer, my brother is.
ჩემი ბიჭი **ათი წლის** ერთ კვირაში **გახდება.**
My boy will become ten years old in a week.

The verbal part of a compound predicate can be the verb **ყოლა/ქონა** (to have): **მაქვს** when the subject of the sentence is inanimate and **მყავს** when it is animate.

ძაღლი (animate) **ჰყავდათ დაბმული** ეზოში.
They had a dog tied in the yard.
მეგობრები (animate) **მყავს მოწვეული** დაბადების დღეზე.
I have friends invited to my birthday.
წერილები (inanimate) დროულად **ჰქონდათ გაგზავნილი.**
They had letters sent on time.

შარშან საინტერესო ***გაზეთები*** (inanimate) ***გვქონდა გამოწერილი.***
Last year we had subscribed to interesting newspapers.

16.2 Adjunct object

The adjunct object and predicate are connected contextually, but the former is not modified by the latter. However, the adjunct object is one of the actants (see 9.1.1, 9.3.1, and 9.6.3.1.) in a sentence and may be either in the dative with postposition or in the genitive, instrumental, or adverbial cases with or without a postposition. Most frequently it is denoted with a noun, pronoun, or gerund, and, less frequently, with other parts of speech. The following chart shows types of adjunct objects and their connection to predicate.

Cases of adjunct object

Cases	*With or without postpositions*	*Examples*
Dat.	**-ზე (on, about, to)** **-ში (in, to, at)** **-თან (with)** **-თან ერთად (together)**	მეგობრებზე (ვისზე? About whom?) ფიქრობდა. He thought about his friends. მთვარეზე (რაზე? To what?) გაფრინდა. It flew to the moon. გიტარაზე (რაზე? On what?) უკრავდა. He played (on) the guitar. ამ ბიჭში (ვისში? In whom) მამამისს ვხედავ. In this boy I see his father. მეზობელთან (ვისთან? To whom?) მივიდა. He went to the neighbour. ცეცხლთან (რასთან? With what?) ნუ თამაშობ! Do not play with fire. მეგობართან (ვისთან ერთად? Together with whom?) ერთად წავიდა. He left together with a friend. ძაღლთან ერთად (რასთან ერთად? Together with what?) სეირნობს. He walks together with his dog.

Cases of adjunct object

Cases	*With or without postpositions*	*Examples*
Gen.	**Without postposition** **-გან (from, of)** **-თვის (for)** **-მიერ (by)** **შესახებ (about)** **მიმართ (towards, to, in someone's address)** **მაგივრად, ნაცვლად (instead of)**	ზღვაში ყოფნის (რისი? Of what?) მეშინია. I am afraid to be at sea. ამ კაცის (ვისი? Of whom?) მეშინია. I am afraid of this man. მეზობლისგან (ვისგან? From whom?) ფული ისესხა. He borrowed money from a neighbour. ქვისგან (რისგან? Of what?) ღობე ააშენა. He built a fence of stone. The indirect object of a tripersonal verb becomes an adjunct object with the postposition *-თვის* in III series forms: შვილისთვის (ვისთვის? For whom?) საჩუქარი უყიდია. He has bought a gift for his child. დაგვიანებისთვის (რისთვის? For what) ისაყვედურეს. You were reprimanded for being late. შენთვის (ვისთვის? For whom?) ყველაფერს გავაკეთებ. I will do anything for you. მათ მიერ (ვის მიერ? By whom?) ჩადენილი უსამართლობა Injustice committed by them ლექტორის მიერ (ვის მიერ? By whom) გაკეთებული კომენტარი The comment made by the lecturer ამ ქალის შესახებ (ვის შესახებ? About whom?) არაფერია ცნობილი. Nothing is known about this woman. მოხსენება გლობალური დათბობის შესახებ (რის შესახებ? About what?) A report about global warming ბევრი რამ გავიგე შენ შესახებ (ვის შესახებ? About whom). I found out a lot about you.

(*Continued*)

(Continued)

Cases of adjunct object

Cases	*With or without postpositions*	*Examples*
		ერთგული იყავი მეგობრების მიმართ (ვის მიმართ? To whom?). Be faithful to your friends. პრეზიდენტის მიმართ (ვის მიმართ? To whom?) გამოთქმული კრიტიკა Criticism expressed in the president's address მინისტრის მაგივრად/ნაცვლად (ვის ნაცვლად? Instead of whom?) მისი მოადგილე გვესაუბრა Instead of the minister, his deputy spoke with us. შენს მაგივრად/ნაცვლად (ვის მაგივრად? Instead of whom?) მე წავალ. I will go instead of you. ბოდიშის მაგივრად/ნაცვლად (რის მაგივრად? Instead of what?) გვეჩხუბა. Instead of an apology, he quarrelled with us.
Ins.	**Without postpositions** -ურთ **(together with)**	An adjunct object in the instrumental case without a postposition denotes the tool of the action expressed with the verb: კალმით (რით? With what?) წერს. He writes with a pen. სამსახურში ფეხით (რით? How?) დადის. He walks on foot to the office. ბათუმში მანქანით (რით? By what?) მივდივართ. We go by car to Batumi. An adjunct object in the instrumental case is used in paronomastic expressions: წერით წერს (as far as writing goes, he writies), ჭამით ჭამს (as far as eating goes, he eats), ხატვით ხატავს (as far as painting goes, he paints) ჭამით ჭამს, მაგრამ მაინც ძალიან გამხდარია. As far as eating goes, he eats, but he is still skinny.

Cases of adjunct object

Cases	*With or without postpositions*	*Examples*
		ხატვით ხატავს, მაგრამ მისი ნახატები არავის//არავის არ მოსწონს. As far as painting goes, he paints, but nobody likes his paintings. პრეზიდენტი მეუღლითურთ (ვისთან ერთად? Together with whom?) მოვიდა. The president arrived together with his wife. მეგობრითურთ მუზეუმში წავიდა. Together with his friend, he went to the museum.
Adv.	**Without postpositions**	An adjunct object in the instrumental case without postposition denotes change or transformation. ჩვენი სოფელი უზარმაზარ ქალაქად (რად? Into what?) იქცა. Our village transformed into a big city. ის მასწავლებლად მუშაობს. He works as a teacher. ჩვენთან სტუმრად მოდის. He comes to visit us. მას ხელმძღვანელად თვლიან. He is considered the leader.

16.3 Predicative adjective

A predicative adjective is a part of the VP in a sentence. The majority of them are denoted with passive voice adjectives mostly in the nominative case. It is differentiated from an attributive adjective by its position in a sentence, which precedes or follows a predicate.

ბავშვი ***დაბნეული*** *იყურებოდა.*
A child looked in confusion.
კაცი სახლში ***დაღონებული*** *დაბრუნდა.*
The man returned home saddened.

In rare cases a predicative attribute is expressed with an adjective:

დედაჩემი ***პატარა*** *დაობლდა.*
My mother was orphaned young.

If the place of an adjective changes, its function will change as well:

ბავშვი **დაბნეული** (predicative adjective) **იყურებოდა.**
A child looked bewildered.
დაბნეული (attributive adjectiveა) **ბავშვი** იყურებოდა.
A bewildered child looked.
გოგონა **ნაღვლიანი** (predicative adjective) **ჩამოჯდა** სკამზე.
A girl sat saddened on a bench.
ნაღვლიანი (attributive adjective) **გოგონა** ჩამოჯდა სკამზე.
A saddened girl sat on a bench.

Attributive adjective

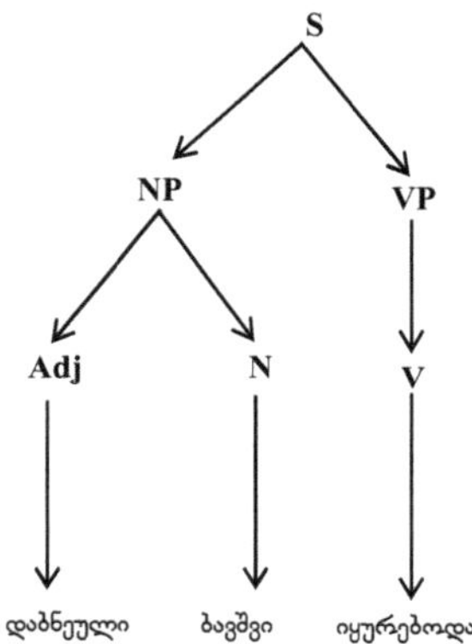

A bewildered child looked.

Predicative adjective

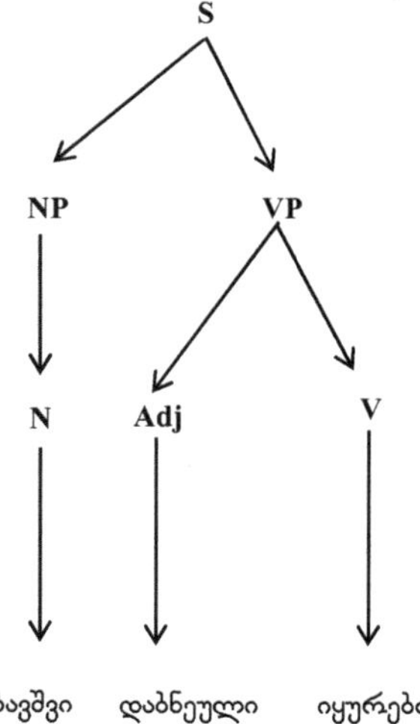

A child looked bewildered.

16.4 Adverbial modifiers

The adverbial modifiers indicate a place, time, cause, reason, mode, or purpose of an action. Most frequently they are denoted with an adverb, but they may be expressed with nouns, gerunds, and participles. Like adjunct objects, they are connected with the predicate only contextually, not formally.

Adverbial modifiers	*Denoted with*	*Examples*
	Adverb of place Dative case without or with the postpositions -ში (in, at), -ზე (about), or -თან (close to, near)	**ახლო-ს** დიდი სასტუმროა. Nearby there is a big hotel. თბილის-ში ჩავიდა. He arrived in Tbilisi. თბილის-თან ახლოს ვცხოვრობ. I live near Tbilisi.
	Genitive case with the postposition -კენ or preceded with an adverb of place that functions as a compound postposition	მატარებელი **მადრიდ-ის-კენ** დაიძრა. The train started towards Madrid. ბავშვები **სახლ-ის გარშემო** დარბოდნენ. The children were running around the house. კატა **მაგიდ-ის ქვეშ** შეძვრა. The cat crawled under the table. **ხ-ის ძირას** გრძელი სკამი იდგა. Under the tree stood a long bench.
	Instrumental case without postposition or with the postposition: -დან (-ით-გან) (from)	**სამხრეთ-ით** თურქეთია. To the south is Turkey. **ტყ-ი-დან** ბიჭი გამოვიდა. From the woods a boy came out. **უნივერსიტეტ-ი-დან მეტრომდე** ფეხით იარა. From the university to the subway, he walked.

(Continued)

(Continued)

Adverbial modifiers	*Denoted with*	*Examples*
Adverb of time	**Adverb of time** Dative case with or without the postpositions: -*ში* (in), -*ზე* (on, at)	***გუშინ*** *ციოდა.* Yesterday it was cold. ***ორშაბათ-ს*** *ბანკში მივდივართ.* On Monday we are going to the bank. ***ნასადილევ-ს/ნავახშმევ-ს*** *შევხვდეთ.* After dinner/supper let's meet.
	Genitive case, sometimes with the postpositions: -*თანავე* (as soon as), *წინ* (before, in front of), *შემდეგ* (after), *მერე* (after), -*კენ* (towards)	***აპრილ-ში*** *უკვე თბილი ამინდია.* In April the weather is already warm. *ხუთ* ***საათ-ზე*** *ვიწყებთ.* We start at five o'clock. *სახლში* ***მისვლ-ის-თანავე*** *დავწექი.* As soon as I came home, I went to bed. *ეს წამალი* ***ჭამ-ის წინ*** *დალიეთ.* Take this medicine before the meal. ***დღე-ის შემდეგ*** *შვებულებაში ვარ.* After today I am on leave. ***საღამო-ს-კენ*** *შევხვდეთ.* Let's meet towards the evening.
	Instrumental case with or without the postposition: -*დან* (from) Adverbial case with or without the postposition: -*მდე* (till, until)	***დილ-ით/დილაობ-ით*** *ბავშვები სკოლაში მიდიან.* In the morning/every morning, children go to school. *ერთი* ***კვირ-ით*** *იტალიაში წავიდა.* For one week he went to Italy. ***ბავშვობ-ი-დან*** *მიყვარს ზოოლოგია.* Even from childhood I have liked zoology. ***პირველ-ად*** *აქ შარშან ვიყავი.* The first time I was here last year. ***საღამო-მდე*** *ეს წერილი უნდა გავგზავნო.* By the evening I should send this letter. ***დილ-ი-დან საღამო-მდე*** *მუშაობს.* From morning till evening, he works. ***გაზაფხულ-ი-დან ზამთრ-ა-მდე*** *ჩვენთან ცხოვრობს.* From spring till winter, he lives with us.

Adverbial modifiers	*Denoted with*	*Examples*
Adverb of manner	**Adverbs indicating manner or frequency** Nominative and dative cases with the postposition: -ვით (like),	*უცბად* წვიმა წამოვიდა. Suddenly the rain started. *ორჯერ* ვიყავი შენთან. Twice I visited you. *შვილ-ი-ვით* უყვარდა. He loved him like his own child. *გიჟ-ი-ვით* დარბოდა. He ran around like a madman. ეს მსახიობი **მზე-ს-ა-ვით** ბრწყინავს. This actor/actress shines like the sun.
	instrumental case	მანქანა დიდი **სიჩქარ-ით** მიჰყავდა. He drove the car at high speed.
	Adverb in the adverbial case denoting the mode of action Nouns, numerals and participles in the adverbial case	ფრანგულად **კარგ-ად** ლაპარაკობს. He speaks French well. ღობე **მწვანე-დ** შეღებეს. They painted the fence green. სტუდენტები **გუნდ-ად** იდგნენ. The students stood in groups. ხმები **ორ-ად** გაიყო. The votes split into two. **ამნაირ-ად** ჯერ არ უმღერია. Like this he has not yet sung. **დაუფიქრებლ-ად** ნუ გადაწყვეტ! Do not decide hastily.
Adverb of cause	Adverbs of cause and nouns in the genitive case with postpositions -გან (from, out of) and გამო (because of)	**რატომღაც** მხიარულ ხასიათზე იყო. For some reason he was in a good mood. **შიშ-ის-გან** კანკალი დაიწყო. He started trembling from fear. **ავადმყოფობ-ის გამო** სკოლაში ვერ წავიდა. Because of illness he could not go to school.
Adverb of purpose	Genitive case with the postposition -თვის (for) and the adverbial case without postpositions	**რჩევ-ის-თვის** მეგობართან მივიდა. For advice he went to a friend. ფეხბურთის **სათამაშო-დ** სტადიონზე წავიდნენ. To play football they went to the stadium.

When adverbial modifiers are denoted with adverbs, they answer the questions that are themselves adverbials:

> **Adverbs of place:** სად (where), საიდან (from where), საითკენ (to where), სადამდე (till where)
> **Adverbs of time:** როდის (when), რამდენ ხანს (for how long), რა დროიდან (from what time), როდემდე (till what time)
> **Adverbs of manner:** როგორ (how), რამდენჯერ (how many times), რანაირად (how, in what manner)
> **Adverbs of reason/cause:** რატომ (why), რის გამო (because of what), რა მიზეზით (for what reason)
> **Adverbs of purpose/intention:** რისთვის (for what), რად (for what), რა მიზნით (for what purpose)

As the two previous charts show, adjunct objects and adverbs may be in the same case and with same postpositions:

ექიმად მუშაობს.	*გზად ნაცნობი შეხვდა.*
He works as a doctor.	He met an acquaintance on my way.

In both these sentences, the nouns are in the adverbial case without a postposition. *ექიმად* is an adjunct object and answers the question *რად* (as what). *გზად* is an adverb of place and answers the question *სად* (where). Sometimes it is not clear if a word with a postposition referring to a predicate is an adjunct object or an adverb of place.

*წიგნი **ჩანთაში** ჩადო.*	*წიგნი **მაგიდაზე** დადო.*
He put the book into his satchel.	He put the book on the table.

The words ***ჩანთაში*** (into his bag) and ***მაგიდაზე*** (on the table) may answer the questions ***სად*** (where), ***რაში*** (into what), and ***რაზე*** (on what).

It is easy to differentiate an adverb of place and an adjunct object when the adverb is a geographic name or a word semantically denoting a space of some kind:

> *ქარი **დასავლეთისკენ** ქროდა.* (Adverb of place)
> The wind was blowing westward.
> ***ფანჯრისკენ** გაიხედა.* (Adjunct object)
> He looked towards the window.

In both sentences, the words with the postposition ***-კენ*** express the direction of the action. ***დასავლეთისკენ*** (westward) denotes a direction in a space, and the appropriate question would be ***საითკენ*** (which way). However, the word ***ფანჯრისკენ*** (towards what) may answer to both questions – **რისკენ** (towards what) and **საითკენ** (which way).

სად დევს წიგნი?	*წიგნი* ***ჩანთასთან*** *დევს.*
Where is the book?	The book is near the bag.

In this dialogue the question **სად** (where) determines that the word **ჩანთასთან** (near the bag) is an adverb of place. The same word independent from this dialogue may answer the question **რასთან** (near what).

In the sentence **კონვერტზე** *მისამართი დაწერა* (he wrote the address on an envelope), the word **კონვერტზე** (on an envelope) may answer the questions **სად** *დაწერა* (where did he write) and **რაზე** *დაწერა* (on what did he write). It is the question asked that determines whether it is an adjunct object or an adverb of place. In either case, both parts of speech belong to the verb phrase.

Chapter 17

Syntactic pairs

17.1 Number of syntactic pairs in a sentence

The number of syntactic pairs in a sentence is always one less than all its parts. A syntactic pair consist of words linked together in a formal-substantive mode or only formally. The formal linkage is underscored morphologically, but substantive connection does not always have morphological support. The formal-substantive pairs consist of a predicate and subject and a predicate and direct or indirect object. The substantive pairs include a predicate and adjunct object and a predicate and any adverb. The substantive and formal linkage occurs between a subject and any attribute defining a direct or indirect object.

In the following sentence there are seven parts and, therefore, six syntactic pairs.

> *ცნობილმა მშენებლებმა ქვის დიდი სახლი მალე დაასრულეს.*
> The well-known builders quickly finished a big stone house.

The syntactic pairs are the following:

1. მშენებლებმა დაასრულეს
   the builders finished (subject and predicate)
2. სახლი დაასრულეს
   finished a house (direct object and predicate)
3. მალე დაასრულეს
   quickly finished (adverb and predicate)
4. ცნობილმა მშენებლებმა
   the well-known builders (attribute and subject)
5. ქვის სახლი
   a stone house (attribute and direct object)

DOI: 10.4324/9781315281131-21

6. დიდი სახლი
   a big house (attribute and direct object)

Separately spelled the postpositions, conjunctions, particles, and interjections are not considered parts of a sentence. Thus, in the sentence *მე **შენ გარდა** არავისთვის მითქვამს ეს ამბავი* (Except you, I have not told this fact to anybody), **შენ გარდა** (except you) forms a single unit, and it is a part of this syntactic pair: ***შენ (გარდა) არავისთვის.***

In the sentence *რა ბიჭი დაბადებულა!* (What a boy that has been born!), the particle **რა** is not an independent part. Therefore, in this two-member sentence, there is only one syntactic pair: რა **ბიჭი დაბადებულა** (subject and predicate).

In the sentence *მშენებლებმა სახლი ვერ დაასრულეს* (The builders were unable to finish the house), the negative particle **ვერ** affects its meaning but not its structure. Thus, we have three members and two syntactic pairs: ***მშენებლებმა (ვერ) დაასრულეს*** (the builders finished) and ***სახლი (ვერ) დაასრულეს*** (finished the house).

Interjections are not considered parts of a sentence either. In the sentence ***ვაი,** როგორ მეწყინა!* (Oh, I was so disappointed!), ***ვაი*** is an interjection expressing sorrow or disappointment, but it is not a member of the sentence, and we have only one syntactic pair: **როგორ მეწყინა.**

17.2 Types of word relations within syntactic pairs

There are three types of connections between the parts of a sentence: the *coordination*, *subordination*, and *substantive linkage*. In a coordinated pair, both members of the unit modify each other; in a subordinated pair only one of them modifies the other; in a substantive pair the constituent members are linked on the bases of their meaning, but there is no formal coordination between them. Such connection exists between an adjunct object and a predicate, or any adverb and predicate. Here are examples of the *substantive linkage*:

ბიჭი მეგობართან თამაშობს.
The boy plays with his friend.

In this sentence the verb phrase consists of the adjunct object and the predicate: ***მეგობართან თამაშობს*** (plays with his friend) – there is no formal coordination between them.

ეს წერილი დილას მოიტანეს.
(They) brought this letter in the morning.

Here the verb phrase includes an adverb and a predicate: დილას მოიტანეს (brought in the morning) – there is no formal coordination between them.

17.2.1 Coordination

The components of coordinated syntactic pairs share their grammatical categories: an attribute and the noun are in the same case (დიდმა სახლმა, დიდმა სახლებმა), and a subject and predicate agree in number. მშენებლ-ებ-მა (=მათ) დაასრულ-ეს (the builders (they) finished) – this is a syntactic pair coordinated in person and number. The suffix -ეს indicates that the predicate denotes the third-person plural and corresponds to the subject in plural form marked with the suffix -ებ.

The predicate takes plural in with more than one subject:

თამარი და ნათია მოვიდნენ.
Tamar and Natia came.

However, an inanimate subject in plural is usually coordinated with a predicate in singular form. In the sentence ოთახში მრგვალი მაგიდები დგას (There are round tables in the room), the subject მაგიდები in plural is marked with -ებ, but the predicate in singular form is marked with the ending -ს.

In the following sentences the subjects are in plural, but the predicates in singular form.

ეს ფაქტები (S) მის დანაშაულს ამტკიცებს (P).
These facts prove his guilt.
მათი წერილები (S) არ მოსულა (P).
Their letters have not arrived.
არქეოლოგიურმა გათხრებმა (S) დაგვანახა (P) ამ ადგილის ისტორიული მნიშვნელობა.
The archaeological excavations showed us the historical significance of this location.

Only in the poetic texts or metaphoric expressions may an inanimate subject agree with its predicate in number. In the following sentences the subjects are inanimate objects, but the predicates are in plural form.

დუმდნენ (P) თოვლით დაფარული მთები (S).
The snow-covered mountains were silent.
კაშკაშა ვარსკვლავებმა (S) გზა მიჩვენეს (P).
The bright stars showed me the path.

ბაღში წითელმა **ვარდებმა** (S) **გამიღიმეს** (P).
In the garden the red roses smiled at me.

If the subject is a collective noun it agrees with the predicate always in singular form.

ხალხი მოედანზე ***მოგროვდა.***
People gathered in the square.
პოლიციამ ***დააკავა*** *ეჭვმიტანილი.*
Police arrested the suspect.
ჩვენი რაზმი გვიან ***დაბრუნდა*** *ბანაკში.*
Our platoon returned to the camp late.

As the previous sentences show, the attributes and nouns they precede, whether it is the subject or object, agree in case but not necessarily in number. Thus, in the syntactic pairs ***ცნობილ-მა*** *მშენებლ-ებ-მა*, *კაშკაშა ვარსკვლავ-ებ-მა*, and ***წითელ-მა ვარდ-ებ-მა***, both the attributes (*ცნობილ-მა, კაშკაშა, წითელმა*) and nouns (*მშენებლ-ებ-მა, ვარსკვლავ-ებ-მა, ვარდ-ებ-მა*) are in the ergative case, but the former are in singular, and the latter in plural forms. However, they agree both in case and number if a noun defined by an attribute is in singular form. Thus, in the pairs ***დიდ-ი სახლ-ი*** (large house) and ***ჩვენი რაზმი*** (our group), the attributes and nouns are both in nominative case and agree in number.

As a rule, the subjects or objects, both the direct and indirect, in plural form marked with the suffix ***-ებ*** do not agree in number with the attribute defining them whether they are in a direct or inverted order: ცნობილი მშენებლები – მშენებლები ცნობილი, დიდი სახლი – სახლი დიდი, etc. Only in the archaic plural forms with the ***-ნ*** and ***-თა*** suffixes is there full agreement both in case and number:

*ცნობილ-***ნ***-ი მშნებელ-***ნ***-ი*	*ცნობილ-***თა*** მშენებელ-***თა***
Well-known builders, nom.	Well-known builders, indirect case
*დიდ-***ნ***-ი სახლ-***ნ***-ი*	*დიდ-***თა*** სახლ-***თა***
Big houses, nom.	Big houses, indirect case

In contemporary Georgian, these forms are seldom used, and even then, attributes and nouns do not agree in number: *დიდ სახლ-თა, ცნობილ მშენებელ-თა.*

17.2.2 Subordination

The parts of the subordinated syntactic pairs have either different or similar grammatical categories that modify each other.

For example, a predicate does not have grammatical case, but it determines the case of the subject. Nouns do not conjugate, but they may determine the person marker of predicate. If a syntactically connected predicate and noun modify each other, their subordination is mutual. In addition, verbs with person markers and nouns may be coordinated with the common grammatical categories.

მშენებლ-ებ-მა (მათ) დაასრულ-ეს – in this pair the subject and predicate modify each other; the subject, *მშენებლ-ებ-მა(მათ)*, *the builders* (i.e. *they*), determines the third-person plural form of the predicate marked with the ending *-ეს*. On the other hand, the predicate, expressed with a transitive active voice verb in the aorist, requires the ergative case of the subject marked with *-მა*.: მშენებლ-ებ-*მა*. In addition, both parts of this pair are coordinated in number. Thus, there are two types of relationship between them, subordination and coordination. Such pairs are defined as subordinate-coordinated pairs.

სახლ-ი (ის) დაასრულეს – here the predicate, a transitive verb in the aorist, determines the nominative case of the direct object, but the latter cannot modify the verb. Consequently, there is no agreement in number between them. Even if a third-person direct object were in plural, it would not change the form of the predicate *სახლ-ებ-ი (ისინი) დაასრულეს*. There is one-sided subordination between them.

The subordination, as a type of syntactic relationship, may exist between two nouns. For example, in the pair *ქვ-ის სახლ-ი*, the noun *სახლ-ი* determines the genitive case of its modifier *ქვ-ის*. In inverted order such pairs agree in case as well: *სახლ-მა ქვ-ის-ა-მ*. Here the noun *სახლ-ი* not only determines the genitive case of its modifier but requires that it should be in the ergative case as well. Thus, *ქვ-ის-ა-მ* has both the genitive and ergative case markers.

17.3 Increasing and decreasing basic parts of a sentence

In the Georgian language, a change in the syntactic structure of a sentence depends on the morphological and syntactic property of the verb denoting its predicate. The predicate causes changes in NP and VP, it increases or decreases the number of the basic parts of a sentence. This makes it possible to determine the rules governing the methods of composing a sentence with simple structure and explains what type of verbs modify the number of main parts and their transformation in a sentence.

17.3.1 *Increasing the number of actants in a sentence*

There are several ways to change NP and VP in order to increase the number of actants. A predicate denoted with a bivalent verb governing two noun phrases – i.e. the subject and the direct object in the verb phrase – can be changed to a trivalent predicate in different ways.

17.3.1.1 *Increasing the number of actants with causative verbs*

In the following base sentence, a predicate is denoted with a bivalent verb:

კაცი დახმარებას ითხოვს.
A man is asking for help.

NP, nom.:	კაც-ი
VP, dat.:	დახმარება-ს + version, bivalent verb: ითხოვს.

If the bivalent verb *ითხოვს* is replaced with a trivalent verb, the structure of the sentence will be changed: *გაჭირვებამ კაცს დახმარება მოათხოვნინა* (the hardship made a man ask for help). Here the causative verb changes the composition of NP and VP. The noun phrase becomes a part of the verb phrase, and the function of the noun phrase is transferred to the new member of the sentence (*გაჭირვებამ*–hardship), which becomes the motivator of the action.

NP = N	(Erg. გაჭირვება-მ)
VP = N+VP	**(**N (Nom. დახმარება) + VP (N (Dat. კაც-ს) + V (Version მოათხოვნინა**)**

The base sentence can be further modified by changing the tense of the transitive verb denoting the predicate: *გაჭირვებას კაცისთვის დახმარება მოუთხოვნინებია* (Apparently, hardship has made a man ask for help). In this sentence, the predicate denoted with a transitive verb in the III series form transforms the morphological indirect object (Dat. კაც-ს) into an adjunct object (in the genitive case with postposition: *კაც-ის-თვის*) – i.e. morphologically the verb does not directly refer to it, but it is still an actant contributing to the verb's valency, and the predicate remains trivalent (see 9.1.1, 9.3.1, and 9.6.3.1.).

NP = N	(Dat. გაჭირვება-ს)
VP = N+VP	**(**N (Nom. დახმარება) + VP (N (Gen. With postposition: კაც-ის-თვის) + V (Version მოუთხოვნინებია**)**.

17.3.1.2 *Increasing the number of actants by changing version*

In the following sentence, the predicate is denoted with a bivalent verb in the subjective version: *კაც-მა ქუდ-ი* **და-ი-ხურა** (the man put on his hat).

NP = N (Erg. კაც-მა)
VP = N+V **(**N (Nom. ქუდ-ი) + V (Version და-ი-ხურ-ა**)**
Neutral Version is კაც-მა შვილ-ს ქუდ-ი და-ა-ხურა.
The man put a hat on his child's head.
VP = N+VP **(**N (Nom. კაც-მა) + VP (N (Nom. ქუდ-ი) + N (Dat. შვილ-ს) + V (Version დაახურა**)**

An indirect object is added to the verb phrase, thus changing direction of the action expressed with the predicate and the correlation between the subject and object.

The objective version: *კაც-ს შვილ-ის-თვის ქუდ-ი და-უ-ხურავს* (A man has put a hat on his child's head). Here the predicate is denoted with a trivalent but bipersonal verb. The indirect object becomes an adjunct object, but it remains a part of the valency of the predicate.

VP = N+VP **(***N (Dat. კაც-ს) + VP (N (Nom. ქუდ-ი) + N (Gen. With the postposition -თვის: შვილ-ის-თვის) + V (Version (დაუხურავს)***)**

17.3.1.3 *Increasing the number of actants with preverbs*

The preverbs have an object modifying function and may affect object role-shifting, thus changing verb's valency semantically, and encoding this change on the morphological level of the language.

The following sentence has a bivalent verb: *კაც-მა* **ა-აშენ-ა** *სახლ-ი* (the man built a house). The valency of the verb can be increased by adding to it a preverb that will cause a change in the structure of the verb phrase. The verb will become trivalent:

1. კაც-მა სახლ-ს ოთახ-ი **მი-აშენ-ა** [the man added a room to (the side of) the house].
   NP = N (Nom. კაც-მა)
   VP = N+VP **(**N (Dat. სახლ-ს) + VP (N (Nom. ოთახ-ი) + V (Preverb: მი-აშენა**)**

2. კაც-მა სახლ-ს სართულ-ი **და-აშენ-ა** (The man built (another) story on (top of the) the house).
   NP = N (Nom. კაც-მა)
   VP = N+VP **(**N (Dat. სახლს) + VP (N (Nom. სართულ-ი) + V (Preverb: დააშენა**)**

As these examples show, the preverbs მი-and და- increased the verbal valency and introduced a new actant in the base sentence, thus shifting the role of the direct and indirect objects.

17.3.2 Decreasing the number of actants in a sentence

A noun phrase and verb phrase may be changed by decreasing the number of actants.

17.3.2.1 *Conversion*

The conversion occurs when an active voice verb in the VP is transformed into a passive voice verb. A bivalent actant active voice verb denoting a simple predicate can be converted into a passive voice verb. Such conversion will change a direct object into the subject, while the VP will maintain only the predicate. The conversion of a trivalent active voice verb will cause similar changes in the NP, but the verb and an indirect object will remain in the VP. In the following sentence, the predicate contains a biactant verb:

მხატვარი ხატავს სახლს.
A painter paints a house.

NP = N (Nom.მხატვარ-ი)
VP = N+V (N (Dat. სახლ-ს) + V (ხატავს)

The conversion of the verb will result in the uniactant predicate:

სახლი იხატება.
A house is being painted.

The direct object (სახლი) becomes the subject of the sentence.

NP = N (Nom. სახლ-ი)
VP = V (იხატება)

In the following sentence, the predicate is triactant:

მე მეგობარი წერილს მიგზავნის.
A friend sends a letter to me.

NP = N (Nom. მეგობარ-ი)
VP=N+VP (N + (Dat. მე) +VP (N (Dat. წერილ-ს) +V (მიგზავნის)

The conversion of the verb will transform it into the bivalent predicate:

მე წერილი მეგზავნება.
A letter is sent to me.

NP = N (Nom. წერილ-ი)

VP = N+V (N + (Dat. მე) +V (მეგზავნება))

The following are the diagrams of changes occurring in a predicate denoted with bi- and triactant verbs:

მხატვარი ხატავს სახლს.

A painter paints a house.

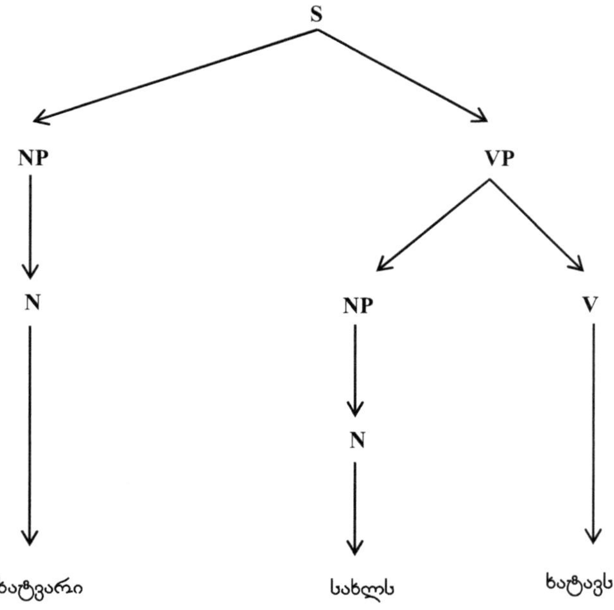

სახლი იხატება.

A house is being painted.

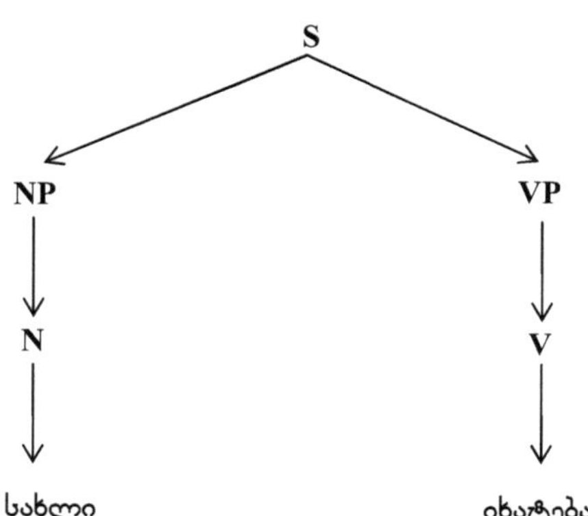

მე მეგობარი წერილს მიგზავნის
A friend sends (is sending) me a letter.

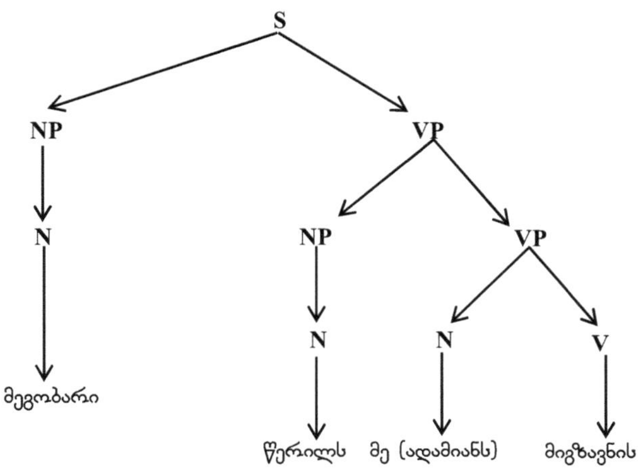

მე წერილი მეგზავნება.
A letter is (being) sent to me.

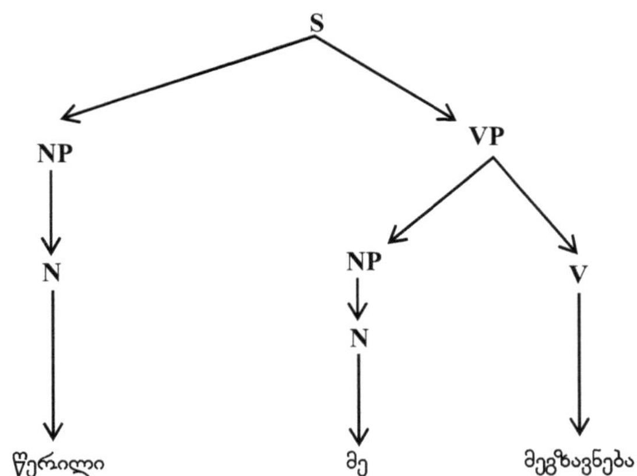

Chapter 18

Modality of sentences

18.1 Declarative sentence

A declarative sentence consists of information which is affirmed or denied. Accordingly, there are two types of declarative sentences – affirmative declarative and negative declarative. A declarative sentence conveys not only a universal truth like *დედამიწა მზის გარშემო ბრუნავს* (The earth revolves around the sun) or *მზე აღმოსავლეთიდან ამოდის* (The sun rises in the east) but also facts and happenings that the speaker believes to be true. For example, *ლუკა სკოლიდან დაბრუნდა* (Luke returned from school) is an affirmative declarative sentence. An opposite statement would be *ლუკა სკოლიდან არ დაბრუნებულა* (Luke has not returned from school). A negative declarative statement includes negations: a negative particle, pronouns, and adverbs.

ჯერ ***არცერთი*** *მოსწავლე სკოლიდან* ***არ*** *დაბრუნებულა.*
So far, not a single student has returned from school.
ჩემი წიგნი ***ვერსად//ვერსად ვერ*** *ვიპოვე.*
I couldn't find my book anywhere.

A declarative sentence can be an answer to a question in a dialogue:

სად ხარ?
Where are you?
უკვე სახლში ვარ.
I am already at home.
Or *ჯერ სახლში* ***არ*** *დავბრუნებულვარ.*
I have not returned home yet.

The last two are declarative sentences reporting a fact, the first in the affirmative and the second in negative mode.

DOI: 10.4324/9781315281131-22

18.2 Interrogative sentence

There are two types of interrogative sentences in Georgian – with an interrogative word and without it. In an interrogative sentence, the question is introduced with the following:

1. Interrogative pronouns: *ვინ* (who), *რა* (what), *რომელი* (which one), *სადაური* (from where), *როდინდელი* (from what time), and so on.
2. Interrogative adverbs: *სად* (where), *როდის* (when), *რატომ?* (why), and so on.
3. Interrogative particles: *თუ* (if), *ნუთუ* (could it be), *ხომ*, *განა*.

The particles ***ხომ*** and ***განა*** have no independent meaning and are used to compose a *tail-question*: ***ხომ*** *გინდა?* (You do want it, don't you?); ***განა*** *არ გინდა?* (You want it, don't you?)

It is the question mark in writing and a stress in oral speech that differentiates an interrogative sentence without an interrogative word from a declarative sentence. The formal relation between the parts of both types of sentences can be the same.

Declarative sentence:	*დღეს ბანკი დაკეტილია.* Today the bank is closed.
Interrogative sentence:	*დღეს ბანკი* ***დაკეტილია'?*** (The stress is marked with an apostrophe.) Is the bank closed today?
Declarative sentence:	*ამ სტატიის ავტორი უცნობია.* The author of this article is unknown.
Interrogative sentence:	*ამ სტატიის ავტორი* ***უცნობია'?*** Is the author of this article unknown?

The stress is placed either on the first syllable of an interrogative word, if it is present, or on the last syllable of the verb denoting a predicate, if an interrogative word is absent.

სა'იდან *ჩამოხვედი?*
From where did you arrive?
თბილისიდან ***ჩამოხვედი'?***
Did you arrive from Tbilisi?
ვი'ნ *ჩამოგიყვანა?*
Who brought you?
მამამ ***ჩამოგიყვანა'?***
Did Father bring you?

რი'თი ჩამოხვედი?
How (by what) did you arrive?
*მატარებლით ჩამოხვედ**ი'?***
Did you arrive by train?

In an interrogative sentence without an interrogative word, the stress is placed on the last syllable of a predicate whether it is at the beginning, in the middle, or at the end of the sentence.

*შენი და გუშინ **ჩამოვიდა'**?*
*შენი და **ჩამოვიდა'** გუშინ?*
***ჩამოვიდა'** შენი და გუშინ?*
Did your sister arrive yesterday?

If the interrogative particle is the last word in an interrogative sentence without an interrogative word, the stress is always placed on the last syllable of the particle just like when the final word is a predicate.

*განა ეს დასაჯერებელი**ა'?*** *დასაჯერებელია ეს განა'?*
Could it be believed? (Could you believe it?)
*ხომ მოხვ**ა'ლ**?* *მოხვალ, **ხო'მ**?*
You will come over, won't you?

Usually, an interrogative word is placed at the beginning of a sentence.

Interrogative phrases are followed by a predicate:

ვინ (subject) *მოუტანა?*
Who brought (it to him)?
ვის (indirect object) *მოუტანა?*
To whom did he bring it?
რა (direct object) *მოუტანა?*
What did he bring (to him)?
რით (relative object) *მოუტანა?*
With what did he bring (it to him)?
როდის *მოუტანა?*
When did he bring (it to him)?
რატომ *მოუტანა?*
Why did he bring (it to him)?
სად *მოუტანა?*
Where did he bring (it to him)
საიდან *მოუტანა?*
Where did he bring it from?

Interrogative phrases may consist of an interrogative word and a noun (a subject or object). Such phrases are also followed with a verb:

***რომელი სტუდენტი** მოვიდა?*
Which student came over?
***ვისი სტუდენტი** მოვიდა?*
Whose student came over?
***რა წიგნი** იყიდე?*
What book did you buy?
***რომელი მსახიობი** მოგწონს?*
Which artist do you like?

18.3 Imperative and exclamative sentences

An imperative sentence expresses a request or command addressed to someone. If it is directed to a second person, whether singular or plural, the verb denoting a predicate is in the aorist.

შენ გუშინ დავალება **დაწერე** (Yesterday you wrote the assignment) – a declarative sentence indicating an action that took place in the past.

დაწერე დავალება! (Write the assignment!) – the aorist form of the indicative mode conveys a request/command that should be done/carried out in the future.

The verbs derived from the root *ვედ-*, *ვიდ-*, and *დი-*are exceptions to the rule since they have different forms in indicative and imperative mood:

> ***ახვედი, ჩახვედი, შეხვედი, გახვედი, წახვედი, ამოხვედი, ჩამოხვედი, გამოხვედი***, and ***წამოხვედი*** (you went up, down, in, out, away, etc.) are the forms of indicative mood.
> ***ადი, ჩადი, შედი, გადი, წადი, ამოდი, ჩამოდი, შემოდი, გამოდი***, and ***წამოდი*** (go up, down, in, out, etc.) are the corresponding forms of imperative mood.

ამ ქალაქში გუშინ ***ჩამოვედი.***
I arrived (came) to this town yesterday. (Declarative sentence)
მალე ***ჩამოდი*** ჩვენთან!
Come to us soon! (Imperative sentence)

If a request or command is addressed to a third person, the verb denoting a predicate is in the optative:

*ეს წიგნი მალე **წაიკითხოს!***
Let (tell) him to read this book soon!
*წერილი დროულად **მოიტანონ!***
Let (tell) them bring the letter on time!

Both sentences are in imperative mood. In negative imperative sentences, the particles **არ** and **ნუ** are used. The particle **არ** and the pronouns and adverbs derived from it are followed with a verb in the optative, which expresses a request/command not to do something:

*არ **დახურო** კარი!*
Don't shut the door!

*ჯერ არ **დაიძინო!***
Don't go to sleep yet!

*არავის (არ) **უთხრა!***
Don't tell anybody!

*არსად (არ) **წახვიდე!***
Don't go anywhere!

The particle **ნუ** and the pronouns and adverbs derived from it are followed with verbs in present or future tenses. In the present tense, the request/command asks to stop an action denoted with a predicate; in the future tense, it functions as the particle **არ** but expresses a request rather than a command not to do something in the future.

ნუ ***ხმაურობ!*** (Present)	*ნუ* ***იხმაურებ!*** (Future)
Stop making noise!	Don't make noise!
ნუ ***ეწევი!*** (Present)	*ნუღარ* ***მოსწევ!*** (Future)
Stop smoking!	Don't smoke!

ნურსად (ნუ) ***მიდიხარ*** *ასე გვიან!* (Present)
Don't go anywhere so late!
ნურსად (ნუ) ***წახვალ*** *ასე გვიან!* (Future)
Don't go anywhere so late!

An imperative sentence may have no verb:

ექიმი ჩქარა!	სიჩუმე!	წყნარად!
We need a doctor right now!	Silence!	Quiet!

Imperative and exclamative sentences end with the exclamation mark. However, there is a difference in their implied meaning and in logical and emotional undertones. An imperative sentence asks or demands that the action expressed with its predicate should be carried out, or it forbids it. An exclamative sentence may express a greeting, advice, encouragement, warning, blessing, curse, etc.

გამარჯობა, მეგობრებო!	*ბილეთები არ დაგავიწყდეს!*
Hello, friends!	Don't forget the tickets!
გაუფრთხილდი დედას!	*დაბრძანდით! მიირთვით ხაჭაპური!*
Take care of Mother!	(Please) sit down! Have some cheese bread.

As was mentioned, the particle **ნუ** conveys a request not to do something denoted by a predicate. It also expresses advice in an exclamative sentence: *ყველას ნუ ენდობი!* (future tense) (Don't trust everybody!). In addition, it conveys good will or a wish when used with a verb in the optative:

ღმერთმა ლხინი და სიხარული ნუ მოგიშალოთ!
May God not diminish (your) joy and happiness!
თქვენი მხარდაჭერა ნუ მოაკლდეს ჩვენს გუნდს!
May your support to our team not lessen!

An exclamative sentence can convey various emotions – satisfaction, approval, surprise, compassion, mockery, indignation, or hatred. In order to stress these emotions, the particles **აი, რა, ნეტავ** are used.

აი ეს მომწონს!
This (is what) I like!
აფერუმ მის ქალობას!
Applause to this woman!
რა ბიჭია, რა ბიჭი!
What a boy, what a boy!
გაუმარჯოს ჩვენს მეგობრობას!
Long live our friendship!
აცხონოს ღმერთმა!
May he rest in peace! (lit. *May God give him salvation!*)

18.4 Interrogative-exclamative sentence

An interrogative-exclamative is a sentence expressing both a question and a strong emotion, positive or negative. It is punctuated with interrogative and exclamation marks. Verbs in such sentences can be in variety of tenses, depending on the intended meaning – surprise, anger, irritation, despair, etc.:

ეს რა ამბავია?!
What's going on here?!
პატარა ბიჭი როგორ უნდა მოგერიოს?!
How can a little boy defeat you?!
თავს არ დამანებებ?!
Won't you let me be?! (i.e. *Don't bother me!*)
რატომ უთხარი?!
Why did you tell (this) to him?! (i.e. *You shouldn't have!*)
რას მელაპარაკები?!
What are you telling me?! You don't say!
სად წავიდე?! ვის მივმართო?!
Where should I go?! To whom should I appeal?!
ამას ვინ იფიქრებდა?!
Who would think of it?!
ამას ვისეუბნები!
Who are you telling this?!
ეს როგორ იკადრა?!
How could he do it?!

Chapter 19

Structure of sentences

19.1 Simple sentences

19.1.1 *Unextended and extended sentences*

An unextended sentence consists only of its main parts. In Georgian language they are the subject, the predicate, and direct and indirect objects. In other words, the noun phrase of an unextended sentence includes only a subject without an adjective, and in the verb phrase, it has neither an adjunct object nor an adverb. An extended sentence consists of main and secondary parts. The following chart shows the difference between these two types of sentences.

Unextended sentence

მოსწავლე მოდის.
A student is coming over.

Extended sentences

გახარებული მოსწავლე მოდის.
A happy student is coming over.

გახარებული მოსწავლე სწრაფად მოდის.
A happy student is swiftly coming over.

გახარებული მოსწავლე ჩანთით ხელში სწრაფად მოდის.
A happy student with a satchel in his hand is swiftly coming over.

გახარებული მოსწავლე ჩანთით ხელში სწრაფად მოდის ჩვენკენ.
A happy student with a satchel in his hand is swiftly coming over to us.

DOI: 10.4324/9781315281131-23

Unextended sentence

მასწავლებელი მოსწავლეს წიგნს უკითხავს.
A teacher is reading a book to a student.

Extended sentences

მასწავლებელი მოსწავლეებს წიგნს ხმამაღლა უკითხავს.
A teacher is reading a book to the students loudly.

ცნობილი მასწავლებელი მოსწავლეებს წიგნს უკითხავს.
A well-known teacher is reading a book to the students.

ცნობილი მასწავლებელი ბეჯით მოსწავლეებს წიგნს უკითხავს.
A well-known teacher is reading a book to the diligent students.

ცნობილი მასწავლებელი ბეჯით მოსწავლეებს საინტერესო წიგნს უკითხავს.
A well-known teacher is reading an interesting book to the diligent students.

ცნობილი მასწავლებელი ბეჯით მოსწავლეებს საინტერესო წიგნს ხმამაღლა უკითხავს.
A well-known teacher is loudly reading an interesting book to the diligent students.

ცნობილი მასწავლებელი ბეჯით მოსწავლეებს საინტერესო წიგნს კლასში ხმამაღლა უკითხავს.
A well-known teacher is loudly reading an interesting book to the diligent students in the classroom.

19.1.2 *Complete and incomplete sentences*

An incomplete sentence lacks a main or secondary part, but it is implied or determined from the context. Such omissions are common, especially in dialogues with truncated responses:

– (შენ) სად მიდიხარ?	– (შენ) დედასთან (~~მიდიხარ~~)?
Were are (you) going?	(Are you going) to Mom?

– (მე) სახლში (~~მივდივარ~~). – დიახ (~~მე დედასთან მივდივარ~~).
(~~I am going~~) home. Yes, (~~I am going to Mom~~).

In this dialogue all sentences are incomplete. They will become complete if the crossed-out words are restored.

19.1.3 *Sentences without or with omitted subjects*

If a subject neither is implied nor can be restored, the meaning of a sentence depends on its predicate. If a predicate is expressed with a zero valent and monopersonal verb its subject cannot be determined: წვიმს (It rains), თოვს (It snows), დაბნელდა (It has darkened), გათენდა (It has dawn), აცივდა (It's gotten cold), დათბა (It's gotten warm). A sentence without a subject may have a verb that theoretically has several actants but nevertheless does not imply an actual subject: გზაში დააღამდა (He was caught by darkness on the road), შესცივდა (He got cold). In both sentences the pronoun მას (he/him) may be inserted, but it is not the subject; it's the indirect object. An imaginary subject is the pronoun ის (it) (darkness and cold), but it is not considered an actual subject.

In a sentence with an omitted subject the predicate makes it possible to determine the missing subject. ბავშვს ახალი სათამაშო უყიდეს (bought a new toy for the child) – in this sentence the subject (მათ/they) can be easily restored because the predicate is denoted with a verb in a third-person plural form and the aorist tense.

19.1.4 *Noun-sentence*

A noun-sentence has only an NP consisting of a subject or a subject with an adjective. These sentences do not have VP, implied or actual. Their NP may be in different cases.

Nominative case: ხაზები . . . (lines), გრძელი ხაზები . . .(long lines), წრეები . . . (circles), ლურჯი წრეები . . . (blue circles), მთები . . . (mountains), მაღალი მთები (high mountains) ღრუბლები (clouds), თეთრი ღრუბლები (white clouds).

Ergative case: *ღვთის მადლმა!*(By grace of God!)
Vocative case: *ღმერთო ჩემო!* (My god!)

19.2 Sentence with coordinated parts

19.2.1 *Coordinated parts*

Parts of a sentence are considered coordinated if they comply with the three basic requirements: they answer the same question, refer to the same part of a sentence, and have the same syntactic function.

Coordinated parts	Sentences
NP = N + N	დედა და მამა დღეს კონცერტზე მიდიან. *Mother and Father* go to the concert today.
VP = V + V	ბავშვები **იცინოდნენ და თამაშობდნენ.** The children were *laughing and playing.*
VP: N (direct object) + N (direct object)	სტუმარს **ყავა და შოკოლადი** მივართვით. We offered *coffee and chocolate* to (our) guest.
VP: N (indirect object) + N (indirect object)	**მოყვარეს და მტერს** ერთნაირად ხვდებოდა. He met a *friend and foe* in the same way.
NP: (adj. + adj.)	**შავი და თეთრი** ფისუნიები ირეოდნენ ეზოში. *The black and the white* kitties were walking around in the yard.
Adjunct objects	ღვინის კასრებს **მუხისგან ან ცაცხვისგან** ამზადებენ. Wine barrels are made of *oak or lime* trees.
VP: (adv. + adv.)	ხეხილი **წითლად, ყვითლად, თეთრად** ყვაოდა. Fruit trees were blooming *in red, yellow, and white.*

In the previous sentences the words in bold letters conform to all three requirements to be considered coordinated. The sentence **დედაჩემის კარგმა მეგობარმა** ახალი წიგნი გამოსცა (My mother's good friend published a new book) is not coordinated although its subject has two qualifiers, **დედაჩემის** (my mother's) and **კარგმა** (good). These definitions are not of the same category; they refer to the same member of the sentence but answer to different questions; დედაჩემის (my mother's) – **ვისი** (whose) – is a genitive modifier, კარგმა (good) – **როგორმა** (what kind) – is an attributive adjective. They define dissimilar features of the subject and therefore cannot be considered coordinated.

19.2.1.1 *Joining coordinated parts*

Coordinated parts of a sentence can be joined with or without a conjunction. They may be joined with the three types of coordinative conjunctions: correlative, separative, and contrastive (see 12.1.). In the sentence **ბნელი, თბილი და წყნარი** ღამე იყო

(The night was **dark, warm, and quiet**), the words ***ბნელი*** (dark) and ***თბილი*** (warm) are joined without a conjunction, while ***თბილი და წყნარი*** (warm and quiet) are joined with the conjunction ***და***.

Joining parts of a sentence with conjunctions

Correlative conjunctions

ჩემმა დამ ბაზარში ყურძენი ***და*** *ატამი იყიდა.*
My sister bought grapes *and* peaches at the market (coordinated direct objects).

კაცი ***თუ*** *ქალი, გოგო* ***თუ*** *ბიჭი – ყველა ზეიმობდა ჩვენი ფეხბურთელების გამარჯვებას.*
Men *and* women, girls *and* boys, everybody celebrated the victory of our football team (compound subjects).

The particle **-*ც*** functions as the conjunction *და*:
*გვილოცავდნენ მეგობრები**ც**, მეზობლები**ც**, ნათესავები**ც**.*
Both friends, neighbours and relatives congratulated us (compound subjects).

ვერც *მეგობართან მივსულვარ (და)* ***ვერც*** *ნათესავთან.*
I can visit *neither* friends *nor* relatives (coordinated adjunct object).

აღარც *ბავშვების სიცილი მახარებს (და)* ***აღარც*** *ბავშვების სიმღერა.*
Neither the children's laughter (and) *nor* the children's singing delights me (compound subjects).

Separative conjunctions

ან *დაგვირეკოს,* ***ან*** *მოვიდეს. //* ***ან*** *დაგვირეკოს,* ***ან კიდევ*** *მოვიდეს.*
He should *either* call *or* visit us (compound predicates).

ხან *წვიმს,* ***ხან*** *თოვს,* ***ხანაც*** *თბილა.*
Sometimes it rains, *sometimes* it snows, (and) *sometimes* it's warm (compound predicates).

გინდა *წადი,* ***გინდა*** *დარჩი.*
Either leave or stay, whatever *you wish*, (compound predicates).

სიცხემ ***არა მარტო*** ***ადამიანები*** *შეაწუხა,* ***არამედ*** ***ცხოველებიც.***
The heat distressed not only people, but animals as well (coordinated adjunct objects).

Contrastive conjunctions

დიდხანს ილაპარაკა, ***მაგრამ*** *ვერავინ დაარწმუნა.*
He spoke for a long time *but* convinced nobody (compound predicates).
ფეხბურთელებმა ***არამცთუ*** *გაათანაბრეს ანგარიში,* ***არამედ*** *ცოტა ხანში კიდეც გაუსწრეს მოწინააღმდეგეს.*
The football players *not only* evened the score *but* in a short time surpassed the opponents (compound predicates).

Sentence with coordinated parts

A noun preceding the conjunction **და** in a pair of coordinated parts can be extended form when in the dative, genitive, or instrumental case:

ამომრჩევლებს და დეპუტატებს// ამომრჩევლებსა და დეპუტატებს *საერთო აზრი აქვთ.*
The voters and their candidates share their views.
ჩემი დის და ძმის// ჩემი დისა და ძმის *მეგობრები ჩემი მეგობრებიც არიან.*
The friends of my sister and brother are my friends as well.
ხალხი ***მანქანებით და ავტობუსებით// მანქანებითა და ავტობუსებით*** *მიემართებოდა ქალაქის ცენტრისკენ.*
People were heading to the city centre by cars and buses.

In a pair of coordinated adjunct objects and adverbs in the dative, genitive, or instrumental case, the one preceding the conjunction **და** will drop its postposition:

*ქალაქ**სა და** სოფელ**ში*** (coordinated adverbs) *ერთნაირად დაცხა.*
It was equally hot in the town and country.
*აქ კერავენ ტანსაცმელს მამაკაცებ**ისა** და ქალებ**ისათვის*** (coordinated adjunct objects in the genitive).
Clothes for men and women are sewn here.
*პრეზიდენტი მეუღლ**ითა** და შვილებ**ითურთ** მობრძანდა შეხვედრაზე* (coordinated adjunct objects in the instrumental).
The president came to the meeting with his wife and children.

Postpositions with particle **-ც** are never dropped:

ქალაქშიც და სოფელშიც *ერთნაირად დაცხა.*
It was equally hot in the town and country.

19.3 Coordinated parts in syntactic pairs

Each component of coordinated parts functions as a member of a syntactic pair. Each coordinated member is linked to another component of a syntactic pair either in a formal-substantive (coordination or subordination) or only formal relation.

19.3.1 *Compound predicates*

There are a few rules to which compound subjects and compound predicates should comply.

> *ბავშვები* ***დარბოდნენ, თამაშობდნენ, ყვიროდნენ.***
> The children were running around, playing and shouting.

All three predicates are denoted with the same types of verbs (monopersonal, intransitive). They modify the case of the subject, while the subject determines their third-person form, and both agree in number.

When compound predicates are denoted with verbs of various valencies, transitivities, or tenses, the case of the subject is determined by the predicate nearest to it.

> ***მოსწავლე*** (ის N – nom.) *სკოლაში* ***მოვიდა,*** *მასწავლებელს წიგნი* ***დაუბრუნა*** (მან N – erg.) *და მეგობრებს რვეულები* ***დაურიგა*** (მან N – erg.)
> **A student** (He N – nom.) **came** to school, **returned** (he N – erg.) a book to the teacher and **distributed** (he N – erg.) notebooks among his friends.

In the previous sentence, the three compound predicates can modify a subject in various cases, but here the subject complies to the nearest of them, an intransitive verb ***მოვიდა***, and therefore, it is in nominative case: ***მოსწავლე*** (ის N – nom.) ***მოვიდა*** (A student came to school).

> ***მოსწავლემ*** *მასწავლებელს წიგნი* ***დაუბრუნა*** (მან N – erg.), *მეგობრებს რვეულები* ***დაურიგა*** (მან N – erg.) *და მერხთან* ***დაჯდა*** (ის N – nom.).
> A student **returned** (he N – erg.) a book to the teacher, **distributed** (he N – erg.) notebooks among his friends and **sat** (he N – nom.) at a desk.

In this sentence the subject is modified by the nearest predicate denoted with a transitive verb ***დაუბრუნა***, and therefore, it is in ergative case: ***მოსწავლემ დაუბრუნა*** (მან N – erg.).

19.3.2 Compound subjects

1. If compound subjects are denoted with animate nouns the predicate must be in plural form.

   დედა და მამა დღეს კონცერტზე მიდიან.
   Mother and Father are going to a concert today.

   ეზოში კატები და ძაღლები დარბიან.
   Cats and dogs are running around in the yard.

2. If compound subjects are preceded by numerals, both the subjects and the predicate are in singular form.

   ხუთი მონადირე ტყისკენ გაემართა.
   Five hunters headed towards the woods.

But:

ხუთი მონადირე და ხუთი მწევარი ტყისკენ გაემართნენ.
Five hunters and five hounds headed towards the woods.

In such cases, the predicate is in the plural as a compound subject.

3. If compound subjects are denoted with the person pronouns, the predicate is always in plural form.

   მე და შენ//მე და მან წელს უნდა დავასრულოთ ამ სახლის მშენებლობა.
   You and I//He and I must finish building this house this year.

4. If compound subjects are joined with a separating conjunction, the predicate agrees in number with the nearest subject:

   ხან ბიჭი მღერის, ხან – გოგოები.
   Sometimes the boy sings, sometimes the girls.

   ხან გოგოები მღერიან, ხან – ბიჭი.
   Sometimes the girls sing, sometimes the boy.

19.3.3 Coordinated direct objects

The case of a direct object is modified by a predicate.

First- and second-person direct objects determine the object person marker of a verb. A predicate and its first- and second-person direct and indirect objects agree with each other in their plural forms.

შვილებმა და შვილიშვილებმა (**მათ** $S_{3\,pl}$) *გა-**გვ**-ახარ-ეს* (**ჩვენ** O_{1d}).
The children and grandchildren delighted us (O_{1d}).

შვილებმა და შვილიშვილებმა (**მათ** $S_{3\,pl}$) *მო-**გვ**-წერ-ეს* (**ჩვენ** O_{id1}).
The children and grandchildren wrote to us (O_{id1}).

1. When the subject is plural and inanimate, the verb indicates the plurality of the second-person object:

   სიმღერებმა და ცეკვებმა (მათ S_{3s}) *აღ-**გ**-ა-ფრთოვან-ა-**თ*** (=თქვენ O_d).
   The songs excited **you** (O_d).

   But: *მომღერლებმა და მოცეკვავეებმა* (**მათ** S_{3pl}) *აღ-**გ**-ა-ფრთოვან-**ეს*** (თქვენ=**მსმენელები** O_{2d}) – The singers delighted you, the listeners.

2. The third-person direct object is modified by a predicate, but it neither determines the person marker of a predicate, nor agrees with it in number.

19.3.4 Coordinated indirect objects

The case of an indirect object is modified by bipersonal intransitive and tripersonal transitive verbs.

1. A first-person indirect object can determine the object person and number markers of a verb in its plural form.

   *დედა **მე და გიას*** (=**ჩვენ**) *შოკოლადებს მო-**გვ**-ი-ტან-ს.*
   Mother will bring to me and Gia (= us) chocolates.

2. If the subject is in singular form, second-person indirect objects determine the person marker of the verb and agree with it in number.

   *მთელი ქვეყანა **შენ და შენს ძმას*** (=**თქვენ**) ***გ**-იყურებ-**თ**.*
   The entire country is looking at you and your brother (= you, plural).

3. When the subject is plural, the second-and third-person indirect objects determine a verb's person marker but cannot indicate its plurality.

   თქვენ სიმღერები გ(O_{2id}) *-ახსენებ-ენ*(**S3pl**) *წარსულს.*
   The songs (S) remind you (O_{id}) of the past (O_d).

ჩემი ძმები **ჩვენს ნათესავებსა** და **მეგობრებს** (=მათ O_{3id}) ხშირად ს(O_{3id}) -წერდ-ნენ(S_{3pl}) წერილს(O_{3d}).
My mother often wrote to relatives and friends (= them, O_{id})

მაყურებლები (=ისინი S) მომღერლებსა და **მოცეკვავეებს** (=მათ O_{3id}) შე-ს(O_{3id}) -ცქეროდ-**ნენ**(S_{3pl}).
The viewers (=they S_{3pl}) were watching the singers and dancers (=them O_{id}).

4. The only exceptions are predicates expressing possession, feeling, or attitudes. The indirect object modifies their person markers and plural form.

   მათ (O_{id}) ანტიკვარული ნივთები აქვ-თ(O_{id}).
   They have antique items.

   თქვენ,ჩვენს მოსწავლეებსა და სტუდენტებს (O_{id}), გ-იყვარ-თ მოგზაურობა.
   You, our pupils and students (O_{id}), love to travel.

   მოსწავლეებსა და სტუდენტებს (=მათ O_{id}) მო-ს-წონ-თ გადაცემა მოგზაურობაზე.
   The pupils and students (= they, O_{id}) like the (TV) program on travel.

19.4 Parenthetical words and phrases

Parenthetical words and phrases give additional information about one of the members of a sentence and can be removed without changing its structure or its overall meaning. They are not considered to be members of a sentence.

19.4.1 *Appositive*

An appositive specifies or gives additional information on the subject, objects, or adjectives in a sentence.

ჩვენი ლექტორი, **პროფესორი რაზმაძე**, ყველა სტუდენტს უყვარდა.
Our lecturer, Professor Razmadze, was loved by all students.

In this sentence, **პროფესორი რაზმაძე** is an appositive – i.e. supplemental attributive adjective. The appositive **პროფესორი რაზმაძე** describes the subject **ლექტორი** (lecturer) that precedes it and is separated from the main sentence with a comma. The subject can have a regular adjective **ჩვენი** (our) a member of the sentence, but it cannot influence the appositive. The appositive gives an additional information about the subject in the overall syntactic structure. The appositive does not necessarily follow the word it specifies, but it should be semantically clear to which member of a sentence it refers.

If the subject, **ჩვენი ლექტორი** (our lecturer), is removed, the appositive will become the subject of the sentence:

> *პროფესორი რაზმაძე* ყველა სტუდენტს უყვარდა.
> Professor Razmadze was loved by all students.

Sometimes an attributive adjective functions as an appositive which specifies or gives an additional information about the subject, object, or a noun part of a compound predicate.

> ეს გიორგია, **ჩემი ძმა.**
> This is George, my brother.

ჩემი ძმა (my brother) is an appositive referring to and specifying the noun part of the predicate **გიორგია** (= გიორგი არის, is George).

> მე, როგორც ახალბედა სტუდენტს, ხშირად მეხმარებოდა ჩემი მეგობარი.
> I, as a newly minted student, was often helped by my friend.

In this sentence **როგორც ახალბედა სტუდენტს** (as a newly minted student) is an appositive giving additional information about the indirect object (მე, I).

If the word, qualified by an appositive, is removed, the latter will become a member of the sentence.

An appositive can be turned into a subordinate clause:

> პრეზიდენტმა, როგორც უმაღლესმა მხედართმთავარმა, ოფიცრები დააჯილდოვა.
> The president, as the commander-in-chief, awarded the officers.

როგორც **უმაღლესმა მხედართმთავარმა** (as the commander-in-chief) is an appositive which can be changed into an adverbial clause of reason:

> ოფიცრები დააჯილდოვა პრეზიდენტმა, **რადგან უმაღლესი მთავარსარდალია.**
> The officers were awarded by the president *because he is the commander-in-chief*.

19.4.2 Free modifiers

A free modifier specifies various aspects of adverbs in a sentence:

> **დილით, მზის ამოსვლის დროს,** *უკვე სტადიონზე დავრბოდით.*
> In the morning, at sunrise, we were already jogging at the stadium.

There are two adverbs in this sentence: **დილით** (in the morning), which is not the main member of the sentence, and **მზის ამოსვლის დროს** (at sunrise), which is a free modifier of time and gives an additional information about what precise time in the morning the action was carried out.

> **ზღვისპირა ბულვარში, პალმების ხეივანში,** *იკრიბებოდნენ მოცურავენი.*
> At the Seashore Boulevard, in the Palm Tree Alley, the swimmers would gather.

In this sentence, the free modifier **პალმების ხეივანში** (the Palm Tree Alley) specifies exactly at which section of the Seashore Boulevard (**ზღვისპირა ბულვარი**) the action was taking place.

19.4.3 Asides

In Georgian some words or phrases express a speaker's attitude or disposition to the facts or ideas formulated in a sentence to which they are attached.

1. Confidence in the truthfulness of an utterance: **რა თქმა უნდა** (it goes without saying, of course), **რასაკვირველია** (of course), **მართლაც** (indeed), **ცხადია** (it's clear)

   რა თქმა უნდა, *ყველას გაგვიხარდა ჩემი დის წარმატება.*
   It goes without saying, all of us were happy about my sister's success.

   ისინი, **რასაკვირველია,** *ჩვენ შემოგვიერთდებიან.*
   They will, of course, join us.

2. Supposition: **მე მგონი** (I think), **როგორც(ა)ჩანს** (looks like), **როგორც ეტყობა** (it seems), **თუ არ ვცდები** (if I am not mistaken), **იმედია** (hopefully, I hope)

   როგორც ეტყობა, *ის მიხვდა თავის შეცდომას.*
   It seems, he understood his mistake.

თუ არ ვცდები, გუშინ კრებაზე განიხილეს ეს საკითხი.
If I am not mistaken, this problem was discussed at the meeting yesterday.

იმედია, კარგად ბრძანდებით.
I hope you are well.

3. Feelings stirred by an utterance ***ჩემდა/ჩვენდა სასიხარულოდ*** (to my/our delight), ***საბედნიეროდ*** (fortunately), ***ჩემი/შენი გულის გასახარად*** (to my/your heart's delight), ***საუბედუროდ*** (unfortunately), ***იღბლად/საიღბლოდ*** (luckily)

საბედნიეროდ, *არავინ არ დაშავებულა.*
Fortunately, nobody was injured.

სამწუხაროდ, *მე არა მაქვს მისი მისამართი.*
Unfortunately, I don't have his address.

4. Source of the information expressed in an utterance: ***ტრადიციის მიხედვით*** (according to the tradition), ***ჩემი აზრით*** (in my opinion), ***როგორც ამბობენ*** (it is said, they say), ***მისი წარმოდგენით*** (according to his view)

ჩემი აზრით, *აუცილებელია ამ ინფორმაციის გასაჯაროება.*
In my opinion, this information must be made public.

როგორც ამბობენ, *მან საქართველოს მოქალაქეობა მიიღო.*
They say, he has received Georgian citizenship.

5. Summarizing comment: ***როგორც უკვე ითქვა*** (as it was mentioned/said), ***მოკლედ რომ ვთქვათ*** (in short), ***თუ შეიძლება ასე ითქვას*** (if it may be said so), ***სხვაგვარად რომ ვთქვათ*** (in other words), ***გასაგებად რომ ვთქვათ*** (to make it clear)

როგორც უკვე ითქვა, *ჩვენ მხარს ვუჭერთ ამ კანდიდატს.*
As it was said, we support this candidate.

მოკლედ რომ ვთქვათ, *ეს საკითხი დაუყოვნებლივ არის გადასაჭრელი.*
In short, this problem should be solved without delay.

6. Sequence of events or facts: ***ჯერ ერთი*** (firstly), ***მერე მეორე*** (secondly), ***პირველად*** (the first time), ***უპირველეს ყოვლისა*** (first of all), ***მაშასადამე*** (that is), ***ამგვარად*** (thus), ***პირიქით*** (just the opposite), ***ერთი სიტყვით*** (in one word, in short), ***სხვათა შორის*** (by the way), ***ყოველ შემთხვევაში//ყოველი შემთხვევისთვის*** (just in case), ***მაგალითად*** (for example)

__ჯერ ერთი,__ ძალიან მომეწონა თვითონ სახლი, __მერე მეორე,__ ულამაზესი ხედი იშლება აივნიდან. __ერთი სიტყვით,__ საუკეთესო ადგილია.

First of all, I liked the house very much; secondly, there is a beautiful view from the balcony. In short, it is an excellent place.

__ყოველი შემთხვევისთვის,__ დავურეკოთ. ეგებ სახლშია.

Just in case, let's call him. Maybe he is at home.

19.4.4 Addressing formulas and expressions

When addressing someone, words should be in the vocative case:

ჩემო ლამაზო გოგო!	*ჩემო კარგო ბიჭო!*
My beautiful girl!	My good boy!
ჩემო საყვარელო დაიკო!	*მეგობრებო!*
My dear (little) sister!	Friends!

In formal speech the standard forms for addressing a man or a woman are **ბატონო** (Sir) and **ქალბატონო** (Madam, Ms.) followed by a personal (not last) name: **ბატონო მერაბ** (Mr. Merab), **ქალბატონო ნინო** (Ms. Nino).

In an informal, colloquial speech, Georgians often use the word *კაცო*, the vocative form of *კაცი* (man). Its lexical meaning has been reduced to an emphatic interjection stressing a statement and can be used while addressing both a man and a woman. It is frequently used after the word **კი** (yes) and **არა** (no) to emphasize the response, negative or positive.

რას ამბობ, __კაცო?!__ ტყუილი იქნება!
What are you saying, man?! It is a lie!
არა, __კაცო,__ გაზეთში წავიკითხე.
Of course not, I read it in a newspaper.
ამ წიგნს ვერ მათხოვებ?
Could you lend me this book?
კი, __კაცო,__ წაიღე, მაგრამ ერთ კვირაში დამიბრუნე.
Sure, take it, but bring back in a week.

There are two idiosyncratic expressions in Georgian often used when addressing someone: *__შენი/თქვენი ჭირიმე__* and *__(შენ) გენაცვალე__*. Etymologically, *__შენი ჭირიმე__* is derived from *__შენი__*

ჭირი მე, which literally means *your woe/plague to me*. In contemporary usage, it means *please*, *be so kind*, and *I beg you*:

> *მაია,* ***შენი ჭირიმე****, არ დაიგვიანო!*
> Maya, *please*, don't be late.
> *არჩილ,* ***შენი ჭირიმე****, ის წიგნი მომაწოდე!*
> Archil, *be so kind*, hand me that book.
> *ხალხო,* ***თქვენი ჭირიმე****, მომეხმარეთ!*
> People, *please (I beg you)*, help me!

The origin of the expression ***(შენ) გენაცვალე*** is more obscure. It might be derived from formulaic words for atonement or good will. Etymologically it means *I stood instead of you, I replaced you (in danger or peril)*. In contemporary Georgian, its meaning depends on the context in which it is used:

> *გიორგი, (შენ)* ***გენაცვალე****, როგორ გამიხარდა შენი ნახვა!*
> George, *my dear*, I am so glad to see you.
> *მანანა,* ***გენაცვალე****, ხვალ დამირეკე, დღეს არ მცალია!*
> Manana, *please*, call me tomorrow, I have no time today.

Quite often, especially in dialogues, it simply makes a request or response to a question sound politer but does not have any particular meaning.

> *დირექტორი აქ არის?*
> Is the manager here?
> *არა,* ***გენაცვალე****, ჯერ არ მოსულა.*
> No, (*sir*, *madam*, *miss*, *my dear*), he has not come yet.

Another word used in a polite request is **გეთაყვა** (please). However, it is a rather old-fashioned expression and seldom, if ever, used in the contemporary Georgian.

> *დაბრძანდით,* ***გეთაყვა!***
> Sit down, *please!*

In addressing formulas still used *by grace* in the ergative case – *მადლმა*:

> ***ძმობის მადლმა****,მხოლოდ სიმართლეს მოგახსენებ!*
> By grace of brotherhood, I will only tell you the truth!
> ***წმინდა გიორგის მადლმა****,ჩვენ არაფერი გაგვიჭირდება!*
> By the grace of St. George, nothing will be difficult for us!

Chapter 20

Complex sentences

A complex sentence includes two or more simple or coordinated sentences.

1. Complex sentences consisting of simple sentences:

   მამა ტელევიზორს უყურებდა, დედა წიგნს კითხულობდა.
   Father was watching television, Mother was reading a book.

   მოუთმენლად ველოდი, თბილისში როდის დავბრუნდებოდი.
   I could hardly wait to return to Tbilisi.

   ადრე მივედით, მაგრამ ბილეთები უკვე გაყიდული იყო.
   We went there early, but the tickets were already sold out.

2. A complex sentence consisting of a sentence with coordinated parts:

   ბიჭი უხმოდ, თავისთვის ტიროდა, მაგრამ მეგობრებმა თვალზე ცრემლი მაინც შეამჩნიეს და ეწყინათ.
   The boy was crying quietly, by himself, but his friends noticed the tears in his eyes and got upset.

   The first part of the sentence (*ბიჭი უხმოდ, თავისთვის ტიროდა*) is connected with adverbs of manner (*უხმოდ, თავისთვის*); the second part is connected with the predicates (შეამჩნიეს და ეწყინათ).

3. A complex sentence consisting of a simple and coordinated sentence:

   რაც უფრო მეტად ნერვიულობდა და ღელავდა ამ ამბავზე, მით უფრო გაურბოდა ჩვენთან შეხვედრას ჩვენი მეგობარი.
   The more he fretted and worried about this problem, the more our friend avoided meeting with us.

This complex sentence consists of two sentences. The first one is a sentence with the compound predicates (*ნერვიულობდა და ღელავდა*); the second one is a simple sentence.

DOI: 10.4324/9781315281131-24

20.1 Complex coordinate sentence

A complex coordinate sentence includes syntactically equal sentences which demonstrate the following:

1. **Simultaneous, sometimes contrasting actions**

   ბიჭები ფეხბურთს თამაშობდნენ, გოგოები მათ ტაშს უკრავდნენ.
   The boys were playing football, the girls were applauding them.

   მთებზე თოვლი იდო, მაგრამ ბარში ვარდები ყვაოდნენ.
   There was snow in the mountains, but in the valley roses were blooming.

2. **Sequence of events, chain of causes and consequences:**

   უცებ მოიღრუბლა და წვიმა წამოვიდა.
   Suddenly the sky was covered with clouds, and it started raining.

The parts of a complex sentence may be connected with or without a conjunction. The conjunctions used most frequently are correlative, separating, and contrastive (see 12.1.).

ჩემი გამოცდები დასრულდა ***და*** *არდადეგები დაიწყო.*
My exams finished and the vacations started.
ყველაფერი ვიყიდე, ***მაგრამ*** *რძე დამავიწყდა.*
I bought everything but forgot (to buy) milk.
ჩვენ კონცერტზე წავედით, ***ხოლო*** *ისინი სახლში დაბრუნდნენ.*
We went to a concert, while they returned home.

20.2 Complex subordinate sentence

The structure of a subordinate sentence:

1. It includes a main and a subordinate clause. The subordinate clause refers to a part of the main clause explaining and specifying it.
2. A main clause includes a word explained and specified by a subordinate clause.
3. A subordinate clause is connected with a main clause with a conjunction.
4. A subordinate clause has relative pronouns and adverbs; they join a main and subordinate clauses and function as parts of a subordinate clause.

ვულოცავ ყველას, ვისაც მუსიკა უყვარს! (I congratulate everyone who likes music!) – in this sentence the subordinate clause explains and specifies the indirect object *ყველას* (everyone). In the main clause, it refers to the relative pronoun *ვისაც* in the subordinate clause. The pronoun *ვისაც* joins the main and subordinate clauses and functions as the subject of the latter.

The main clause may not include the part explained and specified by its subordinate clause, but it can be reinstated.

> *ჩემთვის ცხადი გახდა, რომ ეს შეხვედრა კარგად ვერ დასრულდებოდა.*
> (It) became clear to me that the meeting would not end well.

The main clause, ***ჩემთვის ცხადი გახდა*** (became clear to me), is missing the subject ***ის*** (it), implied by the subordinate clause.

To determine the function of a subordinate clause, especially if the main clause does not include the part to which it refers, a question should be asked so that the omitted word will be the answer.

> *მე ვხედავდი, როგორ ყვაოდნენ ვარდები მეზობლის ეზოში.*
> I saw, how the roses bloomed in my neighbour's yard.

The main clause does not include the direct object (*it*), but it can be restored if asked – ***რას*** *ვხედავდი?* (what did I see?). The subordinate clause explains and determines the missing direct object in the main clause: *მე ვხედავდი* **მას** (I saw *it*). The subordinate clause – **როგორ ყვაოდნენ ვარდები მეზობლის ეზოში** – answers the question ***რას*** *ვხედავდი?* (what did I see?).

> *ივი დარწმუნებულია, რომ ყველაფერი კარგად იქნება.*
> He is sure that everything will be all right.

In this sentence the missing word in the main clause – **იმაში** (sure *of it* – adjunct object) – is defined by ***რომ ყველაფერი კარგად იქნება.***

An attribute denoted with a pronoun in a main clause is explained and specified by an adjective in its subordinate clause.

The stranger stopped near the house where my friend lived.

In this sentence the subordinate clause refers to ***სახლთან*** (near the house), which is specified with the attributive pronoun ***იმ*** (the pronoun ***ის*** in the dative case). Therefore, it is an attributive subordinate clause.

A main clause may have a personal name as its subject or object instead of an attributive pronoun:

> ნინო, რომელიც ბაღში სკამზე იჯდა, ძალიან ჩაფიქრებული იყო.
> Nino, who sat on a bench in the garden, was lost in thoughts.

In this sentence the attributive subordinate clause is ***რომელიც ბაღში სკამზე იჯდა*** (who sat on a bench in the garden), but an attribute defining the subject (*which*, Nino) is missing in the main clause.

There are complex sentences with various types of adverbial subordinate clauses with an adverb of place, time, manner, cause, and intention. Usually, an adverbial subordinate clause refers to an adverb or a word of the same property that is absent but may be restored in the main clause.

> ***როგორც კი*** *დაგინახე,* ***მაშინვე*** *შემიყვარდი.*
> As soon as I saw you, immediately I fell in love with you. (Adverb of time subordinate clause)
> ***იმიტომ*** *დაგირეკე,* ***რომ*** *შენი იმედი მაქვს.*
> I called you because I count on your help. (Adverb of cause subordinate clause)

The following chart lists the indicative words, relative pronouns, and adverbs used in various types of subordinate clauses.

Types of subordinate clauses	*Subordinating conjunction*	*Indicative words: relative pronouns and adverbs*	*Examples*
Subjective	რომ (that), თუ (if)	Relative pronouns ვინც (who[ever]), რაც (what[ever]), რომელიც (which[ever]), in the nominative, ergative, or dative form	*ჩემთვის ცხადი გახდა* ***(ის-subject),რომ*** *ეს შეხვედრა კარგად ვერ დასრულდებოდა.*

Types of subordinate clauses	*Subordinating conjunction*	*Indicative words: relative pronouns and adverbs*	*Examples*
		Relative adverbs სადაც (where[ever]), როცა (when)	It became clear to me that this meeting could not end well. *სადაც გინდა, იქ წადი.* Go where you want.
Direct object	რომ (that), თუ (if)	Relative pronouns ვინც (who[ever]), ვისაც (to whom[ever]), რაც (what[ever]) in different cases: რამაც (to what[ever]), რასაც (what[ever])	***რასაც*** *დასთეს, იმას მოიმკი.* What you sow, you shall mow.
Indirect object	რომ (that), თუ (if)	Relative pronouns ვინც (who[ever]), ვისაც (to whom[ever], whom[ever]), რაც (what[ever]), რასაც (to what[ever])	***იმას*** *გაურბის,* ***ვისაც*** *კარგად იცნობს.* He avoids those, whom he knows well.
Adjunct object	რომ (that), თუ (if)	Indicative words in the dative, genitive, and instrumental case with and without postpositions or the adverbial case without postpositions	*დარწმუნებული ვარ* (***იმაში*** – relative object), ***რომ*** *ეს საქმე მალე დამთავრდება.* I am sure that this business will end soon.
Attributive		Relative pronouns in various cases	*ერიდეთ* ***(ისეთ)****ადამიანს,* ***რომელიც*** *მუდამ დუმს.*

(Continued)

(Continued)

Types of subordinate clauses	*Subordinating conjunction*	*Indicative words: relative pronouns and adverbs*	*Examples*
		ვინც (who[ever]), რაც (what[ever]), რომელიც (who, which[ever]), როგორიც (what[ever] kind), რანაირიც (what[ever] kind), რამდენიც (as many as) Relative pronouns ის (that), იმ (that), ისეთი/ისეთივე (such as, the kind as), იმდენი/იმდენივე (the same amount as), იმისთანა (the kind as) Relative pronouns სადაც (from where), საიდანაც (from where), საითკენაც (to where), როდესაც (when), როცა (when) Conjunctive words ურომლისოდაც (without which)	Avoid (such) a person who is always silent. Avoid the person who is always silent. ***იმ*** *კაფეში წავიდეთ,* ***სადაც*** *გუშინ ვიყავით.* Let's go to the café where we were yesterday. *თქვენ აქ* ***ისეთ*** *რამეს ისწავლით,* ***ურომლისოდაც*** *სიცოცხლე შეუძლებელია.* You will learn things here without which it is impossible to live.
Adverb of place		Indicative words იქ (there), იქით (to there), იქითვე (to there), იქიდან (from there), იქამდე (till there, ყველგან (everywhere)	***იქ*** *წავიდეთ,* ***სადაც*** *ჩვენი მეგობრები არიან.* Let's go there, where our friends are.

Types of subordinate clauses	*Subordinating conjunction*	*Indicative words: relative pronouns and adverbs*	*Examples*
		Relative adverbs სადაც (from where), საითაც (to where), საიდანაც (from where), საითკენაც (to where)	***სადაც*** *არ გელიან,* ***იქ*** *ნუ მიხვალ.* Do not go there, where you are not welcome.
Adverb of time	როდესაც (when), როცა (when), როს (when), რომ (that), ოდეს (when), სანამ (until), ვიდრე (rather than), რა (what), რაკი (since), რაც (whatever), როგორც კი (as soon as), თუ არა (as soon as)	მაშინ (then), მაშინვე (right then), მაშინღა (only then), მას შემდეგ (after that), მანამ (until)	***მაშინ*** *მოხვედი,* ***როცა*** *იმედი უკვე გადაწურული მქონდა.* You showed up (then) when I gave up all hope.
Adverb of manner	რომ (that)	Indicative words ისე (so), იმდენად (so), იმდენჯერ (so many times), ისეთნაირად (in such way), იმგვარად (in such manner)	*შენმა სიტყვებმა* ***ისე*** *შემაშინა,* ***რომ*** *წასვლა გადავიფიქრე.* Your words frightened me so that I changed my mind about going (there).

(Continued)

(Continued)

Types of subordinate clauses	*Subordinating conjunction*	*Indicative words: relative pronouns and adverbs*	*Examples*
		Relative adverbs როგორც (as, so), თითქოს (as if), რამდენადაც (as much as), რამდენჯერაც (as many times as), ვითომ (as if), ვითომც (as if), რაც უფრო (more)	*ისე კარგად ლაპარაკობს,* ***როგორც*** *წერს.* He speaks as well as he writes.
Adverb of cause	რომ (that), რადგან (because, since), ვინაიდან (because), რაკი (since)	Relative adverbs იმიტომ (because), ამიტომ, იმიტომაც, ამიტომაც, მის გამო, იმის გამოც, ამის გამო, ამის გამოც (because)	***იმიტომ*** *ვერ წავედი,* ***რომ*** *ძალიან დაღლილი ვიყავი.* I did not go because I was very tired.
Adverb of intention	რომ (that), რათა (so that)	Relative adverbs იმისთვის (so that), მისთვის (so that)	***იმისთვის*** *გარიგებ,* ***რომ*** *შეცდომა არ დაუშვა.* I am advising you so that you will not make a mistake.

Syntactic tree of a sentence:

ჩემი ბავშვობის მეგობარი, რომელიც ჩემს მეზობლად ცხოვრობდა, ბათუმში გადავიდა.
My childhood friend who lived in my neighbourhood moved to Batumi.

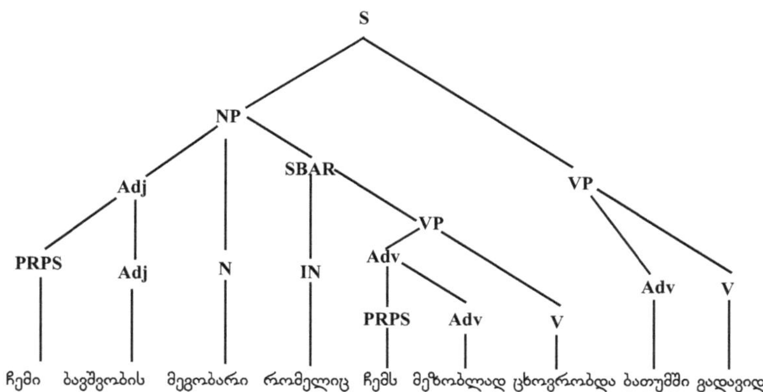

In order to change a complex subordinate sentence to a simple extended sentence, the subordinating conjunctions, relative pronouns, and adverbs should be eliminated so that the subordinate and the main clause can join together as one syntactic unit. In the previous sentence, the subordinating conjunction *რომელიც* should be dropped and the attributive subordinate clause changed into an attribute. This would require changing of the predicate of the subordinate clause, *ცხოვრობდა*, to the participle *მცხოვრები*, which will become an attribute attached to the predicate of the main clause *მეგობარი*. In the main clause the participle *მცხოვრები* will become a part of the noun phrase *ჩემი ბავშვობის მეგობარი* and transform it to *ჩემს მეზობლად მცხოვრები ჩემი ბავშვობის მეგობარი*. All these changes are shown in the following syntactic tree.

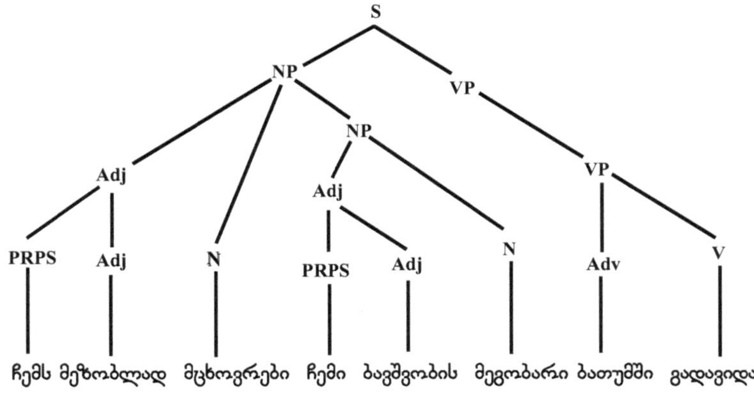

20.3 Adverbial clause of condition

An adverbial clause of condition neither qualifies any member of the main clause nor gives any additional information about them. It stipulates the condition that may or may not allow the action denoted in the main clause to be carried out.

თუ კაცი მოინდომებს, გამოსავალი მოიძებნება.
If there is a will, there is a way.

In this sentence the adverbial clause of condition indicates what is necessary (*a will*) to find the solution (*a way)* to a problem.

An adverbial clause of condition may precede or follow the main clause and is introduced with the conjunctions: *თუ* (if), *თუკი* (if, in case), *რომ* (so that, in order).

ექვსი თვე მაინც უნდა იყო დიეტაზე, რომ წონაში დაიკლო.
You should be on a diet at least six months in order to lose weight.

თუკი ყველა გამოცდას ჩავაბარებ, ორიოდე კვირით იტალიაში წავალ.
If I pass all (my) exams, I will go to Italy for a couple of weeks.

თუ დროზე არ მოვა, არ დაველოდებით.
If he does not show up on time, we will not wait for him.

20.4 Adverbial clause of concession

An adverbial clause of concession expresses a circumstance or condition contrary to the action denoted in the main clause but does not prevent it from being carried out. The verb in an adverbial clause of concession is always in indicative mood.

ძალიან დავიღალე, თუმცა დღეს არაფერი გამიკეთებია.
I am very tired even though I have done nothing today.

In this sentence, the subject (*I*) has no reason to be tired but feels so contrary to the circumstance expressed in the adverbial clause.

An adverbial clause of concession can express a possible obstruction to the action denoted in the main clause but cannot preclude it from happening.

სიმართლეს ***მაინც*** *ვიტყვი, თუნდ მთელი მსოფლიო* ***აღმიდგეს*** *წინ.*
I will tell the truth even if the entire world is against me.

The concessive clause expresses the possible obstacle (the whole world be against) that cannot hinder the action in the main clause (I will tell the truth).

The conjunctions introducing an adverbial clause of concession are **თუმცა**, **თუმცა კი** (although), **გინდ**, **გინდაც**, **თუნდ**, **თუნდა**, **თუნდაც** (even if), **რომ**, **კიდეც რომ**, **რომც** (even if), **რაგინდ**, **რაც უნდა** (no matter). Verbs following **თუმცა** and **თუმცა კი** are in one of the subjunctive moods. A verb in the main clause is often preceded with the particle **მაინც** (still, nevertheless).

> **თუმცა** ძალიან დავიღალე, ამ კონცერტზე **მაინც** წამოვალ.
> Although I am very tired, I will still go to this concert.
> **გინდაც** გვიან დაბრუნდე, **მაინც** დამირეკე.
> Even if you return late, call me nevertheless.
> **თუნდაც** არ გშიოდეს, ჩემი ხაჭაპური უნდა გასინჯო.
> Even if you are not hungry, you should taste my cheese-bread.
> **რაგინდ** ციოდეს, ბავშვებს **მაინც** ეზოში თამაში უნდათ.
> No matter how cold it is, the children nevertheless want to play in the yard.
> თუმცა კი დიდ პატივს გცემ, ამ საკითხში მაინც ვერ დაგეთანხმები.
> Although I respect you greatly, I cannot agree with you on this matter.
> **რომც** ვკვდებოდე, ამ კაცისგან დახმარებას არ მივიღებ.
> Even if I die, I will not ask this person for help.

Sometimes the particle **უნდა** (would, should) is added to a relative pronoun introducing a concessionary clause; the main clause following it will start with **მაინც არ**,**მაინც ვერ** (nevertheless, still, all the same):

> **ვინც უნდა** ეცადოს, **მაინც ვერ** შემაცვლევინებს აზრს.
> No matter who tries it, still they will not change my mind.
> **რასაც უნდა** დამპირდნენ, **მაინც არ** წავალ აქედან.
> No matter what they promise me, I will nevertheless not leave here.
> **რაც უნდა** გააკეთოს, **მაინც არ** დაუჯერებენ.
> No matter what he does, they will still not believe him.

20.5 Adverbial clause of result

An adverbial clause of result defines the result of an action denoted in the main clause and is introduced with the subordinating conjunctions **ასე რომ** (that's why, because of which/that), **რომ** (that, so), and **რის გამოც** (because of which/that).

*გუნდის კაპიტანი ავად გახდა***(მიზეზი), რის გამოც** *თამაში გადაიდო* **(შედეგი).**
The captain of the team fell ill (reason) because of that the game was postponed (result).
*ჩვენი რეისი გადაიდო***(მიზეზი), ასე რომ** *ბერლინში კონფერენციას ვერ დავესწარით* **(შედეგი).**
Our flight was postponed (reason), therefore we could not attend (result) the conference in Berlin.

An adverbial clause of result can be changed into a compound coordinate sentence by using the coordinating conjunctions **ამიტომ** or **ამის გამო** (this is why, therefore):

გუნდის კაპიტანი ავად გახდა, **ამის გამო** *თამაში გადაიდო.*
The captain of the team fell ill, this is why the game was postponed.
ჩვენი რეისი გადაიდო, **ამიტომ** *ბერლინში კონფერენციას ვერ დავესწარით.*
Our flight was postponed; this is why we could not attend the conference in Berlin.

An adverbial clause of result can be changed to an adverbial clause of reason as well. In this case a subordinate clause will define the reason, while the main clause will denote the result of an action expressed with the verb.

Adverbial clause of reason:

თამაში გადაიდო, **რადგან გუნდის კაპიტანი ავად გახდა.**
The game was postponed because the captain of the team fell ill.

In this sentence the main clause, **თამაში გადაიდო** (the game was postponed), conveys the result, while the subordinate clause, **რადგან გუნდის კაპიტანი ავად გახდა**, explains the reason and is introduced with the conjunction **რადგან** (because).

20.6 The compound-complex sentence

20.6.1 *Compound sentence with several subordinate clauses*

A complex sentence may have several subordinate clauses of various configuration:

1. A complex sentence may consist of one main clause with several subordinate clauses:

როცა ტელეფონმა დარეკა, არ ვუპასუხე, რადგან სასწრაფო სამუშაოს ვამთავრებდი.
When the phone rang, I did not answer it because I was finishing an urgent work.

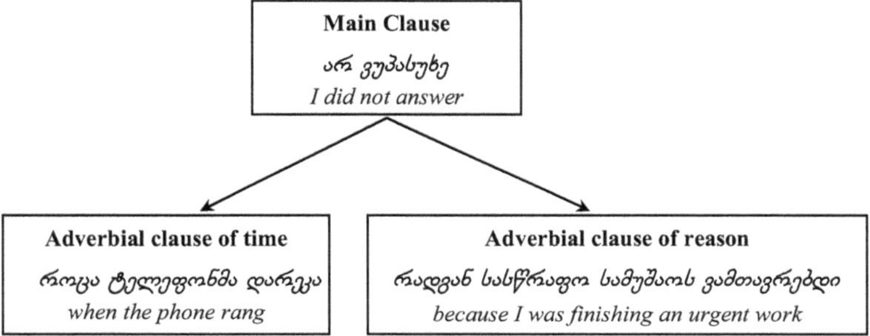

2. In a syntactic structure called a sequential subordinate clause, one and the same sentence can function as the main and the subordinate clause:

თქვენ ჩემგან მოითხოვთ, რომ პატივი ვცე ადამიანს, რომელმაც შეურაცხყოფა მიაყენა ჩემს ოჯახს.
You demand from me that I should respect a person who insulted my family.

The second phrase (II) is a direct object subordinate clause referring to the first phrase (*I*), but it functions as the main clause in reference to the third phrase (III), which is an adjectival subordinate clause and is not related structurally to the first phrase (*I*).

The following sentence has exactly the same structure but with different subordinate clauses.

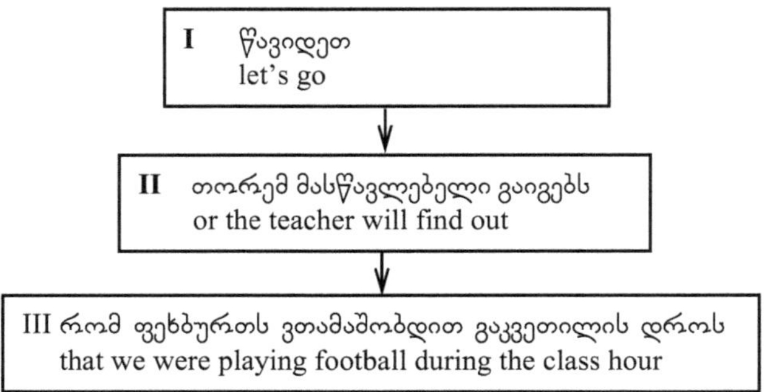

The second phrase (II) is a subordinate clause of concession referring to the first phrase (I, main clause); the latter is in the same relation to the third phrase (III), which, in its turn, is a direct object clause of the second phrase (II) and is not connected structurally to the first (*I*).

20.6.2 Mixed sentences

Mixed sentences include both coordinate and subordinate clauses.

> *ჩემი და, რომელიც ღია ფანჯარასთან იდგა, მოტრიალდა და ჩქარი ნაბიჯით წავიდა კარისკენ, რადგან კაკუნის ხმა მოესმა.*
> My sister, who was standing at the open window, turned around and went hastily to the door because she heard the sound of knocking.

The main clause is **ჩემი და მოტრიალდა და ჩქარი ნაბიჯით წავიდა კარისკენ** (my sister turned around and went hastily to the door). It has two predicates **მოტრიალდა და წავიდა** (turned and went). The phrase **რომელიც ღია ფანჯარასთან იდგა** (who was standing at the open window) is a subordinate clause of subject; **რადგან კაკუნის ხმა მოესმა** (because she heard the sound of knocking) is a subordinate clause of reason.

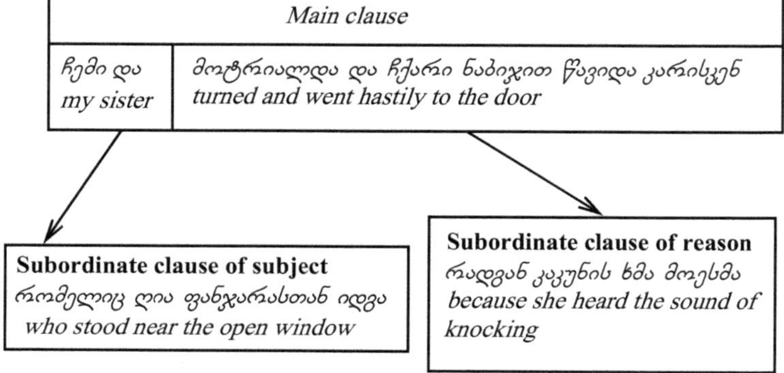

20.7 Direct and indirect speech

Direct speech quotes the words of a speaker verbatim and is often followed by a remark.

დაბრუნდა ჩემი შვილი! – წამოიძახა გახარებულმა დედამ.
My son is back! (*the words spoken*) – the happy mother exclaimed *(remark)*.
A remark added to a direct speech can be as a simple or compound clause. *დაბრუნდა ჩემი შვილი! – წამოიძახა გახარებულმა დედამ.*
My son is back! – the happy mother exclaimed *(the remark is a simple sentence)*.
დაბრუნდა ჩემი შვილი! – წამოიძახა გახარებულმა და აღელვებულმა დედამ.
My son is back! – the happy and agitated mother exclaimed *(the remark is a simple sentence with two adjectives)*.
დაბრუნდა ჩემი შვილი! – წამოიძახა გახარებულმა დედამ, მაგრამ ცრემლი ვერ შეიკავა.
My son is back! – the happy mother exclaimed but could not keep back tears *(the remark is a compound coordinate sentence)*.
დაბრუნდა ჩემი შვილი! – წამოიძახა გახარებულმა დედამ, როცა შვილი დაინახა.
My son is back! – the happy mother exclaimed when she saw her child *(the remark is a compound sentence with a subordinate clause of time)*.

Direct speech may be denoted with the particle-**ო**, which usually refers to a third party supposedly reporting someone's words verbatim:

*დაბრუნდა ჩემი შვილი**ო**. – წამოიძახა გახარებულმა დედამ.*
My son is back – the happy mother exclaimed.

The other particles that mark direct speech are -***მეთქი*** (I said) and-***თქო***, (s/he said) that have a specific function (see 13.5.).

*რატომ არ მოდის-**მეთქი**, გავიფიქრე.*
Why isn't he coming over, I thought to myself.
*შინ მალე დაბრუნდება-**თქო**, დაამშვიდე დედაჩემი.*
I will return home soon, calm Mother down (lit. *He will return home soon, he said, tell Mother/calm Mother down*).
*მოვალ**ო**, შემპირდა იგი.*
I will come over, he promised me *(the speaker is repeating the words of a third party)*.

In dialogues remarks are usually omitted:

შენი შვილი დაბრუნდა!
Your son is back!
მადლობა ღმერთს!
Thank God!

Indirect speech reports the content of someone's utterance. Usually, it is a complex compound sentence in which the main clause is a remark referring to someone's words, while the subordinate clause conveys the content of the utterance.

A direct speech with a remark:

შენი შვილი დაბრუნდა! – მახარა მეზობელმა.
Your son is back! – a neighbour told me gladly.

An indirect speech:

მეზობელმა მახარა, რომ ჩემი შვილი დაბრუნდა.
A neighbour told me gladly that my son was back.

The tense of the verb (in this case *დაბრუნდა*) does not change when a direct speech is transformed into an indirect speech. The remark becomes the main clause, and the direct speech is turned into a subordinate clause in which the possessive pronoun *შენი* (your) is changed to *ჩემი* (my) since now it is the first person who reports someone's (in this case, neighbour's) words.

Indirect speech is not necessarily conveyed with a compound subordinate sentence. It can be conveyed indirectly by changing the verbs in the direct speech into gerunds:

მეზობელმა ჩემი შვილის ***დაბრუნება*** *მახარა.*
The neighbour told me gladly about the return of my son.

Bibliography

Abuladze L., and Ludden A., 2011: *Grundwortschatz Georgisch*. Buske-Verlag, Hamburg. https://buske.de/reading/web/?isbn=9783875488784

Abuladze L., and Ludden A., 2018: *Lehrbuch der georgischen Sprache*. Buske-Verlag, Hamburg. https://buske.de/reading/web/?isbn=9783875488784

Akhvlediani G., 1999: *ახვლედიანი გ., ზოგადი ფონეტიკის საფუძვლები,* რედ. თ. გამყრელიძე. პედაგოგიური უნივერსიტეტის გამომცემლობა, თბილისი

Akhvlediani T., Lezhava I., and Kuparadze G., 2017: *ციური ახვლედიანი, ივანე ლეჟავა, გიორგი ყუფარაძე, ენათა შეპირისპირებითი ფონეტიკა (ქართული, ინგლისური, გერმანული და ფრანგული ენების მასალაზე)*, სახელმძღვანელო უმაღლესი სასწავლებლებისათვის, რედ. თ. ბოლქვაძე, გამომცემლობა "მერიდიანი", თბილისი

Amiridze N., 2006: *Reflexivization Strategies in Georgian*. LOT, Utrecht

Aronson H. I., 1970: Towards a Semantic Analysis of Case and Subject in Georgian. *Lingua (International Review of General Linguistics)*. A. J. B. N. Reichling, E. M. Uhlenbeck, and W. Sidney Allen (Eds.) 25(3): 291–301

Aronson H. I., 1972: Some Notes on Relative Clauses in Georgian. In: *The Chicago Which Hunt: Papers from the Relative Clause Festival*. Chicago Linguistic Society, Chicago, IL: 136–143

Aronson H. I., 1976: Grammatical Subject in Old Georgian. In: *Bedi Kartlisa*. Revue de kartvévlologie, vol. XXXIV. Publié avec le concours du Centre National de la Recherche Scientifique, Paris: 220–231

Aronson H. I., 1982a: *Georgian: A Reading Grammar*. Slavica Publishers, Indiana University, Bloomington

Aronson H. I., 1982b: On the Status of Version as a Grammatical Category in Georgian. *Folia Slavica* 5(1–3): 66–80

Aronson H. I., 1984: On Homonymy in the Georgian Verbal System. *Folia Slavica* 7(1–2): 21–37

Aronson H. I., 1990: *Georgian: A Reading Grammar*. Corrected Edition. Slavica Publishers, Indiana University, Bloomington

Aronson H. I., 1991: Modern Georgian. In: A. C. Harris (Ed.), *The Indigenous Languages of the Caucasus. Volume 1, The Kartvelian Languages*. Caravan Books, Delmar, NY

Aronson H. I., 1994: Paradigmatic and Syntagmatic Subject in Georgian. In: H. I. Aronson (Ed.), *Non-Slavic Languages of the USSR*. Slavica Publishers, Indiana University, Bloomington: 13–33

Aronson H. I., and Kiziria D., 1999: *Georgian Language and Culture: A Continuing Course*. Slavica Publishers, Bloomington

Asatiani R., 1990: *ასათიანი რ., გვარის მორფოლოგიური კატეგორია ქართულსა და ქართველურ ენებში, ტიპოლოგიური* ძიებანი. გამომცემლობა "მეცნიერება", თბილისი: 44–48

Asatiani R., 2005: The Main Devices of Foregrounding in the Information Structure of Georgian. In: *6th International Symposium on LLC*. Springer, Tbilisi and Heidelberg

Asatiani R., 2009: Functional Analysis of Contrasting Conjunctions in Georgian. In: N. Bezhanishvili, S. Löbner, K. Schwabe, and L. Spada (Eds.), *Logic, Language, and Computation*. Tbilisi. Lecture Notes in Computer Science, vol. 6618. Springer, Berlin and Heidelberg: 170–181

Asatiani R., 2010: *ასათიანი რ., წინადადების საინფორმაციო სტრუქტურა: ვნებითი გვარის კონსტრუქციათა პრაგმატიკული თავისებურება ქართველურ ენებში*, ენათმეცნიერების საკითხები, I–II. თბილისის უნივერსიტეტის გამომცემლობა, თბილისი: 135–144

Baramidze L., 1964: *ბარამიძე ლ., ზოგიერთი ტიპის მეშველზმნიან ფორმათა ჩასახვა და განვითარება ქართულში*, თსუ ძველი ქართული ენის კათედრის შრომები, ტ. 9. თბილისის უნივერსიტეტის გამომცემლობა, თბილისი: 95–150

Baratashvili Z., 2013: *ბარათაშვილი ზ., დიათეზა და გვარის კატეგორია ქართულში*. ენათმეცნიერების საკითხები, თბილისის უნივერსიტეტის გამომცემლობა, თბილისი: 66–81

Baratashvili Z., 2019: The Types of the Causative Construction in Georgian. *Bulletin of the Georgian National Academy of Sciences* 13(1): 126–136

Bickel B., and Johanna N., 2006: Inflectional Morphology. In: T. Shopen (Ed.), *Language Typology and Syntactic Description*. 2nd edition. Cambridge University Press, Cambridge

Boeder W., 1968: Über die Versionen des georgischen Verbs. *Folia Linguistica* 2: 82–151

Boeder W., 1975: Zur Analyse des altgeorgischen Alphabets. In: *Forschung und Lehre: Festgruß Joh. Schröpfer*. Slavisches Seminar, Hamburg: 17–34

Boeder W., 2000: Evidentiality in Georgian. In: L. Johanson and B. Utas (Eds.), *Evidentials: Turkic, Iranian and Neighbouring Languages*. Mouton de Gruyter, Berlin: 275–328

Boeder W., 2002: Syntax and Morphology of Polysynthesis in the Georgian Verb. In N. Evans and H.-J. Sasse (Eds.), *Problems of Polysynthesis*. Akademie Verlag, Berlin: 87–111

Boeder W., 2005: The South Caucasian Languages. *Lingua* 115(1): 5–89

Boeder W., 2009: Problems of Mismatch between Syntax and Morphology in Kartvelian, Kadmos. *Journal of Studies of Humanities* #1, Ilia State University, Tbilisi: 60–66

Boeder W., 2010: Mood in Modern Georgian. In: Björn Rothstein and Rolf Thieroff (Eds.), *Mood in the Languages of Europe*. Studies in

Language Companion Series 120. John Benjamins Publishing Company, Amsterdam and Philadelphia: 603–634

Bolkvadze T., 2005: *ბოლქვაძე თ., იდეოლოგიზებული ღირებულებები.* თბილისის უნივერსიტეტის გამომცემლობა, თბილისი

Cherchi M., 1993: Verbal Tmesis in Georgian. *Annali del Dipartimento di studi del Mondo Classico e del Mediterraneo Antico Sezione Linguistics* 16: 33–115

Cherchi M., 1997a: *Modern Georgian Morphosyntax: A Grammatico-categorical Hierarchy-Based Analysis with Special Reference to Indirect Verbs and Passives of State*. Harrassowitz Verlag, Wiesbaden

Cherchi M., 1997b: Verbal Tmesis in Georgian, Part II. *Annali del Dipartimento di studi del Mondo Classico e del Mediterraneo Antico Sezione Linguistics* 19: 63–137

Chikobava A., 1939: *ჩიქობავა არნ., მოთხრობითი ბრუნვის გენეზისისათვის ქართველურ ენებში*, თბილისის უნივერსიტეტის შრომები, ტ. 10. თბილისის უნივერსიტეტის გამომცემლობა, თბილისი

Chikobava A., 1946: *ჩიქობავა არნ., მრავლობითის აღნიშვნის ძირითადი პრინციპისათვის ქართული ზმნის უღვლილების სისტემაში, იბერიულ-კავკასიური ენათმეცნიერება, ტ. I.* საქართველოს სსრ მეცნიერებათა აკადემია. ნ. მარის სახელობის ენის ინსტიტუტი, თბილისი: 91–130

Chikobava A., 1948: *ჩიქობავა არნ., ერგატიული კონსტრუქციის პრობლემა იბერიულ-კავკასიურ ენებში, ტ. 1, ნომინატიური და ერგატიული კონსტრუქციის ისტორიული ურთიერთობა ძველი ქართული სალიტერატურო ენის მონაცემთა მიხედვით.* საქართველოს სსრ მეცნიერებათა აკადემია. ნ. მარის სახელობის ენის ინსტიტუტი, თბილისი

Chikobava A., 1954: *ჩიქობავა არნ., მრავლობითის სუფიქსთა გენეზისისათვის ქართულში,* იბერიულ-კავკასიური ენათმეცნიერება, ტ.V1. საქართველოს სსრ მეცნიერებათა აკადემიის ენათმეცნიერების ინსტიტუტი, თბილისი: 66–77

Chikobava A., 1968: *ჩიქობავა არნ., მარტივი წინადადების პრობლემა ქართულში.* საქართველოს სსრ მეცნიერებათა აკადემიის ენათმეც ნიერების ინსტიტუტი, გამომცემლობა "მეცნიერება", თბილისი

Chikobava A., 1983: *ჩიქობავა არნ., მორფოლოგიური ფაქტის რეინტერპრეტაციისათვის (ქართული ზმნის უღვლილების მასალაზე),* იბერიულ-კავკასიური ენათმეცნიერების წელიწდეული, ტ. X. საქართველოს სსრ მეცნიერებათა აკადემიის ენათმეცნიერების ინსტიტუტი, თბილისი: 32–42

Chikobava A., 1998: *ჩიქობავა არნ., რა თავისებურებანი ახასიათებს ქართული ენის აგებულებას?* საქართველოს მეცნიერებათა აკადემიის არნ. ჩიქობავას სახელობის ენათმეცნიერების ინსტიტუტი. პედაგოგთა კვალიფიკაციის ამაღლებისა და გადამზადების ცენტრალური ინსტიტუტი, თბილისი

Chomsky N., 1957: *Syntactic Structures*. Mouton, The Hague

Chomsky N., 1959: On Certain Formal Properties of Grammars. In: L. Brillouin, C. Cherry, and P. Elias (Eds.), *Information and Control* 2. Academic Press: 137–167

Chomsky N., 1977: *Essays on Form and Interpretation*. Elsevier, North-Holland

Chomsky N., 1991: Some Notes on Economy of Derivation and Representation. In: R. Freidin (Ed.), *Principles and Parameters in Comparative Grammar*. Current Studies in Linguistics, No. 20. The MIT Press, Cambridge, MA and London: 417–454

Chotivari-Junger St., Melikischwili D., and Wittek L., 2010: *Georgische Verbtabellen*. BUSKE, Hambourg

Chumburidze Z., 1976: *ჭუმბურიძე ზ., -ავ და -ამ თემისნიშნიან ზმნათა უღლებისათვის I თურმეობითში,* თსუ ძველი ქართული ენის კათედრის შრომები, ტ. 19. თბილისის უნივერსიტეტის გამომცემლობა, თბილისი: 25–27

Chumburidze Z., 1986: *ჭუმბურიძე ზ., მყოფადი ქართველურ ენებში.* თბილისის უნივერსიტეტის გამომცემლობა, თბილისი

Datukishvili K., 1997a: Some Questions of Computer Synthesis of Verb in Georgian. In: R. Cooper and T. Gamkrelidze (Eds.), *Proceedings of the Second Tbilisi Symposium on Language, Logic, and Computation.* Tbilisi State University, Tbilisi: 83–85

Datukishvili K., 1997b: *დათუკიშვილი ქ., პირის ნიშანთა სისტემა ქართულში,* ზურაბ ჭუმბურიძეს, დაბადების 70 წლისთავისადმი მიძღვნილი კრებული. თბილისის უნივერსიტეტის გამომცემლობა, თბილისი: 63–71

Davitiani A., 1973: *დავითიანი, აკ. ქართული ენის სინტაქსი.* გამომცემლობა “განათლება”, თბილისი

Dixon R. M. W., 1979. Ergativity. *Language, Published by Linguistic Society of America* 55: 59–138

Dzidziguri S., 1973: *ძიძიგური შ., კავშირები ქართულ ენაში.* თბილისის უნივერსიტეტის გამომცემლობა, თბილისი

Enukidze L., 1987: *ენუქიძე ლ., ძირითადი სინტაქსური თეორიები თანამედროვე საზღვარგარეთულ ენათმეცნიერებაში,* რედ. მ.მაჭავარიანი. გამომცემლობა “მეცნიერება”, თბილისი

Fähnrich H., and Sarjveladze Z., 1995: *Etymologisches Wörterbuch der Kartwel-Sprachen*. Brill, Leiden, New York and Köln

Fähnrich H., and Sarjveladze Z., 2000: *ფენრიხი ჰ., სარჯველაძე ზ., ქართველურ ენათა ეტიმოლოგიური ლექსიკონი.* სულხან-საბა ორბელიანის სახელმწიფო უნივერსიტეტის გამომცემლობა, თბილისი

Gabunia K., 2016: *გაბუნია, კ. მარტივი წინადადების ანალიზის პრინციპები თანამედროვე ქართულში.* თბილისის უნივერსიტეტის გამომცემლობა, თბილისი

Gamkrelidze T., 1989: *გამყრელიძე თ., წერის ანბანური სისტემა და ძველი ქართული დამწერლობა: ანბანური წერის ტიპოლოგია და წარმომავლობა,* ა. შანიძის რედაქციით, აკად. გ. წერეთლის აღმოსავლეთმცოდნეობის ინსტიტუტი, საქართველოს სსრ მეცნიერებათა აკადემია. თბილისის უნივერსიტეტის გამომცემლობა, თბილისი

Gamkrelidze T., 1994: *Alphabet Writing and the Old Georgian Script: A Topology and Provinience of Alphabetic Writing Systems*. Caravan Books, Delmar, NY

Gamkrelidze T., 2008: *გამყრელიძე თ.,* ზმნის "პირიანობა" და ენა და ენობრივი ნიშანი, სტატიების კრებული, საქართველოს მეცნიერებათა ეროვნული აკადემია, საქართველოს მეცნიერებათა ეროვნული აკადემია, თბილისი: 113–133

Gamkrelidze T., 2011: *გამყრელიძე თ., ძველი ქართული ასომთავრული დამწერლობა,* საქართველოს ეთნოგრაფიული მემკვიდრეობის დაცვის ფონდი. სერია: ქართველი ხალხის კულტურა, თბილისი

Gamkrelidze T., and Ivanov V., 1994–1995: *Indo-European Language and Indo-Europeans*, vol. I–II. Trends in Linguistics, Studies and Monographs, 80. Mouton de Gruyter, Berlin and New York

Gamkrelidze T., Kiknadze Z., Shaduri I., and Shengelia N., 2003: *გამყრელიძე თ., კიკნაძე ზ., შადური ი., შენგელია ნ., თეორიული ენათმეცნიერების კურსი.* თბილისის უნივერსიტეტის გამომცემლობა, თბილისი

Gamkrelidze T., and Machavariani G., 1965: *გამყრელიძე თ., მაჭავარიანი გ., სონანტთა სისტემა და აბლაუტი ქართველურ ენებში: საერთო-ქართველური სტრუქტურის ტიპოლოგია,. გ. წერეთლის რედ. და წინასიტყვ.* გამომცემლობა "მეცნიერება", თბილისი

Geguchadze L., 2010: *გეგუჩაძე ლ., ქართული ენა სინტაქსის საკითხები.* თბილისის უნივერსიტეტის გამომცემლობა, თბილისი

Gelashvili T., 2019: *გელაშვილი თ., სახელზმნის მორფოლოგიურ-სინტაქსური ფუნქციის ტიპოლოგიური ურთიერთმიმართებანი,* თბილისი

Giorgobiani T., 1997: *გიორგობიანი თ., უკუქცევითობა, საშუალი გვარი ბერძნულში და სათავისო ქცევა ქართულში, საენათმეცნიერო ძიებანი, VI.* გ. გოგოლაშვილი (რედ.), საქართველოს მეცნიერებათა აკადემია, არნ. ჩიქობავას სახელობის ენათმეცნიერების ინსტიტუტი, ბესარიონ ჯორბენაძის საზოგადოება, თბილისი

Gogolashvili G. B., and Arabuli A., 2016a: *ახალი ქართული ენა, წიგნი I, სალიტერატურო ენის მორფოლოგია:* ზოგადი, *სახელი, გ. გოგოლაშვილისა* და ა. *არაბულის რედაქციით.* ივ. ჯავახიშვილის სახ. თბილისის სახელმწიფო უნივერსიტეტი, არნ. ჩიქობავას სახ. ენათმეცნიერების ინსტიტუტი, თბილისი

Gogolashvili G. B., and Arabuli A., 2016b: *ახალი ქართული ენა, წიგნი II, სალიტერატურო ენის მორფოლოგია:* ზმნა, *გ. გოგოლაშვილისა* და ა. *არაბულის რედაქციით.* ივ. ჯავახიშვილის სახ. თბილისის სახელმწიფო უნივერსიტეტი. არნ. ჩიქობავას სახ. ენათმეცნიერების ინსტიტუტი, თბილისი

Gogolashvili G. B., Kvantaliani T., and Shengelia D., 1989: *გოგოლაშვილი გ., კვანტალიანი ც., შენგელია დ., ქართული ენის ზმნური ფუძეების ლექსიკონი (მასალები ქართული ენის სისტემატური კურსისათვის).* გამომცემლობა "მეცნიერება" თბილისი

Gogolashvili G. B., Kvantaliani T., and Shengelia D., 1991: *გოგოლაშვილი გ., კვანტალიანი ც., შენგელია დ., ქართული ენის სახელზმნური ფუძეების ლექსიკონი (მასალები ქართული*

ენის სისტემატური კურსისათვის). გამომცემლობა "მეცნიერება", თბილისი

Gurevich O., 2006: *Constructional Morphology: The Georgian Version.* A Dissertation Submitted in Partial Satisfaction of the Requirements for the Degree of Doctor of Philosophy in Linguistics in the Graduate Division of the University of California, Berkeley

Gvinadze T., 1989: *ღვინაძე თ., ქართული ზმნის ვნებითი გვარის ფორმათა სტილისტიკა.* საქართველოს სსრ მეცნიერებათა აკადემია, ენათმეცნიერების ინსტიტუტი, გამომცემლობა "მეცნიერება", თბილისი

Harris A. C., 1976: *Grammatical Relations in Modern Georgian.* A Thesis in Partial Fulfillment of the Requirements for the Degree of Doctor of Philosophy in the Subject of Linguistics. Harvard University Press, Cambridge, MA

Harris A. C., 1981: *Georgian Syntax: A Study in Relational Grammar.* Cambridge University Press, Cambridge

Harris A. C., 1985: *Diachronic Syntax: The Kartvelian Case.* Syntax and Semantics, vol. 18. Academic Press, Orlando

Harris A. C., 1990: Georgian: A Language with Active Case Marking. *Lingua* 80: 47–65

Harris A. C., 1995a: *Modal Auxiliaries in Georgian.* ალ. კარტოზია (რედ.), ფილოლოგიური ძიებანი, საქართველოს მეცნიერებათა აკადემია, გამომცემლობა "მეცნიერება", თბილისი: 195–207

Harris A. C., 1995b: Georgian. In: J. Jacobs (Ed.), *Syntax: Ein Internationales Handbuch zeitgenössischer Forschung.* Mouton, Berlin and New York: 1377–1397

Harris A. C., 2000: Word Order Harmonies and Word Order Change in Georgian. In: R. Sornicola, E. Poppe, and A. Shisha-Halevy (Eds.), *Stability, Variation and Change of Word-Order Patterns Over Time.* Current Issues in Linguistic Theory, vol. 213. John Benjamins Publishing Company, Amsterdam and Philadelphia: 133–163

Harris A. C., 2003: Preverbs and Their Origins in Georgian and Udi. In: Geept Booij and Jaap Ven Marle (Eds.), *Yearbook of Morphology.* Kluwer Academic Publishers, New York, Boston, Dordrecht, London and Moscow: 61–78

Harris A. C., 2004: *History in Support of Synchrony.* Proceedings of the 30th Annual Meeting of the Berkeley Linguistic Society, Berkeley Linguistics Society, 30, Berkeley: 142–159

Harris A. C., 2009: *Georgian Syntax.* Cambridge University Press, Cambridge

Hewitt B. G., 1987a: Georgian: Ergative or Active? *Lingua* 71: 319–340

Hewitt B. G., 1987b: Review of "Diachronic Syntax: The Kartvelian Case by Alice C. Harris". *Revue des'etudes g'eorgiennes et caucasiennes* 3: 173–213

Hewitt B. G., 1995a: Georgian – Ergative, Active, or What? In: D. Bennett, T. Bynon, and B. G. Hewitt (Eds.), *Subject, Voice, and Ergativity: Selected Essays.* School of Oriental and African Studies, University of London, London: 202–217

Hewitt B. G., 1995b: *Georgian: A Structural Reference Grammar.* John Benjamins Publishing Company, Amsterdam and Philadelphia

Hewitt B. G., 2005: *Georgian, a Learner's Grammar*. Routledge, London

Hillery P. J., 2013: *The Georgian Language*. An Outline Grammatical Summary. ქართული ენა, Made by Vidaba, Minsk

Holisky D. A., 1979: On Lexical Aspect and Verb Classes in Georgian. In: *The Elements: A Parasession on Linguistic Units and Levels*. Including Papers from the Conference on Non-Slavic Languages of the USSR. Chicago Linguistic Society, University of Chicago, Chicago, IL

Holisky D. A., 1981a: *Aspect and Georgian Medial Verbs*. Caravan Books, Delmar, NY

Holisky D. A., 1981b: Aspect Theory and Georgian Aspect. In: P. J. Tedeschi and A. Zaenen (Eds.), *Tense and Aspect: Syntax and Semantics*, vol. 14. Academic Press, New York: 127–144

Iakobidze N., 2018: *იაკობიძე, ნ., ზმნურ შეთანხმებათა სწავლების საკითხი,* ქართველოლოგიის აქტუალური პრობლემები, 7, სამეცნიერო ჟურნალი, საქართველოს საპატრიარქოს წმიდა ანდრია პირველწოდებულის სახელობის ქართული უნივერსიტეტი, თბილისი: 100–108

Imnaishvili I., 1957: *იმნაიშვილი ი., სახელთა ბრუნება და ბრუნვათა ფუნქციები ძველ ქართულში, რედაქტორი ა. შანიძე.* თბილისის უნივერსიტეტის გამომცემლობა, თბილისი

Ivanishvili M., and Soselia T., 2002: *ივანიშვილი მ., სოსელია თ., ქართული პასიური კონსტრუქციის ზოგიერთი მორფოსინტაქსური და სემანტიკური თავისებურება ქართულში, ენათმეცნიერების საკითხები, 4.* თბილისის უნივერსიტეტის გამომცემლობა, თბილისი: 133–140

Javakhishvili I., 1949: *ჯავახიშვილი ი., ქართული დამწერლობათამცოდნეობა ანუ პალეოგრაფია, მეორე გამოცემა.* თბილისის სახელმწიფო უნივერსიტეტის გამომცემლობა, თბილისი

Jorbenadze B., 1975: *ჯორბენაძე ბ., ზმნის გვარის ფორმათა წარმოებისა და ფუნქციის საკითხები ქართულში.* თბილისის უნივერსიტეტის გამომცემლობა, თბილისი

Jorbenadze B., 1980: *ჯორბენაძე ბ., ქართული ზმნის ფორმობრივი და ფუნქციური ანალიზის პრინციპები.* თბილისის უნივერსიტეტის გამომცემლობა, თბილისი

Jorbenadze B., 1983: *ჯორბენაძე ბ., ზმნის ხმოვანპრეფიქსული წარმოება ქართულში.* თბილისის უნივერსიტეტის გამომცემლობა, თბილისი

Jorbenadze B., 1985a: *ჯორბენაძე ბ., ქართული ენის ფაკულტატიური გრამატიკის საკითხები.* თბილისის უნივერსიტეტის გამომცემლობა, თბილისი

Jorbenadze B., 1985b: *ჯორბენაძე ბ.,* ქართული ზმნა, თბილისის უნივერსიტეტის გამომცემლობა, თბილისი

Jorbenadze B., 1988: *ჯორბენაძე ბ., თემის ნიშანთა განაწილებისათვის ქართულში, იბერიულ-კავკასიური ენათმეცნიერება, ტ. XXVII.* საქართველოს სსრ მეცნიერებათა აკადემიის ენათმეცნიერების ინსტიტუტი, თბილისი: 175–186

Jorbenadze B., 1989: *ჯორბენაძე ბ., ქართული დიალექტოლოგია. წიგნი 1.* გამომცემლობა "მეცნიერება", თბილისი

Jorbenadze B., 1990: *ჯორბენაძე ბ., ზმნის გრამატიკული კატეგორიების კლასიფიკაციის პრინციპები ქართულში, იბერიულკავკასიური*

ენათმეცნიერების წელიწდეული, ტ. XVII. საქართველოს მეცნიერებათა აკადემიის ენათმეცნიერების ინსტიტუტი, თბილისი: 11–23

Jorbenadze B., 1993: *ჯორბენაძე ბ., ნაზმნარი მოდალური ელემენტები ქართულში, ქართული სიტყვის კულტურის საკითხები, ტ. X.* საქართველოს მეცნიერებათა აკადემიის ენათმეცნიერების ინსტიტუტი, თბილისი

Jorbenadze B., 1998: *ჯორბენაძე ბ., ქართული დიალექტოლოგია. წიგნი 2.* გამომცემლობა "მეცნიერება", თბილისი

Jorbenadze B., Kobaidze M., and Beridze M., 1988: *ჯორბენაძე ბ., მ.კობაიძე მ., ბერიძე მ., ქართული ენის მორფემებისა და მოდალური ელემენტების ლექსიკონი (მასალები ქართული ენის სისტემატური კურსისათვის).* გამომცემლობა "მეცნიერება", თბილისი

Jorbenadze N., 2008: *ჯორბენაძე ნ., საშუალი გვარის ზმნათა უღლების სისტემა თანამედროვე ქართულში, იბერიულ-კავკასიური ენათმეცნიერება, ტ. XXVVI.* საქართველოს მეცნიერებათა აკადემიის ენათმეცნიერების ინსტიტუტი, თბილისი: 298–314

Karkashadze M., 2010: *ქარქაშაძე მ., ობიექტჩართული ზმნები და მედიოაქტივები თანამედროვე ქართულში, ენათმეცნიერების საკითხები, I–II.* თბილისის უნივერსიტეტის გამომცემლობა, თბილისი: 123–134

Kavtaradze I., 1954: *ქავთარაძე ი., ზმნის ძირითადი კატეგორიების ისტორიისათვის ძველ ქართულში,* საქართველოს სსრ მეცნიერებათა აკადემიის ენათმეცნიერების ინსტიტუტი, თბილისი

Kavtaradze I., 1955: *ქავთარაძე ი., დრო-კილოთა მესამე სერიის წარმოების ერთი თავისებურება ახალ ქართულში, იბერიულ-კავკასიური ენათმეცნიერება, ტ. VII.* საქართველოს სსრ მეცნიერებათა აკადემიის ენათმეცნიერების ინსტიტუტი, თბილისი: 61–79

King T. H., 1994: Agentivity and the Georgian Ergative. In: *Proceedings of the Twentieth Annual Meeting of the Berkeley Linguistics Society February 18–21*. General Session: Dedicated to the Contributions of Charles J. Fillmore, S. Gahl, and A. Dolbey (Eds.). Berkeley Linguistics Society, 20, Berkeley, CA: 327–339

Kiziria A., 1982a: *კიზირია ა., მარტივი წინადადების შედგენილობა ქართველურ ენებში.* გამომცემლობა "მეცნიერება", თბილისი

Kiziria A., 1982b: *კიზირია ა., ქართული ენა,პრაქტიკუმი.* გამომცემლობა "განათლება", თბილისი

Kiziria D., 2009: *Beginner's Georgian with 2 Audio CDs*. Hippocrene, New York

Klimov G., 1964: *Климов Г. 1964: Этимологический словарь Картвельских языков. Издательство АН СССР*, *Москва*

Klimov G., 1998: *Georgij A. Klimov Etymological Dictionary of the Kartvelian Languages, Trends in Linguistics, Documentation 16*. Mouton de Gruyter, Berlin and New York

Kobaidze M., 2007: *კობაიძე მ., ქართული ბრუნებისა და უღლების სისტემის ზოგი საკითხის სწავლების გამარტივების შესახებ. ქართული სალიტერატურო ენის საკითხები: ისტორია და თანამედროვე მდგომარეობა, პირველი კრებული.*

საქართველოს განათლებისა და მეცნიერების სამინისტრო, სახელმწიფო ენის პროგრამა, თბილისი: 158–180

Kobaidze M., 2008: *კობაიძე მ., სტატიკური და დინამიკური ზმნების შესახებ თანამედროვე ქართულში, იბერიულ-კავკასიური ენათმეცნიერება: მემკვიდრეობა და პერსპექტივები, საერთაშორისო სიმპოზიუმი 2, მასალები.* თბილისის უნივერსიტეტის გამომცემლობა, თბილისი: 228–230

Kojima Y., 2005a: Genitive Objects with Some Inversion Verbs in Modern Georgian. In: E. Khintibidze (Ed.), *Proceedings of the Fourth International Symposium on Kartvelian Studies*. Tbilisi University Press, Tbilisi: 59–67

Kojima Y., 2005b: Possessive Verben und Belebtheit im Modernen Georgisch. In: *Georgica 27*. Friedrich Schiller University Jena, Jena: 107–120

Kojima Y., 2007: *Clitics in Modern Georgian*. Asian and African Languages and Linguistics, 2. Research Institute for Languages and Cultures of Asia and Africa, Tokyo University of Foreign Studies, Tokyo: 85–102

Kojima Y., 2010: Two Types of Relative Clauses in Modern Georgian. In: K. Vamling (Ed.), *Language, History and Cultural Identities in the Caucasus*. Malmö University Press, Malmö: 156–167

Kojima Y., 2014: The Position of Rom and Pragmatics of Subordinate Clauses in Georgian: Advances in Kartvelian Morphology and Syntax. In: N. Amiridze, T. Reseck, and M. Topadze Gäumann (Eds.), *Diversitas Linguarum 38*. Universitätsverlag Brockmeyer, Bochum: 141–153

Kojima Y., 2018: Georgian. In: T. Tsunoda (Ed.), *Levels in Clause Linkage: A Crosslinguistic Survey*. De Gruyter, Berlin: 403–450

Kurdadze R., 2005: ქურდაძე რ., ხმოვანმონაცვლე ზმნები ქართულში, თბილისი

Kurtsikidze S., 2006: *Essentials of Georgian Grammar*. With Conjugation Tables of 250 Most Commonly Used Verbs. Lincom Europa, Students Grammars, Munich

Kvachadze L., 2010: *ლ. კვაჭაძე, თანამედროვე ქართული ენის სინტაქსი, რედ. მ. სუხიშვილი.* გამომცემლობა "ცოტნე", თბილისი

Lang E., 1984: *The Semantics of Coordination*. John Benjamins Publishing Company, Amsterdam and Philadelphia

Lazard G., 1998: *Actancy, Empirical Approaches to Language Typology*. Georg Bossong and Bernard Comrie (Eds.), vol. 19. Mouton de Gruyter, Berlin and New York

Lomtatidze K., 1953: *ლომთათიძე ქ., "თბება" ტიპის ზმნათა ისტორიისათვის ქართულში, იბერიულ-კავკასიური ენათმეცნიერება, ტ. IV.* საქართველოს სსრ მეცნიერებათა აკადემიის ენათმეცნიერების ინსტიტუტი, თბილისი: 75–81

Machavariani E., 1982: *მაჭავარიანი ე., ქართული ანბანის გრაფიკული საფუძვლები.* გამომცემლობა "ხელოვნება", თბილისი

Machavariani G., 1953: *მაჭავარიანი გ., ზმნის ძირითადი მორფოლოგიური კატეგორიები ქართველურ ენებში, (საკანდ. დისერტ. ავტორეფ.).* თბილისის უნივერსიტეტის გამომცემლობა, თბილისი

Machavariani G., 1973: *მაჭავარიანი გ., ვნებითის სუფიქსური ტიპის გვნებისის საკითხი ქართველურ ენებში (ვნებითის მაწარმოებელი*

სუფიქსების -ენ,-ედ წარმოშობის შესახებ), საქართველოს სსრ მეცნიერებათა აკადემიის მაცნე, ენისა და ლიტერატურის სერია, №1, თბილისი: 107–121

Machavariani M., 1959: *მაჭავარიანი გ., "უნიშნო ვნებითი" ქართველურ ენებში, ქართველურ ენათა სტრუქტურის საკითხები I.* საქარველოს სსრ მეცნიერებათა აკადემიის გამომცემლობა, თბილისი: 101–130

Machavariani M., 1974: *მაჭავარიანი გ., ასპექტის კატეგორია ქართველურ ენებში, ქართველურ ენათა სტრუქტურის საკითხები IV.* საქართველოს სსრ მეცნიერებათა აკადემიის გამომცემლობა, თბილისი: 118–143

Machavariani M., 1987: *მაჭავარიანი მ., ქცევის გრამატიკული კატეგორიის სემანტიკა.* გამომცემლობა "მეცნიერება", თბილისი

Makharoblidze T., 2005: *მახარობლიძე თ. დესტინაციურ სისტემათა ტიპოლოგია (ქართული და ბასკური მასალა).* თბილისის უნივერსიტეტის გამომცემლობა, თბილისი

Makharoblidze T., 2012: *The Georgian Verb*. Lincom Studies in Caucasian Linguistics 20. Lincom Europa, Munich

Makharoblidze T., 2018: On Georgian Preverbs. *Open Linguistics, De Gruyter* 4(1): 163–183

Margiani K., Kurdadze R., and Lomia M., 2019: *მარგიანი ქ., ქურდაძე რ., ლომია მ., ევიდენციალობის კატეგორია ქართველურ ენებში.* ქართველური ენათმეცნიერების სერია, თბილისი

Marr N., 1908: *Марр Н.Я., Основные таблицы к грамматике древнелитературного грузинского языка. с предварительным сообщением о родстве грузинского языка с семитическими, Изд-во и тип. Имп. Акад. Наук, Санкт-Петербург*

Marr N., 1925: *Марр Н.Я., Грамматика древнелитературного грузинского языка. Изд-во и тип. Рос. акад. Наук, Ленинград*

Marr N., 1931: *Marr N., Brière M., La langue Georgiènne*. Firmin-Didot et Cie, Paris

Martirosovi A., 1956: *მარტიროსოვი ა., წინდებულისა და თანდებულის ისტორიული ურთიერთობისათვის ქართულში, იბერიულ-კავკასიური ენათმეცნიერება, ტ. 8.* საქართველოს სსრ მეცნიერებათა აკადემიის ენათმეცნიერების ინსტიტუტი, თბილისი: 39–46

Martirosovi A., 1964: *მარტიროსოვი ა., ნაცვალსახელები ქართველურ ენებში: ისტორიულ-შედარებითი ანალიზი, ენათმეცნიერების ინსტიტუტი.* საქართველოს სსრ მეცნიერებათა აკადემიის გამომცემლობა, თბილისი

Melikishvili D., 1977: *მელიქიშვილი დ., ინკლუზივ-ექსკლუზივის კატეგორიის გამოხატვის ისტორიისათვის ქართულ ზმნაში, საქართველოს მეცნიერებათა აკადემიის მაცნე.* ენისა და ლიტერატურის სერია 4, თბილისი

Melikishvili D., 1978: *მელიქიშვილი დ., "მიჭირს" ზმნა და მასწავლებლის გასაჭირი, (ინვერსია ქართულ ზმნაში)*. ქართული ენა და ლიტერატურა სკოლაში, 4, თბილისი: 81–93

Melikishvili D., 1995: *მელიქიშვილი დ., შესიტყვების სინტაქსური მექანიზმის აღწერისათვის ქართულში. საენათმეცნიერო ძიებანი, IV.* საქართველოს მეცნიერებათა აკადემიის ენათმეცნიერების

ინსტიტუტი, ზესარიონ ჯორზენაძის საზოგადოეზა, თზილისი: 76–80
Melikishvili D., 2001a: *მელიქიშვილი დ., ქართული ზმნის უღლეზის სისტემა*, "ლოგოს პრესი", თზილისი
Melikishvili D., 2001b: *მელიქიშვილი დ., ქართული ზმნის უღლეზის სისტემა*. თზილისის უნივერსიტეტის გამომცემლოზა, თზილისი
Melikishvili D., 2001c: *მელიქიშვილი დ., ქართული ზმნის უღლეზის სისტემა, ნაწ. II*. გამომცემლოზა "ლოგოსი", თზილისი
Melikishvili D., 2008: *მელიქიშვილი დ., ქართული ზმნის უღლეზადი ფორმეზის გრამატიკული კლასიფიკაციისა და კვალიფიკაციის პრინციპეზისათვის I. ენათმეცნიერეზის საკითხეზი, I–II*. თზილისის უნივერსიტეტის გამომცემლოზა, თზილისი
Melikishvili D., 2009: *მელიქიშვილი დ., ქართული ზმნის უღლეზადი ფორმეზის გრამატიკული კლასიფიკაციისა და კვალიფიკაციის პრინციპეზისათვის II, ენათმეცნიერეზის საკითხეზი, I–II*. თზილისის უნივერსიტეტის გამომცემლოზა, თზილისი: 78–96
Melikishvili D., Humphries J., and Kupunia M., 2008: *The Georgian Verb: Morphosyntactic Analysis*. Dunwoody Press, Chantilly
Melikishvili I., 2013: *მელიქიშვილი ირ., სემანტიკური მარკირეზა მორფოლოგიაში და აქტიურობა-არააქტიურობის კატეგორია ქართველურ ენეზში, კრეზულში: ენათმეცნიერეზის საკითხეზი. თზილისის უნივერსიტეტის გამომცემლოზა,* თზილისი: 15–30
Merlan F., 1982: Another Look at Georgian "Inversion". *Folia Slavica* 5(1–3): 294–312
Metrevei T., 1980: *მეტრეველი თ., ინკლუზივ-ექსკლუზივის კატეგორიისათვის ძველ ქართულში, ძველი ქართული ენის კათედრის შრომეზი, ტ. 23*. თზილისის უნივერსიტეტის გამომცემლოზა, თზილისი: 175–191
Meurer P., 2009: A Computational Grammar for Georgian. In: P. Bosch, D. Gabelaia, and J. Lang (Eds.), *Logic, Language, and Computation*. 7th International Tbilisi Symposium on Logic, Language, and Computation, TbiLLC 2007, Tbilisi, Georgia, October 1–5, 2007. Revised Selected Papers, Springer-Verlag, Berlin and Heidelberg: 1–15
Müller Fr., 1864: Müller Fr., Über den Ursprung der armenischen Schrift, Sitzungsberichte d. *Wiener Akademie* 48
Natadze N., 1956: *ნათაძე ნ., მესამე სერიის დრო-კილოთა წარმოეზისათვის ქართულში, იზერიულ-კავკასიური ენათმეცნიერეზა, ტ. VII*. საქართველოს სსრ მეცნიერეზათა აკადემიის ენათმეცნიერეზის ინსტიტუტი, თზილისი: 81–100
Ninua G., 1968: *ნინუა გ., ზრძანეზითი კილო ქართულ ენაში*. საკანდიდატო დისერტაცია, თზილისი
Nozadze L., 2008: *ნოზაძე ლ., ქართველურ ენათა ისტორიული მორფოლოგიის საკითხეზი*. გამომცემლოზა "უნივერსალი", თზილისი
Oniani L., 1965: *ონიანი ალ., ინკლუზივ-ექსკლუზივის კატეგორიის საკითხისათვის ქართველურ ენეზში, საქართველოს სსრ მეცნიერეზათა აკადემიის საზოგადოეზრივ მეცნიერეზათა განყოფილეზის მაცნე*, 1, საქართველოს სსრ მეცნიერეზათა აკადემიის გამომცემლოზა, თზილისი

Oniani L., 1978: *ონიანი ალ., ქართველურ ენათა ისტორიული მორფოლოგიის საკითხები: ზმნის პირი, რიცხვი, ინკლუზივ-ექსკლუზივი,* გამომცემლობა "განათლება", თბილისი

Pataridze R., 1980: *პატარიძე რ., ქართული ასომთავრული.* გამომცემლობა "ნაკადული", თბილისი

Peikrishvili J., 1974: *ფეიქრიშვილი ჟ., თურმეობითების მნიშვნელობა და გამოყენება ახალ ქართულში, ქართველურ ენათა სტრუქტურის საკითხები, IV.* საქართველოს სსრ მეცნიერებათა აკადემიის გამომცემლობა, თბილისი: 37–53

Peikrishvili J., 2007: *ფეიქრიშვილი ჟ., მესამე სერიის მწკრივები ახალ სალიტერატურო ქართულში.* გამომცემლობა "ჯანსუღ ღვინჯილია", თბილისი

Pochkhua B., 1959: *ფოჩხუა ბ., ხმოვანთავსართული ზმნისართები, ქართველურ ენათა სტრუქტურის საკითხები, I.* საქართველოს სსრ მეცნიერებათა აკადემიის გამომცემლობა, თბილისი: 81–89

Rogava G., 1942: *როგავა გ., კუთვნილებითი აფიქსი-ი ქართველურ ენათა ზმნისა და სახელის მორფოლოგიურ კატეგორიაში (ქცევასა და ბრუნვებში).* საქართველოს მეცნიერებათა აკადემიის მოამბე, № 5, ტ. III, თბილისი: 497–502

Rogava G., 1945: *როგავა გ., აორისტისა და კავშირებითი II-ის ზოგ აფიქსთა გენეზისისათვის -ევ სუფიქთან დაკავშირებით ქართულსა და მეგრულში.* საქართველოს სსრ მეცნიერებათა აკადემიის მოამბე, VI, №8, თბილისი: 647–655

Sarjveladze Z., 1984: *სარჯველაძე ზ., ქართული სალიტერატურო ენის ისტორია.* თბილისის უნივერსიტეტის გამომცემლობა, თბილისი

Sarjveladze Z., and Fähnrich H., 1999: *Altgeorgisch-deutsches Wörterbuch*. Buske, Hamburg

Schmidt K. H., 1962: Zum Passivum in Georgischen und in indogermanischen Sprachen. *Bedi Kartlisa, revue de kartvévlologie* 13–14, Paris: 116–126

Schmidt K. H., 1965: Indogermanisches Medium und Sataviso im Georgischen. *Bedi Kartlisa, revue de kartvévlologie* 19–20, Paris: 129–135

Shanidze A., 1943: *შანიძე ა., აქტივი და პასივი ერთურთის მიმართ მრავალპირიანი ზმნის ჩვენებით. საქართველოს სსრ მეცნიერებათა აკადემიის მოამბე, ტ.4.* საქართველოს სსრ მეცნიერებათა აკადემიის გამომცემლობა, თბილისი: 375–382

Shanidze A., 1961: *შანიძე ა., გრამატიკული სუბიექტი ზოგიერთ გარდაუვალ ზმნასთან ქართულში, თსუ ძველი ქართული ენის კათედრის შრომები, ტ. 7.* თბილისის უნივერსიტეტის გამომცემლობა, თბილისი: 207–238

Shanidze A., 1980: *შანიძე ა., ქართული ენის გრამატიკის საფუძვლები, რედ. მზ. შანიძე, თხზულებანი თორმეტ ტომად, ტომი 3.* თბილისის უნივერსიტეტის გამომცემლობა, თბილისი

Shanidze A., 1981: *შანიძე ა., ქართული ენის სტრუქტურისა და ისტორიის საკითხები, რედ. კ. დანელია, თხზულებანი თორმეტ ტომად, ტ. 2.* თბილისის უნივერსიტეტის გამომცემლობა, თბილისი

Sharashenidze N., 2014: *შარაშენიძე ნ., მოდალობის კატეგორია ქართულში, მისი სწავლების მეთოდები და სტრატეგიები*

უცხოელთათვის. საერთაშორისო ჟურნალი მულტილინგვური განათლებისთვის, 3. თბილისი: 80–90

Sukhishvili M., 1981a: *სუხიშვილი მ., “ანუკამ ილანძღა და ივინა” თუ “ანუკა ილანძღა და ივინა”, ქართული სიტყვის კულტურის საკითხები. წიგნი მეოთხე.* თბილისი: 183–197

Sukhishvili M., 1981b: *სუხიშვილი მ., გარდაუვალ უგვარო ზმნათა სემანტიკისათვის თანამედროვე ქართულში, ქართველურ ენათა სტრუქტურის საკითხები, V.* საქართველოს სსრ მეცნიერებათა აკადემიის გამომცემლობა, თბილისი: 11–14

Sukhishvili M., 1998: *სუხიშვილი მ., თანამედროვე ქართული ენის მორფოლოგია.* თბილისის უნივერსიტეტის გამომცემლობა, თბილისი

Sukhishvili M., 1999: *სუხიშვილი მ., გარდამავალი ზმნები ქართულში, (სისტემისა და ისტორიის ზოგი საკითხი).* გამომცემლობა “მეცნიერება”, თბილისი

Sukhishvili M., 2008: *სუხიშვილი მ., მედიოაქტივთა საქცეო სისტემის საოპოზიციო ცალების ზოგიერთი გრამატიკული და სემანტიკური თავისებურების შესახებ, იბერიულ-კავკასიური ენათმეცნიერება, ტ. XXXVI.* საქართველოს მეცნიერებათა აკადემიის ენათმეცნიერების ინსტიტუტი, თბილისი: 192–203

Tesnière L., 2015: *Elements of Structural Syntax*. T. Osborne (Trans.). Zhejiang University, Sylvain Kahane (Université Paris Ouest Nanterre). John Benjamins Publishing Company, Amsterdam and Philadelphia

Tomelleri V. S., 2009: The Category of Aspect in Georgian, Ossetic and Russian: Some Areal and Typological Observations. *Faits de Langues* 34(2): 245–272

Topuria V., 1942: *თოფურია ვ., III ტიპის ვნებითის წარმოება ქართულში. საქართველოს სსრ მეცნიერებათა აკადემიის მოამბე, № 9, ტ. 3.* თბილისი: 965–972

Topuria V., 1965: თოფურია ვ., ქართული ენა და მართლწერის ზოგიერთი საკითხი. გამომცემლობა “ნაკადული”, თბილისი

Topuria V., 2002: *თოფურია ვ., ფუძედრეკად ზმნათა სუფიქსაციისათვის. შრომები, ტ. 2.* თბილისი: 385–392

Tschenkéli K., 1958a: *Einführung in die georgische Sprache*. Bd. 1. Theoretischer Teil. Amirani Verlag, Zürich

Tschenkéli K., 1958b: *Einführung in die georgische Sprache*. Bd. 2. Praktischer Teil. Amirani Verlag, Zürich

Tschenkéli K., 1960–1974: *Georgisch-Deutsches Worterbuch*. Amirani Verlag, Zurich

Tsereteli G., 1943: *წერეთელი გ., არმაზის ბილინგვა, ნ. მარის სახელობის ენის, ისტორიისა და მატერიალური კულტურის ინსტიტუტის (ენიმკის) მოამბე, ტ. XIII,* თბილისი: 1–84

Tuite K., 1987: Indirect Transitives in Georgian. *Proceedings of the 13th Annual Meeting of the Berkeley Linguistics Society (BLS)* 13: 296–309

Tuite K., 1994: Syntactic Subject in Georgian. In: H. I. Aronson (Ed.), *Non-Slavic Languages of the USSR*. Slavica Publishers, Indiana University, Bloomington: 218–227

Tuite K., 1998: *Kartvelian Morphosyntax*. Lincom Europa, Munich

Tuite K., 2002: Deponent Verbs in Georgian. In: W. Bublitz, M. von Roncador, and H. Vater (Eds.), *Philology, Typology and Language*

Structure: Festschrift for Winfried Boeder on the Occasion of His 65th Birthday. Peter Lang, Frankfurt am Main: 375–389

Tuite K., 2003: *Current Trends in Caucasian, East Euroepan and Inner Asian Linguistics: Papers in Honor of Howard I. Aronson*. D. A. Holisky and K. Tuite (Eds.). Kartvelian Series Markers. John Benjamins Publishing Company, Amsterdam and Philadelphia: 363–391

Tuite K., 2007: Liminal Morphosyntax: Georgian Deponents and Their Kin. In *Proceedings of the 39th Chicago Linguistic Society Conference*. Chicago Linguistics Society 39/1. Department of Linguistics, University of Chicago, Chicago, IL: 774–788

Uturgaidze T., 1976: უთურგაიძე თ., ქართული ენის ფონემატური სტრუქტურა. გამომცემლობა "მეცნიერება", თბილისი

Uturgaidze T., 2002: უთურგაიძე თ., გრამატიკული კატეგორიებისა და მათი ურთიერთმიმართებისათვის ქართულ ზმნაში. თბილისის უნივერსიტეტის გამომცემლობა, თბილისი

Vogt H., 1938: *Esquisse d'une grammaire du géorgien moderne*. Norsk Tidsskrift for Sprogvidenskap 9. Oslo: 5–114

Vogt H., 1971: *Grammaire de la langue géorgienne*. Universitetsforlaget, Oslo

Wier T. R., 2001: *Georgian Morphosyntax and Feature Hierarchies in Natural Language*. A Dissertation Submitted to the Faculty of the Division of the Humanities Candidacy for the Degree of Doctor of Philosophy, Department of Linguistics, The University of Chicago, Chicago, IL

Index

actant: 147–150, 156, 168, 180–181; number of actants 187, 207, 471–473; adjectives: attributive 448–450; comparative and superlative 67–70; declension, preceding nouns 72–76; declension, without nouns 71–72; derivative 64–69; description of 63; function of 448; genitive modifier 450; predicative 459–460; primary 67
adjunct object 456–459
adverbial case: case ending 31, 72, 81, 398, 403; forms 107, 124, 440; function 399, 463–464
adverbs: modifiers 461–465; modify speech 397; primary and derivative 397–401; semantic groups 401–406
Aramaic 7–8
Armazi writing system 7–8
Armenian alphabet 8, 10
Asomtavruli (oldest Georgian alphabet) 8–9, 11
aspect 191–193, 207–208, 214, 252, 266, 284, 354, 373, 377, 379–385, 389, 493

bilingual 7
Boeder, Winfried 9
borrowed: numerals 77, 93; words 17, 37, 45, 228

calendar 8
case markers 28, 59, 397, 470
case, function of 29
Caucasus 3–4
Chan 3–4
Christian 5, 9
Colchian language 4
collective nouns (CN) 316, 319
compounds: closed 144–146; differing stems 139–143; reduplicated stem 138–139; semantics of 137; structure of 137
conjunctions: coordinating: contrastive 420; correlative 416–418; equating 421; separating 418–419
conjunction verbs: aorist 237–251; conditional 219–237; future 218–237; future subjunctive 219–237; future subseries 218–237; imperfect 210–213; medio-active 308; optative 251–265; perfect 265–284; pluperfect 284–297; present 193–208; present subjunctive 297–312; present subseries 193–218
conjunctions: basic and complex 416; contrastive 420–421; coordinating 416; correlative 416–418; equating 421; separating 418–420; subordinating 421–424
consonant: classification 15; clustering 18; clusters 17; pairs 16; single 16–17; triples 15
consonant-vowel-consonant (CVC) 36
contemporary Georgian: compounds 138; noun forms/functions 28, 75; postpositions 410–411; sounds 15; verb forms/functions 151–152, 175, 197, 382; vowel classification 18; word forms, seldom used 386–387, 388, 389, 398, 430, 433, 469, 496
Coptic alphabet 8–10

dative case: functions: 28–30, 42–43, 54, 102, 104, 156, 168, 169, 180, 279, 368, 398, 428, 441, 447, 461–463, 500; declension of: common nouns 32; consonant-stem 33; irregular declension patterns 49; irregular syncopating pattern 39–42; syncopating 34–38; vowel-stem

common nouns 42–45; vowel-stem truncating common nouns 42–51
declension of proper names: consonant-stem personal names 51–52; consonant-stem geographic names 53–54; vowel-stem family names 55–58; vowel-stem given names 54; vowel-stem geographic names 58–62
dialects 3–4, 6
diglossia 5
direct/indirect object: cases 156–157, 377, 473, 478, 485, 499; function 29, 148; markers 153; plural 167, 328; subjective 187, 267; verb modification 169–170, 181, 183, 185
double: consonant 17

ergative case: functions 28–30, 156, 168–169, 182, 204, 279, 285, 299, 361, 377, 428, 451, 469–474, 484, 488, 496, 500
etymology 495–496
evidence 4, 7

flexible stability 5
fricatives 15–16

Gamkrelidze, Thomas 3–4, 8
geminated consonants 17
Georgian: alphabet 7, 11; grapheme development 9; writing 7–8
Georgian language: consonants: clusters 17–18; height 19; pairs 16; triangle of 19–20; triples 15; sound groups 15; vowel classification: backness 18; height 19; triangle 19–20
Gothic alphabet 8, 10
Greek alphabet 7–9

harmonious complex 17

Imerkheuli 6
Indo-European 3
Ingilo dialect 6
instrumental case: functions of 30–31, 411, 458–459, 461–463, 487, 501; truncation 45, 60, 72, 74, 104
intellectualization 5
interjection 437–443
interjection: as grammatical sound 437–438; as noun 441; word or phrase 438–441
Ivanov, V. 3–4

Javakhishvili, Ivane 7–10, 144

Kartli 5, 7–9
Kartveli 5
Kartvelian: languages 3, 5; migrations 4

language: development 4–5; stop-system 3
Laz 3–4

Machavariani, Elene 9
Megrelian 3–4, 6
Mesrop-Mashtots 10
Mkhedruli 9
modernization 5
mood 189–191
morphemes 3, 17–18, 20, 246, 274
morphology (word forms) 21
Mozdokian dialect 6
Mrgvlovani 9
Mroveli, Leonti 8
Muller, Friedrich 10

national identification 5
nominative case: function 29, 155, 158, 168, 180, 377, 453, 459, 484, 488; pronouns 106, 110–111, 116, 134
nouns: adverbial 31; animate/inanimate 23–24; case/number markers 28; collective 26–27; concrete/abstract 24–25; direct/indirect 446–448; function of cases 29–30; grammatical categories 27; human organ 40; instrumental 30; noncount 27; proper/common 25–26; subject 445–446; vocative 31–32
noun phrase 445–452
numerals: cardinal 78–79; declension of: cardinal 89–90; consonant-stem followed by nouns 94–97; consonant-stem cardinal 82–83; consonant-stem fractional 84–85, 97; consonant-stem ordinal 84; consonant-stem quantifiers 85; fractional 92; numeral followed by numerals 98–100; ordinal 91; vowel-stem cardinal 86–87; vowel-stem followed by nouns 92–94; vowel-stem ordinal 87–88; vowel-stem quantifiers 87; groups of, defined 77–78; ordinal and fractional 80–81
Nuskhuri 9

Ossetic 3

Person of the verb 147–158; grammatical person 157, 180; actual person 157, 180
Parnavaz 7–8
Parpets, Lazar 10
particles: action, frequency of 435–436; affirmative 430; approximating 431; emphasizing 432; expressive 433, 434; frequency of action 435; function of 425–426, 436; imitative 434–435; indictive 435; interrogative 426; limiting 427;

negation 428–429; possibility and supposition 434; reported speech 430–431; selective 434; witnessed action 436; wish or desire 433
Pataridze, Ramaz 8
Phereidanian dialect 6
Persian 8
Phoenicians 7
phonetic system 3
phonology: articulation 3, 15–16, 18; nasal sounds 17; pronunciation of sounds 11; sonant sounds 15–17
Plastunkian dialect 6
postpositions: cases 456–459, 461–464; functions of 104, 145, 156, 402–405; types 407–411, 412–415, 487, 501
predicate: compound, structure of 453–455; simple 452–453
preverbs 158–163
pronouns: consonant-stem 111–112; declension of: consonant-stem indefinite 130–131; definite 126–127; demonstrative 112, 114; indefinite 131–133; interrogative 119; possessive 107–110; vowel-stem indefinite 129–130; definite 124; demonstrative 110–111; indefinite 127–129; interrogative 115–119; negative 121–124; personal 101–104; possessive 105–107; possessive-interrogative 120–121; reciprocal 134; reflexive 104–105; relative 135–136
proto-Kartvelian 3–4

Sakartvelo 5
second-person: forms 150, 200, 207, 214, 238, 249, 268, 274–276, 285, 312, 352; pronouns 101–102, 104, 110; subject marker 150–153
Semitic alphabet 7
sentences: adverbial clause: concession 506–507; condition 506; result 507–508; complete/incomplete 483; compound-complex: complex 497; compound predicates 488; compound subjects 489; coordinate 498; mixed sentences 510; subordinate 498–207; with subordinate clauses 508; conjunctions 486–487; coordinated parts 484–485, 488; declarative 476; direct/indirect objects 489–491; direct/indirect speech 511–512; exclamative 481; imperative 479–481; interrogative 79–478; noun-sentence 484; parenthetical words/phrases 491; appositive 491–492; asides 493–495; formulas and expressions 495–496; free modifiers 493; simple extended/unextended 482–483; structure of 482; with/without omitted subjects 484
Slavic (old) alphabet 8
stem of nouns: consonant-stem 32–42; non-syncopating stem 32–33; non-truncating stem 42–45; syncopating stem 33–39; truncating stem 45–50; truncating stem with syncope 50; vowel-stem 42–50
Svan 3–4, 6
symbolism 8
syncopation: clustering 18; nouns 33–35; patterns 36, 39; stem 32–47, 50, 407; vowels 33
syntactic pairs: coordination 468–469; decreasing 473–475; formal linkage of 466–467; increasing 470–473; subordination 469–470; word relations 467

third-person: forms 160, 199, 207, 214, 226, 252, 275–276, 352; object marker 17, 148, 152, 157, 185; pronouns 101, 103–104, 110; subject marker 151–153
tongue movement 16; position 18–19
Tsereteli, Giorgi 7–8, 25
Turkey 3, 461

valency 148–149, 167–168, 307, 471–473
verbal nouns: gerunds 385–389; participles: active voice 389–391; future passive 393–394; medial voice 395–396; negative passive 394–395; passive/past passive voice 391–393
verb phrase 455–466
verbs: ablaut 198–199, 224, 254, 272, 289–290, 292, 304–306; active voice 168–170; active/passive 200–202; aorist 237–238; bipersonal 207, 212, 216, 234, 250, 263, 275; conditional 219; conjugation: aorist 238–240, 243–247, 250; aorist, ablaut verbs 241–243; aorist/medio-active 248–250; bipersonal medio-active 130–231, 293–296; components chart 202; dynamic-passive 260–261; future 226, 228, 233; groups 147, 220–224; imperfect 213; medio-active perfect tense 280–282; monopersonal medio-active 229–230, 262–263, 296; optative 252–253, 257–260, 261, 264–265; perfect subjunctive 299–304, 307–311; perfect tense 267–272, 276–279; pluperfect 285–289, 291–292; present subjunctive 214–218; present tense 193, 195, 199,

203–204, 206; static/static-passive 264–265, 282–283; declension of: intransitive verb subject 155; transitive verb subject 156; direct/ indirect object and number 152–155; feeling 174–175; future subjunctive 219, 231–233; future tense 218; grammatical and actual 157–158; honorific 345–350; imperfect 208–211; irregular: changing stem by aspect 379; changing stem by tense 250; changing stem plural subject 312; changing stems plural direct object 328; medio-active 177–179, 204–205; medio-passive 179–180; monopersonal 206–207; neutral and locative 182–183; object-oriented paradigm 213; objective 185–188; one-stem 195; optative 251, 263; passive voice 170–173, 216; perfect subjunctive 297–299; perfect tense 265–266, 274; person and number 147–150; pluperfect 284; polypersonal 180–181; possibility 173; preverbs, functions of 163–168; preverbs, structure of 158–163; root passive voice 175–176; stems 24, 199, 266, 312, 328, 335, 350, 367, 379; subject and number 150–152; subject and object 155–157; subjective 183–184; tenses and subcategories: aspect 191–193; mood 189–191
version 180–188
voice 178–180
vocal cords 16
vocative case 31, 49, 54, 59–60, 89, 101, 438, 484, 495
vowels: backness 18; front/middle/ back vowels 18–19; height 19–20; long, absence of 20; triangle of 19–20

Zan 3–4

Milton Keynes UK
Ingram Content Group UK Ltd.
UKHW021007121223
434199UK00009B/72